Modern Critical Interpretations

Mark Twain's
Adventures of Huckleberry Finn

Modern Critical Views

Henry Adams
Edward Albee
A. R. Ammons
Matthew Arnold
John Ashbery
W. H. Auden
Jane Austen
James Baldwin
Charles Baudelaire
Samuel Beckett
Saul Bellow
The Bible
Elizabeth Bishop
William Blake
Jorge Luis Borges
Elizabeth Bowen
Bertolt Brecht
The Brontës
Robert Browning
Anthony Burgess
George Gordon, Lord
  Byron
Thomas Carlyle
Lewis Carroll
Willa Cather
Cervantes
Geoffrey Chaucer
Kate Chopin
Samuel Taylor Coleridge
Joseph Conrad
Contemporary Poets
Hart Crane
Stephen Crane
Dante
Charles Dickens
Emily Dickinson
John Donne & the Seven-
  teenth-Century Meta-
  physical Poets
Elizabethan Dramatists
Theodore Dreiser
John Dryden
George Eliot
T. S. Eliot
Ralph Ellison
Ralph Waldo Emerson
William Faulkner
Henry Fielding
F. Scott Fitzgerald
Gustave Flaubert
E. M. Forster
Sigmund Freud
Robert Frost

Robert Graves
Graham Greene
Thomas Hardy
Nathaniel Hawthorne
William Hazlitt
Seamus Heaney
Ernest Hemingway
Geoffrey Hill
Friedrich Hölderlin
Homer
Gerard Manley Hopkins
William Dean Howells
Zora Neale Hurston
Henry James
Samuel Johnson and
  James Boswell
Ben Jonson
James Joyce
Franz Kafka
John Keats
Rudyard Kipling
D. H. Lawrence
John Le Carré
Ursula K. Le Guin
Doris Lessing
Sinclair Lewis
Robert Lowell
Norman Mailer
Bernard Malamud
Thomas Mann
Christopher Marlowe
Carson McCullers
Herman Melville
James Merrill
Arthur Miller
John Milton
Eugenio Montale
Marianne Moore
Iris Murdoch
Vladimir Nabokov
Joyce Carol Oates
Sean O'Casey
Flannery O'Connor
Eugene O'Neill
George Orwell
Cynthia Ozick
Walter Pater
Walker Percy
Harold Pinter
Plato
Edgar Allan Poe
Poets of Sensibility & the
  Sublime

Alexander Pope
Katherine Ann Porter
Ezra Pound
Pre-Raphaelite Poets
Marcel Proust
Thomas Pynchon
Arthur Rimbaud
Theodore Roethke
Philip Roth
John Ruskin
J. D. Salinger
Gershom Scholem
William Shakespeare
  (3 vols.)
  Histories & Poems
  Comedies
  Tragedies
George Bernard Shaw
Mary Wollstonecraft
  Shelley
Percy Bysshe Shelley
Edmund Spenser
Gertrude Stein
John Steinbeck
Laurence Sterne
Wallace Stevens
Tom Stoppard
Jonathan Swift
Alfred, Lord Tennyson
William Makepeace
  Thackeray
Henry David Thoreau
Leo Tolstoi
Anthony Trollope
Mark Twain
John Updike
Gore Vidal
Virgil
Robert Penn Warren
Evelyn Waugh
Eudora Welty
Nathanael West
Edith Wharton
Walt Whitman
Oscar Wilde
Tennessee Williams
William Carlos Williams
Thomas Wolfe
Virginia Woolf
William Wordsworth
Richard Wright
William Butler Yeats

These and other titles in preparation

Modern Critical Interpretations

Mark Twain's
Adventures of Huckleberry Finn

Edited and with an introduction by
Harold Bloom
Sterling Professor of the Humanities
Yale University

Chelsea House Publishers
NEW YORK ◊ NEW HAVEN ◊ PHILADELPHIA

© 1986 by Chelsea House Publishers, a division of Chelsea House Educational Communications, Inc.

3 5 7 9 8 6 4 2

Introduction © 1986 by Harold Bloom

Printed and bound in the United States of America

∞ The paper used in this publication meets the minimum requirements of the American National Standard for Permanence of Paper for Printed Library Materials, Z39.48–1984.

Library of Congress Cataloging-in-Publication Data
Mark Twain : the Adventures of Huckleberry Finn.
    (Modern critical interpretations)
    Bibliography: p.
    Includes index.
    1. Twain, Mark, 1835–1910. Adventures of
Huckleberry Finn—Addresses, essays, lectures.
I. Bloom, Harold.   II. Series.
PS1305.M28   1986   813'.4   86–2578
ISBN 1–55546–013–5 (alk. paper)

Contents

Editor's Note

This volume gathers together what, in its editor's judgment, is the best criticism available upon Mark Twain's masterpiece, *Huckleberry Finn,* arranged in the chronological order of its original publication. The editor is grateful to Eden Quainton for his assistance in locating and judging these essays.

Freedom, Huck's obsession, is explored in the editor's introduction as the rhetoric of the storyteller's own problematic freedom. Leo Marx begins the chronological sequence with his spirited strictures upon the moral inadequacy of the novel's conclusion, in a vigorous argument with T. S. Eliot and Lionel Trilling, two major critics so enchanted by the book that they fell into a defense of its weakest aspect.

J. Hillis Miller's rhetorical criticism contrasts the first-person narrators of Dickens's *David Copperfield* and *Huckleberry Finn,* and concludes that Twain's narrative stance is closer to the endless possibilities of nihilism. Consonant with Miller's reading is Michael J. Hoffman's emphasis upon Twain's irony, with its assault on societal illusions. A similar contemporary awareness of the dubieties of literary language informs the analysis by Neil Schmitz of what he terms "Huckspeech," the rhetoric of a keenly wary innocence.

Another contemporary mode, feminist literary criticism, is exemplified by Nancy Walker, describing the ironies of "women and virtue" in the book. She argues that although the book presents—and ultimately rejects—women in stereotypical roles, nonetheless "the relationship between Huck and women is more complex and dynamic than a simple response to idealized figures." My own favorite among Twain critics, James M. Cox, adroitly reminds us that *Huckleberry Finn* remains "a hard book to take," with the capacity to go on provoking censorship. Cox powerfully defends the book's concluding segment, a defense that shows again why debate about *Huckleberry Finn* never will cease among us.

In this book's last essay, Cleo McNelly Kearns shrewdly demonstrates how Twain's masterpiece exposes the limits and limitations of some widespread current critical modes. Eloquently reminding us that *Huckleberry Finn* moves between the dialectical alternatives of prophecy and of silence, she returns us to the introduction's concerns with the enigma of the storyteller's freedom, and its equivocal relation to our own problematic freedom.

Introduction

> After supper she got out her book and learned me about Moses and
> the Bulrushers; and I was in a sweat to find out all about him; but by-
> and-by she let it out that Moses had been dead a considerable long
> time; so then I didn't care no more about him; because I don't take
> stock in dead people.

Huck Finn's American vision has this in common with Captain Ahab's or Walt
Whitman's, that Huck too would strike the sun if it insulted him. The three best
American books — *Huckleberry Finn, Moby-Dick, Leaves of Grass* — have in common also that they are each the most American of books. Twain's masterpiece is
essentially comic, Melville's is tragic, Whitman's is beyond characterization or
categorization, except that despite its humor and its Emersonian hopes for
America, we remember it best for its dark shadows. *Huckleberry Finn,* shrewd and
grim as it is sometimes compelled to be, remains unique in our national literature
for its affirmative force. Fecund in its progeny — as diverse as Kipling's *Kim,*
Eliot's *The Dry Salvages,* Hemingway's *The Sun Also Rises,* and Mailer's *Why Are
We In Vietnam?* — the book is likely to go on engendering our strongest writers,
with only *Leaves of Grass* as a rival in that role.

What is the secret of an appeal that affected Eliot and Faulkner, Hemingway
and Joyce, with almost equal intensity? Is it because the book tells the truth?
That was the judgment of Lionel Trilling, and I am not moved to dismiss such a
judgment lightly. The book tells a story which most Americans need to believe is
a true representation of the way things were, are, and yet might be. Huck lives in
a complex reality that nevertheless does not negate his freedom. Yet that freedom
is also a solitude, and is purchased by a series of lies, noble in their intention, but
lies nevertheless. Without a family, yet with a murderous father always apt to
turn up again, Huck perpetually experiences a primal loneliness that he both welcomes and dreads:

Miss Watson she kept pecking at me, and it got tiresome and lonesome. By-and-by they fetched the niggers in and had prayers, and
then everybody was off to bed. I went up to my room with a piece
of candle and put it on the table. Then I set down in a chair by the
window and tried to think of something cheerful, but it warn't no
use. I felt so lonesome I most wished I was dead. The stars was
shining, and the leaves rustled in the woods ever so mournful; and I
heard an owl, away off, who-whooing about somebody that was
dead, and a whippowill and a dog crying about somebody that was
going to die; and the wind was trying to whisper something to me
and I couldn't make out what it was, and so it made the cold shivers
run over me. Then away out in the woods I heard that kind of a
sound that a ghost makes when it wants to tell about something
that's on its mind and can't make itself understood, and so can't rest
easy in its grave and has to go about that way every night grieving.
I got so down-hearted and scared, I did wish I had some company.
Pretty soon a spider went crawling up my shoulder, and I flipped it
off and it lit in the candle; and before I could budge it was all
shriveled up. I didn't need anybody to tell me that that was an
awful bad sign and would fetch me some bad luck, so I was scared
and most shook the clothes off of me. I got up and turned around in
my tracks three times and crossed my breast every time; and then I
tied up a little lock of my hair with a thread to keep witches away.
But I hadn't no confidence. You do that when you've lost a horseshoe that you've found, instead of nailing it up over the door, but I
hadn't ever heard anybody say it was any way to keep off bad luck
when you'd killed a spider.

Huck, like any American, does not feel free unless he is alone, and yet solitude makes him fear that he is no part of the creation, however the world happened or came about. His extraordinary pathos results from his ambivalence
towards a freedom he necessarily cannot evade for very long at a time.

II

V. S. Pritchett found in *Adventures of Huckleberry Finn* evidence of an
American limitation, when compared to the more civilized modes of European
literature:

It is not a book which grows spiritually, if we compare it to *Quixote,
Dead Souls* or even *Pickwick;* and it is lacking in that civilised quality
which you are bound to lose when you throw over civilisation — the
quality of pity. One is left with the cruelty of American humour . . .

Pritchett perhaps forgot that throwing over civilization and its discontents is not so easily accomplished. Huck's discomfort with culture is acute, but he is hardly "a natural anarchist and bum" to whom ideas and ideals are "repugnant," as Pritchett thought. Nor is he "the servant of the river-god," which was Lionel Trilling's trope, a mythologization that derived Huck's supposedly "very intense moral life" from his "perpetual adoration of the Mississippi's power and charm." That is to compound Huck with T. S. Eliot, for whom "the Boy is also the spirit of the River." Huck indeed is now part of the American mythology, but hardly because he is the spirit of the river, which is not a god for Twain, whatever it was to be for Trilling and for Eliot. Twain tells us that the Mississippi is well worth reading about, is remarkable, and manifests many eccentricities. Huck too is well worth reading about, is quite remarkable, and is a wonderfully eccentric boy. Critics are fond of finding a moral in him, or at least want to see him as a kind of Sancho Panza to Tom Sawyer's Don Quixote. Tom Sawyer, alas, is something of a bore and not very quixotic, and Huck has little in common with the shrewd and pragmatic Sancho. There is however a touch of the quixotic in Huck, who is a great storyteller, a boy who lies merely to keep in practice.

Huck's fictions are lies *against* time, against an impossible father, against society and history, but not against reason and nature. They are not lies *for* anything; Huck does not seek benefits from them. Like the strong poets, Huck always has the desire to be different, the desire to be elsewhere. Change and travel are necessary for Huck; without them he cannot be independent. But we would do him wrong if we judged him as seeking freedom above everything else. Except for Joyce's Poldy Bloom, Huck Finn must be the most good-natured and tolerant representation of a human being in the fiction of the English language. The freedom he must have, because he is that freedom, is a freedom that he wants for everyone else. It is the freedom of the storyteller, Twain's own freedom.

That freedom, by common consent, has something to do with postponing death, with deferring the fear of dying. Divination, the sidestepping of dangers to the magic, occult, ontological self, is a fundamental component of the urge to tell stories. Huck of course is never going to be an adult, and so never will have to die. Yet that sounds wrong, because Huck rejects a maturation that is merely the death drive. The superego haunts Huck, yet cannot dominate him, because Huck will not surrender his gift for lying. "You don't know about me," Huck begins by saying, and he ends with the insistence that he will be out there ahead of the rest of us:

> But I reckon I got to light out for the Territory ahead of the rest, because Aunt Sally she's going to adopt me and sivilize me and I can't stand it. I been there before.

Huck's discomfort with civilization stems from his wholehearted rejection of guilt, sin, and solipsism, all of them Eliotic attributes, or should one say virtues? We can call Huck's attributes his virtues, because Huck, like his creator, is essentially an enlightened rationalist, though retaining considerable zest for the romance of superstitions. Unlike Eliot, Huck is not a Christian, and his prayer is not, "And let my cry come unto Thee," but something more naturalistic and buoyant:

> Sometimes we'd have that whole river all to ourselves for the longest time. Yonder was the banks and the islands, across the water; and maybe a spark—which was a candle in a cabin window—and sometimes on the water you could see a spark or two—on a raft or a scow, you know; and maybe you could hear a fiddle or a song coming over from one of them crafts. It's lovely to live on a raft. We had the sky, up there, all speckled with stars, and we used to lay on our backs and look up at them, and discuss about whether they was made, or only just happened—Jim he allowed they was made, but I allowed they happened; I judged it would have took too long to *make* so many. Jim said the moon could a *laid* them; well, that looked kind of reasonable, so I didn't say nothing against it, because I've seen a frog lay most as many, so of course it could be done. We used to watch the stars that fell, too, and see them streak down. Jim allowed they'd got spoiled and was hove out of the nest.

This delightful compromise upon a myth of creation is "kind of reasonable," and wholly characteristic of Huck's cheerful skepticism. Even more characteristic is the joy of being that opens Chapter 19 with what must be the most beautiful prose paragraph yet written by any American:

> Two or three days and nights went by; I reckon I might say they swum by, they slid along so quiet and smooth and lovely. Here is the way we put in the time. It was a monstrous big river down there—sometimes a mile and a half wide; we run nights, and laid up and hid day-times; soon as night was most gone, we stopped navigating and tied up—nearly always in the dead water under a tow-head; and then cut young cottonwoods and willows and hid the raft with them. Then we set out the lines. Next we slid into the river and had a swim, so as to freshen up and cool off; then we set down on the sandy bottom where the water was about knee deep, and watched the daylight come. Not a sound, anywheres—perfectly still—just like the whole world was asleep, only sometimes the bull-frogs a-cluttering, maybe. The first thing to see, looking away over the

water, was a kind of dull line—that was the woods on t'other side —you couldn't make nothing else out; then a pale place in the sky; then more paleness, spreading around; then the river softened up, away off, and warn't black any more, but gray; you could see little dark spots drifting along, ever so far away—trading scows, and such things; and long black streaks—rafts; sometimes you could hear a sweep screaking; or jumbled up voices, it was so still, and sounds come so far; and by-and-by you could see a streak on the water which you know by the look of the streak that there's a snag there in a swift current which breaks on it and makes the streak look that way; and you see the mist curl up off of the water, and the east reddens up, and the river, and you make out a log cabin in the edge of the woods, away on the bank on t'other side of the river, being a wood-yard, likely, and piled by them cheats so you can throw a dog through it anywheres; then the nice breeze springs up, and comes fanning you from over there, so cool and fresh, and sweet to smell, on account of the woods and the flowers; but sometimes not that way, because they've left dead fish laying around, gars, and such, and they do get pretty rank; and next you've got the full day, and everything smiling in the sun, and the song-birds just going it!

This is a cosmos that was not made, but "only just happened." It is no part of romance or legend, not myth, but a representation of a natural reality seen in its best aspect, where the days and nights swim and slide by. We hesitate to call this a fiction, since it lacks any residual Platonism. Even Freud had his last touch of Platonism, the transcendentalism that he called the "reality principle." Twain and Huck tell us a story about reality, but without reference to any principle.

III

Eminent critics have disagreed vigorously over the way in which Twain chose to end his masterpiece. That something is seriously wrong with the conclusion is palpable, but what is wrong may only be that in this book no conclusion is possible anyway. T. S. Eliot and Lionel Trilling both argued the formal adequacy of the long episode at the Phelps place, in which Tom Sawyer arrives again to organize the "rescue" of Jim, runaway slave who in some clear sense has become Huck's true family. But the critical decision here certainly goes to Leo Marx, who sees the novel's end as its self-defeat:

Should Clemens have made Huck a tragic hero? Both Mr. Eliot and Mr. Trilling argue that that would have been a mistake, and they are very probably correct. But between the ending as we have it and tragedy in the fullest sense, there was vast room for invention. Clemens might have contrived an action which left Jim's fate as much in doubt as Huck's. Such an ending would have allowed us to assume that the principals were defeated but alive, and the quest unsuccessful but not abandoned. This, after all, would have been consonant with the symbols, the characters, and the theme as Clemens had created them — and with history.

Marx is aware that he asks for too much, but that is the lasting power of the book that Twain wrote until he reached the Phelps place episode. We are so transported by *Huckleberry Finn* that we cannot surrender our hopes, and of these the largest is a refusal to abandon the desire for a permanent image of freedom. Twain could not extend that image into a finality, but the image endures nevertheless, as a permanent token of something evermore about to be.

Mr. Eliot, Mr. Trilling, and *Huckleberry Finn*

Leo Marx

In the losing battle that the plot fights with the characters, it often takes a cowardly revenge. Nearly all novels are feeble at the end. This is because the plot requries to be wound up. Why is this necessary? Why is there not a convention which allows a novelist to stop as soon as he feels muddled or bored? Alas, he has to round things off, and usually the characters go dead while he is at work, and our final impression of them is through deadness.
—E. M. FORSTER

The *Adventures of Huckleberry Finn* has not always occupied its present high place in the canon of American literature. When it was first published in 1884, the book disturbed and offended many reviewers, particularly spokesmen for the genteel tradition. In fact, a fairly accurate inventory of the narrow standards of such critics might be made simply by listing epithets they applied to Clemens's novel. They called it vulgar, rough, inelegant, irreverent, coarse, semi-obscene, trashy, and vicious. So much for them. Today (we like to think) we know the true worth of the book. Everyone now agrees that *Huckleberry Finn* is a master-piece: it is probably the one book in our literature about which highbrows and lowbrows can agree. Our most serious critics praise it. Nevertheless, a close look at what two of the best among them have recently written will likewise reveal, I believe, serious weaknesses in current criticism. Today the problem of evaluating the book is as much obscured by unqualified praise as it once was by parochial hostility.

I have in mind essays by Lionel Trilling and T. S. Eliot. Both praise the book, but in praising it both feel obligated to say something in justification of

From *American Scholar* 22, no. 4 (Autumn 1953). © 1953 by Leo Marx.

what so many readers have felt to be its great flaw: the disappointing "ending," the episode which begins when Huck arrives at the Phelps place and Tom Sawyer reappears. There are good reasons why Mr. Trilling and Mr. Eliot should feel the need to face this issue. From the point of view of scope alone, more is involved than the mere "ending"; the episode comprises almost one-fifth of the text. The problem, in any case, is unavoidable. I have discussed *Huckleberry Finn* in courses with hundreds of college students, and I have found only a handful who did not confess their dissatisfaction with the extravagant mock rescue of Nigger Jim and the denouement itself. The same question always comes up: "What went wrong with Twain's novel?" Even Bernard DeVoto, whose wholehearted commitment to Clemens's genius is well known, has said of the ending that "in the whole reach of the English novel there is no more abrupt or more chilling descent." Mr. Trilling and Mr. Eliot do not agree. They both attempt, and on similar grounds, to explain and defend the conclusion.

Of the two, Mr. Trilling makes the more moderate claim for Clemens's novel. He does admit that there is a "falling off" at the end; nevertheless he supports the episode as having "a certain formal aptness." Mr. Eliot's approval is without serious qualification. He allows no objections, asserts that "it is right that the mood of the end of the book should bring us back to the beginning." I mean later to discuss their views in some detail, but here it is only necessary to note that both critics see the problem as one of form. And so it is. Like many questions of form in literature, however, this one is not finally separable from a question of "content," of value, or, if you will, of moral insight. To bring *Huckleberry Finn* to a satisfactory close, Clemens had to do more than find a neat device for ending a story. His problem, though it may never have occurred to him, was to invent an action capable of placing in focus the meaning of the journey down the Mississippi.

I believe that the ending of *Huckleberry Finn* makes so many readers uneasy because they rightly sense that it jeopardizes the significance of the entire novel. To take seriously what happens at the Phelps farm is to take lightly the entire downstream journey. What is the meaning of the journey? With this question all discussion of *Huckleberry Finn* must begin. It is true that the voyage down the river has many aspects of a boy's idyl. We owe much of its hold upon our imagination to the enchanting image of the raft's unhurried drift with the current. The leisure, the absence of constraint, the beauty of the river—all these things delight us. "It's lovely to live on a raft." And the multitudinous life of the great valley we see through Huck's eyes has a fascination of its own. Then, of course, there is humor—laughter so spontaneous, so free of the bitterness present almost everywhere in American humor that readers often forget how grim a spectacle of human existence Huck contemplates. Humor in this novel flows from a bright joy of life as remote from our world as living on a raft.

Yet along with the idyllic and the epical and the funny in *Huckleberry Finn*, there is a coil of meaning which does for the disparate elements of the novel what a spring does for a watch. The meaning is not in the least obscure. It is made explicit again and again. The very words with which Clemens launches Huck and Jim upon their voyage indicate that theirs is not a boy's lark but a quest for freedom. From the electrifying moment when Huck comes back to Jackson's Island and rouses Jim with the news that a search party is on the way, we are meant to believe that Huck is enlisted in the cause of freedom. "Git up and hump yourself, Jim!" he cries. "There ain't a minute to lose. They're after us!" What particularly counts here is the *us*. No one is after Huck; no one but Jim knows he is alive. In that small word Clemens compresses the exhilarating power of Huck's instinctive humanity. His unpremeditated identification with Jim's flight from slavery is an unforgettable moment in American experience, and it may be said at once that any culmination of the journey which detracts from the urgency and dignity with which it begins will necessarily be unsatisfactory. Huck realizes this himself, and says so when, much later, he comes back to the raft after discovering that the Duke and the King have sold Jim:

> After all this long journey . . . here it was all come to nothing, everything all busted up and ruined, because they could have the heart to serve Jim such a trick as that, and make him a slave again all his life, and amongst strangers, too, for forty dirty dollars.

Huck knows that the journey will have been a failure unless it takes Jim to freedom. It is true that we do discover, in the end, that Jim is free, but we also find out that the journey was not the means by which he finally reached freedom.

The most obvious thing wrong with the ending, then, is the flimsy contrivance by which Clemens frees Jim. In the end we not only discover that Jim has been a free man for two months, but that his freedom has been granted by old Miss Watson. If this were only a mechanical device for terminating the action, it might not call for much comment. But it is more than that: it is a significant clue to the import of the last ten chapters. Remember who Miss Watson is. She is the Widow's sister whom Huck introduces in the first pages of the novel. It is she who keeps "pecking" at Huck, who tries to teach him to spell and to pray and to keep his feet off the furniture. She is an ardent proselytizer for piety and good manners, and her greed provides the occasion for the journey in the first place. She is Jim's owner, and he decides to flee only when he realizes that she is about to break her word (she cannot resist a slave trader's offer of eight hundred dollars) and sell him down the river away from his family.

Miss Watson, in short, is the Enemy. If we except a predilection for physical violence, she exhibits all the outstanding traits of the valley society. She pronounces the polite lies of civilization that suffocate Huck's spirit. The freedom which Jim seeks, and which Huck and Jim temporarily enjoy aboard the raft, is accordingly freedom *from* everything for which Miss Watson stands. Indeed, the very intensity of the novel derives from the discordance between the aspirations of the fugitives and the respectable code for which she is a spokesman. Therefore, her regeneration, of which the deathbed freeing of Jim is the unconvincing sign, hints a resolution of the novel's essential conflict. Perhaps because this device most transparently reveals that shift in point of view which he could not avoid, and which is less easily discerned elsewhere in the concluding chapters, Clemens plays it down. He makes little attempt to account for Miss Watson's change of heart, a change particularly surprising in view of Jim's brazen escape. Had Clemens given this episode dramatic emphasis appropriate to its function, Miss Watson's bestowal of freedom upon Jim would have proclaimed what the rest of the ending actually accomplishes — a vindication of persons and attitudes Huck and Jim had symbolically repudiated when they set forth downstream.

It may be said, and with some justice, that a reading of the ending as a virtual reversal of meanings implicit in the rest of the novel misses the point — that I have taken the final episode too seriously. I agree that Clemens certainly did not intend us to read it so solemnly. The ending, one might contend, is simply a burlesque upon Tom's taste for literary romance. Surely the tone of the episode is familiar to readers of Mark Twain. The preposterous monkey business attendant upon Jim's "rescue," the careless improvisation, the nonchalant disregard for commonsense plausibility — all these things should not surprise readers of Twain or any low comedy in the tradition of "Western humor." However, the trouble is, first, that the ending hardly comes off as burlesque: it is *too* fanciful, *too* extravagant; and it is tedious. For example, to provide a "gaudy" atmosphere for the escape, Huck and Tom catch a couple of dozen snakes. Then the snakes escape.

> No, there warn't no real scarcity of snakes about the house for a considerable spell. You'd see them dripping from the rafters and places every now and then; and they generly landed in your plate, or down the back of your neck.

Even if this were *good* burlesque, which it is not, what is it doing here? It is out of keeping; the slapstick tone jars with the underlying seriousness of the voyage.

Huckleberry Finn is a masterpiece because it brings Western humor to perfection and yet transcends the narrow limits of its conventions. But the ending does not. During the final extravaganza we are forced to put aside many of the mature emotions evoked earlier by the vivid rendering of Jim's fear of capture, the tenderness of Huck's and Jim's regard for each other, and Huck's excruciating moments of wavering between honesty and respectability. None of these emotions are called forth by the anticlimactic final sequence. I do not mean to suggest that the inclusion of low comedy per se is a flaw in *Huckleberry Finn*. One does not object to the shenanigans of the rogues; there is ample precedent for the place of extravagant humor even in works of high seriousness. But here the case differs from most which come to mind: the major characters themselves are forced to play low comedy roles. Moreover, the most serious motive in the novel, Jim's yearning for freedom, is made the object of nonsense. The conclusion, in short, is farce, but the rest of the novel is not.

That Clemens reverts in the end to the conventional manner of Western low comedy is most evident in what happens to the principals. Huck and Jim become comic characters; that is a much more serious ground for dissatisfaction than the unexplained regeneration of Miss Watson. Remember that Huck has grown in stature throughout the journey. By the time he arrives at the Phelps place, he is not the boy who had been playing robbers with Tom's gang in St. Petersburg the summer before. All he has seen and felt since he parted from Tom has deepened his knowledge of human nature and of himself. Clemens makes a point of Huck's development in two scenes which occur just before he meets Tom again. The first describes Huck's final capitulation to his own sense of right and wrong: "All right, then, I'll *go* to Hell." This is the climactic moment in the ripening of his self-knowledge. Shortly afterward, when he comes upon a mob riding the Duke and the King out of town on a rail, we are given his most memorable insight into the nature of man. Although these rogues had subjected Huck to every indignity, what he sees provokes this celebrated comment:

> Well, it made me sick to see it; and I was sorry for them poor pitiful rascals, it seemed like I couldn't ever feel any hardness against them any more in the world. It was a dreadful thing to see. Human beings can be awful cruel to one another.

The sign of Huck's maturity here is neither the compassion nor the skepticism, for both had been marks of his personality from the first. Rather, the special quality of these reflections is the extraordinary combination of the two, a mature blending of his instinctive suspicion of human motives with his capacity for pity.

But at this point Tom reappears. Soon Huck has fallen almost completely under his sway once more, and we are asked to believe that the boy who felt pity for the rogues is now capable of making Jim's capture the occasion for a game. He becomes Tom's helpless accomplice, submissive and gullible. No wonder that Clemens has Huck remark, when Huck first realizes Aunt Sally has mistaken him for Tom, that "it was like being born again." Exactly. In the end, Huck regresses to the subordinate role in which he had first appeared in *The Adventures of Tom Sawyer.* Most of those traits which made him so appealing a hero now disappear. He had never, for example, found pain or misfortune amusing. At the circus, when a clown disguised as a drunk took a precarious ride on a prancing horse, the crowd loved the excitement and danger; "it warn't funny to me, though," said Huck. But now, in the end, he submits in awe to Tom's notion of what is amusing. To satisfy Tom's hunger for adventure he makes himself a party to sport which aggravates Jim's misery.

It should be added at once that Jim doesn't mind too much. The fact is that he has undergone a similar transformation. On the raft he was an individual, man enough to denounce Huck when Huck made him the victim of a practical joke. In the closing episode, however, we lose sight of Jim in the maze of farcical invention. He ceases to be a man. He allows Huck and "Mars Tom" to fill his hut with rats and snakes, "and every time a rat bit Jim he would get up and write a line in his journal whilst the ink was fresh." This creature who bleeds ink and feels no pain is something less than human. He has been made over in the image of a flat stereotype: the submissive stage-Negro. These antics divest Jim, as well as Huck, of much of his dignity and individuality.

What I have been saying is that the flimsy devices of plot, the discordant farcical tone, and the disintegration of the major characters all betray the failure of the ending. These are not aspects merely of form in a technical sense, but of meaning. For that matter, I would maintain that this book has little or no formal unity independent of the joint purpose of Huck and Jim. What components of the novel, we may ask, provide the continuity which links one adventure with another? The most important is the unifying consciousness of Huck, the narrator, and the fact that we follow the same principals through the entire string of adventures. Events, moreover, occur in a temporal sequence. Then there is the river; after each adventure Huck and Jim return to the raft and the river. Both Mr. Trilling and Mr. Eliot speak eloquently of the river as a source of unity, and they refer to the river as a god. Mr. Trilling says that Huck is "the servant of the river-god." Mr. Eliot puts it this way: "The River gives the book its form. But for the River, the book might be only a sequence of adventures with a happy ending." This seems to me an extravagant view of the function of the neutral agency of the river. Clemens had a knowledgeable respect for the Mississippi, and, without sanctifying it, was able to provide excellent reasons for Huck's and Jim's intense relation with it. It is a source of food and beauty and terror and serenity of mind. But above all, it provides motion; it is the means by which Huck and Jim move away from a menacing civilization. They return to the river to continue their journey. The river cannot, does not, supply purpose. That purpose is a facet of their consciousness, and without the motive of escape from society, *Huckleberry Finn* would indeed "be only a sequence of adventures." Mr. Eliot's remark indicates how lightly he takes the quest for freedom. His somewhat fanciful exaggeration of the river's role is of a piece with his neglect of the theme at the novel's center.

That theme is heightened by the juxtaposition of sharp images of contrasting social orders: the microcosmic community Huck and Jim establish aboard the raft and the actual society which exists along the Mississippi's banks. The two are separated by the river, the road to freedom upon which Huck and Jim must travel. Huck tells us what the river means to them when, after the Wilks episode, he and Jim once again shove their raft into the current: "It *did* seem so good to be free again and all by ourselves on the big river, and nobody to bother us." The river is indifferent. But its sphere is relatively uncontaminated by the civilization they flee, and so the river allows Huck and Jim some measure of freedom at once, the moment they set foot on Jackson's Island or the raft. Only on the island and the raft do they have a chance to practice that idea of brotherhood to which they are devoted. "Other places do seem so cramped and smothery," Huck explains, "but a raft don't. You feel mighty free and easy and comfortable on a raft." The main thing is freedom.

On the raft the escaped slave and the white boy try to practice their code: "What you want, above all things, on a raft, is for everybody to be satisfied, and feel right and kind towards the others." This human credo constitutes the paramount affirmation of the *Adventures of Huckleberry Finn,* and it obliquely aims a devastating criticism at the existing social order. It is a creed which Huck and Jim bring to the river. It neither emanates from nature nor is it addressed to nature. Therefore I do not see that it means much to talk about the river as a god in this novel. The river's connection with this high aspiration for man is that it provides a means of escape, a place where the code can be tested. The truly profound meanings of the novel are generated by the impingement of the actual world of slavery, feuds, lynching, murder, and a spurious Christian morality upon the ideal of the raft. The result is a tension which somehow demands release in the novel's ending.

But Clemens was unable to effect this release and at the same time control the central theme. The unhappy truth about the ending of *Huckleberry Finn* is that the author, having revealed the tawdry nature of the culture of the great valley, yielded to its essential complacency. The general tenor of the closing scenes, to which the token regeneration of Miss Watson is merely one superficial clue, amounts to just that. In fact, this entire reading of *Huckleberry Finn* merely confirms the brilliant insight of George Santayana, who many years ago spoke of American humorists, of whom he considered Mark Twain an outstanding representative, as having only "half escaped" the genteel tradition. Santayana meant that men like Clemens were able to "point to what contradicts it in the facts; but not in order to abandon the genteel tradition, for they have nothing solid to put in its place." This seems to me the real key to the failure of *Huckleberry Finn.* Clemens had presented the contrast between the two social orders but could not, or would not, accept the tragic fact that the one he had rejected was an image of solid reality and the other an ecstatic dream. Instead he gives us the cozy reunion with Aunt Polly in a scene fairly bursting with approbation of the entire family, the Phelpses included.

Like Miss Watson, the Phelpses are almost perfect specimens of the dominant culture. They are kind to their friends and relatives; they have no taste for violence; they are people capable of devoting themselves to their spectacular dinners while they keep Jim locked in the little hut down by the ash hopper, with its lone window boarded up. (Of course Aunt Sally visits Jim to see if he is "comfortable," and Uncle Silas comes in "to pray with him.") These people, with their comfortable Sunday-dinner conviviality and the runaway slave padlocked nearby, are reminiscent of those solid German citizens we have heard about in our time who tried to maintain a similarly *gemütlich* way of life within virtual earshot of Buchenwald. I do not mean to imply that Clemens was unaware of the shabby morality of such people. After the abortive escape of Jim, when Tom asks about him, Aunt Sally replies: 'Him? . . . the runaway nigger? . . . They've got him back, safe and sound, and he's in the cabin again, on bread and water, and loaded down with chains, till he's claimed or sold!'" Clemens understood people like the Phelpses, but nevertheless he was forced to rely upon them to provide his happy ending. The satisfactory outcome of Jim's quest for freedom must be attributed to the benevolence of the very people whose inhumanity first made it necessary.

But to return to the contention of Mr. Trilling and Mr. Eliot that the ending is more or less satisfactory after all. As I have said, Mr. Trilling approves of the "formal aptness" of the conclusion. He says that "some device is needed to permit Huck to return to his anonymity, to give up the role of hero," and that therefore "nothing could serve better than the mind of Tom Sawyer with its literary furnishings, its conscious romantic desire for experience and the hero's part, and its ingenious schematization of life. . . ." Though more detailed, this is essentially akin to Mr. Eliot's blunt assertion that "it is right that the mood at the end of the book should bring us back to that of the beginning." I submit that it is wrong for the end of the book to bring us back to that mood. The mood of the beginning of *Huckleberry Finn* is the mood of Huck's attempt to accommodate himself to the ways of St. Petersburg. It is the mood of the end of *The Adventures of Tom Sawyer,* when the boys had been acclaimed heroes, and when Huck was accepted as a candidate for respectability. That is the state in which we find him at the beginning of *Huckleberry Finn.* But Huck cannot stand the new way of life, and his mood gradually shifts to the mood of rebellion which dominates the novel until he meets Tom again. At first, in the second chapter, we see him still eager to be accepted by the nice boys of the town. Tom leads the gang in reenacting adventures he has culled from books, but gradually Huck's pragmatic turn of mind gets him in trouble. He has little tolerance for Tom's brand of make-believe. He irritates Tom. Tom calls him a "numbskull," and finally Huck throws up the whole business:

> So then I judged that all that stuff was only just one of Tom Sawyer's lies. I reckoned he believed in the A-rabs and the elephants, but as for me I think different. It had all the marks of a Sunday-school.

With this statement, which ends the third chapter, Huck parts company with Tom. The fact is that Huck has rejected Tom's romanticizing of experience; moreover, he has rejected it as part of the larger pattern of society's make-believe, typified by Sunday school. But if he cannot accept Tom's harmless fantasies about the A-rabs, how are we to believe that a year later Huck is capable of awe-struck submission to the far more extravagant fantasies with which Tom invests the mock rescue of Jim?

After Huck's escape from his "pap," the drift of the action, like that of the Mississippi's current, is *away* from St. Petersburg. Huck leaves Tom and the A-rabs behind, along with the Widow, Miss Watson, and all the pseudo-religious ritual in which nice boys must partake. The return, in the end, to the mood of the beginning therefore means defeat—Huck's defeat; to return to that mood *joyously* is to portray defeat in the guise of victory.

Mr. Eliot and Mr. Trilling deny this. The overriding consideration for them is form—form which seems largely to mean symmetry of structure. It is fitting, Mr. Eliot maintains, that the book should come full circle and bring Huck once more under Tom's sway. Why? Because it begins that way. But it seems to me that such structural unity is *imposed* upon the novel, and therefore is meretricious. It is a jerry-built structure, achieved only by sacrifice of characters and theme. Here the controlling principle of form apparently is unity, but unfortunately a unity much too superficially conceived. Structure, after all, is only one element—indeed, one of the more mechanical elements—of unity. A unified work must surely manifest coherence of meaning and clear development of theme, yet the ending of *Huckleberry Finn,* blurs both. The eagerness of Mr. Eliot and Mr. Trilling to justify the ending is symptomatic of that absolutist impulse of our critics to find reasons, once a work has been admitted to the highest canon of literary reputability, for admiring every bit of it.

What is perhaps most striking about these judgments of Mr. Eliot's and Mr. Trilling's is that they are so patently out of harmony with the basic standards of both critics. For one thing, both men hold far more complex ideas of the nature of literary unity than their comments upon *Huckleberry Finn* would suggest. For another, both critics are essentially moralists, yet here we find them turning away from a moral issue in order to praise a dubious structural unity. Their efforts to explain away the flaw in Clemens's novel suffer from a certain narrowness surprising to anyone who knows their work. These facts suggest that we may be in the presence of a tendency in contemporary criticism which the critics themselves do not fully recognize.

Is there an explanation? How does it happen that two of our most respected critics should seem to treat so lightly the glaring lapse of moral imagination in *Huckleberry Finn?* Perhaps—and I stress the conjectural nature of what I am saying—perhaps the kind of moral issue raised by *Huckleberry Finn* is not the kind of moral issue to which today's criticism readily addresses itself. Today our critics, no less than our novelists and poets, are most sensitively attuned to moral problems which arise in the sphere of individual behavior. They are deeply aware of sin, of individual infractions of our culture's Christian ethic. But my impression is that they are, possibly because of the strength of the reaction against the mechanical sociological criticism of the thirties, less sensitive to questions of what might be called social or political morality.

By social or political morality I refer to the values implicit in a social system, values which may be quite distinct from the personal morality of any given individual within the society. Now the *Adventures of Huckleberry Finn,* like all novels, deals with the behavior of individuals. But one mark of Clemens's greatness is his deft presentation of the disparity between what people do when they behave as individuals and what they do when forced into roles imposed upon them by society. Take, for example, Aunt Sally and Uncle Silas Phelps, who consider themselves Christians, who are by impulse generous and humane, but who happen also to be staunch upholders of certain degrading and inhuman social institutions. When they are confronted with an escaped slave, the imperatives of social morality outweigh all pious professions.

The conflict between what people think they stand for and what social pressure forces them to do is central to the novel. It is present to the mind of Huck and, indeed, accounts for his most serious inner conflicts. He knows how he feels about Jim, but he also knows what he is expected to do about Jim. This division within his mind corresponds to the division of the novel's moral terrain into the areas represented by the raft on the one hand and society on the other. His victory over his "yaller dog" conscience therefore assumes heroic size: it is a victory over the prevailing morality. But the last fifth of the novel has the effect of diminishing the importance and uniqueness of Huck's victory. We are asked to assume that somehow freedom can be achieved in spite of the crippling power of what I have called the social morality. Consequently the less importance we attach to that force as it operates in the novel, the more acceptable the ending becomes.

Moreover, the idea of freedom, which Mr. Eliot and Mr. Trilling seem to slight, takes on its full significance only when we acknowledge the power which society exerts over the minds of men in the world of *Huckleberry Finn*. For freedom in this book specifically means freedom from society and its imperatives. This is not the traditional Christian conception of freedom. Huck and Jim seek freedom not from a burden of individual guilt and sin, but from social constraint. That is to say, evil in *Huckleberry Finn* is the product of civilization, and if this is indicative of Clemens's rather too simple view of human nature, nevertheless the fact is that Huck, when he can divest himself of the taint of social conditioning (as in the incantatory account of sunrise on the river), is entirely free of anxiety and guilt. The only guilt he actually knows arises from infractions of a social code. (The guilt he feels after playing the prank on Jim stems from his betrayal of the law of the raft.) Huck's and Jim's creed is secular. Its object is harmony among men, and so Huck is not much concerned with his own salvation. He repeatedly renounces prayer in favor of pragmatic solutions to his problems. In other words, the central insights of the novel belong to the tradition of the Enlightenment. The meaning of the quest itself is hardly reconcilable with that conception of human nature embodied in the myth of original sin. In view of the current fashion of reaffirming man's innate depravity, it is perhaps not surprising to find the virtues of *Huckleberry Finn* attributed not to its meaning but to its form.

But "if this was not the right ending for the book," Mr. Eliot asks, "what ending would have been right?" Although this question places the critic in an awkward position (he is not always equipped to rewrite what he criticizes), there are some things which may justifiably be said about the "right" ending of *Huckleberry Finn*. It may be legitimate, even if presumptuous, to indicate certain conditions which a hypothetical ending would have to satisfy if it were to be congruent with the rest of the novel. If the conclusion is not to be something merely tacked on to close the action, then its broad outline must be immanent in the body of the work.

It is surely reasonable to ask that the conclusion provide a plausible outcome to the quest. Yet freedom, in the ecstatic sense that Huck and Jim knew it aboard the raft, was hardly to be had in the Mississippi Valley in the 1840s, or, for that matter, in any other known human society. A satisfactory ending would inevitably cause the reader some frustration. That Clemens felt such disappointment to be inevitable is borne out by an examination of the novel's clear, if unconscious, symbolic pattern. Consider, for instance, the inferences to be drawn from the book's geography. The river, to whose current Huck and Jim entrust themselves, actually carries them to the heart of slave territory. Once the raft passes Cairo, the quest is virtually doomed. Until the steamboat smashes the raft, we are kept in a state of anxiety about Jim's escape. (It may be significant that at this point Clemens found himself unable to continue work on the manuscript, and put it aside for several years.) Beyond Cairo, Clemens allows the intensity of that anxiety to diminish, and it is probably no accident that the fainter it becomes, the more he falls back upon the devices of low comedy. Huck and Jim make no serious effort to turn north, and there are times (during the Wilks episode) when Clemens allows Huck to forget all about Jim. It is as if the author, anticipating the dilemma he had finally to face, instinctively dissipated the power of his major theme.

Consider, too, the circumscribed nature of the raft as a means of moving toward freedom. The raft lacks power and maneuverability. It can only move easily with the current—southward into slave country. Nor can it evade the mechanized power of the steamboat. These impotencies of the raft correspond to the innocent helplessness of its occupants. Unresisted, the rogues invade and take over the raft. Though it is the symbolic locus of the novel's central affirmations, the raft provides an uncertain and indeed precarious mode of traveling toward freedom. This seems another confirmation of Santayana's perception. To say that Clemens only half escaped the genteel tradition is not to say that he failed to note any of the creed's inadequacies, but rather that he had "nothing solid" to put in its place. The raft patently was not capable of carrying the burden of hope Clemens placed upon it. (Whether this is to be attributed to the nature of his vision or to the actual state of American society in the nineteenth century is another interesting question.) In any case, the geography of the novel, the raft's powerlessness, the goodness and vulnerability of Huck and Jim, all prefigure a conclusion quite different in tone from that which Clemens gave us. These facts constitute what Hart Crane might have called the novel's "logic of metaphor," and this logic—probably inadvertent—actually takes us to the underlying meaning of the *Adventures of Huckleberry Finn*. Through the symbols we reach a truth which the ending obscures: the quest cannot succeed.

Fortunately, Clemens broke through to this truth in the novel's last sentences:

> But I reckon I got to light out for the territory ahead of the rest,
> because Aunt Sally she's going to adopt me and sivilize me, and I
> can't stand it. I been there before.

Mr. Eliot properly praises this as "the only possible concluding sentence." But
one sentence can hardly be advanced, as Mr. Eliot advances this one, to support
the rightness of ten chapters. Moreover, if this sentence is right, then the rest of
the conclusion is wrong, for its meaning clashes with that of the final burlesque.
Huck's decision to go west ahead of the inescapable advance of civilization is a
confession of defeat. It means that the raft is to be abandoned. On the other
hand, the jubilation of the family reunion and the proclaiming of Jim's freedom
create a quite different mood. The tone, except for these last words, is one of
unclouded success. I believe this is the source of the almost universal dissatisfaction with the conclusion. One can hardly forget that a bloody civil war did not
resolve the issue.

Should Clemens have made Huck a tragic hero? Both Mr. Eliot and Mr.
Trilling argue that that would have been a mistake, and they are very probably
correct. But between the ending as we have it and tragedy in the fullest sense,
there was vast room for invention. Clemens might have contrived an action
which left Jim's fate as much in doubt as Huck's. Such an ending would have
allowed us to assume that the principals were defeated but alive, and the quest
unsuccessful but not abandoned. This, after all, would have been consonant
with the symbols, the characters, and the theme as Clemens had created them—
and with history.

Clemens did not acknowledge the truth his novel contained. He had taken
hold of a situation in which a partial defeat was inevitable, but he was unable
to—or unaware of the need to—give imaginative substance to that fact. If an illusion of success was indispensable, where was it to come from? Obviously
Huck and Jim could not succeed by their own efforts. At this point Clemens,
having only half escaped the genteel tradition, one of whose preeminent characteristics was an optimism undaunted by disheartening truth, returned to it.
Why he did so is another story, having to do with his parents and his boyhood,
with his own personality and his wife's, and especially with the character of his
audience. But whatever the explanation, the fainthearted ending of the *Adventures of Huckleberry Finn* remains an important datum in the record of American
thought and imagination. It has been noted before, both by critics and nonpro-
fessional readers. It should not be forgotten now.

To minimize the seriousness of what must be accounted a major flaw in so
great a work is, in a sense, to repeat Clemens's failure of nerve. This is a disser-
vice to criticism. Today we particularly need a criticism alert to lapses of moral

vision. A measured appraisal of the failures and successes of our writers, past and present, can show us a great deal about literature and about ourselves. That is the critic's function. But he cannot perform that function if he substitutes considerations of technique for considerations of truth. Not only will such methods lead to errors of literary judgment, but beyond that, they may well encourage comparable evasions in other areas. It seems not unlikely, for instance, that the current preoccupation with matters of form is bound up with a tendency, by no means confined to literary quarters, to shy away from painful answers to complex questions of political morality. The conclusion to the *Adventures of Huckleberry Finn* shielded both Clemens and his audience from such an answer. But we ought not to be as tender-minded. For Huck Finn's besetting problem, the disparity between his best impulses and the behavior the community attempted to impose upon him, is as surely ours as it was Twain's.

First-Person Narration in *David Copperfield* and *Huckleberry Finn*

J. Hillis Miller

David Copperfield (1849–50) and *Huckleberry Finn* (1884), among nineteenth-century English and American novels, are salient examples of masterworks of fiction written as first-person narratives. The first-person novel, in spite of Henry James's distaste for its baggy looseness, is not so much formless as a special case of fictional form. It provides a good example of the interaction of the three aspects of that form.

The distinguising characteristic of the first-person novel is the fact that the narrator in most cases coincides with the protagonist. This does not mean, however, that in this coincidence the structure of intersubjective relations usual in the third-person novel is truncated or collapsed. Rather, it takes another form. In *David Copperfield* or *Huckleberry Finn* the author attempts to come to terms with his own life by playing the role of an imaginary character who in both cases has obvious similarities to the author himself. This imaginary character, in his turn, retraces from the point of view of a later time the earlier course of his life. The interpersonal texture of both novels is made up of the superimposition of two minds, the mind of the adult David reliving his experiences as a child, the mind of Huck after his adventures are over retelling them from the perspective of the wisdom, if wisdom it is, to which they have led. In both novels the older narrator, from the vantage of a later time, watches his younger self engage himself more or less naively in relations to other people. Behind this double consciousness may be glimpsed the mind of the author himself, the Charles Dickens who is reshaping the events of his life to make a novel out of them, the Mark Twain

From *Experience in the Novel*. © 1968 by Columbia University Press. Originally entitled "Three Problems of Fictional Form: First-Person Narration in *David Copperfield* and *Huckleberry Finn*."

who is present in the irony which runs through *Huckleberry Finn* as a pervasive stylistic flavoring. This stylistic quality results from Huck's inability to understand his experiences, either while they are happening or as he retells them, as well as the reader and the author understand them. From author to narrator to youthful protagonist to other characters — the structure of *David Copperfield* or *Huckleberry Finn* is no less than that of *Pride and Prejudice* (1813), *Middlemarch* (1871–72), or *The Golden Bowl* (1904), a pattern of related minds. In both first-person novels the author may be seen going away from himself into an imagined person living in an imagined world in order to return to himself and take possession by indirection of his own past self and his own past life.

If intersubjective relations and relations of the imaginary and the real are so closely intertwined in these two first-person novels, they both provide classic examples of the incomplete circle or spiral form taken by temporality in fiction. The autobiographical novel has exactly the structure of human temporality. It is a moving toward the future in order to come back to what one has already been, in an attempt to complete one's deepest possibility of being by drawing the circle of time closed and thereby becoming a whole. But the circle of time is complete only with my death. As long as I live I cannot reach that future moment when I shall understand myself completely, coincide completely with the hidden sources of my being. Going forward in time through a recapitulation in language of his experiences in the past, the narrator of a first-person novel returns eventually back through his past to himself in the present, but at a higher level of comprehension, it may be, than he had when he began to tell his story. The insight born of the act of retelling may lead the narrator to an authentic understanding of his life, a recognition of its hitherto hidden patterns. On the basis of this recognition he may then take hold of his past life, accept it in a new way in the present, and come to a resolute decision about the future. This revelation, however, is never complete as long as the narrator lives. The spiral is endless. Huck or David could go around and around the circle indefinitely, bringing their past lives up to the present in the light of the new insight gained by the act of retelling, recapitulating their lives over and over without exhausting them or finding that a new circling repetition had brought them back to exactly the same place.

Even so, the moment of return from a journey through the past to the present, when the two levels of the narrator's mind coincide, is the crucial instant in a first-person novel. It is the moment at the end of *Huckleberry Finn,* for example, when Huck speaks in the present tense of his present situation. Having gone through his life up to the present, he sees it whole and sums up what he sees in his decision to run away from civilization. Only in this way can he escape from another repetition of his repetitive adventures, adventures which have rhythmically alternated between solitude and disastrous involvement in society, and are about to culminate, as Daniel Hoffman and others have seen, in a recurrence of the involvement most dangerous of all to his integrity: subjection to the loving-kindness of a well-meaning member of respectable society. "But I reckon I got to light out for the Territory ahead of the rest," says Huck, "because Aunt Sally she's going to adopt me and sivilize me and I can't stand it. I been there before."

At the end of *David Copperfield* David, like Huck, returns after a long looping circuit through his past to present-tense speech about the present. He too looks toward the future on the basis of a clear understanding of the past and makes a decision about that future. But how different is his state of mind! How different is his relation to other people, and how different the resolution he takes! David has experienced in childhood, like other Dickensian heroes or heroines, Oliver, Pip, Arthur Clennam, or Esther Summerson, solitude and deprivation, the lack of a satisfactory place within a family or within society. He has been "a somebody too many" "cast away among creatures with whom [he has] had no community of nature." His search through the adventures he retells is for something which will focus his life and give it substance. Throughout his experiences he is troubled by "a vague unhappy loss or want of something." He seeks something to fill the void in his heart. The novel is his "written memory," in which the adult David, as he says, "stand[s] aside, to see the phantoms of those days go by me, accompanying the shadow of myself, in dim procession." *David Copperfield,* like Thackeray's *Henry Esmond* (1852), contains many references to time and memory. These call the reader's attention to the distance between the present condition of the narrator and that of his past self. They interpose between the one and the other "a softened glory of the Past, which nothing could [throw] upon the present time." Retracing the journey which has led him step by step to the present, David seeks to find the source of the cohesive force which associates each detail with the others and gradually organizes them all, as he retells them, into the pattern which constitutes his destiny.

Is it a private power of feeling in David which does this, a subjective energy of association? The many references to the psychology of association suggest that this is the case. Agnes is "associated" in David's mind with "a stained glass window in a church," just as the image of Ham's anguish after little Em'ly runs away "remain[s]," says David, "associated with that lonely waste, in my remembrance, to this hour," or as David says of Steerforth's death: "I have an association between it and a stormy wind, or the lightest mention of a sea-shore, as strong as any of which my mind is conscious." It may be such associations which gather all the events of David's life together and make them one.

On the other hand, the source of the coherence of David's life may be a providential power which has been secretly working behind the scenes to give an objective design to his life. This is suggested by the way the sea, especially in the descriptions of little Em'ly walking on the causeway by the shore and of the storm in which Steerforth and Ham are drowned, becomes a mysterious supernatural reservoir, an external memory and prevision gathering the past and the future together in a time out of time sustained by God. "Is it possible," asks David as he remembers little Em'ly walking so dangerously close to the sea, "among the possibilities of hidden things, that in the sudden rashness of the child and her wild look so far off, there was any merciful attraction of her into danger, any tempting her towards him permitted on the part of her dead father, that her life might have a chance of ending that day?" Later Ham says "the end of it like" seems to him to be coming from the sea. In Steerforth's drowning "the inexorable end [comes] at its appointed time." During the storm which is to wash the body of Steerforth up at his feet, David feels that "something within [him], faintly answering to the storm without tosse[s] up the depths of [his] memory and [makes] a tumult in them." The personal memory within is matched by a cosmic memory without.

The conflict between these two organizing powers is reconciled when David discovers that Agnes has been all along the secret center of his life, the pivot around which everything else will turn out to have been patterning itself as the circle of his life pervaded by her presence. Agnes is the rock on which he can base himself, the person who will fill the void of his old unhappy loss or want of something. "Clasped in my embrace," says David after his marriage to Agnes, "I held the source of every worthy aspiration I had ever had; the centre of myself, the circle of my life, my own, my wife; my love of whom was founded on a rock!"

In the last chapters of *David Copperfield* the narrator returns, like the narrator of *Huckleberry Finn*, to the present. The young David and the grown-up David coincide, and the narrator speaks for his situation in the present. But far from choosing, like Huck, a solitude which is the only guarantee of an honest life, David has escaped from his solitude into society. He is surrounded by his family and his friends. Far from speaking, like Huck, in the voice of solitude on behalf of the values of solitude, he is now and has been throughout the novel as much the spokesman in the language of the middle-class community for the values of that community as any of the omniscient narrators of Victorian novels told in the third person—the narrators, for example, of *Vanity Fair, Middlemarch,* or *The Last Chronicle of Barset* (1866–67). Though the first-person novel and the third-person novel seem so different, both can become instruments by which Victorian novelists express their sense that authentic life lies in assimilation of the individual mind into the collective mind of society. In marriage to one member of good middle-class society and in a successful career as a writer of novels, like Dickens himself, David has found a way into that society.

Agnes is also for him the mediator of a heavenly light and a promise of heaven. As such, she is the means by which he sees other things and people, judging them according to universal standards. She is the way in which he will rise through society beyond society, not into the solitude of Huck's "Territory," that lonesomeness lacking any vestige of a divine presence, but into the celestial society of Heaven where he can enjoy Agnes's companionship forever.

Huckleberry Finn is an open-ended fiction. Huck's life is not over on the last page of the novel, and his ability to free himself from Aunt Sally and other agents of "civilization" remains in doubt. Dickens, on the other hand, tries to give *David Copperfield* a closed form. He presents the final sentences of David's narrative as a rehearsal of the final moments of his life. The latter will repeat in structure and content the former, realities fading then as memories fade now. The end of the book is an anticipation of the end of David's life, when there will be no more earthly future left. Henry Esmond retelling his life as an old man in Virginia, David speaks as if he were writing from beyond time, as if he were writing from the perspective of death:

> And now, as I close my task, subduing my desire to linger yet, these faces fade away. But one face, shining on me like a Heavenly light by which I see all other objects, is above them and beyond them all. And that remains.
>
> I turn my head, and see it, in its beautiful serenity, beside me. My lamp burns low, and I have written far into the night; but the dear presence, without which I were nothing, bears me company.
>
> Oh Agnes, Oh my soul, so may thy face be by me when I close my life indeed; so may I, when realities are melting from me like the shadows which I now dismiss, still find thee near me, pointing upward!

A modern reader may find it difficult to take seriously the image of Agnes "pointing upward," and Dickens himself was in later novels, most subtly in *Our Mutual Friend* (1864–65), to put in question the strategy by which the conflict between two sources of order is resolved in *David Copperfield*. The contrast between Dickens's novel and *Huckleberry Finn*, however, is a striking example of the different cultural and personal meanings which may be expressed within the form of the first-person novel. In Twain's hands the form is used in a masterpiece in the American tradition of ambiguous personal experience which goes from Hawthorne and Melville through Twain to Faulkner, Hemingway, and Bellow.

As many critics have seen, Huck speaks not the language of the community but a pungent vernacular which can thrive only outside society and is the instrument of a devastating criticism of it. *Huckleberry Finn,* however, does more than juxtapose two ways of speaking, one good and one bad. There are three kinds of language in the novel. Each speaks for a different condition of life. Existence within society is again and again dramatized as speaking a false language, playing a role, wearing a disguise, either wittingly or unwittingly perpetrating a fraud. Honest directness of speech, on the other hand, is possible only between Huck and Jim in their ideal society of two on the raft. This openness and lack of guile is the basis of poignancy in the scene in which Huck feels guilty for having fooled Jim into believing he has dreamed events which have really happened during a foggy night on the river. "It was fifteen minutes," says Huck, "before I could work myself up to go and humble myself to a nigger—but I done it, and I warn't ever sorry for it afterwards, neither. I didn't do him no more mean tricks, and I wouldn't done that one if I'd knowed it would make him feel that way." Huck's sin is to have imported into the Eden-like honesty of social relations on the raft the propensity for lies which is characteristic of life on the shore and which is, moreoever, Huck's only self-defense when he is there. The colloquial rhythm and idiom of his narrative of his life is speech of the raft society. He does his readers the great honor of speaking to them as if they were in collusion with him against the society of the shore and could share with him his true speech.

There is, however, a third language in the novel, a language belonging neither to good society nor to bad society, but to solitude. This language, and the condition belonging to it, are described in two crucial passages in the novel, one near the beginning, when Huck is still living with Miss Watson, and one just before Huck reaches the Phelps Farm and just after he has made his resolution to steal Jim out of slavery again. The same elements occur in both of these passages: an association of isolation with a state of such desolate "lonesomeness" that Huck wishes for death; so complete an openness to inhuman nature and to the presences of the dead within nature that it is as if Huck were already dead; a transformation of language from a means of communication into silence or into an inarticulate murmur, like the speech of elemental nature. The companionship of the dead is a companionship of mute and incommunicable secrets. These texts are of fundamental importance as clues to the quality of Huck's authenticity. They seem clearly related to Twain's deepest sense of his own existence:

> I felt so lonesome [says Huck in the first such passage] I most wished I was dead. . . . [T]he wind was trying to whisper something to me and I couldn't make out what it was, and so it made the

cold shivers run over me. Then away out in the woods I heard that kind of a sound that a ghost makes when it wants to tell about something that's on its mind and can't make itself understood, and so can't rest easy in its grave and has to go about that way every night grieving. I got so down-hearted and scared, I did wish I had some company.

Richard Poirier, in *A World Elsewhere,* has noted how often Huck remains speechless when he is with other people on the shore. He is often a silent watcher and listener who effaces himself as much as possible. This silence is an expression of the onlooking detachment from society which is his natural condition and which is affirmed in his resolution at the end to free himself from civilization. If Huck chooses for silence and solitude, the book allows the reader no illusion about what these mean. They mean loss of language and a kinship with the dead. In solitude one becomes a kind of walking dead man, mute spectator of life. This, however, is preferable to the intolerable falsehood of existence within society.

This stark either / or replaces finally the choice between good society on the raft and bad society on the shore which has apparently structured Huck's narrative. Twain's hesitation before the darker implications of his story may explain that descent to the style of *The Adventures of Tom Sawyer* (1876) in the last episode, so troubling to critics. The Phelps Farm episode, however, plays a strategic role in the progress of the novel. It is the final stage in a gradual contamination of the honest language of the raft by the fraudulent language of the shore. In the end, Huck must choose not between true speech and false speech, but between speech and silence.

If the temporal structure of the novel brings Huck back to himself in the present and to the need for a decision there, the terms of this decision may be identified in its intersubjective structures. In *Huckleberry Finn* Twain plays the role of Huck in order to speak indirectly to the real society of his day, just as he took a pseudonym for his writing, so confronting his readers in disguise. In this novel he is Samuel Clemens pretending to be Mark Twain pretending to be Huckleberry Finn. This playing of roles is also fundamental to the inner structure of the novel, within the mirror-world its words create. Nothing is more natural to Huck, or more necessary, than lying. Repeatedly he leaves the "free and easy and comfortable" life on the raft to involve himself in life on the shore. As soon as he meets someone there he spontaneously makes up a whole history for himself, a name, past life, present situation and intention. Only in this way can he protect Jim and that separate part of himself which can hear ghosts and understands what it would be like to be dead. When he enters society he must enter it in disguise, reborn as someone else. To be within the community is to be a fraud, to pretend to be another person, just as in writing the novel Clemens plays the role of Huck. Even the truth must be spoken by way of fiction. Significantly, Huck's final incarnation is as Tom Sawyer, for his greatest danger is that he will become, like Tom, someone who lives his life as a play and is entirely subjected to one form of fiction: the false idols of society and its romantic traditions.

This pattern of person within person, or of person confronting person by way of a disguise, is also a pattern of imaginary and real. If the novel is a fiction by which Twain attempted to approach his childhood and therefore to reach his own inmost reality, the story itself is constructed as a design of fictions within fictions—the fictions of Huck's lies and disguises, the fictional world taken from novels and historical romances within which Tom Sawyer lives, the no less fictional structures of religious and social beliefs which entrance the Mississippi communities, the frauds perpetrated by the duke and the king. In the travesties of *Hamlet* and *Romeo and Juliet* by the latter, they pretend to be a king and a duke pretending to be the famous actors Garrick and Kean pretending to be Shakespearean characters. These fictions within fictions keep before the reader a picture of interpersonal relations as a complex system of deceit within deceit in which every man lies to his neighbor.

The theme of lies leads back to the paradox of Huck's own language. As Ernest Hemingway, T. S. Eliot, and others have said, Huck's speech is the basis of the book's authenticity. He uses a rich vernacular idiom, couched in indigenous American rhythms, vocabulary, and syntax. His speech grows out of the way of life of a people in a place, and therefore is rooted in reality in a way no abstract language can be. At the same time the novel is full of demonstrations of the hollowness of the language spoken by people around Huck. This is most apparent in the vigorous satires of religious language, but it is also present in the satire of Southern romanticism in the references to Sir Walter Scott and *Lalla Rookh* (both names of steamboats in the novel). A similar theme is expressed in the imprisonment of the Grangerfords and Shepherdsons in linguistic molds which keep their absurd feud going from generation to generation. To belong to Mississippi Valley society is to be unable to speak the truth, to use one form or another of a fantasy language which justifies the greatest cruelties and injustices—slavery, economic exploitation, and the arrogant self-righteousness and psychological cruelties practiced, in Twain's view, in the name of Protestant Christianity.

Though Huck's language is a speech within the community speech, one based partly on the folklore and linguistic vigor of children and Negroes, nevertheless it has grown out of the community language and remains part of it. If it has drawn its strength from its source, it must share also the weaknesses of its origin. Huck's style comes from the popular culture of the Mississippi, but the novel is the exposure of that culture by way of its imitation in its own words. This use of the destructive power of imitative language reveals the silent presence of Twain behind Huck, of the lonesome and silent Huck behind his participation in his culture.

When Huck speaks he too gets caught in the speech patterns of his society. This is apparent in the irony of those many places where the reader can glimpse Twain judging Huck, deploring his enslavement to a false rhetoric. An example is the famous passage in which Huck, in response to a question about whether anyone was killed in a steamboat explosion, says, "No'm. Killed a nigger." The poignant ambiguity of the crucial text in which Huck decides to rescue Jim from slavery lies in the fact that he is forced to express his decision in the language of the culture surrounding him. He must use religious and social terms which reverse Twain's judgment of good and bad in the situation. Worse yet, he is forced to experience the feelings appropriate to the rhetoric of the language he must use because he has no other. As long as he is within society he remains trapped in its language. However he acts, his actions are defined in the community's terms.

Twain and his readers may see in Huck's resolve a heroic act of moral improvisation, an intuition of the truth like that described in W. E. H. Lecky's *History of European Morals from Augustus to Charlemagne* (1869), a book Twain admired. Such a reading sees in Huck the courage to act in accordance with an intuitively perceived moral truth even though it goes counter to the rules of a bad society. Huck, however, does not see it that way at all. He sees his decision to free Jim as the victory of his innate evil over the good teaching of society. It is a conscious choice of damnation. To him it is not the creation of a just moral order in place of the evil one supported by society. His decision to "take up wickedness again" is reprehensible defiance of community laws defending religious right and the sanctity of private property. His act is not a "yes" in obedience to a higher ethical law but a "no" to the yes of a community which he continues to accept. "I was a trembling," says Huck, "because I'd got to decide, forever, betwixt two things, and I knowed it. I studied a minute, sort of holding my breath, and then says to myself: 'All right, then, I'll *go* to hell.'"

Even if Huck succeeds in freeing Jim, this freedom is still a social condition. As the concluding episode of Tom's "evasion" of Jim shows, Jim is as much subject to the sham of his society when he is free as when he is a slave. Only complete isolation is freedom. This is the meaning of the absurdity of Tom's freeing Jim when he is already legally free. Free man or slave, he is still enslaved, like Tom, Aunt Sally, and the rest, by the linguistic and cultural patterns of his society. To negate these is still to remain within them, and so to affirm them indirectly. Whenever Huck speaks he is necessarily subject to this inexorable law. To speak at all he must speak lies, not only because his situation forces him to deception, disguise, play-acting, but because the language of his community is inevitably the instrument of lies. The truth cannot be spoken directly in it, as Huck proves in the soliloquy of his decision to rescue Jim. The choice Huck faces is therefore between false language and no language at all. And this corresponds to the choice between participation in a false society and an isolation from other people which is like death. Society is always imaginary. Solitude is the way to the real. Huck's final resolution, his final integrity, is a choice of lonesomeness and the silence which goes with it: "[S]o there ain't nothing more to write about, and I am rotten glad of it, because if I'd a knowed what a trouble it was to make a book I wouldn't a tackled it and ain't agoing to no more." Then follows his decision to "light out for the Territory ahead of the rest."

To explore in a given novel temporal, interpersonal, and representational structures will lead to an identification of the specific shaping energy which generates form and meaning in the novel in question: the reaffirmation in *David Copperfield*, against alternative possibilities, of a traditional transcendentalism, or the rejection of society and its languages which in *Huckleberry Finn* prepares for the more overt nihilism of Satan's scorn for the "moral sense" in *The Mysterious Stranger* (1916).

Huck's Ironic Circle

Michael J. Hoffman

Twain's Huck Finn extends the implications of the Realist impulse into a unique mode of narrative presentation by employing a vernacular narrator of remarkable descriptive capabilities. Huck Finn sees, feels, smells, and hears everything, and although he often understands very little of what he perceives, he nonetheless speaks in a voice that is obviously "telling it like it is." Having dropped all the pretensions that informed much of Hawthorne and Melville's rhetoric, Twain, using Huck as his narrator, develops an almost perfect instrument for puncturing, through irony, many of his era's dominant illusions.

Huckleberry Finn has been badly misunderstood. It is not a novel about a boy's moral awakening, not a polemic against slavery, not a book about good instincts being stronger than an evil society. In those ways Huck Finn has been overestimated and his creator underestimated. It is now commonplace to lament that the book is best during the center section on the river and that Huck's stature diminishes in the passages dominated by Tom Sawyer. There is no question that Tom Sawyer overshadows Huck when they are together. The prose and the narrative structure are more controlled during the middle two hundred pages. But neither Huck nor the moral dilemmas he has to face is understandable without the opening and closing episodes. For Twain has created an elaborate ironic structure that demands that the reader be taken in by his initial perceptions of Huckleberry Finn. The most important task of Realism was to destroy illusion. It is important that the reader be deceived, so that what happens to Huck later on will shock him into seeing that the problems posed in the book are unresolvable

From *The Subversive Vision: American Romanticism in Literature.* © 1972 by Michael J. Hoffman. National University Publications, Kennikat Press, 1972. Originally entitled "Realism as Vision and Style."

either in fiction or in life. He must not reject those parts of the novel that displease him or whitewash the ending into a demonstration of Huck's essential goodness, thus robbing Twain of his bite and his character of most of his fascinating complexity.

— The dynamic theme throughout *Huckleberry Finn* is the unresolved dialectic between the moral responsibility of the individual and the morality of the society in which he moves and against which he must function. In *Huck Finn* a body of implied assumptions about property, human life, and human behavior is accepted without question by most of the "regular" people who live in the book's fictional country. To be "moral" in this environment is to act according to the community's legislated and unstated ethical codes, regardless of innate instincts or emotions. But underlying Twain's portrayal of Huck is the convention that the morally responsible person acts according to his best instincts and to what *he* feels is right, regardless of what society thinks. Twain presents the first part of his dialectic directly through the inhabitants of his fictional South and the second by implication through a character who lacks the verbal tools needed for properly understanding the moral dilemmas to which he is subjected. The struggle can never be resolved because Huck does not know which side he is on. His upbringing has taken place far enough outside the society to maintain the sweetness of his natural instincts, but enough within it for him to have a "conscience." Huck *believes in* society and its repressive sanctions; at no point does he ever condemn the operations of the social order. Twain condemns them by implication, but Huck assumes that the shibboleths of property and propriety are self-justified. Ironically, Huck sees himself as a kind of outlaw next to Tom Sawyer, who was "brung up" right. Huck has never learned the good and proper ways of behavior, and he can therefore not expect any better behavior from himself. Whenever he breaks one of society's rules—such as setting Jim free—Huck knows he is wrong. The reader knows he is right, but Huck does not.

Since *Huck Finn* is a novel and not a tract, Twain introduces a brilliant literary device to complicate the moral issues and involve the reader in a constant dialectic with Twain the author and Huck Finn the narrator. This device is the deadpan storyteller, whom Henry Nash Smith has described as growing out of the frontier humorist who never cracks a smile at his own stories. Twain carries it a step farther, creating a character who not only does not smile at his own jokes, but does not even know they are funny.

Because the stage comedian faces his audience directly, his listeners know his straight face to be a pose. But through the medium of the printed word and the conventions of written narrative, the writer is at a further remove from his reader and can thus play with the narrator and sit behind him pulling the strings.

Huck Finn has no sense of humor. The fun in the book is all Twain's. All of Huck's remarks have a double edge: on one side Huck's seriousness, and on the other the underlying humor of implication that belongs to Twain. This ambiguity flatters the reader, too, because much as he may admire Huck, he knows that the reader is really a lot smarter than Huck. The reader is, indeed, as smart as the author.

To complicate matters further, Huck almost never makes a moral judgment. He is a magnificent observer, and it is a constant marvel how much he is able to notice and describe in his precise colloquial diction. But he never condemns any of the things the reader and Twain know to be morally reprehensible. In this sense Huck fulfills a Realist ideal by being the detached observer who sees everything and lets the facts speak their own message. The irony experienced here is that Twain judges by implication but never lets Huck make direct statements in support of what the author really feels.

By contrast, Tom Sawyer functions as the perfect representative of his society, made somewhat more palatable to the reader than are the adults because he is the conventional "bad boy." Although mischievous, he accepts without conflict the instinctive and intellectual values of his society. His boyish revolt takes the conventional forms of forming robber bands and running away, but they are only games to Tom, and it is understood that he will eventually become a pillar of the community who will remember with great nostalgia how he "cut up" when he was young. In the opening pages Tom forms his robber band. Huck Finn has finally sickened of the Widow Douglas's "sivilizing" ways and has left the respectable household in old rags to take up residence once again in his "sugar-hogshead." Huck says he "was free and satisfied. But Tom Sawyer, he hunted me up and said he was going to start a band of robbers, and *I might join if I would go back to the widow and be respectable. So I went back* " [italics added].

Two items are of interest here. The first is the obvious contrast between a robber band and the requirement that its members be "respectable." Tom Sawyer could never contemplate being a robber if it meant living permanently outside the law, although Huck can empathize even with murderers. Playing robber is a sufficiently conventional boy's game. But, second, Huck immediately follows Tom's lead and returns to the life he dislikes. It must be remembered that even though he finds "sivilization" personally uncomfortable, he never condemns it. In Tom, Huck sees everything that is admirable in a boy who has the right upbringing and "a character." The passage quoted occurs at the very beginning, yet readers often display surprise when Huck assiduously follows Tom's lead at the end. Since Huck's self-esteem is so low, since he can say of himself, "I was so ignorant and so kind of low-down and ornery," the reader should not be outraged when Huck does Tom's bidding. The irony is that the very elements Huck admires so strongly in Tom lead the reader through unmistakable implication to conclude that Tom is an unmitigated ass. But then, the reader is smarter than Huck.

All of Tom's behavior follows either a social or a literary model—which is exactly how society wants it. If all experience is controlled by codes and models, it is impossible for someone to step in with nothing but his instincts and intuition and act according to private morality. Spontaneity is unpredictable, and neither society nor its representative, Tom Sawyer, can tolerate the spontaneity of Huck. Tom's scheme for setting Jim free is the conventional literary medievalism of his time, and when Huck introduces his more efficient and simple ideas for getting Jim out, Tom accuses him of not wanting to do things "regular." Although Huck is occasionally out of patience with Tom, the worst he has to say is that Tom is "full of principle." He accepts the fact that his own ideas, although better, do not have the requisite style that only someone "brung up to it" can have.

For Twain and most of the Realists society is defined by precisely its emphasis on style and role-playing to the exclusion of the unpredictable. Social behavior is a vast complex of games and unexamined assumptions. In Twain's South property is an unquestioned imperative, and the designation of anything as property, be it inanimate or black, grants an inviolable sanctity to the owner. Huck has been trained enough to know this; he knows, for instance, that when he is working to free Jim, he is doing wrong. His socially trained conscience constantly overpowers his feelings, to the extent that twice in the book Huck actually decides to turn Jim in. It is in the name of property that he feels most guilt and waxes most moralistic. Jim confesses to Huck on the raft his aspiration to hire an "ab'litionist" to steal his wife and children out of slavery. "It most froze me to hear such talk," Huck says. "Here was this nigger which I had as good as helped to run away, coming right out flat-footed and saying he would steal his children—children that belonged to a man I didn't even know; a man that hadn't ever done me no harm." In Huck's socially trained eyes the recipient of this injustice is the property owner. What right has anyone to steal another man's property, even if the "property" is his own wife and children?

All the institutions in a society cooperate to maintain its prevalent standards. It is almost a commonplace since Marx (one of the most important of all Romantic thinkers) to characterize the law as the guardian of the status quo and to see it, not as the disinterested protector of all, but as the tool of those in power. Whether or not Twain was so sophisticated in his thinking, Tom Sawyer, society's golden-haired boy, gives the following rationalization for violating property rights:

It ain't no crime in a prisoner to steal the thing he needs to get away
with, Tom said; it's his right; and so, as long as we was representing
a prisoner, we had a perfect right to steal anything on this place we
had the least use for, to get ourselves out of prison with. He said if
we warn't prisoners it would be a very different thing, and nobody
but a mean ornery person would steal when he warn't a prisoner.

What marvelous legalism; how well Tom has learned his lessons.

As social institutions, both Sunday School and Church lend their weight to
protecting the divine right of property. Huck's skeptical pragmatism constantly
undercuts religion, but the finest use of this kind of irony occurs the second
time Huck contemplates turning in Jim. The Duke and King have just sold Jim
to the Phelpses, and Huck is morally ambivalent about whether to write Miss
Watson and turn in Jim or whether to steal him from slavery. His head is filled
with pulpit rhetoric before he makes his famous decision to go to hell, but the
lines that follow show how strongly Twain indicts all of society's institutions
for sanctioning slavery. A voice inside Huck keeps saying,

"There was the Sunday School, you could a gone to it; and if you'd
a done it they'd a learnt you, there, that people that acts as I'd been
acting about that nigger goes to everlasting fire."

Huck knows, without realizing the irony, that had he gone to Sunday School
more often, he would have had the social code ingrained in him, with little
possibility of his making a mistake or becoming involved in problems of conscience about which he would have to make an unaided moral decision. Religion, like all other social institutions (the nineteenth century realized increasingly that the Church was a social institution), protects property and the
powers behind the status quo.

Aside from indicting social institutions for supporting a corrupt morality,
Twain also demonstrates the power of a culture's overall assumptions to corrupt
even the "good" members. Mr. Phelps is an obviously good and pious man,
who seems to be totally without viciousness. A lay minister who has built his
own chapel, he preaches (without pay) for the neighbors. He runs a house that
the Lord has rewarded with prosperity, in which all blessings are shared generously. But he tries assiduously to return the slave Jim to his owner for a supposed $200 reward. Although he chains Jim to his bed in a dark shack, he feeds
him well and even prays with him. When someone like Phelps, a truly good
Christian in most of the best senses, places property values before humanity, it
is clear how deeply the corruption is rooted.

The doctor who comes to treat Tom's bullet wound also shows a deep
infection with the same diseases. Basically a good man, he is so concerned with

protecting slave property that he will not leave Jim alone with the wounded Tom while he goes to fetch aid, for fear that Jim will run for his freedom—this is after Jim has remained selflessly by Tom's side for several days. The doctor's prejudice in behalf of property (he would surely never admit to being a racial bigot) prevents him from thinking logically, although he has enough fellow feeling to commend Jim to the townspeople as a "good nigger"—in return for which they promise to stop "cussing" him. Jim's selfless behavior in standing by Tom cannot be judged by the same standards applied to a white man's actions. Property and people are not the same.

Twain finds it just as insidious that society rewards style more than substance and that the typical mode of social behavior is the game—behavior acted out according to elaborate and unquestioned rules. For Tom Sawyer everything is a game. In human relations he reduces people to pawns on a chessboard. Even though he knows on arriving at the Phelpses' that Jim has been set free by Miss Watson's will, Tom is happy to keep him a slave for a while in order to play his elaborate masquerade of setting Jim free. For Tom style is more important than any other consideration, and he will violate other human beings continuously in order to follow the rules. Thus, with Huck's complicity, he puts Jim through a series of outrageous tortures. Huck's instincts tell him that Tom is wrong in doing so, and his pragmatic sense tells him that Tom's literary machinations are inefficient, but his "conscience" knows that Tom is right in his style although morally wrong in wanting to set free a slave. Huck does go along with Tom, willing to be an outlaw but unwilling to violate the proper sense of style and incur his friend's disapproval. On a seemingly harmless scale, this is a perfect imitation of adult behavior in that adults do almost nothing but play games.

Colonel Grangerford is the Southern aristocrat par excellence. He has the typical honorific title, dresses in white linen (prefiguring Twain's later uniform?), and maintains a household in which all the traditional amenities are observed, from gracious hosting to keeping a stable of slaves to religious piety and the ownership of traditional American bric-à-brac. He is an admirable figure in all respects, except for being head of a family that has for more than thirty years continued a feud with the Shepherdsons—another aristocratic Southern family—that is utterly bloody, inhumane, and mindless. It is an elaborate game with unquestioned rules. No one knows or cares how it began. When Huck asks Buck Grangerford about the meaning of the feud, he is answered with impatience. The feud is an established mode of behavior—indeed, a social institution—and it makes no difference how it began or what it means. Grangerfords kill Shepherdsons, and Shepherdsons kill Grangerfords. Each side has a real respect for the other; but the other side is distinctly the enemy. Like that of any other institution, the feud's main life force is self-perpetuation. Twain has presented a model of wars as they are begun and sustained.

He would no doubt have included the Civil War in this category; a feud, like a war, is a game. But to call it a game is not to belittle its consequences, since in playing it, people are constantly killed. The only difference between adult games and those of children is that adults play for keeps; it is a matter of degree. Twain poses a problem that is central to the book and to the whole Romantic tradition. How can one, for long, live in and accept a society without playing its games? And having played them, how long can one remain in such a society without becoming permanently infected with its "morality"?

To add poignance and complexity to the question, Twain counterpoises against his society an individual who, for matters of personal survival, tries to escape it. Huck has to leave, not just because he hates "sivilization," but because Pap has locked him up and is beating him. Huck's feelings about "sivilization" are quite complex. Although society "cramps" him and he longs for his sugar-hogshead, he still has a great respect for the people who have "made it." He even adapts quite well, although slowly, to going to school and living with the widow.

> At first I hated the school, but by-and-by I got so I could stand it. . . . So the longer I went to school the easier it got to be. . . . The widow said I was coming along slow but sure, and doing very satisfactory. She said she warn't ashamed of me.

Huck has a strong need to please others. Later, when he turns in the robbers on the reefed *Walter Scott* and thus saves the life of one of them, he also thinks of how it would please the widow:

> I wished the widow knowed about it. I judged she would be proud of me for helping these rapscallions, because rapscallions and dead beats is the kind the widow and good people takes the most interest in.

The irony here is Twain's, not Huck's. Huck wants badly to please good people like the widow, although he wishes to have as little to do with them as he can. Even though Huck has at this point escaped successfully from society, he nevertheless cannot escape from the need to please the guardians of the order.

The truth is that Huck is not a genuine primitive; that role is reserved for his father. Toward the beginning, when Huck is with Pap, they catch part of a log raft that is adrift on the rising river—"nine logs fast together."

> Anybody but pap would a waited and seen the day through, so as to catch more stuff; but tht warn't pap's style. Nine logs was enough for one time; he must shove right over to town and sell.

The true primitive, like the aristocrat, does not postpone gratification. Waiting is a middle-class characteristic. Immediate gratification, that drink right away, is all that Pap worries about. It is Huck who understands postponement and who notices his father's primitiveness.

Huck shares the middle-class beliefs in the rights of property, postponement of pleasure, and the necessity to please others. What he has retained of his father's primitiveness is an impatience with clothes and fancy housing, an intolerance of manners and uncomfortable customs (sitting still on Sundays, going to Church, and attending school), a mistrust of cant (although a belief in it), and an intuitive sense of social types (he sees through the undertaker at Peter Wilks's funeral) and games—although he almost always sees the fault as being his and not society's. It is this peculiar mixture that makes Huck's character so extraordinarily complex and Twain's overall point so difficult to isolate.

On the raft Huck has the illusion that he has finally escaped from the repressive sanctions of his society and can be "free and easy." Here he and Jim can together shed their clothes and go naked. But their action amounts to more than Leslie Fiedler's implications of homosexual miscegenation, even at its most latent. The later nineteenth-century impulse toward Realism was more than a literary method. It was an effort to shed the overriding mediating visions that had grown up since the Renaissance to replace the dying Christian ideology. From the Enlightenment through the Transcendentalist movement there had been a number of attempts to locate a source of meaning and identity either in the empirical world or in an almost Neoplatonic spiritual realm. *Moby-Dick* can be read as a brutal rejection of Transcendental pantheism, although in it Melville still retained the Transcendentalist style. As a later product of the same impulse, *Huckleberry Finn* is written in the spare prose that has come to be associated with "realism." The new ethic is based on the direct confrontation by the individual with the world of fact, image, immediacy. Meaning is to be discovered neither in the perceiving consciousness nor in the world, but in the meeting of the two—both stripped naked. Contrasting the views of nature in Twain and Whitman, it is clear that nowhere does Twain attach the "mystical" significance to the external world that Whitman in his Transcendentalist overview must do. Huck often finds the world marvelous, but *for itself,* and the rest of the time the reality outside himself is simply an arena in which Huck must constantly attempt to solve the problem of being his own man.

What better way of dramatizing the world and the self in naked confrontation than by stripping Huck and Jim of their clothes? Both Carlyle and Thoreau claimed that clothes were the emblems of social roles. The roles endemic to both Huck and Jim are those of free man and black man, master and slave. But stripped of their clothing on the river, floating free of landed social sanctions, the only relationship possible between them is that of two men in mutual confrontation, without the mediating vision of society to dictate their behavior. Their nakedness makes possible the constant empathy, highest of all Romantic ethical virtues, that flows between Huck and Jim. Indeed, it shows how, in special circumstances, the hard fact, the specific image, will triumph over the mediating vision of the social code. When Huck decides to do the "right thing" and turn Jim in to Miss Watson after Jim has been sold by the Duke and King, his thinking, as Henry Nash Smith has shown, takes on a kind of pulpit diction. The voice of religion tells him that "the plain hand of Providence" is "slapping me in the face" and "there's One that's always on the lookout." Thereupon he thinks about the Sunday School and then kneels down to pray—a conventional way of dealing with problems of morality. But his socially trained conscience is not clean, and he realizes he "can't pray a lie." He does the "right" thing and composes the note to Miss Watson; before he goes to post it, however, he thinks awhile and prepares himself to pray again, this time with a clear conscience. But his memory plays a trick on him. He recalls his trip down the river with Jim, the black *man.* He recalls the moonlight and the storms and their "floating along, talking, and singing and laughing." He remembers how Jim "would always call me honey, and pet me, and do everything he could think of for me"; and after that he can neither pray nor turn Jim in, but must now "decide, forever, betwixt two things." He decides, of course, to go to hell, to opt for the life of the "criminal," at least in the eyes of his society— whose values *he does not reject.*

What has made possible the decision that Huck knows is immoral and that the reader knows to be highly moral is that the hard fact, the unmediated world Huck has discovered with Jim on the raft, has overcome the mediating vision, the ideology of society. Here is Twain's major moral point: The only way to overcome the manifestly evil customs of organized society is to strip down the self to face the world and other human beings directly. One must look clearly beyond the self and confront whatever is out there.

Twain has complicated this seemingly standard nineteenth-century literary morality with an irony that has been constantly misunderstood. The rest of the book shows that, although the highly moral state Huck achieves in his decision to go to hell is an ideal for the individual, it is also, like most ideals, impossible to maintain. Huck's falling off from this step of almost Transcendentalist goodness is not Twain's failure of vision, but his further feeling that the forces of society are stronger than the individual's will or his ability to maintain a constant naked confrontation with the world.

The highest moments of Huck's friendship with Jim occur on the raft away from the landed community; here they have no responsibilities to anything but themselves and their own survival. This state, however, cannot last. No one can live outside the social order indefinitely. The first prefiguring of this implication comes with the invasion of the raft by the Duke and King. As con men, they bring on board enough of the grasping venality of the land to show that they are really a part of landed values carried to an extreme. Society has followed Huck and Jim even out on the river, giving a first instance of the true inevitability of the social system.

The King and Duke operate by turning stock responses against the sheep of society. At the revival meeting the King uses conventional religious emotions to fleece the congregation. At Pokeville they both exploit the townspeople's thirst for the salacious in order to take them over. In Peter Wilks's town they manipulate the standard attitudes toward death and mourning to con the dead man's family out of his fortune. Through these role-players par excellence the book conducts its most savage indictment of the social order, although Huck never really condemns them and Twain does so only by implication. And yet, even though the two outrageous but lovable rascals finally get their comeuppance, Huck's sympathies go out to them as he sees them tarred and feathered and ridden out of town on a rail. His instinctive empathy is much stronger than any sense of righteous indignation—a social luxury and an emotion about which Huck knows little. The townspeople's brutality reflects the corruption of society as much as does the behavior of the King and the Duke.

The absolute surprise, however—even though the Duke and King are something of a preparation—is Huck's complicity in Tom Sawyer's outlandish scheme to free Jim. How could Huck, whose morality has been so patently demonstrated, engage in such an action? The truth is that he could have acted in this way all along had the circumstances been right. He has never condemned society or condemned slavery, he has always admired Tom Sawyer disproportionately and patronized blacks (even Jim on the raft), and he has not really been changed by his experiences on the river. This is not a *Bildungsroman,* and Huck Finn has not undergone a moral transformation. It is wrong to insist that he has.

Huck *does* love Jim. But it is only possible for him to feel the emotions for a "nigger" that he might feel for anyone else because he and Jim have left the scene where their interaction was controlled by the socially imposed roles of master and slave. Nonetheless they both carry with them their inbred attitudes. Jim never forgets that he is a "nigger" and that Huck is white. Huck constantly patronizes Jim in his thoughts, saying that you can't teach a "nigger" anything or that Jim is pretty smart "for a nigger." He does not understand that a black man can feel about his family the same way white people do. When Jim mourns the loss of his wife and children, Huck comments, "I do believe he cared just as much for his people as white folks does for their'n. It don't seem natural, but I reckon it's so." Twain is, of course, implying that black people have feelings, but Huck cannot really believe it, much as he likes Jim.

At the end Jim is reduced almost to a parody of the ever-faithful, long-suffering, mindless, and stupid darky. This reversal has disturbed many readers, who insist that Jim is more noble than Twain finally permits him to be. But once again, it is a matter of circumstances. Jim can show great nobility when he does not have to play the slave. Once, however, he is returned to an environment in which the role is forced on him again, he reverts to his lifelong training. Even on the trip down the river Jim has not lost his slave traits. His well-developed sense of inferiority is demonstrated by his stated willingness to accept more abuse from white men than from black and by the pleased surprise in his voice when he states that Jack, Huck's slave at the Grangerfords', is "a good nigger and pooty smart."

It is with the friendship of Huck and Tom, however, that Twain makes his major ironic point about how little, if at all, Huck changes. What Huck admires most about Tom is his sense of style, for it is style that shows the degree of a person's adaptation to his role. Because Huck is so lacking in social self-esteem, he can admire someone like Tom, who is so comfortable and self-assured. Throughout the book Huck invokes Tom Sawyer at key moments, claiming either that Tom would really have done something up with style or that he would have been proud of the style Huck manages to work into a particular action. Huck is never completely his own man, and he never shakes the behavioral model of Tom Sawyer. The only difference on the raft is Tom's absence. It is therefore not surprising that on Tom's return Huck reverts to a kind of discipleship; he has been a disciple all along.

The first shock occurs when Huck tells Tom he is going to try to steal Jim. Tom says enthusiastically, "I'll *help* you steal him!" Huck responds with consternation:

> Well, I let go all holts then, like I was shot. It was the most astonishing speech I ever heard—and I'm bound to say Tom Sawyer fell, considerable, in my estimation. Only I couldn't believe it. Tom Sawyer a *nigger stealer!*

It doesn't matter that he, Huck Finn, is setting free a slave. *He* was brung up wrong; because he knows no better, he has opted for the outcast life; he has chosen to go to hell. But Tom Sawyer is another matter.

> Here was a boy that was respectable, and well brung up; and had a character to lose; and folks at home that had characters; and he was bright and not leather-headed; and knowing and not ignorant; and not mean, but kind; and yet here he was, without any more pride, or rightness, or feeling, than to stoop to this business, and make himself a shame, and his family a shame, before everybody. I *couldn't* understand it, no way at all. It was outrageous.

Tom is everything Huck thinks he himself is not. Therefore Huck is annoyed with Tom for doing something as lowdown and ornery as Huck might do. It is Huck's reaction to Tom's willingness to free Jim that, more than anything else, shows his attitude toward property and slavery to be unchanged.

Being a pragmatist, however, Huck is willing to accept the help and leadership of someone who has know-how and style. He welcomes the help of the young man with the proper literary models. Even when Twain is most ironic toward Tom, Huck never sees through the ridiculousness of his schemes except to say that he is a little "full of principle." Further, Huck can accept Tom's help because he is back on the stable land and is no longer troubled by the immediate problems of survival. He can become a little boy again and imitate adult games because with the Phelpses he is safe. This so-called "regression" is troubling; but Huck has always reacted in this way around Tom, with whom his adventures can be make-belive and never have to be "real." Tom sits on Huck's native instincts, and the latter's ironic veneration for society's ways forces him to obey its rules when he is safely within its bosom. Tom's rules are society's rules, his games a model of society's fantasies, his hypocrisies an image of the only ways society thinks it can be truthful to itself.

Throughout all the incredible machinations of setting Jim free, Huck is never easy about why Tom is helping him. Indeed, his very security in knowing that society is right is shaken. Huck is finally set at ease when he discovers that Tom knew all along Jim was a freed man and that Tom is therefore not guilty of violating the sanctity of property. That Tom is guilty of hypocrisy and willfully violating another human being is not apparent to Huck; these are accepted ways to act in the society in which he was raised. Notes Huck:

> and so, sure enough, Tom Sawyer had gone and took all that trouble and bother to set a free nigger free! and I couldn't ever understand, before, until that minute and that talk, how he *could* help a body set a nigger free, with his bringing-up.

There should no longer be any doubt as to Huck's feelings about slavery and the will of society. Nor do these events violate what has gone before, because Huck's attitude is both prefigured and continuously exposed.

At the end Tom suggests that the two of them "get an outfit, and go for howling adventures amongst the Injuns, over in the Territory, *for a couple of weeks or two*" [italics added]. Like all good citizens, Tom Sawyer contemplates antisocial activities only when they are strictly limited in time. In other words, for Tom, to escape from civilization is only another conventional game—he does not really mean it. However, in the last lines of the book, Huck's famous words are:

But I reckon I got to light out for the Territory ahead of the rest, because Aunt Sally she's going to adopt me and sivilize me and I can't stand it. I been there before.

For Huck the escape is real because civilization cramps him; he does not play games with his freedom. The irony of the book has now come full circle, in that Huck has not rejected society's standards at all. He simply feels personally inconvenienced by such aspects as school, Sunday School, and clothes. But Huck still believes just as strongly that society is right, and he shows that the only way to maintain even the limited freedom that he really wants is to run away. On the last two pages, then, Tom invites Huck to a good middle-class boy's game while Huck desires strongly to escape the constricting amenities of the community.

And the same relationship obtained on the first page of the book. It is part of a pattern established right from the start. Neither character has changed. This irony has proved almost impossible for readers to accept. And yet Twain's point would be so much weaker without it.

Twain has shown that society will almost always bend the individual to its ends and turn him into a cog in the wheel, a role in its collective make-believe. For him the only way to avoid being destroyed by civilization is to maintain a kind of radical innocence and to be, like Huck, an ironic outcast. But Huck does not realize that there is irony in his actions. He does not consciously perceive anything wrong with society. Otherwise he might have turned out like the Duke or the King. Because Huck's instincts are so often at variance with what he knows to be right (and the reader knows to be wrong), he is really two people. But more completely, Huck acts according to the situation, one way within the social order and another outside it. It is therefore important that Twain both begins the novel within society and ends by returning to it. The middle section is the most attractive because, at least in part, it is the most seductive. In it Twain can, in a series of episodes, point out all the ills of a society and can show how attractive life is when lived outside it. And yet he knows that escape is only temporary, that sooner or later one must return and make his peace with the established order. Can one, however, return without being destroyed or turned into just another social cretin?

Twain never answers the question. The novel as the greatest realistic and ironic art form has never found it its task to answer questions; it has always satisfied itself with raising them. Twain poses a problem, posits a possible solution, gives it partial success, and then shows the failure of even a distinct possibility. There are no facile solutions to complex problems. To believe anything else is to believe an illusion.

Huckleberry Finn experiences direct confrontation, but he cannot shake the mediating vision that sees society and its values as instrinsic to the very nature of the universe. The innocent individual can function quite well with a minimum of social stress, but something more is needed for him to combat the day-to-day trials of living in a community. Huck's failure shows that man must learn how to reenter society even though he has found it necessary to leave for a time: if he does not learn, the social order has its own ways of retrieving him. But Twain does not tell how to make this reentry and retain wholeness as individuals. To give such an answer would be to promulgate an illusion, and that would be to abandon the Realist's basic responsibility.

Huckspeech

Neil Schmitz

Due allowance being made for the sounds of language, writing aloud *is not phonological but phonetic; its aim is not the clarity of messages, the theater of emotions; what it searches for (in a perspective of bliss) are the pulsional incidents, the language lined with flesh, a text where we can hear the grain of the throat, the patina of consonants, the voluptuousness of vowels, a whole carnal stereophony: the articulation of the body, of the tongue, not that of meaning, of language.*

ROLAND BARTHES, *The Pleasure of the Text*

My souls, how the wind did scream along! And every second or two there'd come a glare that lit up the white-caps for a half a mile around, and you'd see the islands looking dusty through the rain, and the trees thrashing around in the wind; then comes a h-wack! bum! bum! bumble-umble-um-bum-bum-bum-bum—and the thunder would go rumbling and grumbling away, and quit—and then rip comes another flash, and another sockdolager. The waves most washed me off the raft, sometimes, but I hadn't any clothes on, and didn't mind.

MARK TWAIN, *Adventures of Huckleberry Finn*

First, then, to close the two words: Huck's speech, written as spoken, talked into prose, becomes Huckspeech, a new style in the humorous mode. It signifies, in whichever text it appears, *Ursprache,* Original Language, First Presence of Self-Consciousness, the almost-voice of an almost-child, wary innocence, an almost-innocence. It is written at once in the vulgate, as *common* speech, and in the vernacular, which it assumes in the purest sense of its original meaning, as the homely

---

From *Of Huck and Alice: Humorous Writing in American Literature.* © 1983 by the University of Minnesota. University of Minnesota Press, 1983.

speech of home-born slaves. That is, Huck speaks a familiar speech spoken all around us at all times, the speech of the illiterate, the speech of the preliterate, of the poor, and of children, which, in its proper place, is charming, but which is also, in other places, in the schoolroom, in courts of law, inadequate, wrong, the excluded language of the vulnerable, the ignorant, the innocent. It is emotionally rite and socially rong, a paradox Huck enters when he begins to write his story down, as he would speak it, and the mistakes appear. Speech wrongs writing. Writing wrongs speech. In *Huckleberry Finn,* to use Hosea Biglow's happy phrase, but in a double sense, Huck tries on a "noo soot of close," and the fit is often tight, often smothery. Huck's speech is thus written, miswritten, and becomes Huckspeech, Mark Twain's raft style.

To keep us straight before Huck's funny *felix culpa,* Mark Twain, the sophisticated composer of Huck's naive style, makes certain we perceive his authority as a linguist. There are several dialects spoken in the style: "the Missouri negro dialect; the extremest form of the South-Western dialect; the ordinary 'Pike-County' dialect; and four modified varieties of this last." It is his last word in *Huckleberry Finn,* this brief *Explanatory* which assures us that Huckspeech, which might otherwise seem a loose approximation of the idiom, is in fact worked, composed, *written.* "The shadings have not been done in a haphazard fashion, or by guess-work; but pains-takingly, and with the trustworthy guidance and support of personal familiarity with these several forms of speech." So we are to appreciate the music of the style, the exactitude of its intonation, but for Huck, who writes it, speech, *his* speech, is simply the expression of his feeling, the only language he has, and bereft of aesthetic value. It is the speech of the slave, the abject, those outside, and Huck has had sufficient schooling to know that from the inside, to know at least the meaning of *sivilize.* Jim clarifies the term for him, but so, too, does Pap Finn, who will knock the book from Huck's hand, and curse him for his "starchy clothes." It is a nervous tic, this first and last misspelling, *sivilize.*

In *Tom Sawyer,* where Huck is still very much the pig son of his swinish father, Huck's speech is regarded as a seduction, and prohibited. Why are you late? the schoolmaster demands of Tom, and when Tom confesses that he stopped to talk to Huckleberry Finn on the way to school, the teacher is aghast. " 'You—you did what?' 'Stopped to talk with Huckleberry Finn.' " A severe whipping immediately follows. Huck is "cordially hated" by the mothers of St. Petersburg, who dread his influence, who fear contamination. Pap Finn sleeps with the hogs in the tanyard, and Huck himself sleeps in "empty hogsheads," is the "son of the town drunkard," is "idle, and lawless, and vulgar, and bad," is Pap's piggish boy. Huck's speech is necessarily unclean. The character described in *Tom Sawyer* has indeed a lively career elsewhere in contemporary manuals of sexual hygiene where he appears as the archetype of the evil companion. When J. H. Kellogg (who would later discover the cornflake) cites the thirty-nine "Suspicious Signs" of self-abuse in *Plain Facts For Old and Young* (1879–86), the listing reads as an index of Huckish traits: lassitude, love of solitude, shambling gait, use of tobacco, easily frightened, sleeplessness, confusion of ideas, unchastity of speech. In *Huckleberry Finn* the Widow Douglas and Miss Watson throw the appropriate books at Huck, the Bible and the Speller, and Huck appropriately judges their "book-larnin" with the wry skepticism of his "mother-wit." It is the Writing Lesson, a familiar routine in American humor, and Huck is typically recalcitrant, but the issue of the exchange is problematical. The lesson is learned. In *Tom Sawyer* Huck's illiteracy is the sign of his freedom; he does not go to school, he does not submit to the arbitrary imposition of rules, he possesses the license of speech, but he has come in from out the wet in *Huckleberry Finn,* and he does learn to write. Huck even becomes a good student, winning a "little blue and yaller picture of some cows and a boy" for "learning my lessons good." The lesson is learned, and in writing, looking outside back at the river, at the raft, Huck discovers the magnitude of the lesson.

The simple distinction of vulgar speech and polite writing that constitutes the "funattick" play of humorous writing in the Jacksonian period, a distinction that juxtaposes the stiff, self-conscious, professorial writing of a Parson Wilbur and the rough yarn of Sut Lovingood's unruly speech, is exquisitely complicated in Huckspeech, confused. Perched in writing, barely in writing, Huck is torn between the two systems of value, the two discourses, between Jim and Tom, between Pap and the Widow, and it is the perfect anxiety of this conflict that makes the style of *Huckleberry Finn* different, a transformation. Huckspeech emerges from the humorous style, the style of Lowell and Harris, of Artemus Ward and Josh Billings, overtakes it, reveals its phunny phonocentrism as unfunny alienation, and this is the pain, the hurtful brick, that hits Huck at the start of his narrative, that makes the project of its humor doubtful. In another sense, contextually, the style reflects in its tension Mark Twain's own anxieties as a writer and a humorist. It is, after all, the Mark Twain of *Tom Sawyer,* that affable whitewasher, who is immediately summoned into Huckspeech, judged a liar, and then forgiven. *Huckleberry Finn* effectively begins with a critical reading of *Tom Sawyer,* with a certain knowledge of its mystification.

> You don't know about me, without you have read a book by the name of "The Adventures of Tom Sawyer," but that ain't no matter. That book was made by Mr. Mark Twain, and he told the truth, mainly. There was things which he stretched, but mainly he told

the truth. That is nothing. I never seen anybody but lied, one time or another, without it was Aunt Polly, or the widow, or maybe Mary. Aunt Polly—Tom's Aunt Polly, she is—and Mary, and the Widow Douglas, is all told about in that book—which is mostly a true book; with some stretchers, as I said before.

Huck has read the book, examined this humorous representation of the adventures of boyhood, and seen what it leaves out, what it evades. His critique of Mark Twain's writing is the critique of the pilot in "Old Times." Writers 'modify' the truth. What, then, does Mark Twain stretch, 'modify,' in *Tom Sawyer*? Things. "There was things which he stretched, but mainly he told the truth." Huck understands the necessity for 'white' lies, having witnessed in the great world the prevalence of deception, and yet *this* narrative is reliable. So Huck begins, asserting the difference of his text. So Mark Twain begins, setting Huck free. And the first thing Huck does, at his safe distance, is to give his liberator the lie. It is a hazard, the withdrawal of authority. The humorist is excluded, and so, too, is the work of his humor, stretching the truth. If we are to look at *Huckleberry Finn* as a humorous text, we must then distinguish its humor from the humor of *Tom Sawyer*. Mark Twain's functional shift from third to first person signifies a corresponding shift in his sense of humor. Huck is alone in the liberation of his plain style. It is a large irony, and a severe task. Everything that is repressed in *Tom Sawyer,* or humorously manipulated, returns in *Huckleberry Finn,* amplified—these "things," but by the end of Huck's opening passage, having invoked the truth as his criterion, Huck is without the defenses of humor, bare to his experience.

The humorist, of course, is still there in the text, but he appears in the diminished figure and reckless activity of Tom Sawyer. He is present not as the happy resolver of difficult situations, as the complicit liar, but as a part of the problem, the source of Huck's confinement. That humor which professes the innocence of Tom's play speaks falsely in Huckspeech. It can only speak through its favored creature, Tom, and what an awful constraint it is, to have Tom as a mouthpiece. As we have seen, Huck begins his story by carefully separating himself from the fiction of *Tom Sawyer,* and yet Tom is immediately present to lure him back into the humorous world of make-believe, the safe world where the Dark-Man is always at last locked up, sealed off, killed. We might again ask, after Freud, who speaks in Tom's discourse. It would seem to be the consoling Superego, urging substitution, displacement, sublimation, the Good Genie, except that in Huckspeech the superegotistical voice is fatally compromised. What the humorist says here inevitably appears as contradiction, the sign of danger, not security. "But Tom Sawyer, he hunted me up and said he was going to start a band of robbers, and I might join if I would go back to the widow and be respectable." It is the humorist's consummate trick: no villainy in this villainy, no wrong in this wrong. The overt question of Huck's adventure is whether he can humorously forgive himself, having actually overturned the categories of right and wrong. Within the intersubjective drama of the style another question emerges, whether Huck can forgive Tom's sense of humor.

So Huck begins inside the risk of narrative; so Mark Twain begins an inside narrative. A double set of brackets incloses the proper text of *Huckleberry Finn,* the first and last *sivilize* (the unregenerate expression of preliterate consciousness) and Tom's first and last usurpation of Huck's writing, these reimpositions of motive, moral, and plot, the 'literary' play of his fictions. In Huckspeech Mark Twain appropriates the structure of the humorous style, but not to yield its humor—to question it. The style is placed over the earlier style, like a semi-transparent overlay, and what we see is the subtle disparity, a telling incongruence, how this routine, seemingly so like the other routine, is still different, elaborated. Just as the Widow Douglas teaches Huck about Moses and the Bulrushers, so Huck, after the 'adventure' on the wrecked steamboat, teaches Jim about the wisdom of Sollermun. Mark Twain draws upon familiar forms in both exchanges, on the Writing Lesson and its corollary number in the minstrel show. Here the learned throw books at the unlearned, Parson Wilbur hurls Goldsmith and Pope at Hosea Biglow, and the Interlocutor's stiff question gets a supple response from Mr. Bones. In *Huckleberry Finn* Tom is the principal book-thrower, brick-hurler. " 'Do you want to go to doing different from what's in the books, and get things all muddled up' " he demands. " 'Don't you reckon that the people that made the books knows what's the correct thing to do?' " When Huck teaches Jim about Sollermun, he repeats the lesson of authority he has learned. He throws the book at Jim, but promptly it comes back. " 'Doan talk to me 'bout Sollermun, Huck, I knows him by de back.' " What indeed is the mastery of the Book, the dead letter, over Life? What book will explain to Jim the master / slave relationship, the right of kings to have harems, the right to separate children from their parents? Jim easily deflects Huck's presumption of authority, but he is at the mercy of Tom's books, those romances of captivity and escape, which immure him. Each consequent turn of the exchange in the narrative lessens its humor and increases its seriousness. Within the brackets, the closure of Huck's writing, is the river, the raft, Jim, the scene of Huck's initiation. The knowledge he gains there is played against the lesson he learns in the Writing Lesson, and Jim is the teacher, and Jim's lesson is the hardest.

II

The constant crisis in *Huckleberry Finn* is the urgent issue of direction, of destination. What does Huck want? Where is Huck going? The question of direction is also the crisis of *Huckleberry Finn,* since each literal and thematic interruption of the narrative constitutes a significant rift in the text, and each rift is an ordeal for Huck, an ordeal for Mark Twain. What is the course of *Huckleberry Finn* as a humorous text? Its composition, begun, deferred, written in spasms of energy, indicates the imaginative stresses Mark Twain experienced as a practicing humorist. Any close reading of *Huckleberry Finn* must take into account the bricolage of its construction, its crooked seams, its changing conception of itself. Mark Twain wrote roughly the first sixteen chapters in 1876, breaking off just as Huck and Jim struggle toward Cairo, the missed point of Jim's liberation; then the bulk of the middle section in 1879–80, including Huck's soliloquy on the truth of Jim's meaning; and finally in 1883 the controversial ending. The truth of Jim's meaning, which figures so largely in the politics of *Huckleberry Finn,* which keeps Huck from writing the bad letter, passes through these three sections as the Brick of bricks. Jim is hard perdurable pain, the spook of guilt, unresolved, omnipresent, that figure of suffering which is outside the authority of writing, which, when written (by Tom), can only be wronged. Because Huckspeech is barely in writing, a styleless style 'open' to speech values, to the idiom, to slave talk, Jim 'speaks' in the style, but, as we shall see, mostly between Huck's lines. He is a large brick, indeed the largest brick in American life, and thrown right through the book.

Bang. The task of the humorist, we know, is to wring the bliss of love from the pain of the brick. This transformation is what humor is for. And indeed Huck never ceases to love Jim, never ceases to love Tom. Yet the humorist is not in *Huckleberry Finn* to work this transformation for us. The style excludes him. He can only speak through Tom's foolery, as the poorest of whitewashers, the unfunny humorist. The burden given to Huck is therefore too heavy for his simple discourse to bear, too big for this low style. In the *Biglow Papers,* it will be remembered, Lowell "feared the risk of seeming to vulgarize a deep and sacred conviction" and created Parson Wilbur to convey in appropriate discourse his principled attack on slavery. For Mark Twain, however, the very limitation of the low style is opportune. Such is the beauty of Huckspeech as a humorous style, that it continually breaks down, fails to generate pleasure from unpleasure, fails to find the necessary fiction. Up a tree, Huck watches the Shepherdsons shoot at the wounded Grangerford boys, one of whom is a child. "It made me so sick I most fell out of the tree. I ain't agoing to tell *all* that happened — it would make me sick again if I was to do that." Huck can only endure the slaughter, see it as it is, suffer it. "I ain't ever going to get shut of them — lots of times I dream about them." And how, humorously, to get around the throbbing headache of what to do about Jim. Bricks fly in Huckspeech, and hit, and hurt, a fact which makes Huck long for the comfort of Tom's 'style,' for Tom's manipulative ebullience. Tom will resolve the problem of Jim for us, give us the right ending, but the ending is written in Huckspeech, and Huckspeech is always fated to get this humorous resolution rong. So Jim's ordeal, Huck's guilt, this big brick, comes through the text, misses Tom, who doesn't even see it, slips through Huckspeech, and perversely strikes us as a problem.

Jim is the wrench, the sudden turn, that takes *Huckleberry Finn* out of one humorous mode into another, one not yet mapped or charted, from simple to serious humor. It is a question of direction, a question that could not occur to Tom, but which is for Huck the only question, intricate, delicate, deep, and to which, paradoxically, the text itself is the response. Conjoined on the raft, by the raft, headed South to get North, Huck and Jim are going in different directions. Jim is going to Cairo, into the socio-political world, into *Uncle Tom's Cabin*, or Francis Grierson's *The Valley of Shadows*, where he will find work, try to make sufficient money to buy his family out of bondage, perhaps even associate with Abolitionists. "I owns myself," Jim declares on Jackson's Island, "en I's wuth eight hund'd dollars." Miss Watson's perfidy has taught him to calculate, and Cairo, the free state, is Jim's destination. This is not where Huck wants to go, and it slowly dawns on him, gradually comes to him, that Cairo is where he is going. "We would sell the raft," he reports in Chapter 15, "and get on a steamboat and go way up the Ohio amongst the free States, and then be out of trouble." The "miserableness" of this scheme is soon apparent. With his goal in sight, Jim loosens up; he is free in his speech; he talks openly about his intentions; he speaks as a determined and clearheaded adult, and Huck, alarmed, suddenly beholds their difference. Jim is self-present in his speech, in himself, for himself, and this is not funny, familiar slave talk, nor does this Jim take into account Huck's priorities, Huck's needs.

The raft is for Huck the end of his journey, the place where his "free and easy" river world is regained, but for Jim raft and river are primarily the means of his deliverance elsewhere. It is not as Huck figured it: "'They're after us!'" *They* are only after Jim. It is rather as Jim figured it: "He said that when I went in the texas and he crawled back to get on the raft and found her gone, he nearly died; because he judged it was all up with *him* anyway it could be fixed; for if he didn't get saved he would get drownded; and if he did get saved, whoever saved him would send him back home so as to get the reward, and then Miss Watson would sell him South, sure." Huck faithfully records in italics the careful and suggestive distinction Jim makes, *him,* and almost, at that point, understands *him.* "Well, he was right; he was most always right; he had an uncommon level head, for a nigger." Above Cairo Huck at last completely understands the significance of Jim's flight. The nigger mask is down. "He wouldn't ever dared to talk such talk in his life before." It is the most chilling moment in *Huckleberry Finn*, Jim's brief lapse from the "funattick" play of humorous dialect into the integrity of self-determined discourse, and the quick-freeze of Huck's heart. Here, first in his outrage and then in a single choice, the inversion of white and black, right and wrong, Huck falls from innocence.

In the same movement Mark Twain substantively changes the project of humor. Huck falls out of his humor. He looks upon the jubilant Jim with pure hatred. An ungrateful Jim is going away, and the appropriate racist remark comes promptly to Huck's mind: "'give a nigger an inch and he'll take an ell.'" Everything out there, on the Shore, in the Supplement, is self-alienating, laborious: Civilization, Writing, Authority, clocks, tight clothes, hard chairs. The supple place to which Huck has fled, this found raft, should be the opposed pastoral site, innocent, harmonious, the other-world afloat on the Simple Being of the river, good, and would be, could be, if Jim were to play his part. But just as Huck extricates himself from Tom's fiction, so Jim doesn't fit in Huck's fantasies. A runaway slave constantly living in dire peril is not a good companion for a white boy wanting to lead a free and easy life on a raft. It is a thing Huck never properly sees, that the greatest threat to his raft life, the very center of his narrative, is Jim, not steamboat or charlatan. Jim can share the raft as a domicile, as a hiding-place, but he remains apart from Huck's conception of raft life. For Jim the raft is ultimately a prison as small as the shed in which he is finally kept. He is boarded up on the raft, confined to it, and once Cairo is missed, he is nailed to it, exposed and humiliated on it. So, too, would the raft become a prison for Huck, regressive, a confinement in an earlier mode of self-absorption, if Jim were to leave it. Alone on Jackson's Island at the start of his narrative, and 'free,' Huck is quickly bored. It is truly as the beloved that Jim denies Huck the innocent play of the raft, denies him his 'adventures,' and instead draws Huck from that play into the story of his own unmitigated suffering. As the little Moses cast upon the flood, Huck must go forward into the larger, older, tragic world. So he must fall out of humor, from innocence, and sacrifice the rapture of the raft.

Et in Arcadia ego. It is Huck's line in *Tom Sawyer;* it is Jim's line in *Huckleberry Finn*. It is what they come to mean in each text, the problem of the *other* in paradise, the ignoble savage who wrongs the myth, who refuses to be written in the convenient style. A mythy haze often obscures the particularity of Huck's raft life, the subscription of Jim's problematical presence, and in his haze Huck's motives take on an impossible purity. We are easily pulled into Huck's trance, into the current of this dream, the myth of presence, the myth of origin. The style itself, Huckspeech, so like the raft in construction and motion, takes us there. Tony Tanner's reading of the myth in *The Reign of Wonder* (Cambridge University Press, 1965) is exemplary:

To get at the root significance of this feeling for the raft, for lazying, for nakedness and relaxation it is worth recalling the import of the symbolism of the Sabbath Ritual. The ban on all forms of work not only celebrates God's day of rest after the labour of creation, it symbolizes a state of harmony between man and nature, that paradisiacal state which existed before Adam brought sin and work into the world. Work disturbs the man-nature equilibrium and reveals the extent of our immersion and imprisonment; the almost immobile "rest" of the Sabbath is a temporary escape from time and process, an anticipation of the Messianic time (which is called the time of "continuous Sabbath") of true freedom, peace and harmony.

This longing for the "continuous Sabbath," as Tanner amply indicates, is everywhere in Mark Twain's writing. To get out of work and into play is Tom Sawyer's principal labor. In *Roughing It* Mark Twain lovingly describes the sumptuous leisure of a loose life at Lake Tahoe. Yet the Arcadian desire that creates the paradisiacal scene, delights in Lake Tahoe's pristine clairty, relishes languor, is looked straight through in "Old Times." The knowing pilot realizes the charm of such idyllic representation, but he can no longer take it seriously. Indeed this yearning for a "continuous Sabbath" is generally a humorous topic for Mark Twain, and disposed in contexts that show it as the illusion of travelers, the lust of tourism. For example, Mark Twain takes the raft metaphor to Germany, borrows Huck's raft revery for an imaginary trip down the Neckar, and replays it for us in *A Tramp Abroad* (1880) as a lullaby:

> The motion of a raft is the needful motion; it is gentle, and gliding, and smooth, and noiseless; it calms down all feverish activities, it soothes to sleep all nervous hurry and impatience; under its restful influence all the troubles and vexations and sorrows that harass the mind vanish away, and existence becomes a dream, a charm, a deep and tranquil ecstasy.

For the humorist the raft is now purely the implement of a myth, and so it functions in *A Tramp Abroad*, exhibiting other myths. It floats, unfurls German scenery, is the prop on which Mark Twain humorously rehashes the local river legends: "The Cave of the Spectre," "The Lorelei," "Legend of the 'Spectacular Ruin,'" "Legend of Dilsberg Castle." A grown-up Tom Sawyer at last gets to ride the raft in his style.

Yet there is a moment on this contrived sojourn when Mark Twain brings the Huckish meaning of the raft directly into view. The two gents loll on the raft, "with our sun umbrellas over our heads and our legs dangling in the water," watching naked children cavort on the passing shore.

The little boys swam out to us sometimes, but the little maids stood knee-deep in the water, and stopped their splashing and frolicking to inspect the raft with their innocent eyes as it drifted by. Once we turned a corner suddenly, and surprised a slender girl of twelve years or upwards, just stepping into the water. She had not time to run, but she did what answered just as well; she promptly drew a lithe young willow bough athwart her white body with one hand, and then contemplated us with a simple and untroubled interest. Thus she stood while we glided by.

It is a little vision, almost prurient, and it is Huck's reality, Huck's wide-eyed childish gaze that briefly meets Mark Twain's look in *A Tramp Abroad*. To be naked, to be at ease in nakedness, shy but shameless, this in part is Huck's feeling on the raft, and the luxury of the raft style. The two gents under their parasols contemplate the naked children sporting on the bank, the charm of it, the innocence of it, and then the girl "of twelve years or upwards, just stepping into the water," suddenly appears, and we look, not quite so innocently as before, at her almost-innocence, the "lithe young willow bough." Huck stands on that verge, precariously. At the start of *Huckleberry Finn* Tom summons a relapsed Huck from his "old rags" and "sugar-hogshead," routs him out of the womblike barrel, Huck's home, and drives him back with false promises into the custody of the Widow Douglas. There the "old thing" begins again, the fundamental processes of civilization: tight clothes, regular hours, proper instruction. Huck can read his destiny on his dinner plate, that simple sentence whose parts of speech are meat, potato, vegetable, each portion "cooked by itself." He knows what this "old thing" is: the suppression of instinct, the displacement of desire, division. "In a barrel of odds and ends it is different; things get mixed up, and the juice kind of swaps around, and the things go better." To be sivilized is to be sexually zoned, to be finny is to be sexually latent. A nymph at waterside. Huck's rebellion begins here, with the squirm and discomfort of his body. After supper come the books, the Bible and the Speller; declarations of right and wrong as distinct in their lesson as the segregated food on Huck's plate.

The Writing Lesson indeed takes two forms at the beginning of *Huckleberry Finn*. Miss Watson and the Widow, who have inconsistent interpretations of Providence, throw the Good Book at Huck. Tom asserts the primacy of the bad book. His pirate and robber books authorize his sadistic fantasies and give him the appropriate discourse of mastery: "whichever boy was ordered to kill that person and his family must do it, and he mustn't eat and he mustn't sleep till he had killed them and hacked a cross in their breasts, which was the sign of the band." Miss Watson's notion of Providence and Tom Sawyer's idea of Plot intersect, *Jim,* but at first it is of no matter to Huck since he alertly dodges both Good Book and bad. The lesson of each, after all, is deferral, the emptiness of the signifier. Prayer does not produce fishhooks. No genie comes when Huck rubs his lamp. Tom, who has already courted girls and stolen kisses, stands before Huck in the brightness and malice of his precocity. He tries to show Huck the power of imagination, how metaphor works, how, magically, pleasure can be conjured from nothing, the make-believe of fantasy. "Why they rub an old tin lamp or an iron ring, and then the genies come tearing in, with thunder and lightning a-ripping around and the smoke a-rolling, and everything they're told to do they up and do it." Huck doesn't understand how it works, lamp rubbing, but he thinks the mystery over, and then tries his hand at Tom's magic. "I got an old tin lamp and an iron ring and went out in the woods and rubbed and rubbed till I sweat like an Injun, calculating to build a palace and sell it; but it warn't no use, none of the genies come." Still prepubescent, metaphor-blind, Huck is too literal to take the leap into this form of symbolization, so he throws the lamp aside as "just one of Tom Sawyer's lies." It is a particular type of lie, and it reminds Huck of those he has heard in Sunday School. Miss Watson's punishing God and Tom's pleasing Genie are one and the same, and speak to a single issue: "the self-enjoyings of self-denial."

Huck stands at the verge of all this, the lessons of civilization, the confusions of puberty, quizzically looking in. He dimly understands the value of Tom's style, that it keeps Tom at a safe distance from the real, that it is a strategy, but he has not yet grasped the thesis, the determinant, of that style. The Genie of dissimulated Desire has not yet appeared in his consciousness. Tom knows how to turn broomsticks and laths into guns and swords, how to make the lamp project images, is a bustling, bristling youth, and he calls to Huck, summons Huck, to his Gang. Because Huck cannot locate the pleasure of Tom's play, he repudiates the Gang. Tom is already *there,* a reader of books, a rubber of lamps, fetching "an emperor's daughter from China for you to marry, they've got to do it," already within the cruelty of Miss Watson's guilt, within the murderous rage of the fathers (Pap Finn and Colonel Grangerford), within the confidence game of the Duke and the Dauphin. Huck is still *here,* in Huckspeech, a writing without the defenses of a 'style,' or the tolerance of humorous deception, in a pointless writing that passively floats raftwise, acted-upon, and everywhere breached by the inexplicable. What does Huck want? To evade the meaning of Tom's fiction, to get away from solicitation, whether kind or brutal, to reverse his direction. "I thought it all over, and I reckoned I would walk off with the gun and some lines, and take to the woods when I run away. I guessed I wouldn't stay in one place, but just tramp right across the country, mostly night times, and hunt and fish to keep alive, and so get so far away that the old man nor the Widow couldn't ever find me any more." Huck wants to go nowhere, and be nameless. Here, then, is the providential river. It sends him first a canoe, and then the raft.

So Huck writes, looking back on his first refusal. He is just over the margin into textuality, in this peripheral writing, still essentially *here,* recording his resistance to writing in writing. But on what principle or concept, what sense of the body, does Huck base this resistance? Out of Tom's book, where is he? To fool his swinish father, into whose cruel keep he has fallen, Huck fakes his death with pig's blood, and slips away—a not-Huck into a non-time, back to an island self. On Jackson's Island, where he is 'dead' and safe, 'free' to do as he pleases, Huck directly experiences the "continuous Sabbath" as disappointment. "No difference—just the same thing." Huck has refused to "come to time," to eat the sentence on his plate, to join the Gang, endure his father, but the plenitude of the self he hopes to recover quickly becomes the small measure of his island. "I was the boss of it; it all belonged to me, so to say, and I wanted to know all about it; but mainly I wanted to put in time." Then Jim appears, on the run, in hiding, to offer Huck the first break in the achieved tedium of his self-absorption, and everything complicates. The river, the canoe, the raft, carry him to the figurative center of his narrative, away from the lies of Miss Watson and Tom Sawyer, the supervision of the Widow and Pap Finn, and yet this center is not the place where oppositions are reconciled, the origin of good humor. It is rather the scene of Huck's severest strife, the very stage on which he is compelled to suffer, as a reluctant child, the tragedy of his culture: master/slave, white/black. Huck flees from the lie of civilization, the duplicity of its dualism, from the lie of the adult who clothes his body and conceals his desire, only to discover on the river, in Huckspeech, that the raft, the "free and easy" raft, is *his* lie.

III

The actual raft is a modest affair: "a little section of a lumber raft—nice pine planks." Always specific, Huck gives us its exact size. "It was twelve foot wide and about fifteen or sixteen foot long, and the top stood above water six or seven inches, a solid level floor." Jim builds a "snug wigwam" on the raft, and raises the level of its floor "a foot or more above the level of the raft, so now the blankets and all the traps was out of reach of steamboat waves." Inside the wigwam "we made a layer of dirt about five or six inches deep with a frame around it for to hold it to its place; this was to build a fire on in sloppy weather or chilly; the wigwam would keep it from being seen." So the found raft, a mere floor, becomes a dwelling-place raised above the water, a home with a roof and a hearth, the completion of fire. Having lived in a barrel, in the cleanliness of the Widow's house, in the squalor of Pap's cabin, in a makeshift tent on Jackson's Island, and then in a cave, Huck at last finds the peace and freedom of a dwelling-place. And the food is excellent: fish, bacon, meal, a filched chicken now and then, watermelon, mushmelon, fresh corn. The luxuries Huck and Jim add by scavenging are perfect for the contemplative nature of raft life: three boxes of "prime" seegars, a small batch of books, and a spyglass. In their abode, snug, warm, and dry, they can still feel closely beneath them, a few feet away, the large motion of the "big still river." They travel at night. A watch-light is hung to warn off steamboats. "It was kind of solemn, drifting down the big still river, laying on our backs looking up at the stars, and we didn't ever feel like talking loud, and it warn't often that we laughed, only a little kind of a low chuckle." Such is the meaningful raft Huck constructs in his narrative, plank by plank. It is the place where he dwells, where he is most present, most himself, Huck's Huck. Here for the first time he feels the rapture of intimacy, the highest meaning of dwelling, and this is the beam that holds the raft together for Huck, that makes it resemble (for us) the marriage bed Ishmael and Queequeg fraternally share in *Moby-Dick*. Huck gives us in exact detail the thingness of the raft, its dimension, its equipment, the feel of it, but all this ardent phenomenology ultimately depends on Jim's presence. What the raft means to Huck is not the meaning of the raft in *Huckleberry Finn*.

Indeed Huck's dwelling, this "snug" home, has no foundation, is not grounded. It is rather given over to the "big still river" that runs "over four mile an hour." The river sends Huck the raft and sustains Huck's life on the raft, but the river is also serial time and linear direction, history and geography. It is a relation Huck never seems to understand completely, that position on the river (above Cairo, below Cairo) determines the significance of the raft. "Take it all around," he recalls in Chapter 12, "we lived pretty high." And again in Chapter 18, writing of the resurrected raft, the post-Cairo raft, the doomed raft, Huck declares his devotion: "You feel mighty free and easy and comfortable on a raft." For Jim, who never joins Huck in these rhapsodies, the raft has meaning *only* in relation to the river. On Jackson's Island, before the actual raft appears, he has already tactically concluded that a raft is the safest way to make his crossing: "ef I stole a skift to cross over, dey'd miss dat skift, you see, en dey'd know 'bout whah I'd lan' on de yuther side en whah to pick up my track. So I says, a raff is what I's arter; it doan' *make* no track." Above Cairo, then, the raft is simply a ferry he has fixed up with Huck's help, an opportune mode of transport. His gaze is directed elsewhere, at the muddy expanse of the Mississippi, which he anxiously scans, looking for the "big clear river" that will signify the emptying of the Ohio, his destination, the point of his deliverance.

Below Cairo the raft is briefly a refuge, a relief for Jim who has been hiding in a swamp, and then the stage on which he is at once humiliated and betrayed. The geographical river, the crucial river for Jim, effectively defines the nature and extent of his discourse on the raft. Approaching Cairo, Jim is increasingly contentious in his speech, self-assertive. After Cairo, absurdly floating down river, he lapses into poignant reveries, or is silent, out of Huck's story. "'Goodness sakes,'" asks Huck, and the question is telling, "'would a runaway nigger run *south?*'"

The essential drama of *Huckleberry Finn* therefore occurs on the raft. Huck's adventures on the shore are outlying, contingent, elaborative. He is always right in these episodes, afflicted innocence. On the raft Huck is wrong, Huck falls into contradiction, Huck grapples with the issue of his identity. Here he delivers his finest soliloquy. And there are other performers on this platform, other frames of reference, other speeches. The story Huck wants to tell is the story of a chase—"They're after us!"—and bring Jim as a sidekick into the play of that fiction. So he is always quick to draw upon that dubious pronoun, *we,* and he is proud of the getaway raft. It is finally a nifty little number, trim, with all the accessories. Yet the premise of Jim's tale is the axiom of a different genre in American literature, the beginning of each slave narrative: "I owns mysef." The question for Huck is the extent to which, at the risk of his own fiction, the pleasure of the raft, he will admit into recognition the contraposed existence of Jim's story—hear it, understand it, write it. It is as well the question of the style itself, the risk of *Huckleberry Finn* as a humorous text, whether humor can know suffering without denial or deception, without motive, moral or plot. Huck clings to his idea of the raft; it is the only thing he can properly call his own in *Huckleberry Finn,* the only place where he has a sense of humor, and he clings to his friendship with Jim, which is (for him) the guarantee of the raft's goodness, the assurance of its fun. On the shore Huck is always someone else, disguised, an observer. On the raft, with Jim, he is himself: naked, supple, finny. The two values, raft life and Jim, are incompatible.

In Huckspeech, this low style which is as ramshackle and vulnerable as the raft itself, barely raised above illiteracy, Mark Twain flawlessly spells out the complication of Huck's consciousness. Huck's narrative is first breached from within, by the insistence of Jim's speech, and then commandeered from without, by the insistence of Tom Sawyer's writing, and each time he is pulled toward a fate, a form, that is a denial of his deepest desire. The familiar structure of the conventional exchange in humorous writing, that opposition of illiterate speech and literary writing, *is* the structure of *Huckleberry Finn.* Jim and Tom struggle fore and aft for the mastery of Huck's discourse, the determination of his crossing, while Huck, betimes, simply longs for a "free and easy" life, the impossible rapture of the raft. So Huck writes, and *his* subject is sacrifice. With exacting fidelity and resolution he records at the start of his text the compelling utterance of an escaped slave, the significance of Jim's recitative, and then, across rifts, beyond the raft, the evasive distortions of Tom's literary discourse, Tom's revision of Jim's tale. So the humorist traditionally constructs the exchange in American humor, speech for/against writing, Biglow/Wilbur, Sut/George, and distributes the values. But Huck does not have the stylistic resources of the humorist, the point of a stylus; he has only a clumsy steering oar, and he is too close to his material, which presupposes him, and carries him beyond the reach of his intelligence. In the *Biglow Papers* and *Sut Lovingood's Yarns* the roles of speaker and writer are cleanly distinguished, their value delineated by the "funattick" play in the text. Northern humor, Southern humor: two different versions of colloquial discourse, of its innocence, its ignorance, two different characterizations of the writer who accommodates it, and yet in both texts we remain within the simplicity of the paradigm, inside the economy of the low style. The misspelled sign is the assurance of humorous pleasure. Here, then, is Huck, caught in the middle, who loves Jim and admires Tom, going South to go North, whose dream surely is to reconcile Jim and Tom in his writing and resolve the painful issue of his direction. It is a dream that reflects Mark Twain's desire to unite in a single style the full power of an unrepressed speech with the framing activity of interlocution, to create a "free and easy" writing talked-from the alienation of writing. Huck traverses the humorous paradigm in his text, repeats its routines, misspells, is funny, illustrates Mark Twain's deepening sense of humor, but Jim's story, as Huck reports it, will not translate into Tom's fiction.

In Chapter 12, the fifth night below St. Louis, Jim begins to emerge in his difference. What is at stake is the raft itself. Huck decides to emulate Tom Sawyer and board a wrecked steamboat, the infamous *Walter Scott,* and discovers, to his surprise, that Jim is "dead against it." In the instant the raft becomes political; Huck asserts his mastery, and Jim must feel the restraint of his dependence. "Do you reckon Tom Sawyer would ever go by this thing? Not for pie, he wouldn't. He'd call it an adventure—that's what he'd call it; and he'd land on that wreck if it was his last act." We already know Jim's functional interpretation of the raft; "it doan' *make* no track"; it is for the crossing, and for nothing else. By hindsight we also know that Jim is even now, the fifth night below St. Louis, 'protecting' Huck from the knowledge that Pap, the prime reason for Huck's flight, Huck's 'death,' is dead. Jim needs the raft complicity that Huck enjoys. Each is the other's alibi. Huck does not realize this, but Jim does. His childishness, after all, is largely the product of Huck's childish point of view, which requires Jim's genial sufferance of pranks and abuse. There is another Jim beside Huck's Jim in the ample scan of Huck's writing. On Jackson's Island, before he begins the narrative of his flight, Jim momentarily considers Huck, measures him, and it is the first of a series of such meaningful glances, those wary looks tense with looking. "Maybe I better not tell," Jim says. Here, before Tom's folly, the *Walter Scott,* which has a cheap thriller going on inside, Jim balks, though his dissent is fuzzy. "Jim he grumbled a little, but give in." Huck enters the wreck, finds exactly what Tom Sawyer would find there: a band of outlaws, pistols, treachery, and in the meanwhile the precious raft is almost lost. In the succeeding chapters, as Cairo is neared, Jim's voice gets louder and plainer. A word begins to reiterate, ring, in Huck's discourse — *nigger, nigger, nigger* — and Jim will call Huck *trash.*

Each time Jim asserts his difference, Huck writes *nigger.*

Each *nigger* registers a wrench of Huck's good heart.

Once the raft is recovered, Jim carefully explains the foolishness of the stunt to Huck. He wishes Huck to understand the seriousness of his situation, and so, patiently, he places it all before him. There are different destinies, different dangers, on the raft.

> but he said he didn't want no more adventures. He said that when I went in the texas and he crawled back to get on the raft and found her gone, he nearly died; because he judged it was all up with *him,* anyway it could be fixed; for if he didn't get saved he would get drownded; and if he did get saved, whoever saved him would send him back home so as to get the reward, and then Miss Watson would sell him South, sure. Well, he was right; he was most always right; he had an uncommon level head, for a nigger.

Across *right* and *right,* Huck's grudging admission of Jim's truth, the truth of his blackness, the truth of his otherness, Huck defensively reaches for protection, promptly rings the word, "for a nigger." This *nigger* hangs at the front of the scene; at the rear is still another *nigger:* "you can't learn a nigger to argue." Yet the nigger *has* argued, and this is the sense of Huck's exasperation, that Jim has somehow messed up the scene they were to do, misread his lines, forgotten who he was supposed to be. The story of Sollermun, the master of harems, the careless sire of numerous unrecognized children, the separater of families, the master careless of life, incenses Jim. He refuses to accept Huck's explanation, to get the story straight, because he sees "down deeper" the symbolic dimension of the entire routine. Solomon is not the point, Sollermun is.

> "Doan' talk to me 'bout Sollermun, Huck, I knows him by de back."
>
> "But I tell you you don't get the point."

"Blame de pint! I reck'n I knows what I knows. En mine you, de *real* pint is down furder—it's down deeper. It lays in de way Sollermun was raised. You take a man dat's got on'y one er two chillen; is dat man gwyne to be waseful o' chillen? No, he ain't; he can't 'ford it. *He* knows how to value 'em. But you take a man dat's got 'bout five million chillen runnin' roun' de house, en it's diffunt. *He* as soon chop a chile in two as a cat. Dey's plenty mo'. A chile er two, mo'er less, warn't no consekens to Sollermun, dad fetch him!"

I never see such a nigger. If he got a notion in his head once, there warn't no getting it out again. He was the most down on Solomon of any nigger I ever see. So I went to talking about other kings, and let Solomon slide.

Huck's glance: "I never see such a nigger." Three nights above Cairo, in a dense fog, Huck paddles out in the canoe and is cut off from the raft. He finds himself in a labyrinth, a "nest of tow-heads," and the river, seemingly still, is fierce: "you don't think to yourself how fast *you're* going, but you catch your breath, and think, my! how that snag's tearing along." Huck is here, Jim is there, calling to each other through the fog, whooping, lost. In the morning the fog is gone, Huck finds his way back to the raft, and then plays his last practical joke on Jim. The scene obviously prefigures the oncoming crisis, that tight moment when Huck, again away from the raft, will be asked *the* question about the raft: *whose raft is it?* This much is certain, and the imagery stresses the meaning: white murk, labyrinth, separation, treacherous river, and yet here, too, we see, we overhear, a rhetorical Jim speaking through Huck's text. He readily accepts Huck's teasing suggestion that he dreamed the whole frightening experience of the previous night. He will, in any event, "'terpret" the dream for Huck, and the interpretation is resolutely set forth, specifically pointed. It all means, the tow-heads, the current, the whooping, that they will encounter "quarrelsome people and all kinds of mean folks, but if we minded our business and didn't talk back and aggravate them, we would pull through and get out of the fog and into the big clear river, which was the free States, and wouldn't have no more trouble." The interpretation teaches, anticipates Huck's childishness, reminds him of their direction, their destination. Huck then humorously reveals his fib.

Jim's glare: "he looked at me steadily, without ever smiling." He will not endure now, at all, Huck's play, Huck's innocence, an innocence cruelly insensitive to suffering, blind to reality, the *"real* pint," an innocence that at once evokes and predicts the innocence of Tom Sawyer. The thrust of Jim's rebuke is deep. It drives Huck back again into the role of the pig-son of the hog-father. "Dat truck dah is *trash;* en trash is what people is dat puts dirt on de head er dey fren's en makes 'em ashamed." The mean trashy figure of Pap Finn, still lively in Huck's imagination, who will reappear, dressed-up, rich and powerful, still murderous, as Colonel Grangerford, the *real* killer of Buck, Huck's unrebellious *doppelganger,* is in fact Jim's only card, his only power on the raft. His rebuke is also an appeal. Jim is not yet free of his dependence on Huck, and he will play the card twice, first as rebuke and then as appeal, anxiously singing out to Huck as he paddles forth to meet the slave catchers: "Dah you goes, de ole true Huck; de on'y white genlman dat ever kep' his promise to ole Jim." At the end of the foggy scene, stared-through, Huck is humbled. This *nigger* comes hard to him, hard. "It was fifteen minutes before I could work myself up to go and humble myself to a nigger—but I done it, and I warn't ever sorry for it afterwards, neither." The drama on the raft, of the raft, herein reaches its ultimate confrontation. Jim says *trash* and Huck, shakily, writes *nigger.*

The scene is now set for Huck's sacrifice, but what is sacrificed? Huckspeech, this humorous style so closely attuned to spoken discourse, to raw speech, hits finally the rawest of spoken words in the American lexicon, a bluff reef, and writes it rongly again and again, *nigger, nigger.* "Conscience says to me, 'What had poor Miss Watson done to you, that you could see her nigger go off right under your eyes and never say one single word?' " This potent misspelled word, this disfiguring signifier, effectively sinks the raft, wrecks it, because *nigger* is intransitive. Huck's dream of the raft as a safe refuge from the pains of maturity, as a familial unity, a home with a hearth, cannot accommodate it. Nor can the style, Mark Twain's desire for a "free and easy" writing, a writing released to the current of consciousness, afloat on its copious energy, attuned to its articulation. "Next you'd see a raft sliding by, away off yonder," Huck writes, after Cairo, "and maybe a galoot on it chopping, because they're most always doing it on a raft; you'd see the ax flash, and come down—you don't hear nothing; you see that ax go up again, and by the time it's above the man's head, then you hear the *k'chunk!*—it had took all that time to come over the water." That indeed is the ardor of Huckspeech: writing related to perception as raft is to river, but there is a *nigger* in this idyllic picture, in the writing, and he is now immensely unspoken.

A double irony therefore occurs in Chapter 16, to Huck on the fast foggy river in the 1850s, to Mark Twain writing as a humorist in 1876. Huck's fiction is about to be displaced, his power dispersed, his role altered. The story he wanted to tell is rapidly running into the reality of a slave narrative, which Jim has already sketched out for him in his analysis of the dream. They are going to meet some quarrelsome and mean folks, he tells Huck, and Huck must learn to be quiet, not to talk back, not to aggravate the mean folks. He must learn to behave, in brief, like a nigger. In Chapter 16 Jim gives Huck an ampler prospectus. Jim is going to work, live frugally, "never spend a cent," then buy his wife and children out of bondage, and if that is not possible, steal them. The quick racism of Huck's response: "give a nigger an inch and he'll take an ell" only rationalizes a deeper wrong Jim has dealt him. *There is no mention of Huck in this part of Jim's story.* "Here was this nigger which I had as good as helped to run away," writes displaced Huck, "coming right out flat-footed and saying he would steal his children—children that belonged to a man I didn't even know; a man that hadn't ever done me no harm." It is a shaft, received full by Huck. He looks upon a Jim who is *not* a nigger and sees a man who surely cares for him, but who has his own family, his own children, his own notion of a home and hearth, who is literally dancing to get off the raft, which will be sold, *his* raft, Huck's raft. A man that hadn't ever done me no harm. The only power Huck exercises over Jim, so he realizes ("I just felt sick"), is his ability to wrong him, to give him hurt, to rip that happy world (in which Huck has no place) from Jim just here on the threshold of it. He can turn Jim in.

It is the finest moment in *Huckleberry Finn,* this moment when Huck, who has been so grievously hurt, prepares to give it, to give hurt back. "But I says, I *got* to do it—I can't get *out* of it." The innocence lost here is considerable. Huck sees, without realizing it, that *nigger* is a misnomer, an empty signifier, an alibi. It is not just against his cultural identity as a white Southern boy that he must act, but against the direct pulse of his feeling, the pull of his own desire. He must give up a part of his world in order for Jim to gain his. Whose raft is it? "Is your man white or black?" He's white, Huck responds, he's my father. What next? Nineteenth-century American humorists had made phoneticized spelling, written dialect, the veritable sign of humor: *natur, nater, alluz* the *noo soot of close.* It indicates the space of humor. Josh Billings's *Allminax* immediately tells us what it is. But the cardinal term Mark Twain selects from dialect to center the play of his humor is *nigger,* a bristling word, and it turns irrevocably the play from simple to serious. Huckspeech is a version of niggerspeech, what the vernacular originally means, the speech of the slave, the discourse of the victim. He's white, says Huck, reestablishing his conception of Jim. Later, near the end of his narrative, again on the raft, Huck will attempt to relocate Jim as a *nigger* in his writing, and does indeed write "runaway nigger Jim," but the term won't hold the fullness of Jim's humanity, and Huck remembers the instance in Chapter 16, the choice he made above Cairo. Yet for Mark Twain, writing in 1876, after Cairo, as it were, *nigger* lies heavily in *Huckleberry Finn,* a large and suspicious reef in a text that was to be humorous. The first significant rift in the manuscript occurs here; Cairo is missed, the raft destroyed, Huck and Jim plunged to the bottom of the Mississippi. Mark Twain stops work on the project. The raft briefly reappears in *A Tramp Abroad,*

Mark Twain sits on it telling German tall tales, and then it is again destroyed, steered into a bridge where, flimsy contrivance that it is, it goes "all to smash and scatteration like a box of matches struck by lightning."

IV

Across this rift, the wreckage of the raft, the ending of *Huckleberry Finn* begins. Everything that now happens in the narrative is by way of descent, and haunted by the illogic of the wrong-way passage. The raft is refloated, but its pleasures are now geographically compromised, and it is easily usurped by the duke and the king, bad actors who appropriate the raft as *their* stage, their dwelling. Huck and Jim, whose play is finished, become supernumeraries in this play, extras. It is the raft again that generates the theme of displacement in *Huckleberry Finn,* that infers once more, in a new context, the subliminal horror of being lost to, in, someone else's mad fiction. *Tom Sawyer* and *Huckleberry Finn,* Leslie Fiedler suggests in *Love and Death in the American Novel,* can be seen "as the same dream dreamed twice over, the second time as nightmare," but the "nightmare," properly speaking, is Jim's, and it clicks on as soon as Cairo is passed. The question in this part of *Huckleberry Finn* is the exclusion and relative silence of Jim. All the dangers that befall Huck along the river are resolvable by the simple devices of picaresque fiction: disguise, the apt and convenient lie, flight, the future of the next day, the next episode, except one—the dull, distant, constant pressure of Jim's presence, the exhaustion of his story. Mark Twain's composition of this phase of *Huckleberry Finn* is intermittent, improvisational: mid-October, 1879; mid-June, 1880; the summer of 1883. It is truly a rough piece of steering. For Huck's question is his question: what to do about Jim, whether to go over this reef or around it. The looming spectre of Aunt Rachel in "A True Story," the black speaker whose slave narrative explodes the anecdotal frame of the dialect sketch, reappears in *Huckleberry Finn,* differently, as in a nightmare. She is dressed in a "long curtain-calico gown," and wears a "white horse-hair wig," and her duty here is to howl.

What sense of humor comprehends such pressing pain? In Huckspeech Mark Twain at length turns upon the devices of humorous writing and wrongly writes the illusion of rong riting. That is, Huckspeech at the end of *Huckleberry Finn* is the scrutiny of a humorous resolution, Huck's unblinking eye turned once more upon Tom's metaphors. The whitewashing begins in Chapter 24 on the raft. The duke does exteriors; Tom's specialty is interiors. Through this single ring, this sole utterance, *nigger,* Mark Twain draws, wonderfully convoluted, at once the psychological, the historical, and the stylistic complication of his text. The duke "dressed Jim up in King Lear's outfit—it was a long curtain-calico gown, and a white horse-hair wig and whiskers; and then he took his theatre-paint and painted Jim's face and hands and ears and neck all over a dead dull solid blue, like a man that's been drownded nine days." Huck watches all this, the face, the hands, the ears, the neck, horrified, outraged. Truth floods Huck's discourse in the final sequence of *Huckleberry Finn,* and it makes a high demand of our own sense of humor, of what we can know and humorously suffer. We know how Jim's story is told: "Well, you see, it 'uz dis way. Ole Missus— dat's Miss Watson—she pecks on me all de time, en treats me pooty rough, but she awluz said she wouldn't sell me down to Orleans." Now it must be written:

1. Here a captive heart busted.
2. Here a poor prisoner, forsook by the world and friends, fretted out his sorrowful life.
3. Here a lonely heart broke, and a worn spirit went to its rest, after thirty-seven years of solitary captivity.
4. Here, homeless and friendless, after thirty-seven years of bitter captivity, perished a noble stranger, natural son of Louis XIV.

Similarly the letter of betrayal that Huck writes, but does not send—"Miss Watson your runaway nigger Jim is down here two mile below Pikesville and Mr. Phelps has got him and he will give him up for the reward if you send. *Huck Finn*"—this scarce, scant note, must be rewritten and delivered.

Don't betray me, I wish to be your friend. There is a disprate gang of cutthroats from over in the Ingean Territory going to steal your runaway nigger tonight, and they have been trying to scare you so as you will stay in the house and not bother them. I am one of the gang, but have got religgion and wish to quit it and lead a honest life again, and will betray the helish design. They will sneak down from northards, along the fence, at midnight exact, with a false key, and go in the nigger's cabin to get him. I am to be off a piece and blow a tin horn if I see any danger; but stead of that, I will BA like a sheep soon as they get in and not blow at all; then whilst they are getting his chains loose, you slip there and lock them in, and can kill them at your leasure. Don't do anything but just the way I am telling you, if you do they will suspicion something and raise whoopjamboreehoo. I do not wish any reward but to know I have done the right thing.

UNKNOWN FRIEND

It is the only extensive piece of Tom's actual writing that we have in either *Tom Sawyer* or *Huckleberry Finn,* and everything falls through it, eerily true: the double-talk of duplicity, the judas-sheep, the tinhorn, that thick rich vein of egotistical innocence that allows the ego to have it both ways at once, to be crook and cop. "I am one of the gang, but have got religgion and wish to quit it and lead a honest life again, and will betray the helish design." It is the voice of Conscience in the lowest humorous case, wanting to do the right thing. Mark Twain now restages the routine of the Writing Lesson, which Huck, flinching, has already barely passed through, and Jim becomes the subject. Writing is his agony because he cannot write, because he can only be written and pass into the power of writing. "Jim said it would take him a year to scrab-ble such a lot of truck onto the logs with a nail, and he didn't know how to make letters, besides; but Tom said he would block them out for him, and then he wouldn't have nothing to do but just follow the lines." All the while Jim is written, his story translated into an escapist romance, Huck hears his protest, his outcry: "I doan' *want* none . . . I can't *stan'* it . . . I doan' *want* no sich glory." The idiocy of Tom's script stretches before us — elaborated, drawn-out, painful props; excruciating lines; and as for ink, "the best authorities uses their own blood. Jim can do that." Everything in this script is idiotic, and true, what must be suffered. The slave narrative will be written, stylized, was so written, and the letter of betrayal will be sent, was sent. Tom, after all, has Jim's bill of freedom in his back pocket, the proclamation of his emancipation. And the question was then, and still is (1883) "what it was he'd planned to do if the eva-sion worked all right and he managed to set a nigger free that was already free before?" In Tom's idiocy, a hard logic lies.

Huck rites *nigger* rongly, Tom writes *nigger* properly: "crest, a runaway nigger, *sable*, with his bundle over his shoulder on a bar sinister: and a couple of gules for supporters, which is you and me; motto, *Maggiore fretta, minore atto.*" A sane surreal vision of the actual shines through Tom's usurpation of *Huckleberry Finn*, through Mark Twain's burlesque of romantic fiction. How to liberate the *sable* man who has been emancipated, free the already free? How to make certain that when he enters the 'free' world, he will accept the terms of his freedom? Huck protests, Jim protests; neither of them understand the nuances of such a deliverance. For all his extravagance, Tom has an acute mastery of the primary codes in his culture, so he will insist, he will demand, he will rewrite and revise, to get it right, this necessary script, "because he's [Jim] going out *right,* and there ain't going to be no flaws in his record." The motto he assigns to Jim's Coat of Arms, *Maggiore fretta, minore atto,* means "the more haste, the less speed." This motto, slightly revised, will reappear in Ralph Ellison's *Invisible Man.* It is the sense of a letter of recommendation, a letter of betrayal, that black Dr. Bledsoe sends to white Mr. Emerson, which the Invisi-ble Man naively carries north with him, sealed: "Please hope him to death, and keep him running." Like Tom Sawyer, Emerson likes to think of himself as Huck, likes to play Huck Finn. He says of his friendship with Bledsoe, "With us it's still Jim and Huck Finn. A number of my friends are jazz musicians, and I've been around." Yet Emerson reveals his true character when he arranges for the Invisible Man to take a job in a paint factory where the prime slogan is "'If It's Optic White, It's the Right White.'" "Our white is so white," Ellison's humiliated protagonist is told, "you can paint a chunka coal and you'd have to crack it open with a sledge hammer to prove it wasn't white clear through." Ellison's 'humor' in this part of *Invisible Man* hits like a sledgehammer. The same clarity obtains at the end of *Huckleberry Finn,* but it is diffused through the sweet intonation of Huckspeech. There is Jim, skirted, painted blue, and here is Jim, whose tears Tom will weep, whose passion Tom will feel, whitewashed, become the natural son of Louis XIV, a *sable* man, a colored gentleman.

So Mark Twain humorously writes an unforgivable ending to *Huckleberry Finn.* He does not avoid Tom Sawyer's evasion. It is extended before us, lunatic, necessary, fated, the full paradox of the Reconstruction run through the routine of the Writing Lesson. All the dichotomies of the humorous style: speech / writing, presence / absence, slave / master, low style / high style, even rock-piling / bricklaying, are caught up darkly in this ultimate funny exchange. To please the moralist, *Huckleberry Finn* ought to end in Chapter 31 (before Tom's reappearance) where Huck, still on the privileged space of the raft, but alone now, solitary, bereft, makes a last effort to see (lose) Jim as a *nigger.* Huck will never lose the functional usage of *nigger,* which generally designates, but he has lost the opprobrious usage, the *nigger* that means *I do not recognize you,* and which hits like a thrown brick. His soliloquy juxtaposes heart and conscience, but this is a speech that simply poses an august silence. Huck looks straight at the "everlasting fire" that awaits those who confuse their terms, right and wrong, who flunk the Writing Lesson, and yet before God, that austere Judge, the supreme Teacher, he cannot bring himself to say, meaningfully, the re-quired word, *nigger.* It is a submission his whole being refuses. Huck suddenly has a speech defect; he stutters indeed like Moses on the Mount, refusing: "I was trying to make my mouth *say* I would do the right thing and the clean thing, and go and write to that nigger's owner and tell where he was; but deep down in me I knowed it was a lie—and He knowed it." Here Mark Twain fig-uratively embraces Huck, forgives him. It is a scene that is humorously satis-fying for us, if not for Huck, and yet as a resolution in the narrative of *Huckle-berry Finn* it is obviously inadequate. Huck can't say the word; he can't write the letter; he has made a crossing, but where does all this leave Jim's story? The river has almost reached its full course; History is here, Geography, as the final wall, and the raft is now irrelevant.

Humor transforms suffering, diminishes pain, belittles dread, and this wonder is worked through the agency of a humorist who, in the guise of a tolerant elder, a gentle knower, embraces the wronged self and applies to the wrong, the hurt, a certain compassionate perspective. Or, failing that, the balm of a white lie. Simple humor demonstrates innocence. Serious humor, it might be said, humorously considers that demonstration, the story the humorist tells. How much can humor know humorously, without lying, without evasion? How much at last does Huck know? Before what large losses, overcome by the inexplicable, is it yet possible to forgive, to identify, as Pirandello construes the humorous act, with the unlike and unlovely *other*? That is the question of Huckspeech, in whose circuit Huck becomes Tom, Tom becomes Huck. "The speechform," James Joyce writes in *Finnegans Wake*, "is a mere sorrogate." Huck can't write a lie, and therefore will never write again. Because the crossing is irrevocable, and this text is his crossing, he can only rong once in writing the writer at work, writing, busily engaged in sorrogation. Huck tells Tom "as much of the raft-voyage as I had time to." His only plan for Jim is to repeat the raft-voyage, "hiding daytimes and running nights, the way me and Jim used to do before." Too simple, says Tom, and Huck readily agrees. He realizes that now something must replace this "raft-voyage," stand in its place, refer to it, designate it, but not *be* it. *It* can no longer be. First the raft is taken from Huck, and then his discourse. Tom draws the tropes from his bag of tricks, his 'plan,' the play of his fiction, and Huck, watching the writer at work, admits: "I see in a minute it was worth fifteen of mine, for style, and would make Jim as free a man as mine would, and maybe get us all killed besides." As a style Huckspeech admits everything, even its own failure, its own closure. Sivilize me, Huck writes, I can't stand it. In that last grace-note of the humorous style, *sivilize,* Huck's final resistance, Huck marks the end of his writing.

If, in a second book, some later narrative, Huck is again to rong writing in the text, he must start from a new premise. Everything seen, heard, felt in *Huckleberry Finn,* the literal fullness of its experience, would then have to be critically realized. What is wrong about the rectitude of Tom's writing, the half-truths of Mr. Mark Twain's humorous fiction? Why is it, really, that Tom does not have, properly speaking, a bona fide sense of humor? Tom struts at the end of Huck's book, proud of the bullet hanging on his watch-guard, proud of the formal aptness of his resolution, and bubbling with new plots. Clearly Tom can't wait to go home and exhibit his bullet; yet he suggests parenthetically some "howling adventures" in the Territory. Huck takes him seriously, and will soon step again into the innocence of Tom's play. Perhaps as Huck waits in the wilderness for Tom to appear, and waits and waits, he will begin to invent a theory that explains Tom Sawyer.

Reformers and Young Maidens: Women and Virtue

Nancy Walker

Mark Twain considered it "another boy's book." The Concord, Massachusetts, public library, in 1885, regarded it as "the veriest trash." Daniel G. Hoffman has called it "the most universal book to have come out of the United States of America." The object of praise, banning, and veneration during the hundred years since its publication, *Adventures of Huckleberry Finn* has not commonly been considered a novel about women in nineteenth-century American society. Men occupy center stage in *Huck Finn;* women stand toward the back and sides of the novel, nagging, providing inspiration, often weeping or hysterical. Indeed, Twain's masterpiece would seem a likely reference point for Judith Fetterley's blunt statement: "American literature is male. To read the canon of what is currently considered classic American literature is perforce to identify as male. . . . Our literature neither leaves women alone nor allows them to participate."

As one of several novels commonly thought to address the formation of American attitudes and values, and therefore a "classic" part of the American literary tradition, *Huck Finn* is indeed a "male" novel in several senses. The narrative voice, the specific angle of vision from which the events of the novel unfold, is that of a young boy. Moreover, as a deliberate *Bildungsroman,* the novel traces the moral development of Huck Finn: the traditional passage of the young man from youthful innocence to maturity. Most significantly, the thematic core of the novel embodies a dream of escape to freedom that is both peculiarly American and identifiably masculine. Historically, the political and physical experiences of

From *One Hundred Years of* Huckleberry Finn: *The Boy, His Book, and American Culture.* © 1985 by the Curators of the University of Missouri. University of Missouri Press, 1985. Originally entitled "Reformers and Young Maidens: Women and Virtue in *Adventures of Huckleberry Finn.*"

exploring and settling a wilderness have required a power to initiate and lead social movements that has commonly been granted to men rather than to women. In mythic terms, the typical American hero has, like Huck, resisted the "civilizing" efforts of women and has struck out boldly, often iconoclastically, for a new "territory." For Fetterley, as for other recent critics, the exploitation of the land has come to be seen as analogous to the suppression of women, who are traditionally regarded as both desirable and dangerous. In Fetterley's terms, "America is female; to be American is male; and the quintessential American experience is betrayal by a woman."

Although it would not be accurate to say that Huck Finn is "betrayed" by a woman, Miss Watson's decision to sell Jim down the river—certainly a betrayal of Jim—sets the novel in motion. Were it not for the relationship between the slave and the boy, much of Twain's social commentary would be impossible, and Miss Watson's action allows their relationship to develop, making her a vital element of the plot. Nevertheless, for most readers, the significance of *Huck Finn* requires the male characters to occupy the foreground, leaving the female characters as part of the scenic backdrop. Virtually all readings of the novel, from Leslie Fiedler's assumption of a homosexual relationship between Huck and Jim to discussions of the novel's roots in Southwestern humor, reflect its origins in a male-dominated culture. Even the controversy about the role Tom Sawyer plays in the last seven chapters of the novel centers on the conflict between Tom's romantic swagger and Huck's tenuous moral supremacy: a boy's games versus adult responsibility.

Without detracting from the central role that Huck Finn plays in the novel that bears his name, it is possible to re-view *Huck Finn* as embodying a basic tension between male and female values and roles—a tension that bears directly on Huck's moral growth. Most of the female characters are derived from traditional—usually unflattering—stereotypes of women common to nineteenth-century authors and readers; indeed, the novel could serve as an index to common attitudes toward women as reflected in these stereotypical images. Those few women in the novel who are not merely stereotypes, such as Judith Loftus and Mary Jane Wilks, have more to do with Huck's development than is normally acknowledged. Finally, Huck's ambivalence about women—whom he tends to view as either nagging moralists or paragons of virtue—demonstrates the limited nature of his maturity by the end of the novel. The virtues that Huck begins to develop—honesty, compassion, a sense of duty—are identified in the novel as female virtues. Yet Huck's maleness requires that he ultimately emulate men, that he see women as "other"; and in the end he tries to run from the civilizing presence of women, unable to make the distinction between essential humanity and what society incorrectly considers virtue.

Discussions of Twain's male characters' attitudes toward or relationships with women seem inevitably to address the attitudes of Twain—or, rather, Samuel Clemens—toward women in his own life. Clemens's relationships with his mother, Jane Clemens, and with his wife, Olivia, particularly as they appear to be sources for the female characters in his works (and, in the case of Olivia, to be a "censor" of his work), have been the subject of much biographical and critical study. Although such an approach can invite a confusion of character and author, it may be useful to consider briefly Clemens's view of womanhood, since it is likely that, as the creation of a nineteenth-century male imagination, Huck mirrors some of Clemens's conceptions of the nature and role of women.

Mary Ellen Goad has defined the role that Clemens wished women to play in his own life in order to illuminate his creation of female characters. Goad contends that Twain created patterns of female behavior to which even the actual women in his life were expected to adhere, and that his fictional women were designed as models for the real women in his life:

> Twain viewed the role of the female in a particular, and, to the modern mind, strange way. He operated on the theory that the male of the species was rough and crude, and needed the softening and refining influence of a woman, or, if necessary, many women. The primary function of the women was thus the reformation of man.

This view of woman as the reformer of inherently brutish man was not unique to Twain and had been enhanced by the Victorian insistence on female purity. Ann Douglas argues that between 1820 and 1875 middle-class women and Protestant ministers turned simultaneously to the promulgation of "the potentially matriarchal values of nurture, generosity, and acceptance." Both groups felt powerless to exert influence in overt ways—women because of the removal of key economic activities from the household to the factory, and clergymen because of the legal disestablishment of the church—and therefore adopted the moral suasion of others as their sphere of influence. The fact that this position resulted in women remaining in a real sense powerless coincided with society's efforts to oppress them, according to Douglas, who states: "The cruelest aspect of the process of oppression is the logic by which it forces its objects to be oppressive in turn, to do the dirty work of their society in several senses." The Victorian definition of woman's role as moral guide would account for such characters as Miss Watson and Aunt Sally, part of whose function is "civilizing" recalcitrant boys. In addition, the persistence of this figure in Twain's life and art is explained, Goad says, by the habit that Twain and some of his male characters had of not remaining long in a reformed state. "The business of reform became a game in which one made promises, then suffered periodic relapses, as a sort of recreation."

When Goad discusses the female characters in Twain's work, however, she argues, as so many others have done, that they are merely flat and stereotypical — that in fact they represent one of Twain's failures as a writer. "Twain," she says, "was simply unable to create a female character, of whatever age, of whatever time and place, who is other than wooden and unrealistic." She continues:

> He had evolved over the years a narrow, specialized role for women, and although none of the women he knew fit the ideal, Twain continued to hold it in the abstract. Livy refused to become the narrow, moralizing, reforming shrew that Twain seemed to want, and it is no doubt well that she did, for Twain could not have lived with such a woman. When he was creating a female character in a work of fiction, however, Twain was not troubled by either a refusal to fit a role or the problem of living with someone who did fit the role. He could make a character do exactly what he wanted her to do, and what he wanted was an idealization.

In *Huck Finn,* however, the relationship between Huck and women is more complex and dynamic than a simple response to idealized figures. Changes in our perceptions of the realities of women's lives during the last one hundred years allow us to see that, although Twain may have used idealizations of women as the basis for many of his female characters, those characters play a vital if underrated role in the society of which they are a part; although they may be perceived by the male characters only as occasions for rebellion or opportunities for heroic action, they represent both positive and negative values of that society. For all Twain's mockery of middle-class "respectability," without the real human virtues represented primarily by the women in *Huck Finn* there would be little opportunity for Huck to grow.

With few exceptions, the male characters in the novel are far from admirable by the standards of either conventional or actual morality. They tend to be degenerate, selfish, greedy, and vengeful and are just as stereotypical as are many of the female characters. Pap is an exaggerated version of the "natural man" on the frontier, an illiterate alcoholic such as inspired the temperance movement of the nineteenth century. Though a figure of broad comedy at times, he lives outside society's rules and rejects even its positive values, such as education. Huck's description of Pap in Chapter 5 underscores his subhuman status:

> There warn't no color in his face, where his face showed; it was white; not like another man's white, but a white to make a body

sick, a white to make a body's flesh crawl—a tree-toad white, a fish-belly white.

The Duke and the Dauphin are far more human; they are—initially, at least—rogues rather then bestial villains despite their dishonest schemes. Twain clearly admires their rascality; they are vehicles of satire rather than subjects of horror. Also satirically treated are the Grangerfords and the Shepherdsons, to whom a half-forgotten lawsuit and murder are sufficient to maintain a multi-generational feud. Though Huck describes Colonel Grangerford as a "gentleman all over," we are meant to see the irony of the term "gentle," and Huck is eventually glad to leave his house. Similarly, Colonel Sherburn, for all his insight into the cowardice of a lynch mob, is the cold-blooded killer of the drunken Boggs.

Not all the men in the novel are this recklessly violent, but none except Jim exhibits maturity and virtue. Uncle Silas Phelps is the stereotype of the bumbling, absentminded man married to a woman with a tart tongue; the couple is in the tradition of Rip and Dame Van Winkle and Harriet Beecher Stowe's Sam Lawson and his wife. Tom Sawyer, the classic "bad boy," turns from youthful prankster early in the novel to cunning—if not malicious—torturer during the "freeing" of Jim at the end.

When Huck and Jim lie and steal, they do so to survive, and this behavior seems therefore excusable. Huck's numerous false identities and Jim's posing as a "sick Arab" are ways of avoiding detection and thus contribute to rather than detract from the moral thrust of the novel. The same is true of their habit of stealing, or "borrowing," as Huck prefers to call it:

> Pap always said it warn't no harm to borrow things, if you was meaning to pay them back, sometime; but the widow said it warn't anything but a soft name for stealing, and no decent body would do it. Jim said he reckoned the widow was partly right and Pap was partly right.

Jim's morality thus mediates between the socially unacceptable element, represented by Pap, and the acceptable behavior represented by the widow. Because Jim and Huck steal food and other necessities, rather than the Wilks girls' inheritance, as do the Duke and the Dauphin, this habit, like lying, seems justified to the reader. Huck's most flagrant "sin" is helping a slave to escape, just as Jim's is running away from his owner; ironically, of course, these acts are in Twain's view their greatest moral triumphs, even though they are not sanctioned by the society Twain describes. Only Jim, among the male characters in the novel, exerts a positive influence on Huck. Jim's position outside white society allows him freedom from—if nothing else—both the moralizers and the rascals of that society, and he teaches Huck morality by example rather than by precept.

In contrast to the male characters in the novel, the female characters largely conform to what society—and Mark Twain—expects of them, and this conformity is the source of their often flat, stereotypical presence. Whether stern moralizers, like Miss Watson, or innocent young girls, like Boggs's daughter, the women have been molded by social pressure into representations of several kinds of womanly virtue. As members of the gender responsible for upholding the moral and religious values of civilization, even when those values sanction slaveowning, the women make possible the lawlessness and violence of the men. If we accept the fact that Twain saw men as naturally "rough and crude," then women were either reformers one could tease by temporarily conforming to their rules, or innocent maidens who could restore one's faith in decency and goodness.

Including the deceased Emmeline Grangerford, there are twelve women in *Huck Finn* aged fourteen or older. Of these, some are merely walk-on characters; for example, Emmeline's sisters, Charlotte and Sophia, and Mary Jane Wilks's sisters, Susan and Joanna. Sophia Grangerford, who Huck says is "gentle and sweet, like a dove," is one-half of the Romeo-and-Juliet couple whose elopement triggers a renewal of the feud between the Grangerfords and the Shepherdsons. Twain describes her as the stereotypical young woman in love, blushing and sighing and always "sweet." With Charlotte Grangerford and the younger Wilks sisters Huck has little to do, and Twain seems to use them all merely as parts of his portrait of Southern gentility.

The most obvious "reformers" in *Huck Finn* are the Widow Douglas, Miss Watson, and Aunt Sally Phelps. The widow and Miss Watson are Huck's unofficial guardians at the beginning of the novel; it is their insistence on prayers and clothes that makes Huck feel "all cramped up," and it is from Aunt Sally that Huck runs at the end, with his famous concluding statement, "But I reckon I got to light out for the Territory ahead of the rest, because Aunt Sally she's going to adopt me and sivilize me and I can't stand it. I been there before." Huck's comment that he's "been there before" points to the pattern of reform and backsliding that Goad discusses and suggests that, having escaped the clutches of the Widow Douglas and Miss Watson at the beginning of the novel, Huck has, at the end, endured another period of civilizing at the hands of Aunt Sally. The repetition of the pattern of reform and escape might lead one to believe that all these women are instances of the same stereotype, whereas in fact they represent three different popular images of women in the nineteenth century. There is no doubt that Twain had different models in mind when he created these three characters, and Huck's responses to them emphasize their differences.

The key to the differences among these three female reformers is their marital status. No matter how devoutly some women of the time clung to a state of "single blessedness," marriage was the only widely sanctioned state for an adult woman. American humor in the nineteenth century is filled with satiric portraits of husband-hunting spinsters and widows, and both humorous and serious literature describes the older single woman as straight-laced and narrow-minded. The novelist Marietta Holley, for example, has her persona, Samantha Allen, describe her spinster neighbor, Betsey Bobbet, [in *My Opinions and Betsy Bobbet's,* 1872]:

> She is awful opposed to wimmin's havein' any right only the right to get married. She holds on to that right as tight as any single woman I ever see which makes it hard and wearin' on the single men round here.

Widows had a somewhat better time of it than spinsters in the public eye, as was pointed out by another female humorist, Helen Rowland, [in *Reflections of a Bachelor Girl,* 1909]: "Even a dead husband gives a widow some advantage over an old maid." The spinster, presumed to be unwanted, is presumed also to have ossified. The image of the widow, at one time a wife and probably a mother, is somewhat softer; even as a "reformer," she has a kinder heart. The married woman, assumed to be in her proper element, provides the most contented image of the three and thus is likely to be the mildest reformer of all. The three principal reformers in *Huck Finn* represent each of these three states.

Walter Blair has suggested that the prototype for Miss Watson might have been a spinster schoolteacher who visited the Clemens family in Hannibal. Twain remembered this woman, Mary Ann Newcomb, as being a thin woman and a strict Calvinist. Miss Watson has both of these qualities. Huck describes her as "a tolerable slim old maid, with goggles on," and she threatens Huck with hellfire for his sins. It is not surprising that when Huck, Tom, and the other boys are forming their gang, and Huck has no family to be killed if he reveals the gang's secrets, he offers to let them kill Miss Watson. Miss Watson is a constant nagging presence who is particularly concerned with Huck's manners and his education. It is she, Huck says, who "took a set at me . . . with a spelling-book" and "worked me middling hard for about an hour." She is eternally watchful of his demeanor: "Miss Watson would say, 'Dont put your feet up there, Huckleberry;' and 'dont scrunch up like that, Huckleberry—set up straight.'" In the matter of religion she seems to Huck prissy and sterile. The heaven she describes to him is unappealing: "She said all a body would have to do there was to go around all day long with a harp and sing, forever and ever. So I didn't think much of it." The subject of heaven is one of several on which Huck distinguishes between the Widow Douglas and Miss Watson:

> Sometimes the widow would take me one side and talk about Provi-
> dence in a way to make a body's mouth water; but maybe next day
> Miss Watson would take hold and knock it all down again. I judged
> I could see that there was two Providences, and a poor chap would
> stand considerable show with the widow's Providence, but if Miss
> Watson's got him there warn't no help for him any more.

Dedicated to duty rather than pleasure in a life that apparently has given her little of the latter, Miss Watson imagines an afterlife inspired by her Calvinist
background, one ill-suited to the imagination of an adolescent boy.

Although Huck resists Miss Watson's bleak vision, he recognizes that she
merely wishes to make him a "good" person according to her definition of the
concept, and Twain suggests that Huck understands that Miss Watson is filling
a role determined for "old maids" in American society. Huck's offer to let the
gang kill her if he betrays them may be read in two ways. On the one hand, she
may be an expendable person in his world, but the gang members have specifically required that he have a "family" to kill, and, by naming Miss Watson,
Huck suggests that he accepts her as such. More telling is the famous episode in
Chapter 31 in which Huck wrestles with his conscience about helping a slave to
escape and ultimately decides that he will go to hell. Jim is Miss Watson's property, and the morality he has absorbed—partly from her—tells him he is stealing from her. As his argument with himself gradually builds from practical to
humanistic considerations, he fears sending Jim back to Miss Watson because
"she'd be mad and disgusted at [Jim's] rascality and ungratefulness for leaving
her." When his "conscience" overtakes him, however, he agonizes about
"stealing a poor old woman's nigger that hadn't ever done me no harm."
Despite the syntax of the sentence, it is clear that Huck means that Miss Watson
has "done [him] no harm." Although the reader can easily see the harm done by
the spurious morality of people like Miss Watson, Huck merely sees her as a
"poor old woman," as indeed she is.

Twain makes a clear distinction between Miss Watson and the Widow
Douglas. The widow is a far more gentle reformer than her unmarried sister
and often intercedes between Huck and Miss Watson to mitigate the latter's
severity. Although Twain based the character of the widow on a popular nineteenth-century conception of widowhood, he omitted several of the least desirable characteristics of that image. The most negative presentation of the widow
in American humor is Frances M. Whicher's Widow Bedott, a gossiping
husband-hunter who was the pseudonymous author of sketches in *Neal's Saturday Gazette* in the 1840s. Despite her protestations to the contrary, she is always
on the lookout for eligible men, whom she smothers with terrible poetry and
home remedies. Twain's notes about his immediate prototype for the Widow

Douglas, Mrs. Richard Holiday, suggest that he originally regarded her as a target of similar satire:

> Well off. Hospitable. Fond of having young people. Old, but anxious to marry. Always consulting fortune-tellers; always managed to make them understand that she had been promised three husbands by the first fraud.

Aside from the fondness for young people, the Widow Douglas is considerably modified from this model.

Huck does not resent or pity the widow as he does Miss Watson. He is quick to excuse her behavior toward him, as he does early in the first chapter: "The widow she cried over me, and called me a poor lost lamb, and she called me a lot of other names, too, but she never meant no harm by it." He finds her attitude toward tobacco hypocritical, but is more amused than angry:

> Pretty soon I wanted to smoke, and asked the widow to let me. But she wouldn't. She said it was a mean practice and wasn't clean, and I must try not to do it any more. . . . And she took snuff, too; of course that was all right, because she done it herself.

The widow's method of reforming is to request or explain rather than to scold or nag. Whereas Miss Watson's "pecking" makes Huck feel "tiresome and lonesome," he responds favorably to the widow's kind heart. When Huck stays out all night with Tom and the gang, the two women react quite differently:

> Well, I got a good going-over in the morning, from old Miss Watson, on account of my clothes; but the widow she didn't scold, but only cleaned off the grease and clay and looked so sorry that I thought I would behave a while if I could.

By Chapter 4, Huck has become accustomed to being civilized. When he slips into his old habits, such as playing hooky from school, he welcomes the ensuing punishment: "the hiding I got next day done me good and cheered me up." He retains a fondness for his old life but is pleased by the widow's praise of his progress:

> I liked the old ways best, but I was getting so I liked the new ones, too, a little bit. The widow said I was coming along slow but sure, and doing very satisfactory. She said she warn't ashamed of me.

Huck's response to the Widow Douglas's kindness is important to understanding his later reaction to Jim's essential humanity. From the first pages of the novel, Twain presents Huck as a basically decent boy who is able to respond to loving discipline, and it seems likely that he altered the stereotype of the widow—removing her more laughable traits—in order to allow her to have a positive influence on Huck's moral development. Before Huck sets out on the raft with Jim, Miss Watson and the Widow Douglas are the only representatives of decency in his world. Despite her implicit approval of slavery, the widow has a coherent view of what Huck needs in order to be a "respectable" citizen—a view involving education, cleanliness, and Christian virtues. Were it not for the events that propel Huck into his trip down the river with Jim, he could grow up in the mold of the Horatio Alger hero. The other two major models for Huck's development at this point are Tom Sawyer and Pap; Tom, as the eternal child, would have Huck remain irresponsible and unrealistic, and Pap, in his complete rejection of society's rules and forms, would have him descend into barbarism. It is, after all, from Pap and not from the Widow Douglas that Huck flees in Chapter 7.

The most important lesson that Huck learns from the widow is that it is possible—even desirable—to place another human being's welfare before one's own. Not only has the widow taken the unpromising Huck into her home; she has also demonstrated that she cares about him, that his escapades make her not so much angry as sad. When Huck responds favorably to the widow's efforts to alter his behavior and values, he does so because he realizes his actions have an effect on others. It is this same principle that motivates Huck's final decision to help Jim escape regardless of the consequences for himself. As he is struggling with his conscience, he recalls first the good times he and Jim have had, then the favors Jim has done for him, and finally "the time I saved him by telling the men we had small-pox aboard, and he was so grateful, and said I was the best friend old Jim ever had in the world, and the *only* one he's got now." In his realization of his responsibility for another human being, Huck builds upon the example the widow has set for him; in fact, he surpasses the widow in moral integrity by recognizing a black man as a fellow human being.

Yet Huck's experiences with the third "reforming woman," Aunt Sally Phelps, show the limits of his maturation. The effectiveness of the final chapters of *Huck Finn* has been debated for decades. Those critics who find Huck's acquiescence to Tom's romantic game-playing disturbing in light of his previous maturation on the river probably have the stronger argument, and this objection is strengthened by the presence of Aunt Sally. If Huck ever needs a reformer, it is during the torture of Jim in these final chapters, but Aunt Sally, because of the particular stereotype upon which she is based, is an ineffectual reformer, though reforming is clearly her function.

Aunt Sally and Uncle Silas are a familiar pair in American humor: the harmless nag and the befuddled husband. Aunt Sally is a warm, gregarious woman who whirls around the still center of Uncle Silas. Hers is far from the strict, staid demeanor of Miss Watson; though Uncle Silas is a part-time preacher, Aunt

Sally is untouched by the Calvinist gloom that characterizes Miss Watson's outlook. Apparently happily married to the good-hearted Silas, and the mother of several children, she has a far sunnier disposition than the Widow Douglas and is more likely to be understanding of youthful pranks. When Tom Sawyer kisses her while she still thinks he is the stranger William Thompson, she calls him an "owdacious puppy" and a "born fool," but once she thinks he is Sid Sawyer, she enjoys the joke: "I don't mind the terms—I'd be willing to stand a thousand such jokes to have you here."

But when Huck and Tom—disguised as Tom and Sid—embark on the activities that Tom feels appropriate to freeing a prisoner and begin stealing sheets and spoons and filling the Phelps house with rats and snakes, Aunt Sally shows her temper. Twain's gift for comic exaggeration is nowhere more apparent than in some of these slapstick scenes, and the descriptions of Aunt Sally are strikingly similar to those of Livy, his own "reforming woman," that he included in letters to friends and relatives early in their marriage. In February 1870 he wrote:

> But there is no romance in this existence for Livy. She embodies the Practical, the Hard, the Practical, the Unsentimental. She is lord of all she surveys. She goes around with her bunch of housekeeper's keys (which she don't know how to unlock anything with them because they are mixed,) & is overbearing & perfectly happy, when things don't go right she breaks the furniture & knocks everything endways. You ought to see her charge around. When I hear her war whoop I know it is time to climb out on the roof.

Just as the dignified Livy becomes a comic figure in such descriptions, so Aunt Sally becomes comic and nonthreatening even as she attempts to discipline Huck and Tom. To cover their theft of a spoon, the two boys confuse Aunt Sally as she attempts to count:

> Well, she *was* in a tearing way—just a trembling all over, she was so mad. But she counted and counted, till she got that addled she'd start to count-in the *basket* for a spoon, sometimes; and so, three times they come out right, and three times they come out wrong. Then she grabbed up the basket and slammed it across the house and knocked the cat galley-west; and she said cle'r out and let her have some peace, and if we come bothering around her again betwixt that and dinner, she'd skin us.

Most of the time Aunt Sally's threats are idle, but even when she punishes the boys it has little effect. When the snakes they have collected to put in Jim's cabin get loose in the house, Aunt Sally takes action:

> We got a licking every time one of our snakes come in her way; and
> she allowed these lickings warn't nothing to what she would do if we
> ever loaded up the place again with them. I didn't mind the lickings,
> because they didn't amount to nothing; but I minded the trouble we
> had, to lay in another lot.

Huck's response to Aunt Sally's discipline is to ignore it—it "didn't amount to
nothing"—whereas his reaction to the Widow Douglas's disappointment in his
backsliding early in the novel had been to try to "behave a while" if he could. The
widow touched Huck's humanity; Aunt Sally merely touches his backside with a
hickory switch.

It is difficult, therefore, to take seriously Huck's fear of being "sivilized" by
Aunt Sally at the end of the novel. Not a true "reformer," she is a harmless comic
figure similar to the Livy of Clemens's letters. Given Twain's insistence on the
conflict between Huck's innocence and the corruption of civilization, it is important that Huck thinks he can escape at the end and that the reader knows he cannot—knows, that is, that the "Territory" is simply another civilization. But it
seems odd to posit Aunt Sally as a major representative of civilization—instead
of, say, Miss Watson or the Widow Douglas—unless we understand that
Twain's view of women as the reformers of young men was a product of his own
youthful fantasy, formed in part by the Victorian culture in which he lived. In attempting to claim legitimate—if ultimately ineffectual—authority and self-
esteem in a society that had made them powerless, Victorian women willingly
acceded to a "cult of motherhood," which, as Ann Douglas points out, "was
nearly as sacred in mid-nineteenth-century America as the belief in some version
of democracy." Douglas quotes Lydia Sigourney, who, writing to young
mothers in 1838, urged them to realize their potential influence on their
children: "How entire and perfect is this dominion over the unformed character
of your infant. . . . Now you have over a new-born immortal almost that
degree of power which the mind exercises over the body." All three of the
women who attempt to make Huck conform to society's rules are derived from
traditional stereotypes of women who may superficially be seen as mother figures
from the same societal mold; but Huck's more complex and ambivalent relationships with them point up the different social realities they represent and his own
boyish immaturity at the end of the novel. The fact that Huck can ignore Aunt
Sally's female authority testifies to both his own lack of significant maturity and
Mark Twain's awareness of the final ineffectuality of women in his society.

What growth Huck does achieve comes largely from his perception of
qualities in others that he wishes to assume himself. With the exception of Jim,
all of Huck's important models of decent human behavior are female. Though
the "goodness" of both the reforming older women and the young girls in the

novel is exaggerated for comic or satiric effect, several of the women display qualities that Huck begins to adopt as his character develops before the final chapters. In addition to the Widow Douglas, whose kindness and sincerity are apparent to Huck even as he chafes at the restrictions of his life with her, Mrs. Judith Loftus and Mary Jane Wilks are important influences on his self-definition. Both characters are more than mere stereotypes, and both demonstrate intelligence and courage that Huck does not find in most of the men he knows.

Mrs. Loftus, whom Huck encounters just before he and Jim begin their trip on the raft, is the shrewd, garrulous woman who sees through Huck's disguise as a girl. She shares with common stereotypes of women a love of gossip, but it is her common sense and kindness to which Huck responds. In terms of her age, Mrs. Loftus belongs to the category of "reforming" women; Huck thinks she is "about forty year old." But her advice at this point in the novel (unlike the moralizing of Miss Watson and the Widow Douglas) is the practical sort that Huck needs for survival, and Huck perceives her as strong and intelligent. His clumsy efforts to thread a needle and catch a lump of lead in his lap call forth Mrs. Loftus's scorn, but Twain also emphasizes her kindly attitude toward the boy she assumes to be a runaway apprentice:

> I ain't going to hurt you, and I ain't going to tell on you, nuther. You just tell me your secret, and trust me. I'll keep it; and what's more, I'll help you. . . . Bless you, child, I wouldn't tell on you.

Huck cautiously responds with another lie about his identity, but he is clearly impressed with Mrs. Loftus's perspicacity. When he returns to the raft and reports on his conversation with Judith Loftus, Jim says she is a "smart one."

More importantly, Mrs. Loftus confirms Huck in his maleness early in the novel. Not only does she quickly see through Huck's female disguise; she also outlines for him the male behavior that has betrayed him:

> Bless you, child, when you set out to thread a needle, don't hold the thread still and fetch the needle up to it; hold the needle still and poke the thread at it — that's the way a woman most always does; but a man always does 'tother way. And when you throw at a rat or anything, hitch yourself up a tip-toe, and fetch your hand up over your head as awkward as you can, and miss your rat about six or seven foot. . . . And mind you, when a girl tries to catch anything in her lap, she throws her knees apart; she don't clap them together, the way you did when you catched the lump of lead.

Instead of following Mrs. Loftus's advice, Huck never again pretends to be a girl. He rejects his female disguise after he leaves the Loftus house by taking off his sunbonnet, "for I didn't want no blinders on." A few paragraphs later, at the end of Chapter 11, he joins his fortunes to those of Jim when he says, "There ain't a minute to lose. They're after us!" The male identification forecasts the American male adventure, at the end of which Huck will assume Tom Sawyer's identity and his behavior.

Later in the novel, in anticipation of Huck's final capitulation to Tom's boyish romanticism, comes Huck's rescue of the "damsel in distress," Mary Jane Wilks. Huck's response to Mary Jane is not merely that of the gallant knight to the damsel, however; he is at this point (Chapters 24–30) still on his way to the real moral stature he will achieve in Chapter 31, and Mary Jane is more complex than the traditional damsel. Twain makes her simultaneously weak and strong, so that she in some ways embodies the paradox that Ann Douglas points to in Victorian women who "lived out a display of competence while they talked and wrote of the beauties of incompetence." Though Mary Jane in part matches the sentimental stereotype of the pure, innocent young woman, Huck's view of her includes admiration as well as protectiveness. She combines the piety of the older reforming woman with the absolute innocence of the ideal young girl, but it is finally her intelligence and courage that Huck finds most appealing.

Twain was apparently fascinated with young girls, and he idealized them in both his life and his art. His deep attachment to his daughter Suzy and his intense interest in Joan of Arc are only two examples among many of this preoccupation, and portraits of young female characters in his fiction are often suffused with reverence for their beauty and spotless virtue. Albert E. Stone, Jr., explores Twain's devotion to "young maidens, hovering on the edge of adult experience," and quotes from a fragment that Twain wrote in 1898, describing a recurrent dream of adolescent love:

> She was always fifteen, and looked it and acted it; and I was always seventeen, and never felt a day older. To me she is a real person not a fiction, and her sweet and innocent society has been one of the prettiest and pleasantest experiences of my life.

Most of the young girls in *Huck Finn* are versions of this romantic ideal, including such minor figures as Boggs's daughter, glimpsed grieving over her father's body: "She was about sixteen, and very sweet and gentle-looking, but awful pale and scared." Here an object of pity, the young girl can also be an object of satire, as in the well-known portrait of Emmeline Grangerford. Apparently modeled on Julia A. Moore, a sentimental poet known as the "Sweet Singer of Michigan," Emmeline represents the common stereotype of the morbid female poet, and Twain uses her to satirize sentimental art and the execrable taste of the Grangerford family.

However, it is precisely for her *lack* of sentimentality that Huck admires Mary Jane Wilks. At nineteen, she is the oldest of the three Wilks sisters, undoubtedly older than Huck. The only drawback to her beauty is her red hair, but Huck forgives that: "Mary Jane *was* red-headed, but that don't make no difference, she was most awful beautiful, and her face and her eyes was all lit up like glory." Mary Jane is indeed innocent and trusting. She gives the inheritance money to the Duke and the Dauphin to prove her faith in them and defends Huck when her younger sister accuses him—accurately—of lying:

> "It don't make no difference what he *said*—that ain't the thing. The thing is for you to treat him *kind,* and not be saying things to make him remember he ain't in his own country and amongst his own folks."
>
> I says to myself, *this* is a girl that I'm letting that old reptile rob her of her money!

Mary Jane's goodness bothers Huck's conscience sufficiently that he decides to foil the Duke and Dauphin's scheme by recovering and hiding the money, but he does not tell her what he has done until he realizes that she is upset about the slave family being broken up. In his effort to comfort her, Huck inadvertently tells her the truth, and in a passage that closely prefigures his later decision to help Jim escape, he wrestles with the necessity for truth, still in Mary Jane's presence:

> she set there, very impatient and excited, and handsome, but looking kind of happy and eased-up, like a person that's had a tooth pulled out. So I went to studying it out. I says to myself, I reckon a body that ups and tells the truth when he is in a tight place, is taking considerable many resks, . . . and yet here's a case where I'm blest if it don't look to me like the truth is better, and actly *safer,* than a lie.

The passage describing Huck's parting with Mary Jane in Chapter 28 marks the penultimate step in the moral development that culminates in his decision to risk his soul to help Jim. He is impressed by her willingness to go along with his plan to save the girls' inheritance—a plan that, though involving lies and deceptions, is a model of decency compared with Tom's plan to free Jim—and particularly by her offer to pray for him. Contrasting his sinful nature to her goodness, he thinks:

> Pray for me! I reckoned if she knowed me she'd take a job that was more nearer her size. But I bet she done it, just the same—she was

just that kind. She had the grit to pray for Judas if she took the notion—there warn't no backdown to her, I judge.

By putting himself in a category with Judas and emphasizing Mary Jane's virtues, Huck is playing a game with his reformer: though drawn to the innocence
and purity she represents, he simultaneously insists on his unregenerate nature.
Mary Jane represents the female principle of virtue, always coupled with beauty.
"And when it comes to beauty," Huck says, "and goodness too—she lays over
them all." Huck, on the other hand, is the sinful male, unworthy of but longing for the redeeming power of the woman.

However, Huck is not merely playing a game at this point. His praise of
Mary Jane Wilks is couched in terms that show he has an adolescent crush on
her. She has, he says, "more sand in her than any girl I ever see," and though
she disappears from his life at this point, Huck's memory of her testifies to her
effect on his values: "I reckon I've thought of her a many and a many a million
times, and of her saying she would pray for me; and if ever I'd a thought it
would do any good for me to pray for *her,* blamed if I wouldn't a done it or
bust." Twain combines here the terms of a boy's admiration—"grit" and
"sand"—and the desire to help another person that marks the maturing human
being. Given Huck's uncomfortable relationship with religion, his willingness
to pray for Mary Jane Wilks is a true gift of love. Huck's feelings for Mary Jane
and Twain's depiction of her strength and determination raise her above the
level of stereotype and allow her, like other women in the novel, to be a significant influence on Huck's developing conscience. His offer to pray for her if it
"would do any good" suggests that the idea of self-sacrifice is becoming natural
to him and prepares for his ultimate "sacrifice" of his own soul to help Jim.

A close look at the part women play in Huck Finn's life thus makes clearer
the extent of his moral regression at the end of the novel. In his relationships
with his principal female mentors—the Widow Douglas, Judith Loftus, and
Mary Jane Wilks—he has achieved an appreciation of those virtues that begin to
separate him from the hypocrisy and violence of the society in which he lives.
But his contact with these women has also confirmed that he is in fact male and
must remove himself from what he perceives as a "female" world of conformity
to certain standards of behavior. With the Widow Douglas and Miss Watson
he plays the part of the unruly boy; with Judith Loftus he tries to be a girl and
fails; and with Mary Jane Wilks he assumes the role of the male protector of
female innocence. Finally, with Jim, he arrives at a mature friendship with
another man, one for whom he is prepared to risk eternal damnation. But his
acquiescence to the adolescent behavior of Tom Sawyer in the final chapters
demonstrates just how tenuous and fragile his maturity has been, and his desire

to "light out for the Territory" is youthful escapism rather than a mature rejection of a corrupt society.

Twain's use of nineteenth-century stereotypes of women as the basis of his female characters in *Huck Finn* allows the reader to understand some of the ways a male-dominated culture perceived woman's place and function. Both the men and the women in the novel illustrate the values of a society that has little regard for human dignity, but the female characters also embody virtues that could redeem that society if the women were empowered to do so. The male characters, even the rascals and thieves, are allowed the freedom to accept or reject these values, whereas the women, as members of a subservient group, are obliged to preserve and transmit them. Whether as innocent young girls or as middle-aged reforming women, the female characters are for the most part creations of a male imagination that requires them to inspire men with their goodness or "save" them from their undesirable tendencies. Huck is both inspired and "saved" or "sivilized" in the course of the novel, but finally he exercises the male prerogative of rejection — not of the values of his society, but of the "female" virtues he has struggled so hard to attain. By accepting the limited roles for women that his culture promoted, Twain effectively limits the extent to which Huck Finn can be a moral force in his society. Though they are frequently inspirational or influential, the women in *Huck Finn,* viewed from the male perspective of the novel, are finally powerless — as Aunt Sally Phelps demonstrates — to change the adolescent dreams of the American male.

A Hard Book to Take

James M. Cox

My title may seem at first glance all wrong. If any book has been easy to take for the last hundred years, surely it is *Adventures of Huckleberry Finn.* Read by people of all ?ges, loved throughout the nation, it finally made its way into the academy so that professors of literature — at least a good number of them — have come to take both confidence and pleasure in deeming it a masterpiece of American literature. Yet if Huck's story seems to tell itself upon a current of ease, he says at the end that it was a hard book to write. And it was from the beginning a hard book to take in some quarters. For example, the Public Library Committee of Concord, Massachusetts — home of Emerson, Thoreau, and Hawthorne — banned it. The *Boston Transcript* approvingly reported the committee's judgment that the book was rough, coarse, and inelegant, "the whole book being more suited to the slums than to intelligent, respectable people." The *Springfield Republican* condemned the book on the ground that it was trashy and vicious. Recalling that, eight years earlier, Mark Twain had shown a singular lack of propriety at the Whittier birthday dinner, the *Republican* averred that the book degenerated into "a gross trifling with every fine feeling."

It became so easy to flog those dear old genteel custodians of New England culture for their utter failure of taste, that a generation of academic custodians of literary culture could forget how long it took for Mark Twain to displace the New England worthies in the schools. They could forget, for instance, that Jim's observation about Frenchmen and the French language is not quite so hilarious to Frenchmen (so I have been told) as it is to us; they could forget that the jokes

From *One Hundred Years of* Huckleberry Finn: *The Boy, His Book, and American Culture.* © 1985 by the Curators of the University of Missouri. University of Missouri Press, 1985.

on religion might not be so funny to a devoutly Primitive Baptist; or that the exposures of village cruelty and Southern mores, pursued with the zeal characteristic of so many published interpretations of the novel, might prove a trial to the humor of rural conservative Southerners. These could be forgotten because the enlightened audience of today does not have to worry about any of these groups. The French, who are far away in their own language, will just have to take the little joke (it is really quite a big one), or, if they cannot, somehow mute the joke in translation; the primitively religious do not really count any more than the Southern rural conservatives. They can stay in their communities, for one thing; for another, they can probably find other books to ban since by nature they distrust the literary imagination. Such was the essentially complacent attitude of the academic establishment that put Mark Twain among the major American writers.

I am part of that establishment, and I have helped put to rout the last traces of the genteel remnant in the academy. Even those professors, refined in taste or devoted to the art of real artists (artists like Henry James or Dante), who used to dismay us with their scorn of the ending of *Huckleberry Finn,* have now been worn down or fatigued by our adroit defenses of the ending. And so they are silenced, as they should have been silenced in 1950 when T. S. Eliot, the very embodiment of high art, affirmed that the book — the whole book, ending and all — was incontrovertibly a work of art. But then we who subsequently went on defending the ending should have also rested, at once silent and content in the knowledge of Eliot's magisterial affirmation. But how could we have known that Eliot's judgment, like so many of his decisions, was to be the literary law of the land, making our subsequent interpretations nothing more than glosses on an approved text.

Despite our confident assurance about the book's quality, there has been, in the last fifteen years, another group — steadily increasing in numbers — that finds the book hard to take. I mean of course black Americans. Since they do, our complacency is, or should be, shattered. We used to be able to assure them — when they were little more than token presences in what we are pleased to call the world of higher education — that they could surely see that the book was in no way really prejudiced against Jim or the Negro (as we used to say before Malcolm X sought to set us free). The presence of the word *nigger* throughout the book, we would go on to say, merely reflected the time and place of the novel and was a manifestation of Mark Twain's celebrated realism. To take the term personally or negatively was to fly in the face of the whole intention of the novel. Editions of the novel that took up the matter at all did what they could to defend Mark Twain, or, in one instance that I remember, to declare complaints about Mark Twain's usage irrelevant, since the author's good racial intentions were manifestly visible.

However much we may recognize those good intentions, we nonetheless know, both historically and personally, that racial objection to that word is not irrelevant. If Mark Twain could use the word in the nineteenth century with a certain freedom and could not use all the four-letter words we have lately allowed to pass the censor, we feel a greater inhibition about that word than we can quite believe Mark Twain ever felt and certainly more hesitation about it than about the four-letter words we are using more easily. Let me come closer home. Almost every student of Mark Twain has felt that he exaggerated the matter of social censorship on writers. To be sure, we know that the Gilded Age had overrefined standards of taste and usage. But even Brooks and DeVoto, both of whom lamented the stifling pressures of New England gentility, ultimately concluded that Mark Twain, more than his society, was primarily responsible for the censorship against which he railed.

The fact remains, however, that *Huckleberry Finn,* alone among the masterpieces of nineteenth-century American literature, remains to this day threatened with censorship. School boards in New York and Pennsylvania have recently considered removing it from assigned reading lists; and recently the Mark Twain High School (of all names!) in Fairfax County, Virginia, within a stone's throw of the nation's capital, found itself determined to remove the book from circulation. There were the usual high-minded editorials defending the book and lamenting the bigotry that keeps failing to understand it. Yet for all the familiar defenses and for all my belief in freedom of the press and my love for the book, I know in my heart that, if I were teaching an American literature course in Bedford Stuyvesant or Watts or North Philadelphia, I might well find myself choosing *Tom Sawyer* or *A Connecticut Yankee* rather than *Huckleberry Finn* to represent Mark Twain.

Such a decision would not necessarily be reprehensible. After all, Huck himself often acted precisely along such lines. He had learned from Pap that the best way to get along with scoundrels like the King and the Duke (and Pap, too, for that matter) was to avoid trouble with them. Even to remember the novel is to remember that Pap had something to teach Huck by precept as well as by forceful presence. He taught Huck to "take a chicken when you get a chance, because if you don't want him yourself you can easily find somebody that does, and a good deed ain't ever forgot." Those who find such wisdom immoral would do well to remember that Thoreau thought the wood he stole made the sweetest fire.

To say a word for Pap may seem to many readers of the book — and good

readers—nothing short of sacrilege. Yet entertainment of Pap's humanity—
which is, after all, immensely entertaining—can provide an avenue for compre-
hending as well as acknowledging the power and wisdom of the book. On the
one hand he is fiercely cruel, and his cruelty runs directly athwart two of the
sacred values the book exploits. First of all, his treatment of Huck convicts him
of child abuse; but more important, he is a classic exemplification of racial
bigotry. Set against the values the book seems so clearly to uphold, these two
forms of behavior characterize Pap as a reprobate.

At the same time, Pap is truly a performer. His speech against the government *is* hilarious as long as we can bring ourselves to laugh at it. But the matter
of that speech crosses our sense of humane and rational ideals enough to make
us displace our humorous response with a harsh moral judgment when we are
writing criticism approved for publication in the journals. Even so, the humor
is undeniably present right through Pap's performance. For if Pap is a miscreant,
he is also helplessly humorous. Listen to his lament:

> "A man can't get his rights in a govment like this. Sometimes I've a
> mighty notion just to leave the country for good and all. Yes, and I
> *told* 'em so; I told old Thatcher so to his face. Lots of 'em heard me,
> and can tell what I said. Says I, for two cents I'd leave the blamed
> country and never come anear it agin. Them's the very words. I
> says, look at my hat—if you call it a hat—but the lid raises up and
> the rest of it goes down till it's below my chin, and then it ain't
> rightly a hat at all, but more like my head was shoved up through a
> jint o'stove-pipe. Look at it, says I—such a hat for me to wear—one
> of the wealthiest men in this town, if I could get my rights."

For all its irony, the passage discloses Pap's incomparable stage presence. In
playing, or rather replaying, his public speech before Huck, Pap is in all prob-
ability exaggerating, yet the exaggeration is an integral part of his histrionic
sense of himself. His unforgettable description of his hat brings him to the edge
of a self-consciously humorous grasp of his own image that all but betrays the
limitations of illiteracy and cruelty in which his character is conceived. At such
a moment the performer is at the brink of eluding the ideational constraint
upon his character.

When, in his next breath, Pap launches into his matter of the free Negro
professor whose presence in his memory outrages him, we are at the true
threshold of the novel. The measure to which the humor—continuing throughout the passage—will be drowned out depends on the indignation the critical
audience feels in relation to the matter of the speech. Since that matter is directly

racist, it possesses both the volatility and the simplicity to reduce as well as to define its audience. Listen again:

> "Thinks I, what is the country a-coming to? It was 'lection day, and I was just about to go and vote, myself, if I warn't too drunk to get there; but when they told me there was a State in this country where they'd let that nigger vote, I drawed out. I says I'll never vote agin. Them's the very words I said; they all heard me; and the country may rot for all me — I'll never vote agin as long as I live. And to see the cool way of that nigger — why, he wouldn't a give me the road if I hadn't shoved him out o' the way."

In the public and social terms of the novel — let us say in its relation to the national conscience — the irony is sufficiently savage to cut athwart the irrepressible humor that continues to ripple the current of Pap's speech. Though the humor reinforces, it nonetheless qualifies the irony of the performance. Thus when Pap says he was about to vote if he "warn't too drunk to get there," his acknowledgment of his condition is at once in character yet again brings him to the threshold of a self-consciousness that belies his relentless hostility to blacks. I don't mean at all that Pap himself is any freer from his bigotry by virtue of his humor; I do mean that in his act of performance — and in Mark Twain's management of that performance — his admission (or is it his boast?) of his drunkenness is very much designed to draw a laugh. It is surely so designed by Mark Twain; even Pap, who remains throughout his replay of his speech insistently aware of his own performance, is all but masterfully producing one of his effects. When he subsequently tumbles over the tub of salt pork, barking his shins, and then, rising and cursing, proceeds to give the tub an unfortunate kick with the foot that has two toes "leaking out the front end" of its boot, he bursts forth with an agonized string of curses that he later says "laid over anything he done previous." Consciously casting himself in the role of a master performer, Pap sees himself as an actor in the great tradition of Sowberry Hagan.

I begin with Pap because his presence and identity are characteristic of a central aspect of the novel. The more seriously we take the matter of the book — I mean the matter of race and slavery — the less we are likely to want the humor to rise to the surface of this passage. If we refuse the rise of humor, in the system of emotional exchange that runs through the book the indignation at Pap's brutality and racism has freer play. Acknowledging the humor — which is to say *experiencing* it — involves an instinctive recognition of Pap's humanity. For if Pap is fierce in being, he is a delight in peformance. The delight comes first of all from the exposed ironic relationship between his attitudes and his behavior. Equally important, it comes from the economy of pity we enjoy upon seeing him so justly and so visibly in pain. We are, by virtue of the irony, spared the expenditure of sympathizing with him.

The pity we save at Pap's expense we fairly lavish on Jim as the novel proceeds. Seeing the terms of this emotional exchange is to see Pap's vital function and placement in the book. In terms of affect, he is the figure who opens the way for Jim to be a center of sympathy; in terms of theme, his behavior and his departure make it possible for Jim to displace him as Huck's loving father. Even more important, Pap's inimitable performance literally initiates the racial theme just as Pap himself literally drives Huck out of the childhood world of Tom Sawyer and into the arms of the escaped Jim. The two fugitives—the one from Pap, the other from Miss Watson—find in each other the resources that lift their journey into mythic significance. Borne southward on the great river into the very heart of slavery, they nonetheless embody in their relationship what is probably the most powerful expression of our national dream of freedom.

Yet the fact that the direction of this dream of freedom is into the land of slavery should keep us in touch with the profound contradictions of the book. The novel generates a wish for both freedom and brotherhood embodied in a magically simplified image of human relationship between a black man and a redneck boy. But that simplification, as Pap's presence already indicates, is built upon a series of remarkably complex trades and exchanges. Thus, we can see that, although Pap's speech exposes his viciousness, the matter of that speech would or could still offend a particular audience. That very speech is one I could easily imagine *not* reading to a high-school class in Harlem. Yet if I can imagine such self-censorship in the face of external social pressure, I can just as easily imagine a self-indulgent public emphasis on the negative character of Pap in order to expose his bigotry to the lash of criticism—censoring in the process the humor that is so irrepressibly present in the speech. To censor the humor is to deny Pap the humanity he ineffably possesses.

Even more important, failure to recognize his humanity results in a corresponding reduction of Jim's humanity. For if Pap is often reduced to his racism, Jim is just as often simplistically elevated into sainthood. Here again the simplification results from a refusal to see the humor of Jim's performance. For Jim, like all the characters in this novel, is in the business of humorous performance. If Pap's humor threatens to redeem him from simple racism, Jim's humor threatens him with a minstrel identity. It is just this identity that makes modern audiences—whether black or liberal white—uncomfortable. Thus it is not only the word *nigger,* so liberally distributed throughout Huck's narrative, that publicly troubles us. It is the role Jim plays, or is forced to play. Yet diminishing that aspect of Jim's character results in an emphasis on his goodness, generosity, and essential humility. To be sure, Jim manifestly possesses these qualities in abundance, but they come to the fore almost inevitably at the expense of his intelligence. In other words, the more Jim is made a saint the more he is likely to be the humble victim lacking any semblance of the shrewd humanity Huck so amply possesses.

Yet surely Jim is shrewd, as shrewd as Huck. If we take the incident in Chapter 2, in which Tom lifts the sleeping Jim's hat and hangs it on a tree above his head, we cannot be quite sure, in this world where everyone is involved in tricks, deceit, and confidence games, that Jim is even asleep. If we see in Pap's racism the traces of a humorous consciousness of his own performance, we should be able to detect in Jim's gullible account of being bewitched the apparition of a master of the tall tale. To exclude such a "superstitious" presence is to settle for Huck's complacent feeling of superiority to Jim's gullible belief in superstition. Using this episode as the most genial and disarming initiation into Jim's relation of narrative and relation to the narrative, we can go much further. We know and admire Huck as a liar but are prone never to realize that Jim lies to Huck about Pap's death. He does not elaborate a lie about it; he simply conceals his knowledge from Huck. Though one of his motives for evading Huck's query about the dead man in the floating house may be his tender wish to spare Huck the knowledge of being an orphan, Jim has good reason to suspect that a Huck free of his Pap might leave him high and dry.

The possibility that Huck will abandon or betray Jim is, after all, at the very center of the whole journey — and the two fugitives can never believe in each other sufficiently to annihilate it. That possibility is, after all, nothing less than the likelihood that the social reality from which they both are fugitive will intrude at any time to split asunder their precarious pastoral on the raft. Given this reality, Jim and Huck have confidence in each other at the same time they con each other. There is no better revelation of their relationship than the sequence extending from Huck's apology to Jim after deceiving him about the fog (in Chapter 15) to his wonderful lie to the slave-hunters in the very next chapter.

The fact that two pages after he humbles himself to Jim — that action for which Huck has received so much critical praise — he begins to think about turning Jim in should give us considerable pause. Is Huck's reversal merely a reflection of Mark Twain's carelessness, or is it Huck's own inconsistency of character? Or, more likely, is his rising social conscience integrally related to his sense of guilt at having mistreated Jim about the fog? It is hardly accidental that at the very moment Huck has "matured" in our own eyes by having recognized Jim's humanity he should begin to think about being a good boy in relation to the authority of his own society.

The problem, of course, is that if Huck's determination to be kind to Jim makes him a good boy in our eyes, his wish to be a good boy in his own society puts Jim in great jeopardy. But the paradox runs much deeper. For the fact of the novel is that the passage in which Huck apologizes to Jim literally marks Huck and Jim's passage by Cairo, the Ohio, and freedom. Put another way, the good feeling evoked by Huck's sincere apology literally masks the fact that Jim has irrevocably passed his chance for freedom. As if this were not enough, Huck no sooner ends Chapter 15 asserting that he was glad to have apologized to Jim and "didn't do him no more mean tricks" than he is inwardly planning to turn Jim in. Surely this would be the meanest trick of all. Yet Huck himself betrays no consciousness of his contradiction. Fearing immediately after his apology that they might miss Cairo, Huck proposes to go ashore to discover their exact whereabouts. As he prepares for this excursion, he becomes uncomfortably conscious of Jim's bold anticipation of being free. Troubled by his complicity in Jim's determination to be free, he accuses himself of ingratitude to the respectable people who have tried to help him. His sense of his own wrong is sufficiently acute to repress for the moment the moral enormity of turning Jim over to the authorities. And so, just as our serious approval of Huck's apology to Jim keeps us from seeing that freedom was being lost at precisely that moment, Huck's serious recognition of his own criminal activity is sufficient to keep him from seeing that he is about to do Jim the meanest of mean tricks. Mean tricks are of course in the world of Tom Sawyer and childhood; and Huck, doubtless feeling and even liking his own maturity as much as we feel and applaud it, cannot see this adult effort to be socially responsible as a mean trick. Besides, Jim is talking bolder, and why shouldn't he? Not only does he think freedom is around the bend; he has also just put Huck in his place. As for Huck, if he has humbled himself to Jim, small wonder that from his new perspective Jim suddenly seems proud.

These observations in no way denigrate the nobility of Huck's apology, but they do gauge the emotional exchange in the book. The smoothness, swiftness, and disarming flow of Huck's narration conceal the snags, reefs, and channel crossings that the narrative is constantly negotiating. Moreover, our tentative scrutiny of this particular sequence in the novel prepares us for the wonderful exchange Huck has with the slave-hunters he is about to meet. Even before he can shove off in the canoe with the ostensible mission of finding out just where he and Jim are on the river—and with the secret intention of reforming himself by turning Jim over to society—Jim just may have divined what we might call a honky in the woodpile. Listen to his heartfelt farewell to Huck and to the response it arouses in Huck:

"Pooty soon I'll be a-shout'n for joy, en I'll say it's all on accounts o'Huck; I's a free man, en I couldn't ever ben free ef it hadn't ben for Huck; Huck done it. Jim won't ever forgit you, Huck; you's de bes' fren' Jim's ever had; en you's de *only* fren' ole Jim's got now."

I was paddling off, all in a sweat to tell on him; but when he says this, it seemed to kind of take the tuck all out of me. I went along slow then, and I warn't right down certain whether I was glad I started or whether I warn't. When I was fifty yards off, Jim says:

"Dah you goes, de ole true Huck; de on'y white genlman dat ever kep' his promise to ole Jim."

In this exchange we have the full force of the idyllic myth: Huck, the good-hearted boy possessing an innocence tied to irony and cunning; and Jim, the long-suffering man who is equally innocent, but whose innocence is expressed in terms of gullibility and humility. At the same time, we have a Huck with bad intentions and a Jim voicing praise sufficiently intense to betray an intelligence that knows betrayal may be at hand. Such an analysis of their exchange does not deny so much as it qualifies their affection for each other. That is why both language and drama are profoundly in harmony. Jim's speech, with an auditory trace of confidence in its performance, is penetrating Huck's vulnerable psyche precisely because the speech is penetrating and the psyche vulnerable.

Huck has no sooner heard Jim's farewell praise than he is confronted by the very society to which he has intended to hand over Jim. It comes in the form of two men hunting not one but five fugitive slaves. With Jim's affectionate voice still sounding in his ears, Huck, unable to tell the two men the truth, helplessly drops into one of his best lies. When he lied to Judith Loftus, he had been caught in the lie (or did he let himself be caught?) and then, in the teeth of her pleasurable self-congratulation at having caught him, he told her a bigger and bolder lie. This time he lies by implication and withdrawal. Asked whether the man on his raft is black, Huck hesitantly replies that he is white. And to the series of questions that follows, Huck says that the man is his father and is sick. When he adds blubberingly that his mam and Mary Ann are also sick and that no one will help them, the men themselves begin to fill in the blanks, concluding that the whole family has smallpox. If Judith Loftus had helped Huck out when, realizing he was not a girl, she supplied him with the details of the identity (an apprentice who had been badly treated) on which he in turn built his second lie to her, the slave-hunters do even better. Keeping their distance to avoid the disease, they are nonetheless so touched by Huck's narrative (which they themselves have fearfully concluded) that they give Huck forty dollars.

And Huck takes it. When he returns to the raft so near at hand, Jim is there to praise Huck's performance as much as he had earlier praised his character:

> "I was a-listenin' to al de talk, en I slips into de river en was gwyne to shove for sho' if dey come aboard. Den I was gwyne to swim to de raf' agin when dey was gone. But lawsy, how you did fool 'em, Huck! Dat *wuz* de smartes' dodge! I tell you, chile, I 'speck it save' ole Jim — ole Jim ain't gwyne to forget you for dat, honey."

They take the money and share it in a moment worthy of the King and the Duke, yet you may be sure that there has been little criticism directed toward pointing up that analogy. As for the two slave-hunters, they have never to my knowledge been given their share of moral credit for their all but spontaneous and certainly heartfelt contribution to Huck's welfare.

Of course they do not know, as we do, that Huck is concealing Jim. Yet they are charged with their intention of hunting runaway slaves at the same time that they are robbed of the moral credit they deserve for sympathizing with what they believe to be Huck's stricken plight. Reflection on the slave-hunters and their fate at our hands, and further reflection on this whole episode, affords an opportunity to ask some genuine moral questions about *Huckleberry Finn*. Having already seen the humor in Pap's racism, the confidence in Jim's gullibility and in his loyalty, the abrupt reversal between the Huck of the apology and the Huck intending to betray Jim to the authorities, and the way in which the emotion of Huck's apology literally displaces the fact that these two travelers have forever passed by Cairo and freedom — having seen so much, we are faced with the forty-dollar charity display of the slave-hunters. We cannot help applauding Huck's dodge as much as Jim applauds it. Yet even allowing for the fact that the men are slave-hunters and that their charity has about it a strong element of payoff in order to avoid the plague they have imagined, they still seem to me a wonderful snag in the moral current of the narrative. Aren't they really as good as anyone in the book? Is there anyone else's charity that is really superior to theirs? And aren't Huck and Jim, by taking their money, just as bad as the King and the Duke, who are waiting in the wings? Of course these questions go against our feelings — they go against the master current of the fiction. Yet not to ask them is to settle for a far tamer stream than the shifting, magnificent Mississippi that absolutely underlies the book.

These questions point us back to a particular kind of moral and emotional exchange that is always going on in the book. The value we are holding to as if it were the measure of all others is, of course, Jim. Huck's relation to and involvement in Jim's freedom lift him out of the childhood world and lift his lies from what we might call the world of low picaresque into what we want to see as the realm of higher humanity. The antislavery sentiment affixed to Jim and his freedom functions as an absolute moral yardstick by which to measure other values. Thus our sense of Pap's anguish is crowded out by our indignation at his racism; thus the slave-hunters' sympathy for Huck's fictive family is set at naught because they *are* slave-hunters; and thus the King and Duke cease to be amusing once they go beyond fleecing the rural, evangelical, and illiterate white communities strung out along the river and take up the business of trading off the Wilks slaves. And Huck himself ultimately loses value when he goes along with Tom's travesty of freeing Jim according to the rules.

Yet Huck has always done all he could to go along with the more powerful forces he confronts — and so many of those forces are more powerful than he, a mere orphan adrift upon the mighty river. His great value lies precisely in his negative relation to the banks of both right and wrong between which both his narrative and his life so beautifully and powerfully run. Look at his own appraisal of the incident involving the slave-hunters:

> They went off, and I got aboard the raft, feeling bad and low, because I knowed very well I had done wrong, and I see it warn't no use for me to try to learn to do right; a body that don't get *started* right when he's little, ain't got no show — when the pinch comes there ain't nothing to back him up and keep him to his work, and so he gets beat. Then I thought a minute, and says to myself, hold on, — s'pose you'd a done right and give Jim up; would you felt better than what you do now? No, says I, I'd feel bad — I'd feel just the same way I do now. Well, then, says I, what's the use you learning to do right, when it's troublesome to do right and ain't no trouble to do wrong, and the wages is just the same? I was stuck. I couldn't answer that. So I reckoned I wouldn't bother no more about it, but after this always do whichever come handiest at the time.

This, it should be emphasized, in his reflection on the action he has all but helplessly had to take — an action which, *negative* in its nature, leaves him feeling *bad* and *low*. Out of that depression and regret he would like to think that had he done the opposite he would have felt better, but he knows that he would have felt no better (he does not say he would have felt worse); and so he concludes with the determination to do in the future only what is handiest or easiest. Thus the essential pleasure principle of ease and handiness that he affirms arises out of a helpless action — and the minute we pursue the origins of that action we are led back to Huck's bad intention of betraying Jim, back from that to his apology for having lied to Jim about the fog, and on back to the encompassing narrative fact that the fog itself along with Huck's apology constitute Mark

Twain's own dodge for eliminating the possibility of an Ohio ending for his novel. Yet if the episode of the fog, Huck's lie to Jim, and his subsequent apology literally displace their loss of freedom, this narrative sequence just as surely constitutes Huck's much approved "moral growth" that forms the basis for the serious sentiment on which the novel depends.

There, it seems to me, is a fairly clear analysis of the sequence leading to Huck's affirmation of his pleasure principle. His pleasure principle, of course, involves a bold program, so bold that he himself cannot keep it up, and no reader of the novel should have to be told where he fails. The failure is, as a matter of fact, at the heart of his greatest success — the moment when he determines to set Jim free. That moment is a remarkable variation on both the action and reflection we have just examined. This time, however, Huck is alone, the King and the Duke having "stolen" and sold Jim for "forty dirty dollars," to use Huck's description of the transaction when he learns of it. Realizing Jim's plight, Huck thinks at first of writing Miss Watson, on the premise that Jim will be treated better upriver than where he now is. He decides on second thought not to write because he fears that Miss Watson might vengefully sell Jim back downriver. But then the greater fear of what people will think of *him* for abetting a fugitive slave gets the better of him — and out of that fear emerges his conscience to upbraid and shame him for his wickedness until he finally decides to write Miss Watson of Jim's whereabouts. In the midst of the flush of self-approval that follows hard upon the completion of his letter, the image of Jim looms in Huck's mind as a rebuke to his first act of writing. Benignly presiding over and pervading Huck's highly compressed mental rehearsal of the journey, Jim stands as the figure against whom Huck, remembering incident after incident of their journey, cannot harden his heart:

> and at last I struck the time I saved him by telling the men we had small-pox aboard, and he was so grateful, and said I was the best friend old Jim ever had in the world, and the *only* one he's got now; and then I happened to look around, and see that paper.
>
> It was a close place. I took it up, and held it in my hand. I was a trembling, because I'd got to decide, forever, betwixt two things, and I knowed it. I studied a minute, sort of holding my breath, and then says to myself:
>
> "All right, then, I'll *go* to hell" — and tore it up.

No attentive reader of the novel can ever wish that Huck had concluded otherwise. Yet his choice, if we take it seriously — and if anything in the novel is to be taken seriously, surely this decision is — seems to run directly athwart his prior determination to do whatever came easiest and handiest. The more seriously the decision is taken — the more it is seen as Huck's "crisis of conscience" — the more disappointing the ending of the novel will be. For instead of living solemnly by his decision, Huck merely submits to Tom Sawyer's extravaganza of freeing Jim. Moreover, Tom's farce is predicated on his concealed knowledge that Jim is already free — and freed by Miss Watson, of all people! She, the moralist of the old order, who has been advertised in the fiction as the person who would sell Jim down the river, turns out to make the will that legally sets him free. How could Mark Twain play such a mean trick? The least he could have done was to plot his novel better and make Jim the property of the Widow Douglas.

Of course he had given us this authorial warning through a G. G., Chief of Ordnance (could those initials stand for General Grant?):

> Persons attempting to find a motive in this narrative will be prose-
> cuted; persons attempting to find a moral in it will be banished;
> persons attempting to find a plot in it will be shot.

Given such a series of threats, we had perhaps better not even wish for a plot, let alone seek one. Here again, it is worth noting that Mark Twain is not deny-ing the presence of motive, moral, or plot but asserting the danger of seeking for them. We do not wish to take this warning seriously, yet all the criticism written about this narrative, including this essay, is testimony to the book's resistance to motive, moral, and plot.

What, after all, is the almost universal disturbance about the abortive end-ing but a complaint about Mark Twain's rather high-handed (or was it his casual, or worse, his unwitting?) dismissal of whatever motive, moral, or plot his narrative had generated? And the ending does indeed seem to abort the motive (Huck and Jim's wish for freedom), the moral (the triumph of the natural good intentions of a sound heart over a deformed conscience), and the plot (a young picaro's account of his discovery of a slave's humanity and his sub-sequent attempt to steal the slave out of slavery). In those last ten chapters Huck and Jim no longer visibly wish for freedom but become passive slaves to Tom Sawyer's "plot"; Huck's sound heart is so still that he seems as heartless as Tom Sawyer; and the act of stealing a slave becomes Tom's charade of enslaving a free man.

No wonder such an ending has driven critics of sound mind to distraction. If it has never really bothered children, there is not all that much evidence that so many of them actually read it. It bothered Leo Marx enough to make him mount an attack on Lionel Trilling and T. S. Eliot, who he felt had not been bothered enough by it. And it has more recently motivated John Seelye to re-write the book under the title of *The True Adventures of Huckleberry Finn*. Putting in all the four-letter words that Mark Twain left out, Seelye, obeying liberal and even radical intentions, has Jim killed so that Huck, speaking in the dark, can conclude the narrative with these words: "I didn't care whether the goddam sun ever come up again."

The happy effect of Seelye's tour de force, giving us a dead rather than a free Jim, should enable us to realize that such a substitute ending, though it may satisfy those who long for something more serious than Tom's farce and something more real than his fantasy, is little better than a conventional happy ending would have been — an ending that would have had Huck, not Tom, free Jim — and not a *free* Jim either, and certainly not according to the rules. To have accomplished that, Mark Twain would have needed to put the fog and apology far enough upstream (since no one would want them removed) to leave Huck time and space to have his crisis of conscience above Cairo. Or, if he had them pass it in order to have his great Arkansas scenes, he would have needed to have them use that forty dollars they got from the slave-hunters to buy passage on a steamboat (as Jim suggests at one point) and come to freedom in style. But we couldn't stand that ending either, because then the slave-hunters would have provided Huck and Jim's passage to freedom. The more anyone thinks about such substitutions, the more Mark Twain's mean trick of an ending seems as good as we are likely to get. He had Tom give Jim forty dollars for being such a good prisoner, and Tom even hoped to take Jim back on a steamboat and have a circuslike celebration in St. Petersburg.

Mean trick though Mark Twain's ending may be, it is probably the best ending we shall ever have. By making us wish for something else, it remains its own discordant reality principle. If we want Huck to have freed Jim, we just want Huck to be a charitable good little abolitionist. Mark Twain might just as well have sent him across the yard in Hartford to Harriet Beecher Stowe's house to ask for Eva, the good little Christian. If, however, we continue to look at the novel in terms of emotional exchange, we can see that Mark Twain determined to save both Huck and Jim at the expense of Tom Sawyer. In the world of literary interpretation, poor old Tom never has got over that decision, and he never will. In the light of those interpretations, we have to see that Mark Twain so loved Huck and Jim that he sacrificed Tom Sawyer for them.

To review Mark Twain's mean trick and his sacrifice of Tom is to be taken back once more to Huck's mean trick and his apology. Remembering just how that remarkable sequence displaced the actual passage by Cairo and the irrevocable loss of freedom ought to instruct us about the implicit vision behind the mean trick of the ending. Surely this second trick discloses that, far from being free, humanity is in slavery. The travesty of Jim's "freedom" in the closing narrative movement reveals in a way that no other ending could that he is not free and will not be. Why else and how else could we, after one hundred years of the book's life, keep being drawn into the splendid lie of a young boy deciding to steal a slave out of slavery? Let me offer three tentative reasons for our being sold by as well as sold on the book. First, deep down we know and know socially every day that neither we nor Jim is free despite the fictions of history and the Thirteenth Amendment; second, we do not even want Jim to be free, in order that we can continue to enjoy the perennial self-approval of freeing him; and third, we tell ourselves he is free because we, like all the characters in the book, want to be lied to. If that last is what the King and Duke know so well, it is also what Huck knows. The lie is, in a world of lies, what comes easiest and handiest to mind and mouth. Knowing so much, Huck, like the King and the Duke, can easily enlist the help of his interlocutors. As he says of Aunt Sally and Uncle Silas when he lies to them about having been on a steamboat that blew its cylinder head, "If I'd a called it a bolt-head it would a done just as well."

The truth we most deeply need to believe in a free country is that we are free — and freedom in this country, first defined as freedom from tyranny, came to be defined as freedom from slavery. Freeing the slaves — emancipation — was the great international and political movement in the West in the nineteenth century. Predicated on the twin humanitarian emotions of indignation at the cruelty to the downtrodden of the earth and sympathy for their plight, emancipation volatilized the American dream of freedom into the war that freed the slaves. Having lived on the great Mississippi that had run directly between freedom and slavery and having come across that river to take up residence next door to Harriet Beecher Stowe — the very embodiment of Christian indignation and sympathy — Mark Twain knew that the current of that emotion was as powerful and deceptive in history as the current of the river. But beyond that he knew that official religions, national claims to truth, moral interpretations of history, the Christian conscience, and even God himself were lies. If he himself had a great sympathetic heart, he had also seen every form of fraud and was himself, as he well knew, hardly exempt from greed and mendacity.

Nietzsche, it is well to remember, during the very years in which Mark Twain was writing *Life on the Mississippi, Huckleberry Finn,* and *A Connecticut Yankee,* was projecting a whole long series of notes, aphorisms, and speculations for a book to be called *The Will to Power.* He saw and felt, with perhaps more clarity and intensity than Mark Twain could see, the lie of the nineteenth century. Indeed his book in every respect constitutes fine parallel reading with *Huckleberry Finn.* One quote from it will suffice to show how Nietzsche defined the lie:

The holy lie therefore invented (1) a *God* who punishes and rewards, who strictly observes the law-book of the priests and is strict about

sending them into the world as his mouthpieces and plenipoten-
tiaries; (2) an *afterlife* in which the great punishment machine is first
thought to become effective—to this end the *immortality of the soul;*
(3) *conscience* in man as the consciousness that good and evil are permanent—that God himself speaks through it when it advises conformity with priestly precepts; (4) *morality* as a denial of all natural
processes, as reduction of all events to a morally conditioned event,
moral effects (i.e., the idea of punishment and reward) as effects per-
meating all things, as the sole power, as the creator of all transformation; (5) *truth* as given, as revealed, as identical with the teaching
of the priests: as the condition for all salvation and happiness in this
life and the next. [Friedrich Nietzsche, *The Will to Power,* trans.
Walter Kaufmann and R. J. Hollingdale (New York: Random
House, 1967)]

Nietzsche concluded that the origin of this holy lie was nothing more or less
than the *will to power.* That will was at once the motive and the end of the institutions of knowledge, morality, imagination, and society, which is to say that
it was the motive of schools, churches, literature, and nations. He longed for a
great human being who lacked "the virtues that accompany respect and 'respectability' and altogether everything that is part of the 'virtue of the herd,'" who
"when not speaking to himself wears a mask," who "rather lies than tells the
truth," and whose strength of will is "the freedom from any kind of conviction."

Surely anyone familiar with Mark Twain's overt attitudes and expressed
observations knows how much he shared Nietzsche's premises. Indeed, Huck
Finn is in an uncanny way Mark Twain's expression or version of Nietzsche's
great human being. For Mark Twain recognized that the holy American nation, having fought out the battle of good and evil along the lines and under the
terms of freedom against slavery, was itself moving toward the goal of imperial
power. And if we survey our progress in the one hundred years since the publication of *Huckleberry Finn,* we see how much we are at the threshold of George
Orwell's *1984,* in which the Ministry of Truth projected the following slogans:

WAR IS PEACE

FREEDOM IS SLAVERY

IGNORANCE IS STRENGTH

In Orwell's world, Winston Smith, under the vigilant electronic eye of
Big Brother, is commissioned to rewrite history each day, first by removing
every aspect of it that fails to conform to the originating policy changes of the
Ministry of Truth, and second by translating the narrative into Newspeak—a

language designed to purge ambiguity, to eliminate irregular verbs, and to use nouns, verbs, adjectives, and adverbs interchangeably so as to annihilate as much as possible the distinctions between act and thing, and between individual and class. In addition, Newspeak built up a vocabulary of compound words with the design of making the political component the absolute dominant power of language. Here good and evil, as defined by the state, could instantaneously be communicated into conceptual linguistic designations such as *goodthink* and *crimethink, crimesex,* and *goodsex,* all for the purpose of regulating the lives of the citizens of Oceania.

Having lived through 1984, we may feel sufficiently unthreatened by Orwell's book to contend that history is not corroborating his dystopic vision. Yet each day the paranoid camera eye is projected through an electronic image of a world where an incredible array of missile clusters, called densepacks, are being projected into a projectile called the Peacemaker; where the way to arms reduction lies in the production of more arms; and where the institution for waging absolute destructive war is called the Department of Defense. And all this defense is being stockpiled to keep our national freedom secure from the slavery of rival political ideologies.

The discordant reality principle of Mark Twain's ending in its very act of travesty exposes an implicit vision profoundly related to Nietzsche's holy lie and Orwell's Big Lie. Mark Twain, who had lived across the division of his own nation, could see the holy lie of religion as well as the big national lie of freedom. Yet however much we might see Mark Twain's relation to Nietzsche and Orwell, we unfailingly know that neither the narrative nor the narrator of *Huckleberry Finn* can quite be subordinated to that relationship. By way of pointing up the difference that qualifies the relationship, we can take another passage of the book which, appearing only five pages after Huck's much heralded crisis of conscience, records an exchange between Huck and Aunt Sally just after he lies to her about being on a steamboat that blew its cylinder head. Showing immediate concern, she asks,

> "Good gracious! anybody hurt?"
> "No'm. Killed a nigger."
> "Well, it's lucky; because sometimes people do get hurt."

That brief exchange, surely one of the most universally approved passages in the book, is usually quoted to illustrate the instinctive heartlessness of a slaveholding society. Yet the exchange raises all the moral questions of earlier passages we have examined. How, after all, *are* we to take Huck in the exchange? In light of his long experience with Jim and his recent declaration of love for him, is Huck consciously going along with the value system he knows Aunt

Sally to believe in? Is he deliberately or merely instinctively withholding that part of himself that is dedicated to freeing Jim? Or is he impervious to an awareness beyond his individual experience with Jim that "niggers" count as people? Or has he literally forgotten his relation to Jim in this new tight place in which he finds himself? If he continues to refer to Jim as a nigger—which he does right through to the end—can he really think that Jim counts as a person? All these questions point to vital aspects of Huck's character that assume negative relations to a positive and principled desire for Jim's freedom, leaving only our wish that Huck remember his knowledge of and experience with Jim—for if Huck remembers he does not show it. As for Aunt Sally, her earnest remark that people sometimes do get hurt all but convicts her of the cruelty from which we might wish to exempt Huck. Yet the fact remains that both she and Huck are unquestionably kindhearted characters, and *both are momentarily sacrificed in order to produce the vividly savage satire upon the society in which both helplessly exist.* Both, in other words, are made by Mark Twain to perform the little drama intended to expose the cruelty of a benighted society.

To subject this passage to the scrutiny that we have directed upon other memorable and much-approved passages is to come full circle back to the fact that this is a hard book to take. For we see once more that directing satiric scorn harshly upon the slaveholding society robs Aunt Sally of her good intentions and even throws Huck's good heart into question. Moreover, the satiric irony of the passage, no matter how manifest, cannot really make up for the *matter* of the passage—the fatal word—to a black audience. To the audience content to feel a pleasurable thrill at seeing the slaveholding society of the old South or the segregated society of the intermediate South flogged once more, we should be able to say, in the presence of the new South, that they are taking pleasure in flogging a dead horse. Rather than continuing to do that, such an audience ought to be glad that a new black audience is rising in force to object to the book. Such objection is assurance that the book is alive in a living, shifting society and cannot be complacently approved by the new academic tradition that has replaced the old genteel tradition.

Is there a way out of these mean tricks that begin to bare themselves wherever the book is indulgently approved? Just possibly. If we go on to read the lines directly and happily following that famous passage, we find Aunt Sally going on to say,

> "Two years ago last Christmas, your Uncle Silas was coming up from Newrleans on the old *Lally Rook,* and she blowed out a cylinder-head and crippled a man. And I think he died afterwards. He was a Babtist. Your Uncle Silas knowed a family in Baton Rouge

that knowed his people very well. Yes, I remember now, he *did* die. Mortification set in, and they had to amputate him. But it didn't save him. Yes, it was mortification—that was it. He turned blue all over, and died in the hope of a glorious resurrection. They say he was a sight to look at."

There again is the beautiful principle of emotional exchange at work. If we are indulgently indignant at the cruelty of the slave society, we do not even want to remember the poor Baptist. Certainly we are not meant to sympathize with his fate. But if we care about the humor of the book we cannot do without him. Aunt Sally in this instance is made a little more stupid than she really is, but her sentimentality and kindheartedness are somehow retained in Mark Twain's determination to move from the savage irony of satire into the dissolution of helpless humor. There is no sign that Huck laughs at this turn of events. He is as silent on the subject as he is about his knowledge of Jim, but the humor of his narrative is undeniably there. If we do not helplessly laugh it is only because we have been unduly arrested by our pleasure in the satiric cruelty that initiates the exchange.

Huck's apparent lack of memory about Jim and his deadpan about the humor are surely the great redemptive facts about this book. Like Nietzsche's great human being, Huck retains a true freedom from all conviction. He truly does belong on the current of the Great Mississippi running between the banks of good and evil, between freedom and slavery, and still running in its lower reaches, between banks where slavery is on both its sides, toward an open sea. We have to recognize, or surely would want to, that even when he chooses to go to hell, he is even then somehow, like the running river, taking the path of least resistance. It is surely easier and handier for him to betray Miss Watson than to betray Jim. His lies are, in their final analysis, better than the truth that our own socially and morally approving conscience would confer upon him. If the people in the black audience find the fatal word and the stereotypical minstrel characterization of Jim hard to take, they are only telling us that we ought to find its manifest and indulgent good intentions as well as its implicit nihilism —a nihilism utterly but oh so humorously explicit in its final sentences—harder to take than we do.

It would not be so bad if the book were banned in the public schools. Then we might read it anew and find another passage as central as the much-quoted passages I have cited. When Huck first embarks upon the river after his escape from Pap and before he meets Jim, he writes (for he is a *writer,* we must remember):

> I didn't lose no time. The next minute I was a-spinning down stream
> soft but quick in the shade of the bank. I made two mile and a half,

and then struck out a quarter of a mile or more towards the middle
of the river, because pretty soon I would be passing the ferry landing
and people might see me and hail me. I got out amongst the drift-
wood and then laid down in the bottom of the canoe and let her
float. I laid there and had a good rest and a smoke out of my pipe,
looking away into the sky, not a cloud in it. The sky looks ever so
deep when you lay down on your back in the moonshine; I never
knowed it before. And how far a body can hear on the water such
nights! I heard people talking at the ferry landing. I heard what they
said, too, every word of it. One man said it was getting towards the
long days and the short nights, now. 'Tother one said *this* warn't one
of the short ones, he reckoned — and then they laughed, and he said it
over again and they laughed again; then they waked up another
fellow and told him, and laughed, but he didn't laugh; he ripped out
something brisk and said let him alone. The first fellow said he
'lowed to tell it to his old woman — she would think it was pretty
good; but he said that warn't nothing to some things he had said in
his time. I heard one man say it was nearly three o'clock, and he
hoped daylight wouldn't wait more than about a week longer. After
that, the talk got further and further away, and I couldn't make out
the words any more, but I could hear the mumble; and now and then
a laugh, too, but it seemed a long ways off.

How much is beautifully there. The fugitive boy in the stolen canoe running
away upon the running river with no time to lose, yet time enough in the idle
moment to see the depth of the heavens above him, and ears acute enough to
hear the conversation far across the water. And then the wonderful conversation itself with the stupid jokes — showing that for every two people who share
a joke there is likely to be a third who finds nothing funny, and showing too
humanity's inveterate need to repeat itself in an act of performance. And the
stupidity and the corny jokes made incredibly humorous as Huck's written rehearsal redeems those dear old yokels. And finally the voices fading, leaving the
mumble and the laughter trailing in the wake of the passage. With no time to
lose, how much is gained!

On a great muddy river where, unlike the blue stillness of Walden Pond,
the water's action makes reflection impossible just as its color hides its depth,
the instinct of both Huck's deviant language and deviant character is equal to
the mulatto solution of the current. That is why Huck's being and language are
magically and mysteriously identical with the current, and also why the humor
he both evokes and records keeps him free from the principle of freedom, the

principle that in the economy of moral exchange always threatens to create two rednecks for every slave it frees. Mark Twain knew as well as we know how utterly necessary that principle is for American society. It was the principle we believe we believed in enough to fight the one war when God was truly on our side. Yet the war was bloody and divisive, involving catastrophic loss of life. The humor of *Huckleberry Finn* literally displaces that loss with a gain of helpless and overt pleasure. Such pleasure, a manifest and true expression of the pleasure principle at the heart of all life, serves to disarm the pleasure of principle that is the armor of adult society. The point is that it disarms it but does not overtly attack it. No adult society can do without the pleasure of principle, which, after all, is at once the purpose and conscience of civilization. Mark Twain believed in it enough to sacrifice Tom Sawyer to it—and we cannot forget that Tom was the character through whom he had discovered Huck Finn. Yet he would not sacrifice Huck to it. Instead he let Huck reject civilization and the adult conscience in the very last pages of his book—an ending that is, as Eliot so rightly realized, as perfect as any in literature.

Holding to the beauty of this humor, yet remembering always that humor involves an exchange that threatens somebody, we should be able not only to stand but to understand civilization's impulse to ban the book. The banning would express society's discomfort with the book just as Huck's rejection of civilization is an expression of his discomfort with adult society. Even if the book were banned in all the schools, we would only be reminded that its very language was proof from the beginning that it never was for the schools. When the book was banned in Concord, Mark Twain applauded the action on the grounds that it would sell thirty-five thousand copies. As both inventor and publisher of *Huckleberry Finn*, he lived in a world where abrupt exchanges were conducted in as well as between the realm of the moral indignation and the arena of the marketplace. Huck observes at the outset of the novel that he doesn't like the widow's food because everything is cooked by itself. He likes things cooked together, as if in a barrel of odds and ends, where "things get mixed up, and the juice kind of swaps around, and the things go better." Later, observing the early morning sun shining through the forest leaves on Jackson's Island, he notes the freckled places in the gloom, which "swapped about a little, showing there was a little breeze up there." Lost in the fog on the river and calling out to Jim, he cannot place Jim's answering whoops because he "never knowed a sound dodge around so, and swap places so quick and so much." Finally at Aunt Sally's, when he discovers that he is supposed to be Tom Sawyer and almost slumps through the floor in relief, he regrets that "there warn't no time to swap knives" as Uncle Silas forcibly hustles him into his new identity with a barrage of questions that he happily *can* answer. Swapping, it turns out in this humorous and devious world of moral relativity, leads to possibilities of taste, beauty, anxiety, and pleasure.

Having experienced the manipulative, shifty, shrewd, and humorous exchanges constantly taking place both on and beside the moving Mississippi, we should be able to contemplate with a degree of equanimity the possibility of widespread removal of *Huckleberry Finn* from school and library shelves. In the face of such censorship, we would still be left with the happy choice of pursuing the pleasure of principle with a serious—even outraged—public defense of the book against those who found it hard to take, or indulging the pleasure principle by reading the book in private where we could blessedly take it easy.

The Limits of Semiotics

Cleo McNelly Kearns

It is sometimes claimed that modern literary theory is an impossibly esoteric affair, offensively elitist in its barbarous jargon. The truth is that such theory has always been more acceptable to the ruled than the rulers. Oppressed peoples are natural hermeneuticists, skilled by hard schooling in interpreting their oppressors' language. They are spontaneous semioticians, forced for sheer survival to decipher the sign systems of the enemy and adept at deploying their own opaque idioms against them.
— TERRY EAGLETON, *New York Times Book Review*, 9 December 1984

"Dah, now, Huck, what I tell you?—what I tell you up dah on Jackson islan'? I tole you I got a hairy breas', en what's de sign un it; en I tole you I ben rich wunst, en gwineter be rich agin; en it's come true; eh heah she is! Dah, now! doan' talk to me—signs is signs, mine I tell you; en I knowed jis' 's well 'at I 'uz gwineter be rich agin as I's a stannin' heah dis minute!"
— JIM, *Huckleberry Finn*

Tom's most well, now, and got his bullet around his neck on a watch-guard for a watch, and is always seeing what time it is, and so there ain't nothing more to write about, and I am rotten glad of it, because if I'd a knowed what a trouble it was to write a book I wouldn't a tackled it and ain't agoing to no more. But I reckon I got to light out for the Territory ahead of the rest, because Aunt Sally she's going to adopt me and sivilize me and I can't stand it. I been there before."
— HUCK, *Huckleberry Finn*

Jim's outburst, "signs is *signs,* mine I tell you," in the final chapter of *Huckleberry Finn,* proclaims his status as the novel's semiotician par excellence. Indeed, his general performance in that role seems to confirm at least some of Terry Eagleton's

---

Published for the first time in this volume. © 1986 by Cleo McNelly Kearns.

claims for the "spontaneous" semiotic activities of the oppressed. Throughout the novel, Jim displays dazzling powers over signs, decoding in his own inimitable way texts as diverse as the natural indices of the body and the complex stories of the Bible. He finds signification everywhere, from the hair on his breast to the figments in dreams, and his ability to "read" these signs gives him a sense of control over his own fate which helps him survive the multiple indignities of life as a slave. Jim reads signs intensely, both to ward off the despair of his and Huck's situation and to challenge Huck's (slight but important) advantages of greater knowledge and greater mobility. As he does so, Jim becomes the novel's own model of what it means to read in semiotic terms, helping us to bring into focus through his "opaque idioms" the advantages and limitations of an acute attention to signs.

Those limitations, however, become more and more evident the more Jim's practice as a semiotician comes under scrutiny. In the first place, Jim is himself a sign, a sign produced by Huck's narrative. His "sign-reading" abilities are very much those assigned to the stereotypical stage darky, full of a superstition which is the more fascinating for its occasional flashes of insight or retrospective justification. Only the gaps, the fissures, the "breaks" in Huck's own presentation of Jim, the places where his sense of Jim's skill as a sign-reader breaks down or is transformed into something else, allow another dimension of Jim's character to appear and offer a genuine challenge to Huck's own reading of their situation. At these moments—the moment on the raft when Huck challenges Jim to interpret a fictive dream and the moment when his consciousness of a danger neither he nor Jim can control causes him to tear up his own piece of sign-making, the note turning Jim in—can Jim's presence in the novel indicate a real and liberating sense of power. This power is expressed not through the prognosticating and passive activity of sign-reading or semiotic decoding, but either through a genuine act of hermeneutic interpretation, one which affirms the moral and social responsibility of the interpreter and his prophetic role in making the meaning he purports to "see," or through a complete rejection of all sign-systems whatever for a liberating, if evasive, silence.

Jim's form of prophetic interpretation not only transcends semiotics, but is framed by Huck's skeptical and evasive response, which makes a counter-claim for another kind of attitude to semiotics, a rather Joycean "silence, exile and cunning." Huck's tacit rejections of Jim's semiotic skills, and his own violations of all forms of coding, from the expectations of his mentors to the activity of writing itself, indicate a very different sense from Jim's of semiotic constraints. Jim seeks to transcend those constraints on behalf of a social and fraternal concept of liberation: Huck seeks to escape them on behalf of an individual and self-authorizing freedom. The tension between the two is at the heart of the novel and informs its interpretation both within and without the text.

Like those who dabble in divination, itself an instance and a telling paradigm of semiotic activity, Jim often operates, superficially at least, on the assumption that meaning is already coded in and that he gets his authority only as a "reader" of what is already there. This assumption usefully averts the crippling anger and despair generated by the powerlessness of his position, but it also reduces his function to that of mere prognosticator or diviner, a kind of tool of the texts he reads. While he does find relief in semiotic activity, then, Jim does so at the risk of submitting himself to the control of a system of identities—signs is signs, x is y—which are already fixed in advance. In assuming this position, Jim not only underestimates his own power and responsibility, but puts himself in constant danger of becoming nothing more than a comic butt. His audience, which includes Huck, Tom, and the reader, recognizes his prognostications to be naive, and they see all too clearly, in Jim if not in themselves, the motives of self-defense and self-aggrandizement that prompt such reductive semiosis. It is only in those moments when he (and we) abandon "spontaneous semiotics" and take on the full responsibilities of a wider and deeper kind of interpretation that any possibility of liberation from racial stereotype and oppression can be glimpsed in the discourse of the novel.

Furthermore, as this novel makes abundantly clear, the existence of many "natural" strategies of interpretation is not in itself a guarantee of liberation, and the variety of these strategies may involve more vital issues than a casual embrace of theory-at-large would allow. Jim, after all, is not alone on his raft, and his experiments in interpretation do not go unchallenged, either by his enemies or by his friends. Huck himself, for instance, offers another, very potent alternative to the "spontaneous semiotics" and "opaque idioms" of Jim's usual mode of interpretive activity. While Huck is, for the most part, lost in wonder at Jim's semiotic skill, and more than vocal in his admiration for it, he also constantly tests that skill and seeks to reveal its narrow base. Faced with Jim's apparent and insistent faith in the complete, direct, reciprocal, and transparent relationship between sign and meaning, Huck constantly deconstructs this semiotic activity by bringing into play a deeper skepticism and a far more radical sense of the unrepresentability of any signified by any material sign. Huck is, furthermore, vexed in a way Jim is not by the implications of determinism in semiotics. He recognizes that both he and Jim are far more implicated in the making of the codes they pretend merely to "read" than his partner would seem to admit, even though this recognition leaves him, too, in an uncomfortable position of entanglement and uncertainty. The two interpreters are, then, often engaged in a struggle for mastery between different and incommensurable ways of reading, one which, as each of them comes to recognize, makes any easy resolution by "natural," "spontaneous," or semi-conscious theories out of the question.

This struggle is motivated in part by some degree of competition for mastery over the narrative itself. There are times, for instance, when it is unclear, from a genre point of view, whether this novel is meant to mimic the narrative of an escaped slave or the deposition of a boy on trial for abetting that slave (See Harold Beaver, "Run, Nigger, Run: The *Adventures of Huckleberry Finn* as Fugitive Slave Narrative." *Journal of American Studies* 8 (1974): 339–61). Beneath this generic difficulty lies a tension between the two figures of Huck and Jim which makes us wonder whose story this really is, after all. Huck has control over the actual writing, it appears, but Jim often has a far superior grasp of the action and a deeper understanding of its significance for their fate. As long as Jim remains only a decoder of signs these deeper dimensions do not come into play. When, however, he is able to rise to Huck's challenge and to use his deeper powers of interpretation and prophecy to transcend the role of mere semiotician, he becomes Huck's great antagonist—becomes, indeed, *so* strong that he very nearly usurps Huck's role in the story altogether.

Jim's exuberant assertion that "signs is *signs*" indicates, then, one attitude toward signification: an affirmative and hopeful attitude insisting on the fullness and richness of the sign, with its promise of future meaning and future wealth. This attitude is in part Huck's construct, however, and is undercut by moments when his own sign-making activity breaks down, revealing a deep skepticism both about the adequacy of signs and about the codes on which they depend. These two attitudes are juxtaposed throughout the novel, contributing both to its comic effects and to its near brushes with tragedy, as issues at stake in questions of interpretation become more and more vital to each character's life and fate.

These two attitudes toward semiotics are worked out in terms of a running analogy between monetary relations, prediction, and textual interpretation. Money is useful here because it shows both the great power of signifying systems, able as they are to convert one kind of value into the terms of another, and their inherent limitations, the danger of collapse as those values prove incommensurable after all. All signs, like all currencies, can be inflated with values they cannot sustain or used reductively to indicate conversions that cannot be performed. Indeed, the central problem on which this novel rests is precisely a problem of such reductions: the reduction in this case of a human being to a unit of monetary worth, a slave. Prediction, too, can be inflated or reduced, especially in the form of divination, which denies human freedom and reduces those who indulge in it to the level of pawns in a rigged game. Analogous, as well, are the most debased forms of textual interpretation represented here: the overly literal readings of religious fundamentalism and the overly spirited ones of romantic fiction, each of which falsifies the value of the signs with which it deals either by inflation or by reduction. To these are opposed the true use of money, the genuine function of prophecy, and the sane, contextually rooted interpretation of literary and religious texts. These are distinguished from the false use of signs by their assumption of freedom of the will and their dedication to that fully realized political and ethical liberation which is the novel's ever-receding goal.

We can trace this interweaving of money, prediction, and textual interpretation throughout the novel. It is no accident, for instance, given their counterposed attitudes toward signs, that the story begins with Huck trying to give up a fortune and ends with Jim looking forward to one. In Chapter 2 the analogy is even more fully worked out. Here Huck and Tom steal three candles from under a sleeping watchman's nose, leaving a five-cent piece for pay. The watchman turns out to be Jim, and Tom compounds the mischief by taking Jim's hat off while he sleeps and hanging it on a tree over his head. When Jim wakes up, the boys are gone, and he begins to make quite a reputation for himself by claiming that "witches" have charmed him and ridden him down to New Orleans and back and even around the world, hanging his hat on a limb to show "who done it." In this inventive semiotic scheme, the five-cent piece becomes the gift of the devil, having curative powers as well as powers of command over the witches. Money is closely related to magic, and Jim is their would-be master. The whole business makes him quite a celebrity—the founder, indeed, of his own little community of interpretation—and he is, Huck tells us with a note of childish jealousy, "most ruined" for a "servant" on its account.

At first look this is a simple piece of local color and class and race stereotyping. We see Jim as a caricature, a stage darky, a superstitious, comic, and pretentious character, just about to get "above" himself—and very much the butt, rather than the equal, of Tom's boyish pranks. The events of the story do, however, in some ways confirm, figuratively speaking, Jim's sense of himself and of his adventures. He does indeed get "taken for a ride" by a certain kind of white-boy witchery, a ride which takes him very nearly to New Orleans and enlarges his scope as if he had indeed gone "around the world." His recovery from that ride and his mastery over it are also very much dependent on the possession of that "five-center piece." Money is a talisman of command over the manipulations to which Jim will be subject as the tale goes on. Even at their most apparently simplistic, Jim's semiotic interpretations have an unconscious or subconscious truth, a truth which is part of their charm. At this point he does not surpass that charm, but remains enmeshed in the code he purports to read. This reading is consoling and enabling, helping Jim and us to believe that his fate is not entirely sealed, that he can understand, anticipate, and circumvent trouble, and that good fortune, however far in the future, is destined to be his.

It does not, however, allow Jim to engage consciously in creating the meanings to which he points, and its illusions eventually prove more disconcerting than enabling.

The complex connection between money and signs becomes even clearer in Jim's next appearance. In Chapter 4 Huck has just discovered that his father is back in town and looking for him — no doubt for access to his little fortune, won in the earlier tale *The Adventures of Tom Sawyer.* Here Huck provides the first of many tacit and complex reversals in the strength and weakness to be gained by the activity of semiotics. The incident opens with Huck seeking Jim's advice. It seems that Jim is in possession of a hair-ball which predicts the future, but which requires, Jim claims, a little wherewithal in order to prompt its powers. This claim leads to a strong suspicion that Jim himself has an all-too-materialist analysis of the nature of sign-reading, but Huck is by no means an easy mark for this game. He tries to avoid being taken for all he has by remaining discreet about the full dollar in his pocket and proffering a visibly spurious counterfeit quarter instead. Accepting the premise of the hair-ball's powers, he *explains* that the quarter is counterfeit, but suggests that maybe the hair-ball won't know the difference! This piece of innocent but self-defeating guile (who does Huck think he's kidding, the hair-ball or Jim?) is, however, completely outdone, both morally and in terms of the comedy, by the talisman's owner, who promptly scoops the scene by advancing a plan for *improving* the counterfeit so that it will pass in the local market.

In undertaking this task, Jim makes himself Huck's confederate rather than his antagonist in this game of true and false significations, and indicates, by the same token, his complete ease with apparently contradictory signifying codes. While the rationalist reader is busy working out who believes what here, Jim moves with ease from the code of soothsaying, where he clearly believes his words to be true, to the code of money, where truth-value is irrelevant, as long as the sign is superficially credible. Combining these codes, he proceeds, in cooperation with the hair-ball, to deliver a prophecy which is partly a perfectly accurate guess as to the nature of Huck's father's actions, partly an expression of the rather Manichaean dualism associated with divination, and partly the healing and consoling message of an older person to a younger one. (According to the hair-ball, Huck's father has two angels hovering around him, one white and one black, and their alternation of ascendancy dictates his instable actions; Huck himself will have both trouble in his life and "consid'able joy," and is destined either to be hanged or drowned. The prophecy at this point is somewhat muddled, but we may note that hangings and drownings do lie ahead in this tale as its violence and danger increase.) In this scene, then, a spurious coin becomes, by a semiotic operation, "as good as real," and likewise a spurious bit of fortune-telling becomes "as good as true" as the false coinage of superstition is redeemed by Jim's practical wisdom. Here Jim has begun to demonstrate powers of conversion, conversion of false coinage into true, of monetary relations into relations of collaboration and friendship, and even, to some extent, of superstitious divination into prophetic wisdom. The coin, however, is still counterfeit at base, and the limits of the power of semiotics to convert one sign into another at will are beginning to become apparent.

As the novel progresses, Jim is more and more construed by Huck as the master semiotician. "Jim knew all kinds of signs," Huck says, "indeed, he knew most everything." In Chapter 8, Huck even presses Jim for some insight into the semiotic theory on which he works. His first concern is why Jim constantly draws attention to *bad* signs, rather than *good* ones. Jim's answer is incontrovertible and pragmatic: the only reason to interpret signs is to prompt corrective action, and in the case of good coming, it is better to let well enough alone. There are, besides, "mighty few" good signs, and the most useful ones are those that predict something far off—like wealth. "You see," Jim explains, "maybe you's got to be po' a long time fust, en so you might git discourage' en kill yo'self 'f you didn't know by de sign dat you gwyne to be rich bymeby." Signs are useful for their pragmatic impact on the present, as forms of encouragement or despair.

Jim uses as a case in point here the prophecy of his own riches as indicated by the hair on his breast, and Twain takes the occasion for another comic excursus on the complex relation of signs and money. This time the signs are linguistic and even literary, rather than magical, and they provide a lesson in the limitations, as opposed to the strengths, of Jim's semiotic powers. Jim, it appears, once had fourteen dollars, but he took to speculation and lost it all. Jim's form of speculation was a series of bad investments which were bad in part because they rested upon deep confusions of figurative and literal meaning. He invested, he tells Huck, first in "stock." The "stock," however, turns out to have been "livestock"—in the form of one cow, which died. He then put the money in a bank scam, itself a literal misreading of the nature of the banking enterprise by a fellow-slave, and invested the putative return in a wood-flat which was stolen, while the 'bank' went bust. Finally, prompted by a dream, he offered ten cents to a fellow named Balaam, who had taken literally a preacher's injunction that money given to the poor would come back tenfold. Needless to say, there was no immediate return. The apotheosis of this continual, comic melange of figurative and literal meanings comes when Jim remarks, ironically, that in spite of all these failures, he must already be rich because he owns himself, and he is, after all, worth eight hundred dollars on the open market. "I wisht I had de money," he concludes. The underlying lesson of these misadventures is the frequent untranslatability of one kind of sign into another, of money into real goods, of words into their literal counterparts, or of cash value into flesh and blood. Too reductive a semiotic equation, "signs is signs," x is y, will eventually break down, both in theory and in practice: a lesson Jim has yet to learn.

Twain liked to read aloud this excursus on signs and money together with a later passage in the novel, also revealing of Jim's semiotic strategy—the very funny exchange between Huck and Jim as each tries his interpretive powers on a classic text, one of the Biblical stories of Solomon. Solomon comes up in Chapter 14, in the context of Huck's reading to Jim from books all about "kings, and dukes, and earls and such." The conversation calls into play the conflict between at least three different codes of signification: Biblical fundamentalism, romantic adventurism, and proverbial wisdom. Jim, like a zany student, poses a marvelously off-the-wall but cogent question, one which links money with a different kind of social and economic power. "How much do a king git?" he asks. Huck, caught off guard, provides a makeshift answer, in the course of which the notion of a harem comes up. Jim adroitly elicits a definition of this hitherto unknown term, and then masters it by a neat analogy. (This analogy can only be described as "metaphysical": a harem must be like a boiler room, the latter equally noisy, but more productive, and you can shut it off. The conceit of the harem-boiler room will later reach nightmare proportions in Richard Wright's *Native Son*.) Jim then turns his attention to his own ingenious interpretation of the passage from 1 Kings 3:16–18 which describes how Solomon found the true mother of a child by threatening to cut it in half. This project, Jim argues, was criminal folly; why didn't Solomon first "shin aroun' mongs' de neighbours" and *find out* to whom the child belonged before indulging in this cruel form of experimental vivisection? Charged by Huck with completely missing the point—the child wasn't *really* going to be cut in half—Jim rises to heights of dialectical casuistry that leave us gasping: "De 'spute warn't 'bout a half a chile, de 'spute was 'bout a whole chile; en de man dat think he kin settle a 'spute about a whole chile wid a half a chile, doan' know enough to come in out'n de rain."

This dazzling rejoinder is a classic semiotic response, a manipulation of signs as it were in air, with little responsibility toward that complex relation between literal and figurative meanings they entail. Necessity is here the mother of invention, for Jim, as Huck presents him, is clearly compensating for lack of knowledge by the overwhelming exercise of his interpretive ingenuity. At the same time, he demonstrates unconsciously that all semiotic activity is far more context-bound than it appears. An equation within a code in one situation is no equation at all in another. Jim's method of resolving the dispute over the child comes as deeply out of the tribal and proverbial context of a close-knit slave community as Huck's does out of the fundamentalist Biblical culture to which he has been half-exposed. The two codes are incommensurable, and the significations of one do not convert easily into those of the other. Confronted with this lack of fit, Huck, his whole being actively and consciously bound up with the contradictions between these codes, experiences an understandable despair, and he inaugurates that strategy of withdrawal he will later pursue to the end. "I see it warn't no use wasting words," he concludes, and, taking refuge in a raw and unmediated privileging of one code over the other, "you can't learn a nigger to argue." He is himself the "divided child" over which they have been arguing, and he cannot heal that division with signs, but only with his own particular version of silence, exile, and cunning.

There are, however, problems with Jim's semiotic play here and with the stock role Huck makes him occupy. Indeed, in asserting him as the novel's great semiotician, Huck is exposing Jim to ridicule as the perfect type of the superstitious darky. In light of this stereotype, the ability to read "signs" appears less as a skill than as an illusion, a pretension produced by events and motives that a more liberal, more sophisticated, and perhaps more cynical audience can understand better than either character. After all, we know, because we have followed Huck and Jim through the story, the rational causes of the events they experience, and we can imagine, all too easily, the psychological needs and defenses which give rise to these grand and reductive semiotic equations. Huck's glorification of sign-reading in Jim, then, takes place to the disadvantage of his own reliability as narrator, as well as playing to a stereotype that can only confirm the audience's superiority, rather than involve that audience in the dangers, responsibilities, and inadequacies of submission to a genuine, but flawed, process of interpretation.

As the novel progresses, Jim steps out of his two-dimensional stereotype and begins to assert this genuine hermeneutic power. He does so by breaking through Huck's expectations of him to inaugurate a very different kind of interpretive activity from sign-reading or prognostication. (How this effect is created through the constructs of Huck's discourse is, of course, a mystery of Twain's craft; *that* such an effect is created seems beyond dispute.) A particularly sharp demonstration of the difference between semiotic divination and prophetic interpretation comes at the novel's turning point, in Chapter 15, in which Huck's relation to Jim reaches a moral crisis. During the events of this chapter, the friends are separated by fog, as Huck's canoe breaks from the raft and is swept to the other side of an approaching island. Later, Huck manages to return to the raft and finds Jim asleep, with one oar broken and a litter of dirt all around him to testify to his efforts to find the boy again. When Jim wakes up, Huck, possessed for the moment of the spirit of adventurist elaboration that animates Tom Sawyer, tries to tell him that this separation and struggle have been only a dream. Jim is hard to convince, but once duped, he sets himself to interpret this so-called "dream." He does so with his usual brilliance. The dream is a *warning,* a warning of danger ahead, and of the necessity for waking up and paying attention to signs, so the two can get out of the fog and into the "big clear river" again. Jim is not, in figurative terms, entirely wrong here. Huck's lie and the fictional experience it refers to *are* a kind of warning, a warning of the fog of false consciousness which can divide the two and make them lose their ethical moorings.

Both lie and fiction, moreover, seem to call out for decipherment, the need for which Jim himself insists upon. The events of the so-called dream are, Jim claims, important calls to action, and if the two of them didn't "try hard to make out to understand them" the dream events would take them *into* bad luck instead of keeping them out of it. Jim concludes with a major semiotic equation, itself one of his not infrequent excursions into literary troping. He identifies, Huck tells us, the "big clear river" figuratively with "the free States." Jim reads signs here as a writer of fictions might read them, with a kind of literary sensibility that is revealing but also artificial. Furthermore, his reduction of signs to pragmatic indications involves all kinds of logical contradictions he does not explore.

Huck, however, at once tries to puncture this literary mode of signification and to reveal its lack of ground. He is apparently operating under the not-unfamiliar critical assumption that simply by pointing to a text's base in a fiction he can deflate its semiotic claims. "Oh well, that's all interpreted well enough, as far as it goes, Jim," he says, "but" (pointing to the leaves and rubbish and the smashed oar, incontrovertible proofs of the fictionality of the dream, not to mention of his own cruel and self-aggrandizing lie) "what does *these* things stand for?" Jim gazes at the evidence of the facts, a harder set of signs than he has hitherto confronted, and a set which makes the question of the human intentionality behind them explicit. He is at first stunned, and simply looks back and forth. At this moment of defeat, far from giving up, however, Jim, in a remarkable *coup de théâtre,* abandons the mode of semiotics proper for the greater mode of interpretive insight and prophetic power. With superb dignity, he shifts the ground of argument from the dubious discourse of divination to the compelling one of moral truth, a truth which includes the human subject as an essential element. Turning to Huck, he asserts an interpretation stronger than any he has made, one which draws its strength not from reductive identities, or from some elaborately literary turn of speech, but from the force of his own perception of the *willed* nature of the situation. Looking from the things on the raft to Huck he says:

"What do dey stan' for? I's gwyne to tell you. When I got all wore out wid work, en wid de callin' for you, en went to sleep, my heart wuz mos' broke bekase you wuz los', en I didn' k'yer no mo' what become er me en de raf'. En when I wake up en fine you back agin', all safe en soun', de tears come en I could a got down on my knees en kiss' yo' foot I's so thankful. En all you wuz thinkin 'bout wuz how you could make a fool uv ole Jim wid a lie. Dat truck dah is *trash;* en trash is what people is dat puts dirt on de head er dey fren's en makes 'em ashamed."

This speech has a ring of authenticity which lifts Jim permanently out of the category of stereotype and makes him one of the strongest characters in American literature. The word *trash* here is one indication of that strength, for it is about the most telling term Jim could have chosen to bring Huck to his senses. It has a literal and a figurative application, and for once they cohere. Huck is "trash" in the literal sense, a part of the flotsam and jetsam the current has swept back to the raft. He is also "trash" in figurative terms; he is under-animated, so to speak, by any human difference or power of self-determination which would distinguish his attitudes from the detritus of those of the worst of his class, race, and time. There lingers behind this word a hint of the only term of abuse that outweighs *nigger* in contempt, *white trash.* This term of abuse represents social degradation without the alibi of racial discrimination, and it has great pejorative force. Huck escapes this appellation only by a hair's breadth, perhaps—indeed, only by virtue of Jim's own restraint, which will not allow him to stoop to a particularized application of the universal human law of brotherhood.

In making this interpretation of the bits and pieces on the raft, Jim deliberately exaggerates the language of signification. "What do dey stan' for?" he repeats after Huck, with scornful emphasis, "I's gwyne to tell you," and he does, with great underlining of the copula, the primary linguistic indicator of reductive equation: "Dat truck dah is *trash;* en trash is what people is dat puts dirt on de head er dey fren's." The repeated, sarcastic "is" serves to draw attention less to Jim's office as a semiotician than to the fact that there are limits to that office. Here, the need for a specialist in signs becomes itself an indication of shame, of the lack of a fully developed and awakened consciousness. "We hold these truths to be *self-evident*" begins the founding document of Huck and Jim's conflicted nation. For some things—liberty, equality, and fraternity, for instance—Huck does not need a reader of hair-balls or an interpreter of dreams, but a prophetic reminder of the free will in which signification must be grounded and the goal of liberation which it must seek.

Huck is forced, as it were, by Jim's strength here to acknowledge his greater power and moral force, though he narrates this acknowledgment with the faintest trace of defiance, as if aware of an internal and external voice of pride which regards such an acknowledgment as a shame rather than a virtue. In general, Huck is careful to evade or avoid such moments of conscious fraternity, abjuring all forms of consensual relationship whether of brotherhood, sisterhood, adoption, or even the subtle but implicit contract between writer, reader, and character. Huck associates these consensual relationships very much with the realm of women and slaves, which he wishes to leave behind for a direct, unmediated experience of male freedom. Huck is always looking for, losing, and reasserting interpretive priority — over himself, his own life, and the facts of his narrative as well. Like his blood father, he rejects domestication, and in his strategies of evasion he keeps alive — like Joyce's Stephen, like Rimbaud — the possibility that he will become the real master of his own debatable Territory. On that Territory, so unlike the fluid, changing River, he will, in some receding future tense, be able to make his mark and write the story of his own dominance, a dominance not only over Jim, over Tom, Aunt Polly, and the Widow, but even, at times, over the author and audience of his tale, whose expectations only complete silence will allow him to evade.

Throughout the novel, Huck constantly acts out the contradictions of this relationship to the very sign-systems which allow him to speak. At one point or another, he breaks every code of signs he can encounter or imagine, from speech to writing, from the letter he himself has composed turning Jim in to the signifying systems that make possible the novel he writes. At the same time, he revels in all of these modes, exploiting them to the full for a number of cross-purposes, ranging from the preservation and maintenance of his own distinct and superior identity to the defense of his relationship with Jim. To write and to speak are, for Huck, ways of asserting in the face of Jim's often superior power of interpretation a countervailing mastery over signs. They are also ways of rescuing, in the face of a society which would annihilate both Huck and Jim, the individuality that gives them life and the fraternal bond that holds them together. Huck can no more escape these activities than he can fly, for his entire narrative is constructed by them: on the one hand, by a certain "literariness" (which we may read sometimes as static on the line created by Twain himself, sometimes as the precociousness of a boy just becoming aware of an audience for his charms) and on the other hand, by the lively presence of one of the most purely *spoken* voices in all literature.

Speech and writing are, as Huck comes to learn, inextricably tied to and entangled in codes of signification which leave no place for his own experience and which threaten his exclusively boyish and anarchic little world. Rather than bend and reform these codes, as Jim seems to do, by sheer force of will and interpretive strength, Huck chooses to step outside them altogether and to break with the matrix of civilized behaviors they inevitably entail. Writing, as Huck has occasion to know, and as he tells us in the opening paragraphs of his tale, is not innocent. It is, on the contrary, fraught with lies or "stretchers." Huck accepts this as part of the game, but he worries about it nonetheless. Furthermore, Huck's own writing is, as we have seen, rather deeply motivated by a struggle with Jim over narrative priority and interpretive power, a struggle which causes him to lose confidence, now and then, in their common ground. Finally, Huck has had what social workers love to call a 'bad history' with many forms of writing. He has been early exposed to that highly reified and dangerous reading of the Bible produced by fundamentalist literalism, and his later experience of tales of romance as interpreted irresponsibly by Tom has proved a dangerous substitute. In every case, writing has left Huck no space for his own commitments and experiences, but rather with a sense of codes and systems which are threatening, but which he cannot quite dismiss from his mind. Speech proves equally deceptive, for, among other things, in this realm Jim is supreme, and he consistently gets the upper hand—and by beating Huck at his own game.

Huck's rejection of writing and speech marks another limit of semiotics, a limit marked not by its transcendence into strong interpretation, but by its fall into silence. We have already seen how, when confronted with Jim's dazzling powers of dialectic over the Solomon story, Huck decides that it is useless to waste words arguing with "a nigger." Just as he withdraws from speech when confronted with Jim's superior power, so Huck withdraws from writing when confronted with the superior power of "sivilization." In a direct attack on signs, he simply tears up his own letter turning Jim in. Huck's wrestling-match with his conscience in this case is typically confined, as is much semiotic activity, to a set of yes-or-no acceptances of a particularly literalistic and reductive code. He cannot, it seems, learn to bend, break, or transcend this code so as to make it adequate to his ethical and political needs. (It is Jim's function in the novel precisely to raise and keep alive the hope of this revisionary interpretive activity.) Huck's decision to tear up his letter represents both a genuine step forward in maturity and comprehension and a gesture of despair and blind will, one not unlike his refusal to go on arguing with Jim. These withdrawals reach their climax when Huck decides to "light out for the Territory" and stop writing altogether—the only point at which his decisions and thoughts become genuinely unanswerable, either within the novel or without.

Of course, this attack on signification conceals a deep uncertainty in Huck about his own powers of persuasion and, as many would argue, a regressive and self-defeating desire to escape from consensual reality as well. Huck's decision, however, calls into question not only "sivilization" but "civilization" (a distinction that, like the *a* in Derrida's *differance,* can *only* be represented in writing). Among other things, it throws into relief the assumptions and reading strategies of that largely liberal, white, and Northeastern audience for which this book would seem to be written. This audience, with its confident expectation that the moral code is self-evident, that the characters will receive their just deserts and that the tensions between Jim, Huck, and society can be dissolved in conventions of genre, receives from Huck's decision to "light out for the Territory" a genuine moral shock. This shock marks an absolute limit of the power of semiotics to resolve all forms of difference, and it keeps alive the possibility of Huck's own individual freedom to operate outside the codes and bonds of a previously established system.

We cannot forget, however, in the sensation of this shock, the continued power of Jim's role in the narrative. The final pages of *Huckleberry Finn,* pages in which Jim makes his famous assertion that "signs is *signs,"* are pages of very rapid denouement, which describe the continued turns of a wheel of fate that Huck's abrupt departure does not entirely stop. Here, in quick succession, Jim learns not only that he is free and has, under the terms of Miss Watson's will, been free for some time, but also that his freedom is to be underwritten by Tom Sawyer to the tune of forty dollars. (We are tempted to interpret, retrospectively, the moment of Miss Watson's death as precisely the moment Jim utters the word *trash* on the raft.) Confronted with this offer, it is true, Jim does not respond with anything like what a weaker or more stereotypical character might have said in a more sentimental tale. He utters no Beecher-Stoweish "Praise de Lor'," no "bless yo' soul, Marse Tom," no "shucks, ole Jim ain't worth so much turr'ble fuss as all *dat."* Nevertheless, his "signs is *signs,"* and his prediction of future happiness and wealth, although they may indicate a kind of poetic justice, ring hollow with the hollowness of a repeated stereotype, a hollowness Huck's silence — for he does not say a word here — tends to underline.

Jim makes a partial recovery from this stereotypical role when he is able to interpret another set of signs in an apparently more genuinely liberating way. Just here, at the climax of the story, Huck tells us that he remembers his absent father, authorizer of all kinds of signs, as deeply terrifying a figure to Huck's mind now as when he lay in wait unexpectedly in his son's room at the very beginning of the tale. Jim, however, seems able to reinterpret Huck's experience so as to defuse this threat. First, he reminds Huck of a body they had found on the river whose face Huck "didn't want to see." "Doan' you 'member de house dat was float'n down de river, en dey wuz a man in dah, kivered up, en I went in en unkivered him and didn' let you come in?" he asks. Then he reveals its 'true' meaning: "Well, den, you k'n git yo' money when you wants it; kase dat wuz him." Here, as Tina Zworg has pointed out, Jim's interpretive skill enters Huck's narration on a conscious level and enters the reader's as well, giving us the power either to go back and recover a deeper sense of it on our own from "between the lines" of Huck's story or to continue to block its implications by "lighting out for the territory." Jim reveals that he has defied what is for Huck and for all weak interpreters a great taboo; he has "unkivered" the dead, and in doing so he has demystified once and for all an obscure and threatening entity so as to master it, to render it harmless, beyond any further capacity to frighten or disturb. Like the famous "Mistah Kurtz—he dead," in Conrad's *Heart of Darkness,* but in celebration rather than dismay, Jim's "dat wuz him" predicts a great hope: the death of an old, violent, patriarchal order and the promise of a new, fraternal one—but only if we will consent to forget Huck's construction of this story and his continued skepticism and fear and to reinterpret it in Jim's own light.

Huck's response to this news, however, is by no means as ecstatic as Jim's careful, therapeutic, and self-assured questioning might lead us to expect. Rather, as he has on similar occasions, Huck chooses silence as a response, passing instead to a curt and somewhat caustic wrap-up of what has happened to Tom since these revelations took place. Huck's silence, his change of subject and his decision to "light out for the Territory" express not only a touch of boyish annoyance at Jim's and Tom's claims to have known more about his life than he does, but a skepticism towards all forms of interpretation, from semiotic decoding to genuine prophecy. It is Huck, after all, who, even if only mimicking Jim's restraint, has witheld from *his* audience the crucial information of the father's death until the last moment, and it is in part a way of setting Jim up for deflation (for surely things cannot work out quite as well as they here seem to) that Huck has allowed him to break the news in the tale. Now, dropping Jim completely, and leaving Tom dangling his watch-fob in a haze of rather contemptible self-congratulation, Huck takes the occasion to express, as succinctly as possible, his jaundiced attitude toward the whole business of narration and interpretation. Not only is there "nothing more to say," he tells us, but he is "rotten glad of it," because if he had known what a trouble it was going to be to write a book, he wouldn't have done it in the first place, and he certainly isn't going to undertake it again. Instead he will "light out for the Territory" and forgo any situation, even the situation of writing, where he has "been before."

Huck's skeptical and evasive response to Jim, to Tom, and even to his own good fortune here, suggests a countervailing hope to Jim's—the hope of a willed and even willful priority, a total and utterly individual future command over audience, character, and even the author of his own tale. The novel is indeed constructed by the difference between these two definitions of liberation—liberation as brotherhood and equality and liberation as self-authorizing paternity and priority. Both of these kinds of liberation move the novel beyond the limits of semiotics to prophecy on the one hand and silence on the other. To choose between these alternatives is to lose sight of Twain's point: their complete contradiction of and their absolute necessity to one another.

Chronology

1835	November 30, Samuel Clemens is born in Florida, Missouri, to John Marshall Clemens and Jane Lampton.
1839	Family moves to Hannibal, Missouri.
1847	John Marshall Clemens dies; Samuel leaves school and begins career as a printer.
1853–54	Clemens travels as a journeyman printer to St. Louis, New York, Philadelphia, and Iowa.
1856	Plans trip to South America. Stops in Cincinnati and writes *The Adventures of Thomas Snodgrass*.
1857	Apprenticed to a river pilot.
1861	Volunteers for a Confederate Civil War brigade; leaves after a few weeks. Heads for Carson City.
1862	Works as a miner and reporter. Adopts the pen name Mark Twain.
1864	Travels to California; meets Bret Harte.
1866	Sent to Sandwich Islands as a feature writer.
1867	Publication of *The Celebrated Jumping Frog of Calaveras County and Other Sketches*.
1869	Publishes *The Innocents Abroad*.
1869–71	Writes for the *Buffalo Express*.
1870	Marries Olivia Langdon.
1871	Moves to Hartford where he will live and write for the next sixteen years. In Hartford he will also embark on several business ventures and accumulate debts.
1872	Publishes *Roughing It*.
1873	*The Gilded Age*.
1876	*The Adventures of Tom Sawyer*.
1880	*A Tramp Abroad*.
1884	*Adventures of Huckleberry Finn*.
1889	*A Connecticut Yankee in King Arthur's Court*.
1892	*The American Claimant*. Disastrous investment in typesetting scheme.

1894	*Puddn'head Wilson.* Twain departs on a worldwide lecture tour to pay off debts.
1896	*Joan of Arc.*
1898	Finishes paying off debts.
1900	Writes "The Man That Corrupted Hadleyburg."
1904	Twain's wife dies.
1906	Begins working on autobiography. Publishes *What is Man?* privately and anonymously.
1907	Receives honorary D.Litt. from Oxford University.
1909	Daughter Jean, the last of his four children, dies.
1910	April 21, Twain dies, leaving many unpublished papers, among them the incomplete drafts of "The Mysterious Stranger."

Contributors

HAROLD BLOOM, Sterling Professor of the Humanities at Yale University, is the author of *The Anxiety of Influence, Poetry and Repression,* and many other volumes of literary criticism. His forthcoming study, *Freud: Transference and Authority,* attempts a full-scale reading of all of Freud's major writings. A MacArthur Prize Fellow, he is general editor of five series of literary criticism published by Chelsea House.

LEO MARX is Professor of English at Massachusetts Institute of Technology. His books include *The Machine in the Garden* and an edition of *Huckleberry Finn.*

J. HILLIS MILLER is Frederick W. Hilles Professor of English and Comparative Literature at Yale University. His books include *The Disappearance of God, The Form of Victorian Fiction,* and *Form and Repetition.*

MICHAEL J. HOFFMAN is Professor of English at the University of California, Davis. He is the author of *Gertrude Stein* and *The Subversive Vision: American Romanticism in Literature.*

NEIL SCHMITZ is Professor of English at the State University of New York at Buffalo. He is the author of *Of Huck and Alice: Humorous Writing in American Literature.*

NANCY WALKER is Executive Assistant to the President of Stephens College in Columbia, Missouri. A teacher of American Literature, she has published on Dickinson, O'Hara, and Irving.

JAMES M. COX is Avalon Professor of English at Dartmouth College. He is the author of *Mark Twain: The Fate of Humor* and of an edition of critical essays on Robert Frost.

CLEO McNELLY KEARNS is Associate Professor of English at Rutgers University, and the author of the forthcoming *"What Krishna Meant"*: *Indic Philosophy and Religion in the Work of T. S. Eliot.*

Bibliography

Anderson, Frederick, ed. *Mark Twain: The Critical Heritage.* London: Routledge and Kegan Paul, 1971.

Ashley, L. F. "Huck, Tom, and Television." *English Quarterly* 4 (1971): 57–65.

Banta, Martha. "Rebirth or Revenge: The Endings of *Huckleberry Finn* and *The American.*" *Modern Fiction Studies* 15 (1969): 191–207.

Barchilon, Jose and J. S. Kovel. "*Huckleberry Finn:* A Psychoanalytic Study." *Journal of the American Psychiatric Association* 14 (1966): 16–18.

Bier, Jesse. *The Rise and Fall of American Humor.* New York: Holt, Rinehart and Winston, 1968.

Blair, Walter, ed. *Mark Twain's Hannibal, Huck, and Tom.* Berkeley: University of California Press, 1969.

Budd, Louis J. "Introduction." *Adventures of Huckleberry Finn: Facsimile of Manuscript.* 2 vols. Detroit: Gale Research Co., 1983.

———. *Our Mark Twain: The Making of His Public Personality.* Philadelphia: University of Pennsylvania Press, 1983.

Carkeet, David. "The Dialects in *Huckleberry Finn.*" *American Literature* 51 (1979): 315–32.

Carrington, George G., Jr. *The Dramatic Unity of* Huckleberry Finn. Columbus: Ohio State University Press, 1976.

Egan, Michael. *Mark Twain's* Huckleberry Finn: *Race, Class, and Society.* London: Published for Sussex University Press by Chatto and Windus, 1977.

Emerson, Everett. *The Authentic Mark Twain: A Literary Biography of Samuel L. Clemens.* Philadelphia: University of Pennsylvania Press, 1984.

Ensor, Allison. *Mark Twain and The Bible.* Lexington: University of Kentucky Press, 1969.

Fetterley, Judith. "Disenchantment: Tom Sawyer in *Huckleberry Finn.*" *PMLA* 87 (1972): 69–74.

Fiedler, Leslie. "Literature and Lucre: A Meditation." *Genre* 13 (1980): 1–10.

———. *Love and Death in the American Novel.* New York: Stein and Day Publishers, 1975.

Gerber, John C., ed. *Studies in* Huckleberry Finn. Columbus, Ohio: Charles E. Merrill Publishing Co., 1971.

Gollin, Richard and Rita Gollin. *"Huckleberry Finn* and the Time of the Evasion." *Modern Language Studies* 9 (1979): 5–15.

Gunn, Giles. *The Interpretation of Otherness: Literature, Religion, and the American Imagination.* New York: Oxford University Press, 1979.

Kaplan, Harold. *"Huckleberry Finn:* What it Means to be Civilized." In *Democratic Humanism and American Literature.* Chicago: The University of Chicago Press, 1972.

Johnson, James L. *"Adventures of Huckleberry Finn."* In *Mark Twain and the Limits of Power: Emerson's God in Ruins.* Knoxville: University of Tennessee Press, 1982.

Kolb, Harold H., Jr. "Mark Twain, Huck Finn, and Jacob Blivens: Gilt-Edged, Tree Calf Morality in the *Adventures of Huckleberry Finn." Virginia Quarterly Review* 55 (1979): 653–69.

Lauber, John. *The Making of Mark Twain.* New York: American Heritage, 1985.

Lynn, Kenneth S. *Visions of America.* Westport, Conn.: Greenwood Press, 1973.

Mark Twain Journal, 1936–.

Mark Twain Society Bulletin, 1978–.

Miller, Lee. "Huckleberries and Humans." *PMLA* 87 (1972): 314.

Pettit, Arthur Gordon. *Mark Twain and the South.* Lexington: University of Kentucky Press, 1974.

Pinsker, Sanford. "Huckleberry Finn, Modernist Poet." *Mississippi Quarterly* 24 (1983): 261–73.

Rubin, Louis D., Jr. "Mark Twain's South: Tom and Huck." In *The American South: A Portrait of a Culture,* edited by Louis D. Rubin, Jr. Baton Rouge: Louisiana State University Press, 1980.

Schmitz, Neil. "The Paradox of Liberation in *Huckleberry Finn." Texas Studies in Literature and Language* 13 (1971): 125–36.

Sattelmeyer, Robert and J. Donald Crowley, eds. *One Hundred Years of* Huckleberry Finn: *The Boy, His Book, and American Culture.* Columbia: University of Missouri Press, 1985.

Simpson, Claude M., ed. *Twentieth-Century Interpretations of* Adventures of Huckleberry Finn: *A Collection of Critical Essays.* Englewood Cliffs, N. J.: Prentice-Hall, Inc., 1968.

Smith, Henry Nash. "Guilt and Innocence in Mark Twain's Later Fiction." In *Democracy and the Novel: Popular Resistance to Classic American Writers.* New York: Oxford University Press, 1978.

————, ed. *Mark Twain: A Collection of Critical Essays.* Englewood Cliffs, N. J.: Prentice-Hall, Inc., 1963.

Trilling, Lionel. *The Liberal Imagination: Essays on Literature and Society.* Garden City, N.Y.: Viking Press, 1966.

Young, Philip. *"Huckleberry Finn:* The Little Lower Layer." In *Three Bags Full: Essays in American Fiction.* New York: Harcourt Brace Jovanovich, 1972.

Acknowledgments

"Mr. Eliot, Mr. Trilling, and *Huckleberry Finn*" by Leo Marx from *American Scholar* 22, no. 4 (Autumn 1953). © 1953 by Leo Marx. Reprinted by permission of the author.

"First-Person Narration in *David Copperfield* and *Huckleberry Finn*" (originally entitled "Three Problems of Fictional Form: First-Person Narration in *David Copperfield* and *Huckleberry Finn*") by J. Hillis Miller from *Experience in the Novel,* edited by Roy Harvey Pearce, © 1968 by Columbia University Press. Reprinted by permission.

"Huck's Ironic Circle" (originally entitled "Realism as Vision and Style") by Michael J. Hoffman from *The Subversive Vision: American Romanticism in Literature* by Michael J. Hoffman, © 1972 by Michael J. Hoffman. Reprinted by permission.

"Huckspeech" by Neil Schmitz from *Of Huck and Alice: Humorous Writing in American Literature* by Neil Schmitz, © 1983 by the University of Minnesota. Reprinted by permission of the University of Minnesota Press.

"Reformers and Young Maidens: Women and Virtue" (originally entitled "Reformers and Young Maidens: Women and Virtue in *Adventures of Huckleberry Finn*") by Nancy Walker from *One Hundred Years of* Huckleberry Finn: *The Boy, His Book, and American Culture,* edited by Robert Sattelmeyer and J. Donald Crowley, © 1985 by the Curators of the University of Missouri. Reprinted by permission of the University of Missouri Press.

"A Hard Book to Take" by James M. Cox from *One Hundred Years of* Huckleberry Finn: *The Boy, His Book, and American Culture,* edited by Robert Sattelmeyer and J. Donald Crowley, © 1985 by the Curators of the University of Missouri. Reprinted by permission of the University of Missouri Press.

Index

Also by Barbara Bush

C. FRED'S STORY

MILLIE'S BOOK

Barbara Bush (signature)

A Memoir

❦

Barbara Bush

A LISA DREW BOOK

Charles Scribner's Sons

New York   London   Toronto   Sydney   Tokyo   Singapore

Lisa Drew Books
Charles Scribner's Sons
Rockefeller Center
1230 Avenue of the Americas
New York, NY 10020

SCRIBNERS and colophon are registered trademarks of Macmillan, Inc.

A leatherbound signed first edition of this book has been published by The Easton Press.

Book design by Laura Hough

Manufactured in the United States of America

10   9   8   7   6   5   4   3   2   1

Library of Congress Cataloging-in-Publication Data
Bush, Barbara, date.
    Barbara Bush : a memoir / Barbara Bush.
        p.   cm.
    "A Lisa Drew book."
    1. Bush, Barbara, date.   2. Bush, George, date.
    3. Presidents' spouses—United States—Biography.   I. Title.
    E883.B87A3   1994
    973.928'092'2—dc20
    [B]   94-13829
                                                                   CIP

ISBN 0-02-519635-9
     0-02-519275-2 (Signed edition)

To faith, family, and friends; and to George Bush, who taught me that these are the most important things in life.

Contents

Preface

I have loved writing this book and know that it is a story of a life of privilege—privilege of every kind. If I didn't know it before, I certainly do now. No man, woman, or child ever had a better life.

Lisa Drew, my editor with Scribner's, passed a message to me after reading five chapters that said she would only allow me to use one "wonderful" a page and one "precious" a chapter. Later Jean Becker added "close friend" to that list. "Nobody has that many good and close friends," she said.

Not bad to have had a life that was filled with *wonderful* people and happenings, *precious* family, and many *close friends.* That's the life that first my family, and then for much longer, that wonderful, precious, close friend, George Bush, have given me and I'm grateful for it.

I wrote every word in this book myself from copious diaries, tapes, letters, and a very selective memory of the early days. It is the truth as I see it.

It might amuse the reader to know that I wrote in my diaries about more good meals that I have eaten (and am wearing today) and that many pages were filled with resolutions not to eat so much and remorse over my lack of self-discipline. I have spared you that.

I also note that we seem to weep a lot in this book. We are an emotional group and rather like a good tear or two. Please also notice that we cry when we are glad *and* when we are sad. Love brings a tear. Friends bring a tear. A smile, sweetness, even a kind word brings a tear. In a life of privilege there are lots of tears.

I have left out so many friends and happenings, but I hope they will forgive me. Time and space have run out. I hope you know who you are and how much we love you.

I want to thank lots of people for putting up with me, especially Jean Becker, who not only researched this book but also reassured me, did the first editing, checked me on truth and spelling, and laughed in all the right places. I certainly want to thank Lisa Drew, my editor, for her third attempt to make a writer of me. (She was there also for *Millie's Book* and *C. Fred's Story.*) I suspect that Lisa wanted more from me, but she applied no pressure to write about things I did not feel were appropriate or things that might make a book sell, but also might hurt.

I also want to thank everyone at the George Bush Presidential Library Center, especially Mary Finch, for helping us track down the facts.

And to the hero of this book, what can I say? George Bush knows how I feel. He is the hero. Incidentally, at my request, he read the book before it went to print. I wanted him to save me from myself, as I would not knowingly hurt someone. He made no deletions and the only additions he made were so typically George. He added many complimentary adjectives, often added praise for a fellow worker or shared the credit with others. I, of course, gave it to him alone. He is my hero.

Barbara Bush
March 1, 1994

BARBARA BUSH

A Memoir

Prologue

January 20, 1993. We were going home. For four extraordinary years, home had been the White House, but when we woke up that morning, it felt like a foreign place. Our bed, along with our tables and chairs, already were in Texas. George had been telling people that I almost had gone, too. He was right. Once we lost the election, I had tried to ignore the hurt and turned my mind toward Houston and a new life.

George, on the other hand, was presidential until the very last moment. He worried about the staff and where they would go. And he had to cope with the larger problems of Iraq, Somalia, and Bosnia.

We started that day as we did every morning, waking up about 5:30 A.M., ringing the bell for the butlers, and drinking coffee in bed while we read the papers. Our phone started ringing almost immediately with our children checking in to make sure we were okay.

Later in the morning, George called me from the Oval Office and asked if I wanted to walk around the South Grounds with the dogs just one more time. It was a glorious, sunny day. The dogs ran and chased squirrels and dashed around looking for who knows what. The pleasure George got from his dog Ranger taking flying leaps over imaginary logs cannot be described. We talked about the ducks that had been nurtured in the South Grounds fountain the past spring and summer and wondered if they would all come back to roost that spring. If they did, how would the White House groundskeepers cope with all those little families? We walked past the tennis court and the horseshoe pit, where you could always hear the clink of shoes at lunchtime. We wondered if Bill Clinton would keep up the White House horseshoe tournaments. It was a great way to get to know the ninety-three people who kept the People's House in such beautiful shape. We walked hand-in-hand by the swimming pool and the cabana, the Oval Office and the Rose Garden, sharing happy memories. Even writing about that day, the house, and the very thoughtful staff brings a warm feeling to me. We always have lived in happy houses, but nothing matched this special place. The problems George faced there were unbelievable, but the staff surrounded us with goodwill, warmth, and caring. They gave the President of the United States exactly what he needed: a happy, tranquil home.

We had put off the good-byes to the residence staff and grounds-keepers as long as we could, but at 10:00 A.M., it was time. We had been dreading it. Chief Usher Gary Walters, head of the household, led off with a funny, warm essay about all the new phrases they had learned from George. It read in part: "We thought that 'Pops' were either soft drinks or a breakfast cereal, but we found it to be a term of endearment. We also thought that 'Eeooooh' was something you said when you hit your thumb with a hammer—not 'Where's Ranger?' We learned that the real name of the presidential retreat in the Catoctin Mountains was Camp Marvin, not Camp David, and that a six-pack does not necessarily refer to beer, but is the means to becoming the horseshoe king."

Ron Jones, a houseman and a great horseshoe competitor, presented George with a trophy made in the carpenter shop. The staff also gave him the flag that was flying over the White House on January 20, 1989, and one that had been flying there that morning. Nancy Clarke, the genius in the flower shop, gave me a beautiful doll in a large Lucite case—a reminder of all the beautiful dolls and other decorations her staff had made for Christmas each year. We had so much fun together decorating the house for formal state dinners and holidays. (I should say she and her shop worked; I admired.) We were too choked up with emotion to say what we felt, but I think they knew the affection we had for them all.

Vice President Quayle and Marilyn and George's chief of staff, Jim Baker, and Susan arrived, along with my outstanding chief of staff, Susan Porter Rose. We talked for a few moments, and then right on time—at least I thought it was right on time—the Clintons, Gores, and the other guests arrived. I say that because I read in the paper that they were late. I don't think that was true. The ladies looked great and both wore hats. It reminded me of how critical everyone had been about Marilyn Quayle's hat four years before, and I wondered if Hillary and Tipper would get away with theirs. The time probably dragged for the newcomers, but it raced for me. When we were told we must leave for the ceremony, I rushed around, through the Red Room then back into the Blue Room, to hug the butlers, out of sight of everyone else. How dear they had been to us and our family.

From then on, it was all downhill. The hard part for me was over. I rode to the Capitol with Hillary, and the conversation was relaxed and easy as we talked about the long day ahead. It could have been an awkward time, but I think we were both determined it would not be. People waved at the new First Family, as they should have, and everyone looked very happy.

Then came the moment when the mantle was lifted from the back of my superb husband and placed on Bill Clinton's. It will come as no surprise that I felt a lesser man by far had won the election, but that was behind us now. The speeches were fine. Bill Clinton's was short and sounded very familiar—like John F. Kennedy's, but not quite as eloquent.

We said good-bye to Senator Bob Dole and Elizabeth, Senator Alan Simpson and Ann, the Clintons, and the Gores. The loyal Quayles flew with us to Andrews Air Force Base, where we hugged good-bye. After a great send-off from staff and supporters, we flew to Houston on *Air Force One* surrounded by friends. From my staff we had Susan Porter Rose and Laurie Firestone, both remarkable women who had been with us for twelve years. My great and dear friend Andy Stewart was there along with Richard Moore, the former ambassador to Ireland, and so many others. Every person on that plane was someone we hold very dear.

The press complained bitterly to me that they were not being allowed to send a press pool. That amused me, and I told them that any one of them who had voted for George should speak up then or forever hold his peace. The silence was deafening.

During the flight we watched a film put together by Dorrance Smith, a Houston childhood friend of our children, and more recently George's communications director and tennis opponent. It was very funny, very tongue-in-cheek. He had interviewed many of George's staff, and two of our children, Marvin and Doro. It poked fun at us, and it lightened the day.

We arrived in Houston to a great airport rally and immediately saw so many old friends. We said good-bye to the people who had flown down with us, as most of them were going back to Washington with the plane.

Our new life began.

We did not expect the welcome we received. Everywhere we looked were yellow ribbons. Stores and motels had WELCOME HOME on their marquees. There were billboards with WELCOME HOME, GEORGE AND BARBARA. There were even homemade signs on the backs of pickup trucks. People stood and waved flags along the entire route.

When we pulled up to our rented house, the neighbors were all out to give us a big welcome. It was so sweet, and made everything look brighter and better.

There were even more surprises ahead. We walked into a house that was unpacked and filled with plants and flowers. Paula Rendon, our beloved housekeeper; dear Don Rhodes, who had been with us for years; and our friend and neighbor Jack Fitch had worked like dogs sorting out what should be stored and what should be opened. Jack's wife, Bobbie, organized the neighborhood to put flowers in the house and in the garden. What a wonderful way to come home.

January 21, 1993—What a difference twenty-four hours make. We awakened at our usual time of 5:30 a.m.—but we had no bell to ring and no butlers. We got up, walked and fed the dogs, picked up the papers, and carried coffee upstairs to read in bed.

So here we are—almost full circle—taking care of ourselves again and loving it. How did we get here, and where are we going . . .

2

Growing Up

Where to start? I was born in New York City in 1925, the daughter of Marvin and Pauline Pierce. Our family had just moved out of the city to Rye, but my mother returned to the same doctor and hospital where my sister, Martha, five, and my brother Jim, three and a half, had been born.

Rye was a wonderful place to grow up. It was tiny in those days, and we knew most of the eight thousand people who lived there. It had a bakery, a meat man, a greengrocer (no supermarket), a movie theater, and a library which we visited often. We went to the movies almost every Saturday afternoon, usually children's adventure stories.

It was then, and still is, a bedroom community to New York City. Daddy worked for the McCall Corporation (he became president of the company in 1946), and every day he walked fifteen to twenty minutes to the train station for the commute into the city. He loved the ride. In the morning he would read his paper, and in the evening he'd ride in the Club Car, where the men had a drink and played bridge. We didn't know him at the time, but George's father commuted on the same train, getting off two stops farther down in Greenwich, Connecticut. Some of my happiest times were walking with Daddy to the station in the morning, and then I would take the bus to school.

Everyone in Rye knew everyone's business. I remember one humiliating incident when I was ten years old. I had walked downtown, bought a can of Marshmallow Fluff, and happily ate it all the way home. By the time I got there, my mother already had received three phone calls from people saying they had the cutest thing to tell her: Barbara was walking down the street covered with Marshmallow Fluff, eating right from the can with her fingers. Mother did not think it was quite so cute. To add insult to injury, I was violently ill. I haven't eaten it since.

Indian Village—the name of our section of town—was a true neighborhood. We knew everybody and all their families and dogs. The houses were modest by Rye standards, but I know our house seemed enormous to my parents after a New York City apartment. Years later when I visited the house with my brother Scotty, I was surprised how much smaller it was than I remembered.

The bedrooms and bathrooms especially were squeezed into a small space. Once, when George and I were visiting after we were married, Mother asked him not to go to the bathroom at night because he woke her up when he flushed the toilet. George, already inventive at twenty-one years of age, went out the window! That would have killed Mother, but her request was outrageous.

My memories of that lovely little house are only good ones. Our living room was full of bookshelves, and although I do not ever remember Daddy with a hammer in his hand, he was a graduate of MIT and claimed he made those shelves. He always said he had trouble making them even, so he tucked in a match someplace and all was well. There was a set of "My Book House," the *Encyclopaedia Britannica,* and several other collections. We were a family of readers, and many evenings were spent with everyone enjoying a favorite book or magazine. I also believe we had a radio in that bookcase which we listened to a lot in those days. I especially remember "The Shadow."

The best food in the world came out of our kitchen. I don't remember that Mother cooked, but she knew good food and trained the helpers very well. Thursday and Sunday afternoons were their days off. I don't remember what happened on Thursdays, but on Sunday evenings we picked up dinner. We ate a big meal at lunch, usually a baked chicken with the world's best stuffing and mashed potatoes. On Sunday night, we would have graham crackers and cream. What a glorious dish that was. Even talking about it puts on weight. Everything we had was rich and, I now know, bad for us. Daddy and I were the only ones with a weight problem; Scott and Martha were really skinny. I remember my mother saying, all in one breath, "Eat up, Martha. Not you, Barbara!"

We ate meals as a family in those days—a wonderful tradition few families now enjoy. My mother sat at one end, my dad at the other, and Martha, Jimmy, Scotty, and I fell in on either side. Daddy always took the gravy spoon and made a little bowl in the mashed potatoes and then let the gravy fill it. Mother would scold him for very bad manners and for eating so much potatoes and gravy. On Friday we always had fish just in case one of us brought a Catholic friend home. (In those days, Catholics were not allowed to eat meat on Friday.) Scotty got lamb chops because he did not like fish, and since he was sick as a child, he got away with it.

Being kept home from school was fun. Sometimes we got to lie in Mother's bed and listen to the radio. There were all sorts of great, sort-of-forbidden programs like "Stella Dallas" and "Helen Trent." If you were getting over a tummy problem (probably from gorging on something like Marshmallow Fluff), which your mother mistook for the flu, you got milk toast. It was delicious. You toast some white bread, butter it while hot, sprinkle it with white sugar, and pour hot milk over it. Then you eat it immediately. It was just as good for you as graham crackers and cream, I'm sure.

〜 My dad was a smiling man, about six feet tall. He had a great sense of humor and everyone liked and respected him. He was the fairest man I knew until I met George Bush.

Daddy worked hard his whole life, starting in high school. His father, Scott Pierce, was born in Sharpsville, Pennsylvania, where the very wealthy Pierces had the big houses and had started the churches. They lost all their money in the 1890s, and my grandfather never recovered. He sold insurance in Dayton, Ohio, but the family lived humbly. Daddy and his sister, my Aunt Charlotte, supported Grandfather and Grandmother Pierce financially for years. They did it willingly and with love. My mother did not feel quite so loving about it. She would tell the story about how during World War I, when Daddy was serving in Europe, my grandfather took up golf and wrote Daddy all about his golf game. That irritated Mother no end, but I never heard my dad criticize his father.

Daddy was really bright and graduated Phi Beta Kappa from Miami University in Oxford, Ohio, while at the same time waiting tables and tending furnaces. He also earned nine letters playing on all the athletic teams. Toward the end of his life, he was made Miami's first "M" man, a very special occasion attended by all his children. Miami is where Daddy met and fell in love with Mother, who was studying to be a teacher. It's also where he became friends with Colonel Red Blaik, who went on to become Army's great football coach. Red was Daddy's friend for life, and years later, I was thrilled to be at the White House when President Reagan honored Red with the Medal of Freedom.

When I was about four or five years old, my father would take me with him on business trips to Dayton, the site of a McCall plant. We would catch the overnight train from the Harmon, New York, railroad station. In those days, the sleeper had a female attendant who would undress me and put me to bed. In the morning, Grandfather or Grandmother would meet me and take me home by bus. I don't ever remember them owning a car. In the summer the house was so hot my funny little grandfather would sleep in the basement to keep cool. The rest of us died of the heat. My grandmother, Mabel Marvin Pierce, was a country girl and both she and my Aunt Charlotte put up with no nonsense. They called a spade a spade. Aunt Charlotte, who never married, taught school around the country. In later years, she would sometimes stay with our children when George and I went on a trip, although they didn't like her very much because she was too strict. One night, our boys apparently were misbehaving badly at the table, and in desperation my bright schoolteacher aunt told them if they didn't stop she would leave the table. So of course, they just got worse, and she left. They still laugh about that. I know she was a wonderful teacher, because many people over the years have told me she taught them fifth grade, and they loved her.

When she died she left each of Daddy's children $6,000. That was a great gift to me. We had five children at the time, and we could only afford necessities for the family. But George said, "This is for you alone. Do not spend it on groceries or something for the children." I wonder if he regretted saying that. That $6,000 really spread itself thin, because whenever I wanted something for myself I'd just think, Aunt Charlotte would want me to have this . . . and this . . . and this . . .

୶ My mother was a striking beauty who left the world a more beautiful place than she found it. She grew lovely flowers, did the finest needlepoint I have ever seen, and knew how to keep an exquisite home.

I understand her better now than I did then. I certainly did not appreciate all the pressures she must have felt until I also became a mother. She taught me a great deal, although neither of us realized it at the time. Probably her most important lesson was an inadvertent one. You have two choices in life: You can like what you do, or you can dislike it. I have chosen to like it.

My mother, on the other had, often talked about "when her ship came in" she was going to do such and such or buy such and such. She was a lucky woman who had a husband who worshiped the ground she walked on, four loving children, and a world of friends. Her ship had come in—she just didn't know it. That is so sad.

She was a wonderful gardener and was, in fact, famous for her green thumb. Our house had an unfinished basement that would often flood in heavy rain (it also had rats), but one year Mother grew endives—that wonderful white vegetable that grows in damp, dark places—down there. Another year Mother sent off for tons of earthworms and nurtured them in our basement, using them to aerate her garden soil. She also had a compost heap—although not in the basement. My sister Martha tells the story of when she took Mother up to Greenwich to meet her future mother-in-law and aunt, two very stylish older ladies, and a woman rushed up to Mother and exclaimed, "Oh, the compost and worm lady!" Martha was humiliated. I suspect Corinne and Madeleine Rafferty thought she was charming. Mother was very active in the Garden Club of America and was the conservation chairman for a while.

She grew up one of four children in Marysville, Ohio. Her father, James Robinson, was a lawyer who served on Ohio's Supreme Court in the mid-1920s. Her mother, Lulu, was a tall, thin woman who changed after my grandfather died. Up until that time, she was a very sweet, sedate lady who baked bread and looked after her husband. After his death, she learned to drive and with several friends drove a small trailer around the United States, Canada, and Mexico. My mother and her sisters complained about their driving and safety. I only knew her after her husband died, and I loved my Grandmother Robinson more than my other grandparents.

Mother was close to her sisters but her only brother, Jim, was an alcoholic who caused nothing but heartbreak. At one time he was married to Aunt Peggy, and they had a son, Jimmy. After my uncle ran away with his secretary, Aunt Peggy left with Jimmy, and we have absolutely no idea where she went or what happened to them. My uncle surfaced off and on, always in trouble and often drunk.

⤳ Mother did most of the scolding in the family. My brother Jimmy got the most spankings. Yes, my mother spanked us and pretty hard with either the back of a hairbrush or a wooden clothes hanger. I bet that Jim would agree with me that we were never spanked without deserving it. I know I deserved my spankings. And we were never really hurt—mostly hurt feelings and probably a little mad that we had gotten caught. I spanked my own children, but not as hard as my mother did. On the other hand, they were not as naughty. I can't remember anything I ever did that was really bad, but I suspect I baited my mother and was rude and sulky.

My older brother and sister fought a lot. Martha was thin but tall, and Jimmy was feisty. She would kick him, and he would pick up the child's chair by our fireplace and fend her off like a lion tamer. I must have been a real pill, for I either told on them or called my friends to come and watch.

Our neighborhood had few children Martha's age, and she grew up somewhat of a loner. She was a great student and a raving beauty in her teenage years. The boys all adored her. She used to compete in the Manursing Island swimming and diving meets, and we were very proud of her. People wore rubber bathing suits in those days, and those suits had to be handled with care; I seem to remember her bathing suit ripping during a Fourth of July or Labor Day meet. She has been a great sister and shares my love of reading. She once told me that she got one of those college reunion questionnaires, and one of the questions was "How many books do you read a year?" Well, she figured she read probably close to 260, but felt that would be bragging, so she knocked off 110 books. The reunion newsletter reported that the average number of books read was eight a year. There was a footnote that said, "One liar claims to have read 150!"

I both was terrified of Jimmy and looked up to him—he was,

after all, my older brother. My friends and I followed him around constantly, which drove him crazy. I was such a pest. Once, on my eighth birthday, he told me he was going to kill me, and I believed him—probably because I deserved it! I spent the entire day hiding under the front porch. He grew up to be a great athlete, and Daddy was very proud of him at the Saturday football games at the Taft School in Watertown, Connecticut. He loved fishing and hunting and was well known in that world.

Scotty was born when I was five. He broke his arm at age two, and the family discovered he had a "cyst" in his arm. That started some five years of operations. The surgeons took bone chips from his hip and both shins and implanted them in the arm. He spent forever in the hospital after the operations, and then months in bed at home with one cast, or sometimes two casts, on. I really don't know what he had, but it was an enormous worry for our parents, not only emotionally but financially. Mother really carried the load. She commuted to the hospital in New York City daily and was worried to death all the time. I don't remember ever being told that we couldn't do this or have that because of Scott, so our parents must have done a great job of sheltering us from their worries. I remember Mother reading the Wizard of Oz books to him, and eventually he learned to read them himself. One of the presents he got was multicolored strips; we made paper chains and hung them from the four posters on his bed. I seem to remember armies of soldiers all over his bedspread, too. I'm sure he complained, but I don't remember it at all. I only remember him as being a great pleasure. Finally, the last operation succeeded, and Scott also went on to become a great athlete. If the four of us voted on "Who do you feel the closest to, who's the kindest, etc.," I suspect we all would say Scott.

꧁ I had five good friends in our neighborhood: Lucille Schoolfield, Posy Morgan, Kate Siedle, June Biedler, and Joan Herman. We played all the time. Twice a year Daddy would bring home an outdated McCall's pattern book, and my friends and I would have such fun. We would choose a mother, father, and a family and cut them out and play paper dolls by the hour. Lucille and Kate were a year older and a grade ahead. Lulu was clearly our leader. She decided what games we would play and who would play what part, although she never made herself the heroine. She had a glorious imagination. The School-fields' house was bigger and quieter and always open to us. We would play the Victrola and sing sad cowboy songs. To this day I can sing "The Red River Valley" and "Jesse James." We also listened to many of Joe Louis's fights on the radio in Lulu's basement.

The Schoolfields were originally from Knoxville, Tennessee, and often served southern dishes. I remember on their dining room table they had a silver basket with a handle. The basket was filled with flowers or fruit. Lulu insisted her mother give me one as a wedding present, and I still have it. In the backyard they had a rope tied to a tree, and we would jump for hours and chant: "All in together girls, never mind the weather girls, etc."; or "Teddy Bear, Teddy Bear, touch the ground. Teddy Bear, Teddy Bear, turn around. Teddy Bear, Teddy Bear, walk upstairs. Teddy Bear, Teddy Bear, say your prayers. Teddy Bear, Teddy Bear, get into bed. Teddy Bear, Teddy Bear, lay down your head. Teddy Bear, Teddy Bear, turn out the light. Teddy Bear, Teddy Bear, say good-night."

When Scotty had his operations, we had to be careful he didn't catch any diseases. So when I got sick with the usual childhood ailments, I moved in with the Schoolfields. It was so great to be sick there. Mrs. Schoolfield, who died while George was vice president, was like a second mother to me.

✎ It was a very carefree childhood. One of my first memories of something really awful happening was when Charles Lindbergh's baby was kidnapped and killed in 1932, and that really frightened us. I can remember being thrilled whenever we spotted Amelia Earhart, the first woman to fly the Atlantic solo, at the Manursing Island Club. She lived for a time in Rye and was a huge celebrity, so we were devastated when she disappeared in 1937. Likewise, we couldn't believe it when the *Hindenburg* exploded that same year, especially since we had loved watching the huge blimp fly over Long Island Sound. Many years later George told me that he had seen the Hindenburg the day it went down.

As we grew up, we all went to Miss Covington's Dancing School. She was a formidable, well-corseted woman who carried a clicker and spoke in a commanding voice. A Westchester County phenomenon, she went from Scarsdale to Bronxville and other cities nearby. In Rye we met in the Episcopal Church Activity Center on Friday afternoon and evening. The younger you were, the earlier you went. So Friday was wash-your-hair and put-on-your-party-dress day. I remember owning one silk dress during those years, maybe two, bought strictly for those Friday afternoons. I was one of the tallest girls in my class and probably should have been corseted myself. Miss Covington had us all line up in rows, and we practiced for half the lesson what we learned last week and the step we were going to learn that week. Then the dread moment would come when Miss Covington clicked her clicker. The boys would be seated on one side of the room and the girls on the other. "All right," she would yell. "Cross your feet and put your hands in your lap." Every now and then she would slip up and yell, "Cross your hands and put your feet in your lap." She would be furious and click away at our giggles and snickers. She then announced in her loud voice that there were several more girls than boys and she needed two or three girls to volunteer to take the part of boys. Most of the boys hated dancing school. Some of them got sick on dancing school day or hid in the bathroom until their parents came to pick them up. I always raised my hand to play the part of a boy. That way I avoided being the last girl chosen, or rejected altogether. Finally, Mother absolutely forbade me to raise my hand again. She used to come and sit in the balcony with the other mothers and watch the lesson. She was by far the prettiest woman there, but she was the only mother who didn't wear a hat and that humiliated me. I would ask her to please wear a hat and be like other mothers. I must have been the biggest pain in the world.

∝ I went to the Milton School, a public school, through the sixth grade, then Rye Country Day School through the ninth grade, and Ashley Hall in Charleston, South Carolina, for the tenth, eleventh, and twelfth grades. My mother, who grew up in Ohio, always felt that East Coast people thought everyone from west and south of the Hudson River was a hick. That offended her, so my sister and I went south to Charleston for school. I also believe it was cheaper than some of the eastern schools, but that was never discussed. Although my family certainly was much luckier and better off than so many others at that time, I know we pinched pennies during the Depression. But Daddy left his business problems at the office, and family worries were kept behind bedroom doors.

I loved going to school at Ashley Hall, where I grew up quite a bit. I was a true square, making good marks and never breaking the rules. I swam a lot and acted in school plays, which I loved. I was so shy at the time and never could have gotten up and given a speech, but somehow, acting was different. George still teases me that as the angel in the Christmas play, I had the only speaking part.

꙰ Ninth grade was the year I discovered that doing things with boys was just as much fun as doing them with girls. My friends and I eased very gently into traveling in a group with both boys and girls. It was so much easier then than it is now. Drugs, sex, and violence were not constantly thrust at us by television.

All during my fourteenth year, we rode bikes every Saturday afternoon to somebody's house or just rode around picking people up and then dropping them off again after a fun and exhausting day of bike riding. I had no special beau in those days, but was part of the group.

When I came home from Ashley Hall for my first school break, I started going to vacation dances. Our little group went from dance to dance, sometimes with dates. I had several boys whom I liked, who had written me from their schools, and who were kind enough to take me to dances. We were still too young to drive, so our fathers or theirs took us to the dances and drove us home. I honestly think we had much more fun than our children did at the same age. We did not stick with just one person. We danced with anyone who asked us, and there were boys who cut in and we danced away. Eventually I had a special boy whom I liked, but we were very shy and certainly never kissed. I think one reason I liked him was that my mother and older brother thought he was a jerk. He was, but a sweet one.

One thing I rarely did during my teenage years was drive. We had only one car, and with two parents and two older siblings, I never got the chance. My mother was so smart. She would let me have the car if I would do a few errands, and the list always included a personal female item. I hated asking the druggist or clerk for such things, so therefore did not want to use the car very much.

       ◦ Just before Christmas vacation in 1941 the Japanese bombed Pearl Harbor. Although fighting had been going on in Europe for several years, war seemed very far away. This astonishes me today, but then it was true.

It wouldn't be too long, however, before I realized how closely the war would touch my life—and how important this particular Christmas vacation would be.

3

Love and War

It was the Christmas when I was sixteen—1941—and I was having a wonderful time. I was at a vacation dance in Greenwich, Connecticut, seeing friends I hadn't seen since summer and wearing a pretty, bright, new red-and-green dress. Jack Wozencraft, a boy I had grown up with, cut in on my dancing partner and took me to meet a wonderful-looking young boy he said wanted to meet me, a boy named Poppy Bush. We danced a little, and it was fun talking to him. He asked if I'd mind sitting out the next dance as it was a waltz and he didn't know how. He told me he was a senior at Phillips Academy Andover, and I told him I went to school in Charleston. I honestly cannot remember any more of our conversation than that, but we did chat for about fifteen minutes. He asked me what I was doing the next night, and I told him I was going to a dance in Rye.

I went home and sat on my mother's bed, answering all her questions about the dance. We always had to go into Mother's room and talk when we got home. Otherwise, she could not sleep and, I believe, she was smart enough to know that in the night, you are willing to tell all. If she waited until the next day, she knew she'd get one-syllable answers. Always from Daddy's bed we would hear, "Can't this wait until morning?" Mother knew it couldn't.

On this night I told her I'd met the nicest, cutest boy, named Poppy Bush. By the time I got up the next morning, Mother—who should have been an FBI agent with her superior intelligence network—knew that Poppy was a wonderful boy who came from "a very nice family." That was enough to almost do him in!*

The next night Poppy did show up with his sister and several friends. He asked me to dance, and my older brother cut in almost immediately, saying: "Aren't you Poppy Bush? Please go over and wait on the side. When I get rid of her, I want to talk to you." I could hardly believe it! Jim barely tolerated me on good days, and here he was dancing with me when I would much rather be dancing with my new friend. And he acted like I'd be difficult to "get rid of." Jim wanted to ask Poppy to come to Rye on the following Thursday night and play in a basketball game between prep school boys and the local Rye High School championship team. Pop said he would love to. Then he asked me for one more dance, and also asked me to go out with him after the game. To my horror, the whole family turned out the next Thursday for the basketball game. I was absolutely sure it was to look over my new friend.

The Rye championship team won the game, Pop met my family—all of them—and we went out. Poppy told me later that he had begged his mother to let him use the Oldsmobile that night because it had a radio and their other car did not. He was so afraid we would sit in stony silence and have nothing to say to each other. For years he has teased me that there was no silence that night and I haven't stopped talking since. All I know is that I liked him a lot.

He went back to his school, and I went to mine. We wrote letters all winter. Only one day of our spring vacations overlapped, and he and a friend took me and a houseguest of mine out to a movie.

I was so excited when he invited me to come to his senior prom. I stayed with Prissy and Pen Hallowell, a house master and his wife, who were great friends of my sister, Martha. Poppy walked me all around the campus and introduced me to his friends. The other girls seemed so sophisticated to me—they obviously had been to a senior dance before. I hadn't and had just turned seventeen that very week.

---

* I should explain the name "Poppy." George was named after his maternal grandfather, George Herbert Walker. He had four very young uncles who called their father "Pops," although maybe not to his face. So they called their nephew "Little Pops," which soon became "Poppy." Poor George hated it as he got older, but it was hard to break such a long-standing habit. We had been married some seventeen years when a man told me he thought it was so cute the way I called George "Poppy" when we had so many children. That cured me—almost. You'll see "Pop" in some of my diary entries throughout the book.

"Sweet Sixteen and never been kissed" has been written about me, and it was true. But after the dance, Pop walked me home and, in front of the world, leaned down and kissed me on the cheek. I floated into my room and kept the poor girl I was rooming with awake all night while I made her listen to how Poppy Bush was the greatest living human on the face of the earth.

Pop graduated and joined the Navy on June 12, 1942—his eighteenth birthday. Most of his friends waited for a year or two, but Pop wanted to go right away. He went to basic training, and I had a summer job working at Lord & Taylor department store in Greenwich. We wrote letters back and forth. On the way back to school that fall, I stopped off for a few hours in Chapel Hill, North Carolina, where he was training. Travel was curtailed in those days, and I was very lucky to get on a train that stopped at North Carolina. Before I went, he wrote and asked me to please tell everyone I was eighteen years old. He was the youngest man in flight training school and got teased all the time. As we walked around campus, we met a few of his friends and not one of them asked me how old I was, although I tried to work it in several times. After that visit, Pop wrote my mother and asked her to please send him a picture. She sent one that was several years old and featured my cairn puppy, Sandy. Poor Poppy. That picture made it look like he was dating a twelve-year-old. Shortly afterward, I had a graduation picture taken and at least it was without the dog.

George got his Navy wings in Corpus Christi, Texas, in June 1943. At age eighteen, he was the youngest pilot in the Navy at the time.

I graduated that same June and was accepted at Smith College. None of my family came to my commencement because travel was "unpatriotic"; most trains and planes were reserved for troops and military personnel. Much to my mother's distress, I worked that summer in a nuts and bolts factory in Port Chester, New York. I rode my bike to work with a boy I knew, and both of us were "gofers," doing the most menial of jobs. Yet, we were constantly told we were helping our country as the company did some war work.

By this time, my sister, Martha, had graduated from Smith, married Walt Rafferty, and had a baby girl. Walt had joined the Marines and was in Camp Pendleton, California, waiting to be sent overseas. Martha had gone out to say good-bye, and they had been in a holding pattern for several months. They missed their baby, who had stayed back east. The baby's German nurse was afraid to go on the train to California alone—she thought people would think she was a spy—so I was tapped to accompany them. I was very excited, as I had never been west of Dayton, Ohio. What I remember most was body-surfing in the Pacific Ocean and being terrified of the big waves. Walt eventually shipped out to the Pacific and landed on Guadalcanal. Many of his friends died in the war, and his brother Kevin, a pilot, was lost in Europe.

Pop was due home on leave for seventeen days. His mother invited me to come to their home in Maine and stay with them throughout the leave. I guess Mrs. Bush had all sorts of reasons to invite me, but I suspect they wanted to see as much of their son as possible before he went off to war. By having me there, it meant Pop would spend less time going back and forth. That was my first trip to Kennebunkport, Maine, and my first glimpse of our beloved Walker's Point.

All the way up on the train, Poppy kept telling me about his wonderful family—and scaring me to death. I knew, of course, they would hate me. George is from the biggest, closest family. His grand-mother and grandfather were alive, and all six of their children were there with spouses. George's family lived next door in a considerably smaller house than it is now. About eight of us shared the only bathroom.

Because of gas and tire rationing, the Bushes had a horse-pulled wagon. The horse's name was Barsil. George's brother Pres used to tease me and call me Barsil, and that is how I got my nickname, Bar.

It was a wonderful visit, with lots of undercurrents. First, we knew Pop soon would head overseas—either the Atlantic or the Pa-cific. And there was the budding romance. Did they like me? Did I like them? I know the answer to that one—yes. But they were over-whelming. The teasing was enormous from everybody, except George's mother. She was the most wonderful woman and had an extraordinary ability to see good in everyone without sounding insincere or like a Pollyanna.

When she told my mother I was a great cook, I thought I'd die laughing. My mother said something like, "Oh?" Mrs. Bush recounted the story of the night she and her husband were going out for dinner and she didn't have time to make dinner for Bucky and Johnny, Pop's brothers who were about four and ten at the time. According to Mrs.

Bush, I stepped right up and said I'd take on that little project and made the most delicious peanut butter and jelly sandwiches for all. My mother's face was worth seeing.

We rode bikes, went to the beach, played tennis, collected sea glass and seashells, and had marvelous picnics. At night, Poppy and I walked on the rocks and watched the moon come up, and we were finally alone. I can't speak for George Bush, but I fell madly in love. We got secretly engaged.

The time came when Poppy had to go back to his ship and I went to Smith College. George wrote and he called some, but not much. Telephone use was limited because of the war, although servicemen had priority.

Smith then had around two thousand women undergraduates, and it was the first time I had been in a racially mixed school. I had some very exciting times just finding my way around campus. It must have been a lean year, because I not only made the freshman soccer team, I was captain. I lived in Tyler House with my great roommate, Margie Boyce, and many other girls who quickly became good friends.

However, in the fall of my first year the most unpleasant thing happened. A pretty little sophomore came to me and said, "I've looked the freshman class over and have chosen you to go with me on a blind date to Amherst." I made some excuse and thanked her. I wasn't the least bit interested in going on a blind date. I was in love with George Bush, but it was a secret. This happened several more times, and then she stopped asking me. My roommate, Margie, came to me and told me my secret was out. She said that nasty sophomore decided I didn't like men and told everyone that Margie and I were lovers. To protect herself and me, Margie told everyone that George Bush and I were engaged. I was shocked by all of this. What a protected life I had lived. As far as I knew, I had never been the victim of gossip before. It was a lesson then—and now—that you shouldn't believe everything you hear.

Poppy and I decided to announce our engagement at Christmas. When I called to tell my family I had a surprise—and to ask permission—they said, "So, you're going to marry Poppy. How nice." I couldn't believe they weren't surprised. "You fool," my brother Jimmy said. "Anyone within a mile of you two knew you were in love."

I went with George's mother to the Philadelphia shipyards for the commissioning of George's ship, the U.S.S. *San Jacinto*. The *San*

Jac, a converted cruiser, looked enormous at the time, but compared to today's aircraft carriers, it was tiny. George flew a Grumman Avenger, an awkward plane compared to jets now. How he landed that big thing on that tiny deck is a wonder. He gave me my engagement ring on that trip, before he headed for the Pacific.

I went back to Smith, where I drifted through the rest of my freshman year and summer school. I was hoping to graduate in three years, but I did not put my heart and soul into my studies. I'm not too proud of that, but it was true. My poor dad spent a lot of time explaining to Miss Corwin, the freshman dean, that my marks were bad because my fiancé was on a ship in the Pacific. I'd like to say that was true, but I also just did not work. My dear father, who had worked his way through high school, college, and graduate school, must have suffered.

I certainly did miss George (for his sake, I'll quit calling him "Poppy"), and I was really worried about him. We listened for every piece of news from the Pacific, and rumors ran wild. Edward R. Murrow had a radio report that we all listened to and it almost made us feel like we were there. Well, we certainly weren't there compared to today's news reporting. Every word he said was censored, and we heard lots of "This is Edward R. Murrow from someplace in the South Pacific" or from some other theater of the war. No names and no places. The reporters in those days were much more careful than they are now about not giving away too much information in combat situations.

George wrote faithfully; sometimes I would receive many letters in one day, and sometimes a month would go by with no word. All mail was censored. No hints were allowed as to where they were. We all read between the lines as best we could. He received mail in the same fashion. (Unfortunately, in all our moves over the years, I've lost his letters.)

George was due to come home in the fall of 1944, and I was leaving Smith to get married. The plan was for me to return to college when George returned to his fleet. We heard nothing from him that September, but that was not unusual. Mail was slow. Then one day I got a letter from Doug West, a pilot in George's squadron, who told me George had been shot down off the island of Chichi Jima in the Bonin Islands. Doug said he had buzzed overhead and had seen George swimming toward the raft. (I later learned it was thanks to Doug that

George had even found his raft; Doug buzzed it with his plane, pointing George in the right direction.) Doug also said that he and another plane had strafed an enemy boat that had set out after George from the Japanese-held island.* I called Mrs. Bush, who had just gotten the same notice and was calling me. We were frantic, but Doug's letter held out hope that a submarine had been alerted and might have rescued George. I really don't remember the next three days—they are just a blur—but the Navy got a message to the Bushes that George had in fact been picked up and was in Hawaii for some R&R before being returned to the *San Jac.* His two crew mates, however, had been lost. George could have gotten home leave if he wanted, but he was anxious to get back to his ship. Of the original fourteen pilots in his squadron, four were dead.

I continued making wedding plans, addressing the invitations, and buying my trousseau. Mother begged and borrowed shoe coupons from friends since shoes were rationed during the war.

One might well ask why our parents would sign permission slips for us to get married at the ages of nineteen and twenty. I know that our children have asked that question. The answer: In wartime, the rules change. You don't wait until tomorrow to do anything.

Just before I was married, Daddy invited me into New York City for lunch. This was an enormous treat for me. I rarely went into the city, even though we lived so close, and I hardly ever got to be with my dad alone. I will never forget that luncheon. He talked to me about marriage and the commitment it meant. He told me the largest cause of divorce was money or the mishandling of money. That shocked me, for my dad absolutely idolized my mother, and yet she constantly spent more money than Dad made. I got up my nerve and asked him about that. He said Mother was different. He budgeted the money that he could afford for her allowance, and then gave her half. Then twice a year—at Christmas and at their anniversary in August—he bailed her out and she thought he was a hero! I think that he learned the hard way that no matter what he gave her, she was going to spend twice as much. The top drawer of the nightstand next to Mother's bed was full of unpaid bills. I thought she kept that a secret from Daddy, but he knew. He had just given up trying to get her to live within her

---

* We later read in *Life* magazine that the Japanese had committed acts of cannibalism on this same island.

budget. Several years later, when Mother died, vendors from around the country came to Daddy with unpaid bills. Thanks to her example, I have tried to pay my bills as they came along.

He also told me that the three most important things you can give your children are: the best education, a good example, and all the love in the world. He certainly lived by that rule and gave us all that and more, including trust. George has done the same with our children.

George's return date kept being put off. We eventually scratched December 17 from our wedding invitations and wrote in January 6. He finally called from Hawaii to say he was on his way home, waiting for a military flight. On Christmas Eve, he called from New York City, and I met him at the train station in Rye. What a Christmas present!

On New Year's Eve, we went to Miami Beach for his brother Pres's wedding to a wonderful girl, Beth Kauffman, which began a lifetime friendship between the two of us. Then it was our turn.

We were married January 6, 1945, in the First Presbyterian Church in Rye. Aunts and uncles and cousins by the dozens came on both sides and as many friends as possible. Needless to say, there were many more women than men at the wedding. My brother Jim was not there as he was in the service and couldn't get leave. It was a lovely, cold day, and I remember standing in the back of the church with my dad. The bridesmaids were just about to start down the aisle when the church door blew open and there stood Gerry Bemiss, a childhood friend of George's, in a Navy uniform. He said he was in the wedding, but my dad said that he wasn't, that it was too late. Wrong. Gerry whipped out of his winter gear and was racing down the aisle before the bridesmaids. I was told that George's smile when he saw Gerry was wonderful. We had a lovely reception, and then headed for New York City for the night. Before leaving town, we saw *Meet Me in St. Louis* at Radio City Music Hall and then took the sleeper to the Cloisters in Sea Island, Georgia. We had such a nice time there. Most of the people were older, but we did meet some other honeymoon couples. We swore that we would return often. So much for resolutions. We finally went back to that lovely place in 1991 for a wonderful weekend.

For the next eight months we moved around the country while George's new squadron formed and trained. Sometimes I could go with him and sometimes I couldn't. We went to Grosse Ile Air Base in Michigan and lived in rooms in Wyandotte and Dearborn. The first room we rented was dark, and the landlady took great pleasure in my mistakes. I made many. I heard her say one day to a friend on the phone, "You should have seen what she did today. She washed all her silk underwear and it shrank." I did, and it did, but how mean of her not to tell me how to wash it. We moved over to Dearborn and stayed with the dearest family, Joe and Grace Gorgone and their children. We have stayed in touch all these years, until Grace died in March 1993. She taught me some of the things my mother thought I should be able to pick up by reading—things like how to cook, clean, and wash clothes.

We were moved to a base in Maine and lived in several rooms in the Lewiston-Auburn area. George's mother came to see us and told my mother we lived in the red light district. Rooms were hard to find in base towns. We had a small, one-room efficiency apartment with a kitchen in a closet and a Murphy-in-a-door bed. It smelled of other people's cooking, and there was really very little to keep me busy all day. So I wandered the streets and read a lot. I'll never forget the day George came home early because Franklin Roosevelt had died. We were sick. Neither one of us had ever voted—we were too young—and we probably would have voted for the other fellow, but Roosevelt was our President, the Commander-in-Chief of a country at war, and we joined the world in mourning. We felt truly lost, very young and alone. Who had ever heard of Harry Truman?

The next time I joined George was in Virginia Beach. I had been warned by an older friend from Rye that I should go down early to get a place. She also suggested that we try to join the Princess Anne Country Club, which had several very inexpensive service member-ships available. We ended up with a tiny basement apartment in a really big private home right across the street from the club, and for six dollars, we became members of this little gem of a place. The food was good, and the golf course was beautiful. The woman we rented from, a Mrs. Grandy, was an absolutely crazy woman. We had a tiny bathroom across the hall from our little room. Mrs. Grandy rented out space on her living room floor and said that our bathroom went with it. So I instantly became the cleaner of a public bath. She had wild, dyed red hair and wandered around that big house in her nightgown. There were hundreds of stories about her, and I believed them all. The one I liked best was the fact that she hated hairy men and made her late husband sit in a bathtub of Neet hair remover. We never heard how he died, but we guessed it was a very painful death.

It was a fun summer. We sat on the beach, partied, and entertained guests. George's sister, Nancy, came to visit and lived on the beach. We warned her about the sun, but she said she didn't burn. Famous last words. We sent her home on the train with a burned face and closed eyes.

George took up golf with Max Moore, another young pilot, who has remained a friend for life. The boys would send me into the fairway about three hundred yards ahead. Then one of them would hit, and I'd hear a yell: "Left." Then I'd charge into the woods to the left and try to find the ball. Those two lost more golf balls than you can believe. We laughed our way through the summer with Jacquie and Doug West, Milt Moore, Jack and Bea Guy, and Max Moore.

But again, the undercurrents were strong. George and his new squadron, VT 153, were getting closer and closer to going back overseas, probably to be involved in the anticipated invasion of Japan. By now I realized that what my dad had told me before I married was true. He said that every day you stay married, you fall more and more in love with your husband or wife. It was certainly true in my case, and I did not want George to return to the war. Many of our friends were dying. V-E Day came and went, and yet the Japanese fought on. Then the atomic bombs were dropped on Hiroshima and Nagasaki. Horrid as those bombs were, they saved many, many American and Japanese lives. I've always respected Harry Truman for making that courageous decision. I was also very grateful.

V-J Day arrived in August, and the rejoicing on the streets in Virginia Beach was loud, wild, and fairly liquid. And why not? There was a lot to cheer about. Before the day ended, George and I went to a little church to thank God for ending that war and to pray for all who had not lived. What a waste of so many good men and women, including many friends.

❧ Because George had been in for three years, and had served overseas in combat, he was one of the first in his squadron to get out of the service. He had two air medals, a Distinguished Flying Cross, and a wife, and he was headed to Yale University.

George had been accepted into Yale his junior year in high school, but his family felt he was too young. So four years later, in 1945, George and I moved to New Haven, Connecticut, for his freshman year of college. The GI Bill paid for his tuition, and he had some savings from his years in the Navy.

We went to all the football games and joined his family and friends at tailgate parties in the stadium parking lot. George played his beloved soccer his freshman year, but did not continue as it took too much time. He became a member of Delta Kappa Epsilon fraternity and was chapter president for a short time. He really worked hard.

I, on the other hand, played bridge and went to movies with some of George's more frivolous friends. I did work half a day at the Yale Co-op and audited a course (nicknamed Pots and Pans by the students) given by John Phillips, an authority on American furniture and silver. I did not go back to Smith, and Yale did not take women at the time. I could have commuted to Connecticut College, but I hated to ask my dad for the tuition. I had every opportunity to finish my education, both then and in later years. George would have been very supportive. I chose, instead, to have a big family.

We lived in three different places the two and a half years George was at Yale. The first was a shotgun apartment on Chapel Street, a tiny, adorable place we loved. The front faced the avenue, with the trolley going up and down our street. Two doors down was a funeral home. Somebody has to do it, I know, but I have been a little cynical about funeral homes ever since. We often saw the men standing in the back of the building in shirtsleeves, kicking the hearse's tires, chewing, smoking, spitting, laughing, and joking. Five minutes later, these same men appeared in the front of the building with the hearse with their Digger O'Dell suits and long, funereal faces.

On Thanksgiving, George invited ten of his best friends at Yale from Andover days to have dinner with us. Travel was still difficult, the boys could not get home, and rationing was still on. I do not remember too many of the details, but I know we had a turkey and we did not have a dining room. We sat on the couch, chairs, and the floor. I remember pulling out every pan we owned and getting every dish, piece of silverware, and glass dirty. After dinner, they went home and we fell into bed exhausted. It took me three days to get those things washed. Today, I can clean the kitchen up after feeding fifty in less time than it takes to say "Thanksgiving."

We had a wonderful black standard poodle puppy named Turbo. We were devoted to him. He was a great dog and went to work with me. He would stay behind the counter until George's last morning class, then George would pick him up and take him on to his next activity.

George played baseball for Yale and was a great fielding first baseman. There are lots of jokes about his hitting ability, but the truth is, George hit when the chips were down. I should know—I kept score. He never missed playing in a game the three seasons we were there, and his team won the Eastern Championship for two of the years. I sat behind third base, with family members of the other players and some faithful Yale baseball fans. Finally, one game, Ethan Allen, the Yale coach and a former big league player, asked me to sit behind home plate, where they had a safety net. I was huge and weighed more than a Yale linebacker. Yes, I was pregnant with our first child. The Chapel Street landlord liked dogs, but not babies. So we moved to Edwards Street, where they did not like dogs, so Turbo went to live with George's mother and father in Greenwich. The baby did not come and did not come. George's mother finally gave me a good dose of castor oil and that baby came all right—I'm tempted to say covered with glory. The baby was a lovely little boy, but sad to say, he did not weigh sixty pounds. That is what I had gained and that was what I had to lose. George and I were mad about our baby, whom we named George Walker Bush. My mother said she hated to be in the room with the baby, for if she took her eyes off him, George looked hurt.

In the fall we moved into our third and last New Haven home, on Hillhouse Avenue. The president of Yale University lived next door in a tremendous old Victorian house. The houses on either side belonged to the university and had been converted into housing for students who were married and former military. George and I shared the first floor with two other families. We were so lucky, for we had three tiny rooms and a tiny bath. That was the key—our own bath! We shared a kitchen with the other two families. There were two of everything, and since the other two families did not speak to each other for various reasons, George and I had a third of one refrigerator and a third of the other. They scheduled their mealtimes so they would not be in the kitchen at the same time. And the communal bath was a source of great contention. It was fairly amusing. I think there were

nine families and eleven children living in that house. Longtime friends
Bill and Sally Reeder lived on the third floor with their twin sons,
Boots and Shack. Our second year in the house, we lost one of our
kitchen mates, thank heavens, and we had some peace. In their place
came Patsy and Jack Caulkins with their little boy, Corky. They have
been very dear, close friends for the last fifty years. Communal living
has its ups and downs, but since I'm a people person, I loved it. It was
hard for George to study there, but he certainly managed. He won a
number of awards and was Phi Beta Kappa his senior year. It was
during George's Yale years that we began a lifelong relationship with
Bill Trent, then head of the United Negro College Fund (UNCF).
George was involved with the school's annual charity fund drive, and
UNCF was one of the beneficiaries. George brought Bill home after
one of the meetings, and a friendship was born.

Bill and his wife, Vi, invited us to come to their home in Harlem
for dinner following a baseball game between Yale and Columbia
University. Most of George's family was at the game; I sat with Bill
and Vi. The family all looked us over, but George's Ganny Walker—
who truly was a dear woman—said in a loud stage whisper as she
walked by, "It's all right. They look like Indians." I was embarrassed,
but Bill and Vi understood; they had lived a life of segregation.

This very special man died in November 1993 after spending a
lovely Thanksgiving at home surrounded by his wife of fifty-nine years
and his children. He truly was a great American.

∽ Recently, I learned my father was just as proud of George
then as I was. I came across a letter Daddy had written a childhood
friend, updating him on the Pierce family. He wrote about us:

> My second daughter, Barbara, went to Smith College for a
> year and a half and then married in January 1945 a young
> fellow named Bush, to whom she had been engaged for two
> years while he was flying a torpedo bomber in the Pacific.
> He won the Distinguished Flying Cross and altogether is a
> great guy. They are still living in New Haven where he is
> attending Yale until his graduation in June. He is by all
> odds the biggest man on the campus, having been the last

man tapped for Skull and Bones and having been awarded a faculty prize for having done the most for Yale. He is captain of the baseball team and a hell of a good first baseman. They also have a baby and I hope I live long enough to see George Bush [our baby] playing one end for Yale and Kevin Rafferty [Martha's baby] on the other.

4

Striking Out on Our Own

George interviewed for jobs all winter and spring of 1948. We had spent most of his savings from Navy days, and we needed to get on with real life and make a living.

It was very important to George that he like his work. He told me he had thought about it a great deal while standing night watch on the submarine deck after being rescued. He had decided he did not want to work with intangibles; he wanted a product he could see and feel. I think that meant he did not want to be in the investment or banking business like so many of his family. His dad was a partner with Brown Brothers, Harriman and Company, and his grandfather was the founder of G. H. Walker and Company.

We looked into farming briefly and read some books by Louis Bromfield. Thank heavens we did. It saved us from racing off into a life we were unqualified for and which is hard work. Bromfield made farming sound very romantic and idealistic. But he also made it clear that in order to be a success, you needed a lot of money to invest, which we didn't have. So realism overcame idealism, and we looked elsewhere.

Numerous companies came to New Haven to interview Yale graduates, but there were many applicants for every job. The country was gearing down in peacetime, military plants were cutting back, and there were many out-of-work servicemen. I do remember that Procter & Gamble interviewed George, and they turned him down.

George had several good choices, but ended up accepting an offer from Dresser Industries, a holding company that had several oil-related subsidiaries. The CEO was Henry Neil Mallon, a classmate of George's father and a dear family friend. I had heard stories about "Uncle Neil" almost from the moment I met George. He and Prescott Bush were certainly about as different as two men could be. George's father was six feet four inches tall with a full head of black hair and a take-charge attitude; Neil, a bachelor, was about five feet nine inches, bald, and a modest, quiet man. Yet, both men were very successful in their own fields and were the best of friends. Every family should have an "Uncle Neil." The most thoughtful man alive, he always seemed to have time for everyone.

One story will explain why the Bush kids loved this dear man. When they were about ten or eleven years old, George and his older brother, Prescott, were playing catch as Neil watched. One of the boys threw a wild ball, and it shattered the car windshield. George's father came charging out the door, bellowing at Poppy and Pressy that they knew better than to play ball near the house. Neil quickly stepped up and took the blame, saying he was the one who threw the ball!

Neil's excitement about George coming to Dresser was contagious. He wanted George to have experience with all the various companies, starting with Ideco (short for International Derrick and Equipment Company) as Dresser's only trainee.

So the day after graduation, George headed for Odessa, Texas, in a little, two-door, red Studebaker, a graduation present from his mom and dad. He stopped on the way in Birmingham, Alabama, to see his Yale baseball teammate, Frank Quinn (who had signed with the Boston Red Sox for $100,000) play minor league ball.

Our son, Georgie, and I went to Maine and stayed in "the big house" with Gampy and Ganny Walker. As always, they spoiled us to death. It was a happy time—except I missed George. He promised me he would send for us the moment he found a place to live. I remember he wrote his grandparents to thank them for putting us up. He also told them he was so happy he had gotten a great education at Yale, because he was putting it to good use. He knew this for a fact, because his boss, Bill Nelson, told him he was the best warehouse-sweeper-outer he had ever seen. He also was very good at painting oil field equipment in temperatures that reached 105 degrees at noon. As you can tell, George started at the bottom.

Odessa was a boomtown and there was little or no housing available. Midland was twenty miles down the road, but that's where the white-collar workers lived. The blue-collar workers, like us, lived in Odessa. A week after his arrival, George finally called to say that he had found a tiny place and we should come down. He said it was a sorry little house—and it was—but Georgie and I were so excited about being with him. This was an adventure the three of us had signed up for together.

We stepped off the plane—after a twelve-hour flight in those days—to a whole new and very hot world. Odessa is flat as a pancake and as different from Rye, New York, as any place imaginable. Nothing comes easy to West Texas. Every tree must be cultivated, and every flower is a joy.

As far as my mother was concerned, we could have been living in Russia. Who had ever heard of Odessa, Texas? She sent me cold cream, soap, and other items she assumed were available only in civilized parts of the country. She did not put Odessa in that category. I loved being given all that stuff, but eventually had to write and tell her we had big, beautiful supermarkets, which Rye did not have at the time.

George had rented a two-room apartment on East Seventh Street. We first shared a bath with a very nice couple from Oklahoma, Valta Ree and Jack Casselman, who had a similar apartment on the other side. When they moved out, three females moved in: a grandmother of thirty-eight, a daughter of twenty, and a three-year-old. The two older women had questionable occupations, and we saw very little of them, day or night. To use the bathroom, we walked in and locked the door on their side; then when we were done, we unlocked their door before going back to our own room. The big key here was remembering to unlock the other door as you left. Our neighbors' many gentlemen callers had a hard time remembering that, which caused a small amount of friction. We would be locked out of our own bathroom! Otherwise, sharing a bath did not seem strange to us—we had done it most of our married life. We also felt lucky, because most of our neighbors did not have bathrooms at all, just outhouses. The family two doors down not only had an outdoor toilet, but mules and some other livestock. The overwhelming smell drove the neighborhood wild. We also had the only refrigerator on the street. As life is relative, we lived pretty well.

Speaking of smells, I still blush when I remember awakening soon after our arrival to the strong odor of gas. I woke up George,

Georgie, and the Casselmans and made everyone leave the house before it blew up. The Casselmans were dear and patiently explained to me that the wind had shifted and I was smelling fumes from the nearby oil-related plants.

~~~ Some wonderful things happened in Odessa, and we certainly grew up a little more. George and I learned a whole new outlook on life. Texans are apt to think that the "Texas way" is best. One day at work a man said to George, "Say, you're a college grad, aren't you?" When George told him he had gone to Yale, the man thought a minute and said he'd never heard of it. He mumbled something that sounded like "Too bad." George got the distinct impression he felt sorry for him. So much for eastern elitism. It didn't count much in West Texas.

Texas was "high and dry" then—literally. You could not buy liquor by-the-drink over the counter. You either belonged to a private club or bought a bottle and "brown-bagged" it. Some counties were absolutely dry—you couldn't even buy a bottle. Nearby Midland County was "dry," and Ector County was "wet." So people drove to the Ector County line to Pinky Roden's liquor store—a rather profitable business. It wasn't until 1970 that a liquor-by-the-drink bill passed, much to our dismay, which I'll explain later.

We drank little or nothing, but I remember one night when George brought home a man named Smitty, an Ideco salesman from Oklahoma. Smitty was a real good ol' boy, and when George offered him a drink, Smitty picked up our one bottle of bourbon and took a big swig. He then passed it to me. Out of the corner of my eye I saw George watching to see what I'd do. He had a big grin on his face. I let the men pass the bottle. Poor ol' Smitty eventually was "run off," caught by the boss for having very light fingers, and George poured him on the train for Oklahoma after emptying his pockets of Ideco supplies.

We had another very interesting visitor in the fall of 1948, whom I wrote home about:

> Friday Pop did not come home for lunch as he had to meet a man who was coming in from Dallas—a Mr. Rabacheck from Yugoslavia. He does not speak English. Just "hello,"

"okay," "good morning," etc. We find some West Texans are not only Eastern-prejudiced, but also "furiner"-prejudiced. No one in the store wanted to have anything to do with Mr. R. He has visited all the Dresser Companies and has been wined and dined by the presidents and vice presidents of these companies. He gets to Odessa and they act like he has a disease. Consequently, Pop has been with him constantly since Friday. He is an excellent engineer. Pop says Mr. R. was very apologetic that he couldn't speak better English so he could talk to Bill Nelson. (This was all with the help of a dictionary and the hands.). Pop looked up the word "shy" and told him that Bill was shy, but the truth of the matter was that Bill did not want to have anything to do with a "furiner" and a "commie."

Mr. R. wanted to know how to skid a rig from well to well without breaking the derrick down, moving it and reassembling it again. This is a very complicated process, and Pop had to ask for answers to almost everything that Mr. R. asked. Something gets lost in the translation. It has been good for Pop, but not so great for Mr. R.

Friday night we took him to the football game. He was fascinated and a charming guy. Last night he wanted to see "cowboy," so we took him to see a western movie. He loved it.

He and Pop went out to different rigs Saturday, Sunday and Monday and today, and will probably go out until he leaves on Wednesday.

He came back here last night after the movie and we had a very interesting talk. It was rather like playing The Game. [We would guess what each other meant, using our hands, facial expressions, and the dictionary.]

Both George and I really liked this man a lot. It broke our hearts when he said good-bye to us, clutched his heart, and said "Friends." George and I felt sad that because of his country's policies, we could not really be friends. As I write this in 1993, his beautiful country is under terrible civil strife, and I think of this warm man and his family.

⤳ My letters home during this period are boring, filled with stories of Georgie—a much beloved and slightly spoiled little boy. They sound lonesome for family and family news, although the people we met both at church and at work were very nice to us. One of the many things we have learned in all our travels is that it's the people who count. West Texans were the best. Most people everywhere are interesting, and if you can't find a friend, then maybe there is something wrong with you. For our brief stay on East Seventh Street, the Casselmans were friends. And our housemates from Yale, Bill and Sally Reeder and their twin boys, lived in Midland and we saw them several times.

We had our first Christmas away from family. We got many packages from home and decorated our new little apartment on East Seventeenth Street—still considered on the wrong side of the tracks, but we had our own bath.

On Christmas Eve, Ideco opened the doors to its shop and had an open bar for all its customers. George and another fella were put behind the bar to pass out Christmas cheer. Each "good ol' " boy had a drink, and you had to have one with him. George started sipping early, and at dusk Christmas Eve, store manager Leo Thomas drove up to the house in a pickup truck and dropped George off—literally. He opened the back of the truck, dumped George in the yard, and drove away. It was a long time before I let George forget it. Maybe that's why my letters to my family were so boring. I left out the more interesting things happening to us!

⤳ In the spring of 1949, George, Georgie, and I moved to California, where George first worked as an assemblyman at Pacific Pumps, and then became a salesman for Security Engineers Company, a manufacturer of drilling bits. Both were Dresser companies. We lived in a motel in Whittier, the beautiful Pierpoint Inn in Ventura, a rented house in Bakersfield, and finally came to rest in an apartment in Compton. By this time I was very pregnant with our second child.

That fall my brother Jimmy married Margie Dyer in Cleveland, Ohio. I went east for the wedding and had a great time with my family and friends. She was a lovely bride, and we were all so happy that my precious, funny, slightly wild brother had found the rock of Gibraltar to settle down with. She has remained a great beauty and a great wife.

At that time, George was working in the Pacific Pumps factory seven days a week, eight-hour shifts. A week or so after the wedding, George came home early one day and had the terrible job of telling me that my mother and father had been in an automobile accident. My beautiful mother had been killed immediately, and my dad was in the hospital. After much discussion with my sisters and brothers, we got the message from Daddy that I was not to come home. He did not want the baby endangered. What a lonely, miserable time that was. I was so glad I had been home for the very happy family wedding. Sudden death is a terrible shock—but then all death is a struggle and a shock. My younger brother, Scott, a freshman at Yale, heard the news on a car radio. Jim and Margie came home from their honeymoon, moving in with Daddy for several years until he remarried. My sister, Martha, and her great husband, Walter, took charge of all funeral plans. And I sat in California.

George was wonderful. His bosses gave him the next day off, and he called several friends from Yale and Smith who were living in the Los Angeles area. Margie and Dick Jenkins, David and Suzy Grimes, and Barbara and Bill Mannon were marvelous to me, and all have remained friends for fifty years. Certainly, George and I could not have lived the life we have without friends.

We had a lovely little apartment, living near a couple with four small children. They seemed so very nice. She agreed to keep Georgie when I went into the hospital to have the baby. About a week before the baby was born, we heard screaming, banging, and shouting. Then four little children came tumbling out of that apartment and said, "Call the police. Dad is killing Mother." We brought the children in and called the police. They arrived, knocked on the door, and the noise suddenly stopped.

In a few minutes the wife came to the door bleeding, with a blackened eye and a red, tear-stained face. She said there was no problem and became angry with us because we called the police. It was so ugly and awful. The police finally went away, and we tucked the children in for the night. Eventually the husband drank himself into a stupor and the wife's father and brothers came, put the drunk on the floor, and moved the family out. George and I grew up a little more.

For prenatal care, I was going to a clinic where you saw whichever doctor was on duty. So I didn't meet the doctor who delivered our little girl until the night of her birth, December 20, 1949. I can't remember his name or what he looked like, but I remember thinking he was a knight in white armor, a prince, and a saint. Any woman in labor feels all that and more about the doctor who delivers her baby.

We named our daughter Pauline Robinson Bush and called her Robin. We were considering calling her Pauline Pierce Bush until George's mother said the poor child would go through life as P. P. Bush and that would never do. That was so unlike Dotty Bush—it's funny the things you remember.

George brought Robin and me home Christmas Day. You can't ask for more than that. Daddy gave us a Hoffman television set—a big, heavy rectangular thing with a tiny little yellow screen—and our friends came over for Milton Berle, which was fun. My sister, Martha, visited us for a few days that Christmas, which was wonderful. Daddy and Scott went to a fishing lodge in Florida for the holidays, and Scott told me that they were very lonely. We all missed Mother as she really loved Christmas.

Fortunately, Scott wasn't lonely for long. He married his childhood sweetheart, Janice Chamberlain, when she graduated from Mount Holyoke College and he from Miami University in Oxford, Ohio. They have been a team for some forty years and have four wonderful children.

And there is another happy footnote: In June 1952, my father found a wonderful woman named Willa Martin, a writer with the Associated Press and an artist of some renown, from Greenville, South Carolina. She brought many good things to the family when they married, not the least of which was her niece Patty, who eventually married George's youngest brother, Bucky.

⤳ In 1950 George was transferred back to West Texas, but this time to Midland. He was back working for Ideco as a city salesman, calling on oil companies mostly located right in town. I was glad, as he had traveled a great deal in California. At first we stayed in George's Courts, a motel right on Main Street in downtown Midland. The first morning, George went out to get some milk for the baby, but he came rushing back into the motel and changed his clothes. He had on Bermuda shorts, and the truck drivers were whistling at him. I don't believe he wore shorts ever again, except to play tennis.

We stayed there until we were able to settle into our very first house. It was located on East Maple Street in a section of town called Easter Egg Row. Every brand-new, identical house was painted a different wild color and cost just under $8,000. We loved that marvelous little home.

Many Easterners had come to Midland to get in on the oil boom— John Ashmun, Toby Hilliard, Dottie and Earle Craig, Hopie and Jimmy Ritchie. There were Texans, too, like John Overbey, Marion and C. Fred Chambers, Steve and Anne Farish, Liz and Tom Fowler, and Betty and Murphy Baxter. There were Oklahomans like the Liedt-kes—Betty and Hugh, and Bessie and Bill—and Jimmy and Jocie Hewgley, Marian and Bill Bovaird, and many more. We all had been uprooted; we all had young children; and we all were having a lot of fun. The women joined the Midland Service League, and the men played touch football in the Martini Bowl. We all worked in the Little Theater and the YMCA and volunteered at the hospital. Most of us were active in church; George was an elder, and we both taught Sunday School at the First Presbyterian Church. We took turns having cookouts on our tiny patios or in backyards and watching each other's children. When the chips were down, all of us were there for each other.

George was working very hard trying to support his growing family. After several years of working for Dresser, he decided to go off on his own. He went to see Neil Mallon, and in his usual supportive fashion, Neil said that if he were young again, he'd do the same thing. So in late 1950, our neighbor across the street, John Overbey, and George went into business together, forming Bush-Overbey Oil Development Company, Inc. George's wonderfully loyal Uncle Herbie Walker helped him finance his part of the deal.

George worked even harder and spent a lot of time traveling, looking for good oil deals and financing. A few years later, in 1953, Bush-Overbey joined forces with the Liedtke brothers, Hugh and Bill, calling their new company "Zapata." (They took the name from a Marlon Brando film playing in downtown Midland at the time, *Viva Zapata!*) It was truly an exciting time, a life filled with risk and hope.

We moved again, into a slightly bigger house, on West Ohio Street, and we all had more babies. For us, it was John Ellis Bush, born in February 1953. We called him Jeb.

Life seemed almost too good to be true.

 5

Robin

So I am glad not that my loved one has gone,
But that the earth she laughed and lived on was my earth, too.
That I had known and loved her,
And that my love I'd shown.
Tears over her departure?
Nay, a smile
That I had walked with her a little while.*

Jeb was just a few weeks old when Robin woke up one morning
and said, "I don't know what to do this morning. I may go out
and lie on the grass and watch the cars go by, or I might just stay in
bed." I didn't think that sounded like a normal three-year-old and
decided she must have what my mother called "spring fever." I took
her to our excellent pediatrician, Dr. Dorothy Wyvell. She examined
Robin, took some blood, and told me she would call me after the test
results were in. She suggested I might want to come back without
Robin, but with George. That sounded rather ominous to me, but I
wasn't too worried. Certainly Robin had no energy, but nothing
seemed seriously wrong.

Dr. Wyvell called, and George met me at her office in the late
afternoon. Dorothy was not one to pull any punches. She told us Robin
had leukemia. Neither of us had ever heard of it, and George asked her

---

* Sent to us by a friend after Robin died.

what the next step was; how did we cure her? She talked to us a little about red and white blood cells and told us as gently as possible that there was no cure. Her advice was to tell no one, go home, forget that Robin was sick, make her as comfortable as we could, love her—and let her gently slip away. She said this would happen very quickly, in several weeks. We talked a little more, and George asked her if she would talk to his uncle, Dr. John Walker, at Memorial Sloan-Kettering Hospital in New York City. She readily agreed. Uncle John also thought Robin had little chance to live, but he thought we should by all means treat her and try to extend her life, just in case of a break-through.

I drove home, and George had to return to the office for just a minute. On the way, he stopped at Liz and Tom Fowler's house and asked Liz please to come over to be with me. By that evening our living room was filled with close friends, all offering to help. I remember being so surrounded by love that I did not really believe what the doctor had told us was true. She just had to be wrong. But either way, we knew we had to do everything we could to save our beautiful child.

It's funny how you remember such unimportant things at moments of stress. Our minister, Dr. Matthew Lynn, and his wife popped in. They were offered a drink, and I will always remember his answer. He said, "Not *now*, thank you, George." Tommy and Matthew Lynn would no more take a drink than fly, but by saying "now," he made everyone feel comfortable. Such a silly, small thing to remember.

The very next day George and I flew to New York City, leaving Georgie and Jebby with different friends, and checked Robin into Memorial Sloan-Kettering on Sixty-eighth Street. At first, no one there believed that our little hospital in Midland had done the testing correctly. Robin's white blood cell count was just too high—the highest they had ever heard. Unfortunately, it was correct, and they immediately put Robin on medication. We moved into Ganny and Gampy Walker's beautiful apartment on Sutton Place in New York and stayed there off and on until October 1953, when our little one passed away with both of us standing by her side.

It was an extraordinary experience, and in a strange kind of way, we learned how lucky we were. We met people there who had only one child. We had three. We met people who did not love each other. We loved each other very much. (I learned later that 70 percent of people who lose a child get divorced. I suspect this is because their love for each other was found wanting and they did not communicate.) We had the most supportive family, and we shared. We had friends who helped us. Financially, we were very lucky, as our insurance covered almost everything.

And last, but not least, we believed in God. That has made an enormous difference in our lives, then and now.

I became very close to the parents of the other patients. Not only did we spend hours together, but we understood each other. So many of them had serious financial problems, which made the ordeal even tougher. Sloan-Kettering did not charge those who couldn't pay, but there were so many other expenses involved. I remember one precious little boy named Joey, whose mother had a big family in upstate New York. Her husband was a laborer and was trying to cope with schools, bills, and meals. She worried all the time. She had no Ganny Walker to put her up nine blocks from the hospital, and no Mom Bush to help with the children. (Mrs. Bush had sent one of her boys' childhood nurses, Marion Fraser, down to Texas to take care of our boys.) Joey's mom had a cheap room out in the Bronx and commuted every day on the bus and subway in her bedroom slippers. She had the face of an angel, a big warm heart, and enormous faith in God. As Joey's time drew near, I met her one day in the parents' room and asked about her son. "Joey's bad, Barbara," she said, adding: "Do you remember in the Bible where it says, 'Let the little children suffer and they will come unto me'? Joey is really suffering." I loved that courageous lady, and I loved Joey. God bless him.

Years later, when I did a little work for Ronald McDonald Houses, I always thought of Joey's mother and how much they would have helped her. Ronald McDonald Houses not only provide inexpensive rooms and transportation to and from the hospital for whole families, they also allow parents who are going through the same thing to be together, to support and care for each other. It's a wonderful program that really helps families in need.

George was just getting started in business, so he rushed back and forth between Midland and New York. He came east whenever he could, and we talked on the phone every evening. I missed my baby Jeb and Georgie at home, but George was with them as much as possible.

Friends and family made such a difference. There were so many who cared and helped. Lud Ashley, George's classmate and great friend from Yale days, was a bachelor then living in New York City. He quietly checked in all the time. I did not know just how much until very early one morning a night nurse said, "What does your husband do, Mrs. Bush? I meet him every morning around 2 A.M. when he comes in to check on Robin before going to bed." I said that it couldn't have been my husband because he was in Texas. It was Lud Ashley.

One day, when Robin was very ill, I remember going out onto the cold roof off the parents' room to be alone for a tear or two. I found Lud huddled outside, freezing. He hadn't wanted to intrude, but he wanted to be there if needed. Lud went on to be a Democratic congressman from Toledo, Ohio, and has remained a great friend.

People really wanted to help. One friend of George's, Jimmy Markham, felt so bad that he appeared with his most valued gift—a beautiful, pedigreed, tricolored collie pup. With "Mark" came a list as long as your arm of things that this dog needed. Needless to say, the last thing on my mind was the care and feeding of this big, gawky puppy. We got the basics and put Mark in our backyard in Midland. When we returned in October, we had the world's most beautiful gentle dog. We all loved him. He was dognapped several years later, breaking our hearts.

Back in Midland, George dropped by church every morning at 6:30 A.M. and prayed for Robin. He said at first only the custodian was there. Then one morning he felt a presence, and our minister, Matthew Lynn, had started joining him. They never talked, just prayed. That meant a lot to George.

One day George got several phone calls from friends who had heard radio personality Paul Harvey talking about a doctor in Kansas who had a cure for leukemia. George spent the day following up, and after about five hours, he finally got the doctor on the phone. The poor man was distraught. He did not have a cure—just another medicine they were testing. He had spent the day talking to other parents who were desperate to help their loved one. He did tell George that Sloan-Kettering was a great hospital and if there was a breakthrough, they certainly would know it. I'm sure Paul Harvey, whom George now knows and respects, had no idea what anguish he caused a small group of parents. He raised our hopes only to have them dashed.

Robin was wonderful. She never asked why this was happening to her. She lived each day as it came, sweet and loving, unquestioning and unselfish. How we hated bone marrow tests. They were so agonizing for all ages. She had many painful blood transfusions, and family and friends quietly slipped into the hospital and replaced the blood supply. Several times I was called to come pick up my sister or a friend who had passed out while giving blood. The hospital asked people to try to get replacements for the blood that was used, and thanks to many dear people, I honestly think we fulfilled our obligation.

Robin would go into remission, and once in a great while, we were able to take her as an outpatient to Ganny Walker's. Gampy Walker was a scary old man, but he was putty in Robin's hands. He taught her to play a simplified game of Gin Rummy, which she misunderstood to be Gin Mummy. She then changed it to Gin Poppy, after her beloved father.

Sometimes we went to the Bush house in Greenwich, and in the summer, we went to Maine for a brief period and Robin got to see her brothers. She had their pictures taped to her headboard at Sloan-Kettering and every single doctor and nurse heard about those "superman" brothers of hers.

We took her home to Midland for a short stay. That was the farthest the hospital had ever allowed a patient to go, but the doctors knew Dorothy Wyvell could take care of Robin. Still, it was scary to be so far from the hospital. Hugh Liedtke and George were building their new business, and George must have been exhausted with work, worry, and travel, but somehow he managed to do it all. Hugh's wife, Betty, who had children of her own, saved my life. She spent hours each day with us, thinking up ways to get Robin to eat and make her laugh. She was loving and funny and no matter how bad it got, she came. I don't know how she knew, but if I got frightened, she was there.

Leukemia was not a well-known disease. Many people thought it was catching and did not let their children get near Robin. In those days, cancer in general was only whispered about, and some people just couldn't cope with a dying child. It was not an easy time for our friends or us.

I made up my mind that there would be no tears around Robin, so I asked people who cried to step out of her room. I didn't want to scare our little girl. Poor George had the most dreadful time and could hardly stand to see her get a blood transfusion. He would say that he had to go to the men's room. We used to laugh and wonder if Robin thought he had the weakest bladder in the world. Not true. He just had the most tender heart.

Rightly or wrongly, we did not tell six-year-old Georgie that his sister was dying. We hated that, but we felt it would have been too big a burden for such a little fellow. On the other hand, there could be no more roughhousing since leukemia patients easily hemorrhage, so we had to keep a close watch on them when they were together.

One day, back in New York, George's father asked me to go with him to the graveyard in Greenwich. He wanted me to see where he would be buried. The lot he picked was lovely, on a nice hillside with trees. He was such a dear man, and he picked out a modest headstone that said BUSH—about three feet tall and four feet wide. On one side of the headstone was a freshly planted lilac bush; on the other side, a dogwood tree. It was a sunny, bright day, and Dad pointed out some enormous mausoleum-type buildings or large headstones. Then he said, "I knew old so-and-so. He certainly thought highly of himself, didn't he, Bar?" That darling man bought that lot so Robin would have a place to rest.

Eventually the medicine that was controlling the leukemia caused other terrible problems. We called George, and by the time he got there after flying all night, our baby was in a coma. Her death was very peaceful. One minute she was there, and the next she was gone. I truly felt her soul go out of that beautiful little body. For one last time I combed her hair, and we held our precious little girl. I never felt the presence of God more strongly than at that moment.

We loved our doctors at Sloan-Kettering and have kept up with them. Joe Burchenbal, Lois Murphy, and Charlotte Tan were so bright, caring, and dedicated. Lois and Charlotte were Robin's doctors and became dear friends of ours, although they tried to stay detached. They just could not get too involved emotionally. At that time no leukemia patient had recovered. Today, if caught in time, recovery is fairly common, thanks to many dedicated doctors and researchers.

The nurses also were very special to us. I wondered at their ability to put in day after day with sick and dying children, and then go home to face all the problems that come with raising a family. They were, and are, exceptional.

      We called our families and told them the news and went to Greenwich for a memorial service. (There would be no funeral; we had signed papers giving Robin's body to research.) Those few days are a little vague, but several things come to mind.

The day after Robin died, George and I went to Rye to play golf with Daddy, at his suggestion. As we drove out on the parkway, I was shocked that the leaves were at the peak of their fall beauty. I remember realizing life went on, whether we were looking or not. I also remember changing my shoes in the ladies' locker room and seeing a childhood friend, Marilyn Peterson. We talked briefly, and I did not mention Robin. I wondered later if she thought it was strange that we were playing golf the day after our baby died. I, for one, was numb.

The next day there was a memorial service for Robin with family and only a few dear friends. Upstairs in our bedroom, I could hear the family gathering below and told George I did not think I could face all that. He was so dear and special and became the rock of our family. For one who allowed no tears before her death, I fell apart, and time after time during the next six months, George would put me together again. He looked out the window, and seeing my sister, Martha, and her husband, Walt, walking up the driveway, said, "Sure, and with the O'Raffertys, it is going to be a grand wake." Sounds dumb now, but believe me, it did the trick. I giggled through my tears and went down.

The minute the service was over, George and I raced home to Midland. (George's mother and Lud Ashley laid our little Robin to rest several days later when the hospital released her body.) We wanted to be the ones to break the news to Georgie. As we drove up to his school, Georgie was walking down the covered walk carrying something into his classroom. He ran and asked his teacher, "My mom, dad, and sister are home. Can I go see them?" We felt devastated by what we had to tell him. As I recall, he asked a lot of questions and couldn't understand why we hadn't told him when we had known for such a long time.

We picked up Jebby at Betty and Hugh's, and George made us all go by several friends' houses just to say hello and get over that first awful moment of seeing each other after a death. That started the most painful period of adjusting to life after Robin.

We awakened night after night in great physical pain—it hurt that much. I hated that nobody mentioned her; it was as if she had never been. I know now that it was because our friends did not want to hurt us, but you don't think too clearly after a death. Several times Georgie helped break the ice. At a football game George had taken him to, Georgie suddenly said he wished he were Robin. George told me all his friends stiffened with uncomfortable embarrassment. When he asked Georgie just why he wished he were Robin, he said, "I bet she can see the game better from up there than we can here." Another time, he asked his dad if we had buried Robin lying down or standing up. Again, shocked silence. George said that he wasn't sure, but why did Georgie want to know. He said he had just learned that the earth rotated, and he wanted to know if she spent part of her time standing on her head, and wouldn't that be neat? He made it okay for our friends to mention her, and that helped us a great deal.

Midland was a small town, and many, many people called on us. It was exhausting, and once I complained to George about it. People I hardly knew came by. I caught one friend practicing in front of a mirror her sad facial expressions and what she was going to say to me. I backed out of the living room and came in again. She struggled through something that came out like this: "At least it wasn't your firstborn and a boy at that." I was speechless. George pointed out that it wasn't easy for them and that I should be patient. He was right. I just needed somebody to blame.

I wanted to get back to real life, but there is a dance that you have to go through to get there. When I wanted to cut out, George made me talk to him, and he shared with me. What a difference that makes. He made me remember that the loss was not just mine. It was his, Georgie's, and Jeb's, our friends' who loved her, and all our family's so far away. He did it subtly, but with love. Many times he held me in his arms and let me weep myself to sleep. In those days there was no Hospice program, which I certainly needed. Thank heavens George was always there for me.

Hugh Liedtke came up with the brilliant idea of setting up a foundation for leukemia research in Robin's name, which helped me enormously. We called it the Bright Star Foundation.

I devoted my time to our children, spending every single moment with Jebby, and then with Georgie when he came home from school. One lovely, breezy day I was in our bedroom when I heard Georgie talking to a neighbor child who wanted him to come over and play. Georgie said he wanted to, but he couldn't leave his mother. She needed him. That started my cure. I realized I was too much of a burden for a little seven-year-old boy to carry.

For a year I devoted my time to starting a little woman's exchange shop for the Junior Service League. I worked at that project night and day, and everyone helped me. We made very little money for the league, and when I retired in 1955 to have yet again another baby, the store closed. I think the shop was just another way that our supportive hometown helped me cope with death.

We named our beautiful, smiling little boy after Neil Mallon. Less than two years later, in 1956, Neil was followed by Marvin, named after my dad. Just as an observation—men are funny. We wanted to name the other boys after Daddy, but he always said that we should not because Marvin was a dreadful name. Well, when George and I called and told him that in spite of him, we were going to name the baby Marvin Pierce Bush, he cried. He really had not meant it when he said no.

⌒ George and I love and value every person more because of Robin. She lives on in our hearts, memories, actions, and through the Bright Star Foundation. I don't cry over her anymore. She is a happy, bright part of our lives.

After George's mother died in 1992, I was given an envelope with George's name on it. It contained the following letter, which George had written his mother several years after Robin died and which she had saved all these years:

Dear Mum,

I have jotted down some words about a subject dear to your heart and mine. It is fun to fool around and try in one form or another to express thoughts that suddenly come up from way down deep in one's heart. Last night I went out on the town and on my way home—late—I said to myself, "You could well have gone to Greenwich tonight" . . . this thought struck me out of the blue, but I felt no real sense of negligence. The part I like is to think of Robin as though she were a part, a living part, of our vital and energetic and wonderful family of men and Bar.

Bar and I wonder how long this will go on. We hope we will feel this genuine closeness when we are 83 and 82. Wouldn't it be exciting at that age to have a beautiful 3 ½-year-old daughter . . . she doesn't grow up. Now she's Neil's age. Soon she'll be Marvin's—and beyond that she'll be all alone, but with us, a vital living pleasurable part of our day-to-day life. I sometimes wonder whether it is fair to our boys and to our friends to "fly-high" that portrait of Robin which I love so much; but here selfishness takes over because every time I sit at our table with just our candlelight, I somehow can't help but glance at this picture you gave us and enjoy a renewed physical sensation of closeness to a loved one.

This letter . . . is kind of like a confessional . . . between you and me, a mother and her little boy—now not so little, but still just as close, only when we are older, we hesitate to talk from our hearts quite as much.

There is about our house a need. The running, pulsating restlessness of the four boys as they struggle to learn and grow; their athletic chests and arms and legs; their happy noises as the world embraces them . . . all this wonder needs a counterpart. We need some starched crisp frocks to go with all our torn-kneed blue jeans and helmets. We need some soft blond hair to offset those crew cuts. We need a doll house to stand firm against our forts and rackets and thousand baseball cards. We need a cut-out star to play alone while the others battle to see who's "family champ." We even need someone . . . who could sing the descant to "Alouette," while outside they scramble to catch the elusive ball aimed ever roofward, but usually thudding against the screens.

We need a legitimate Christmas angel—one who doesn't have cuffs beneath the dress.

We need someone who's afraid of frogs.

We need someone to cry when I get mad—not argue.

We need a little one who can kiss without leaving egg or jam or gum.

We need a girl.

We had one once—she'd fight and cry and play and make her way just like the rest. But there was about her a certain softness.

She was patient—her hugs were just a little less wiggly.

Like them, she'd climb in to sleep with me, but somehow she'd fit.

She didn't boot and flip and wake me up with pug nose and mischievous eyes a challenging quarter-inch from my sleeping face.

No—she'd stand beside our bed till I felt her there. Silently and comfortably, she'd put those precious, fragrant locks against my chest and fall asleep.

Her peace made me feel strong, and so very important.

"My Daddy" had a caress, a certain ownership which touched a slightly different spot than the "Hi Dad" I love so much.

But she is still with us. We need her and yet we have her. We can't touch her, and yet we can feel her.

We hope she'll stay in our house for a long, long time.

Love, Pop

6

Oh, the Glamorous World
of Politics

In the years that followed we moved into a slightly larger house, near McCall Park, where we could watch Georgie play Little League baseball. We got a puppy named Nicky—a "gift" from Saint Nicholas—who lived to be nineteen years old. He was sold as a poodle, but as he got older, we discovered he was a mixed breed. He looked like a lamb.

Every other summer we went to Maine. It was just too far and too expensive to take the whole family every year, and several times I was pregnant. George went more often, if even just for a day or two, to talk to his biggest investor, Herbie Walker, or to attend a family wedding or funeral. George has made it to Maine at least one day every summer of his life except for a year during the war.

Georgie started our children's tradition of going to Camp Longhorn in the Hill Country of Texas for a month in July. Now George's twins go, too. They all became "aterwaytogoers"—short for "That's the way to go!"—which we all shouted on Parent's Day.

One summer, George's brother Buck and his friend Fay Vincent, who later became Commissioner of Baseball, came to Texas and spent their college vacation working in the oil fields.

In 1957 we rented the Pierce house (no relation to my family) in Kennebunkport for a month. It is a wonderful house that sits on the rocks just past St. Ann's Church on Ocean Avenue. Our boys were eleven months and two, four, and eleven years old. George wisely thought it would be no vacation for me without help, so he hired two

50

young black women to go up with me: Julia May Cooper, who already helped me part-time, and a woman she knew, Otha Fitzgerald. Six of us—Julia May and Otha, the three younger boys, and I—drove cross-country. George, who was going to fly up later with Georgie, had planned very carefully the places where we would stop at night to avoid any racial incidents. Fortunately, we had no problems and the trip east was painless.

We had a great month, and then since Georgie's school started early, he flew back to Texas with his dad and Julia May. Otha, the three little boys, and I would drive. We planned a fun trip, with stops in Niagara Falls and several other places. I learned to tuck the boys in the back of the station wagon asleep around two A.M., stop for breakfast when they woke up, and then drive until about noon. I would check into a motel with a pool, the boys would spend the afternoon swimming, and after an early dinner, we all went to bed to start again at two A.M. It may sound crazy, but that way, we usually missed traffic and the boys didn't get too restless. All went well until we got to the South. The racial showdown in Little Rock, Arkansas, over school desegregation had erupted, and tension was high. Otha was not welcome in any restaurants, motels, or hotels. That dear woman insisted I take the children into restaurants alone and leave her in the car. That was unacceptable to me, so we all picnicked together from food bought at 7-Elevens. Sleeping also was a problem, and again, she insisted we go ahead and check in and she would sleep in the car. I wouldn't go in without her. Finally, we stopped at a Howard Johnson between Tulsa and Oklahoma City and found that they would both feed us and let us spend the night. It just so happened that one of their restaurants between New York City and Washington had refused service to a black man, and when he turned out to be a diplomat, it caused an international scandal. From that moment on, Howard Johnson across the country were integrated.

Otha and I had very long, interesting conversations on that trip. Once again, I grew a little more—a lot more—and my eyes were opened to an aspect of life that was inconceivable to me. I was so ashamed of our system that could tell this fine woman she was not equal. When we got home, Otha moved to East Texas to take another job and we lost touch. Twenty years later, when George and I were attending a National Federation of Republican Women's Convention, I was told there was a delegate by the name of Taylor who wanted to speak with us. It was Otha, now married. We have stayed in touch ever since.

Looking back, I'm not sure if I really appreciated how protected my life was—and always had been—from such ugliness. I thought I was very much aware of what was going on in the world. For example, during the early 1950s, I can remember the terrible "Red Scare" going on in the country. We were convinced there were Communists everywhere (there were some legitimate spies), and everyone was glued to the TV and radio listening to Senator Joseph McCarthy conduct his hearings. But seldom did I have to deal with such issues personally. I was much more concerned with my family and keeping house.

⮑ By this time, George was president and CEO of Zapata Off-Shore Company, a subsidiary of Zapata Petroleum. Their venture into offshore drilling was exciting and new. The rigs they ordered were a revolutionary tripod design by R. G. LeTourneau, weighing about nine million pounds and costing up to six million dollars. Before you could borrow money in those days for something that big, that expensive, and that risky, you had to prove you had a certain number of contracts lined up. (By way of contrast, George and I recently saw several eighty-million-dollar rigs in "mothballs" in Galveston, Texas, built with no contracts at all.) So George and Hugh Liedtke worked very hard, nationally and internationally, getting work. They were very successful and had four to five rigs operating.

In 1959, Zapata Petroleum Company amicably split, with George taking over Zapata Off-Shore. There was only one problem: landlocked Midland is nowhere near "offshore," and it only made sense for us to move to Houston. When George first mentioned it, I felt a sinking feeling. I loved Midland and our friends and did not want to leave that cocoon of warmth and love. Midland had been home for almost eleven years. We—especially George—had been such a part of the community: raising money for the church and the little theater; helping establish the first Midland YMCA and starting a bank; building the Republican party, including twice heading the Eisenhower/Nixon campaigns; working for the cancer drive; serving on the United Way Board. How could we leave?

George and I also had one other very small problem: I was pregnant again. How could I leave the wonderful doctors, Walter Parks and Garland Lang, who had delivered Neil and Marvin?

But George couldn't work three hundred miles from home, so we headed for Houston to look for a house.

We stayed with Baine and Mildred Kerr, who certainly made our life easier and were to become great friends. A lawyer, Baine had done legal work for both Zapata companies. He found 1.2 acres of marvelous wooded land just around the corner from their new house. We bought the lot, contracted with their builder, and went back to Midland to await his blueprints. Sitting with the boys one day, we planned what we wanted. George told young George to go measure Jeb's bedroom. When he came back with the measurements, George said, "Write down 'four rooms twelve-by-twelve.' " We went through our whole house that way and sent the measurements down to Houston. The builder sent word back that our proportions were a little off: The first floor would have filled a half block; and the second floor was about the size of a pinpoint. That's why you hire professionals.

George moved first to set up his office, and I stayed in Midland until he insisted I join him to supervise the new house, meet my new doctor, and find new schools. The boys would finish up the school semester in Midland with our wonderful baby-sitter, Mrs. Lois Rogers. She and her husband later moved to Houston for three months to help out with the move and the new baby. I was hoping they would stay with us forever.

Once in Houston, I awakened several times feeling almost nauseated over leaving Midland, yet I was too busy to be really homesick. Anyway, what a waste to miss what you can't have.

George and I moved into a "swinging" apartment house built around a swimming pool. Most of the residents were young working people, and we could hear them partying all night long. I got to know them very well when I sat at the pool. What a different world it was from ours. It actually was a lot of fun, and once again, we made new friends. Marion and Dave Arnspiger, who attended our church, were living there while waiting to get settled into a house, and a young Al Vargo, who now owns and runs one of the best restaurants in Houston, lived nearby.

The house and the baby got finished at the same time. On August

18, 1959, Dorothy Walker Bush—named for George's mother—was born, weighing in at nine pounds, eleven ounces. We called her Doro. Aunt Charlotte, who had come down for the birth, told me that when George went to look at Doro in the nursery, she found him with his head against the window, tears of joy running down his face.

George moved us into the new house while I was in the hospital. When I came home, I found very neat rooms with no clutter. Mrs. Rogers, who had just arrived from Midland, said that she didn't know Mr. Bush could do housework. He certainly could, and he had done a great job. Except that it took months for me to find everything. George had unpacked by putting things in the nearest closet, with no regard for what the item was or what room it would be used in.

The Rogers family did finally leave, and we answered a newspaper ad to sponsor a lady from Mexico to help with the housework. That was one of the best things ever to happen to the Bush family. A tiny woman named Paula Rendon came to live with us, and she's still here! She started out as Doro's nurse and is now our housekeeper and a member of the family. She has a tremendous family of her own, and she rules them and us with an iron hand. (Although she spoils George to death.) She has been just as at home in the Waldorf Towers, the Vice President's House, and the White House as she is in Houston.

That fall, the boys went off to their new schools—Georgie to the Kinkaid School; Neil and Jebby to Grady Elementary public school—and Marvin and Doro were home with me. One night in November, I went to bed exhausted as I had played golf for the first time since Doro was born. George stayed awake a little later reading *The Caine Mutiny*. Georgie was not home; our four youngest children were asleep in their rooms on the second floor; and Tom Devine, a friend visiting us from New York, was asleep in the guest room on the first floor, where our room was. George heard a tiny cough on the intercom and decided he'd better check the baby. A "blue norther" had blown in and we had turned our heat on for the first time. Something had been put in backward, and the whole upstairs was filled with smoke. George yelled for me, put Doro in my arms, and ran for the other children. He got them all out, breaking a window for air as he carried them downstairs. Groggy and asleep, they did not awaken until George put their feet on the icy cold pavement. We were told if George had been fifteen minutes later, our four youngest children would have been dead from smoke inhalation. Thank God he heeded that tiny cough. After that, we put ladders on the outside of our house on both ends so that our children could get out and, if need be, we could get in. People thought we were crazy to invite burglars like that, but we were never robbed and we certainly slept better after the ladders were in place.

The boys all became very active in Little League and school activities. I spent half of the next ten years doing what every mother in America does: taxiing children to the doctor, the dentist, birthday parties, baseball games, tennis matches, and so on. When I look at my date book entries from those years, they're all baseball games and what fields they'll be played on. The boys were good players, and I felt torn in two, racing from game to game. When they weren't playing organized ball, they were in our backyard. We had a pool, a small baseball field, trees to climb, and tires hung for all the children to swing on. The Kerrs had three boys and, much to our great pleasure, a little girl named Mary a year younger than Doro. The boys played in the nearby bayou and had several hair-raising experiences, most of which ended with trips to the emergency room for stitches.

For several Christmas Eves, all these little wild men turned into angels when the Bush-Kerr children put on a Christmas play for the adults. Those are the wonderful memories you just never forget. Fortunately, the grandchildren have continued the tradition and entertain us every year.

And of course the children got all the childhood diseases. It was during a siege of the chicken pox that Neil, who was about six years old at the time, was in my bed one day, and I asked him to read to me. I discovered that not only could Neil not read, he didn't have a clue. Yet, he was getting all A's at school, including in reading. I spoke with his teacher, who told me I was dead wrong; Neil was one of her better students. So I went to his class to see this "great little reader." It was a fascinating study in manipulation. The teacher had the children read a line or two, and when she got to Neil, he flashed that great smile of his and paused. A student helped him with the first word, the teacher the next, and so it went. Neil had been faking his way through reading—not uncommon for children with reading problems—and nobody had noticed.

Neil was diagnosed as having dyslexia. Grady Elementary had no courses for children with this problem, but Kinkaid had a wonderful reading teacher who was willing to help Neil. Marvin hadn't started school yet, but we had been told he was more than ready for first grade, so I enrolled both boys in Kinkaid. Then I learned you get a discount for a third child, so I enrolled Jebby also. While all this was happening, George was in some far-off place trying to find work for his oil rigs. He came home and he couldn't believe it: four of his children were in private school. My math confused him; I was convinced we were saving money.

For the rest of his school days, Neil had to work very hard. We spent hours reading together as he struggled with every word. But thanks to wonderful teachers, and a little boy who refused to give up, Neil eventually earned his undergraduate and master's degrees in business administration at Tulane University—and in just five years.

By this time, Georgie had followed in his father's footsteps and was attending Phillips Academy in Andover, Massachusetts. How we missed him. Every day I walked down the driveway to meet the mailman to see if he had written. I was homesick, but the child obviously wasn't. Finally, the mailman, John Taylor, rang the doorbell and thrust a letter into my hand with a big smile on his face. He knew how much I missed Georgie. Fortunately, he didn't hang around to see me open the letter. It started out, "Last weekend was the greatest in my life . . ." I burst into tears. Our boy had the "best weekend of his life" without us! How silly that seems now and just a tad selfish.

If I had any complaints in those wonderful early days in Houston, it was that George and I didn't have time to do a lot together. He was busy building a business, which involved a lot of travel, and we had five young children and a new house, which meant a lot of expenses. Needless to say, we rarely went out.

One of the reasons I fell in love with George was that he was so kind and nice. He always thought of the other fellow. Sometimes that caused me some pain and jealousy, which I'm now ashamed to admit. I just didn't think there was enough time for us.

I remember one incident that for years made me feel guilty and now I think is funny. We had a friend whom we both adored and admired, a smashing, bright young widow. George and I both worried about her, so he decided that the next time he was in New York City, he would round up all the eligible bachelors he could find and give her a dinner at the "21" Club. For weeks before the trip, George reported to me the progress of his dinner plans as he lined up ten attractive available men. I must confess that I was so jealous that he was giving this splendid dinner at "21," where we could never afford to go and I, for one, had never been. Of course I never said a word but just listened to his planning, getting more and more envious.

The morning after the big dinner, he called me heartbroken. Our widow friend had breezed into the dinner quite late, with a date, and stayed barely long enough for a drink before rushing off to the theater, leaving George with a large dinner bill and his bachelor friends. I told George I was sorry his plans were for naught. Deep down, I was thrilled. I'm not very proud of that, and George didn't find out until recently just how jealous I had been.

It was during this period of our lives when George decided to get more involved in politics. He always had been interested: His dad was a United States senator from Connecticut at the time, and George had been politically active in Midland. In February 1962, just before Doro and I left to visit Mom and Dad Bush for a week in Florida, George asked me how I'd feel if he became chairman of the Republican party of Harris County. He said he really wanted to do it, and I said fine. So off Doro and I went for a great little vacation, and when we got back, George was in the meanest political battle of his life. I was so naive; I had assumed that he had been invited to be chairman. It never occurred to me that he had to run. I can't really remember who the opponent was—maybe I'm purposely forgetting—but it was ugly. Harris County, with 210 precincts, is one of the largest in the country. George, usually with me along, managed to visit all of them. The evenings could be long and tedious. That's when I took up needlepoint, just to keep from looking and feeling bored to death. After all, I had heard George's speech two hundred times! Not only did needlepointing do the trick, it was a good icebreaker. Fellow stitchers always wanted to know about my project and tell me about theirs.

George was elected, along with our dear friend Nancy Thawley as vice chair. The county executive meetings were a circus, and George was like a ringmaster. We went into each one with fear and trembling, and he always pulled it off. The party even took on the old courthouse crowd and won a redistricting suit that would have great impact on our lives in a few years.

In 1963 George decided to make a run against incumbent U.S. Senator Ralph Yarborough, who was up for reelection in 1964. Texas Democrats were very divided at that time. Yarborough was battling with Governor John Connally, and polls showed that Vice President Lyndon Johnson was at an all-time popularity low. It looked like a long-shot opportunity for a Yarborough upset.

Eventually four people got into the Republican primary race: Jack Cox, who had made a good run against Connally in the last governor's race; Dr. Milton Davis, a thoracic surgeon who claimed to be "grass roots"; Dr. Robert Morris, who was originally from New Jersey; and George. I hate primary campaigns, as you are fighting people in your own party. George appeared all over the state debating these men or joining them on the speaker's platform. My blood boiled at half the things they said about George. There was some discussion about making George wear a cowboy hat to make him more "Texan." George rejected the idea, saying he didn't want to resort to gimmicks.

I remember one meeting at a Republican picnic in Fort Bend County. We had a great chairman there, Mary Ann Napier, who requested we get there early and mix and mingle before the speeches. With five-year-old Doro along, we worked the crowd and ate the barbecue. Jack Cox appeared with great fanfare just as he was being introduced for his three-minute speech. Some celebrity had died that day, and Jack dramatically praised the man and called for a moment of prayer. Before we could even bow our heads, he said, "Thank you," and started his harangue. He certainly wasn't going to waste any more of his precious three minutes on that poor dead soul. That always amused me.

I was not so amused, however, on another evening, when we were sitting in a darkened auditorium listening to candidates for every conceivable office. Someone gave me a stack of papers and said, "Take one and pass it on, please," which of course I did. When the lights came on, I had a handful of hate literature about George, calling him a "tool of the Eastern establishment"; a "Rockefeller plant largely financed by the Eastern group who are leading the 'Block Goldwater' movement"; and "a stockholder in Brown Brothers, Harriman." That was the name of George's father's firm, but they were referring to Ambassador Averell Harriman, a liberal Democrat. No doubt, this was the world of the ultraconservative John Birch Society, who thought Houston was way too liberal.

One day we received a flyer in the mail that said I was the daughter of Marvin Pierce, president of the McCall Corporation (true), which published *Redbook* (true), and everybody knows *Redbook* is a tool of the "commies." Huh? I countered by reminding people that McCall also published *The Blue Book*, the John Birth Society's handbook. Another flyer, addressed to all Republican voters, said I was "an heiress who spent all her time on the Cape"—meaning Cape Cod. I wrote my dad that to my knowledge I had never set foot on the Cape and to please write immediately if I was an heiress. He sent my letter on to Aunt Charlotte with the note that she must never let it be known she voted for FDR! He added that they had given up publishing *The Blue Book* because it was losing money.

Several times we had hate letters under our door in the morning. That was scary since the person who put them there had to walk up a long driveway.

During the campaign I went east to visit family, who quickly let me know George was too conservative. What a world: George was too conservative for the East and too liberal for Texas. I always have been proud of the fact that George thought each problem out separately and did not take a party line. If I had to label George, I would say he was a fiscal conservative and a social liberal. I know that others might disagree. As for George, he says "Labels are for cans."

On November 22, 1963, George and I were in the middle of a several-city swing. I was getting my hair done in Tyler, Texas, working on a letter home. Here are some excerpts:

> Dearest Family,
>
> Wednesday I took Doris Ulmer out for lunch. They were here from England and they had been so nice to George in Greece. That night we went to . . .
>
> I am writing this at the Beauty Parlor and the radio says that the President has been shot. Oh Texas—my Texas—my God—let's hope it's not true. I am sick at heart as we all are. Yes, the story is true and the Governor also. How hateful some people are.
>
> . . . Since the Beauty Parlor the President has died. We are once again on a plane. This time a commercial plane. Poppy picked me up at the beauty parlor—we went right to the airport, flew to Ft. Worth and dropped Mr. Zeppo off (we were on his plane) and flew back to Dallas. We had to circle the field while the second presidential plane took off. Immedi-

ately Pop got tickets back to Houston and here we are flying home. We are sick at heart. The tales the radio reporters tell of Jackie Kennedy are the bravest I've ever heard. The rumors are flying about that horrid assassin. We are hoping that it is not some far right nut, but a "commie" nut. You understand that we know they are both nuts, but just hope that it is not a Texan and not an American at all.

I am amazed by the rapid-fire thinking and planning that has already been done. L.B.J. has been the president for some time now—2 hours at least and it is only 4:30.

My dearest love to you all,
Bar

Certainly this was not the world's most brilliant letter, but it reflects a little of my feelings at that time. George canceled all his political activities for the next few months.

In a letter I wrote on November 30, I complained to my family that all the press talked about were fanatics on the far right, even though word was out that Oswald was playing games in both Cuba and Russia. They just couldn't stand the thought that the assassin was someone leaning left.

George eventually won the hard-fought primary contest, and we formed the greatest team for the general election. Locally, I joined a group of supporters, organized by our friends Jack Steel and Bobbie Fitch, who went door-to-door handing out literature. I'll never forget one night when I was teamed up with Jack, working what could be called a "redneck" neighborhood. I didn't want people to know I was the candidate's wife—we wanted honest reaction from the voters—so my name tag just said BARBARA. Everyone assumed I was Jack's wife and called me Mrs. Steel. One lady spit in her flowerpot the whole time we tried to talk to her; one man answered the door in his underwear and didn't seem to mind one bit. Jack and I got so tickled it took everything we had not to laugh until we got back out on the street. That same night, the "Bush Bandwagon" bus, which was supposed to go around and pick everybody up, couldn't find us, and we sat on a curb under a streetlight waiting and waiting. Oh, the glamorous world of politics.

Another time when George and I were at a reception in San Antonio, I heard several times, "Would the lady in the red dress please get out of the photo?" I suddenly realized they were talking about me! They didn't have a clue who I was.

That was the year of the famous mushroom cloud TV ad, where the Democrats were trying to play off people's fear of nuclear war. Locally, I heard our opponent say something like, "George Bush doesn't care if our small children are exposed to leukemia." I can't remember if I heard this on TV, or if maybe I heard it while driving by an outdoor rally. You can't imagine how shocked we were by that. In the speaker's defense, I'm sure he didn't know about Robin.

With or without such campaigning, Kennedy's death drastically changed the political world, and with Johnson at the top of the Democratic ticket, we did not have a chance to beat Yarborough. After we lost, George called and wrote thank-you letters to console the fabulous people who had worked so hard.

He went back to devoting his energies to Zapata, and the company continued to grow. In September 1965, disaster struck: Hurricane Betsy ravaged the Gulf of Mexico, and a rig the size of a football field completely disappeared never to be seen again. Luckily, the workers were evacuated by boat and helicopter and nobody was hurt. Several days later George came home and told me his eyeballs hurt from looking for the rig all day by helicopter. He also described the small towns in Louisiana he had flown over, saying they looked like those playing card houses we used to build, then push one card and they all fell down. I don't know if he hurt more from the devastation he saw in those little towns or the devastation his company felt from such a mammoth financial loss. But he rallied the troops; they dug their heels in and rebuilt. As usual, George put more stock in the people than the equipment. He wrote in Zapata's annual report that year: "We are lucky to have the finest offshore drilling crews in the business. This year 23 more men completed their fifth year with the company, a record of which we are very proud."

Houston got a new congressional seat in 1966 and, thanks to George's redistricting suit, there was a chance a Republican could win. George decided to make another run at elected office. His chief opponent was the very popular district attorney, Frank Briscoe, a conservative Democrat. He ran as a native-born Texan and tried to paint George as a carpetbagger. It really worried me until George told me that three fourths of the people living in the new Seventh Congressional District were newcomers, too. Besides, by this time, we had lived in Texas nearly eighteen years!

I'll never forget driving Doro and one of her friends to school one day, listening to the two of them talk in the backseat. Doro's friend said something like, "I saw your daddy on TV last night." To which Doro very nonchalantly replied: "Oh, you know, it was about that erection that he's going to have."

Frank was actually a very nice man and well liked, but thanks to a lot of hardworking volunteers, friends, and George Bush, George won. This was quite a win for us. George was the first Republican elected to Congress from Harris County, and one of just three Republicans in the entire Texas delegation: Bob Price had been elected in the Texas Panhandle; and our dear friend John Tower was one of Texas's U.S. senators. Jim Collins of Dallas eventually would become the fourth, after winning a special election.

The night of the big win, Jack Steel and Sarah Gee came to George and asked him if he would do them a big favor. They had been the most extraordinary volunteers, and George certainly would grant them anything. They asked if they could continue to run his office as volunteers. What a favor! They lined up some of the very best people, and for years this little army has helped George over and over again. They did such a great job, along with a superb Washington staff, that George was unopposed when he ran for reelection two years later. Many of these same people are volunteering in George's office today, helping him answer his enormous stacks of mail. Jack, who personifies the very definition of "best friend," comes in every day, at age seventy-five. I do not know what we would have done without these dear friends (see Appendix A).

Once again, we had hundreds of decisions to make. Would I move to Washington? Would the kids move? Would we see more of George if we stayed or moved? Would we keep our big Houston house or move into something smaller? What about Washington; houses were so much more expensive in Washington than Houston. If we moved, where would the children go to school? How would George organize his office? What about Zapata? These are problems that all new congressmen and congresswomen face, and today, I think it's even more complicated with so many two-career families.

As for Zapata, George already had resigned as head of the company to devote himself to the campaign. It had been a tough call to make, but the one he thought most fair to the company and the campaign. Now he decided it was best to get out altogether. We also decided the entire family should go to Washington. So we sold our house, bought a lovely town house as a home base in Houston, and headed for Washington.

7

A Different World

W e bought a house in Spring Valley, a lovely section of Washington with lots of trees and houses built in the 1920s and 1930s. George bought it over the phone, sight unseen, from Senator Milward Simpson of Wyoming, Al Simpson's father. It was a really old house—such a change from our home in Houston where everything worked. One day I came downstairs to find George sitting in the living room under an umbrella. A bathtub had leaked right through the ceiling. I would have laughed, except that's how the whole house was. Only three of the children were with us: George W. was at Yale and Jeb stayed at Kinkaid in Houston, living with Baine and Mildred Kerr, before going on to Andover.

George's campaign manager, Jimmy Allison, helped set up the office. Aleene Smith, who had worked at Zapata and the Republican party of Harris County office, moved to Washington with us, and George hired Rose Zamaria, who had headed the office of Houston Congressman Albert Thomas, the powerful Democratic chairman of the House Appropriations Committee until his death. Rose knew The Hill and George's constituents, and Aleene knew George Bush. These two amazing women, both used to ruling the roost, worked very well together and became best friends. Aleene is retired and lives in Florida with her husband, Hargrove; Rose moved to Houston with us and ran George's office there until March of 1994 before returning to Washington.

Eventually, Don Rhodes, a volunteer during the campaign, moved from Houston to Washington to become part of the team and has been with us ever since. Like Paula, he has become part of the family.

⌒ Washington was a whole different world for us: exciting, overwhelming, intimidating, interesting, exhausting. Looking back on my diary entries, I'm not sure when we slept. Here's some of what I wrote that very first month:

January 3—Drove up to the house and there were the moving men shoveling the snow. Moved in all day. House was frozen. Piano didn't fit in the living room. House without carpets seemed tiny and cold. Moving men invited to spend the night by G. He cannot stand an empty bed! Only had sheets for two beds and so had to race to Sears to buy sheets, etc. before it closed. BOYS ACCEPTED AT ST. ALBANS!!!!

January 4—Up at 4 a.m. for me. From 7 to 10 moving men and George and I unpacked boxes and there was no damage. George and I left at 10:30 for two days of briefings for new Republican congressmen and wives (or husbands). Invaluable for me.

January 5—Wives had a panel the second afternoon telling us what to expect. I now expect to be without a husband most of the time!!! Mrs. Les Arends, Betty, a great beauty, spoke on protocol and was lovely to look at. Her speech was ridiculed in the papers and although she claimed later to have been misquoted, it caused great excitement among the ladies. She gave calling cards a great play. All this surely went out with the horse and buggy. She also told us that she "tagged" her gowns so she wouldn't wear the same thing with the same people twice. She told us that she took out all the hems from store-bought clothes and hemmed them by hand. Talked about long gloves, etc. I must confess that we were worrying about schools and making ends meet, etc. [This same dear lady wrote me a note in 1993, enclosing a copy of a letter she sent to Ross Perot. It said: "Dear Ross, I hope you are happy about what you did to your country. You ASS. Love, Betty." I guess she decided to heck with calling cards and white gloves!]

January 9—TV connected. Went to Yarborough reception . . . met the Vice President (Hubert Humphrey). Jack Steel killed us by going up to the Vice President and saying to him, "Mr. Vice President, you remember me? Jack Steel?" The Vice President gave him the biggest jolly and a two-handed clasp. I later said to Jack, "I didn't know that you knew the Veep." And of course Jack answered, "I didn't, but you saw the welcome he gave me."

January 10—Ate with GB in Capitol Dining Room and went on into the State of the Union Address. Great thrill to see all the dignitaries. Sat in far left corner and therefore could not see the speaker or the President, but could see the Congress . . . G and I loving all the excitement!

January 12—I took a cab to the Capitol with evening clothes over my arm. G and I rushed over to the Capitol Hill Club. We were just getting settled, talking to nice people when George grabs my arm and says that we are at the wrong reception and so we race to the Rayburn Building to the reception the 89th Congress was having for the 90th! BOTH receptions very nice.

January 15—Walked in the afternoon and attacked by strange dog. He followed us for hours and G finally returned him to address on his collar. Belonged to the new Secretary of Commerce. They were thrilled to get him back.

January 25—ANNOUNCEMENT MADE OF G'S APPOINTMENT TO WAYS AND MEANS!!!

January 26—Kids like Washington. Already have many friends. That night we went to Rolly and Kay Evans' house for a black tie dinner. We were crowded into a dining room with round tables. I sat next to Senator Ed Muskie from Maine. We had a lovely talk about Kennebunkport where he has a house . . . George and I were the only Republicans. Also at the party were Ambassador and Mrs. Harriman. He spoke so well of Mom and Dad. Mrs. Harriman, when the ladies were having coffee, said to me, "I've known many Republicans. Now let's see . . . there's John and Lorraine Cooper. Everyone likes them, and oh, yes, that man who died, Chris Herter and his wife, and I remember Dotty and Pres!!" She was so proud to be able to think of three Republican couples . . . also at this party were Joan and Teddy Kennedy. She is a very lovely-looking person. I found her very friendly, a bubbly type person. I like her. Teddy, in fairness, I did not talk to, but also wasn't charmed by. He had much more of Bobby and less of Jack.

January 29—Still cold. We all get dressed for church and then can't find it.

February 2—GB and I were at The Shoreham at 7:30 a.m. for our first Presidential view. The Congressional Wives Prayer Breakfast. G went to the men's breakfast where 1,100 men gathered. He says that he was not impressed because the TV lights and cameras took away any spiritual meaning to the breakfast. 500 ladies gathered on our side and it was lovely. Mrs. Humphrey, VP's lady, read a text, and Mrs. Johnson gave a truly meaningful short message. Last night G came home in the rain to pick me up. I have given up on these unending receptions, but this one given by the President of the American Bankers Association was supposed to be filled with Texans just dying to see G. We arrived . . . to find thousands of people and the only Texans we saw were other Texas congressmen looking for Texans!

I tried everything once. I went to briefings at the State Department, Republican meetings, Congressional Wives meetings, luncheons, and dinners. Texans came to visit at the drop of a hat. George and I decided early on that we should not go to any embassies—there were no votes there. Considering our later life in the diplomatic world, that's funny. But you have to learn in Washington that you can't do everything. Like all of life, you have to set your priorities, and it took me a while to discover that.

At a dinner party one night, when we were still sorting out which parties to attend and which to skip, I sat next to a man who almost immediately started talking about how sad it was I had missed the "Days of Camelot." I listened while he criticized the Johnsons for every known fault until he said, "I hate all Texans." When I told him I was a Texan, he said something like, "Well, you know what I mean. You were born and brought up in the East." I said that he was right, but that he was talking about my children, who were lucky enough to be born Texans. I turned my back and never spoke to that whining, pompous man again. Looking down on the Johnsons was a favorite of this particular group. As part of the clique who had hung around the Kennedys, they viewed the President and First Lady as "gauche outsiders." George and I cut "inside Washington" dinners off our list.

Because George was the first freshman in this century to be put on the prestigious House Ways and Means Committee, we were on everybody's "list." I was flattered to be invited to small lunches with the cabinet's and other leaders' wives. We would have cocktails and lunch, then I would have to race for one of my many car pools. After about three months I told George I didn't think I could do these luncheons; they were just too time-consuming. He laughed and said that they were given by lobbyists' wives—people who were trying to get to him through me—and of course I didn't have to go. So I cut out lunches. Several of my friends didn't and at least one became an alcoholic.

One of the groups I did join was the International Club II, of which George's mother had been a founding member. The club was made up of twelve congressional ladies: six from each party, which were evenly split between the House and the Senate; and ten embassy wives whose husbands were all ministers, the rank just below ambassador. The club was started to make foreigners feel at home in our country. I liked this group a great deal for several reasons. Most of the other clubs took ambassadors' wives only; we took the number twos. Also, our club let the women whose husbands retired, died, or went on to other jobs stay in the club as associates. Some of the other current or former members were Abigail McCarthy (Eugene), Bethine Church (Frank), Betty Ford (Gerald), Helen Jackson (Scoop), LaDonna Harris (Fred), and Lady Bird Johnson. We must have had more people whose husbands were running for president than any other club, and three eventually made it. We would eat one month at a congressional home, and then the next at a diplomat's home. I tried hard never to miss one of these meetings. In later life, I met many of the embassy wives in their homelands where their husbands were foreign ministers, protocol chiefs, and so on.

George went home almost every weekend that first term, but the children and I could go only during school vacations. It was a strange life, but an exciting one. I decided the children should see all the sights. So every single weekend, I dragged those poor young people around Washington, taking hundreds of pictures. It got so bad that Neil and Marvin begged not to go, and I took pity on them. Doro was not so lucky. I remember one Sunday the two of us took a Park Service tour around the White House. We stood at the foot of the South Lawn with our faces pressed against the fence while the guide told us some interesting fact of history. At that moment the door opened and people came out. We strained to see who was lucky enough to have been in that glorious house. Years later, whenever we walked down to the fence on the South Grounds with our dogs, I thought about little Doro and me on the outside looking in.

All those pictures I took came in very handy later. I put together several slide shows and raised money for different causes by showing them to schools, garden clubs, civic groups, churches, and so on. It certainly was an easy way to give a speech. The slides were almost a protective shield, something you could hide behind—just like writing a book with a dog.

⌒∾ We lasted in that old house for only a year and then bought a wonderful new, four-story town house right across the street from Supreme Court Justice Potter Stewart and his wife, Andy. Through the years Andy and I became very close, and she is absolutely the best friend anyone could have. She and Potter would walk down the street every single Sunday for soup or whatever on our back terrace or in the basement playroom. George always gathered the most interesting group of people of all ages for Sunday lunches. One such couple was columnist Bill Safire and his wife, Helene. Unfortunately, when George became President, Bill turned on him with a vengeance.

We loved that house and our new neighborhood. Congressman Jerry Pettis from California and his beautiful, bright wife, Shirley, lived right next door. She is one of the most beautiful women I have known. Even when she is sick, she manages to look lovely and glamorous. In spite of that, we also became the best of friends. Since George and Jerry were elected to Congress at the same time, Shirley and I took in many meetings together.

We made so many other new good friends during this period of our lives. Among George's closest colleagues in the House were Sonny Montgomery, a Democrat from Mississippi; Lud Ashley, a Democrat from Ohio; John Paul Hammerschmidt, a Republican from Arkansas; Bill Steiger, a Republican from Wisconsin; and Tom Kleppe, a Republican from North Dakota. There were so many others, but these men stand out in my mind.

George also thought highly of Wilbur Mills, chairman of the House Ways and Means Committee. Other new congressmen told George their committee chairmen never let them talk or left when they presented their thoughts. However, Wilbur listened to the lowest ranking member, Democrat or Republican, and stayed until the end of the most boring hearing and made sure every member could question the witness. Our shock when Wilbur Mills did all those crazy things with that burlesque queen cannot be described. How could this fair and decent man be such a Jekyll and Hyde? As it turned out, he was a closet drinker. He and his darling wife, Polly, overcame their problems, and we were so proud they were our friends.

An informal group of wives of the 90th Club (our husbands were members of the Ninetieth Session of Congress) got together to study issues. All of us were brilliant, of course, but Janet Steiger—who later became the first woman chairman of the Federal Trade Commission—

seemed to understand the issues better than most and would usually lead the group. We eventually filtered down to eleven women, remaining very close, dear friends and trying to stay in touch all these years. The other "ladies of the club" are Shirley Pettis Roberson, Olga Esch, Louise McClure, Loret Ruppe, Joan Winn, Antoinette Hatfield, Carol Vander Jagt, Dee Collins, and Mary Jane Dellenback. Some of these women went on to do some pretty impressive things on their own.

There were so many other dear friends, but these people have remained such an interesting part of my life.

The year 1968 began with me taking a very important step: I gave up smoking. I had been a smoker since age eighteen and knew I should quit but just never did. A few months earlier, I had gone into the hospital for a small operation and woke up several times in the middle of the night alone. I can remember really wanting a cigarette, and although I was still groggy from the medication and had an IV in my arm, I made it into a chair and lit up. At that very moment, a tiny nurse came into the room, got me back in bed, and before charging out of the room, informed me she'd be back to talk to me in the morning. True to her word, after she got off duty, she took the time to come in and read me the riot act. She told me that I was addicted and a disgrace. Addicted? Me? I couldn't forget that nurse, and on New Year's Day I quit. It was terrible. For about six weeks I would wake up in a cold sweat. Sometimes I dreamed that I was having a cigarette and would awaken in panic. I had trouble staying in one place and was restless. I'm not trying to show how brave I was, but how addicted I was and how hard it is to wean yourself off a bad habit. I'll always be grateful to that little nurse. George Bush never smoked, but he never complained about my bad habit. I am very antismoking now; in fact, George says I'm a bore about it. He's right. I am only critical of the people I care about.

This was a very interesting time to be living in Washington. The Vietnam War was debated at all the dinner parties, and the whole country worried about racial and student unrest. Here is part of my diary entry from April 5, 1968, to show a little of what it was like then:

In truth I cannot begin to write the horrors of the day. Memphis, Tennessee, has been having the most awful garbage strikes led by Dr. Martin Luther King, Negro Nobel Peace Prize winner . . . Standing on a balcony last night Dr. King was gunned down by an unknown man. The reaction to this killing may turn out to be very bloody. A newsman at 11:30 called from the Houston Post. I asked about Houston and he said, "Small stone throwing and small groups wandering around the city." I am frightened.

Took children to school. Worked in tiny garden getting the flower beds ready for plants. I took Neil to his knee doctor only to discover that the entire city was rioting about 5 blocks away. We could see smoke, etc. It took us an hour and a half to get home. George called from Texas to see if we were all right. . . . All day our lovely city burned, and all night. A curfew was put on, no liquor sold, no gasoline unless in cars and no guns. We went to bed in shock.

Later that month, Congress passed the civil rights open housing bill, the most controversial bill George voted on while in the House. He voted yes, despite the fact that mail from his constituents ran heavily against it. What made him feel particularly strong about this was that so many young black men were fighting in Vietnam for the cause of freedom, yet were denied freedom when they came home.

I was proud of the stand he took, but upset by how personal and mean his mail was, including from supporters who said they were shocked and disappointed. I remember that we went to a Peter Sellers movie the night of the vote, just to be able to laugh.

I was even prouder a week later when George flew to Houston to face a hometown crowd. He was introduced to loud boos, but at the end of the speech, during which he told them he "put human rights above property rights," he had won them over and they gave him a standing ovation. Still, I was very relieved he had no opposition for reelection that fall; it would have been a tough campaign.

༄ We had settled into a nice routine in Washington. In between carpooling the children to school, I took care of the house, attended various lunches and meetings, tried to lose weight, and even took to coloring my hair.

One of the funnier luncheons I attended was at the White House. I discovered that most of the attendees were world-renowned doctors and nurses, all women, in all different fields of medicine. Several people asked me what I did, and I began to wonder myself. You can imagine my surprise when Mrs. Johnson got up and said that there were twenty nurses among the congressional wives, including Mrs. George Bush of Texas. I got to attend this fascinating luncheon under false pretenses! I learned later that a computer had mistakenly identified me as a nurse. I'd like to add here that Mrs. Johnson was a very gracious First Lady and a wonderful hostess. This particular luncheon was just a few days after President Johnson had shocked the nation with the news he would not run for reelection, and I marveled at her composure.

That summer was filled with presidential politics, including the National Republican Convention in Miami. Here are some excerpts from one of many letters I wrote that year to George's cousin, George Walker, who was serving in Vietnam:

Dear George,

It was my first convention and very, very exciting for me. We stayed at The Barcelona Hotel on Collins Avenue at about 42nd Street. The world's rudest people work there, but the location was just great . . . I loved seeing all the big GOP names at the Republican Gala the night before the Convention opened. We sat at a table right next to the Nixon girls, David Eisenhower and his Mom and Dad. The girls were darling and the minute I introduced myself they quickly said they'd like to meet Pop . . . I had flown down in a plane load of Reagan supporters and they were so eager for me to meet the Reagans. Since we sat near them, I took advantage and went over to meet them. I found them both very attractive. She is tiny and really a very lovely natural beauty. I thought that he should get a lot of credit for hanging in there after losing on the first ballot. He kept his troops very happy and allowed harmony to prevail . . .

Bill Steiger decided his first morning there that GB had a good chance of being the VP candidate and so turned all his attention to this one project. He spent the rest of his time lining up delegates on the floor, making telephone calls, etc. A very few people put out a great deal of effort and the long and the short of it was that although this may never seem possible to you, your cousin almost became the candidate for Vice President. . . . I must confess that up until the last morning I thought it was such a long shot that I didn't worry. I'm sorry for Pop for he would have loved it so. I am glad for the five little Bush children. . . .

Love,
Bar

Since George was unopposed in 1968, he worked hard for the Nixon-Agnew ticket. I sat in Washington with the children, biting my nails while George traveled all over the country campaigning. I certainly was glad when it was over and Nixon had won.

During George's second term, I began writing a monthly newspaper column called "Washington Scene" for the Houston newspapers. It was lots of fun, and although the writing was not brilliant, the columns gave people back home a glimpse of life in Washington. Here's a column dated March 1969:

Early March saw the annual White House Congressional Reception. I cannot describe the excitement we felt from the moment we drove in. George, at my request, parked on the circle and we walked across the lawn to the diplomatic entrance hall where the Marine Band was playing. Can you picture the setting? The men looking SO handsome in black-tie and the ladies in long gowns and the Marines in their red uniforms!

We gathered in the East Room, bright and gay with the flags of the 50 states, visiting with friends. The excitement when President and Mrs. Nixon were announced was electric! There was an Honor Guard, "Hail to the Chief" was played, and they walked slowly through the room to the receiving line followed by Vice President and Mrs. Agnew.

There was a large buffet in the State Dining Room, but George and I did not linger there. The whole beautiful house was open to the guests and we took advantage of the opportunity to look around. The rooms were filled with lovely flowers and each room had a large crackling fire in the fireplace. Every room has well passed the test of time since James Hoban designed the house 170 years ago. I kept thinking of the feet that had walked these same steps before us: every president since John Adams, foreign kings and queens, great world statesmen, outstanding men and women in every field and walk of life.

The gifts given to the President on his trip to Europe were on display upstairs. We did NOT try out the Lincoln bed as I read another guest did, but we did look at paintings and at the Gettysburg Address written in Lincoln's hand. We did see the magnificent Yellow Oval Room, the Treaty Room, and the family living and dining rooms. We, as Americans, can all take pride in this beautiful house for it belongs to us all.

March saw Neil and Marvin Bush confirmed in the magnificent Washington Cathedral with 26 of their classmates by Bishop Paul Moore. The size of this cathedral and the glorious voice of the all-boys choir must surely add to the awe and beauty of any confirmation. Happiness for a mother is seeing her boys confirmed!

March saw our son George home for a weekend from flight school in Valdosta, Georgia. Happiness for a mother is also having a boy home from the service!

March saw George going home to Houston for two weekends and spending the week days in the Ways and Means Committee hearings as they struggle through the tax reform legislation. . . .

The end of March—best of all—saw the Bush family home in Houston for Easter with four of their five children!

That summer, the Bushes almost missed the main event of the year, on July 20, when man landed on the moon. We had spent the day boating on the Potomac River and had stopped to eat dinner on the way home. When we came out of the restaurant, we had locked our keys in the car. We eventually got the car unlocked, raced home, and with the rest of America, watched with pride and awe as Neil Armstrong made that first historical step.

One last note on 1969: After several years of failing health, my father died. During the last months I spent a great deal of time traveling between Washington and Rye to be with him, and it was very difficult to watch him slip away. He truly was a hero of mine; a daughter could not ask for a better father.

⇗ The year 1970 began with George considering another run at the Senate against Ralph Yarborough. George found being a member of the minority party in the House very frustrating. As head of his own business, he was used to making decisions. In the best of times, things moved very slowly in the House and almost never for minority members. So at the urging of friends and supporters, he decided to get into the race.

With all of that going on, the last thing on my mind was our twenty-fifth wedding anniversary in January. You can't even imagine my shock when George managed to pull off an enormous surprise party at the Bayou Club in Houston with so many of our friends and family. Even when we got there and I saw many people we knew walking in, I thought it was just a coincidence.

George's schedule that whole year was unbelievably busy, with him trying to run a Senate race in Texas and be a member of the House in Washington. We were both very disappointed when he was going to be out of town on April 4 for the wedding of Mildred and Baine Kerr's son to the daughter of William S. White, a well-known and highly respected newspaperman who was a close friend of Lyndon Johnson. It was to be a small wedding in the Whites' Washington, D.C., apartment with many festivities planned around the day. We offered to do anything we could—George W. was a member of the wedding party—and Mildred and Baine asked if we could have a buffet luncheon the day of the wedding for all the people coming from back home.

George had to be in Texas that day for an event that he just could not cancel. I hated having a party without him, but these were our dearest friends and I really wanted to help. For the first time I hired a caterer, filled the house with flowers, and actually was beginning to feel ready.

At the last moment we got a message from Jack Valenti, President Johnson's former aide and now head of the Motion Picture Association, that ex-President Johnson would love to come to the lunch—if invited. That put a whole new light on the party. I panicked and called George, saying he couldn't invite the Johnsons, or if he did, he should cancel his event and come right home. George laughed and said that of course we should invite the Johnsons—after all, they had been so nice to us when they were in the White House—but that he couldn't possibly come home.

A former President coming to our house for a buffet luncheon and no George? I was terrified.

The day of the big event arrived, and the Kerr party came in enormous black limousines that they had hired to taxi their friends around Washington. This caused big excitement on our little Palisade Lane. By the time the former President arrived in his big limo, our neighbors were out in full force, led by Andy Stewart sitting on the curb in her gardening clothes watching all the cars go by.

Lyndon Johnson held court in our little library and could not have been a better guest. Years later, after *Millie's Book* came out, Jack Valenti sent me a picture of the former President scratching our dog Nicky's ear, with a note that said, "Millie is not the only Bush dog who has been a confidante of a President."

Doro and little Mary Kerr were awestruck and followed the Johnsons everywhere. They were in deep shock, however, when they saw the former President take our newspaper from the front yard as he was leaving.

The day still was not over. George got home that night just in time to throw on rented white-tie dinner clothes so we could race over to the White House to meet the Duke and Duchess of Windsor. We had not been invited for dinner, but had made the second cut, for after-dinner drinks and entertainment.

All went well until George looked for the shirt. The aide who had rented the outfit had forgotten to get one. So George, who certainly wears some strange clothes at times, said that it did not matter, put on a plain white shirt, and away we went. All night long we could see men studying George's neckline with interest, amazement, and some jealousy, I believe. Could they have thought they were outdated? George couldn't have cared less. We were amused that although he was eyed strangely all night, no one mentioned the outfit.

As for me, I had bought a new dress for the occasion—at that time, the most expensive dress I had ever owned. The entertainment was Bobby Short, and his date had on the very same dress! My, what an impression the Bushes of Texas must have made that night.

At one point during the evening, President Nixon came up to us and said, "George, you and Barbara know the Duke, don't you?" Before George could answer, he went on, "He has asked about you. Go talk to him." I believe that the President had exhausted his "small talk," of which he had a limited supply, and just wanted to share the load. We had met the Duke and Duchess once at a small dinner at Lloyd Smith's home in Houston several years before. We were equally sure that the Duke did not remember or ask for us.

I remember at the Smith dinner being surprised by how tiny the Duke and Duchess were and how charming she was. The ladies retired upstairs for coffee and the men to the salon for cigars. (I'm not really sure what the men did, but that sounds like what one would do if you had a Duke for dinner.) The Duchess of Windsor held forth upstairs in a very warm and amusing fashion. I was charmed.

But back to the White House event. On the way to the car, George fell ill and got sick all over his rented cutaway. (Shades of things to come?) What a day it had been.

On May 4, 1970, the terrible confrontation took place in Ohio on the campus of Kent State between students and the National Guard, with four young people being killed. The tragedy rocked the country and lit a fuse on campuses everywhere. I was driving home from a meeting one late afternoon and ran into a large traffic jam on the Key Bridge. As I sat patiently in my car, I realized a frenzied gang of students was working its way down the bridge. When they got to my car, one of them yelled, "We got one here," and before I knew what was happening, my car was rocking and what seemed like a hundred mean faces were leering in the windows at me. A young man thrust a microphone in my car window and said, "What do you think about Nixon who killed the students at Kent State?" I was scared to death and started to speak, "I don't t-h-i-n-k . . ." and then burst into tears. The young man with the mike took one look and quickly told his friends that I was crying and to back off. They did and moved on. The faces all suddenly looked like young, caring kids instead of the mean-faced monsters I had seen one second before. I honestly think they all pictured their own mothers in the same situation. They had picked me out of the crowd in the first place because my Texas license plate said "House 7."

I was spending as much time in Texas as possible helping George campaign. I will never forget one memorable day. First, as I was getting off the plane in Marshall, Texas, my heel caught on the steps and I literally fell off. I'm sure that made quite an impression on our supporters who were kind enough to greet me at the airport.

The day only got worse. I recently had decided to do something with my hair, which to me looked dead. So I tried a new hair color product, a rinse called "Fabulous Fawn." Well, as the day got hotter, and when the air-conditioning quit working on the plane, "Fabulous Fawn" began to trickle down my back. All day I looked like I had a dirty neck. I think that was the last time I ever colored my hair, and I decided to let nature take its course.

I remember another slightly more glamorous day on the campaign trail when we traveled with the Agnews. I was amazed that during the long flight between Texas and Washington, the Vice President never once read, wrote, or worked. He played gin rummy. I liked them both very much. They were very relaxed and absolutely put on no airs.

Once again, lightning struck to completely change the political picture. This time, our friend Lloyd Bentsen ran against Yarborough and beat him in the Democratic primary. This hurt us badly, but we still thought we could win. Then those smart Democrats put a liquor-by-the-drink bill on the ballot, and the Democrats who otherwise would not have voted turned out in record numbers. Losing is not fun at all, and this was harder than ever. Election night, as we were walking out of the hotel where George had spoken to his loyal supporters, Doro burst into tears. We tried to tell her it would be okay, but she sobbed, "Oh, no, it won't. I'll be the only girl in the fifth grade whose Daddy doesn't have a job."

The next day I went to play tennis with several of my close friends, but every time I thought of George Bush sitting at home calling people and thanking them, I'd start weeping. We finally gave up and went in to have coffee and lunch.

Incidentally, no more brown-bagging it in Texas. We could now buy liquor over the counter by the drink.

8

The United Nations

A fter the election, George and I returned to Washington to finish out his career as a congressman. George was very disappointed. He always had wanted to be in the Senate, especially since the days when his father had served there. Now the big question for us was: What next?

Many people felt President Nixon owed George, because he had asked him to give up his safe House seat to run for the Senate. George did not feel that way. It had been his choice to get into the race. Nevertheless, rumors flew all over Washington about who would get what jobs, including George. The President once hinted that maybe George should move to Connecticut and run against Senator Abraham Ribicoff in 1972. That had zero appeal. I was ready to suggest we go home to family and friends and live happily ever after.

However, George knew exactly what job he wanted: Ambassador to the United Nations. Family friend Charley Bartlett had suggested it once, and after much thought, George decided it was where he could serve the President and the country best. He discussed it with White House Chief of Staff Bob Haldeman and many others, but not directly with President Nixon.

Finally, the call came for George to come to the White House, and the President offered him a job as special assistant to the President. George said he would do whatever was asked of him, but added he was sorry that the President didn't like the UN idea. He said he felt he could have served the President well there, especially since incumbent

Ambassador Charlie Yost was a liberal Democrat and really didn't represent the administration's views. A few minutes later, President Nixon called George back into the Oval Office and said, "I've thought about our conversation—you have the UN job."

This story tells you something about the presidency: Very often the people around the President do not present the case for someone else very well—or maybe at all.

It also makes one wonder: In light of what later happened in the Nixon White House, were we not the luckiest people in the world?

At the time, I knew nothing about the United Nations other than what was in the newspapers. So I looked it up in the children's World Book encyclopedia, and once when I was in New York City, I cruised by in a cab. I didn't dare go in, since George had not yet been confirmed.

In late February, our friend and neighbor Associate Justice Potter Stewart conducted the swearing-in ceremony at the White House, with Mom and Dad Bush in the audience. While we were waiting in the Red Room, Potter told me President Nixon always said the same thing when he saw him: "Of course, I know the Justice. He is the youngest Justice on the Court." Just then, President Nixon walked in and said, "Oh, Justice Stewart, how are you? Barbara, did you know that the Justice is the youngest Justice on the Court?" It was hard not to laugh. In later years, Potter would swear George in as Director of the CIA and as Vice President of the United States. That lovely man died before George became President.

Shortly before the swearing-in, we went on an orientation trip to Europe to visit some of the UN agencies and world organizations. The U.S. government would pay first-class for George and an aide, Paxton Dunn, but George would have to pay for me. There was lots of teasing about how we would go. George said he and Pax would send me back messages from first class to coach, or maybe I could come up and visit first class once in a while. They also told me not to worry: They would wait for me to get off the plane.

Of course, we all flew coach class. Paxton was a very good sport about it, and was also a great guide through the State Department maze. All went well until we arrived in Austria on a tiny European plane. As we exited from the rear with the other coach passengers, we saw a band playing at the front of the plane, along with a small delegation headed by a very official-looking mayor. At first we wondered who was getting such a grand welcome. Then George spotted the American ambassador among the welcoming party. What a dilemma! Do we leap back on the plane and get back off through the first-class exit, or do we creep up on them from behind? We bit the bullet and chose the latter course. Ambassador John Humes was kind about our unusual arrival. He kept mentioning how great we were to save the government so much money. Although we always were concerned about saving government dollars, I must admit we were more worried about saving our own!

In Paris, we stayed with an old Bush/Walker family friend, Ambassador Dick Watson. While there, I went with a darling young woman, Eva Prohme, whose husband worked at UNESCO (United Nations Education, Scientific, and Cultural Organization) to my first couture house; I have forgotten the name. The room was crowded, but it quickly became apparent that the others were straphangers and the whole show was for me. They must have been told I was a rich Texan who certainly would buy out the place. Three beautiful models were in and out of some eighty dresses in just about an hour. It was so embarrassing for me and certainly for my young guide. We did not know how to get out of there. Finally, when the high-pressure saleslady turned her back, Eva and I slipped away in giggles—and feeling very guilty, I might add.

It was a fast, exciting trip for me as we whipped through many of the European capitals. But I soon realized that trip was just the beginning of two wonderful years for us. I will leave the politics to George and tell you instead about the personal side of being at the United Nations.

Our first look at apartment 42A in the Waldorf Towers—the UN ambassador's official residence—was slightly frightening. The Towers was a formidable place to live. Ambassador and Mrs. Yost had just been relieved of their post in a cruel, awkward fashion. They very kindly invited us for lunch, but I remember them as dour people. He later did the unforgivable: Not only did he stay in New York, but he wrote anti–U.S. policy articles for *The New York Times* op-ed page. Soviet Ambassador Yakov Malik would wave them in George's face in Security Council meetings and say, "See, George, just how wrong you are. Your colleague says . . ."

The residence is a large, roomy apartment with five lovely bedrooms. We used one of the large bedrooms for a study/dressing room for George and often tucked one of our boys in there when they came for a visit and we had a crowd. One bedroom was a guest room (we had lots of guests), and Paula and Doro had the other two. Doro was an adorable, chunky twelve-year-old at the time. She missed all her friends from Washington, but Paula kept her from being lonely, and her older first cousin, Peggy Pierce, often came for the night to keep her company. And of course she had lots of friends from the United Nations school. At that time, it was in an old warehouse on Fifty-fourth Street, and I could walk her there if the weather was pleasant. Our three younger boys were all away at school, but they visited often with friends.

The apartment had a lovely front entrance, a small octagonal room with one of what seemed like hundreds of original Gilbert Stuart portraits of George Washington (he must have turned them out like rabbits!), a lovely den with a fireplace, and a mammoth living room that was forty-eight feet long. The Yosts had their own furniture in the apartment, and when they left, it left also. The hotel sent up some sorry replacements: white satin couches and chairs and two large round mirror-topped coffee tables. They cannot be as ugly as I remember them, but they were hideous. At the first of our many receptions, these coffee tables caused no end of excitement. Women's skirts that year were just shorter than the coffee tables, and to my horror, I realized that you could see right up the ladies' skirts if you were standing across the table from them. The tables left the very next morning.

I worried about furnishing an apartment that big and making it look warm and inviting. I borrowed some beautiful paintings from the Metropolitan Museum: *Tennis at Newport* by Bellows; a lovely Mary Cassatt; a glorious, small John Singer Sargent of two ladies lounging on a very green lawn; and many others. Much to everyone's dismay, I returned two beautiful Monets. I would love to be surrounded by Monets, but felt that since we do not subsidize our artists as so many countries do, the least I could do was display American art. When criticized, I would answer, "When the French start hanging American artists, I'll think about hanging French paintings."

Mildred Kerr came to visit while I was worrying about furnishing the living room. She noticed all the beautiful glass objects (supplied by the Steuben Glass people) and told me she had seen a big Steuben bowl filled with eggs that looked very cozy. Maybe eggs would add color to that cold-looking room. So out we went and bought seventeen colored stone eggs, put them in a bowl, and stepped back to admire them. Well, in a room that size, they were absolutely nothing. They looked like a grain of sand on a big beach. However, as a result, people thought I collected eggs and brought them to me as gifts, which I thought was rather funny. But at the same time, people also would "borrow" an egg every now and then, so I remained pretty constant—eggwise.

As I mentioned earlier, living at the Waldorf could be intimidating. At the time, it was home to Mrs. Douglas MacArthur; actress Carol Channing; former Senator Bill Benton; former postmaster general and confidant of Franklin Roosevelt, Jim Farley, with whom we shared several fun dinners; Mrs. Edwin Hilson, a great friend of the Eisenhowers; benefactress Mrs. Charles Engelhard; and many others. The first time I went to the grocery store and brought back bags of groceries in my arms, I felt a slight panic. Would they lead me to the service elevator? Would somebody tell me that their clientele did *not* carry groceries up in the tower elevators, much less through their lobby? They did no such thing, and by the time we left after two years, I felt that everybody in that sumptuous hotel was a friend. I mean everybody—the permanent residents, doormen, elevator operators, the manager, and on and on. George and I grew very fond of Jean Mac-Arthur, Mildred Hilson, and Jane Engelhard, who was a great supporter of the White House Endowment Fund and remained faithful twenty years later when I revived it.

You'll be happy to know that Jean took us to the "21" Club several times—the source of my great jealousy years earlier. She had her own table, and when we arrived, she would be there to greet us. Always in front of her would be a stem glass with a pale liquid and an olive in it. It seemed so amazing to see this tiny little southern lady drinking a martini straight up, and even more amazing when she would request another. After we got to know her quite well, we discovered that she was having water with an olive. She wanted her guests to feel free to order whatever they wanted.

Apartment 42A also was the place where the Secretary of State entertained when in New York City, and Secretary William Rogers used the apartment several times. I remember being told about many things that the Secretary did or did not like. So you can imagine my surprise one night when Bill and Adele Rogers took us out for dinner and he ordered lamb. I had definitely been told that the Secretary hated lamb. I mentioned this to Bill, and he laughed and asked what other things he "disliked." When I repeated the list, he really laughed. Not a bit of truth in the list! That is so typical of getting information secondhand.

One luncheon the Secretary gave at 42A will always remain indelibly—maybe I should say "pressed"—in my mind. It was in the fall, during the busiest time. I had arranged the flowers, chosen the menu, and gone gaily off on my own schedule. George told me the luncheon had gone well. Paula, close to tears, had a different story. Just before the luncheon, the chief of protocol came in and announced the tablecloth looked wrinkled. So the waiters pressed it right on the table. After the lunch was over, and the dishes and cloth were removed, we saw marks left by a hot steam iron on our beautiful table. But we were told that if you rubbed the table with ashes and camphor, the marks would disappear. So Paula and I collected ashes from the ashtrays and took turns rubbing with ashes and Campho-Phenique. I really don't know if the mixture did it, or if we did by rubbing so hard and long, but it worked.

We loved Bill and Adele Rogers. Later, I did a little work with her in the literacy field. She volunteered in public schools in both New York City and Washington, D.C., as they commuted back and forth for many years.

One thing we learned to hate at the United Nations were the words "We don't do it that way." An example: Immediately after we arrived, all the ambassadors from other countries wanted to pay a courtesy call. When George got the call that one was on his way up the elevator, he would start down the hall to meet him. An aide said, "Oh, no, Mr. Ambassador, we don't do it that way. I meet him at the elevator and bring him to you." George met every ambassador at the elevator, whether he was from Great Britain or Ceylon (now Sri Lanka). They fast learned that George does things differently and his own way. And they loved it. There were eleven floors of State Department people at the U.S. Mission—for the most part, very able and dedicated people. George brought Tom Lias, Jane Kenny, and Aleene Smith with him from his congressional office. Our dear Don Rhodes went to work for Congressman Charles Sandman of New Jersey.

At the time, New York City's mayor was John Lindsay, who was married to George's childhood friend Mary Harrison. We both loved

Mary, but grew to think that John was the most conceited, arrogant man ever born.

The Mayor of New York and the U.S. Ambassador to the United Nations often co-hosted events. John came late to everything—and sometimes did not come at all. Then he would look at anyone—Mary, me, a member of his staff, or a member of George's—and say "Get me coffee" or whatever without a please or thank-you.

John's slogan for New York was "Fun City." Aleene and her husband, Hargrove, had fun with that. For instance, one day walking to work, a car came very close to the curb and splashed filthy water all over them. They would say, "Welcome to Fun City." Tom Lias judged his days in Fun City by whether it was a "one-dog day," "two-dog day," and so on—depending on the number of dog piles he stepped in on his way to work.

⁓ George loved to entertain and came up with some extraordinary and fun ideas. Sometimes, however, they would backfire.

When the movie *The Godfather* came out, people were waiting in lines for hours to see it. George thought it would be fun to have a private showing, so he rented a little theater and invited around one hundred people. They were thrilled—until the movie came on.

Sitting through this bloodthirsty film, showing the worst of America, I suddenly saw it through the eyes of our foreign guests. They already thought our streets were unsafe, and here we were showing them a film that seemed to prove them right. After the movie, I assured them that this kind of thing didn't happen anymore. As we walked out of the theater, the early-morning editions of the newspapers were already on the street, with screaming headlines: MOB KILLINGS IN NEW JERSEY!

Another time, during the Security Council meetings in the fall when many heads of state and foreign ministers were in town, George woke up on a Sunday morning with the idea that British Foreign Minister Sir Alec Douglas Home and Lady Home might like to get out of the city and go to Greenwich for lunch and a nice walk. I quickly said that he could not call their Ambassador, Sir Colin Crowe, at six A.M. Not only was it too early to call, it was certainly too late to extend a luncheon invitation to a very popular foreign minister. He called anyway, although he did wait until seven A.M. The Homes and the Crowes loved the idea. So George got on the phone and arranged for us to have lunch with his aunt and uncle, Mary and Herbie Walker, followed by a walk through the beautiful Audubon Society Park.

Well, we forgot to find out if it is open on Sundays in October, and when we got there, it was closed tighter than a drum. That didn't stop George. He hoisted Lady Crowe and Lady Home—skirts and all—over the fence, along with the rest of us, and we took a glorious walk through the park. That is until the park manager challenged us with his dogs. George quickly ran ahead and explained who we were, and we finished our walk—leaving by the proper gate this time. One of the Foreign Minister's security men from Scotland Yard later told George this was "a first" for him. Well, I guess so!

One August weekend, I invited the French and Italian ambassadors and their wives, whom we liked very much, to come to Maine and get away from the ghastly summer heat. George loved the idea, especially since they all played tennis. Later George came home laughing, saying his office had seen a cable about the improvement of the relationship between France and the United States. The proof the cable cited was the fact that the French ambassador and his wife were visiting the U.S. ambassador in Kennebunkport!

This story might answer a question I'm asked all the time: Did anyone tell you what to do, or give you any guidelines, when your husband was in government? The answer is no. Certainly I was given advice on protocol, and occasionally on what to wear or not to wear, but, for the most part, I just depended on the manners my mother taught me.

George's Uncle Herbie was a small partner of the New York Mets baseball team, and we occasionally took some ambassadors and wives to dinner and a game at Shea Stadium. Baseball is not an easy game to explain to foreigners, but peanuts and hot dogs were a refreshing change from all the black-tie, six-course meals.

Speaking of six-course meals, we usually served four, and I would worry whether we were doing enough. George just would not put up with any more, and he said there was a direct correlation: The poorer the country, the grander the meal. So we weren't surprised when Burundi served a seven-course meal.

Once we took a group of ambassadors and their wives for a briefing at NASA and dinner in Houston. We also hosted a Texas barbecue on the eleventh floor of the U.S. Mission and took them around Manhattan Island on a boat.

George's biggest party success was one he had for "The 10 Most Overrated Men in New York City"—at least according to *New York* magazine. George promptly invited all ten men—well, the nine others—to come to a reception in their honor. He asked Dick Schaap, the author of the article, to join us, along with quite a few ambassadors and their wives. I can't remember the others, but I do know that Senator Javits was on the list, and although he was a fine man, he had no sense of humor about his selection. He said he "wouldn't dignify the article by attending." At the party, George jumped up on a chair, called us all together, and gave out some funny awards. Our Russian friend, Ambassador Malik, confused by the party, was overheard asking another ambassador more familiar with the West, "Vat is dis '*overrated*'?" George loved that.

Dick Schaap was brave enough to attend. George said in his little award ceremony that "only modesty kept Dick himself off the list." Dick later wrote that he came to the party in fear and trembling and believed that his worst fears had been realized when the first people he saw, being a man of Jewish faith, were ambassadors from Arab nations!

George wasn't the only member of the family who enjoyed entertaining. I invited several of my Washington groups to New York for a day. They were to take the train, tour the residence, have a light lunch, and get a briefing and tour of both the U.S. Mission and the United Nations. The first group came, about forty in all.

Since the kitchen in our apartment looked like an L-shaped Pullman train kitchen, I decided to have the Waldorf serve a light lunch: chicken salad, lobster salad, hot rolls, white wine, and then some sort of yummy dessert. The whole day went well. Several weeks later, George asked me how it had gone—and then told me that the bill from the Waldorf was $900. I burst into tears and told him I had two other groups coming. He said I shouldn't worry. But I did, and Paula and I worked up a light lunch for sixty people in that tiny little kitchen that cost considerably less and tasted just as good.

Although we entertained a lot, we also were entertained a great deal. We went to several receptions every evening, many dinners, and quite a few lunches. I loved all that. In fact, I was born to the job: I love people and adore eating. For George, these social functions were work. At the ambassadors' level, much of the real work of the United

Nations was conducted at these social functions. Especially if there was a problem between two countries, the only communications the ambassadors had with each other were "after hours." Your guest list often was composed of people who wanted to meet but couldn't on an official level.

We were on the reception circuit one December evening, racing from party to party. As it was close to Christmas, I had on a bright red suit—really bright red. Suddenly we pulled up to a building that looked different, and I asked what reception this was. George grabbed my arm and said that this was a call we had to make. As we ran up a flight of stairs, he explained that a brand-new ambassador, a former president of a Central American country, had died shortly after arriving at the United Nations and was lying in state here until arrangements were made to send him back home. At that moment, we literally ran into a room filled with people dressed in black and clearly mourning. We were led right up to the open coffin, where people were posing for pictures with their fallen leader. Yes, posing for pictures, putting their arms around the casket and putting their heads near his and having their pictures taken. Tears were everywhere—and so were TV cameras. It never occurred to George that I might not have been appropriately dressed in my bright red. To him, being there is what counts, not one's clothes.

I cannot tell you how many times during our UN years I wished I spoke French or Spanish. I had studied French as a child and learned some Spanish after moving to Texas, but was proficient at neither. I've decided people who are musically inclined are also better at languages. I am tone-deaf and can't carry a tune, so that was my excuse. I did find that the Spanish-speaking people were thrilled when I tried to speak their language, but the French always acted like I was attempting a language they had never heard. George didn't care. He went right ahead using his schoolboy French.

I learned that a touch, many smiles, much interest, and lots of honest affection were a universal language.

Being the host ambassador kept George very busy. When the elderly ambassador and his wife from Cyprus were attacked, robbed, and had their shoes thrown in the Central Park lake one evening, it was George's fault for not making the park safe. When a bomb was placed next to the embassy door of a small African country, it was George's fault. And when the Soviet Embassy had a shot fired into it from a nearby rooftop, just missing a Russian family, it was George's fault. He spent hours working on these housekeeping, rather than policy, problems.

I volunteered one morning a week at Sloan-Kettering Memorial Hospital—not with the children but with adults. I loved it. The hospital had the most marvelous staff and an esprit de corps that made being there a joy. My job was the Art Cart—hardly a big job, but worthwhile. The cart had many pictures, classic and modern. We were assigned a floor and told what rooms to call on. Then you asked the patients what they liked and if they wanted the art changed in their rooms. All of this was really a cover. Mostly our job was to get to know the patients, see if they were happy or lonely, and generally to spread good cheer. I became very attached to many of the patients and even taught one sweet military wife to needlepoint. Many times I would bring the patients souvenirs from dinners and other UN events.

One day the hospital asked me to call on a lady who was very much in the dumps. They confessed that the only spark they had seen was when they told her that the wife of the U.S. Ambassador to the United Nations was working at the hospital. I called on this lady many times and dropped names and events like mad. She loved it.

I felt very guilty and disappointed when I had to miss my Thursday morning at Memorial. Often I would race from the hospital to a luncheon. Our foreign friends found volunteer work really strange, but certainly commendable. They always said "it would never work in our country."

In those days, about 80 percent of the people who were treated at our hospital went home either in remission or cured, never to return again. Several times we had friends come through the hospital. The saddest for us was when George's wonderful dad got a persistent cough and was sent to Memorial. He was in the hospital about three weeks as I remember, being tested, operated on, and then sleeping away his life. He died October 8, 1972. He was a magnificent man who brought great pleasure to his family. He and Mom had been married fifty-one years and were a great team.

Dotty Bush planned his funeral with their children. I remember several things about that service. First, she told us to wear color. Death was a beginning and not an ending. She wrote the eulogy herself, and it was so loving and hit the mark. She made her children sit with their own families. She said she wanted their friends to see what grand families Pres Bush had. She sat with the pallbearers, who were their grandsons. Several of our boys were pallbearers—maybe all of them—but the one I remember was Jeb. He was a student at the University of Texas, nineteen years old, six feet four inches tall. Remember, this was the early 1970s. He, of course, did not have a dark suit. He told me not to worry—he'd borrowed one. I should have kept worrying. It was black corduroy. He is the most handsome man (at least according to his mother), and that saved him. Otherwise, he would have looked like a card shark from Las Vegas.

After the church service, we all walked over to the cemetery and buried Pres Bush next to our little Robin. George and I felt very fortunate we were living in New York during the last year of Dad's life.

ᘓ So much of what we did during the United Nation's years was fascinating, but a number of events or periods stand out in my mind.

The fall of 1971 was not to be believed. Witnessing the election of new Secretary General Kurt Waldheim, the China vote, and the constant meetings of the Security Council were extraordinary.

The Dual Representation Policy (some erroneously referred to it as the Two China Policy) was a very difficult time for the U.S. Ambassador to the United Nations, but it was interesting. The United States wanted Taiwan to keep its UN seat despite the entry of the People's Republic of China into the United Nations. We lost by a narrow margin—59 to 55—but it was a major setback for the United States. The night of the vote, I was seated with a few other American wives in the General Assembly. Once it was clear that we had lost the vote, the room went wild. Seated right in front of me were some people from the Tanzanian Mission. They turned and jeered and spit at me. I truly was shocked by the hatred they felt for us. It was so sad to see the lovely foreign minister from Taiwan walk out of the United Nations, his back straight and head held high. It was equally dramatic to see the new ambassador from the People's Republic of China walk in that first time.

The very next day, I was scheduled to attend a luncheon the African wives were having for me. I told George I didn't think I'd go. He insisted that I go and said they would be nice. How right he was.

The wives were so sweet and lovely and we even shared a tear or two, although for the most part they were on the other side of the China issue.

The People's Republic of China delegation was the rage of New York. They lived in a hotel and their every move was reported. What they wore and what they ate became front-page news. The fact of the matter was they were very nice people just trying to feel their way along.

Shortly after George's dad died, he asked his mother if she would mind including the Chinese in one of our family Sunday lunches. Although still in mourning, she was a dear and immediately agreed. She would have a buffet and let the grandchildren help as usual. At that time, the Chinese men and women all dressed alike in Mao suits, so Mrs. Bush greeted us in black pants and a black sweater. She wanted the Chinese to feel at ease and at home. We were late getting there, and her dinner sat for a little too long in the warming oven. When our lunch was served, I heard the foreign minister ask Mrs. Bush what something was. Her answer: "Minute Rice." We had a hard time explaining to the Chinese what that was—and why we were giggling. Poor Mom. The rice was so overcooked that even the Chinese did not recognize it. I never loved that courageous little woman more than that day.

꙳ Another outstanding, very educational experience for us was a trip to Africa in February 1972. George went first to Somalia and then on to Ethiopia, where the Security Council was to meet. I joined him there.

The altitude in Addis Ababa was devastating to many of us. Sleep was impossible at eight thousand feet. The Security Council met all day and half the night. During the day we visited the marketplace, and it was teeming with poor-looking people who thrust things at you to buy. The pressure was enormous.

From there we went on to Khartoum, Sudan, where we caught up on our sleep. Since we did not have relations with the Sudan at that time, we had to deal through the Dutch Embassy. We stayed in our chargé d'affaires's guest house. Curt and Sally Moore were truly wonderful people. She was the principal of the American School—according to her, because they couldn't find anyone else, but I doubt that. She was a very bright, strong woman. We did take a lovely boat trip up the Nile and saw where the White Nile meets the Blue Nile. We saw an oxen water bucket routine that was exactly as it was done in 1500 B.C. The irrigated land around the river was green and fertile. All the rest was sand. The Sudanese are very beautiful people. At that time, the Sudanese ladies were circumcised, which was common all over Africa. It was a very depressing country. We saw many dead or starving animals. I don't know how these people eked out a living.

There is a tragic footnote to this visit. We eventually normalized relations with the Sudanese, and at a going-away party for the Moores in March 1973, the Black September Terrorists took incoming Ambassador Noel and outgoing Chargé d'Affaires Moore hostage and eventually killed them both. George and I attended their joint funeral on March 7 in Washington, D.C.

We went on to Kenya for a lovely visit. We drove out of Nairobi through beautiful rolling residential countryside, past tea and coffee plantations and into the mountains. Suddenly, far below us, we saw the Rift Valley spread at our feet. Nairobi is about five thousand feet high. We climbed to eight thousand feet and then dropped about three thousand feet into the valley. We saw many deer, monkeys, impala, the yellow-billed stork, those tiny little deer called dik-diks, and giraffes eating those marvelous thorn trees. But the most exciting part of this day trip was Lake Nakuru, where we saw the most fantastic sight. Nakuru is an alkaline lake filled with green algae, on which pink flamingos feed by the millions. From a distance, it appears the lake has pink beaches. Not true—just miles of beautiful flamingos, moving like ballet dancers.

On to Lusaka, Zambia, where we immediately took a side trip to Victoria Falls and got soaked. We walked out on a bridge that formed the line between Zambia and Rhodesia (now Zimbabwe). Since our government had asked us not to go into Rhodesia, we stopped in the middle of the Knife Edge Bridge and looked at the glorious falls.

We were then taken to the Quadrapoint, where Namibia, Rhodesia, Botswana, and Zambia meet. We jumped on a very primitive river ferry, which was really a small converted steel barge. As we approached Botswana, we could see a welcoming party of officials waiting and, twenty feet away, another kind of welcoming party behind barbed wire: Rhodesians with guns and cameras. Fortunately, they shot only the latter. We nervously took pictures back.

We spent the night at the Chobe Game Preserve. We took a boat trip looking for hippos, saw none, but loved the extraordinary river. We drove through the preserve and saw many families of baboons and hundreds of elephants bathing, rolling in the dust, and squirting their young. We passed a baby rhino with parents and friends and saw some waterbucks. The Zambians had gotten their independence in the 1960s, but were still struggling when we visited. At the time, the country had only one hundred college graduates and one Zambian doctor.

Next was Zaire, where we visited a space satellite station funded by the Export-Import Bank. This was our first visit with President Mobutu, who wears a leopard skin hat and carries a tribal stick. He is very flamboyant, but charming. Years later he visited us for dinner in Maine one night on his way to a meeting in Montreal. He speaks no English, and we speak little French. George's mother came for dinner with us and enchanted him and her grandchildren as she reached way back to her school days and spoke French very well.

Next stop: Libreville, Gabon. Our embassy was a lovely, modern home with nice gardens on a tall hill looking down on all sides at native huts and shacks. I found it fascinating, but felt uncomfortable in a "Marie Antoinette" way, watching the women trudge by carrying tremendous loads on their heads.

Our entry into Lagos, Nigeria, probably influenced my feeling about that country. The traffic was horrendous. The city was filthy. The river was polluted. There were no closed sewers, no water, and sometimes no electricity. The streets were teeming with people— some dressed, some half dressed, and some relieving themselves. The roads were lined with shacks. I saw beggars, people sleeping on the streets, and garbage everywhere. Never had I seen such filth. The very worst was that a lady gave birth on the street outside our car and no one seemed to care. People just stepped over or walked around her.

Chad was more of the same—poor. The minister of health told me they could keep the clinic open with a mere $100. The capital, Fort Lamy, was a dry, dusty city. We ate lunch with President Tombalbaye, who was assassinated several years later in a coup.

We left that fascinating continent thinking Africans were the world's warmest, friendliest people who had more problems than we could believe.

∽ We met many world leaders and interesting, exciting people during the two years we were at the United Nations. Ali Bhutto, then deputy prime minister of Pakistan and later prime minister, made an enormous impression on George when he spoke before the Security Council. Ambassador Toukan from Jordan was a very dear man. We became close and George even helped his daughter, Alia, who was in her early twenties, get a job at American Express. I think she was in the secretarial pool and sat in the fifth desk from the back. The ambassador and his family were recalled to Jordan after a year. The beautiful Alia went on to become the third wife of King Hussein. On a state visited to the United States, Queen Alia told George that right after her engagement, the women she had worked with at American Express all chipped in and called her in Jordan.

During this same period, we went up to the Rockefellers' country place, Pocantico Hills, on the Hudson River for a luncheon David Rockefeller gave a visiting dignitary. It was a lovely day, and we ate outside around the pool. Sitting at our table was Najeeb Halaby, who at that time was CEO of PanAm, and his daughter, Lisa. A child of the 1970s with long hair and sandals, she stood out in this crowd of older, well-dressed people. But she grew up to be a beautiful young woman who went to work in Jordan and became Queen Noor, the fourth wife of King Hussein, after our little friend Alia was killed in a helicopter accident.

I have to tell you another story about that lunch. I distinctly remember that Pat Patterson, whose husband was head of Chase National Bank, was at my table. She sat next to a man from a South American country who spoke with a heavy accent. I heard him say to Pat, a gorgeous redhead, "Do you like New York?" She immediately went into all the virtues of New York City. When she finished telling him about the opera, the theater, museums, and so forth, he said, "And sex?" Pat, a normally sophisticated woman, looked nonplussed, but before she could answer, he added, "Sex Fifth Avenue; don't you like shopping?"

∽ Toward the end of our United Nations days, and shortly before the 1972 election, George and I were in Austin, Texas, where he was speaking. As we were getting ready to fly home in a private plane to Houston, George decided to call President Johnson to see if we could make a courtesy call. He told me he didn't want to give him any warning. That way the President could say that he was sorry, it was too late to make plans. Instead, he said to come ahead.

Besides being President when we arrived in Washington, Lyndon Johnson had served in the United States Senate with George's dad. Pres Bush used to say, "I rarely agree with Lyndon on anything politically, but he always kept his word to the Senate and he was a great majority leader." We landed right on the LBJ Ranch landing strip. There were Lady Bird and Lyndon in a big white Lincoln. He immediately asked us if we'd rather go to the ranch house or drive around the ranch. Before we could answer, he chose to ride around the ranch. Lady Bird and I were put in the backseat and the men got in the front with Lyndon at the wheel. We charged over hill and dale without any thought to trails or roads. I decided that it must be a manicured ranch, for we hit no potholes or rocks as we raced through the tall grass spotting and chasing deer. George and the President talked a mile a minute about domestic successes and problems. The President told George that he had resigned all the boards he was serving on and put Lady Bird on some. He talked at length about the LBJ Library and invited George to speak there. He told us that he was thrilled that Barbara Jordan was there, or was going to be there. He knew that George had great respect for Barbara and had served with her in Congress. At one point we stopped on a hillside and looked at a great Hill Country scene. A man appeared at our car window and asked what we would like. Drinks appeared for all and we were off again. It was a marvelous experience. When we got back on our plane, both George and I felt that LBJ knew he did not have long to live and was paving a smooth way for Mrs. Johnson.

George worked very hard at his UN job and was superb. We went to the UN as critics and left as critics—but much less so than when we arrived. The United Nations has done so much good in fields like drugs, population, health, and environmental problems. And I guess that we will never know the wars that didn't happen because of the United Nations.

I take great pride in the fact that twenty years later, the United Nations came into its own when Iraq invaded Kuwait, and the world formed a coalition to protect one country from being invaded by another. George worked long and hard to form that coalition and to keep it together during the months before UN troops freed Kuwait. George Bush taught us how to keep the peace.

9

Surviving Watergate

President Nixon easily won reelection in 1972. I campaigned with other cabinet wives and had a very good time doing it. Sometimes we went out in teams, and I was fortunate to campaign in Texas with Jill Ruckelshaus and Lenore Romney, both women of great stature and knowledge. Jill's husband, Bill, had run for the Senate from Indiana and was head of the Environmental Protection Agency. Lenore's husband, George, was Secretary of Housing and Urban Development and had been Governor of Michigan. Lenore herself later ran for the United States Senate. Jill and Lenore did the heavy lifting, with me usually introducing them to Texans and our wonderful Texas to them. I take no credit—but get lots of joy—from the fact that Jill and Bill Ruckelshaus eventually moved to Houston.

Sometimes the re-elect committee sent me out alone, and that was not as enjoyable. I respected the President, but he did not make it easy to like him. He just did not know how to deal with small talk. I like him much more now twenty years later.

I loved Pat Nixon, who was a sensational, gracious, and thoughtful First Lady. She was personally involved in acquiring some of the White House's most treasured and historic possessions, including original furniture from previous administrations. It was her idea to have the White House lit at night, and she also started the annual Spring and Fall Garden Tours. She worked tirelessly promoting volunteerism, a cause she believed in deeply.

Immediately after the election George attended a cabinet meeting in Washington. The President thanked them for all their hard work and left the room. Then Chief of Staff Haldeman, speaking for the President, asked the entire cabinet to have their resignations on the President's desk as soon as possible. They were shocked. Eventually there would be a total of eight new cabinet members.

George Shultz, who remained Secretary of the Treasury, talked to George about being his number two, an idea George liked a lot. However, it had been rumored in the papers that President Nixon was going to ask George to be chairman of the Republican National Committee. When the call came for George to meet with the President at Camp David, I sent him off with the strong urging not to accept the RNC post if offered. I just felt it would be a terrible experience. Party politics are very dog-eat-dog, and I knew he would have to travel a great deal. Of course, that's exactly what the President asked George to do, and of course, he took it.

Our diplomatic friends' reaction was very interesting. They thought being chairman of the RNC was not only a great job but a step up. I could understand the Chinese thinking that, since Chairman Mao's title was head of the Communist party. But several other ambassadors told me that leading one of our two great political parties was an honor. Several lectured me on the fact that our country's strength comes from having two strong parties. In contrast, many of their countries had many parties, resulting in coalition governments. In retrospect, I agree with them and understand their envy of our party system. I strongly believe people should pick the one that most closely fits their political philosophy and then try to work within the party. So many people criticize our system of government or the people who run it; yet, they never would think of attending a precinct meeting. They complain that the party has gone too far left or right and then announce that they are Independents. I think that is a cop-out.

In December, George went to Washington for a meeting and had lunch with our friend Congressman Bill Steiger of Wisconsin. Bill suggested they wander over for an informal visit to the Republican National Committee headquarters. What a shock. Not only did no one welcome them; they were ignored. Many people had their feet on the desks, and the building seemed filled with staff with nothing to do. The offices were messy and dirty. George realized he had an unpleasant task ahead, but he excelled at this kind of challenge.

So after a round of going-away parties in New York, we headed back to Washington. Our house was rented and the tenant did not want to leave until his lease expired in six months. Once again, I went house-hunting, and found a great furnished house on Cathedral Avenue convenient to the children's schools.

The Republican National Committee met on January 19 and unanimously elected George its new chairman. As we visited with the committee members, they all seemed to have the same complaint: unhappiness with the Nixon White House staff, whom they found arrogant and inaccessible.

On January 20 we attended the second inauguration of Richard Nixon and Spiro Agnew. We sat with the cabinet and went to the luncheon in the Capitol Rotunda with the President and Vice President and their families, and the House and Senate leadership. Then we sat on the presidential platform to watch the parade. At that point life seemed challenging and very exciting.

George and I dropped in at the RNC to get warm for a moment, and we were surprised to find that it was almost closed. We couldn't believe it. Not only was a Republican president being sworn in, the city was teeming with party members, including all the committeemen and women. We had heard that the morale was low, but so was the service they were giving. Life was getting more exciting and challenging by the minute.

That night we attended a dinner given by Ross and Margot Perot for the three Texans serving in Washington: Anne Armstrong, a counselor to the President who later became Ambassador to Great Britain; Bill Clements, an Assistant Secretary of Defense who later became Governor of Texas; and George. It was an extraordinary dinner attended by the Joint Chiefs of Staff, many senators and congressmen, Billy and Ruth Graham, a Medal of Honor winner, an escaped POW, a Vietnam widow, the son of a general killed in Vietnam, Governor and Mrs. Reagan, Supreme Court justices, and many friends. It opened with a blessing, which is unusual for a Washington dinner, and the entertainment was the Naval Academy choir. Ross Perot certainly knew how to put on a party, and it will come as no surprise that he gave a little speech.

George and I then went to the Inaugural Ball at the Kennedy Center, where we were supposed to be hosts. Our only role was to greet the Nixons and the Agnews when they arrived and lead them to the stage. We never could work our way through the crush that night and were so far away that we barely heard the President's remarks. It taught me a good lesson: Don't buy new clothes for that event. (Okay, I did break that rule in later years.)

꩜ It immediately became a busy year. President Johnson died suddenly on January 22, Neil's eighteenth birthday. We were so glad that we'd had that nice visit at the ranch in the fall.

On January 23 President Nixon spoke to the nation at ten P.M. and announced that we had peace at last in Vietnam. It was a very emotional time for our country. The war had lasted such a long time and in the process, had torn us apart. Finally, our servicemen and servicewomen could come home. I wrote in my diary:

January 23—It seemed so ironic that President Johnson died some 28 or 30 hours before the peace announcement. It would have pleased him so. No man wanted peace more. I think back to the United Nations. Vietnam hung over our head. It affected every talk, every negotiation. For so many reasons we are thrilled about the peace. Think of Sybil Stockdale . . . knowing that her (husband) Jim will be home soon. [George and I had gotten to know and like Sybil Stockdale through George's involvement with POWs and MIAs. In fact, I wore her husband's POW bracelet. We were disappointed in 1992 when Jim agreed to be Ross Perot's running mate.]

January 25—Mrs. Johnson was absolutely magnificent. She smiled at everyone, thanked everyone. She was quoted as saying that she was sure she would have those great waves of sorrow, but right now she was just grateful for 38 years. They really laid Lyndon to rest in great style.

February 12—THE FIRST POWS ARE OUT!!!! OUR MAN JIM STOCKDALE LIMPED OFF. THANK GOD.

There is one more diary entry from this time period I must share with you, if only because it amused me when I came across it in 1993:

February 1—First time I had my hair blown dry. It was very easy but I'm not sure it will catch on. Didn't do much for my hair.

꩜ As much as we loved our stay in New York, it was great to return to Washington. Doro was happy to be back at her school with friends, and although the Waldorf was an elegant place to live, we loved being in a house again. Neil, who had boarded at St. Alban's while we were at the United Nations, moved home and became a day student, and Marvin was just a short distance away at Woodberry Forest School near Orange, Virginia. He absolutely loved that school and it started a lifelong love affair with Virginia, where he still lives with his family. George W. was at Harvard Business School and Jebby was at the University of Texas in Austin.

I should note that as close as Marvin was, 1973 was the year of the Arab oil embargo and we suffered through long, long gas lines. It made going to see him almost impossible. Several times I barely made it home; my gauge was right on Empty. It was an inconvenience for almost everyone but absolutely devastating for those whose livelihood depended on the availability of gasoline.

We were especially thrilled to be with Neil that year. Everything was coming together for him. He was elected a prefect (class officer) at his school, and through much hard work, he made the honor roll and was named all-city second string in basketball—quite an honor in a city like Washington. Neil had overcome his learning disability and now could read with the best of them.

Dotty Bush, George, and I were in the audience on Prize Day when Neil won a coveted award. No child ever worked or tried harder to please, so this was truly a joy for us all. And we were all thrilled when he was accepted at Tulane University. He had come a long way from the day when we discovered he could not read.

After graduation, Neil took a group of four girls and four boys to Maine for a house party. Thank heavens I am too old to chaperone another one of these. It was agony. They were good kids, but the sloppiest, messiest children I have ever seen. Maybe since they had done the wonderful thing of graduating for us, they felt they could be rude. I put up with it for as long as I could, but when they didn't stand up when George's mom came into the room, I said, "Up, up!" and gestured with my hands. Later I overheard the girls imitating me, and I must say, I must have sounded pretty bad.

One of the children was the daughter of Spiro and Judy Agnew. The Vice President was going through a dreadful time in the press and the rumors about him were running wild. I was so touched by the way the older children protected Kim; politics can be brutal to children.

Agnew finally resigned in October, and President Nixon appointed Jerry Ford Vice President. He was a popular man with House and Senate members of both parties and a reassuring, healing choice for the country.

     In June, on my forty-eighth birthday, the family surprised me with a month-old blond cocker spaniel. After much thought, we named the puppy after C. Fred Chambers, a dear friend of George's. Our dog Nicky had gone to live with Paula's family in Texas when we moved into the Waldorf, and I really needed a dog. It was Marvin's idea, and George asked our friend Don Rhodes to take him dog-shopping. Don said Marvin looked deeply into the eyes of dozens of dogs until he finally found the perfect pup—C. Fred. It was an absolutely perfect birthday present.

I was keeping very busy. I had rejoined my International Club; saw a lot of my 90th Congressional friends; spent day after day with Andy Stewart; had twelve to twenty-five people over every Sunday after church for cookouts; carpooled; and worked as a volunteer at the Washington Home, which was a nursing home. And of course I worked for the party. Although I was one of the founding members of the Republican Forum, which educated party members on the issues, I can take very little, if any, credit since others did all the work.

Once a month Andy and I attended the Washington World Affairs Council luncheon, where Mrs. Virginia Bacon, widow of a New York congressman and an old grande dame, invited fascinating speakers to tell us about the world. They were very informative luncheons, but the thing I remember most was the fact that Mrs. Bacon put her head back and slept soundly and noisily through every speech. It was amusing to watch the speaker when he or she realized that Mrs. Bacon was asleep and then tried to act like it didn't matter.

I also joined the Theater Group, which I continued off and on throughout all our Washington days. It was an interesting group of eight or ten women made up of Supreme Court justices' wives, ambassadors' wives, historians, Democrats and Republicans, small business owners, and a housewife or two thrown in, all active in the community and all bright women. In those days we attended matinee performances and saw some wonderful plays, including *Macbeth* and *The Day After the Fair.*

Once a week in the early morning, I played tennis with Meredith Homet, Milly Dent, and Ann Buckley. I also played with Barbara MacGregor, Joanne Kemp, Martha Bartlett, and many others. All of our husbands held various positions in Washington.

Meanwhile George was keeping the most extraordinary schedule. In the first eleven months after taking over the party, he traveled 97,000 miles in thirty-three states, giving one hundred and one speeches, conducting seventy-eight news conferences, and making eleven national TV appearances. Watergate haunted him and permeated absolutely everything. Scores of Republicans were deserting the President. It got so bad that my childhood friend Milly Dent, whose husband, Fred, was Secretary of Commerce, became my only tennis partner. We couldn't find two others who did not think President Nixon was lying. It was a very unpleasant time for everyone.

Top Nixon aides Bob Haldeman, John Ehrlichman, and John Dean, and Attorney General Richard Kleindienst resigned April 30. George told me that the morning of the announcement, Bob said something to him like this: "I'm all right, George. Jo and I were sitting around the breakfast table this morning, reading our lesson from the Bible, and we came across the passage where it says [again I am paraphrasing], 'If *you* know that you have not sinned, then nothing else matters.' " I mention this because after twenty years, I have come to the conclusion that none of these people think they did anything wrong. It certainly is a different way of thinking.

Fortunately for George, his counterpart at the Democratic National Committee was Bob Strauss. He was a worthy opponent who played fair. We have counted Helen and Bob Strauss as dear friends for many years. When George was President, he sent Bob to the Soviet Union as ambassador at a very crucial time. He was the right man in the right place to help protect American interests as the Soviet Union fell apart.

Our household was jumping during Christmas vacation that year. All the children came home, including Jeb with the news that he wanted to marry a young woman he had met during a high school program in Mexico. This came as no surprise to us as Columba was the only girl he had ever dated. I remember one episode that made it clear to me that she certainly was a great influence on Jeb. We were notified that because of his academic record, Jeb had made Phi Beta Kappa. I called to say how thrilled we were, and he told me he had done it for

Columba because he wanted to prove he was serious. She thought he was a rich man's son and a playboy. That vacation I went with Jeb when he bought a tiny engagement ring. I wrote in my diary:

Jeb and I went in the afternoon to Boone & Sons and bought a ring and had my Grandmother Pierce's wedding ring fitted to Columba's size. When he has a wedding date he'll then get it marked. I am praying that he'll be as happy as Grandmother Pierce was and I am . . . How I worry about Jeb and Columba. Does she love him? I know when I meet her, I'll stop worrying . . . I am praying to be like Dotty Bush but it will be hard.

Jeb and Columba were married February 23, 1974, in a small family wedding in the chapel at the University of Texas. Only Columba's mother and sister, George's mother, and our immediate family plus Paula, our housekeeper, were there. Jeb was our first child to get married, and he and Columba reminded me so much of George and me. Jeb was just twenty-one, a year older than his father had been, and Columba was my age, nineteen, and they still had college to finish.

We were not an easy family to marry into. I had found the big Bush family a little overwhelming twenty-nine years before, so I could imagine Colu's feelings! To complicate things, she spoke very little English then, although she became fluent very quickly. She was a superb campaigner in Spanish and English in all our presidential campaigns; has helped with the Mexican Ballet Folklorica, Mexico's national ballet company; and has sponsored Mexican artists in this country. She also has given us three of the most attractive, bright grandchildren. She has made Jeb very happy, and we love her dearly.

⟳ The wedding was a happy interlude in a year dominated again by Watergate. On January 14, I wrote in my diary: "I am worried about George as he does not love his work. How could he? All this scandal."

I will never forget those marvelous Nixon daughters and how hard they worked for their dad. Julie called George once and asked him why he wasn't defending her dad more. She didn't realize it, but she had caught him, exhausted, in an airport going from city to city doing just that. He told me that she sounded just as frustrated as he felt.

Of course I thought George did a terrific job keeping the party out of the mess while still defending the President. He told me that the White House asked him to do things he just wouldn't do. They weren't illegal; they were just wrong. For example, they asked him to send out strongly worded letters he didn't believe in. He got memos from White House aide Chuck Colson saying, "The President wants you to . . ." George would ask Chuck to have the President call him. President Nixon never did, and George never did what Chuck asked. White House staff often quote the President, and one would do well to be sure that the President wants what the staffer wants. This is not a partisan statement. Both Democratic and Republican staffers have the same proclivity: a desire to appear on the inside track close to the President.

Certainly Chuck Colson was not alone in outrageous requests. I remember him because he totally turned his life around and has done the most remarkable job helping felons discover new and productive lives.

George wrote President Nixon a letter in August saying that he regretfully had to tell him that he felt the President must resign for the good of the country. The President continued to insist to George in private that he had done nothing wrong and asked George to help raise money so he could buy television time and take his case directly to the American people. On August 8, I was in Maine with the children when George called me from California, where he was fund-raising, and told me President Nixon would announce to the nation he was resigning and asked me to meet him in Washington the next morning. He flew all night, and on August 9 we met Dean Burch, a counselor to the President, and his wife, Pat, at the White House mess for breakfast. At ten A.M. we joined the White House staff and cabinet members in the East Room. The Nixon family came in, and the President told us good-bye. It was a sad moment in our history. One of the brightest men of our time was brought down by a stupid cover-up. The buck does stop with the top man, and President Nixon and the country paid the price. Tears flowed down all our faces. We went down to the helicopter pad on the South Grounds and awaited the First Family. Who will ever forget that moment when the President turned and gave that final wave?

We went back into the White House to attend the swearing-in of Gerald Ford as the thirty-eighth president of the United States of America. We had lunch with the Burches, after which Dean went to

President Ford's first staff meeting. He later commented on the difference between it and President Nixon's. President Ford asked each person in the cabinet to stay on and told them he was grateful for their help.

I will never forget that day: We saw a president resign and a new president sworn in. It was amazing how gently and quickly the executive branch switched gears. As we were walking to lunch, we noticed that even the White House pictures had changed: Photos of the Nixons were gone and the Fords already were on the walls. We are a great country, and the wonder of the smooth transition will stay with me forever.

China

After the change of presidents in 1974, George felt Jerry Ford needed his own spokesperson at the Republican National Committee. I also suspect he was exhausted. George always said dealing with Watergate was like dealing with a centipede: The other shoe kept dropping.

He had worked hard to keep the party away from the scandal and the scandal away from the party. In a letter he wrote me from Denver in the fall of 1974, he said: "I can't do this job much longer, if it is to be done well. It will need new blood after the elections." He suggested to President Ford that the RNC co-chair, Mary Louise Smith, be appointed. She was, doing a great job as the first woman to head a national party.

George had worked closely with Jerry Ford during his years in Congress and as chairman of the party. So when he went to Washington to talk to President Ford about the future, the President kindly offered him just about any job he wanted. We were vacationing in Maine at the time, and when George returned, he told me he hoped I would understand, but he had turned down all the stylish embassies (including London and Paris) and asked for the post in the People's Republic of China—if I agreed. He'd had all he wanted of constant receptions and dinner parties at the United Nations, and felt the People's Republic was where the action was, where one-fourth of the world's population lived.

To say that I was speechless is an understatement. Evidently

President Ford told George he would give him that job, but he must be ready to stay for two years. The more George talked, the more excited I got. I missed being with George—he had traveled a great deal as RNC chairman—and the thought of having him to myself sounded like the answer to my prayers.

Besides that, it was a new adventure for us both. I remember as a little girl digging in the sand on the beach and being told that if we kept digging, we'd go right through the earth and come out in China. And there we would find little Chinese boys and girls digging in the sand trying to find the United States. That beach in Rye, New York, was the closest I ever thought I'd get to China!

The United States and the People's Republic of China had a special relationship in 1974. Although Richard Nixon had opened the door a crack on his historic visit in 1972, we did not have formal diplomatic ties. There was no embassy, but a liaison office. George's title would be Chief of the U.S. Liaison Office to the People's Republic of China.

As we sat with our children on the porch of the gray house* in Kennebunkport, George told them he had a new job, but they had to guess what it was. We would still be on that porch if George hadn't given them some heavy hints!

I was so grateful that Doro, who was fifteen, already had decided on her own to go to boarding school. At first, I didn't want her to go away—she was my baby! But now it was for the best, because there were no classes for foreign children her age in China. I was glad she was going to boarding school because she wanted to, not because she had to.

That fall was very busy. We got Doro and the boys ready for school. I studied very basic Chinese language at the State Department's Foreign Language School, and we were briefed by the State Department. The Chinese based in Washington gave us a party, and we gave them a party. And then there was the packing. We sent two shipments, one by sea and one by air.

Earlier, George had broken the news to me that C. Fred could not go to China. I asked the State Department people, and they said there were American dogs in China. Then I asked the Chinese, and they said there were many foreign dogs there. That settled it—C. Fred was

---

* I'm referring to a house that we owned for about ten years. We did not buy Walker's Point, our current residence in Kennebunkport, until 1980.

going! I shipped seventeen cases of his special dog food—then George had to let him go; he had too big an investment in dog food not to. We never regretted taking him. There were lonely times, and both George and I enjoyed curling up with a good book and C. Fred at our side.

Finally, in early October, the big day came. George and I took off for China via Alaska and Japan. C. Fred, who had traveled many times to Maine in the bowels of an airplane, was in his little box in the luggage compartment. I walked him in Alaska on the tarmac and never saw him again until he was delivered to me in China.

In Japan, we were met by our ambassador and his wife, dear friends, Marie and Jim Hodgson. We were told that C. Fred was to go into quarantine while we were there, but not to worry, he would be exercised daily. We spent two wonderful days in Japan and then flew off to Beijing,* stopping briefly in Shanghai.

We had read in all the books about the great cleanup in China and the fact that we would see no insects. The first thing I saw in Shanghai was a fly—but I must admit I saw very few after that first stop. In Shanghai we were isolated from the Chinese people in a special room until we flew on to Beijing. This was a sign of things to come.

George had told the liaison office staff not to come to the airport, but he invited them instead to come to a reception at our residence— within an hour of our arrival! Who but George Bush would have done that, but it was just the right thing to do. So over they came with their wives and children—fifty-three in all. They were an amazing, brave little army of Americans. Most of them had come with David Bruce, George's distinguished predecessor, to open the office. Now many of them were leaving, moving onward with their careers. C. Fred was brought in with our luggage, and you have never seen a happier little dog. After looking at him and his cage, I suspected that he had spent five days locked up without any care. He was very dirty in an equally dirty cage and soon had the first of many baths in China.

After the reception, George and I had dinner at the home of John Holdridge, the deputy chief of mission, and his wife, Martha. They had an apartment in one of the buildings set aside for foreigners. Mr. Guo, our driver, honking the horn the whole way, wove through a

---

* Beijing was then still spelled Peking, but for the sake of consistency, except in diary entries, I'll call it Beijing.

crowded, poorly lit street, barely missing pedestrians and people on bicycles. George said to me, "You studied Chinese. For heaven's sake, tell him to put on his headlights. We're going to hit somebody." My two months of Chinese didn't teach me to say anything even close. We quickly told the Holdridges of our hair-raising drive, and they told us it was against the law to use headlights. Everyone in China drove with one hand on the horn and one foot on the brake.

John and Martha were real pros. I was so lucky to have this bright woman as a friend and a guide. They went on to a brilliant career with the State Department.

Our residence and George's office were inside the same, small compound. We had an apartment upstairs consisting of a large sitting room/dining room, four bedrooms, and two enormous baths. The toilets had "The Victory" written in English on their sides. The Chinese tend to name all their goods, but sometimes you wonder just how they think these names up.

The staff consisted of Mr. Yen, the head of our household; the number two, Mr. Chen; two ladies who did the dusting and ironing; and two cooks. Not one spoke a word of English. Thank heavens Mr. Yen was replaced by Mr. Wang after several weeks. He was a fine young man who spoke some English. He was also politically very correct—he always carefully touted the party line. The cooks were excellent, although the one who knew how to cook Western food didn't do it very well, so George and I ate Chinese food and loved it. The first time we ate in our upstairs dining room, we had a beautiful meal. I think the cooks were trying to please us and show off. At one point we were served some delicacy that almost did us in: rubbery, gray-looking things about two inches long with slippery-looking spikes all over them. George and I debated what to do with them. Should we eat them so that we wouldn't hurt their feelings? Should we flush them down the toilet when the cook was out of the room? After much discussion, George said that we better just leave them on our plates so they wouldn't think we liked them and serve them again. We later learned they were sea slugs, or sea cucumbers, and the Chinese believe they are a great treat. Whenever we had Chinese guests, our chef insisted we serve them. To add insult to injury, sea slugs cost $25 a pound. When we were served them at banquets, we bit the bullet and ate them.

Although we ate what seemed like a lot of food, we both lost weight. I believe that was because the Chinese eat a low-fat diet and no dairy products, which only made sense since they had no refrigerators or iceboxes. We did have delicious yogurt and fresh milk delivered to our residence daily. The yogurt came in blue Chinese jars, and the unhomogenized milk came in bottles just like we used to have in the United States in the 1920s and 1930s.

The household staff arrived at eight A.M. and left at four P.M., unless we had a party in the evening, and then they were paid overtime. The Chinese prided themselves—in fact, boasted—about having no unemployment. Judging from our household, we could see why. They had two or three people doing something one person could have done. As head of the household, only Mr. Wang had any incentive to work hard and see that the job was well done. The cooks worked hard, but only prepared one meal a day. The rest did the minimum. We heard story after story about three people vacuuming at the Peking Hotel: one to plug the machine in, one to turn it on, and one to push the darn thing. I know for a fact that when I went to the government bank to cash a check, two people made the calculation on abacuses. The result was passed on to two other people who counted out the money and passed it to me. And peering over all of this was a supervisor.

The household staff rode bikes to work from great distances and through all kinds of weather. Several days a week after work, they all had to attend block meetings where they heard "the party line."

The Chinese were bombarded with propaganda wherever they looked and wherever they went. There were billboards that sent some pretty strong and strange messages: DIG TUNNELS DEEP, STORE GRAIN EVERYWHERE AND NEVER SEEK HEGEMONY. Sometimes they said charming things: BEWARE OF THE IMPERIALIST DOGS WHO INVADED VIETNAM. Since George and I did not read Chinese, the signs looked rather pretty to us.

The propaganda continued on trains, parks, and often on the streets. A loud, shrill voice would come bellowing out of microphones placed high on light posts, exhorting people to work hard for the Chairman. The first week we were in Beijing we went to the Western Hills for a long walk with the Holdridges. When we were close to the top, the loudspeaker came on and really shocked us. You just can't get away from it. Evidently, a little boy quite far down the path felt the same way: He put his fingers in his ears.

It didn't take us long to fall into a routine. George, C. Fred, and I awakened at six o'clock or so. One of us walked the dog and picked up the yogurt. That was breakfast. We listened to the Voice of America, which drifted in and out, and sometimes BBC. That was the most frustrating experience. We would hear: "Today, tragedy hit . . . [fade out] . . . this well-known American was beloved by one and all." We would worry until George saw the cables, hoping it wasn't one of our friends. When something bad did happen, we would get phone calls. I especially remember when our former next-door neighbor and friend, Congressman Jerry Pettis, was killed in an airplane crash, and we felt bad for his wife, Shirley. And when a good friend of our children's, Lisa Rimmer, was killed in a car accident, how we ached for them. Those were the times when home seemed far, far away.

George walked over to the office around seven-thirty. He came home at eleven A.M. for our Chinese lesson with Mrs. Tang, whom we liked very much. Like so many Chinese, she had a warm personality and a good sense of humor. Half our lessons were spent laughing at each other's terrible accents and mistakes.

We had lunch right after our lesson, then George went back to the office. If we weren't going out to one of many marvelous restaurants, the cooks left our dinner in a thermos. We might have soup, hard-boiled eggs, and sliced bread. We would spend the evening reading unending books about the history of this massive country, or George would read cables from home.

Every night I set out about ten P.M. with C. Fred on a leash and walked around several large blocks. I was never afraid. We walked by the embassies of Cuba, North Vietnam, Romania, Great Britain, Egypt, and others. Incidentally, all of the embassies had People's Liberation Army guards outside their gates. Never in fourteen months did those bright-looking young men ever relax, smile, or speak to us. In fact, no one did. There was a constant swishing on the streets of the bicycles going silently by all night long. An occasional truck or car went by. There were absolutely no privately owned Chinese cars in the country when we lived there.

But we would get lots of looks—all at C. Fred. There were dogs in the country, but not many. In the 1950s, the Chinese had killed most of the dogs because they were considered scavengers and thieves, stealing food from the people. The Chinese especially had never seen a dog like C. Fred, who had beautiful blond curls. Sometimes we would hear them say something that sounded like "mao." We realized they thought poor C. Fred was a cat—an insult he found unbearable. I learned to say in Chinese: *"Ni bu pa. Ta shi shau go. Ta bu yau ren."* ("Don't be afraid. He's a little dog. He doesn't bite people.")

In the spring, we would see a lovely sight on our evening walks: young men and women standing close together in the park, sometimes holding hands. The need to have a little privacy must have been intense.

The first full day we were in China, George took me to the Friendship Store, where foreigners and high-ranking Chinese shopped. We bought two "Flying Pigeon" bicycles. As Beijing is flat as a pancake, it is the only way to go. I was also lucky enough to find a new friend named Lois Ruge, an American married to a German reporter. She not only played tennis, but had taught herself Chinese and knew Beijing like the back of her hand. We played tennis and explored the city on our bikes. She made my life so much happier. I would retrace our bike trips with George on his afternoons off. We would take our bikes to the Forbidden City or the old theater district to browse through shops or markets. We would park our bikes and some very old lady would give us two wooden tags with the same number. One went on the bike and one you kept. I often wondered as we rode along with hundreds of Chinese if we were the only people riding for fun. I'm sure they thought we were crazy.

One thing I noticed as I rode around Beijing: There weren't many white-headed people around. I asked the wonderful beauty parlor man if there was something in the water or diet that kept their hair from turning white. He laughed and told me there was "something in a bottle that kept them from going white." He went on to say that "one bottle serves all," meaning every head in China was black and there were lots of dyed heads around. That really surprised me, for this was in the days when everybody looked alike in baggy Mao suits. Thank heavens—they were human.

George rapidly found people to play tennis with and had games with the Chinese at the International Club. It was their job to play with us, and it was also a rare opportunity to mix with the Chinese. The ambassador from Canada played fairly well, but George was the best among the diplomats.

On Sundays, George and I attended church above the old Bible Society Building. We loved that dear church. There were only seven

Chinese who attended, three of whom had been pastors in other Protestant churches in the old days before the Communist takeover. The
service was held in Chinese, but we all had our own Bibles and could
for the most part follow the service. I especially loved the hymns. We
all shouted out our songs in our own language—French, English, and
Chinese. With the exception of Easter, when the church was packed,
we were a small army of Christian soldiers, maybe twenty on a good
Sunday.

In the summer of 1975, Doro was christened in that little church
in the most beautiful service. Due to deaths, politics, long distances,
and floods (literally), her baptism had been put off four times. This was
hard to explain to ourselves, much less the Chinese. So Doro became
the first American to be baptized in China since 1949. Marvin stood
in as a proxy for her godparents, Spike Heminway and Mildred Kerr.

We revisited our church on a trip back in 1989, when George was
president. The congregation had moved into a big church and was
crowded with Chinese people who even stood in the street. It was an
emotional homecoming.

And as incredible as this would have seemed during our China
days, our three ministers from that church visited us at the White
House. We all certainly had come a long, long way.

One of the decisions George made soon after our arrival was that
we should socialize with the Chinese as much as possible. Up until
then it had been U.S. policy not to attend the various National Day
receptions, since we did not have formal diplomatic relations. George
disagreed, feeling that any contact we had with the Chinese—and
representatives from Third World countries—was important. He felt
we should not isolate ourselves. The first reception we attended was
given by the Algerians in the old section of the Peking Hotel. We
created quite a stir when we walked in.

To describe this reception is to describe them all. The reception
had four waves. Wave number one was a group of sixteen chairs which
remained unoccupied until the top Chinese guests appeared. The
minute they did, our hosts stepped out of the receiving line and sat
down in the chairs, alternating every other one with the eight Chinese.
The most enormous amounts of food were served and consumed.

Wave number two consisted of diplomats and ambassadorial
rank, and wave number three were diplomats of lesser rank (like us).
Waves number two and number three watched the action of wave

number one, with everyone analyzing how high the Algerians rated, based on the rank of the Chinese who had shown up. Wave number four was the most interesting. In marched a large group of Chinese who looked like a rent-a-crowd. In the back of the room were forty food-filled tables. The Chinese immediately surrounded the tables and did some serious eating. We tried to talk to them, but they did not come to talk. They came to eat.

Our receptions were not too much better. We gave many for visiting American delegations, and George worked out a system where the Americans came early so they could ask us questions and tell us a little about home. Then the Chinese would appear and it was business as usual.

We also gave many receptions for various Chinese groups who were headed for the United States. In our first month we had back-to-back receptions for the Chinese Plant Photosynthesis Study Group and the Pharmacological Theory Study Group of the Chinese Medical Association. If these men spoke English, I might have found it pretty heavy sledding. But since they didn't, you can imagine what fun it was.

How we loved our "responsible person," Mr. Wang. One evening after a deadly reception for two groups going to the United States—the Chinese Solid Physics Investigation Group and the Chinese Art Delegation—I spoke to Mr. Wang. First, I told him the food was beautifully presented. But didn't he think we had just a few too many canapés? The table had been loaded with food and, although our guests ate and ate, we had lots of food left over. Mr. Wang thought over my suggestion of "a few too many canapés" and came back with "No, I think we just had too few guests." I couldn't argue with that.

When we first got to China, our colleagues told George the Chinese accepted only one out of ten invitations. So George, the great entertainer, thought up a million reasons to invite them to the residence, so they actually ended up coming over quite a bit. Our diplomatic corps colleagues, not knowing George's trick, complained about the number of times we had the Chinese.

⟳ We barely had arrived in the country when it was time to get ready for a visit from Henry Kissinger. A trip by Henry Kissinger was a thing of wonder. He traveled with an enormous staff, and both he and they were very demanding. He is a brilliant man with a large self-proclaimed ego, and therefore one put up with some nonsense. He also was and is very entertaining and great fun to be around.

He came three times while we were in China. Later, when George visited foreign countries as the vice president or president, he kept the Kissinger demands in mind and tried to make it easy on our embassies.

On the first trip Henry brought not only Nancy, but also his two very attractive and bright children, David and Elizabeth. Nancy is a fascinating woman—such a series of contrasts. When we visited a hospital or commune, followed by her large press contingent, she certainly did not look the part in her long mink coat, glamorous hairstyle, constant cigarette smoking, and very bored look. When we got the inevitable lecture on productivity of the commune, always ending with the glories of Chairman Mao—the "line"—Nancy would look up and ask the most intelligent questions. She was clearly very interested and interesting.

During our commune visit we saw a dairy farm, and I was appalled to see their milk cows had horns. We city mice in Rye, New York, did not know our farmers dehorn their milk cows so they won't get hurt or hurt each other. I was really proud of Nancy, for while we were viewing the cows, with the TV cameras whirring away, we saw a number of them being mounted. Nancy never flicked an eyelash. That's savoir faire. We finally got to the last part of the briefing—the cows who were producing. The Chinese told us their cows were such good producers that they had to be milked three times a day. I have never seen such full bags. Several of the poor old girls were literally on their knees. I wouldn't put it above the Chinese to have put off milking those poor cows just to prove they had upped productivity. Every place we visited, whether it was the engine factory in Harbin, the Peking Duck farm outside Beijing, or the rug factory in Tientsin, they all had increased productivity thanks to the glorious leadership of Chairman Mao.

To our great pleasure, the Kissinger family joined us for Thanksgiving lunch. We had not been there long enough for a turkey to arrive, so we pretended the chicken course was a turkey. It was a happy lunch, even for C. Fred. For every five candied nuts Secretary Kissinger ate, he gave C. Fred one. George teased me about that, saying I would kill him if he did that. True. If poor C. Fred were here today, he would tell you he was always on a diet.

Several things happened during the Kissinger visit that confirmed our suspicions we were being spied on. Our first week there, I

Life has barely begun, age one.
(Family photo)

PUBLIC SCHOOL MILTON POINT N.Y.

I guess they forgot to tell us to smile. I'm the chubby little girl standing in the middle, with the white Peter Pan collar. (Family photo)

One of my favorite pastimes—
eating. I'm at the far left,
with Susan Kennedy, Wease
McDowell, and Shirley Ayres.

One of the first dogs in my
life, Sandy. My mother sent
George a copy of this photo
when he was in the Navy.
(Family photo)

Playacting with friends Posy
Morgan and Kate Siedle. I'm
on the far left. (Family photo)

With Father and Mother on
my wedding day, January 6,
1945. (Family photo)

The bride and groom.
(Family photo)

With Yale housemates Jack and Patty
Caulkins and David Grimes. Patty's
chocolate chip cookie recipe was
destined to become famous.
(Family photo)

Easter 1948 with my family. Standing
behind the couch are my brothers Jim
and Scott. Sitting on the couch are,
from left, George, me holding George
W., Mother, Daddy, my sister Martha,
and her husband, Walt Rafferty, with
their daughter, Sharon. (Family photo)

This was taken not too long
after we moved to Midland,
Texas. (Family photo)

Holding Robin, with George W.,
October 1950. (Family photo)

Robin with her daddy, 1953.
(Family photo)

Playing golf with the world's best in-laws, Dorothy and Prescott Bush.
(Family photo)

George in his very first political campaign, the 1964 Texas Senate race. With him is our good friend Will Farish. (Family photo)

The boys think they're being funny, imitating their father on the campaign trail, 1966. From left: Doro, George, Jeb, Marvin, George W., Neal, and me. (Family photo)

The Ambassador to the United Nations and
Mrs. Bush. (Family photo)

The Great Wall of China.
(Family photo)

In Tibet in the fall of 1977,
drinking the horrid tea. I love
the child peering at us from
behind the quilt.
(Family photo)

Welcoming the hostages home from Iran, January 27, 1981. Tip O'Neill is on the far right. (White House photo)

Something certain has Lady Bird Johnson and me tickled, September 1981. (White House pho

Our dinner with the Ceauşescus in Romania, September 1983. Not exactly what you would call a cozy evening. (White House photo)

Sneaking in a nap during the 1984 campaign. (White House photo)

Doing a little garden wc
Kennebunkport while ta
a break from the 1988
campaign. (David Valde

The Reagans meet our
grandchildren George P.,
Noelle, and Jebby as they leave
the 1988 Republican National
Convention and we arrive.
(White House photo)

Addressing the 1988
Republican Convention.
(White House photo)

Kicking off the inauguration festivities with the Quayles. (White House photo)

Granddaughter Barbara Bush shares a secret during the inaugural gala, while twin sister, Jenna, and Gampy watch. (David Valdez)

I get the first kis[s] the new Presiden[t] the United State[s] (Susan Biddle)

Walking the parade route. You can tell it was cold and windy. (David Valdez)

Would you have gues[sed] the shoes underneath $29? (Mike Sargent)

Everybody wanted their picture taken on the Lincoln bed. Here George does the honors for then Congressman Edward Madigan of Illinois and his wife, Evelyn. He later became secretary of agriculture. (Mike Sargent)

Holding an AIDS patient at Grandma's House in Washington, D.C., March 1989. Looking on are the heart and soul of Grandma's House, Joan McCarley and Debbie Tate. The baby died a few weeks later. (Carol Powers)

Watching the
President give a [
conference from t
Ushers' Office in
the White House
(Carol Powers)

I was thrilled to be honored
along with George and (not
pictured) President François
Mitterrand and Chancellor
Helmut Kohl at Boston
University's commencement in
1989. (Carol Powers)

The Harlem Boys
Choir lights up t
East Room. Betty
is sitting behind
(Carol Powers)

One of my best friends, Andy Stewart. What you don't see are all the people gathered for her surprise birthday party on May 9, 1989. (Carol Powers)

Doing a little play-by-play during a Texas Rangers baseball game.
(Carol Powers)

Millie and the childre[n]
on the South Lawn o[f]
the White House[.]
(Mike Sargen[t]

George and Ranger bonded
early on. (Carol Powers)

could tell that one of the household staff, because of the information he knew, had read a note on my desk from George. That did not worry me, but it helped me decide not to keep a diary. So for the fourteen months we lived there, I wrote long letters home to our families and several friends and sent them in the diplomatic pouch, being careful to never leave them sitting around. These letters were saved for me.

But during the Kissingers' stay, the spying was even more evident. Nancy told me she had said to Henry one afternoon in their room, "I wish the Chinese would let the children be in the car with us. It would be more relaxing, and we are not seeing them enough." When they went out for dinner that evening, the Chinese greeted them with: "We have put David and Elizabeth in the car with you. We thought you might enjoy that."

George and I also were staying in guest quarters near the Kissingers, to cut down on the commuting time. The thoughtful Chinese had supplied our rooms with absolutely everything a person could want: slippers, bathrobes, every kind of nail polish made in China, facial creams, perfume, toothbrush, toothpaste, face powders, and on and on. The tables were filled with cigarettes, matches, candies, nuts, fruits, postcards, writing paper, ink, and stamps. While waiting for the next event, I sat down to write some postcards. I mentioned the one thing they had forgotten was glue to affix the stamps to the cards. When we returned to our rooms after the event, there was the glue!

Another time, while riding my bike with Lois, I left my glasses in one of the many shops we had visited. I had no idea which one. My glasses were back at the residence before I was.

When the Kissingers went home, I left with them to be with our children for Christmas. Although this was planned for months, I was heartsick. I had never been so far away from George and could hardly stand saying good-bye to him. On the other hand, we both missed our children, and George could not leave the post so soon after arriving. So I went without him, spent a day or two in Washington, and then went to Houston to check on our newlyweds, Jeb and Columba. Friends called from all over, and many invited me out. I especially remember a lunch with Rogers Morton, the Secretary of the Interior, who invited me to have lunch in his private dining room. I thought he wanted to hear all about living in China. But he showed no interest and led the conversation toward politics. In the course of talking, it came out that George had written Rogers and asked him to please give me a call. He told him that we had never been apart for Christmas or for such a long time. It also turned out that George had written all those nice people who had invited me for meals, the theater, and so on. And here I thought I was incredibly popular!

George also had written our children: "Take care of your mother at Christmas. If she seems down once in a while, hold out your hand to her. Make her very happy . . ." There has never been a nicer, more thoughtful man.

Meanwhile, George's mother and his Aunt Margie Clement went to stay with him for Christmas. They had a wonderful visit and wowed everybody. Dotty Bush, at seventy-three, rode my Flying Pigeon all over Beijing. George took them on a trip south to Nanking, among other places.

When the children went back to school, I went back to China. We had our first of many, many houseguests, Neil and Anne Mallon. Everybody wanted to come to China. It was all so new and exciting. But in all honesty, it was easier to get a dog into the country than a person. One could come only if invited by the ambassador to stay in his residence. So from the Mallons on, we had wall-to-wall houseguests, and we loved it.

Back in the States, Don Rhodes helped people get their visas and arrange their trips. He must have told people we needed cheese and tennis balls. Well, that was true—but not for long. Soon, we were up to our elbows in both. It made us pretty popular with our diplomat friends from other countries who needed either or both.

There were certain things you had to show your houseguests, such as the wonderful Forbidden City. To do the city justice, you really needed several visits. I went so many times that I took to sitting on a wall in a lovely sunny spot and reading Chinese history or just people-watching while our guests toured. The Forbidden City has to be the most fascinating, most beautiful, and the largest museum in the exact middle of a city in the world. Once, when I told an exhausted guest that it covered 250 acres and included 9,000 rooms, I quickly added that all the rooms weren't open. I overheard her say to her husband, "Thank God, I thought she was going to make us walk through them all." My enthusiasm apparently had outlasted her feet.

The ceremonial palaces were spectacular. I found the little ones where the empresses and the concubines lived the most interesting. Some of them were filled with period furniture; others were little

museums that housed jades, jewels, embroidered costumes, and porcelains. They also had marvelous gardens filled with tree peonies,
lilacs, and fruit trees, depending on the season. The pomegranate
plants in huge pots are a very clear memory.

But I especially remember the people. The Chinese walked around
the Forbidden City staring not only at the signs but also at the
Westerners—sometimes two feet from your face. There is no Sunday
"day off" in China, so one-seventh of the people are off every day,
walking through the parks and, for a few pennies, around the Forbidden City or the Temple of Heaven.

Another great favorite and a must-see was the beautiful Summer
Palace. It was about twenty minutes out of the city, close to the
Western Hills. In the winter the lake froze, and people ice-skated.

And, of course, there was the Great Wall of China, which was
about forty minutes out of town. Our favorite thing to do was to go to
the Great Wall and stop on our way home for a picnic at the Ming
Tombs. I loved this, for we could take Freddy with us. He would sit in
the car with Mr. Guo while we charged up the Wall. It was quite a hike
and sometimes scary as the angles are so steep. Our guests usually went
up the left side, which was steeper, but gave a much better view. The
wall is about sixteen feet across with a four-foot stone wall on each side.
There are stopping places along the way where you can get some great
pictures. The guests I remember with the greatest affection were those
who did not carry too much luggage in the way of cameras and other
equipment. I remember one houseguest who insisted on wearing high
heels up the Great Wall as I was to take their Christmas picture at the
top. George and I were fairly amused to see when their card arrived I had
cut the picture off at her knees—not on purpose.

How I loved the tombs. With Freddy on a long leash, we would
walk by the famous Avenue of the Animals—glorious statues of huge
animals, seated and standing, and wise men or guardians who lined the
road. This was a great "photo op" for our guests. We'd climb back into
the car and drive to the only tomb that had been excavated, the Ding
Ling. (Honest, that is what it was called. *Ling* means "tomb" in Chinese.) That was where all the tourists went. First we would explore this
wonderful tomb, visit the museum, and see the artifacts buried with the
emperor. Next, we would go off to one of the other twelve tombs that
had not been touched. Many times broken pieces of tile from a fallen
altar or the tomb would just be lying around on the ground. One of our

more famous houseguests went out to the tombs and brought back some large pieces of the tile. This was reported to me, and I hardly knew what to do. So at lunch, I made up an awful story of the British houseguest who was stopped at the airport for trying to carry out some antiquities—to be exact, pieces of a monument. I went into detail of how embarrassing this had been and just how long the Chinese had detained him. After the guest left, we found a bag of the yellow tiles in the guest room, and I sneaked them back to the tombs.

All our guests wanted to visit schools, communes, and one of the beautiful areas of China outside Beijing. Some got to go, and some didn't. We had a twenty-mile limit as to where we could travel without permission, and sometimes I think the Chinese decided who could travel and who couldn't on a whim.

Even the Chinese could not travel without passes, and there were checkpoints at every village. That's how you controlled 800 million people. (Today, their population is estimated at 1.2 billion.) They were taking no chances after the violence and upheaval of the Cultural Revolution.

Pat Moynihan and two of his children came to visit on his way home from his ambassador's post in India. Pat is a fascinating man and very good company. One afternoon, George invited our little embassy family to come hear Pat tell us about India. I remember two things about his talk. He spoke exactly fifty-five minutes, the length of a college class, and he felt very strongly our foreign policy was ignoring India and that was a mistake.

One morning during Pat's stay we went to visit a Revolutionary Street Committee. Among the many things we did there was visit a home where there was a young teenage girl about Maura Moynihan's age. The two girls quickly got to be friends and ended up holding hands as they sat side by side on the bed. They did not speak the same language, but they certainly communicated. They examined each other's clothes and discovered they had the same socks. They giggled over the bulge under the Chinese girl's socks—long winter underwear. It looked homemade and very warm. On looking around, I found that everyone had a bulge under their socks. No wonder I was freezing. The two girls from such different backgrounds sitting there holding hands was very sweet.

We also visited a schoolroom that day. Quoting from a letter written home:

We visited a nursery where there were children up to the age of 3. The room was divided in half. One half was a raised platform covered with a blanket and had a railing to keep the babies from falling—rather like a giant playpen. Tucked in that nursery were about 20 babies and three old crones, probably my age. The other part of the room had a few baby cribs with sleeping babies, or babies nursing on mothers who had rushed in from the fields. When we walked in, several of the older babies were standing at the railing and applauded. To save time, let me just say that we were applauded over and over again.

We went on to a kindergarten where about 35 children, ages 3 to 5, were sitting in the barest room on three crude long benches about 6 inches from the ground. There were two young teachers and absolutely no teaching props. Up they jumped, applauded, and then a tiny little thing with her hair in two black pony tails said something like our "a one and a two" and all 35 belted out a song that would have done Judy Garland proud . . . when she was 16! You have never seen anything like it. Then the little leader sang an unending song about a happy little worker and the glories of the Chairman, and we were dragged away from those lovely looking children. Their teeth are good, their smiles broad. You can't fake that.

We visited several more classes that morning and it was more of the same. The art class was made up of 40 little fourth-graders copying line for line a picture drawn on the blackboard of a happy little worker tilling the fields for Chairman Mao.

When we got home Pat Moynihan said the school visit depressed and frightened him.

It was a depressing morning, but old China hands will tell you that these same children would not have even been in school 25 years ago.

At Easter, our dear friends John and Betty Rhodes—John was Minority Leader in the House—came on a trip with the Leader of the House, Carl Albert, and his wife, Mary. It's no secret Carl had a drinking problem in those days, which I understand he overcame.

More power to him. At a banquet for him and his party, Carl argued with the Chinese and was really insulting. At one time during the evening he was told he would meet the next day with the foreign minister. This was not a high-enough ranking official for Carl, and he explained to the Chinese that the whole U.S. government was controlled by the Congress and that made him one of the most important men in the country. What a frightening thought! He went on to say that he should be seeing some "big" Chinese leaders. (I guess they believed him: He saw Vice Premier Deng Xiaoping the next day.) As the toasts went on, his mood shifted and he was soon ignoring the high-ranking Chinese and flirting outrageously with Nancy Tang, the charismatic interpreter who became well-known during the Nixon visit. You could tell she was very embarrassed. (Having said that, I should say that Carl and Mary are dear friends, and Carl subsequently overcame his drinking problem. He served his country with great distinction, and we respect him very much.)

Both couples stayed in the former Indian Embassy in the old Legation Quarters, which the Chinese had reclaimed and turned into offices or guest houses. Looking at old maps of the city, it was easy to see why these places had irritated the Chinese. The foreign community had made its own rules and acted as though the natives were visitors, keeping them out of large sections of the city. That probably explains why when we lived there, the foreign embassies were surrounded by Chinese apartments and hovels. Yet, the Chinese were careful to never let us know where they lived or let our children play together.

⁓ Weather-wise, we thought we were the best prepared people to live in Beijing. It is hot and humid in the summer—the so-called rainy season—and cold and dry and dusty in the winter and spring. It sounded very much like Houston and Midland to me. But then spring arrived and I realized even I wasn't prepared for this. The Chinese pulled out all their grass to keep down the insect population. But it also created a big dust problem. Then you add a cold wind from the Gobi Desert, and you are talking dust storms beyond anything Midland ever dreamed about. It was really bad. We could not keep clean, and poor old golden Freddy became a gray dog. He had more baths than any dog ever had to suffer, but he was our bedmate and we had to draw the line someplace.

Shortly after Easter we went to Canton to visit the Trade Fair and then went on into Hong Kong. It was exactly like going from a black-and-white movie into Technicolor. We returned to China on the famous train that drops you at the bridge at the border. You detrain, walk across the bridge, go through a checkpoint, and climb on the next train. For years this was the only way you could enter Red China, and it was dramatic. As we were crossing into the People's Republic, we could hear singing voices and, "just by chance," there was China's greatest asset: schoolchildren marching home for lunch being led by a child carrying a red banner. They all belted out a welcoming song. A lot of poverty and broken windows were disguised by these precious little children.

Both trains were comfortable, and the roadbeds very smooth. But the bathrooms on both cars were beyond belief. Really bad. All through the station we were followed by the loud singing and music of the revolutionary opera at a very high pitch. Much to everybody's horror, it was piped into the train as well. The next hour and a half was spent viewing the most beautiful truck gardens, rice paddies, tree-planting and irrigation projects, and spotless little compounds. I was a little cynical as everyone we saw was really hustling. This was just not true elsewhere. As there were only two trains a day coming from the border, I wondered if the Chinese didn't pick up the pace just a little around train time.

Marvin was going to graduate from high school that spring, and as the date drew nearer, I got bluer. Marv understood it was a long way, and he and his brothers and sister were coming to China in June. Yet, George and I were having a problem with letting him graduate without one of us being there. I can't tell you how happy I was when George said I must go home for a week and surprise him. Don Rhodes told Marvin to go to the airport to meet a good friend of ours. I walked right by both him and Neil, who were scanning faces for our friend. Suddenly I heard, "Mom, what are you doing here!?"

The children and I left for China about the same time, but I flew back as I came, and they took the slow route: first to Houston to see Jeb and Colu, and then on to Hawaii for a day or two, then finally Beijing.

We had a great time exploring China together. We all had bikes. The children thought the public baths smelled and that some of the food was "gross." I'm afraid I had romanticized just a little. I especially remember one day when we rode our bikes through a commune, on our way to the Summer Palace. Those loudspeakers were blasting away at the happy little workers in the fields. George drove out to meet us and treated us to the best lunch at "The Pavilion for Listening to Orioles." Either the eighteen-mile ride out had gotten to Doro or she just wanted her father to herself, for she tucked her bike in the trunk of his car and rode back to town with him.

One evening we drove out to the Ming Tombs and had a picnic at the Mao Ling, a lovely old fallen-down tomb. The diplomatic choral group sang before and after dinner to about one hundred friends tucked here and there among the ruins. It was lovely as the sun set, with the Ming Temple set back among the pines. A dear young Mexican couple ended the evening by singing some plaintive Mexican songs, and we all hummed along. It was our nicest evening in China, I believe.

George took us all to Beidaihe (called Pietaiho then), a large seaside resort that grew up at the turn of the century for the missionaries and Western diplomats. It is on the Bo Hai Sea, just southwest of Qinhuangdao, a large seaport. We were given villa number 12, which turned out to have four bedrooms and four clean baths, which is not a given in China. The cottage had a large veranda, and a lot of time was spent reading in the lovely wicker furniture for which the town is famous.

George had brought several Frisbees with him, and we all threw them on the beach. The Chinese gathered to watch this and got as close as they could, but would not enter in. So sad.

We had a very nice young man assigned to our house who, we discovered the hard way, slept two feet from our bedroom and bath. We literally could hear him breathing. He also practiced the violin in the bathroom, which had a nice, close, damp quality to it. I think several ladies slept off our courtyard. I saw them several times shoveling coal into a furnace that George thought heated our water.

About fifty feet from our house, between us and the sea, was a twenty-four-hour manned guardhouse. We were ever conscious of being observed. The question was: Are we being guarded or watched?

Young George ran for miles every day until he came to signs that said: NO LOITERERS BEYOND THIS POINT. This translated meant: "This is the beach for our foreign friends" or "No Chinese allowed." The diplomatic world hates being segregated. It's so odd: Before the Communist takeover, the Chinese were not allowed on the beach by the foreigners, and in the 1970s they didn't allow the foreigners to mix with them. Therefore, we are still segregated. We have been told that Beidaihe is now used by the Chinese as a rest place for workers and many of the villas are now owned by factories and communes.

We also took the children to see where the Great Wall rises out of the sea and starts its meandering trip across the north of China for 2,000-plus miles.

On the third of July, we had the usual agonizing reception: Guests stood around until the Chinese arrived and sat in the only chairs and ate; our top-ranking staff talked to theirs; and their rent-a-crowd ate us out of house and home. On the actual Fourth of July, we all were up early, decorating the whole liaison office with red, white, and blue bunting and paper streamers. It was the hottest day, and all day long a storm threatened, but it held off. George had all four Bush children out working, along with the Thayer children. By this time, Harry Thayer, who had worked with George at the United Nations, had replaced John Holdridge as deputy chief of mission at the liaison office. Those great kids manned the hot dog and hamburger stands in the most unbearable heat, and the diplomats came en masse, along with the Chinese, for great American food and fun. George had spent months getting all the right ingredients together for this big day and it was a smashing success. The next morning, the same little army of "volunteers" came back as the cleanup squad.

⌒ Traveling through China was always an adventure. The children and I took off late on the fifth of July for a trip to Nanking, Wuxi, and Shanghai. It was a hot, sweaty but wonderful trip. We visited all the usual things and laughed our way through these marvelous historic cities. We discovered that our Chinese guides usually knew much less of their history than we did. We also discovered that Beijing was China's window to the world, and the quality of life goes downhill outside the capital city.

The Chinese say "Women hold up half of the world." That means that women are equal. I would say their women were equal to men on the ditchdigger level. In 1975 you saw many women laying pipes, sweeping the streets—in fact, doing heavy work. But how many women did you see ruling the country? None. Well, maybe one.

Chairman Mao's wife, Jiang Qing, was said to wield great power at this time.

Family planning in the cities was fairly successful, but less so in the countryside. We were told at a commune that they gave incentives for male and female sterilizations. A woman was offered forty days with pay and extra rice and brown sugar rations. A man was offered fifteen days with pay and no extra rations. You can imagine the family pressure on the woman to have the more serious operation.

George and I and a houseguest, Greg Petersmeyer, who later did a wonderful job heading the Points of Light Foundation for George, and dear Bill Thomas, our economic officer, took a great trip as guests of the Chinese to Dalien, Harbin, and Daqing. The Chinese had created Daqing by arbitrarily picking up people—some with their families and some without—and putting them down in this godforsaken, brutally cold place. The residents told us they could see their families two weeks out of the year.

Our friend Jack Steel from Houston, Bill Thomas's wife, Sarah, and I took a trip to Datong on the northern border and visited the caves and tunnels where they stored grain. This pathetic little underground city would not have withstood a conventional bombing, much less missiles. We went by train and slept together in a tiny compartment. We panicked that a fourth would be put in the car with us, but it didn't happen.

I took another train trip, to Loyang and Sian, with two women who worked in the liaison office. There in Sian, by the old Bell Tower, we saw miles of eighteen-year-olds being lined up to "go to the countryside." We asked our interpreter if they looked forward to that. He said no. They knew they had to go and they also knew most of them would spend the rest of their lives there. They could come back only if they were voted back by their peers—whatever that means.

Out the window of our train we saw carts being pulled by camels, donkeys, oxen, and people. We saw people riding their bikes with terrified, wiggling little pigs tied to the sides—shades of "this little pig went to market . . ."

It was interesting to see how everyone's impressions of China were so different. In May 1975 we had two couples visiting at the same time. One morning, one of the women said to me: "Bar, you know the thing that I notice in China? I don't see the children playing. They seem so sad to me." That very afternoon, the other wife and I were walking home when she said, "Do you know what I find so surprising about China? I didn't expect to see such happy children!" These two ladies saw the exact same places, but through different eyes. Remember that my memories of China are through my eyes.

⤳ In October, George and I took part in one of China's big national celebrations—Liberation Day. (The other big day there is May Day.) Here are parts of a letter written to the children on October 2, 1975:

> Another exciting day or two in our life in the PRC, the 26th Anniversary of the Liberation. For days we have seen activity in the parks. The Temple of Heaven has been closed. Disappointing for our latest houseguests. Our celebration started with an invitation from Chou En-lai to a banquet on September 30th. As we do not attend the banquets for visiting heads of state as our colleagues do on a weekly basis—a welcoming banquet and a farewell banquet—we were really looking forward to the evening. Our buddies dread them for they have little notice and are expected to cancel any other plans, and also because they are seated by protocol and sit with the same people week after week, whether they speak diplomatically or personally or not, and because the speeches are long and very often dull.
>
> We were told to leave a little ahead of time, for on this evening the crowds would be large. George's driver has to be a genius. He maneuvered us through more cars, more people on bikes, more standing pedestrians, more buses than we had seen in our whole stay in the PRC. By the end of our drive we were driving through a human tunnel. We could hear people saying *"Meiguo Ren,"* meaning Americans. We saw nothing but warm, friendly faces or faces filled with curiosity. Thank heavens that we feel absolutely no fear and have no reason to.
>
> How to describe the city? Oh to be a writer, for it was lovely. As we passed the Friendship Store, the International Club and the tall apartments built for foreigners, we got our first hint. The buildings were outlined from head to toe,

from stem to stern, and balconies in-between, with white light bulbs. As Peking is a flat city, these buildings can be seen for miles. The Railroad Station was particularly spectacular as it has twin pagoda-like towers. A plain square building becomes a thing of splendor when draped in white lights. Some of the buildings had gentle swags, some designs around the roof line and some red stars. The Peking Hotel, for instance, went from three rather different, rather ugly sections (one section built by the Russians, one by the French, and finally a tall new Chinese section) to a fairyland building with the two outside sections outlined, and the French middle section covered with swags and designs. It was lovely.

To understand the scope of what we are talking about in Peking, one must know that Tiananmen Square is 98 acres big. On the north, outlined and lighted, is the Gate of Heavenly Peace that leads into the Imperial City and on into the Forbidden City. Chairman Mao's tremendous picture dominates this gate. On the south can be seen the southern gate that is all that is left of the Tartar Wall, a tremendous building that is four or five stories high. It has a lovely roof line. Also on the south is the Marco Polo Shop and several other buildings, all with the bright white light outline. On the east is the National Museum which has not been opened since we have been here. On the west is the Great Hall of the People where we had our banquet. I believe that all the street lights were on when usually only two of three layers are on. The first is a big globe; the second has five globes; and the third—the one they use on special days—has nine globes. Also, there were large characters in red lights. As we can't read Chinese, these look very beautiful, such lovely shapes and all. The five big, and I do mean big, pictures on Tiananmen Square are Chairman Mao facing south, and Lenin, Stalin, Marx and Engels, two on the left and two on the right, facing north. For these few days only, a sixth big picture is put up right in the middle of the southern part of the square, that of Sun Yat-Sen. If this year is like past years, he will disappear in a few days. I still can't understand the great love for him, even though he was the first president of the republic. But he also was the man who tapped Chiang Kai-shek (who opposed the Communist takeover of China) to succeed him.

On to the banquet . . . 4,500 people. There were some tourist delegations in the darndest outfits. Of course some were fine, but some were outrageous. Just because the Chinese aren't dressy does not mean that they aren't the neatest, cleanest people you have ever seen. I was thrilled to hear people in front of us speak French. What a relief. They had on filthy, frayed clothes, tangled hair, tight pants over female rumps, run-down heels on their shoes, dirty toenails showing through their sandals, etc.

Every inch of the room was taken up. There were two orchestras in the balcony instead of the back of the room. We were about three-fourths of the way back and therefore could not see the Head Table guests, as it was not raised. The betting was that the Premier would not attend and he didn't. Deng Xiaoping was the top ranking man. Prince Sihanouk and wife, as visiting Head of State from Cambodia, were the guests of honor.

The room itself cannot be described. It is really tremendous, has spectacular lighting, including TV lights that look like part of the wall decoration when turned off. I counted 27 chandeliers on the three balconies, 90 lights that were three feet across in the three sections of the room under the balconies, and heaven only knows the number of lights in the main center section. The room must be four stories high.

The National Day was a joy. Very much a repeat of May Day. It did seem to me that there were more exhibits, more decorations, many more of the masses let in. We had tickets allowing us to go into eight parks. As I understand it, the Chinese needed tickets to get into a park and certainly we saw many people standing outside the parks watching the foreign guests go in. We went to the Summer Palace in the morning.

We got home at 1 P.M., picked up our lunch, had a quick nap and then rode our bikes down to the parks on either side of the Forbidden City. Many children dancing, acrobats, magicians, stand-up comics, adult ballet and opera singers, plus exhibits galore. We wandered around and made the mistake of staying until 6 P.M. when it suddenly ended. We were two of hundreds of thousands who rode our bikes home. It is quite a sensation to find yourself riding 10, 20 and 30 abreast like that. The worst place is at the street lights. Those little Chinese ladies who ride on men's bikes have trouble getting on and off at the stop. Their feet do not touch and so they fall off and swing on in a very set fashion. We were too tired to ride to the Workers Stadium for more acrobatics last night and that really is sort of dangerous at night in a crowd that size.

All summer long we had seen sunflowers growing on every available inch of space around the hovels and homes. Fall was the season when their heads were cut off and they were put out to dry for the oil from the seed or just for the seeds themselves. They were dried on rooftops, and it looked like a van Gogh painting. It was also the season of harvesting that long, wonderful Chinese cabbage. For a few weeks in the fall, the streets were packed with mule- and horse-pulled wagons, three-wheeled bikes with a platform on the back, hand-pushed wheelbarrows and trucks, all coming in from the countryside filled with cabbage. It was then piled high on the streets before being toted to the different homes, often to be dried on roofs or on a small apartment balcony to be used during the cold winter months. I wondered how much soot and dust they ate along with it.

The pomegranates were on the enormous potted plants in the Forbidden City and the persimmons were ripe at the Temple of Heaven. And the leaves were turning red at the Western Hills. There was a sign that said: DO NOT PICK THE RED LEAVES. And the Chinese came down the hill with their arms filled with red leaves.

      On November 2, George got a "for eyes only" cable asking him to come home and head the CIA. We were riding our bikes home from church when he was notified. What a shock. The CIA! What would our high school and college-age children think? At that time, the CIA was going through a very unpopular period and was highly criticized for abusing its power. We talked it over at length and then decided to call our oldest son, George, and ask him to feel out his brothers and sister very discreetly. He called back and said, "Come home." I often have wondered if George really asked for their opinions or if he just waited a reasonable period of time and called back with his opinion. Let me add that George Bush, the dad, was thrilled. He had the utmost respect for the CIA and the men and women who served so valiantly there. I was torn. I missed the children and home very much, but I was enjoying our China experience. However, I knew it was always smart to leave a place while still wanting to stay.

Before heading home, we had President Ford's visit on our plate. That meant an enormous advance team came for Thanksgiving, which was fun. The trip itself went well, mainly because the Fords are such nice, generous, easy people. The logistics were fascinating, for the President had agents, Betty Ford had agents, Susan Ford had agents, and Henry Kissinger had security. The motorcades often came from different directions and caused traffic jams beyond belief.

Another thing I remember from their visit was how rude our press was to the Chinese. Mrs. Ford and I, accompanied by several high-ranking Chinese women, visited the Forbidden City. The American press pushed and shoved, trying to get at Mrs. Ford. They especially pushed the Chinese out of the way, not realizing their rank since everyone in China dressed alike, regardless of who they were. I was embarrassed.

There were many going-away parties before we left. Because of the isolation from the outside world, there was a special bond among the foreigners who lived in China during that period. I especially remember the Russian ambassador teasing George about his new "spy" job. You're tempted to think of that childish taunt "It takes one to know one!"

On December 10, we left this fabulous, fascinating country with few regrets. We had been privileged to live there, and now we were looking forward to home, a new job, friends, and especially our precious families.

Keeping Secrets

Dear Pres, Buck, Nancy, John,

Pardon the joint message. It occurs to me that my controversial new job may cause concern—if not to you, to some of your kids. No I can't see (5-year old) Billy bitching about the CIA to his peers, but for the older ones, it might not be easy.

I did not seek this controversial job. It came to me—one week ago—short fuse reply.

It's a graveyard for politics, and it is perhaps the toughest job in government right now due to abuses of the past on the one hand, and an effort to weaken our capability on the other. Besides, it's not always a clean and lovely business.

I am convinced it is important.

I know we will be thrust into ugly controversy—my intentions and character will be questioned.

But overriding all this is what I perceive to be a fundamental need for an intelligence capability second to none. It's a tough, mean world and we must stay strong. My year here has given me a chance to think and to observe. We have got to stay strong.

When the cable came in I thought of "Big Dad"—what would he do, what would he tell his kids—I think he would have said, "It's your duty."

It is my duty and I'll do it.

I love you all.

Pop

George wrote this letter to his four siblings from China, explaining how he felt about his new job. As you can see, he expected tough times ahead.

We hadn't been home one week when the Senate confirmation hearings began on George's appointment. I sat and listened and of course was furious at anyone who spoke against him. The final witness was a young man who was a member of the Socialist Workers' Party. The TV lights were turned off, and Senator John Stennis of Mississippi was the only member of the committee who sat through the testimony. In fact, the only people in the room were me, Senator Stennis, George, the witness, and some TV technicians. The young man was against George, and I fumed as I listened to his untrue and irresponsible accusations. Then suddenly I found myself thinking: What a great country we live in. Here is a United States senator giving this man a chance to say exactly what is on his mind. This couldn't happen in China.

During the debate on the Senate floor, Senator Frank Church led the attack against George (really against the CIA); and Texas Senator John Tower led the charge in his favor. Our friends Bill and Janet Steiger went with me to watch the vote. I hated it as "Nay" after "Nay" resounded across the floor. The minute enough votes were cast to confirm George, John Tower turned and gave me a thumbs-up. And a minute later my friend and fellow International Club II member Bethine Church rushed over, gave me a hug, and said that she wanted me to know Frank did not mean it personally. I don't think the average American understands that in Washington you can be friends with your political opponents. Bethine and I remained close, even when she moved back to Idaho after Frank's death.

George was to replace William Colby, who had been a controversial director. However, he and his wife, Barbara, could not have been nicer and even gave us a dinner party before George took over. On January 10, 1976, our much beloved friend and neighbor, Potter Stewart, once again swore George into a new job, this time with President Ford looking on. George also was very pleased that his former boss on the Ways and Means Committee, Wilbur Mills, and his wife, Polly, attended. They had been through their own personal hell, and George insisted they be invited.

The news coverage was something else: *The Washington Post* ran a front-page, above-the-fold picture of me kissing Jerry Ford; *The New*

York Times ran a front-page, above-the-fold picture of me kissing Potter. For months, every time I saw Potter, he sang "I Wonder Who's Kissing Her Now?"

George was thrilled with his new job, despite the fact that the CIA was under fire and morale within "the community" was at an all-time low. There also was a great deal of fear. Richard Welch, the CIA station chief in Greece, had just been assassinated on the front steps of his house. This gentle Greek scholar's cover had been blown, along with many others', by a traitorous, tell-all book written by former CIA agent Philip Agee.

George and I went on a morale-boosting trip to Europe shortly after his confirmation, and security was unbelievably tight. We traveled commercially with an assumed name—I believe we were the "Rushes." When we landed in Munich, Germany, we disembarked before the plane taxied into a ramp and were immediately put into cars and driven to the hotel, skipping Customs. It amused me that after all this secrecy, as we marched into the lobby, we heard loud and clear bellowing across the lobby: "It's the Bushes! Hello there, George Bush." It was Sir George Weidenfeld, a British publisher and the husband of our friend Sandra Payson. So much for all that subterfuge.

Several times we stayed in the private homes of CIA employees because the security was better. Because of Agee's book, the houses had to be heavily guarded. I came to love these courageous people and their brave families, and George came to believe that CIA employees were the most dedicated and brightest in the government. Their main job was to collect information, evaluate it, and pass it on. They certainly did not do all the things you see in cloak-and-dagger spy movies.

Back home, I threw myself into life in Washington. I resumed my volunteer work at the Washington Home, a nursing home where I had worked previously, and especially enjoyed getting to spend time again with my dear little friend Frances Hammond. She had broken her body in a dive into a swimming pool many years before, leaving her a paraplegic, and although every inch of her hurt, she never ever complained. She thought only of others and was an inspiration in courage.

Her one relative was a son who had gone to the Naval Academy and was stationed quite far away. I often took C. Fred to sit on the terrace with Frances. All of the residents loved Freddy. We forget that people in homes miss children and animals, and I'm so glad many institutions today have "pet" days. Anyway, I used to do Frances's fingernails and we'd sit and visit. She had many other friends, but none who loved her more. She remained an important part of my life until she died in November 1983.

I also put together a slide program on China and traveled around the country showing it to civic groups, schools, and churches; at fund-raisers for different charities; and at political gatherings. China was still a "hot" item. I tried to have a fast-moving program with *no* pictures of George, me, the children, or even C. Fred. I wanted to be completely nonpartisan so civic groups would feel comfortable inviting me to speak.

I rejoined my International Club, met with our 90th Club congressional friends, played tennis, entertained many, many houseguests, and kept very busy. Although the children were scattered at various schools and jobs, they came home often to visit.

Yet, I was very depressed, lonely, and unhappy.

It still is not easy to talk about today, and I certainly didn't talk about it then. I felt ashamed. I had a husband whom I adored, the world's greatest children, more friends than I could see—and I was severely depressed. I hid it from everyone, including my closest friends. Everyone but George Bush. He would suggest that I get professional help, and that sent me into deeper gloom. He was working such incredibly long hours at his job, and I swore to myself I would not burden him. Then he would come home, and I would tell him all about it. Night after night George held me weeping in his arms while I tried to explain my feelings. I almost wonder why he didn't leave me. Sometimes the pain was so great, I felt the urge to drive into a tree or an oncoming car. When that happened, I would pull over to the side of the road until I felt okay.

Years later, I did tell my doctor, and he asked why I hadn't sought help. He said that there are several treatments for people with problems like that—in many cases quite easy ones—and it could have been caused by a chemical imbalance.

It seems so simple to me now: I was just the right age, fifty-one years old, for menopause; I could not share in George's job after years of being so involved; and our children were all gone. I was a classic case for depression. My "code" told me that you should not think about self, but others. And yet, there I was, wallowing in self-pity. I knew it was wrong, but couldn't seem to pull out of it. I wish I could pinpoint the day it went away, but I can't. All I know is that after about six months, it just did. I was so lucky.

But I do not consider those miserable six months lost or wasted; I became much more sympathetic of people with emotional problems. I used to think that you could control your emotions, that you just needed to think of others and not yourself. I still think that is one of the secrets to happiness, but I also realize you cannot handle everything alone. And when things go out of control, you should seek help. Certainly if I could do it over again, I would.

While all of this was going on, the 1976 primary season was swirling around us. We were completely out of it, since George's job was not political. I wrote in my diary that spring:

The primaries seem insane at times. The words get so mean and bitter. Then I say to myself, Don't ever complain about a free election. This couldn't happen in China.

On February 24, I wrote in a letter to Mrs. John Sherman Cooper, wife of our ambassador to East Germany:

The Democrats are having a fascinating political season. I wish you could have heard them this morning, the morning after (the New Hampshire Primary), on the tube. (Jimmy) Carter, having come in first, was "elated." (Mo) Udall, having come in second, was "ecstatic." (Birch) Bayh, who came in third, was "joyful." (Fred) Harris, who came in fourth, "couldn't believe the friends he had made." And lastly, Sarge (Shriver) was "overcome by the good feeling he had gotten from all the good people in New Hampshire."

Jerry Ford had his own tough fight with Ronald Reagan in the primaries, and although he won the GOP nomination, he lost in November to Jimmy Carter. A day or two after the election, George said that I better head down to Houston and house-hunt yet again. Typical George; he already had invited guests to a home that didn't exist! The recently widowed King Hussein of Jordan was going to be in Houston for his annual physical in March, and he had accepted George's invitation to dinner.

I looked at about thirty houses and fell in love with one on Indian

Trail. George flew down with me on the first of January to sign the papers—*then* he went to see the house. He could barely hide his shock at discovering that it had no garage and needed to have the kitchen gutted and completely replaced. I found a fantastic man, Bob Wilson, who agreed that he would have the house finished in time for our dinner party, and he did.

That didn't prevent the evening from being a borderline fiasco. First of all, it had to be kept a secret in order not to compromise His Majesty's security. As I made plans for the evening, I kept reading all the things that His Majesty was going to be doing at the exact same time of our party. I would ask George, "Are you sure the King is coming here?" He assured me that he was.

So I hired a caterer, had an instant garden put in our backyard, bought new terrace furniture, had the pool cleaned, and sat back to enjoy the dinner.

George had invited guests from all over the country whom he thought the King might enjoy seeing. Before anyone arrived, the heavens opened up with a fierce storm. My new garden washed right into our clean pool, along with the garden furniture. Meanwhile, the plane from Washington carrying our very important guests, former Vice President Nelson Rockefeller and his wife, Happy, and Ambassador Henry Catto and his wife, Jessica, was circling over our heads, trying to land. Of course His Majesty would appear early. Thank heavens for Jessica's lovely mother, Oveta Culp Hobby, who arrived on time and entertained us. Just to make it a perfect evening, the food was cold, not very tasty, and poorly served. I was talking to Nelson (who had finally arrived an hour late) on my left when I heard a little commotion on my right. I caught Nelson's eye and he said, "Don't look now, Barbara." Sissy that I am, I didn't. The waiter had dropped a steak in the King's lap. His Majesty was very kind, but I'm sure he put it down as an evening to be gotten through.

Although we missed our Washington friends, we loved being home in Houston again. The most exciting thing to happen to us was becoming grandparents: George Prescott Bush had been born in April 1976, and Noelle Lucila Bush was born in July 1977, both to Jeb and Colu, who were living in Houston at the time. How we loved having those two darling little babies around.

I still did some traveling, showing my China slides and raising money for various charities, and George had joined several corporate boards and worked for a bank. Mainly, he traveled around the country making speeches and consulting with friends, laying the groundwork for a presidential race. You could say he was "testing the waters."

At one point during this period George and I found ourselves in a most unusual situation: We were alone. Paula had gone on her month's vacation, and the children were either grown up or away at summer jobs. I must confess it was like a second honeymoon, and we were loving our quiet, relaxed time together.

He went away on an overnight fishing trip with his friend Fred Chambers, and they came home as excited as two little kids, showing off a cooler full of redfish. I told George I would fix it for dinner. Well, I knew nothing about scaling, cleaning, or cooking fish, so I got out *The New York Times Cookbook* and set about following the instructions for baked stuffed redfish.

I chopped, seasoned, and stuffed this awful-looking thing half the afternoon. I set the table with our finest, including candles, and when George came home, I was feeling pretty happy with myself.

The big moment came for our main course, and I had a dreadful time getting the smelly, slippery thing on the platter. George, not knowing I had spent hours on this project, took one look and said with a twinkle in his eye, "You don't think I'm going to eat this sh-t, do you?" I burst into tears. My sense of humor had deserted me.

That was almost twenty years ago, and he has raved over everything I have cooked ever since. That expression has become a password between us that always brings a giggle.

⤳ In the fall of 1977, George and I returned to China as guests of the Chinese government. Also in the delegation were our good friends and George's former business partner Hugh and Betty Liedtke; Dean and Pat Burch; our friend and Texas state Representative Chase Untermeyer; Jim Lilley, who had served with George in China; our friend James Baker, who had just headed President Ford's reelection campaign; and David Broder of *The Washington Post* and his wife, Ann. But the most interesting member of the delegation was Lowell Thomas, the eighty-seven-year-old broadcaster and world traveler, and his new bride, Marianne. (I should note that Susan Baker stayed home with their new baby girl, Mary Bonner Baker, who is George's godchild.)

What a grand trip: Beijing, Chengtu, Chungking, a boat trip

down the Yangtze River through the gorges, and Kweilin. But the highlight was visiting Tibet in the company of Lowell Thomas. In 1949, Lowell and his son were the seventh and eighth Americans to visit this remote country, and for years he was called "the last American out of Tibet." On that journey over the Himalayas, he fell from his horse and broke his hip and had to make a seventeen-day trip by litter to India and safety. China annexed Tibet two years later and closed the door. The next group of Americans to visit was a group headed by former CIA Director and Secretary of Defense James Schlesinger in 1976—and now us. We were told I was the third American woman ever to put foot on Tibetan soil.

We were all so excited about visiting this remote, mountainous country, home to the exiled Dalai Lama. Unfortunately, in my case, that didn't last long. The 12,800-foot altitude of the city of Lhasa was difficult to handle. I wrote in my diary on September 30:

I had such a sick headache that I wanted to die. Dean Burch slept. He is not at all well. Lowell, at 87 years of age, seems to be in better shape than any of us. In the morning we all walked as though we were walking on egg shells, being given oxygen off and on . . . We took off for the Norbu-Linka Park (Pearl Park), the summer palace of the Dalai Lama, 360,000 square meters, built by the 7th Dalai Lama in 1755. . . . We were given a choice of barley beer or Yak butter tea. (The former looked and smelled like urine and the latter like tea with some rancid fat on the top.) Both were nauseating. Our old friend, the sea slug, has appeared again. When feeling well, they are dreadful; sick, they are revolting.

. . . I am beginning to believe Lowell when he says that Tibetans don't bathe all winter long. I just wonder, "Do they bathe in the summer?"

On October 2, I wrote about our visit to the Potola, the Dalai Lama's hilltop palace:

It was a beautiful day and we all set off looking forward to seeing this wonder of wonders that sits on a lone hill dominating this whole city . . . There are 13 floors, 178 meters high—two-thirds as high as the Empire State Building (Lowell's offering). 420 meters east to west, 330 north to south. 130,000 square meters, wooden and stone structure, walls 3 meters thick, built in conformity of the hill. Most ancient and well-preserved building in Tibet, started in the 7th Century.

... The weather in Tibet is crazy. It is cold in the shade, and the sun is the hottest that I have ever felt. I got sunburned. The air—what little there is of it—is the clearest I have ever seen.

... This is the only place that I have ever been in where I felt the people were oppressed. I felt that we were in an occupied country. It is not a comfortable feeling.

As the plane left Tibet, most of the party missed the clear, crisp air. Dean Burch and I got steadily better as the cabin became pressurized, thank heavens. For those who also suffer the same "altitude sickness," I have discovered recently that pills from your doctor, lots of fluids, and moving slowly really do help.

The trip down the Yangtze River was marvelous. One evening George invited Lowell to tell us about his first trip with his son, Lowell Jr., to Tibet. He took us around the world, dropping famous names as he went. We were fascinated. I'm not sure he ever got around to telling us about Tibet, but the tales of Indian maharanees who wanted to marry him; Franklin Roosevelt, a friend and neighbor near Hyde Park in New York; Lawrence of Arabia; and kings and queens he knew were marvelous. Incidentally, one by one, our Chinese hosts, not the least interested, got up and crept out.

Another night we had a musical evening with David Broder organizing a song-and-dance group. It was pretty bad. The Chinese took on this challenge, and different members recited some heavy poetry and one sang an aria from a Chinese opera. It was a highlight as we cruised down that magnificent river that for so many years divided the country. (The first bridge across the Yangtze was built after the revolution in 1949.)

Another time we were sitting in the stateroom when we looked out, and there was Lowell jogging in *very* slow motion around the wet and slippery deck. He was an amazing man and knowing him was a treat. We kept up a wonderful correspondence, and we loved his letters and notes that continued right up until his death. George and I attended his funeral in 1981, and I was amused to see that his coffin was draped not with a flag but with some exotic cloth that he must have received from a king or emperor. He was a true adventurer!

The day after we got home from our China trip, George W. came to Houston with a beautiful young woman and announced they were getting married. Laura Welsh and George had been grammar school classmates in Midland but had not been aware of each other. They were married in November, right in the middle of George W.'s campaign for Congress. The next year, he would win his primary fight, but he lost the general election.

Laura is a very special person, and I always thought that being an only child with few cousins, she was amused by us. In our very competitive, large family, she does not compete. She walks, reads a lot, has great taste, is excellent company, and like Columba, was a fine addition to our family.

꿈 As we entered 1978, it became more and more apparent that George would run for president in 1980. On March 3, I wrote Frances Hammond at the Washington Home:

> What a man is my great George. He is getting better about "blowing his own horn," a thing we were taught as children to never do. But a thing that you must do if you want this job. He is uniquely qualified, and I am more than willing to tell people why. The one thing that he has done that none of the rest of them have done is he founded and made a success of a company that has business around the world. He knows what it means to meet a payroll, work with all government rules and regulations, and he also knows how to wrestle with tough problems and make it work. You don't need a lecture about my George, but when you add his business experience to his many government jobs that he did well, it just adds up to the right person at the right time for the job.

We had a late summer meeting in Kennebunkport with Bill Steiger, Dean Burch, Jim Baker, and others where the possibility of a George Bush run for the presidency was seriously discussed. Strategy and timing were debated. It was decided that if George was going to make the run, he must step up his travel and start lining up teams in every state.

One of the questions people asked George was how he could run with no constituency. He would answer that he had "a big family and lots of friends." I know people laughed, but how did George eventually win? He has a big family and lots of very loyal friends who know George is the best friend someone can have.

That fall George suggested that since he would be on the road, I should accept Bill and Sarah Thomas's invitation to visit them in China, where they still served in the U.S. mission. I invited George's sister, who lives in Massachusetts, to go with me. As I sat in a New York City airport waiting for Nan Ellis to join me, I began to think: What do I actually know about her? We meet at big family gatherings, but how do I know I will be able to share a room with her for three weeks and end up liking her?

Almost as soon as she arrived at the airport, she asked me the time. My heart sank as I thought: My gosh, she does not wear a watch! For three weeks she'll be asking me "What time is it?" Nan could tell that I was appalled and quickly assured me, "I will never ask you the time again and I will never be late." She didn't and she wasn't. She then announced several rules that she felt very strongly about. I remember two. "Never use my hairbrush. You may use my toothbrush, but never the hairbrush." And: "Wash out the bathtub after your bath." I agreed to the rules and added: "Never ever use my toothbrush."

She was the best traveling companion and went from being my sister-in-law to a dear and close friend.

On January 5, 1979, George filed his intention to form a Presidential Search Committee. It wasn't as strong as actually announcing he was a candidate (he would do that in May), but it meant he was very serious about running. We were on our way.

12

Hitting the Campaign Trail

It didn't take long for me to find out just how frustrating this campaign would be at times. On March 9, 1979, I was asked to participate in a national press conference at the Waldorf in New York with the other candidates' wives. A better name for it would be a "Cattle Show." We were not going to be allowed to speak! I had the best candidate, but in a beauty contest or best-dressed competition, I didn't have a chance. The other wives were Nancy Reagan; Joy Baker, wife of Senator Howard Baker; Jackie Fernandez, wife of Ben Fernandez; and Elizabeth Dole. We were asked to pose together over and over. Crazy!

Campaigning was exhausting. George was flying from one end of the country to another and then back. He was getting advice from everywhere. Some friends were telling him to smile more; some were saying to smile less. I remember one day thinking I would love to fix his hair, but I didn't want to join the chorus of criticism!

The receptions, lunches, and dinners were endless. Some would be wonderful and lift your spirits. But there were many others where we were told 400 people would come and maybe 150 would show up. I was never sure what to do at many of these affairs, and I often felt like I attracted the people who had been drinking too much. It also seemed that the worse the day was, the better the chance our motel room that night would smell of stale cigarette smoke or we would take a bumpy plane ride to the next stop.

We still found lots to laugh about, though. One night, we were awakened at four A.M. by our message light flashing on the phone. We immediately thought of the children, picked up the phone in fear and trembling, and found instead that some unknown couple in room 210 wanted us to come down for a drink. The hotel had forgotten to pass on the message until the wee hours of the morning. I lay in bed thinking about calling and telling them we accept, or just getting up, getting dressed, and appearing at their door. I fell asleep giggling.

Another night, I awakened to hear George answering the door. There was this tiny little girl asking if he was Mr. Jones and had he sent for her? George sent the poor little thing away and told me she was a hooker. Later someone suggested that it might have been a setup.

On Ash Wednesday, we were in Mexico to speak to the Young Presidents' Organization. We were very excited to find that Billy and Ruth Graham were there and invited them to take a boat trip with us. While picnicking on a military beach, Billy saw his hotel down the way and decided to jump ship and work on his speech. He was wearing George's borrowed bathing suit and no shoes. He ran into military police who would not let him walk up the beach, and Billy Graham had to walk down the burning hot highway barefoot and in swimming trunks.

In July 1979 we took a brief break from the campaign trail and traveled to the Middle East. President and Mrs. Sadat of Egypt were absolutely charming and invited us to their lovely home in Alexandria on the Mediterranean, sending a helicopter to Cairo for us. In conversation, he took us around the world and gave George his evaluation of what was happening. He spoke in a soft, clear voice and we were spellbound.

In Israel, we met with Prime Minister Begin, who was pleasant but not forthcoming. I believe he didn't think George had a future. However, we did have a glorious tour of Jerusalem and met with the mayor, Teddy Kollek, in what was to be the first of many meetings George had with this respected leader.

⁀ Long before the campaign began, I had put some hard thought into what my role would be. I knew people would ask me what my cause was, and I still wasn't sure about that.

Rosalynn Carter was interested in mental health; Betty Ford, arthritis; Pat Nixon, volunteerism; Lady Bird Johnson, the beautification of America. I had to know exactly what my cause would be. For many years I had volunteered in hospitals and nursing homes, such as Sloan-Kettering Memorial Hospital in New York City and the Washington Home in Washington. I loved doing that, but I felt there was now a real opportunity to pick a cause that would involve a larger group of citizens. During the summer of 1978, while jogging in Houston's Memorial Park, I thought about all the things that worried me: the environment, the homeless, teenage pregnancies, hunger, crime, and on and on. I felt the subject I chose should help the most people possible, but not cost the government more money and not be controversial. A president has enough troubles—he does not need a wife to stir up more controversy for him.

Sad to say, there were plenty of problems filling those criteria. Finally, after much thought, I realized everything I worried about would be better if more people could read, write, and comprehend. More people would stay in school and get an education, meaning fewer people would turn to the streets and get involved with crime or drugs, become pregnant, or lose their homes. It seemed that simple. I had found my cause.

So the campaign was told that literacy was my interest—but we forgot to mention I knew absolutely nothing about the subject, at least not yet. One day, my traveling companion, Becky Brady, and I took off for a swing through the Midwest, including a stop at Cardinal Stritch College in Milwaukee. We were met by a Sister Camille, who led us into a meeting saying, "We are so excited about your visit. I have collected literacy experts from all around Milwaukee, some forty-five of the most informed people, and they are waiting to hear you. We are just thrilled!"

At that moment I could have killed Margaret Tutwiler, who had just come on board to do George's scheduling and who had sent me off on this trip. (It certainly was unfair to blame her, but at the time, she was the only candidate.) All the experts sat in two large rows, forming a semicircle around two chairs in the middle. Sister Camille and I plunked ourselves down, and she introduced me by saying, "Well, here she is. We can't wait to hear what you have to say."

I was lucky, for it suddenly came to me what to do. After saying a very few words, I asked them a question: "If you were married to the President and had the opportunity to really make a dent in the field of illiteracy, what one thing would you do? How would you go about it? We'll start on the right and go around the room. Each person, please tell me how you'd approach this."

Well, you can guess the rest. They started talking, and by the time we got halfway through, Becky told me it was time to go on to the next event. I thanked them all, and we were out of there. We got back in our minivan and laughed ourselves silly. As wife of the Vice President, I went back to Cardinal Stritch College to give the commencement address and receive an honorary degree. I'm not sure I deserved the degree, but I certainly did learn something there: People would rather hear themselves talk than someone else. So when in doubt, keep quiet, listen, and let others talk. They'll be happy, and you might learn something.

By the way, the Margaret Tutwiler I mentioned is the same marvelous woman who went on to become the spokesperson at the State Department during George's presidency. She was a great scheduler for us during the campaign, although George used to tease her unmercifully for being the world's worst speller.

In a campaign you came to expect the unexpected. One time, George and I were together at a rather unusual fund-raiser: a dance, where the top prize was dancing with us! Thank heavens I danced with a gray-haired gentleman. What if I had gotten a rock-'n'-roller? George joked with the audience that he had heard first prize was dancing with him; second prize was dancing with him twice; and third prize was dancing with him all night. Then he introduced me to give a few remarks. I could have killed him; I had absolutely nothing prepared. Then it hit me. I went to the microphone and said: "I hope I win first, second, and third prize," and sat down.

You also learned how to keep a stiff upper lip when things didn't go as planned. I remember one tough day in Massachusetts traveling with one of our local campaign workers, a young man named Ron Kaufman. The "crowds" were pitiful; we rarely hit double digits. Poor Ron was trying to keep my spirits up, and he promised that the last event would have probably 150 people. There were exactly four, three of whom were staff. Nevertheless, the four people saw my entire China slide show.

Ron Kaufman, by the way, was one of the many young people we met in the 1980 campaign who became a friend for life. He headed up the Political Affairs Office at the White House and guided us through many political mine fields.

⤺ One of the real joys of the campaign was our children. They all put their own lives on hold to campaign for George. George W. was just coming off his run for Congress in West Texas, and although he needed to get on with making a living, he campaigned as much as he could. Jeb and Colu were living in Venezuela, where he was a branch bank manager, but he gave up the job to come home and work full-time in the campaign. It was an enormous sacrifice financially, and an enormous gift to his dad. Neil campaigned hard in New Hampshire and Marvin in Iowa, both boys taking time off from school.

Doro told her dad she wanted to leave Boston College and work in the campaign. George, who adores her and could deny her nothing, surprised me and asked her what she could do; what could she bring to the ball game? He said she must have a talent and therefore should go to typing school so she could really help and not just be the daughter of the candidate. To our amazement, Doro enrolled in a nine-month course at Katherine Gibbs, certainly one of the finest, toughest secretarial schools. I know that George only meant for her to go to a three-month school to learn a little typing. So off came the blue jeans, on went the stockings and skirts, and she gave up summer vacation in Maine. I wonder if Doro ever realized she did way more than her father had in mind. When she finished the course, she worked in the Bush for President headquarters in Boston and did an outstanding job.

One very good thing came out of that campaign. The children treated me like an adult for the first time. Before that, they asked me all the "peanut butter and jelly" questions and George all the "steak and potato" questions. Then they discovered I could campaign with the best of them. My thinking about them changed, also. They no longer were children. They were able, bright, loving, loyal young men and women. They still are. They have been tested time and again, and always have made us very proud.

Cousins, nieces, nephews, brothers, and sisters from both sides of the family were involved in the campaign, which was wonderful. Sometimes, however, it could be very misleading. While driving through Massachusetts early in the campaign, I was so excited to see a George Bush for President bumper sticker. I drove up to catch the car, and there was the husband of one of George's cousins. Another time, driving through Iowa, I was listening to a radio talk show when a young man called in and said he was for George Bush because he was a great man and had a great family. Again I was so excited—until I recognized Marvin's voice!

        One thing I had to get used to during the primary was being followed by press. The "Today" show was planning features on each wife and asked permission to follow me. They came along one whole day through New Hampshire, attending coffees and other political events. I wore an open mike on my belt, so everything I said and everything said to me was on tape. I constantly pointed to the open mike, telling people they were on tape. Nevertheless, people said dreadful things I otherwise would have ignored—but I certainly did not want, by keeping silent, to leave the impression I agreed with them. Although the TV technicians assured me they turned off the tape when I went into the bathroom, I still ran the water in the tub or sink.

It was an exhausting day, climaxed by a half-hour interview with Jane Pauley. She was so pretty and sweet-looking—and managed to absolutely devastate me. We had a polite little interview until her last question, which went something like this: "Mrs. Bush, people say your husband is a man of the eighties and you are a woman of the forties. What do you say to that?"

Why didn't she just slap me in the face? She was darn lucky I didn't burst into tears and say that was the worst question I had ever heard! I was speechless and heartsick. I finally answered: "Oh, you mean people think I look forty? Neat!" I went on to say, "If you mean that I love my God, my country, and my husband, so be it. Why, then I am a woman of the forties." The interview was over practically before it started. After she left, while I was still rocking from the question, I told Becky I was sure I hadn't understood her question. It was so hurtful. A crew member spoke up and said, "Oh, you understood her okay." He conveyed the impression that it was not unusual for her to be so ugly.

To add insult to injury, we got a phone call saying the whole day's tape had been ruined and they'd like to spend another two days with me in Illinois. Since the other wives' interviews were "in the can," the office felt I must do it.

So we started over again with fear and trembling. The first day was an unbelievably bad one. Nothing went right. It snowed, and we traveled all day in a tiny plane, landing in small airports that usually closed immediately after we took off. Because of the weather, the people who were supposed to meet me were often late or didn't show up at all, so the cameras got pictures of me trudging through the snow alone. During a college visit, I was asked all the tough questions and harangued for not speaking out on the issues myself. It was the worst possible day. Jane flew in and met me at a high school to redo the interview. She started out by saying something like, "Mrs. Bush, some days on the campaign trail everything seems to go wrong . . ." I waited for a real zinger, but surprisingly, the interview was all sweetness and light. Several weeks went by, and then it was my morning on the air. I was very nervous, sitting alone in a California hotel room. Although the interview began with the footage of me walking alone through airports and Jane asking her "everything goes wrong" question, the next seven minutes were spent with the "Today" show allowing me to say in every way possible just how great George Bush is. It was amazing. The man who edited the tape really did me a favor. I honestly feel he did it on purpose. I think he felt we had bonded on those bumpy, scary flights through the storm; that we had been good sports by spending two more days with them after their tape had been bad; and that Jane had been cruel in that first interview. Who knows what he thought or why it turned out so well. When the seven minutes were over and the show went back to New York, Bryant Gumbel said, "The Bush campaign should have paid for that segment." Lucky me.

About this same time, I had a very hurtful conversation with a very loved sister-in-law who told me she had attended a dinner where some of the family had talked about "What are we going to do about Bar?" Huh? That really hurt. They discussed how to make me look snappier—color my hair, change my style of dressing, and, I suspect, get me to lose some weight. I know it was meant to be helpful, but I wept quietly alone until George told me that was absolutely crazy. He has always made me feel loved and just right for him. I certainly did not expect all the personal criticism when he announced for the presidency.

On this same note, one day after speaking at a New York City luncheon, I went to see a well-known speech consultant who was going to critique my speaking. I was very hesitant about all of this. The consultant greeted us kindly and truly gave me a pretty fair mark on the public speaking, but she had a dress consultant with her. That very young woman had on hideous pink tights and an off-colored weird dress; wild, long, frizzy hair; not to mention a very made-up face with emphasis on lavender eyelids. She started in: My clothes were all wrong; I should color my hair . . . I stopped her there. People had gotten to know me with white hair and it would be fake to change it now. She then said that if I wouldn't tint my hair, I must shave my dark eyebrows—they did not go with my hair. While I was still rocking from that ridiculous suggestion, Becky said we had to leave that very moment because we were late for our next meeting. We hardly got out of there before we doubled up with laughter.

Becky and I often got the giggles. Once we were touring the Springfield, Massachusetts, area with a large entourage, and I had just spoken to a group of GOP women and done a couple of press interviews when a tiny lady came up to me and asked if she could "read" my wrinkles. She counted six wrinkles on my forehead and said: "You've had six traumas and handled them well." Looking at the sides of my eyes, she counted five wrinkles and said: "You've had five children." Then I knew she had read my biography, and I knew the next thing in it was the line "The Bushes have lived in twenty-seven homes in seventeen cities." Unfortunately, Becky managed to drag me away to the next event and I never got to hear the rest of the wrinkle-reader!

Becky was the first of many aides who have become so dear to me. She was followed by Nick and Kitty Brady's daughter Kim. (No relation to Becky, who was the granddaughter of our longtime friend and former RNC chairwoman Mary Louise Smith.) Kim could head a company anytime she wanted, she is so organized and certainly a considerate, thoughtful young woman. She was followed by Elizabeth Wise, who looked like a Botticelli painting and was so smart I felt like the dog was being wagged by the tail. We loved that tiny, dainty, smart young woman. Casey Healey from Oklahoma came next and was beloved by all ages, and she was followed by Peggy Swift, who has all the above abilities, plus is a great beauty. At this writing, Nancy Huang has been my aide for six months, and I don't believe I've ever seen her frown, she is always so upbeat. Beside all her other talents, she is a computer genius and has saved me from disaster several times writing this book. I have shared everything with these young women, and they know more about us than anyone else in the world. Not one has betrayed our trust and friendship. They traveled around the world with me, held my hand throughout sickness and many a terrible faux pas on my part. We have had unending days and many funny times. They have remained loyal and even-tempered throughout—heaven only knows how. Both George and I love them and would do anything we could for them.

⮑ One of the best things about being on the campaign trail was seeing old friends along the way. I especially remember spending two days in Michigan with dear Patsy Caulkins—one of our housemates from Yale—and her sister-in-law, Chrissie Finkenstaedt. They were helping out with the trip, although neither one of them had organized a political event, or attended one to my knowledge. The "pros" said that the trip would be a failure, since they did not know how to raise a crowd, and so forth. So we spent two days going from town to town attending some of the best coffees and receptions we had in the primary. These young women didn't know that what they planned couldn't be done, so they just did it! Incidentally, we won the Michigan primary, which, in all honesty, was due to George Bush, a very popular Governor Bill Milliken, and many other hard workers, including the present governor, John Engler.

In reading my notes on the primary season in 1980, I am once again reminded that the more things change, the more they stay the same.

In the Republican primary, a candidate must always prove just how conservative he is. George has always been accused of being a liberal in conservative clothing in the primary, and a conservative in liberal clothing in the general election. I was always so proud of George. He stuck with what he believed, whether or not it was popular. He never paid attention to the polls.

Also during that campaign, I was quoted as saying about John Anderson, who lost the GOP primary and went on to run as an Independent: "I think being an Independent is a cop-out. The strength of the United States is in the two-party system. You pick the party that is close to you philosophically and try to change the things about it you don't like." Like I said, the more things change, the more things stay the same. A three-person race does not give the winner a clear mandate.

One of the big issues in the 1980 primary campaign was abortion. It seemed that's what we were asked most about. Just how committed was George to being anti-abortion? Very committed. He did believe, however, that abortion was acceptable when it came to rape, incest, and the health of the mother. His views were not acceptable to the true believers on either side of the issue. One of the public misconceptions about George was that he changed his opinion on abortion. He never did. He was always opposed. I think the misunderstanding came from the fact that as a congressman he had been very active in promoting family planning and had supported Planned Parenthood before abortion became their battle cry. That's where he parted ways with them.

In all our years of campaigning, abortion was the toughest issue for me. Everyone, it seemed, tried to make me say how I felt about the issue, hoping to catch me disagreeing with George. I honestly felt, and still feel, the elected person's opinion is the one the public has the right to know.

I never questioned George's conviction and certainly shared his concerns about abortion being used as a contraceptive. There is no question in my mind that the law permitting abortions has been abused. We both agree that the estimated 1.6 million abortions performed in the United States every year is unacceptable.

For me, abortion is a personal issue—between the mother, father, and doctor. If a minor is involved, you can add parents to that list also.

It should be allowed in the first trimester only.

Abortion is not a presidential matter.

Education is the answer.

Morals cannot be legislated.

On the campaign trail, abortion met us everywhere. We were greeted outside the first primary debate in New Hampshire with large pro-Reagan signs and signs that said: GEORGE BUSH—MURDERER. Reagan supporters also took out many ads saying George was for abortion and Reagan was against. It was very untrue and unfair.

Once, when I was campaigning in Maryland with Helen Bentley, the tough but very nice congresswoman from the Baltimore area, the press asked her: "You are a well-known advocate of women's rights. How come you are anti-abortion?" I loved her answer, although I never saw it in print. She said simply, "It's against my religion." George Bush could give the same answer.

Both George and I felt strongly about our positions but respected each other's views; there was no point in discussing it every time it came up.

∽ By the end of the primary season, it was evident 1980 was not our year. After the high of an upset win in Iowa, we lost New Hampshire, and although we rebounded to win several more important primaries, Ronald Reagan was well on his way to winning the nomination.

During the campaign, Neil had met and fallen in love with a darling young schoolteacher from New Hampshire, Sharon Smith. He not only won her vote, but thank heavens, her heart, too. In the summer of 1980, they got married in Kennebunkport at tiny St. Ann's Church, where George's mother and father had been married more than sixty years before. We had the reception on the lawn at Walker's Point with family and friends. It was a very happy time, and they left for Europe on their honeymoon having been assured by us we were going to the Republican Convention to bow out of politics with style, and then go home to Houston.

∽ We went to the convention with the plan of asking George's delegates—he had the second-highest total—to get 100 percent behind Ronald Reagan. I dreaded the trip, but must confess it was fun. I joined a team that went from delegation to delegation speaking well of Ronald Reagan. I remember that Cap Weinberger, later Secretary of Defense, was on the team. He was a gentle, kind man who made it very easy for me. Maureen Reagan was also on the team, working very hard for her dad. She was a piece of work who came on like gangbusters.

I truly began the convention thinking, Hurrah, no more politics! But as the week went on, I found myself getting very competitive. George was by far the best man for vice president. Groups were forming for Jack Kemp, Paul Laxalt, Howard Baker, and, of course, Jerry Ford. The next thing we knew, George was in the running, too.

The keynote address at the convention was to be given by our dear friend Guy Vander Jagt. Guy and Carol had come to Congress the same year we did and we are good friends. His speech was being highly touted. Guy is a great orator and prides himself on using no notes. He was fast becoming a dark horse candidate, and a lot was riding on his speech. The night he was to speak, the convention ran overtime, so the keynote address was put off for one day so it could be in prime time. This built up expectations even more. George was to follow Guy, so he was put off twenty-four hours also.

I remember walking over to the convention hall that night with Susan Baker and Pat Burch and discussing the interview we had just heard with Walter Cronkite and Jerry Ford. Jerry hinted he would consider being the vice presidential candidate, under the right circumstances. We were confused about what was happening. We walked past people working for Jack Kemp, who were handing out Kemp posters and yelling "Stop Bush." What was happening?

Guy started his speech with that beautiful, strong voice and he talked and he talked and he talked. He recited from memory parts of the Bible and some poems, and he talked very movingly about his forebears. When he got past the thirty-minute mark, I knew that George's speech would be well received, for it was short. I don't know how long Guy talked, but it was very, very long. With each word he helped George.

George's time finally came. The whole convention hall seemed blanketed in homemade BUSH signs, which our friends and supporters had spent the whole night painting. George gave a fine speech. I learned later that just before he spoke, he had been told Jerry Ford was Reagan's choice for vice president.

We went right back to the Pontchartrain Hotel and our whole floor was filled with many close friends and family. It was like a funeral. George found Jeb in our bedroom really upset. "It's not fair, it's not fair," he said. George and I put on old clothes, and I urged him to let us pack up and get out of there. George gave both Jeb and me a talking-to: "We came to this convention to leave politics with style and we are going to do it." Almost immediately, the phone call came to our room from Ronald Reagan and the rest is history.

By the way, the next day in Austria, a honeymooning Neil and Sharon saw George's picture on the front page of a local paper. Neil excitedly grabbed a paper and tried to figure out what it said. When the owner of the newsstand realized the man in the photo was Neil's father, he translated the article. That's how Neil and Sharon found out it wasn't over yet.

On September 3, 1980, my first day of campaigning for Ronald Reagan and George Bush, I flew to New Orleans under the protection of the Secret Service. This began a twelve-and-a-half-year relationship with some of the world's finest, most professional men and women I have ever met. Over the years, people often would ask us if we didn't get tired of being constantly under surveillance. We never did. In fact, it amazed me whenever I heard someone complain about these brave people. Their only job is to see that you are safe. They are ready to risk their lives—and many of them have—for whomever they are protecting.

I wonder if many people know that the Secret Service also investigates financial crimes, such as counterfeiting and credit card frauds. Protecting presidents and vice presidents and their families, presidential candidates, and visiting heads of state is only one of their roles. I often felt it almost was insulting for these highly dedicated and trained people to follow me around. They surely were bored.

Becky and I soon realized it embarrassed the Secret Service to see us struggling through airports with our luggage. Their job was to protect me, not wait on me, and they certainly could not carry bags. I told Becky that from now on, the advance people (the campaign workers who went out ahead and set up events) should have someone meet us who could help with luggage. That made such a difference after all those months of carrying our own bags.

Getting back to that first day on the campaign trail—it was very different. I knew everything about George Bush and very little about Ronald Reagan. For quite a while there were "Reagan people" chaperoning George and me, to be sure we were toeing the line. I am not sure that they knew us well enough yet to realize that loyalty, decency, and honor are George's code. I believe that for the most part, they came to respect George.

What made it easier for us was that our primary campaign manager and dear friend Jim Baker was now a senior adviser in Reagan's campaign, and ours was being run by Dean Burch. Dean was very smart and had such a great sense of what was right. The two campaigns were in perfect sync.

I campaigned twenty-seven days in September alone, touching down in sixteen states and thirty-seven cities all over the country. Sometimes I campaigned with George and sometimes by myself. I met Nancy Reagan on the trail only once, campaigning with her in Baltimore. People wanted to see, meet, and touch her. She was more than nice to me.

I was asked over and over again about what Reagan felt about this or that. Since I really did not know the Governor, this was difficult for me. But it was fairly easy to talk about Jimmy Carter's inflation, Jimmy Carter's interest rates, Jimmy Carter's unemployment, Jimmy Carter's failed foreign policy. However, I was used to campaigning for George Bush, which was a cinch, and not against the opponent. I certainly prefer the former.

When it came to being interviewed, I was always afraid that I was going to hurt, rather than help. One day I was going on a radio call-in show, and the topic under discussion that day was a statement made by the head of a large Protestant church group. He was quoted as saying: "I never get over how strange it is at political meetings. We have a Catholic priest, a Protestant minister, and a Jewish rabbi pray, when everybody knows that God doesn't hear Jewish prayers." I panicked. What a terrible thing to say, and I didn't want to get involved in any way. If asked, I would say how outraged I was by that kind of bigotry. I thought that I might give a Helen Bentley answer—"That kind of talk is against my religion"—which it is. But the wonderful talk show host, a man named Mike Miller, not only did not involve me in the discussion, he did not take phone calls while I was on the air. I went back to the hotel relieved, but almost sick with rage at a statement like that.

∽ There is sort of a pattern to campaigning you fall into. When something doesn't follow the schedule, you remember it. One day I raced into a meeting where I was told absolutely no speeches; just mix and mingle. I was met at the door, led right up to a standing mike, and handed a card. It read: "1. Thank hostess. [No name on card.] 2. Thank party chairman. [No name on card.] 3. Party line. [That I could wing.]" Not my finest hour.

Another time I was expecting to speak and was greeted at the door by a nice-looking man who said, "Did they tell you to speak well of Apple?" I looked at my notes—no Apple. He said, "Apple is our one hope and bright light. Rave about Apple." Well, I added Apple and gave him a big plug. After the reception, one of our people asked me who Apple was. I sought out my man and asked him and he, of course, said, "Me."

You do meet all sorts of people on the campaign trail. As George and I stood in receiving line after receiving line, having pictures taken with supporters, I often thought about Rosalynn Carter, who once innocently had her picture taken with Jim Jones, the man who led the cult to Guyana and forced them to drink poisoned Kool-Aid. As I shook people's hands, I would think, Is this a good guy? Is he a mass murderer? It could happen.

᧬ We campaigned in backyards, ballrooms, courthouses, bowling alleys, at a cider and doughnut farm, hot dog plants, high schools and colleges, retirement homes, and hospitals. You name it, we were there.

Jeb and Columba stayed active in the campaign, but our college-aged children had gone back to school, campaigning on the weekends only. I called Doro one morning to check in, and she told me that nobody at Boston College was for Reagan-Bush. She had joined the campus campaign and was doing all the work. However, when the Reagan-Bush campus chairman had asked her "Where's your Reagan-Bush pin?" she answered him, "Are you crazy? I'm trying to make friends on the campus!" She is such a warm, funny child.

᧬ I remember the day that I knew Ronald Reagan was going to win. I was in Detroit with a couple of free hours, waiting for George to get into town. I had the evening news on and saw Jimmy Carter denying he had called Ronald Reagan a racist. Then the news showed a tape of President Carter in a black church saying Ronald Reagan was a racist. For the first time I saw the "dark side" of Jimmy Carter. One of the things he had going for him was that he was a good, decent man, but for that one moment he also was a man who told a lie and felt hate. He had an indefensible record, so his people ran an underground smear campaign about Ronald Reagan. They said he was a racist, and pulled out another old campaign threat: Ronald Reagan would do away with Social Security. In truth, he and George actually strengthened the Social Security system while in office.

On Election Day we gathered our family and friends in Houston to wait for the results. I went running in Memorial Park and came across members of our traveling press corps playing softball with some of our staff. Several press people told me that the election was over; the exit polls were showing that Reagan-Bush was going to win big. I still couldn't believe it. We had worked so hard—yet it seemed so sudden. In May, we had bowed out of politics forever; six months later, I was the wife of the Vice President-Elect of the United States of America.

13

Around the World and Back

The next two and a half months were spent hiring a staff, getting ready to move yet another time, deciding what to do about our homes in Texas and Maine, and celebrating Christmas.

I have read that Nancy Reagan considered me lucky because I was not a newcomer to Washington and knew what to expect. That is very true. But I also knew enough to hire the most perfect person to be my chief of staff, Susan Porter Rose. Susan knew Washington and knew her way around the White House. I met her when she was a very young woman working for Pat Nixon. She went on to be Betty Ford's scheduler and then worked in the Justice Department during the Carter years. Susan has the most extraordinary sense of what is right and thinks things through with great care. I don't. Therefore, we made a great team for twelve years. Susan saved both George and me from many mistakes, and for that we are both eternally grateful. She also ran the very best office and hired the very best staff, many of whom would stay with me for the next twelve years. Susan is married to Jonathan Rose, whose father, Chappy, was a friend of George's dad. Both Mr. Rose and Jon were highly thought of by all.

The day after the election, Joan Mondale called me in Texas and couldn't have been nicer. She offered to show me the Vice President's House any time I wanted to see it, and she received me with great kindness several weeks later. My wonderful friend Andy Stewart went with me. Andy is one of those people who pull out a tiny camera to record moments of history. She humiliated me during the visit by insisting that Joan and I pose shaking hands upon arrival and several other times during the tour. That's when I knew Joan was sincerely a nice person—she agreed to pose over and over.

Joan is a great supporter of the arts, and the house was filled with the most modern work. Andy would back us up to some amazing piece of neon art that she (and I) thought was hideous and insist that we pose. She knew that George would last about five minutes with most of the pieces in the house. Let me add as a footnote that we know absolutely nothing about modern art, so this should be taken as a knock at our ignorance rather than a slap at Joan's taste. (I should also add that you rarely see any of the pictures Andy takes; she keeps them in drawers or under beds.)

∽ The moment the election was over, George generously suggested I go to New York City and buy some "designer" clothes. He didn't want me to have to hear about how "dowdy" I was. So I took Laurie Firestone, the magical young woman who was our social secretary for the next twelve years, and bought some clothes from Bill Blass and Adele Simpson (both of whom had visited China while we were there), and Diane Dickinson. Later I would meet Arnold Scaasi, and for the next twelve years I bought my clothes from these very talented people. I never was criticized, but I didn't draw raves either. Nobody noticed what I wore. All I know is that I felt terrific. All these designers were very kind to me, but Arnold became a close personal friend and a supporter of my literacy causes.

On that first visit I bought a great purple dress and a red coat to wear to the Inauguration, a pretty bright blue coat with a white dress, and several other things. Thank heavens Nancy Reagan slipped the word to me that she was wearing red. In my excitement I had forgotten that I was not the "mother of the bride" and never thought to ask! So I wore the blue coat instead and it was fine. All our children had to buy long evening clothes, and we had great fun doing it. They looked beautiful.

That red coat and purple dress gave me a good laugh later in the year. In May, the Archbishop of Canterbury visited Washington, and George and I attended a service at the Washington Cathedral with His Royal Highness the Prince of Wales. An unusual cold front had come through Washington, and I decided to wear that outfit one more time before putting it away for the summer. As we were standing for the procession, young Prince Charles leaned over to George and said, "Your wife, sir, is very appropriately dressed." We turned and looked, and there came the bishop followed by twenty-eight primates—all gowned in purple vestments with red overrobes.

Inaugural Week could not have been more exciting and fun for us and our children. Of course everything did not go perfectly. At the Texas Ball, held a few days before the Inauguration, I tripped and hit my leg as George and I were announced onstage. It stunned me for a minute, then I was okay. While George was speaking, I noticed that something felt slightly funny. I turned sideways and looked down, and I was standing in a nice little pool of blood. The military aide who had been assigned to me for that week only, a Navy lieutenant named Todd Bruner, looked like he might faint. (Todd's parents were not only our good friends in Kennebunkport, but his dad, Laman, was our minister.) The minute the speeches were over, the Secret Service quietly took me into the nearest ladies' room. As the women came out of the stalls, they were slightly taken aback to see men in their room and rushed out gasping. Dr. Bill Hughes, ABC News reporter Ann Compton's husband, came to my rescue and sent me to the emergency room at Georgetown University Hospital. The Secret Service really didn't want George to go for fear rumors would start about his health. I insisted he go, and he was the rage of the nursing staff. It was Saturday night, and they had a full load of stabbings, but all was momentarily forgotten while they sought autographs. And no rumors started, thanks to the big Band-Aid I wore over my fourteen stitches throughout the Inauguration. When we went to the star-studded Inaugural Gala, we sat across the room from the Reagans in great thronelike chairs. The doctor had told me to put my foot up, but I couldn't. I was afraid I'd look like Henry the Eighth.

We began Inauguration Day at St. John's Episcopal Church for a service with the Reagans, our joint families, and friends. The minister, John Harper, and his wife, Barbie, were old friends of ours as we are Episcopalians. Every president since James Madison has worshiped at St. John's, located across Lafayette Park from the White House.

Then it was on to the White House. Fritz and Joan Mondale met us at the North Portico entrance and were warm and gracious. They had been most helpful during the transition, despite the fact this couldn't have been an easy time for them.

The Reagans arrived, and it was a long, tense forty-five minutes. We did not sit down, but just "hung around" waiting for the trip to the Capitol. Rosalynn Carter spent the time telling the White House staff good-bye. Nancy and I discussed that when we faced being in her position—in four or eight years—we would not drag it out like this. And we didn't. However, twelve years later, I would be much more understanding of Rosalynn. In 1993, although we had already said our good-byes to the staff, I was still much more concerned about them than the incoming administration.

I rode to the Capitol with Joan Mondale, driving past crowds of cheering people. For the first time, the Inauguration was to be held on the west side of the Capitol, looking out toward the Mall and the monuments. With thousands watching, and surrounded by family and friends, our dear friend Potter Stewart swore George in as the forty-third vice president of the United States, and Chief Justice Warren Burger swore Ronald Reagan in as the fortieth president. We were especially grateful that George's mother was there to see him sworn in, as she would be in 1989 to see him become president. To add to the excitement and the drama, we got word that the fifty-two American hostages held in Iran were released while President Reagan was giving his Inaugural Address.

George saw our house for the first time when we drove up after the Inaugural Parade. We arrived exhausted, and were about to host 150 family members for a light dinner! However, we found C. Fred and Paula in the house, our clothes all unpacked, and a great buffet supper on the dining room table. Laurie Firestone, Paula, and a group of volunteers had performed this miracle.

After the dinner, and after every family member had had their pictures taken with the new vice president, George and I climbed into bed for a nap. We awakened and looked out our bedroom window to see lighted on the horizon the Capitol and the Washington Monument with fireworks over the Mall. It was magical. That view, which we had only in the winter, never failed to thrill us. In the summer, we looked out over a carpet of green, and when it rained—summer or winter—the colored car lights on Massachusetts Avenue looked like a shimmering jeweled necklace winding up the hill.

For the Inaugural Balls, I had a glorious new gown—bright blue, made of the most heavenly silk with big puffy, long sleeves. I felt like a bride in all my new finery. I still blush when I think of this, because when the pictures came back, they were not so glorious. The light hit that silk in all the wrong places, and I had two big shiny balls on the top and a big round tummy—highlighting my finest points!

Our very first week in office, President Reagan asked George to meet the hostages at Andrews Air Force Base and escort them to the White House for their official welcome home. The entire route into town was lined with people waving flags, cheering, and even weeping. The strangest assortment of people were hugging each other—all ages, all shapes, all sizes, all races—all Americans whose prayers had been answered. Inside the bus was a quiet disbelief. The hostages just couldn't believe that we had prayed and cared for them; that we had counted "Day 1, Day 2," up to the last day, "Day 444." As we got closer to the District, the hostages were overwhelmed by the yellow ribbons and growing crowds. Their leader, Bruce Laingen, wrote "thank you" on a tiny piece of paper and held it up to the window. I found a bigger piece and gave it to him, and he taped a big "thank you" on the window. He left it on the bus, but I took it and mailed it to him a month later, thinking he might like a remembrance of that historic day.

⤫ Once the excitement died down, I turned my attention to the house. It had been built in 1893 at a cost of $20,000 on the seventy-seven-acre U.S. Naval Observatory grounds for the in-resident admiral. In July 1974, it became the official residence of the vice president.

Virginia Senator Harry Byrd, who was on the congressional committee charged with finding a house, told me that Admiral Elmo "Bud" Zumwalt was the occupant when they decided this would be the perfect home for the vice president. Harry said Zumwalt did not seem too thrilled with the idea that the Navy's house was going to be confiscated. However, Harry didn't realize just how strongly the Admiral felt until his next election. Bud Zumwalt ran against him. Incidentally, Harry was one of only fifteen or twenty people who told me that they "personally" were responsible for getting that house for the vice president's residence. Must have been a big committee.

I first saw the house when Nelson Rockefeller was vice president (they did not live there but used it for entertaining), and I remember thinking it was nice but small. It was actually bigger than I thought, and I loved it. "It's a house that sort of talks to you," I wrote in my diary. But it also needed a lot of work. Everything was off center—the fireplaces, chandeliers, windows, arches, and so on. And there was a terrible conglomeration of furniture and artwork. It had been perfect for Joan Mondale's purposes. She used it very much as a museum and sponsored American art and artists. I was into literacy. She had teen-aged children. Mine were all grown and living away from home. Our needs were different. However, we both shared a great love of books, and there was one addition to the house the Mondales made that I loved: a library of books by and about vice presidents, their wives, and later, their dogs.

I got lots of help with the redecorating. I was especially grateful to the outstanding decorator, Mark Hampton, and Dottie Craig, an old friend from Midland days. Mark not only found some beautiful rugs and furniture for us, he donated his time and profit. He is great fun to work with as he uses what you have, and he and his wife, Duane, have become good friends of ours. Mark also has served on the Committee for the Preservation of the White House, worked on Blair House (the president's guest house), and helped us redo the Oval Office and the family rooms at the White House. At this writing, he is helping Ambassador Pamela Harriman with our embassy in Paris and with our new home in Houston.

Dottie Craig's part in the redecorating really was almost a gift from God. George had been asking me just how I was going to pay for all this, and I told him not to worry, that I knew it would all work out. One day my phone rang and it was Dottie. "Bar, I know from George W. that you are redoing the VP House. I am without a project and would love to help raise money." I don't know what I would have done if she hadn't called, and I certainly don't recommend this kind of financial planning to others. Dottie raised all the money we needed (she'd be the first to say she did it with lots of help), and then eight years later, helped me resurrect the White House Endowment Fund. Dottie and Earle are presently serving on the Board of Trustees of the George Bush Library Foundation.

After the house was redecorated, I wrote in my diary: "The rooms say, 'Please come sit down,' rather than, 'Please stay out.'"

We lived in that graceful, charming house for eight years—the longest we have lived in any one home in our forty-nine years of married life. We especially loved the large veranda that wrapped around the front of the house. We ate many meals there, watching grandchildren swing or C. Fred, and later Millie, chase squirrels and explore.

Talking about redoing the house does bring up a subject that I have wanted to comment on. Nancy Reagan got lots of criticism for redecorating the White House when we all should have been on our knees thanking her. She raised the money privately and not only redecorated but restored the White House, including modernizing the bathrooms and fixing faulty wiring. As her successor, I was eternally grateful to her for that.

ꕔ March 30, 1981, began as a fairly typical day—even quiet compared to most. My schedule read:

FYI   Cherry Blossom Festival
11 a.m.   Washington Performing Arts Society Volunteer Reception (&NR)
12:30 p.m. Cabinet Wives Lunch, National Trust Historical Preservation (&NR)
3 p.m.   San Antonio Art Institute Tour/Tea

After lunch, Nancy Reagan ("&NR" on my schedule means it was an event with Nancy) went back to the White House and I went home. Working at my desk with the TV on mute, I looked up and found myself looking at a newscast: a lot of racing around; a shot of the President being pushed into the car; someone lying on the ground. I couldn't believe what I was seeing. My heart ached so for Nancy. I knew that the best thing I could do for her was to stay away; what she needed was a best friend. Dear Andy Stewart came right over to be with me. George was in Texas and called me several times during his flight home. I really needed to be near his voice, and he must have sensed that. The TV kept saying that after he landed, he was going to take the helicopter right to the White House. He told me that was not true; he was going to land at our house and then drive to the White House. George felt strongly that only the President should land at the White House in a helicopter. There are exceptions, but George knew that he needed to send the message that Ronald Reagan was still responsible in every way to run the country. Ed Meese, one of the President's senior staff, stopped by the house before he went up to the helicopter pad to meet George. He was obviously worried sick and yet took time to stop by the house to reassure me. I especially remember the hug he gave me with tears in his eyes. We walked up to the helicopter pad together to wait for George. When he landed, he gave me a hug and then left with Ed for the fifteen-minute drive to the White House.

George was asked over and over again what he felt and thought when he heard about the assassination attempt. His answer: "I worried about my friend who was hurt."

There were two big weddings that summer: Prince Charles married Lady Diana, and on June 13, Marvin married Margaret Molster in Richmond, Virginia. Margaret is from a large, loving family—not as large as George's, but few are—and she and Marvin attended the University of Virginia at the same time. They both had many mutual friends and have shared them with us. We watched the royal wedding at a breakfast at the British Embassy. Ours looked like much more fun. Betty Molster, Margaret's mother, worked really hard before we all arrived, and then when we got there announced that if it wasn't done, it wouldn't get done. She was going to relax and enjoy it. She taught me a good lesson: Everyone has more fun if the hostess is enjoying herself.

Early during the vice presidential years, I got a letter from a woman saying she had read that I did needlepoint and played tennis. She then asked: "Do you also sit home and eat bonbons?"

It probably seemed that way to some, but the eight years George was vice president were, I believe, the busiest of my life—more so than the White House years in many ways. I hate quoting statistics. I agree with Mrs. Robert Taft, Sr., who once said: "All statistics are hard to swallow and impossible to digest. The only one I can ever remember is that if all the people who fell asleep in church were laid end to end, they'd be a lot more comfortable."

But I'm going to chance it anyway. In the 2,923 days of the vice presidential years:

- 1,629 days were spent out of Washington traveling, including visiting all fifty states and sixty-five different foreign countries, many of them more than once.
- George and I traveled an estimated 1.3 million miles, which is about fifty-four times around the world.
- When I was in town, I hosted 1,192 events at the Vice President's House and attended 1,232 other events in Washington.

Whew! Lucky for you, I'm not going to describe every single mile or share every speech. But it was an extraordinary eight years, and I would like to share with you some of the people we met, some of the places we visited, and some of the wonderful experiences we were lucky to enjoy.

~ *June 30, 1981*—At President Reagan's request, George and I attended the inauguration of President Marcos of the Philippines. Clare Boothe Luce and Efrem Zimbalist, Jr., and his wife were in the delegation. We were all amazed that Clare never slept on the entire seventeen-hour trip. She talked—maybe entertained is a better way to describe it—the whole way over and back. George and I had a private cabin, but we all took turns listening and enjoying her. What a remarkable woman: a famous beauty and seductress; wife of legendary Henry Luce, founder of Time/Life; author of *The Women*; congresswoman; ambassador to Italy; and a delegate to the United Nations. Clare, whose tongue was finely honed, was very opinionated, generous, charming, and amusing.

We arrived late on a Sunday night and left at six A.M. Tuesday, our visit cut short by a typhoon in the forecast. Imelda Marcos, a charmer in her own right, met us upon arrival and took us straight to the famous Malacanang Palace (home to Imelda's 1,060 pairs of shoes), where we were staying. Before being allowed to go to sleep, she said she had two dresses for me and asked if I'd try them on to see if they fit. Neither dress would have gone over my thigh, much less my body. Imelda said not to worry, a seamstress would fix that. She must have worked all night and the next day, because just as I was getting dressed for the ball the next evening, the dress Imelda insisted I wear was delivered. I certainly didn't want to wear it, but felt that I must. It was a disaster. It was a long sheath of a dress with a slip top, which was covered by a capelike overtop. Every time I raised my arms to eat or dance, this cape thing rolled back up my arms to expose my slip. The dress did not move when I moved, so I had to turn my whole body with every gesture. To add insult to injury, the dress was about two inches too long and my every step looked a little like a goose step—a kick and a scoot.

Among the other guests were many friends from the United Nations days who were there representing their countries. I asked one of the ladies if Mrs. Marcos had given her a dress, and she assured me that she had, but of course she hadn't worn it. My only comfort was that when I told Nancy Reagan about the dress, she told me that the same thing happened to her. I don't mean to sound ungracious; I know Mrs. Marcos was just being generous.

It was a well-known fact that she was a compulsive shopper; it certainly was obvious from our rooms. There were several dozen large baskets of food stacked on the floor, all wrapped in cellophane. Much to our horror, they were put on our plane when we left. They were filled with stale chocolate, cans of diet food, popcorn—you name it, we had it.

While we were there George praised Marcos for lifting martial law, which we had been pushing him to do for years. The press crucified George for this because of continuing human rights violation charges. But they neglected to mention why George felt he must praise Marcos: to encourage him to continue moving in the right direction; and because, at that time, it appeared Marcos was the only person standing between his country and a Communist takeover. I guess the reporters' parents never told them that the "sin of omission" is as bad as a lie.

We had a great visit while we were there with General Carlos Romulo and his wife, Beth, dear friends from our UN days. Rommy was a great hero in World War II, along with President Marcos, and was a compadre and friend of General Douglas MacArthur. I think in light of the later troubles in the Philippines, we forget the enormous courage of these people and the losses they suffered side by side with our own troops.

However, as Imelda escorted us around, we would pass high wooden fences behind and through which we could see abject poverty. I wrote in my diary: "I have a feeling that I'm looking at a Marie Antoinette. Someone who is living pretty highly while others are suffering . . . I fear that they will have another Iran or Nicaragua here."

I take little credit for predicting Marcos's overthrow; it did not take a rocket scientist to see it coming.

The actual inauguration was held early in the morning because of the immense heat. Thousands of people were bused in, and the square was packed. The visiting dignitaries were on a stage overlooking a large crowd held back by security men holding hands. On the right, in the middle of the crowd, I noticed one of our tall Secret Service agents. In that group, he literally stood out in a crowd. During Marcos's address, a man suddenly broke through the hand-holding security line and charged across the square waving a tube. He got within five feet of Marcos before our tall agent, jumping over twenty or so people, managed to put both arms around him and carry him off. It must have embarrassed our hosts that their own men hadn't responded. Considering the fact that Imelda had been slashed by a machete several years before in just such a situation, their security should have known something could happen. We were so proud of our brave, disciplined agent. As it turns out, the tube held only a petition, but no one could have known that at the time.

We came home from that trip to our new summer home, Walker's Point in Kennebunkport, which we had purchased after George dropped out of the presidential race in 1980. George's Uncle Herbie Walker, a great friend and business backer in earlier days, had died and the Point was for sale. It had been in George's family since the turn of the century. Several commercial groups wanted to buy it, but George's mother would not sell her little acre that sits right in the middle of the Point. On a government salary we felt we couldn't afford it, but in June 1980, we were out of politics, so George bought it. Suddenly, in August, we were back in politics. So to meet our financial commitments, we sold our dream house in Houston and bought a small lot, and we also sold the gray house in Kennebunkport where we had summered for ten years. As it turns out, the Point was a smart buy for us as our happy gray house would have been impossible to protect. It was right on the street, and people often walked up on the porch and looked in the windows.

We are so lucky in Maine to have great friends who also are great builders. Longley Philbrick had worked on Walker's Point in 1925 when the porch was incorporated into the house as a living room. In

1981, Longley and his son Danny restored Walker's Point and helped us make many changes in the structure of the house. At this writing, Danny and his son Terry are restoring Mrs. Bush's bungalow.

Longley is gone, but the family, headed by his wife, Mary, represents everything that is great about America. They love their country, their God, and their family. They are fair, honest, and hardworking.

Walker's Point always had been an important part of George's life. For the next twelve years, it would be the perfect refuge from our high-profile lives and is now our summer home.

During the vice presidential years we had several terrific Memorial Day house parties in Maine. They were great fun for us as we gathered some of our favorite people, many of whom had not met each other before but are now friends. Political party affiliations made no difference in this house party. Among the many people who came were Louisiana Senator Bennett Johnston and his wife, Mary; Wyoming Senator Alan Simpson and Ann; Ambassador Fred Zeder and Martha; Betsy and Spike Heminway, from Kennebunkport and Greenwich, longtime friends of ours and our children; Malcolm Baldrige, Secretary of Commerce, and his wife, Midge; Pat and Dean Burch; Bobbie and Jack Fitch and Daphne and Bob Murray, all from Houston; former Houston neighbor Charles Neblett, a brilliant brain surgeon, and his wife, Sally; and Dick and Sally Novetzke (she later was named ambassador to Malta). These are all people that George and I love and enjoy.

One Memorial Day weekend, Mac Baldrige and George spoke at the First Congregational Church service on Sunday. Mac told about when he was a soldier during World War II, holding a hill on an island in the Pacific. During the day, a group of Japanese women started up the hill with water jars in their arms. Mac, as the leader, had to make the decision: Were they really women, or were they armed men? They got closer as dusk came, and Mac decided that he couldn't take a chance, so they opened fire and killed them. The next morning the Americans rushed down the hill and found that they had made the right decision— they were fully armed Japanese men.

Mac then skipped to several months later when he was with the occupation troops in Japan. They saw pictures of Americans as villains with long noses and mean faces—just as we saw Hirohito in our country. Worse, he saw that the average person was afraid of him and other Americans. He suddenly saw the Japanese as human beings. He ended his very moving talk by saying that we must learn all people are the same, and wars must end.

Several years later our dear friend Mac suffered a massive heart attack while taking part in a rodeo. Every Easter, our friend Annie Cluff gives an Easter lily in Mac's name at the First Congregational Church, and just recently we found two new hymnals in our pew given by Annie: one in Mac's name and one in ours.

September 10, 1981—I went to Sandra Day O'Connor's Senate hearings on her appointment to the Supreme Court, which was very exciting since she was the first woman nominated. Potter Stewart had resigned from the court after serving twenty-five years. When he was sworn in in 1956, he said that he would resign after that period of time and he did. I believe that he hoped that other older justices would do the same, but they didn't.

Sandra is everything that I admire in a woman. She and her husband, John, have three fine sons and have struck a balance in their two careers that is enviable. I was very happy to attend her swearing-in on September 25.

There are several stories that I love about Sandra. One concerns a graduation speech that she gave. She said that she never thought that she'd be a Supreme Court Justice. She just tried to do the best she could in everything she did: the best student, the best daughter, the best wife, the best mother, the best lawyer, and so on. I rather liked that because I have always felt that's what George Bush did. He just did his best at everything he took on. The mountain seems easier to climb if you take one hill at a time.

The other story I love about Sandra has to do with golf. She took up the game so she and John could enjoy it together. She took lessons and hit balls on the practice tee for several years before she ever played a game on a course. What marvelous discipline.

I played tennis with Sandra at seven A.M. once a week during both the vice presidential and White House years. She was always on time, a good sport, very competitive, and played a much better game than I did.

One morning I noticed that her hair was causing her great trouble. It was too long, and she kept poking it up. As with many busy women, she had a sense of priorities and her hair was not on that list.

I mentioned to her that she badly needed a cut and my hairdresser had a shop near her on the Hill. I told her that I would call her office and give her secretary the number.

She called me that afternoon and said, "I had my hair cut, and I feel like a new person. Thank you so very much."

Several days later I got a note from her husband:

> Dear Barbara,
>
>   I married Sandra 27 years ago, and once, the year after we were married, she had her hair styled. She's never done it since. When I came home, I said: "Wow. What happened?" She said: "Barbara Bush told me to have my hair cut." If I ever find myself in trouble with Sandra, may I call on you?
>
> John

In spite of the hair story, Sandra and I have remained friends. I only wish that my children and other friends were as obedient when I make suggestions.

꙰ *October 4, 1981*—I came home to find George in the living room talking with a very nice man, the vice president of Egypt, Hosni Mubarak. A few days later, he was president of his country. On October 6, Anwar Sadat was assassinated, shot down during a military parade. That brave, courageous man was one of the heroes of the twentieth century, and the two or three times that I met him were very special. President Mubarak has been a great leader for Egypt, and he and his wife, Suzanne, have become dear friends of ours. Their job has not been an easy one, and the stand that he took years later during Desert Storm showed great courage.

It was thought too dangerous for the President or Vice President to attend Sadat's funeral, so President Reagan invited the former presidents to go, and they all accepted. The Reagans very kindly invited me to join George and the President's top three aides, Jim Baker, Mike Deaver, and Ed Meese, at the White House when President Reagan symbolically gave the presidents a letter to carry to the funeral. We watched from a window as President Reagan and Nancy greeted the helicopter on the South Grounds. It was certainly a historic moment.

There stood the four living presidents of the United States. It all rather amused me. I don't really think they liked each other very much. Ronald Reagan had challenged Jerry Ford in a nasty Republican primary fight in 1976. Jimmy Carter was beaten by Ronald Reagan in 1980. Jimmy Carter had beaten Jerry Ford in 1976. Many people believe Jerry Ford lost the election because he pardoned Richard Nixon. And there they all stood together. Rosalynn came also, and I don't believe that she and Nancy liked each other very much. Those tense fifteen minutes were up fairly quickly, and the helicopter took off for Andrews Air Force Base.

I was especially curious about who sat in the President's cabin. I was further amused to discover that it was "none of the above." Al Haig, who was Secretary of State, and Cap Weinberger, who was Secretary of Defense, did. And to be truthful, I don't think they liked each other very much either. Henry Kissinger was also on the trip. Now Henry and Al Haig had worked for Presidents Nixon and Ford, and, of course, Al worked for Henry. I don't know how much they all liked each other, but it was fun to speculate. And speculation it is—and a little fun I had.

  October 17, 1981—President and Mrs. Mitterrand of France came to the United States to celebrate the two-hundredth anniversary of America's—with France's help—victory at Yorktown, ending the Revolutionary War. George and I were asked to have a dinner for the Mitterrands one evening of the visit. The inn where we were holding the dinner sent us three menus to choose from. They sounded great, but all were French cuisine. I sent back a request that we have American food, and they came back with a delicious menu of pumpkin soup served in pumpkins, turkey, and other uniquely American foods. I was very pleased. You can't out-French the French, and we do very well on our own.

The next evening the Reagans had a sensational dinner with all the pomp and ceremony one could imagine. We made a dramatic entrance through men and women in colonial costumes, with flares to light our way. I never tried to out-Reagan the Reagans, either.

This was the beginning of a warm relationship George had with Mitterrand. For some reason, President Reagan and Mitterrand did not strike up a friendship, and it is pretty hard not to like Ronald Reagan.

November 19–23, 1981—Loret Ruppe, the able director of the Peace Corps and my dear 90th Club friend, invited me to go to Ghana to help celebrate the twenty-fifth anniversary of the corps. We had the most marvelous trip. Before we went, I called an old friend from our UN days, Shirley Temple Black, and asked her for any advice she might have since she had served there as ambassador. She came up with the same suggestion as others: Get some wedge-heeled shoes, as many of the parties were outside and the ground at this time of the year was soft from the rain. In regular heels, you would sink into the ground. So Becky, my aide, was sent out on a search, and after much looking did find some beige patent leather shoes with a wedge heel. What a laugh. All the ladies in Ghana wore the highest heels. We also were there during the driest, hottest time of year. The ground felt like rock, and not only did I look really dowdy, the patent leather cooked my feet.

One day we went out into the countryside, where we met with an *asantehene,* who is a chief of a tribe. This gentleman was a great big man with a very cultured voice; he was dressed in tribal robes and covered with gold toe and hand rings, chains, and other finery. (I also saw pictures of him in his white wig and barrister robes.) Then the ceremony started. Very dramatically we were led in to sit under an awning, then the tribes came in, dancing and singing to beating drums. The women came first, followed by the children and finally the men. It was hotter than one could believe. Finally the Asantehene was carried in with much pomp, and he sat opposite me under another tent. Little boys shimmied up long poles, teetering above our heads, and men and women did strange dances.

Out of the middle of all this came a man covered with white powder. The crowds parted, and he took center stage, dancing around and around in a frenzied fashion and swinging a feathered thing over his head and down on the ground. I'm not sure when it came to me that the feathered thing was a live chicken. I think it was just before this crazy man put its head in his mouth and bit if off. He then rubbed the blood on his body as his followers threw more white powder on him. Yuk. He got closer and closer to me until someone yelled at him, and they led him off. Becky almost fainted from the heat and disgust.

During all this I sat next to the governor of the state. He had on the darndest costume. He told me with pride that he had gotten the material in Europe. It was a simulated leopard skin that was made of something like oilcloth. He wore it like a toga, and it was dripping wet. I can't think of a more miserable outfit to wear—or to sit next to—in that kind of heat.

Another day we visited several villages where we saw the work our Peace Corps volunteers were doing. They were all ages, shapes, sizes, and colors. What extraordinary men and women. They are the very best aid that we give, I believe, for they teach people to do for themselves. It is not a handout, but a hand up. George and I have visited Peace Corps workers around the world. They sometimes live under the most destitute conditions but they always do a great job. I hated leaving them so far from home and tried to either write or call their relatives when I got back to the States. I will confess that I didn't always tell their families that their child or parent was living under the most primitive of conditions.

December 1, 1981—I was invited to put the star on the top of the national Christmas tree on the Ellipse in front of the White House. I went up in a cherry picker with a dear man named Joe Riley, who was and still is the chairman of the Annual Pageant of Peace. This ceremony is not to be confused with the annual lighting of the Christmas tree. The tree is the same, but the events are two weeks apart. The President has the honor of doing the latter. For the eight years George was vice president and the four he was president, up I went in that cherry picker. It was a wonderful, fun event. Over the years, Joe and I took many of the grandchildren—Jenna and Barbara, Sam and Ellie, Walker and Marshall, Lauren and Pierce—and several schoolchildren to help us. Some years were bumpy and some smooth; we went rain or shine. Sometimes I felt a little like Mary Poppins.

It struck me that I worked so hard all year long for literacy and got little or no press coverage, and then I would do something frivolous like going up in a cherry picker and my picture is seen around the world. So one year I took Rita and Rex Saurus, two puppets who encourage children to read. I had met Rita and Rex at a Reading Is Fundamental (RIF) event, and then saw them several times around the country. I am a huge fan of RIF and believe it is a very effective way to put books into the hands of children, many of whom never had the joy of owning a book. You can find RIF in schools, migrant workers' camps, homeless shelters, and soup kitchens, just to name a few. Although it gets some federal funding and many grants, it's largely a volunteer effort.

My dear friend Anne Richardson took over the leadership from its founder, Margaret McNamara. It has grown from Margaret taking her children's old books to a public school into a nationwide effort that gives away an estimated ten million books a year.

∾ *April 23–25, 1982*—During a visit to Japan, George and I had lunch at the Imperial Palace with Emperor Hirohito. While waiting for him to appear, I remember standing in front of some closed double doors and thinking that behind them stood the man we thought of as the devil when we were growing up. This was whom, rightly or wrongly, we blamed for Pearl Harbor. When the doors opened there stood a tiny, gentle-looking being.

During that most memorable lunch, I sat next to the Emperor and found the conversation pretty heavy sledding. I would say, "I went to the school your grandchildren attend this morning." He would smile and say, "Yes." He had a "yes" or "no" answer for everything with an occasional "thank you" thrown in. We were sitting in the glorious, relatively new palace, so, desperate for something to talk about, I said that the new palace was lovely.

"Thank you," he answered.

Then I tried, "Is it new?"

"Yes."

Finally I tried: "Was the old palace just so old that it was falling down?"

He turned with a charming smile on his face and said, "No, I'm afraid that you bombed it."

I turned to my partner on my left.

∾ *September 1, 1982*—Doro, who had graduated from Boston College in June, married Bill LeBlond on a cold, rainy day in Kennebunkport at little St. Ann's Church. This is our summer church in

Maine, open only from the Fourth of July to Labor Day. George's parents and Neil and Sharon were married there, several of our children were christened there, and various other family functions have taken place in this beautiful stone church.

We were to have a reception under a big tent on the lawn at Walker's Point. We awakened that day to not only rain, but a fierce rain that came in at an angle. I will never get over being grateful to Jane Weintraub, formerly Jane Morgan, a Kennebunkport friend and neighbor and a marvelous entertainer. She came by that morning around nine A.M. to see if she could help. I was suffering over just what I should do. Should we move the party into the Boat Club? Should we take a chance and stick with the tent? George was calling the Coast Guard for weather reports on the hour when Jane said: "Make up your mind at ten o'clock. We move to the Boat Club or we don't and then sit back and enjoy it." We did just that, moving to the Boat Club. We stopped the florist from decorating the tent, and she and my boys moved the tables and chairs and the flowers. It was a day of hard work for all.

I was amused because many "Bush-watchers" had gathered across the bay with chairs to see the Vice President's daughter get married. They did not get the word and watched the empty tent for hours in pouring rain.

In spite of the weather, it was a happy wedding. Bill's parents are dear friends, and we love Billy. Sad to say, the children did not stay married. They had two very beautiful children, Ellie and Sam, and have behaved in a way that should be a manual when that awful thing, divorce, happens to others. The happy ending is that they both have remarried lovely people, and Sam and Ellie have two sets of parents, siblings on both sides, and more grandparents who love them than any other children I know.

~~~ *October 3, 1982*—George and I had the great pleasure of dedicating the Betty Ford Center in Palm Springs, California. George said in his speech what we both felt:

> In 1978 Betty Ford discovered that she had become dependent on alcohol and drugs. I can state the case plainly because Betty has already had the courage to do so.

. . . She transformed her pain into something great for the common good. Because she suffered, there will be more healing. Because of her grief, there will be more joy.

. . . Our nation has produced great men. It has also produced great women. Our gracious First Lady stands among them.

November 9–24, 1982—George led a delegation on an African trip, including Dr. Ben Payton of Tuskegee and Dr. Louis Sullivan of the Morehouse School of Medicine, representing two prestigious, predominantly black schools. We had some funny things happen on that trip. At one luncheon, our hosts wanted to make us feel at home so they played American music—"Ol' Black Joe," "Carry Me Back to Old Virginny," and some other gems. I caught Louis Sullivan's eye, and he winked at me.

In Zaire, both men went with me to visit a literacy program at a university. A lady named Alice Anderson had come to Zaire for a short visit, saw a great need, and stayed on for the next twenty years to teach people to read. We attended a graduation, where I gave a small talk and handed out certificates. Then some of the students read a short story telling us what reading meant to them. Their reasons resembled what I heard from adult literacy students in our own country: They want to get a job; they want their children to be proud of them; they want to read their Bibles, and so forth. Then one woman got up and said: "I needed to read. My husband kept getting letters. He said they were business. Now I can read . . . now I know." She left the clear impression that her husband had been up to no good, and she had put a stop to that!

Shortly after we returned from that trip, Dr. Sullivan invited me to join the Morehouse School of Medicine Board of Directors. I accepted and spent six very happy years with some of the finest men and women I have ever met. Although I was concentrating most of my time on literacy, there is a very good argument that a healthy child is a better learner, so there was a definite connection.

It is not easy trying to start and support a medical school. Louis Sullivan did and did it well. It was a constant struggle, especially when we had no alumni to draw from. I traveled with Louis and fellow board member Bob Froehlke to many cities across the United States to fund-raising lunches. The need for a school like Morehouse is very apparent. There are many rural and inner-city areas in our great country that are medically underserved or not served at all. Morehouse doctors are being trained to go into these areas.

Although I went off the board when George was sworn in as president, I certainly didn't lose interest. I went back in October 1989 to give the convocation speech, which said in part:

> Compared to white children, black children are twice as likely to die in the first year of life; three times as likely to have their mothers die in childbirth; and five times as likely to become pregnant teenagers . . . boarder babies, throw-away kids, crack babies. It doesn't sound urgent enough to call these children the "medically underserved." The children George and I have seen at Covenant House, Grandma's House, Martha's Table, and at D.C. General Hospital are literally fighting for their lives. Their fight is our fight . . . and that fight is the mission of Morehouse.

It always amused me that I got credit for Louis's being asked to join George's cabinet as Secretary of Health and Human Services. George introduced me to Louis, and I got invited to join his board because I was George Bush's wife. They certainly got that one wrong, but I was always glad to get the credit. Lou and Ginger were a great addition to the Washington scene, and he was an outstanding HHS secretary. Lucky for the school, he has returned to Morehouse.

In the middle of our trip to Africa we got the word that Soviet leader Leonid Brezhnev had died. There were many cables sent back and forth about who would go to the funeral. We heard that all the former presidents and secretaries of state wanted to go with George. There was so much pressure being put on the White House and State Department that it was decided "none of the above"; Barbara Bush would go and then nobody could gripe. What a break for me. The fact that I had only summer clothes with me and this was November in Moscow made no difference. We called Laurie Firestone and she bundled up boots, gloves, dresses, and a winter coat along with George's clothes and saw that they were put on Secretary of State George Shultz's plane.

We left most of our traveling party in Africa and flew off to Moscow for the most extraordinary day or two. On our arrival, Secretary Shultz boarded our plane with our winter coats, which we put on over our summer clothes, and we went right away to view the body, lying in state at the Kremlin. We walked up a glorious, winding staircase with the most haunting music wafting downward. Above our heads were large wall sconces, all wrapped in black net. Russians were standing about four deep. I will have to confess that I saw no people weeping for Brezhnev, in contrast to China, where the people kept their heads down and looked mournful at Chou En-lai's funeral. The people we saw were all types, some very well dressed and some not so well dressed.

Suddenly we were at the top of the staircase, and there in a bier directly in front of us, slightly tilted upward, was the body of the former chairman. To our left was a symphony orchestra all dressed in black and the source of the plaintive music. The whole casket was covered with a blanket of flowers, and his medals were displayed at the front. To the right sat a sweet, sad little group, and George rightly judged an older lady to be Mrs. Brezhnev. He told her that he was an American expressing the grief of our people, and she answered back something about our two peoples wanting peace. It was amazing that before this funeral, we Americans were not even sure that there was a Mrs. Brezhnev.

The next morning our ambassador's wife, Donna Hartman, bundled us up, and George, George Shultz, Ambassador Arthur Hartman, and I went off to the funeral. It was the most beautifully orchestrated event I have ever attended. I wrote in my diary:

We got to Red Square, got to a certain spot and were let off. We came out behind Lenin's Tomb and the next thing I knew, they came up and said: "This is the place where you stop." They let George Bush through and then there was some discussion as to whether or not I could go through. Finally they said: "Yes, because she is part of the delegation." And Secretary Shultz was sort of pulled through. They cut off Arthur Hartman and my Secret Service, but they had a better view than us, to be honest. They could see

Castro, Arafat and the rest. They had put on the left all the countries who were sort of friendly to them, and on the right countries like us and Great Britain, Italy, Australia and Ireland.

In the middle of the square was an orchestra that stood at the ready without moving or playing for an hour. Directly in front of us stood the most elite, Aryan-looking troops I have ever seen, all facing us. I was amazed. This in a country that prides itself on having some forty minorities.

As we stood talking with our friends from Great Britain, Ireland, and Italy, we heard a great commotion in the crowd, and pushing by us went Imelda Marcos. She had on the most extraordinary floor-length mink coat with a herringbone pattern. Very soon after she passed an aide came back and said, "The First Lady of the Philippines would like the Vice President of the United States to join her in the front row." George thanked him and turned him down. George Shultz and I told George that was lucky for him. Had he accepted, it would have been the end: George Shultz would not have let him back in the country, and I certainly would never have let him back into the house. How we later laughed over that.

The funeral started on the hour, and in came the casket drawn by a tank, solemnly followed by Brezhnev's family, who were walking. The orchestra started playing the most beautiful lugubrious music. The casket was turned to face the tomb, where the hierarchy of the Soviet Union was standing. There were no women near the top. We saw Gromyko, that great cold warrior, and Andropov, the former head of the KGB and the newly designated leader of the USSR. There were many speeches, and we all huddled around an interpreter with the Irish delegation. The speeches said very little about Brezhnev and lots about the future. The casket was taken around behind the tomb, followed by family and then the diplomats. I was cut away from the men and led toward the cars, where Arthur Hartman and I waited for the two Georges. The minute the casket disappeared, the whole tone of the day changed. The music was one of victory and jubilation. One of our Western friends rather cynically said, "The King is dead, never to be mentioned again."

Much to his surprise, George saw Mrs. Brezhnev lean over the coffin and make the sign of the cross. After the funeral was over, both

Georges were led up a staircase into a great hall in the Kremlin where they shook hands with the top leadership of the country, including Andropov.

Just fourteen months later, George would attend Andropov's funeral and meet his successor, Chernenko, and then a year later, he would go to his funeral, where he met Mikhail Gorbachev. George developed a friendship with Gorbachev and to this day has enormous respect for this thoughtful man who really changed our whole world for the better.

It was shortly after the Chernenko funeral that people started introducing George as the man with the motto "You die, I fly."

I was amazed recently to read that Vice President Gore announced that he didn't do funerals. I really feel that is shortsighted. George met with many current or future heads of state at the funerals he attended, enabling him to forge personal relationships that were important to President Reagan—and later, President Bush.

July 10, 1983—George and I hosted a clambake at Walker's Point for the governors and their families who were attending a governors' conference in Maine. (Many years later, Bill Clinton would remind Chelsea that she had met us that day.) There were so many governors and family members that we had to make a rule that no straphangers—meaning staff members—were allowed. Those with babies under age two could bring nannies, but that was it.

Our children helped with tours of the Point, and then we had a typical Maine clambake with clams, lobster, fresh Maine corn, coleslaw, salad, ice-cream bars, and of course hamburgers and hot dogs for those who can't face shellfish.

George's mother joined us on the lawn for lunch and met all the governors. Governor George Wallace came with his new, very sensual third wife, I believe. (I know that she was sensual; it's which wife she was that I'm unsure of.) She had on a very tight dress, was very well endowed, and had her hair pouffed up with much teasing and hair spray. By comparison, the rest of us looked a little underdressed in pants and cotton shirts. The Governor was in his wheelchair, pushed by an Alabama state policeman. They both were very pleasant and polite to Mrs. Bush. After the lunch, when we were alone, Mrs. Bush said, "George, I just can't see what that nice man sees in that woman." George didn't have the heart to tell her.

George liked and felt a lot of sympathy for George Wallace. Whether or not you agree politically with a person is certainly no excuse for taking the law into your own hands.

ᗗ *August 6–8, 1983*—In the middle of a trip to the western states, George decided that we should go camping in Glacier National Park in Montana. I was thrilled as I had never visited a national park. George also decided that we would sleep in a tent in the woods. The others in our party had a choice of a tent or a camper with running water, indoor plumbing, and air-conditioning. Not for us. We wanted to be communing with nature. So our little tent was set up quite a way from the others; we zipped ourselves in and climbed into our sleeping bags with many giggles. It didn't take long for us to realize that for security reasons, our tent was ringed with lights some thirty feet away. We felt like we were sleeping in the middle of Times Square. Then the roots under our sleeping bags started to torture our backs. It was very hard to sleep. Finally George got up to go to the bathroom in the woods to discover that behind every light and tree was a Secret Service agent. It was one of the most miserable nights of our lives. The next night two tiny mattresses appeared under our sleeping bags, and a jar appeared for George's nocturnal use. I walked half a mile to the camper, followed by an agent. I was tempted to stay.

Nevertheless, that was really one of the most fun trips we took. Wyoming Senator Alan Simpson and his wife, Ann, were with us, and as always, they were great fun to be with. The park was beautiful, and the National Park Service people were splendid.

ᗗ *September 11–21, 1983*—George and I took an amazing ten-day trip to northern Africa, visiting Morocco, Algeria, and Tunisia, and then went on to Yugoslavia, Romania, Hungary, and Austria, refueling at Ireland on the way home. In every country we were received graciously by the leaders of the country. We had dinner with King Hassan in Morocco, lunch with President and Mrs. Bendjedid of Algeria, and an unusual luncheon given by President and Mrs. Bourguiba of Tunisia. He was a national hero who many years before had been the "father of his country." By 1983 this fine man was very old and senile. His doctor had put him on a diet, so all during lunch he ate from my plate. When it came time for his toast, with the TV cameras running, he fumbled and yelled. His glasses slid down his nose, and he shouted that he was going blind until his wife leaned across the table and pushed them up. When George got up to give his toast, this poor man interrupted, ranting and raving until he was quietly pulled down. It wasn't funny, just sad. What was amazing was, on the evening TV news, he looked perfectly in control.

In Yugoslavia, Kim Brady, my personal aide, became very ill and ended up having her appendix out. Luckily, it was a very good hospital and her doctor had been trained in Houston. How I hated to leave her there, but her mother was en route to be with her and the ambassador, David Anderson, and his wife, Helen, were wonderful. Before leaving, we had dinner with the Foreign Minister, Lazar Mojsov, and his wife, old friends from the United Nations.

Then it was on to Romania for an unbelievable twenty-four hours. We were warned that President and Mrs. Ceauşescu were very strange people. We weren't surprised, then, to find that the plans for meeting with them were loose and different. Our events in Bucharest were few and very limited. I visited a pleasant outdoor museum promoting their handicrafts. We noticed that the streets were large, broad, and very empty. The people were downcast, drab, and unhappy looking. In most cities around the world, you would see people walking around outside after work enjoying life. Not here. It was a dreary place.

The tentative plan was for George to meet with Ceauşescu, then there would be a dinner. The problem was that no one knew who was invited. I was told early in the evening that it was going to be just George and me and the dinner would be held at the Lodge, an informal place. So I dressed and settled down with a book. I waited and waited. Then the word came that the plans had changed and we would be eating at the official residence. So I changed into a short black taffeta dress with a little velvet trim. I was picked up by a sturdy interpreter with a nice smile and henna-colored hair, which finds such favor in Eastern European countries. She took me to a large house where we sat in the front hall for an hour and had a strained chat. The hour was getting later and later. I could hear men's voices in the background and recognized George's, otherwise I would have felt that I was in the wrong place. At about 8:45 P.M., a plain-looking, very informally dressed woman walked down the staircase and was introduced as Mrs. Ceauşescu. We sat in the stiff front hall and talked. She had no small talk, spoke not a word of English, and did not initiate one word of conversation. After forty-five tense minutes, the door opened and out walked George and President Ceauşescu, thank heavens. At ten o'clock we went into a magnificent dining room with a long table that probably seated sixteen or eighteen people. Down one side were four place settings with about three feet separating each one. I sat on the end, followed by the President, then George, and finally, waaaaaaay down on the other end, Mrs. Ceauşescu. No sooner had we gotten seated than the press were led in for pictures. I looked down the table and saw George smiling and the two of them looking grumpy as if they smelled something bad. So all the pictures that appeared in the papers reflected that we were having fun and they were not.

A seven-course meal followed, starting with bowls of caviar served by four men in lavender livery. There were plates of bread, butter, fruit, and cheeses at each place. At one time during the lavish meal, a London broil was served, and after I took a tiny piece, my lavender-liveried waiter said: "Oh, go on, take some more, it's good," in an obviously Brooklyn accent! What in the world an American was doing serving our dinner I never did find out. I couldn't believe all the grandeur in a country where people were lining up for every bite they ate and where we had been told the shortages were almost overwhelming.

All during the dinner Ceauşescu talked and talked and talked and George listened. When George tried to answer or talk, Ceauşescu interrupted. We were stunned by his ego. She spoke once only, and he turned and said something that was not interpreted, but the tone of voice led me to believe it was something like "Be quiet!" Years later it would be clear that we had been with two of the most evil people in this world.

The visit to Hungary was very typical of the many trips we took during the vice presidential years. I visited schools, hospitals, museums, and met with the leading women of the country while George met with the heads of state.

∽ *October 23, 1983*—Tragedy struck when 241 of our Marines, who were part of a multinational peace-keeping force, were killed in

Beirut by a kamikaze terrorist attack. The country was stunned. George was going to make a top-secret trip to the war-torn country to boost the remaining troops' morale. He told me he would go to the office and leave from there, taking only Admiral Dan Murphy, Shirley Green, and Jennifer Fitzgerald of his staff. We were supposed to go to the Pakistan Embassy that night for a dinner given for us by General Zia. George asked me to go alone and told me to sidle up to the General and explain just how sorry he was and that he would know the next morning why he wasn't there. Thank heavens that I did not have to go to the Embassy. The nice Chief Justice Warren Burger went in George's place. I could never ever have kept from showing how frightened I was.

George told me that his trip was very safe and that I must not worry, but that for the sake of security, I must be very, very discreet and not tell another living human.

Several times during the day I got calls from the White House switchboard asking me if George was home. Each time I said no. The operator mused once, "Well, we show him still at the office, but he isn't answering." I kept my regular schedule and went to a Ronald McDonald House event and later to a Daughters of the American Revolution tea where they very kindly gave me a medal for my work with literacy. I felt funny not saying a word to Susan Porter Rose or Andy Stewart, to whom I tell everything—almost.

That night I sat at home alone doing needlepoint, worrying and praying. The phone rang, and it was Steve Rhodes, a wonderful man who worked for George and who also was a friend. He said that he had been trying to reach George all day. I lied and hated it. I told him that George was in a very important meeting and I expected it to run very late.

The next morning when I awakened, I saw George in Beirut on TV. One minute later he called. He had told me that he would call the minute the plane left Beirut, and he did. I called his mother immediately so she would not worry when she saw him over there. I was so grateful. I will confess that keeping secrets is an enormous burden for me. Having George in danger is almost unbearable.

≈ *February 11–12, 1984*—We went to England and stayed at Winfield House with our wonderful Ambassador Charlie Price and his wife, Carol. Carol is the person in the world that you would most like to stay with. She is the best hostess, very thoughtful, and runs the most comfortable household. They hosted a glorious black-tie dinner, including on the guest list many Americans who came to England especially for the evening and some who were in Europe for a vacation or business. One of our more stylish friends wore the darndest dress for a thin, over-thirty—well, maybe over-fifty—socialite. It was a green chiffon sheath with a bib top and spaghetti straps. The side view on an eighteen-year-old would have been provocative; on an aging lady who was prone to flamboyant gestures, it was embarrassing.

The next day, Margaret and Denis Thatcher gave a large lunch at No. 10 Downing Street, the home of the prime minister. George sat next to Denis, and I noticed they were sharing a big laugh. George told Denis to tell me the joke, which he did immediately. "George asked me if I hadn't enjoyed the dinner at the U.S. Embassy the night before," Denis said. "And I replied that I had; but that I had sat next to [the woman in question] and quite frankly, I got awfully tired of looking at her left tit." I was so surprised that I burst out laughing; not a small giggle, but a loud laugh. At which time Margaret turned to George and said, "Isn't it nice that Denis and Barbara get along so well?" That got the three of us really laughing.

On that same visit the Thatchers invited us and the Prices to Checquers. It was a joy to see this exciting country estate, which is the British equivalent of Camp David. We were greeted by our host and hostess, given a cup of tea, and led to our rooms. Margaret made sure that I was comfortable and had plenty to read; gave me the guest list for dinner, saying that she had picked dinner partners that she thought I would enjoy; then rushed off to discuss armaments and other issues with George. Amazing. I remembered being very moved and touched by her thoughtfulness and thinking that she combined all that was good about being a woman in public life. She was proud of both her ability and of being a woman.

While they talked, Denis squired Carol Price and me around, showing us, among many things, trees that foreign heads of state had planted. Although I later went back to Checquers with Norma Major, George never went as president and so did not plant a tree there. On Sunday morning while the leaders worked, Denis, Carol, and I went to a lovely tiny church that sat on top of a hill and that had a spire that was taller than the church was wide or long. Denis told me not to worry—the service would not be too long. And believe me, it wasn't.

The poor minister had barely gotten into his sermon when Denis made a loud "Ahem," raised his arm, and looked pointedly at his watch. It worked. The sermon drew rapidly to a close.

Every time I saw Denis, I loved him more. When George and I first met the Thatchers, George was still in Congress, and Margaret came to Houston to give a speech. I was so impressed with her knowledge and presentation. But Denis I found rather rude, especially when he made several disparaging remarks to me about Americans. But I learned over the years that he has a wonderful sense of humor and is steady as a rock. Plus, he's a good sport. Many times he found himself the only male in a roomful of "spouses."

April 3, 1984—C. Fred officially became a famous dog and an author with the publication of *C. Fred's Story.* I don't know who was more surprised—him or me.

It all started many months earlier when we were having dinner with Nelson and Sandy Doubleday at the Vice President's House. Nelson backed into C. Fred, and George said, "Don't kick that dog. He is writing a book." Nelson took George seriously, and several weeks later asked me to talk to Lisa Drew, an editor at Doubleday. I certainly did not know when I met this bright, feisty, funny lady that she would edit three books for me, help me with a foundation, and become a good friend.

Up until this point, I really just had been *talking* about writing a book with Freddy. I wanted to raise some money for literacy, and that was just one idea that I had. Lisa came to call on me when she was in Washington, and we were on our way. I'm not sure that Lisa ever had a handwritten manuscript sent to her before, but I do know that after she saw mine, she requested a typewritten one. Thank heavens, our dear friend Jane Kenny typed it for me. We had a lot of fun with that book and raised around $100,000 for Literacy Volunteers of America and Laubach Literacy Action, the two national programs I had been working with.

About half the money raised came from donations people sent in. One day George called and asked if I was seated. He knew I'd fall down otherwise when he told me that he had opened a letter from someone whom we had never met, a Mr. Joseph Uihlein of Grafton, Wisconsin, but who was a friend and classmate of George's uncle, Dr. John

Walker. He had sent a check for $25,000 for LVA along with a letter saying he liked the book. In my wildest dreams I never thought the book would make $25,000, so the whole experience was very happy for me. On a smaller scale, quite a few other people sent in checks and contributions.

We had several book parties in public libraries, including the kickoff at the New York City Public Library. I am a big supporter of libraries, which play such an important role in our educational system. Many of them sponsor literacy classes and programs to get children hooked on books early in life. Sad to say, if there is a money crunch, the libraries are the first to feel it—just when their services are the most needed. Many city libraries have numerous programs that can really help, such as English as a Second Language classes, seminars on job hunting, coffee kitchens for mothers, story times for children, art appreciation classes, and on and on.

In conjunction with the book parties, I also went on a media tour to talk about the book. I didn't mind doing that as I really wanted to talk about the problems of illiteracy in this country. I wanted people to know that we had a literacy problem and to urge them to be part of the answer, whether they donated money to local programs that worked, volunteered their time, or just made darn sure that they were reading aloud to their children and grandchildren. It gave me an opportunity to urge people to support their public libraries and to take an interest in their children's schools by volunteering, running for the school board, or just attending PTA meetings. My mission was to make literacy an important value in every household.

So the day after the first book party, I appeared on the "Today" show to be interviewed by my old friend, Jane Pauley. She raced on the set, and as she was putting on her mike, she said something like, "Let's make this fun and not talk about literacy." Not talk about literacy? No way. That was what I was there for. Her first question was, "Mrs. Bush, why would a dog write a book?" Knowing that this might be my only chance, my answer was that he was worried about illiteracy in our country, and then I got in as many facts as possible before I let her get another word in edgewise.

∽ *May 7–20, 1984*—George and I took a fascinating trip to Japan, Indonesia, India, and Pakistan.

In Japan we lunched with Prime Minister and Mrs. Nakasone, a very attractive couple, and their children. We also had a reunion with Mike Mansfield, a former senator and our ambassador to Japan, and his wife, Maureen. I believe that when they thought up the word *gentleman,* Mike was the model.

In Indonesia our host was Vice President Wirahadikusuma. I just put this in because I loved thinking about saying to a store owner: "Just charge it to Umar Wirahadikusuma, please." We called on President and Mrs. Suharto, and most important, we saw our former colleagues from our days in China, Martha and John Holdridge; John was now our very able ambassador in Indonesia.

In India, George and I had dinner with Indira Gandhi at her house. Also in the group were Mrs. Gandhi's son, Rajiv, and his wife, Sonja. I wrote in my diary:

The Prime Minister's house was modest, really nice. Rajiv and Sonja live with Mrs. Gandhi. Sonja runs the household and Mrs. G. pretty much tells her what to do. They have a staff of servants. A lovely garden with many lilies out the window in full bloom. Sonja, who is from Italy, tells me she has vegetables growing in the back of the house. The minute we arrived Mrs. Gandhi and George went to another room to talk privately. Sonja and Rajiv have been married 16 years and have two children, a boy age 13 and a girl 12. The boy was with us briefly. Mrs. G. seems very affectionate towards him. We keep hearing that she is gearing this son to succeed her. Seems very hard for me to believe. He seems soft to me . . . just a little overweight and elite and effete to me. He also seemed feminine in that he was interested in gardens, schools and things I was interested in. He was educated in a public (our private) boarding school in India where his son is now, on to Cambridge where he met this very beautiful Italian girl. They are very attractive, very compatible, very easy to be with, loving, a gentle kind of man . . .

The five of us had a very pleasant dinner talking of many things. I was surprised to hear that Mrs. Gandhi's husband was not related to Mahatma Gandhi; I knew that she was Nehru's daughter. We discussed the awful dowry system that was causing such a scandal in India at the time. Then we learned that all the Gandhis had chosen their own mates. (Unfortunately, she was divorced.) After dinner George and Mrs. Gandhi retired again, and the young couple and I returned to garden talk.

Back on the airplane I was asked by the support team to give my impression of Rajiv because he was little known to Americans. His late brother, who had been killed in a plane accident, had been the apple of his mother's eye and had been the one being trained to take over. I told them my thoughts. To this day I blush about that. I could not have been more wrong. Several months later his mother was assassinated by some of her own guards, and Rajiv took over. From the moment of her death, he was strong, brave, and wise. He didn't just reach into thin air and find strength when he had to; he had it all along, and I was just too naive to see it. Later, when they were in the United States, we were thrilled to escort Sonja and Rajiv to Houston for a visit to NASA. The tragedy is that this fine young man was assassinated by a fanatic. George and I felt a personal loss.

We then went to Pakistan, where we were guests of President Zia. He had the most beautiful eyes I have ever seen, and was very sweet to a very nice, but very plain, wife and a retarded daughter he took many places with him. He also had put to death our friend, Prime Minister Bhutto. Just ten years before we had been guests of Bhutto, stayed in the same guest house with the same household staff. What a strange world. Not too many years later, Zia himself would die in a plane crash under very suspicious circumstances. What to believe? Was he a good man or a devil? I remember thinking after he died that I hoped someone took care of his wife and child. Bhutto's beautiful daughter, Benazir, then became prime minister and visited us while we were in the White House. She now also is embroiled in political problems involving her own family.

Next we visited the Khyber Pass, which historically had been the gateway into India. History tells us this was where Alexander the Great and, much later, Genghis Khan came through the rough and impassable Hindu Kush mountains to conquer India.

Now it is the border between Pakistan and Afghanistan, and at the time of our visit, a very dangerous place to be. We were eye-to-eye with Soviet and Afghan Communist troops, and we were told not to put one foot over the border or we might be shot. We visited a forward base for the Pakistani forces who were defending against possible Afghan aggression.

From there we went to one of the largest camps for political refugees from Afghanistan, located between the pass and Peshawar. The land was barren, with no trees or grass in sight. We were told that men and women lived in separate sections—almost separate worlds. Theirs is a male-oriented society where the men take care of the women, and we were told that the first thing the Communists did when they attacked a village was to kill males of all ages and rape the women and girls. The women often fled over their mountains with improper clothing, dragging or carrying their children with them. Many died, and many others buried their babies along the way.

George went to an enormous tent where he addressed thousands of men, and I was led into a smaller tent where about one hundred of these "women without men" were seated. I looked carefully around the tent and saw empty faces and dead eyes. To my horror, I was introduced to speak.

I fumbled around, telling them that we had brought them food and medicine. I put my hand over my heart and told them that President Reagan and the people of the United States were thinking about them and cared. I smiled and stepped back. Nothing. Absolutely no response.

Then someone whispered in my ear to keep talking because George was still speaking. We could hear roars of cheering coming from the men's tent. So I tried again. This time I asked them to tell us about themselves. The first woman told us a hideous story of death and destruction. Again, I told her we sympathized and cared. Those dead eyes came alive, her voice got strident, and she was screaming at me. I asked the Pakistani interpreter just what the woman was saying, and she said in a soft voice, "She says she is grateful to you and thank you." The next woman and the next and the next all told similar tales and looked beseechingly at me. Again they would scream at me and wave their arms. And again the interpreter would tell me they were saying things like, "She wants to thank the generous people of the United States for their kindness."

Finally it ended, and when we got into the car, my American interpreter told me the women really were saying things like, "We don't want your sympathy. We want guns. Our lives are worth nothing. We want weapons to go kill the Communists. We want to go home."

I have thought about these women a lot, and sometimes I think being told that you can never go home again must be the toughest thing in the world.

⤳ *June 12, 1984*—For George's birthday I invited the Reagans to come by for a surprise drink with us. They had just returned from the annual Economic Summit meeting in Europe and, as usual, the President was full of marvelous stories. He told one about how rude Canadian Prime Minister Pierre Trudeau had been to Margaret Thatcher. When President Reagan mentioned it to her, she said: "Don't worry. We women are used to men who don't mature."

14

The Poet Laureate (Retired)

The campaign in 1984 was a relatively simple one for the President of the United States. The economy had recovered with a bang, and Ronald Reagan was riding a great high.

It was not so easy for the Vice President. George had been the butt of the liberal press's frustration over Reagan's popularity, and he was running against history in the making: Geraldine Ferraro, the first woman to be a candidate for vice president for one of the major parties. I'm sure that we will mature as a country when it comes to a woman running against a man, but in 1984 it was very difficult. There seemed to be a double standard: one for her and one for George.

Case in point: One of the nicest events in Washington is the Italian-American Dinner, held every fall. Either the president or vice president usually attends, and in an election year, so do the candidates. It's a black-tie event that draws a very large crowd from across this country and from Italy. In 1984, George and I arrived first, soon to be joined by the President and Nancy in a holding room. Normally the president arrives later, so we should have been able to go right into the dinner. However, we were told that Mrs. Ferraro's dress had been left on the plane, and we would have to wait. After about twenty minutes, the President and George decided that two thousand people should not be kept waiting any longer, so we went in. Not too much later, the Mondales and Geraldine appeared—the women, I might add, in short silk dresses although the rest of us were in formal clothes. Had she been a man, she would have come in her suit and apologized and explained that her bags were lost. Everyone has lost bags and would have understood. She then proceeded to talk throughout President Reagan's speech. She was playing by women's rules. By the way, she got a polite hand and the President brought down the house.

That night was the first time I had seen Geraldine in person, and I wrote in my diary: "It was good to see that she didn't have wings and a halo and her feet were on the ground."

Another case in point: George was campaigning in the shipyards the day after their debate. He was working his way down a group of longshoremen when one man held up a sign saying: GEORGE, YOU KICKED A LITTLE ASS LAST NIGHT! The man followed George all along the line, and as George was getting in the car, he leaned over and repeated what that longshoreman said in a low voice. This was picked up by a TV boom mike and made a big splash for days on the news. Geraldine and her followers claimed that it was a sexist expression. Baloney. I will say that it is not my favorite, but as the mother of four competitive boys, I know what that expression means and, I suspect, so does Geraldine.

I campaigned all over the country for the ticket with great pleasure until one fateful day when George and I were flying to New York City. I was in the press section of the plane laughing and joking with Terry Hunt of the Associated Press and Ira Allen of UPI about the debate the night before between the President and Fritz Mondale. Fritz had needled the President about his elite, rich vice president. It really had burned me up because we all had read that Geraldine and her husband, John Zaccaro, were worth at least $4 million, if not more. The press were teasing me about it, and I said something like, "That rich . . . well, it rhymes with rich . . . could buy George Bush any day." It was not a nice thing to say. But we all laughed and went on with a jovial give-and-take.

George and I did a joint event in New York and then parted ways. I was on my way to the airport when Kim Brady told me that my statement was running every few minutes on the radio and would shortly be on TV. We arrived at the airport, went into a holding room, and I immediately called Geraldine and apologized. She was very gracious about it. I certainly wasn't lying about being sorry. I would rather die than hurt George Bush in any way and what I had said in jest was ugly. I called George to confess. He was so dear, saying that he had heard it, but not to worry. Worse things had happened. As we were talking, Kim came into the room and told me that there were press waiting for me outside the boarding gate for our flight to Buffalo. Then I was really upset. I told George, and he said that I should call him back in five minutes, that he was with Dick Moore and they would think of something. When I called back, he said he was on an open phone, but that Dick's advice was to "remember Halloween." So I marched out smiling and said that I had talked to Ms. Ferraro, apologized for calling her a witch, and that she had graciously accepted my apology.

Everything said on the campaign plane was supposed to be off the record unless specified otherwise. It was dumb of me to believe that. I do not blame the press for reporting it because I should have known better. But they should know that I never again felt free to be relaxed with them. The other reason I regretted saying it was that it was not nice and I choose to think that I am not like that.

I can laugh about this incident now, but at the time it was agony. For several years I thought it would be engraved on my tombstone. My family teasing called me the "Poet Laureate" of our household.

Another torturous event of the campaign for us was marching in the annual Columbus Day Parade in New York City. The sparsely attended Labor Day Parade had been a large embarrassment to the Democrats, so this time they bused people in. The streets of New York were filled with their supporters carrying Mondale/Ferraro signs. They yelled and jeered at George and me. We were saved by the beautiful Sophia Loren, who, as grand marshal, marched right in front of us. Nobody would dream of booing her.

At one time during the parade we were told that we shouldn't worry, "our people" were "up around Fifty-second Street." When we got there, we saw one Reagan/Bush sign carried by our cousins, Debbie and Craig Stapleton, with their daughter, Wendy, on Craig's shoulders. Those dear, loyal people ran up and appeared on every corner as long as we stayed in the parade. It was so bad that one of the organizers felt sorry for me and came back and said, "Mrs. Bush, don't worry. George McGovern won the 1972 Columbus Day Parade."

Because Geraldine was the first woman chosen to run for vice president, the national media assigned many women to cover both her and our campaign. It was a hostile press on our plane, and the camaraderie of earlier campaigns was gone. A CBS reporter told George that was not true of the Ferraro plane, where, according to him, women reporters often went to the front and helped with strategy. At one of the debates, the women of the press cheered when they thought Geraldine had scored a point. Another time they gave her a standing ovation. After the debate, the press reported that she won; the polls said George won.

So the 1984 campaign was not much fun for us. But it wasn't any better for the Mondales and the Ferraros/Zaccaros either: The former because he was running against a very popular president, and the latter because they were plagued by ugly rumors. Our personal experiences with both of them and their families were extraordinarily nice.

More important, we won another four years.

Once again we got ready for an Inauguration, and once again I was destined to sport a bandage with my fancy clothes. In early January, while George and I were in Florida visiting his mother, I got hit by a car while taking a walk. For some reason, the driver tried to pass another car on the right, driving up on the grass where I was walking with a Secret Service agent. Of all the people in America to hit, she picked the wrong person! I was surrounded by law enforcement officials. However, I begged them not to arrest her because I did not want to make a scene. Because of my black-and-blue and bandaged arm, I could not wear the short-sleeved red gown I had for the balls.

The 1984 Inauguration was unique in several ways. First of all, January 20 fell on a Sunday, so there were two swearing-in ceremonies. The Sunday ceremony was a small, very moving family affair at the White House. Both the President and Vice President took the oath on the steps of the Grand Staircase on the State Floor surrounded by family and friends. All the cabinet, Supreme Court, and top staff members were invited. It was a marvelous treat for our family as they also stayed for a buffet luncheon served in the glorious State Rooms. At one time the President came over and sat with Mrs. Bush and me, which was a very kind thing for him to do.

The big outdoor swearing-in was going to be held the next day, but Mother Nature intervened with a record cold spell. The ceremony was moved into the Rotunda of the Capitol and the parade was canceled—a huge disappointment for the high school marching bands. However, their lips would have stuck to their instruments. Each congressman and senator was given two tickets, and only our families and very closest friends were allowed in the room. I was amused to see that some of the members of Congress had wedged in their wives and several children. It was jammed.

Two of our grandchildren, George, eight, and Noelle, seven, were going to see their grandfather sworn in. The winter weather didn't bother them one bit. Born in Texas and now living in Florida, they had never seen snow, and we had great fun watching them slide down the hill behind the Vice President's House.

Noelle watched the video *Annie* six times that week and knew every song and dance. The day of the Capitol ceremony, we went to St. John's Church with our adult children and the Reagans. The plan was for Paula to bring George P. and Noelle straight to the Capitol. Columba had bought a darling dress for Noelle and asked Paula please to comb her hair and tie it with a bow. The little group got to the Capitol, but we noticed Noelle had no sash on her dress and no bow in her uncombed hair. We later learned that Noelle had been in the middle of her seventh viewing of *Annie* and refused to leave before it ended. She locked herself in the third-floor bathroom, and poor Paula was desperate. The military aide assigned to bring the children to the ceremony had to take the door off the hinges. They got her out in the nick of time and raced to the Capitol, dressing her on the way.

⁓ With the campaign and Inauguration behind us, it was back to business as usual—if that's what you can call life when you hold public office. Anyway, once again, I'd like to share with you some stories about George's second term as vice president.

⁓ *January 30, 1985*—George and I attended the annual "Salute to Congress" dinner, which honors the new members. One of my dinner companions was Sam Donaldson, whom I wrote about in my diary: "Much to my shock I really enjoyed him. He seems like such a devil and such a mean guy (on the tube). He was a very interesting partner."

Sam told such a funny story, which was verified by my partner on the left, Senator Alan Cranston of California. At one of those deadly receptions before the dinner, Jay Rockefeller, the newly elected senator from West Virginia, came up and introduced himself to Sam. He then went on to say, "Sam, tell me about yourself. I want to get to know you.

Are you from humble beginnings?" Sam's answer: "Compared to you, Senator, I guess you could say that I came from humble beginnings."

During our presidential years, Sam and Diane Sawyer did one of their "Prime Time" shows live from upstairs at the White House. At one point, Sam and I were touring the Yellow Oval Room with Millie at our heels. Sam asked me how Millie liked living in the White House at the exact same moment she decided to clean up a little. I gave her a gentle nudge with my foot, and the White House switchboard immediately lit up with people saying: "Who does Sam Donaldson think he is, kicking Millie?" Poor Sam, he does have an image problem.

After we finished the show, George invited Sam and Diane to have a glass of wine while their crew removed some of the tons of equipment they had brought in. The most amazing conversation followed. One said to the other: "I thought I handled the Lincoln Bedroom well, didn't you?" Back came, "Yes, but didn't you think I was good in the Long Hall?" Back and forth they went, complimenting each other and themselves for several moments. The other "spear carrier" and I were amused and thought to ourselves: Who says that politicians are egotistical? I very much would like to add that Diane has always been a favorite of ours and still is. She and Sam are just human—very human.

George and I went to hundreds of dinners during our political years. Typical of many of them was one I went to one night when George was out of town. This had been sold to me as an early evening with few speeches. The man who gave the invocation set the tone. He prayed for the whole world, person by person. I sat next to the ninety-year-old man who was being honored that night. I discovered that he had taken a taxi to the dinner and told him that I would give him a ride home. After a long dinner, the chairman stood up and gave a longer talk. The hour was getting late, and both my partner and I were getting very restless. When the chairman called on his committee heads to give their annual reports, we moaned and settled down for a miserable additional hour. Just then a Secret Service man slipped me a note: "Mrs. Bush, we have to go. Our job is to protect you and you are being bored to death. Let's go." It was signed "USSS" (United States Secret Service). I made my apologies, grabbed my new ninety-year-old friend, and left. Lest I leave the wrong impression, the note was written by my aide, Kim Brady; not the Secret Service.

March 3–12, 1985—George and I went to the Sahel countries in

Africa to take food and medicine to drought victims. Much of the aid we took was gathered by AmeriCares, and Bob Macauley, its founder, accompanied us on our plane. This amazing man had gotten tired of fighting red tape and had organized the most comprehensive program that brings immediate relief to those in need around the world. He sees a problem; begs, borrows, or steals the food, medicine, doctors, nurses, planes, or trucks that he needs; and takes off for whatever part of the world needs help. George and I are AmeriCares' biggest fans.

On this trip we visited large refugee camps in Sudan where they were trying to save the lives of drought victims and refugees from Ethiopia. There were so many unforgettable impressions: everything and everyone covered with dirt and flies; a seven-year-old who weighed twenty-seven pounds, the same as our grandson Sam LeBlond, who wasn't a year old yet; a four-pound baby whose mother had died shortly after the birth and who now was lying at the feet of her dying grandmother on a filthy mattress. I held that little baby and was told that she had no chance of living. The newcomers to the camp were so thin and malnourished that it was like looking at X rays instead of bodies. Five times a day relief workers would spoon a mush made up of milk, sugar, and oil into these people's mouths, and we were told that in several weeks, many of those listless blank-eyed children would be running and playing. The dedicated volunteer nurses, doctors, missionaries, and Peace Corp volunteers who worked surrounded by filth and the dead and dying were the most giving group of people I had ever met.

We also went to Mali, taking food and medicine to drought victims there. Lala, the wife of President Moussa Traore, was my hostess. She really touched me. She was a large, smiling woman who'd had nine children, the first when she was thirteen years old. She was caring and so sweet. I sat next to her at a banquet and watched her stuff three morsels of beef surrounded by at least an inch of pure white fat into her mouth. To her, it was a treat. I really loved her and have thought of her often.

After Africa, we went to Switzerland, where George made an impassioned appeal at a United Nations Famine Relief Conference. That evening we met up with a congressional delegation at a reception given by our close, dear friends, Katy and Sadruddin Aga Khan. Texas Senator John Tower and his wife, Lilla, were there. She told me that she thought George was all wrong: "I don't believe in feeding those people. They should learn to take care of themselves." I have to confess that I had been so moved by what I saw that I just said, "Lilla, go away." Starving babies and we shouldn't feed them?

~ *July 1, 1985*—We were in the middle of a swing through Europe when the President asked George and me to go to Germany to meet the hostages from the TWA hijacking incident. The entire world had watched as that plane had been held captive on a runway in Beirut. What joy it was for them and their families they were finally free.

Sadly, however, George and I also had gone to Andrews Air Force Base to meet the body of Seaman Robert Stetham, who had been killed in cold blood by the hijackers when they discovered he was in the service. His family had a rich military tradition, and I'll never forget his mother and father and siblings standing there on the tarmac at Andrews with us. They were grief-stricken, yet proud. As the casket came off the plane, his younger brother, in his dress Navy uniform, saluted his hero brother as tears ran down his face.

~ *July 13, 1985*—A few weeks later, we were in Kenne-bunkport for a weekend when George got a call saying the President was going to undergo surgery to remove a polyp in his colon. George decided to return to Washington in spite of opposition from Chief of Staff Don Regan, who thought it might hype the public's perception of the seriousness of the operation. I wrote in my diary:

> We wondered, of course, all day about how things were going in Washington. Pop called several times and told us the President came through the operation. And a very historic thing happened and, thank God, George went down there because the President signed a paper transferring the power to the Vice President, and I think it held true for the seven hours that he was being operated on. Evidently Don Regan went in and talked to him and decided he was in total control, no more effects of the anesthesia, thus rescinded the power after seven hours. Pop played tennis, stayed out of sight, and tried to keep a low profile. But he was president for seven hours.

We stayed glued to TV the whole weekend. After we knew that the President was fine, Marvin and I got the giggles. The descriptions of the bowel and all its processes were on every station with graphic drawings. What I didn't know was that Marvin was getting more and more frightened. Every symptom that was described was exactly what he was going through, although he hadn't told any of us. So thanks to the very personal press coverage and Ronald Reagan, he went to see Dr. Tabb Moore, an excellent doctor and a former neighbor of ours. Marvin got temporary relief from his problems, then went his merry way, pretty much ignoring all Tabb had told him.

Marvin was diagnosed as having colitis, a devastating autoimmune disease. After a miserable winter of cramping, racing to the bathroom, and bleeding, he went into the hospital in the spring of 1986 to try to control this dreaded illness. He continued to lose weight and to lose ground. Margaret spent night after night at his bedside. No man ever had more friends and, if there was an up side to this ailment, it was then that both children surely learned how loved they were. I knew that Margaret and Marvin really loved and valued their friends; now we learned that their friends felt the same.

After weeks in the hospital, a forty-five pound weight loss, and consultations with specialists, our doctors told us that they were going to reevaluate Marvin at the end of the week. On May 7, 1986, I was on my way to Santa Fe, New Mexico, to do a charity fund-raiser for my dear friend Marion Chambers. I would be back in twenty-four hours. We had an interim stop in St. Louis, and after the plane doors had already closed, the Secret Service told me the Vice President was on the phone and needed to speak with me right away. They reopened the door, and my heart sank when George told me that Marvin's vital signs were failing and I should come home. No trip was longer. I tried to pretend that I wasn't afraid. Nothing could happen to our precious boy. I was praying that he would be all right. I was so afraid that I would see George at the steps of the plane, because that would mean something awful had happened. He was not there. I raced to the hospital to find George sitting at Marvin's beside, with his hand on his arm. Marvin told me later that he knew he was dying when two things happened: His dad spent the day by his side, and Jeb called to just pass the time of day. He ended his call with "I love you, Marvin." My boys don't say things like that to each other. They just know it and act it. That day, Jeb said it.

Marvin had several blood transfusions to give him enough strength to go through an operation. The next day he had a temporary colostomy. That is a terrible shock to anybody, but to a very athletic young man it is a bitter pill to swallow. The other choice was death. I suspect that sometimes in those next few days Marvin thought that he would have preferred the second choice. The pain was bad, and he was depressed. Thank God for Margaret, who was so strong and very supportive.

They had a double worry as they were also at the end of a long period of trying to adopt a baby. They were so eager to adopt. Anyone who has ever been through that process will tell you that the strain of all the interviews and then the waiting is so hard. To have gotten this far and to lose the baby would have been such a disappointment.

Ten days after the operation Marvin's doctor brought in an attractive young man who talked to Marvin about his similar operation and the fact that he'd just run in a marathon. Marvin later told me that this man really helped him see that life was not over. Another person who was very helpful was NFL player Rolf Benirschke, later the daytime host of "The Wheel of Fortune," who had had a similar operation. His calls meant a great deal to Marvin and to all of us.

The convalescence was long because he had lost so much weight and blood. I never saw anyone work harder at getting strong. At first he joined me in long six-mile walks at the Naval Observatory. His good friend Jeff Austin hit tennis balls right to him so he wouldn't have to run. Dorrance Smith, who then was producing David Brinkley's show on ABC and later came to the White House with George, kept him supplied with good and interesting books. Other friends helped in different ways.

Within the year, it was decided that Marvin could not do away with the colostomy, so back he went for more surgery to remove what was left of his colon. Again, we were worried.

About this time, the Pope came to visit the United States. President Reagan welcomed him in Miami and we were to bid him goodbye in Detroit. George invited the family to join us there and as many as possible came. We also urged our housekeeper, Paula, to come with us. We were puzzled when she said no, especially since she's a devout Catholic. Finally, one day I had an idea, and said to her that it was too bad we only would be able to shake the Pope's hand instead of really talk to him. Suddenly, she decided to go. I think she was afraid he was going to quiz her about her religion!

The day finally came and we all waited anxiously for the Pope to arrive. One by one we walked up to meet him, all of us sounding tongue-tied. He is such a charismatic man and so gentle-looking that we were in awe. After the receiving line it was suggested we have a group photo taken. When that was done, Paula broke ranks, went right up to the Pope, and said in Spanish, "Papa, the Vice President's son is going to have a very serious operation. Will you pray for him?" He put his arms around her, calling her "Little Mama," and assured her that he would. At that, he and George left to talk in private. The rest of us closed ranks around Paula, just like a football huddle, tears spilling down our faces. This dear little woman had overcome her fear to speak up for Marvin. It was so sweet and touching.

The prayers must have worked. Marvin came through the operation fine, and although he suffered through a lot of pain, he got back in shape quicker than before. Today, his tennis game is superb, better than ever, and he's improving at golf.

But more important, Marvin is trying to use his experience to help others as the spokesman for the Crohn's and Colitis Foundation of America. Through humor and sensitivity, he has helped people of all ages learn to live with the "bag" which replaces your bowels. The late Tip O'Neill, a truly dear man and former Speaker of the House, underwent this same surgery, and every time we saw him, he let us know in his wonderful Boston accent how much a phone call from "your Mahvin" helped him recover.

And there's more happy ending. In June of 1986, Marvin and Margaret adopted a baby girl, Marshall Lloyd Bush. She and her little brother, Walker, who joined our family in 1989, are special children and have brought such joy into our lives. I never see them that I don't thank God for Marvin and Margaret, who are loving parents. I might add that I'm very grateful to the Edna Gladney Home in Fort Worth, Texas, where they adopted their children.

⤳ *October 10–20, 1985*—En route to China and Hong Kong, we stopped to refuel on Saipan in the Mariana Islands. George loved revisiting the islands that he had flown over during World War II and seeing the relics left behind by the Japanese.

During our stay, I dedicated a hospital, the Commonwealth Health Center, which certainly was not an uncommon event for me. But this particular occasion really touched me. I wrote in my diary: "It's kind of a funny feeling knowing that there'll be a plaque somewhere in the middle of the Pacific with your name on it, Barbara Pierce Bush. It's stretched my life a little and made me feel very humble."

❧ *January 6, 1986*—I would just like to share with you my diary entry for that day:

Sunday and Monday I worked around the house, trying to get rid of Christmas . . . Monday we were going to the NBC dinner. First I was told that I was to wear a daytime dress, then they revised the schedule to a cocktail dress. I talked to Doro in the morning in Maine. Just sort of spent the day getting things together and getting back into regular life . . . I put on a black skirt and brocade top. Did not wash my hair . . . Just as we were going out, Marvin called and said that the stole that was left at our house did belong to Ulla Wachtmeister (the wife of the Swedish ambassador) and could we drop it by her house as she was leaving town the very next day. George said that was easy as we were dining right across the street. He said as he got into the car, "Gosh, I have to call the office. This is the annual NBC Dinner, there is some news breaking and before I get there I better be briefed." So he tried to call the office and the line was busy. Meanwhile the Secret Service got on the phone to tell the police escort that we were going to make an interim stop at the Swedish Embassy. Just as we pulled up, George's phone call came through, and he asked me if I'd mind running the stole up to the door. I rang the doorbell. They opened the door and . . . I looked up and there were Jeb and Colu. I couldn't believe that they knew the Swedish Ambassador. Then I saw Doro with tears running down her face . . . it was a 41st wedding anniversary surprise party! And in all honesty it was the biggest surprise in the world. George Bush was so thrilled as were Ulla and Willie . . . That morning George had called Doro and said, "Call your mother before you leave. Otherwise, you know your mother, she'll call, and the baby-sitter will tell her that you are on your way to Washington." So she did call me. During the day Libby Crudgington (Doro's friend) had called me and asked for Doro. She said the baby-sitter had told her that Doro was in Washington. I had said, "Dumb baby-sitter. She has gone to a hockey game in Boston." . . . Andy came by for tea . . . I just called Marion Chambers (in Texas) to see how she was just as she was rushing out the door to come see us. She said that she was afraid that I was going to make her miss her plane.
    . . . There were all those people, Bob and Georgette Mosbacher, Bobbie and Jack Fitch, Mildred and Baine Kerr and Hugh and Betty Liedtke . . . I

mean there was the most extraordinary group of people . . . Bob and Marion Blake from Lubbock, Marvin and Margaret, Doro, Jeb and Colu. Neil, Sharon, George and Laura didn't come . . . it's a long way and too expensive.

There were many many more friends there: the Drapers, Nan Ellis without Sandy and Betsy Heminway without Spike to just name a few. And my dear Andy. I couldn't believe that she didn't tell me. She said that she knew that I didn't know because I had not washed my hair.

. . . Jack Fitch had brought up lots of blown-up pictures and Marvin had gone over on Sunday and helped with the seating . . . there were poems, slide shows, songs and on and on. It was one of the loveliest evenings of my life.

A lot of people couldn't believe that I was surprised. I did joke about it and say, "Wouldn't you be surprised if it was the second time in forty-one years of married life that your husband had remembered?" But the truth is we have never needed parties to celebrate.

George really had worked hard with the marvelous Wachtmeisters to pull it off. (There wasn't even such a thing as an NBC dinner!) I could write a book about the parties and nice things he has planned for others. Maybe that is what I am doing right now.

∽ *July 4, 1986*—It was a very special July Fourth celebration that year for our entire country. I wrote in my diary:

The Statue of Liberty celebrated her 100th birthday. The Bushes and the Jim Bakers with (their daughter) Mary Bonner and our Noelle spent the 4th in Kennebunkport and then flew down to New York City for the closing ceremonies. 55,000 people at Giants Stadium (The Meadowlands). The whole week had been an extravaganza beyond belief. They had fireworks, lit the Lady and Tall Ships.

The finale, which we attended and George took part in, was unbelievable. They had 350 Elvis "look-alikes." More like impersonators as there were men and women, black and white. We were all given a light and a separate lens. At the given moment we all turned on our lights and we turned into a red, white and blue flag with stars, and LIBERTY was spelled out. Dancing girls came out by the thousands, and when they flipped their capes, they were the American flag and they made the flag wave to the cheers of the crowd. Liza Minnelli, Shirley MacLaine and John Denver sang, backed by a cast of thousands. Our two little girls were not the only ones who loved that show.

After the evening was over, the pilots of the helicopter flew around the Statue of Liberty at 11 P.M. It was so beautiful. We could see the New York skyline outlined in lights and the Tall Ships in the harbor. One of those magic moments in life.

꿈 *July 25–August 5, 1986*—I will never forget my visit to the Wailing Wall in Jerusalem during our trip through the Middle East. George was led off to the men's side of the wall, and I was taken to the women's. We both were touched by the sight of people praying and tucking notes into the wall. I left a note: "Please, dear God, let us have peace. Protect my little family. Your devoted servant, Barbara."

꿈 *January 19, 1987*—Just as we were going to bed, C. Fred seemed to have a horrible spasm. His little legs went out from under him and he looked awkward. He couldn't move. His beautiful brown eyes looked so trustingly at us. George moved our loyal little friend onto a blanket and we brought him in by my side where we could comfort him. He didn't move all night. Whenever we turned on the light to check on him, his eyes were open and he was looking so puzzled. It was almost as though he expected us to make it all right. Eventually we both fell asleep for a few hours. In the morning we awakened and there was our little friend sleeping normally. He jumped up for his morning walk and all seemed well. In the middle of the morning Laurie called and said it had happened again in the garden. We went straight to the vet's, where he told me that Freddy was having a stroke. He said that he might come out of it and maybe would have several more months experiencing these strokes intermittently. I could not let my best little pal suffer, and with tears running down my face and the doctor's, I held Freddy in my arms and the doctor gave him a shot. It was very peaceful and that twisted, tormented little body relaxed and rested.

I was devastated, but reminded myself that the loss was not just mine, but George's and Don Rhodes's, too. It was also an opportunity for me to prove what I always have said: I value all people more than dogs. I may sometimes like the dog better, but people are and should be more important.

I came home and called George to tell him what I had done. He said I'd made the right choice. I also called Susan Porter Rose about something else, burst into tears, and told her what had happened. She advised me not to tell people that I had put him to sleep. She said that we would get letters about how mean I was. I did it because I loved him.

We cover sadness in our family with humor sometimes. I was just giving myself a real talking-to about not being mournful when the door burst open and our son, George W., arrived from Texas for the night. He had been forewarned not to mention Freddy, so he rushed in saying, "Mom, I'm so sorry, doggone it!" Funny. Even I had to giggle.

George immediately called our friend Will Farish and asked him if he had a puppy or knew where we could find a young dog. We had fallen in love with Will's black-and-white springer spaniels when we had visited Will and Sarah on their Beeville, Texas, ranch after Christmas. Several days later he called and said they had a perfect dog for me, but there were several problems. For starters, the dog was a girl. We'd never had a female dog, but that seemed fine. Then came the zinger: She wasn't black and white; she was liver-colored. She was a little over a year old. Will said that she had been trained as a huntress, but that she was such a loving dog they thought she'd be a better house dog. She sounded perfect.

We had a small problem with Don Rhodes. He truly was C. Fred's best friend. I loved Freddy best, but he loved me second best. Don was his first love. George told Don that we were getting a new dog. I suspect that Don thought I had not let enough time pass between dogs, because he came to my door one night, leaned in, and asked, "Let me ask something. If the Vice President died, would you get a new husband?" And I answered, "You bet, if I could get one just as good." Don did not think that was funny, stomped out, and did not speak to me for several days.

On February 13, Will delivered Millie to the steps of *Air Force Two* after a speech George had given. Millie turned out to be my dog in about five minutes. Don Rhodes likes her, but not like Freddy. He did forgive me—I think.

All this reminds me of another dog story. It sounds so silly, but it was about to cause a real family disagreement.

One early morning in Maine I was sitting in my bed reading the morning paper and having a cup of coffee when the bedroom door burst open. George's wonderful Uncle Lou Walker was standing there looking really upset. He said, "Bar, we have all agreed that you will make the final decision on a family argument. I know just how much you loved C. Fred and so I will accept your words. You alone understand how much I loved my dog, Gilbert, who died this past winter. Grace and the girls say that I can't give flowers in her memory this Sunday in church. Don't you think that is all right?" My heart sank. Of course he couldn't give flowers in her memory in church. I could just hear Laman Bruner saying, "The flowers this morning are given in loving memory of John Smith, adored father of Betty and Jim Smith, and Gilbert Walker, most beloved dog of Grace and Louis Walker!" The whole congregation would laugh us out of church or be insulted and furious. Grace and the girls would be humiliated. I said, "Lou, just tell me one thing. Did Gilbert accept Jesus Christ as her savior?" That seemed to end that.

⌒ *September 24–October 3, 1987*—We visited Poland during a fascinating time in their history, when Lech Walesa was becoming a national hero and Solidarity was becoming known worldwide. I wrote in my diary:

I got in the car with Mrs. Jaruzelski. She is very nice and about 59–60. Very friendly. She has a trim little figure and wore a pale green dress. She has very blond hair and speaks English . . . better than we thought. She teaches German at the University. She told me that without her job she could not exist because he is gone so much. He, of course was (General Jaruzelski), now head of country and chairman of the (Communist) Party . . . She told me that she was reading in English, through her interpreter. (I noticed that she didn't really need her.) She told me that she'd just finished "Home Front." I said that I'd never heard of it. She said, "You know, it was written by Mrs. Reagan's daughter. Is it true?" It was that horrible book that Patti Davis had written. I said no, that it was a novel. It was not true and it was not a success in our country. Ye Gads! I asked her how she had seen it, and she said that a friend had sent it to her. Some friend.

I had another strange encounter with another wife of a Polish official. I told her that the American people really like the Polish people. She returned with: "Why?" (Hardly encouraging to a long conversation, but I persisted.) I reminded her that there were so many Poles in America that Chicago is the second largest Polish city in

the world. Her response was "You only got the peasants and igno-
rants." So much for composer Ignace Paderewski, baseball greats Carl
Yastrzemski and Stan Musial, Duke basketball coach Mike Krzyzew-
ski, Maryland Senator Barbara Mikulski, Illinois Congressman Dan
Rostenkowski, and many others.

It was on this trip that we met with the courageous Solidarity
leaders, including Lech Walesa, at a dinner given by our talented
ambassador, John Davis, and his wife, Helen. Many of the men had
spent years in jail as political prisoners and yet they fought on. The
next morning George went to lay a wreath at the grave of the martyred
priest Father Popieluszko. As we were getting ready to leave, Lech
Walesa slipped into our car, and right behind him, wedging into the
front seat with our driver and agent, came an enormous man that only
Hollywood could have cast to be a spy. Lech said that this man
followed him everywhere to keep watch on him. The day before,
Jaruzelski had told us that the Solidarity movement was almost dead.
Well, the ride to the church was lined with thousands upon thousands
of people waving Solidarity and American flags, cheering Lech and
George.

⤫ *December 8, 1987*—It had been a very tough year for Nancy
Reagan. She had a breast operation in the fall, and her mother died
three days after she got out of the hospital. Two of her husband's
Supreme Court nominees had been rejected, and the Iran-Contra investigation was in full swing.

On top of all this, Mikhail and Raisa Gorbachev arrived for their
first visit to the United States. Excitement ran high. Since the men's
meetings were closed to the press, the ladies' activities became a big
news item. The press had noted an antagonism between the two First
Ladies. There was some truth in that. It was what I call a "chemical
thing," plus a cultural difference.

I recorded the following on my tape recorder as I walked Millie
around the Observatory grounds on December 11:

The arrival ceremony was very exciting. You could certainly tell whose
husbands weren't running for president. I wore a very Republican cloth coat,
and Nancy wore her mink. Mrs. Gorbachev, who had stepped off the plane
the night before in what the press described as an "indescribable" fur, had on

a very long, very chic, brown or liver-colored broadtail coat . . . belted in the back, collar turned up.

. . . We went right into the Green Room, where we were offered tea and coffee. Under her coat she had on a beautiful white wool suit. Her feet were demurely crossed at her ankles. Her coloring is marvelous . . . paper says "henna" hair, but I'd say much softer. She is a lovely looking creature, smaller than the size twelve we are reading about, more a six or an eight. She is a prettier package than the pictures show. I don't know how old, but think the paper said fifty-three or fifty-five. That's funny, for we really don't know if Nancy Reagan is sixty-five or sixty-seven and she won't tell. I guess Raisa won't tell either.

Mrs. G. never said (to Nancy), "I hear you have been sick. How are you?" Or, "I was sorry to hear about your mother." She started right in on, "We couldn't understand why you didn't come to Iceland" (where the husbands had met recently). Nancy started to say, "But I thought that only men were going . . . " She never had a chance because Mrs. G. interrupted and went on, "You would have liked it. People missed you." Nancy tried again, but Mrs. G. interrupted again, "It was so interesting," and on and on.

Mrs. G. moved immediately into their twenty-year housing project or program and told us there were no homeless in Russia. (Several days after the G's left town, our papers were full of stories about the thousands of homeless in Russia.) She said everyone had a place to spend the night in Russia. Clearly a jab at us.

She then went into the Civil War—yes, the Civil War—and slavery. Evidently Russia had freed their serfs about the same time.

From there she moved rapidly into the homeless widows caused by World War II, hoped we would never experience a war in our country. I was tempted to tell her that we had seen many widows and orphans in Afghanistan refugee camps in Pakistan . . . RECENTLY.

At one time Obie Shultz leaned over to me and whispered, "Nancy doesn't like this conversation." I whispered back, "Who would?"

Mrs. G. took over the whole conversation.

Finally Nancy said, "I'm afraid that I am keeping you from your schedule." Mrs. G. said, "Oh, that's all right." That should have told us how little staying on schedules meant to them. They were late to almost everything on that first visit.

. . . George and I went to the East Room on the State Floor for the signing of the INF (Intermediate-range Nuclear Force) Treaty. I was flattered to be included. Nancy, Mrs. G. and I were the only spouses there. Everyone else had worked on the treaty. We were packed in like sardines. It was thrilling.

On that first visit we were all impressed about how well briefed the Gorbachevs both were on all of us. At the receiving lines, both at the State Department luncheon and the White House Dinner, they had something personal to say to each guest. That's pretty impressive. It also made the receiving line take hours. Jane Muskie told me that she and Ed got to the State Department at 12:30, lunch was served at 1:45 and she got home at 5 p.m. Wow.

On December 9, I wrote:

The Russians had the return dinner for the Reagans at the Russian Embassy on 16th Street. The embassy was built around 1909 by Mrs. Pullman, the railroad king's widow, for her daughter and son-in-law. The latter was a congressman. It was sold to the Russians in 1913 and they moved in around 1930. It is very ornate and has grand, gilded chandeliers, mirrors, etc.

They had 72 people and served 9 courses: caviar to start with (it came around twice), crab, fish soup, suckling pig, baked fish, maybe veal, sherbet, fruit and blueberry pie . . . It was a lovely, but very long dinner. Then they had entertainment . . . a rather formidable (stands for large-chested) young opera star who sang song after song, popular romantic songs—maybe well-known is a better description than popular. George said that he took a chance, and after quite a few songs said to Mrs. G. while looking at the singer with a twinkle in his eye: "I think I am falling in love." The interpreter struggled through the translation and Mrs. G. thought a minute and then said with a perfectly straight face, "I think you better not. This is an election year. Remember Gary Hart." George says that she didn't have a twinkle in her eye. It was a flat statement. She certainly was well briefed and knew a lot about us and our politics.

. . . I went to the going-away ceremony on the South Grounds in the pouring rain. The Reagans were smiling and the Gorbachevs looking straight ahead and very serious . . . for home consumption?

. . . I drove to the airport that evening with Mrs. G. She had been well briefed on me and had me down as a housewife. She asked me if we ever served pies? I said that we did and she then gave me her recipe for blueberry pie: "You take a cup of flour, a cup of cream and a cup of blueberries and mix 'em up and you have a pie." Even I know that will not make a pie. I put my hand on her knee and said, "Mrs. G., I am not a great cook. I can feed 50,

but no one would ever rave over my food. Tell me about your average day."
She did.

After that we had the darndest conversation. I asked her if she knew that Nancy Reagan had a serious cancer operation a month ago. She said yes, but that in her country they would not talk about it and the doctor would be in trouble for mentioning it . . . that it was very difficult for a woman to have a breast removed. I said that in our country the press would know if the First Lady disappeared for several weeks and would want to know her whereabouts. That brought about a big discussion about the press's right to know personal things . . . like Gary Hart's personal life. It was hard to explain that Gary Hart invited the press to follow him and examine his life. And they did. I found myself defending the press and finally said, "We get so angry with the press for their probing personal questions but would die for their right to ask them." She then asked, "What if the First Lady had an abortion?" I said that the First Lady wouldn't have an abortion and that breast cancer and an abortion were certainly two very different things. I then said that we felt that Nancy Reagan had been very courageous, and that by going public she had saved many lives by influencing women to have mammograms. We arrived at the airport before we could pursue this anymore.

It occurred to me later that women in Russia do not have the machines that we have to cope with mammography or delicate radiation. Therefore encouraging women to go for these procedures is not a part of their lives.

We had many more visits with Raisa over the years, and I grew to like and respect her. She was the first wife of a Russian leader to surface into the public eye. It was not easy for her. She was a pacesetter. She once asked me why Nancy Reagan didn't like her. I said that I was sure that Nancy did like her. She said that she had read otherwise in Nancy's book. I was hard put to answer, but she almost answered her own question by saying that she did not know our customs and that she was trying to learn. She did dominate the conversation, but maybe she thought that was what she was supposed to do. Who knows?

I never saw her in such stylish clothes again. I was amused to note that on that first trip her skirts got shorter and shorter to match Nancy's. They must have had a seamstress working late at the embassy.

I believe that the Russian people did not like the wife to be front and center. We heard that she got off the back of the plane at home, and I read that when NBC's Tom Brokaw interviewed Gorbachev, before the Russians showed it on their TV, they deleted the part where Gorbachev said that he discussed everything with his wife.

This is an interesting subject. A spouse has a fine row to hoe. Denis Thatcher played it just right, in my eyes. He was supportive of Margaret always, and yet had a life of his own.

I am not too sure that the American public likes the spouse to be too front and center. The jury is still out on this, but in January of 1994 when I am writing this, Hillary Rodham Clinton is certainly very much a part of her husband's decision-making process. She seems much the stronger of the two. Does it make him seem weaker? I am afraid that when problems or controversy occur, and they will, the finger will be pointed at Hillary. I am not saying this is right or wrong. It just occurs to me that the American people also are going through an adjustment.

⤳ One last note on 1987: George became an author, writing his autobiography, *Looking Forward,* with the help of our great friend Vic Gold. George donated his share of the profits to the M. D. Anderson Hospital for its work in the field of leukemia, and the United Negro College Fund.

⤳ Before I talk about George's last year as vice president, which was dominated by the 1988 presidential race, I'd like to make a few general observations about that eight-year period.

The 1980s was the decade that televangelists truly came into their own. I am not going to attempt to pass judgment. So many of them bring hope, love, and God into American homes. We all have aging shut-in relatives who are nourished by these people. But we also know that there are some greedy charlatans out there who take advantage of vulnerable people and who seem to put self above God and the people they say they are hoping to help.

I bring this up because we had a reception for a group of televangelists during the VP years, including Jimmy and Tammy Faye Bakker and Jimmy Swaggart. I wrote in my diary: "I'm offended when they think they are the ones who discovered God when He has played such an important part in our lives. I was amused when Jimmy

Swaggart said on that visit that whoever likes country music was immoral. GB's response: 'Well, that does me in.' "

It hurts me when I see Billy Graham grouped in with these fakes. George and I have known Billy and Ruth Graham for many years, and they have had a very positive spiritual influence on our whole family. We have had several wonderful evenings where our extended family has sat around Billy and asked him questions that worry us about death, life, and the Bible. We have learned a lot about each other in these sessions, and more important, about God and our relationship to Him.

Religion has played such an important part in our lives. It's a very personal thing with us, but I know we could not have survived the difficult times without our faith and the support of our religious family. Whether we were worshiping in our enormous church in Houston, St. Martin's; our two tiny churches in Kennebunkport, First Congregational Church and St. Ann's; the tiny little chapel at Camp David; or St. John's Church, across from the White House, we always have felt we were a part of a very special community.

∽ One of my greatest pleasures during the 1980s was getting involved with the literacy cause and witnessing firsthand the exciting things beginning to happen. People began to see the potential problems of an uneducated work force, and businessmen and politicians began to be aware of the problem. This did not just happen. It took men like Harold McGraw, retired CEO of McGraw-Hill, Inc. Harold and his wife started the Business Council for Effective Literacy, seeded with a million dollars of their own money, and for ten long years he stood on the literacy soapbox. He talked many companies into having on-site continuing education classes or supporting literacy programs in their communities. He made the point that it would save them money in the long run. He also lobbied Congress hard. With no personal agenda, Harold played an invaluable role in making people aware of our silent, hidden problem.

I was lucky to work with so many people who understood the problem and wanted to help make a difference. One of my favorite literacy stories is about a gentleman named Gary Stein who works with the Houston Food Bank. We met while I was taping a public service announcement for a food drive, and he wrote me the following in his thank-you note:

Illiteracy should also not be allowed to occur in America. I know that eliminating this terrible condition is your personal battle. I would like to offer a suggestion which has resulted in a win-win situation for our company, a Houston-based steel distributor with about 100 employees, and an illiterate individual.

Recently a slip-up occurred in our hiring procedures, and a totally illiterate man—we'll call him "Tim Jones"—was hired. (Someone else had filled out his job application.) Ordinarily a false application would be grounds for immediate dismissal.

However, I intervened and told our plant manager that we would allow Tim to stay employed *if* he would enroll immediately in a reading program at Houston Community College. He would be required to bring regular progress reports and report cards to his foreman. Tim accepted our offer.

The results after several months were:

1. The company has gained a motivated, loyal, extremely hardworking employee.

2. Tim Jones has gained some literacy in school and on the job and is eager to learn more. In fact, he informs us he is saving to hire a private tutor.

3. A man was taken off of the welfare rolls and now has a well-paying job with a future.

But best of all, this was accomplished by individuals without government involvement or special programs. Just a simple concept under which everyone wins—the company and individual . . . imagine how much impact could be made in working for greater literacy if more companies would try this with only *one* new employee.

Many states were establishing literacy councils and I worked with some wonderful people, but I particularly recall working with the present governor of Illinois, then the secretary of state of Illinois, Jim Edgar. He and his staff were very able and eager workers in the field. Three Secretaries of Education also were most helpful: Ted Bell, Bill Bennett, and in George's presidential years, Lamar Alexander.

Perhaps the biggest success story was Project Literacy U.S., known as PLUS. A private/public partnership between PBS and ABC, it was an unprecedented coming together of public and commercial TV. Margot Woodwell of PBS's WQED in Pittsburgh and Jim Duffy, Anderson Clark, and Jack Harr of ABC were the prime movers behind the extraordinary project. PLUS launched a major public awareness campaign on literacy and helped organize communities to deal with their individual needs. It also set up a referral network which brought together all the different groups working for literacy.

ABC also started sponsoring the Reader of the Month, many of whom became real success stories and went on to join national literacy councils. One Fourth of July, I left my family in Maine to fly to St. Louis to take part in their annual celebration under the Arch. Attracting a million or more people, it's considered one of the biggest Fourth of July events in the country. ABC was going to broadcast the celebration live, so millions more would see it this year. I had agreed to a walk-on part where I would introduce a darling Reader of the Month. "Mr. Smith" was a retired truck driver who had driven for forty years although he was illiterate. He decided to learn so he could read his Bible. On this particular show, he was going to read the Preamble to the Constitution. We had a little practice session in the afternoon, and although it seemed to me that he could not read at all, I was assured by the production people that he was just nervous and that by that night he would be able to read. He didn't seem nervous to me. In fact, he seemed very relaxed. That night he sat having refreshments and laughing with the many actors, singers, and dancers who were entertaining this huge crowd that spread as far as the eye could see. Our big moment came around eleven P.M. I went out on the stage and said my words, which I had put to memory just in case I couldn't see the cue cards. Then this lovely old man came out, smiled, hugged me, and we waited, arms around each other. Nothing, absolutely nothing, came out. He did look adorable. So after an agonizing standoff, I said: "Let's all join Mr. Smith in saying the Preamble to the Constitution," and we did, all one million of us. It truly was a magic moment.

We encouraged all sorts of literacy programs. We visited senior citizens' homes with reading classes. We supported English as a Second Language programs for immigrants who wanted to learn. We visited Head Start and Even Start classes. We tried to help alternative school programs for kids at risk like Cities in Schools. We encouraged programs that worked with mothers who had dropped out of school. We tried to help programs that taught new mothers not only parenting skills but the importance of reading to their children. We supported the March of Dimes Reading Olympics, which I liked for it not only encouraged children to read, but to help others. We went to schools to try to motivate reading, and spoke to civic clubs to encourage people to volunteer. Nothing is sadder than an adult student getting up the nerve to come to a class and finding no tutor available. We visited homeless shelters and food banks, such as Martha's Table in Washington, where they not only feed the body, but they feed the mind by reading to children. We wrote articles for newspapers, newsletters, and magazines trying to raise awareness and encourage volunteerism. We answered enormous amounts of mail and became somewhat of a clearinghouse for literacy. In the eight vice presidential years, I participated in 537 literacy-related events and another 435 events related to volunteerism. At times it was exhausting but it was always exhilarating. I always felt like I got more out than I put in.

I have saved the most important highlight of our VP years until last. Our family grew by leaps and bounds—two new in-laws, whom I've already mentioned, and eight new grandchildren: George and Laura had the twins, Jenna and Barbara in 1981; Jeb and Columba had their third child, Jebby, in 1983; Neil and Sharon had Lauren in 1984 and Pierce in 1986; Marvin and Margaret adopted Marshall in 1986; and Billy and Doro had Sam in 1984 and Ellie in 1986.

Each of the grandchildren has a letter from their Gampy, written when they were born. Following is what George wrote Lauren on June 28, 1984:

Dear Lauren,

You're just a few days old. Already you have made your old grandparents very, very happy. We saw that picture of you in the Daily News and in the N.Y. Post. That's pretty good coverage for a 3 day old.

You are a lucky girl. You have a loving Mother who is always thoughtful and nice; and you have a Dad who his brothers and sister named "Mr. Perfect."

Anyway, Lauren, we can't wait to see you. We want to see you smile, to hold you, to love you.

It's a funny thing—when you get older, even if you have an exciting life surrounded by interesting people and having the chance to meet all the world leaders—even with all that—what counts is family and love.

We love you more than tongue can tell.

Devotedly,
Gampy

15

The 1988 Campaign

The 1988 campaign started, I believe, January 21, 1985, the day after the Inauguration. As early as May 30, 1986, I wrote in my diary: "George is obviously the most qualified person for the job. Do I want him to run? Absolutely not!"

I am surprised that I wrote that, but there it is. I may well have been tired that day, or maybe that's truly how I felt. Thank heavens I didn't feel that way very often. I do feel that campaigns are too long, but how are you going to keep people from running? I don't care if it is for dogcatcher, city council, governor, or president, someone will start early and then the others have to jump in. I am writing this in January of 1994, and about ten Republicans are running for 1996. I suspect it won't be long before we have eight Democrats.

For the first couple of years, the campaigning consisted of getting out and meeting as many people as possible and attending receptions and dinners. By 1987, it was in full swing. That was the year our son George moved his whole family to Washington to work in the campaign, which was such a gift to us both.

Finally it was 1988, which started off with a bang. On January 25 we went up to the Capitol to have dinner with our houseguests, Bud Wilkinson and his wife, Donna, and then to attend the State of the Union Address. George was scheduled to have an interview with Dan Rather before the President's speech. It was billed as a political profile, which they had done on all the other candidates and which had been benign stories devoid of controversy. However, CBS opened with a six-minute "exposé" on George's alleged role in Iran-Contra that was filled with false assumptions. It was just plain ugly. Then came nine minutes of Dan grilling George. There were raised voices on both sides. At one point George said: "You have impugned my integrity . . . if this is a political profile for an election, I have a very different opinion as to what it should be." George rarely gets angry, but Dan kept on about Iran-Contra with the most vicious slander, never listening to an answer. At one time George interrupted Dan and said: "It is not fair to judge my whole career by a rehash on Iran. How would you like it if I judged your whole career by those seven minutes when you walked off the set in New York." (He was referring to an incident several years earlier when Dan had done just that, resulting in dead air.)

After the interview each side accused the other of an ambush. Our campaign felt CBS purposely misled them on the content of the interview; CBS said that the Bush campaign deliberately planned an attack. I do believe we came out the winner: CBS reported getting complaint calls; ours were of support.

I was there and, believe me, there was no plot or plan to attack. But you can just take so much. I really do feel that CBS news programs often start an interview with an unflattering opener, and in this case, an untrue one. This puts many interviewees on the defensive. George often has to remind me of that when I see an interview featuring a political opponent and I'm taking some comfort in their unease. George forgives to a fault, but he will never trust Dan Rather again.

The year 1988 was so different from other campaigns, mainly because George had a full-time job in addition to being a candidate. The vice president, despite all the jokes, has many duties. At least George did. Not only was he President of the Senate, but President Reagan put him in charge of regulatory relief, narcotics interdiction, and antiterrorism, to name a few.

Although I had no official job, I had certain responsibilities that continued, campaign or not. We were very busy. I can't even find a diary for the primary season, which maybe is my excuse for a sometimes faded memory.

I do remember that the field of candidates was enormous on both sides, which is typical of a year when there is no incumbent running. There were eight major Democratic candidates, four of whom were members of the U.S. Senate. The one I knew best was Paul Simon from

Illinois. He shared my interest in literacy, and we had attended several breakfast meetings together at the Department of Education. I'm not sure if he remembers, but twenty years earlier we had worked together as volunteers in a public school. On a personal basis, I thought he did a great job. We disagreed on the means to solving the problem—he wanted to pump more money into everything—but his heart certainly was in the right place.

Then there was Gary Hart. Since I was the president of the Senate Ladies, I had known his wife, Lee, although she had not been an active member. Lee was always polite to me and seemed very nice. She went on television several times defending her man, and I was sorry to see her put in that position. They have disappeared from public view—I hope, to live happily ever after. I had met Senator Hart many times. He was a very attractive man, and he was certainly the front-runner on the other side. Behind every candidate there is an army of believers who work their hearts out, and his must have been very disappointed in him. He threw away a good shot at being president.

Senators Al Gore and Joe Biden made a try and ran into problems—Joe's self-inflicted, and Al just died for lack of attention. I ran into Al's father on the campaign trail and had a nice visit with him on a plane. He had served with George's dad in the U.S. Senate.

Congressman Dick Gephardt from Missouri ran. He won Iowa and was a "flash in the pan," although I'm sure that he thought he had what was called "BIG MO." We certainly knew that feeling from 1980.

Two governors ran: Bruce Babbitt of Arizona and Mike Dukakis of Massachusetts. Neither of them seemed to have a chance either—in the beginning.

And then there was Jesse Jackson. Jesse is a big man who fills a room. He must be a chore for the Democrats. He has his own agenda and has never missed a funeral, a strike, or a march. He certainly must be the man they wrote the joke about: "Where is the most dangerous place in the world? That spot between Jesse Jackson and a camera." That being said, Jesse could charm the paper off the wall. His wife, Jacqueline, is a lovely woman, and he has very bright, articulate children. It always amused me that with all his talk, he sent his children to private schools. And it always saddened me that Jesse did not get out of politics and use his charismatic talents to turn kids off drugs and into school. We have seen what he can do; he had and has the ability to really make a difference. With his golden tongue and pied piper quality, kids listen to him. George has told me over the years that when Jesse gave him his word, he kept it. I must confess to liking him.

On our side of the political aisle, it was not so simple, at least from our viewpoint. Certainly Kansas Senator Bob Dole and televangelist Pat Robertson were the main competition, but former Congressman Jack Kemp, former Delaware Governor Pete DuPont, and Al Haig were right in there for every debate. It is always unpleasant to run against members of your own party, and this election was the worst. Because George was considered the front-runner, the others all took dead aim at him and hit the target hard. Much of it was ugly, and rumors ran wild.

The debates were a nightmare, but then they always are. The very first primary debate that took place in Houston in the fall of 1987 is especially memorable. That "man of the people," as Pete DuPont called himself, especially went on the attack, accusing George of not having an agenda. George turned to answer him and said, "Well, Pierre . . ." and that was the end of that. But then it was the others' turn to take a swipe. Al Haig went ballistic on George. All in all, it was hard, as Joanne Kemp was and is a great friend, and I have the utmost affection for both Elizabeth Dole and Pat Haig. I just hate Republican primaries and love Democratic ones!

The first big contest was the Iowa Caucus, where we had upset Ronald Reagan in 1980. What a difference eight years make. The farm economy was faltering, and as we drove through town after town, we would see boarded-up stores and farms that needed paint. As in so many businesses across the country, people had borrowed heavily with no collateral, so when the economy took a natural, cyclical downturn, they could not meet their obligations. So the climate in Iowa was not great for George Bush. We could understand Bob Dole's victory; he was "the farmer's senator." He also is a tough opponent. He has a razor-edged tongue and wit that is better aimed at someone else.

However, Pat Robertson's second place finish to our third was a shock. With his religious overtones, Pat brought a whole new dimension into the campaign. In fact, after his surprising showing in Iowa, he said, "God deserves credit for the victory." I had the same reaction to that as I do to televangelists in general: God is important in our lives, too; it's just more personal. Anyway, with the "700 Club" appearing daily on TV and radio, Pat already had a national following, and he is a personable, soft-spoken man who appeals to many people.

We left Iowa before the count was in, but we knew what was coming. The plane trip to New Hampshire was awful. Lee Atwater, our very bright campaign manager, was down in the dumps, as was the rest of the staff. I finally said that they must cheer up. How could they expect George to campaign with so many people around him singing the blues? George was looking forward, not back, although how he kept so stable, I'll never know.

We landed at the airport, and there was Governor John Sununu. What a man. He gave me a hug and whispered in my ear, "Don't worry. He'll win New Hampshire. 'Mr. Fix-it' will see to it."

The next week I asked and received permission from George never to sit in on a meeting or watch television. So after a full day of campaigning, usually on my own, I would join George and the others for dinner and then retire into our bedroom to read "no-think" books. I believe that I read six or seven that week. I could hear the others talking in the living room night after night, but I stayed away.

One evening as I was returning from an exhausting schedule, ABC's Carole Simpson stopped me and said, "You know your husband is losing the state, don't you?" I said that I didn't—and didn't she know that nobody was allowed to talk to me about the campaign? She apologized and scooted away. I have always laughed about that. Of course she didn't know, but I can't campaign with all that doom and gloom. We had the best guy, and I knew it. And so did many others. That marvelous baseball great Ted Williams campaigned with George, and he loved that. Longtime friend Nick Brady was there, and family and friends came from all over once again to stump the state. In a mall one day, trudging through the slush, was Barbara Franklin, carrying a BUSH sign and handing out literature. Barbara had held a key position in the Nixon White House as well as sitting on many prestigious corporate boards, and here she was carrying a political sign for George. This very able woman was the Secretary of Commerce at the end of George's administration.

On Primary Day I went from polling place to polling place to thank our supporters who were carrying signs and handing out literature. I saw tons of young people with Dole signs and ran into Pete DuPont and his family doing what I was doing. How I worried that day. I just knew we were going to lose. In the early afternoon George called me and said, "Come back to the motel. We are winning!"

All week John Sununu had been winking at me, saying we were going to win. We did, but it was not without a lot of bitterness from Bob Dole. The polls had showed him closing fast, but when the votes were counted, George got 38 percent and Bob got 28 percent. A year or so later I told John just how much his enthusiasm meant to me. He laughed and said that he was faking, that he never dreamed we were going to win.

New Hampshire had some real problems for us. Former Governor Hugh Gregg, father of then-Congressman Judd Gregg and now Senator Gregg, had been our campaign manager in 1980 and was our dear friend. The Greggs and the Sununus had a lot of personal animosities that I didn't understand. That put us all in a very tense situation. We liked them all so much and still do, particularly John and Nancy Sununu, who went through hell for George later on. John is a hero of mine. He's such a bright man, such a funny man. Unfortunately John does not suffer fools gladly and is sometimes his own worst enemy.

We spent the day after New Hampshire in Washington, and then spent the next three weeks crisscrossing the country, usually apart. George was great about calling, so we stayed in touch. The Super Tuesday primary took on enormous importance. I bumped across the country visiting some eighteen states, and George did more. We all spent long hours.

But it paid off. On March 8, George took all sixteen states and 57 percent of the votes cast, winning more primaries on a single day than any U.S. politician ever. The press called it a "knock-out blow." And it was. We coasted through the rest of the primary season, watching as Michael Dukakis emerged as the winner on the other side.

During the Democratic Convention in July, George and Jim Baker went fishing in Wyoming, where George finally rested. He was in heaven: fishing with a friend and no TV. I was in Kennebunkport with family and for some reason settled down to watch Ann Richards's (she's now the governor of Texas) ugly, devastating attack on George. I watched about ten minutes and turned off the tube with a sick feeling in my stomach. How naive of me to think that I was going to enjoy watching people trash George for three days! It hurt. What was worst, by the end of the convention, the Gallup Poll had us trailing Governor Dukakis 55 to 38 percent.

We headed to New Orleans to our own convention with no known vice presidential candidate. George whispered to me on the plane that he was going to ask Dan Quayle to be his running mate, but he had not told anyone else. He had looked over a field of very well qualified men and women and after much thought, felt Dan had much to offer. He was highly respected by members of the Senate. He had co-sponsored with Senator Ted Kennedy the Jobs Training Partnership Act, which was helping unemployed and laid-off workers get back into the job market. He was bright and, George felt, the right age. Some of George's closest advisers had worked with Dan and recommended him highly. I might add that some of those advisers developed a little amnesia when the going got tough.

Upon arrival we were greeted by the Reagans, who had been at the convention and were flying to California. We then went right away to a private home, where George got on the phone to all the potential candidates and tried to find Dan Quayle, which he eventually did. No one else was allowed to use the phone; George didn't want anyone letting the word out before the official announcement.

I can't resist saying a word or two about "leakers." All politicians are blessed with them, I don't care who they are. A leaker is a person who puts self above the candidate or boss. Leakers think they will get better treatment by the press. Maybe they do, but they get no respect from me.

In direct contrast to a leaker is someone like Craig Fuller, George's chief of staff during this period. He did not travel with George all the time, but I loved it when he did. Craig always put George first. He did not react to every little bump in the political road; instead, he stayed calm and seemed relaxed and confident. I liked him before the campaign and absolutely loved him during it. He quietly did his job and did it well. I thought that perhaps he deserved to continue on as chief of staff in the White House. I don't know if he wanted the job, but he carried on well after he knew he wasn't going to get it and agreed to head the transition team. Now a highly successful businessman, he and his wife, Karen, have remained really good young friends of ours.

New Orleans was a great place to have a convention; almost everything is within walking distance. We made a grand entrance on a riverboat, where George announced Dan as his running mate. I heard later that Dan and Marilyn had trouble getting to the platform because they looked too young and no one realized why they needed to be up there. I wonder if they had anticipated the beating they would take for the next four years if he would have accepted the job. I hope so.

My memories of the convention are kind of a blur. Our dear friend Jane Morgan Weintraub sang at the luncheon honoring me. She came out of retirement to sing as she had long since concentrated on being a wife and raising her three little girls. Her voice always reminds me of honey or velvet, it seems so pure and easy to listen to. She and her husband, movie producer Jerry Weintraub, have a house in Kennebunkport, and we have been friends forever.

Doro introduced me at the tribute lunch and looked absolutely perfect to her old mother. George came as a "surprise" and teased me unmercifully. I recall asking him to please sit down and look at me with the same adoring eyes I had for him when he spoke. There were always innuendos that we were not lovey-dovey enough in public. That is not us. We don't need to be public about our affection; it's just there. I know that perception is very important in public life, but I also know that people can spot fakes. It may take a while, but eventually they do. We both resisted the "handlers'" request that we hold hands or whatever.

The whole convention was a happy family time. All our children and brothers and sisters had worked hard for George, so the night of the big roll call vote, our family was very well represented. First, Colu gave the second nominating speech for George. She had not eaten a thing all day and really was nervous, but she did it with style and, as I remember, partly in Spanish. When it came time for the roll call vote, all five of our children represented their states: Neil, Colorado; Jeb, Florida; Doro, Maine; George W., Texas; Marvin, Virginia. In addition, George's sister, Nancy Ellis, announced Massachusetts. Several states passed so that our Texas could put George over the top, which meant poor Marvin, when he announced Virginia's vote, gave it long after the celebrating and hoopla were over. He claims only the janitors were left to applaud him. Colu's role especially was a surprise. Earlier that year, she had quietly gone off and become an American citizen without a word to us. We never would have asked her as she has a great love for her native land, Mexico. It was a very touching gesture on her part.

On the last night of the convention there was a lot of pressure being put on George to make "the speech of his life," since we were behind in the polls. I don't know how he does it, but George seems to be able to stand the heat and even enjoy it. He did look so handsome and gave a magnificent speech.

The next day, the polls showed us almost in a dead heat. On to the next leg.

      The official kickoff for the general election campaign was Labor Day, the beginning of the end of months and months and months of campaigning. Both Kitty Dukakis and I had agreed to write a weekly column for *USA Today*, which forced me to keep scrupulous notes. So probably the best way to describe the frantic pace and nervous energy of the next nine weeks is to share with you excerpts from my diary.

September 4—How to pack for these long trips where you spend every night in a different bed? Well, first of all, at the age of 63, I announced that I no longer carried bags through the airport. I learned this from George. At the age of 60, George had announced that he no longer ate broccoli.* So I decided that I no longer carried luggage through airports and my life was much happier. The advance people took care of it.

    . . . First I pack books; second, needlepoint; third, toiletries; and fourth, clothes. I am trying to go all black, or blue or brown, thus cutting down on shoes and handbags.

Labor Day—Packed all the wrong clothes. We did four outdoor events in record heat wave from San Diego to Los Angeles with a stop in between at Disneyland. Should have worn picnic dresses to all four.

    (Went to) Chesapeake Bay Fish Company. Two attractive young owners, third generation proud. After touring the plant where GB got a lesson in filleting, we went to an outdoor rally. Stood on a stand with maybe eight workers, men and women, with ships of all sizes in the bay behind us with balloons and large BUSH FOR PRESIDENT banners. The "Good Duke" was with us all day, a quiet and decent man. [George Deukmejian, governor of California. I'm afraid that in my mind the "Bad Duke" was Mike Dukakis. This was nothing personal—I had never met him. But in politics, the opponent is always the bad guy.] A few protesters. Bob Grady, a speech writer, noted that he recognized some of Dukakis' paid workers among the protest-

---

* This became public knowledge several years later, and the National Broccoli Growers delivered two tons of the stuff to the South Grounds of the White House. Millie and I were the designated receivers. Some we kept for the White House mess and the rest we sent off to homeless shelters and soup kitchens.

ers. . . . It was hot, hot, hot. After the rally we heard that a man was picked up with a stun gun on his back.

. . . We went to an enormous rally at Disneyland (built-in crowd, of course) to send off the American Olympic Team to Korea. They are all shapes, sizes and colors, and they are all the best in their field . . . George gave a very moving speech . . . full of pride and love.

An amusing note: Sheila Tate told me that they did not want the picture of the week to be GB and Mickey Mouse, the Disneyland logo. They wanted George and the athletes. So I stood on George's name tape to keep two people between G. and Mickey, and several times George moved to my other side. Not an easy man to control.

On to the Los Angeles Police Academy annual picnic. A young policeman named Pratt had just been killed in the line of duty. His wife was pregnant with their fourth child. I hate to hear the police abused when you think that they risk their lives daily for us.

September 6—Awakened at 4:15 Los Angeles time (7:15 EDT), so I guess you could say we slept in. Read papers. Good pictures of GB. Was thrilled to see that the N.Y. Times is running three articles, PRICE OF ILLITERACY TRANSLATES INTO POVERTY AND HUMILIATION, on the front page. Left at 7 a.m. and flew to Oregon, where we were met by Antoinette and Mark Hatfield.

. . . We went to the Northwest Ironworks, where George toured the USNS Andrew J. Higgins and then on to a staging area to address the workers. I would have to give this a mixed review—at best. Big organized labor force with a large loud Dukakis cheering section. The press loved it, *BUT* so did George. His adrenaline flowed, and he kept on top of the situation. We heard from some workers and members of the press that he was gutsy to speak to people who were not for him. Some even asked if the campaign had planned it that way so it would show just how good George was. Well hardly! But he did a great job and went in to have lunch with some workers who invited him to join them.

. . . Flew on to Everett, Washington, where we visited the Fluke Plant. There we got away with a classic campaign boo-boo. At one point GB spoke with the word "Fluke" right above his head. I am sure that when the advance "how-to" book is written, this will be featured as "how-not-to."

. . . (Went to) airport rally where George gave a Distinguished Flying Cross to a Mr. Harry Lewis. It had gotten lost and he'd never received it. He

was in the same task force as G.B. in WWII. I got weeping because he looked
so moved . . . talk about unsung heroes.

September 7 —. . . Flew last night to Louisville, Kentucky, arriving
hotel at 11:45 for bed. No windows to open so it was either cold or stuffy.
There is no happy medium. Walked almost three miles in a nice residential
community called Hurstbourne. A darling young woman rushed out of her
house with a camera, BUSH sticker, and a young daughter by the hand. She
said that it was her daughter's first day of school and could she take her
picture. Then the car pool arrived with six little girls, and the young woman
got all their pictures. It brought back memories of putting five little Bushes
in school the first time. I could hardly wait for them to get home to tell me
about it. I can even remember my mother taking me to the Milton School for
the first day of the first grade. Suddenly I looked around and she was gone.
No good-byes, and I felt abandoned. But I had such fun and truly loved
school that I had forgiven her by the time I got home. I think in our own
children's case they never looked back.

. . . To the American Legion, where George got a great reception . . . he
gave a very moving speech, but in the middle of it, got off the track on Sept.
7th being the anniversary of Pearl Harbor Day. We all got confused, and he
could hear a titter run through the audience and quickly said, "Did I say
September 7th? I meant December 7th." But for a while the press made so
much about it. He recovered and all was well.

. . . On to a Victory '88 fund-raiser . . . to a G.O.P. Headquarters . . .
back to a late lunch . . . flew to Baltimore. Airport rally . . . George spoke to
a B'nai B'rith, enormous convention in Baltimore Convention Center . . .
home to meetings for GB at the house. SPR (Susan Porter Rose) came by to
tell that I was going to be followed by Dave Montgomery (Fort Worth
Star-Telegram) on the morrow. I miss the good old days when (my aide)
Casey and I just took off.

September 9—Met George in York, Pennsylvania, for a rally. There was
a woman picked up the night before who said that she had a friend who told
her that he was going to shoot George Bush at the rally. They ran his name
through the computer, found his picture, a man with a gold tooth, and I was
told that the spotter on the rooftop with a telescopic lens had spotted him
with his gold tooth and a red shirt in a crowd of two to three thousand
people. The Secret Service had followed him for several blocks, picked him

up only to find they had the wrong man. They were back trying to find him again.

. . . Finally we were introduced and it was thrilling. I wish I hadn't known about the man with the gold tooth. [I've been asked if I worried about this kind of thing a lot. The truth is, no—not unless we knew something specific. You just can't let yourself think about it.]

. . . There were thousands of people, lots of BUSH signs and, of course, a few for DUKAKIS or a few anti-Bush signs. Lots of press, lots of color. Big American flag on Court House, flags, cheerleaders with pompoms, bands, football captain, balloons, etc. George gave a fired-up speech, they barely let him talk with cheering. Steve Studdert (with the campaign) was in front like Cecil B. DeMille directing, "take a pompom," "move the Senator," "get behind George," etc. Lee Greenwood sang his song, "I'm Proud to Be an American"; the crowd went wild. Steve was wildly trying to get my attention to get me to move George next to Lee and then to move me and the Senators next to him . . . You just have to have a sense of humor, not to mention nerves of iron.

September 11—We asked the Quayles for lunch with their little people, three very nice children. They have a boy about 14, Tucker; a boy Ben, 11; and a daughter Corinne, 9 . . . it is so different for Marilyn than it is for Kitty Dukakis, B.A. Bentsen or me. She still has to worry about riding lessons, homework, dentists, etc. Quite a juggling act.

September 12—Northern Kentucky Senior Citizen Center . . . welcomed by a kazoo band playing "Yellow Rose of Texas." Adorable. One man with thimbles on all his fingers playing a metal washboard, antique bottles, etc. . . . One elderly citizen to another:

"Which one is Mrs. Bush?"

"The one with the white hair."

"They all have white hair."

"Which one *is* Mrs. Bush?"

[This reminds me of a funny story that happened after George became President. He was talking at a Veterans Hospital about health care reform when an elderly gentleman in the back kept yelling, "What's all this crap? When is Ike coming?"]

. . . Hyatt Regency, Chicago. Biggest suite I have ever seen . . . George got in from a big rally in Illinois and a full day. I could barely speak to him

I was so tired, but I loved showing him the bathroom in our suite, sauna with seats for four or more, Jacuzzi for two to four and every fancy soap you have ever seen and lotions. I filled the "lake" as I called the tub and took a hot bath. George took a sauna. I was asleep before you could say "Jack Robinson."

I am torn over the soaps and lotions. Do I want the hotel people to think I need soap, shampoo and lotions? Not really. But do I take them? Yes, I do. I have a nice collection at home right now, and every now and then I send them down to the shelter in Washington. I keep thinking that a clean piece of soap all your own must be nice.

September 13—Executive Club of Chicago breakfast. Sat one away from Johnny Johnson, the publisher of Jet and Ebony and founder of a cosmetic company. He grew up in Arkansas, the son of a widowed black woman. He told me his mother worked as a domestic and saved her money to move her family to Chicago so her son could go to school. Arkansas was not educating teenage blacks 55 years ago. He started a Black Digest on a shoestring that grew into Ebony and Jet and, I guess, a lot of other things. He reminded me of Frederick Douglass. If you want to do something badly enough, it can be done. A great man. It does show what a positive influence a good parent can have on a child. His mother set an example and instilled a work ethic in him that money can't buy.

We drove through Illinois . . . listening to country music, reading and occasionally looking out at miles of rolling countryside. Whenever we went through a town there would be people with homemade signs or just plain waving, standing on the street or running out to greet the Vice President. At one place we passed a graveyard, and there stood a young woman with her head bowed putting flowers on a grave. Even in the middle of a big campaign, life does go on. That young woman somehow or other put things in perspective.

September 14—How George loves the West Coast because he can call anybody he wants when he wakes up. I have to hold him at bay on the East Coast. By the time we left our rooms (in Los Angeles) at 7:40 he had called his office, his mother, his sister, and Nick Brady who had gotten through the Senate confirmation committee 15 to 0.*

---

* When Jim Baker resigned as Secretary of the Treasury to be George's campaign chairman, President Reagan appointed Nick to replace him.

. . . I took my soaps, lotions, shampoos, etc. (to Christian Mission) and dumped my filled purse on the table. They all laughed at me. Evidently a hotel does supply them with all the above, but they said they could use all they could get.

. . . George didn't sleep well because he was worried about his speech before the San Francisco Economic Club, thought it was too negative about Dukakis. I urged him to rewrite it. George got up at 5:30 and did rewrite his speech. I heard him tell Jim Baker that he just had to be himself. I know that George got where he is today by trusting his own instincts and he usually is right. Let others knock Dukakis. Dukakis is knocking Quayle a lot. I don't think George has mentioned Bentsen once. Frankly, we are not hearing much about Lloyd either.

September 16—Cleveland, Tennessee . . . There I ran into Kids-on-the-Block again. They are a great group of puppeteers who teach kids about the handicapped, drugs, sex education, etc.

Chattanooga, Tennessee . . . We met with PROJECT READ volunteers and students. They were a good group of 225 tutors teaching 280 students . . . they have a waiting list. This always saddens me. Imagine, people get up their nerve to ask for help and we can't help.

Home to stacks of mail.

. . . On the way home in a light rain we spotted those cardboard figures that people have their pictures taken with. There was the President, Dukakis, George, Nancy and the latest, I believe, Tom Selleck. We stopped the car, jumped out and had our picture taken for $5 with "George." It caused lots of excitement among the tourists. I took a picture of the vendor and his pretty little wife with the real George. Back in the car, as the picture developed, we saw why people were so surprised that George is so tall. He just towered over the cardboard George by at least 4 inches.

. . . George called the two former presidents to see if they had any advice for the debates. President Nixon said, "Just be yourself." Jerry Ford said, "Take your time before you answer a question. Take a deep breath and think and then answer." Both good advice.

All through the campaign I read to relax . . . "Lilly: Reminiscences of Lillian Hellman," by Peter Feibleman. Amazing just how much I dislike her lifestyle and still like so much of her writing. She is like Truman Capote in that respect. I hated his lifestyle and yet thought "In Cold Blood" absolutely beautifully and chillingly written.

. . . Doro called late Tuesday night. She was *so* upset. She'd been to a big GOP dinner and the entertainers were so vicious that John Engler (our Michigan chairman) had taken her from the room. She said that they said ugly things about Dukakis and GB, but they were really mean about me and Kitty. They had someone in a white wig debating Kitty. In the debate I used not only all the four letter words, but also made an ugly hand gesture to K.D. Doro was so upset, but I must confess to laughing. It reminded me of a night in Indiana recently. I was the guest speaker at that tremendous fund-raiser they have every year. I was one of five speakers, so why they felt they needed to hire a comedian, I will never know. This man was so tasteless and just plain crude that I got the giggles from embarrassment and from catching the eye of my dear friend Mary Jo Bradley. It was horrid, so very bad and the worse he got, the worse I got . . . almost hysterical giggles. I had to put my head down. I know that 1,500 Indianians thought I thought he was funny and liked him.

. . . Jim Baker and I were talking about how you can't control some things. He told me that when Susan Baker and Tipper Gore were exposing the dangerous, sick, ugly words that were hidden in the rock and roll music that the kids are listening to, Hustler magazine had a picture of the two of them as "A—h-l-s of the Month." Apparently they have one every month. That is too much. Can you imagine lovely Susan Baker or Tipper Gore being treated that way?

September 23—Woke up at 6:30. Went down in my bathrobe to walk Millie. Got caught. There were press all lined up for George's breakfast with (Soviet Foreign Minister) Shevardnadze. Then later they were moved from the front gate to the front lawn with a direct view into my dressing room. I crawled to the closet for my clothes. What has happened to my usually peaceful private home?

. . . Lots of questions about debate coming up on Sunday. "Was I nervous?" "Was I giving George advice?" The answers were all the same— "No" and "No."

. . . Lots of phone calls wishing GB good luck in the debates. They have been hyped to a make-or-break situation. Polls showing GB slightly ahead after being *WAY* behind. They are expecting a hundred million people to watch this debate. Amazing. I do not envy GB.

September 25—We slept until 6:30, which is pretty good for us.
On board the plane the press had a gift for George. Everyone had signed

a Christmas card. Pearl Harbor on September 7th—therefore this was Christmas Day. All signed with funny messages. GB loved it.

. . . Walked through the Convention Hall (in Winston-Salem, N.C.), where the debate was to take place. There was the Dukakis podium three inches shorter than George's. When the big moment arrived the Dukakis people carried in a carpeted thing that looked like a pitcher's mound, making Dukakis now 6 inches taller in perception—a 3-inch shorter podium and a 3-inch riser. I am amazed. He is shorter and it ought not matter. They clearly think it does. (When the two candidates were announced from different sides, they both walked across the stage to shake hands. George tripped over the hidden box!)

September 26—I thought that George won hands down. The polls, pundits, commentators, etc., seem to feel that no one made a knock-out punch, but the undecideds leaned slightly towards George. "Too close to call" was the consensus. One reporter wrote, "I went to bed thinking Dukakis had won and woke up to find that the American people thought that George Bush had won."

September 28—George P. and Noelle joined us in Bloomington, Illinois, on a bus tour. The three sisters, our dear friends Loretta Lynn, Crystal Gayle and Peggy Sue, were with us all day to sing and warm up the crowd. It was such fun because they sang in the bus.

. . . We were told to move over to the window and wave as the press truck pulled up for a "photo op." So we all moved over to the right side of the bus, opened the windows and leaned out smiling and waving. The truck moved up and as they got alongside us, the press said with one voice, "Pardon me, sir, do you have any Grey Poupon?" We died laughing.

September 30—Last day of the month. 40 more days to go, but who's counting?

October 3—Hardly slept knowing that we had a long day ahead, flying to California to welcome the shuttle home. This will be an exciting day. It will end for me in Yakima, Washington, at 9:20 p.m. (12:20 EDT). Arrived at Edwards Air Force Base in California. Driven immediately to Shuttle Landing viewing area on lake bed, an immense 50-mile space, flat as a pancake, hard clay bed . . . On the exact moment that we should have, we heard Discovery break the sound barrier twice and then we saw the shuttle. It circled the sky and then came down at a 27-degree angle that looks like it is going to crash into the earth . . . with perfect timing the plane "flared" and set down exactly where they wanted it to. When you consider that the shuttle has no power, it is on glide, it is a miracle. Some of that same feeling of pride that we felt at the Olympics. The USA certainly got a gold medal on this flight. There was great rejoicing among everyone here. It had been 2½ years since the Challenger blew up. (This was the first shuttle flight since Challenger.) A promise kept, I felt. "Back to the Future" pins were handed out.

. . . George and I went into a holding room, really a men's locker room. He went into a tiny back room and promptly fell asleep. I read my book, "The Duchess of Windsor: The Secret Life," by Charles Higham. Fascinating, but not fascinating enough to keep me awake. She certainly was a racy, determined devil!!!

Reading, California. Big rally, streets lined to and from with warm cheering crowds. George Deukmejian told us in the car going back to the airport that he felt *VERY* good about the crowd reaction.

October 5—34 more days to go!!!!
Slept like a baby, but awakened with clenched teeth and a headache. This will be a tough day. Dan Quayle will be debating Lloyd Bentsen. The latter is so confident, saying things like, "Day I'll be eating Quayle," etc.

. . . New NY TIMES poll. Gap is closing. GB 3 points ahead, down from last week.

. . . Flew home, getting home in time for last hour of the V.P. debate. Lloyd got in one, really telling shot at Dan on JFK. He was lying-in-wait for him. Rather interestingly, I wonder just how well Lloyd knew JFK. The Kennedys hated Lyndon, and surely Lloyd was for his fellow Texan. Ah, well, it does not matter. He got his shot in.

October 8—During the morning our house was really buzzing. First a CIA briefing. Then, to action. Our dining room had to be seen to be believed. Two podiums set up, cameras, TV monitors, table for questioners, red, green and yellow lights for timing and warning on answers. It was set up just as it will be on the night of the debate, TV lights and on and on. In the living room there were 14 people with pads on their laps, all watching the monitors and the simulated debate. (Richard) Darman is the "Bad Duke" and George answering the questions put to him by Margaret Tutwiler, Craig King, Jim Pinkerton and Bob Goodman (moderator). Amazing production. The next debate is on Thursday or Friday . . . depending on the World Series . . . let's get first things first!!!

. . . Finished "Breathing Lessons" by Anne Tyler. Loved it. Started Eric Segal's "Doctors."

October 10—New Atlanta poll out today. Showing George ahead in the South by 12%—49% BUSH, 37% DUKAKIS. Showed 14% ahead in Texas and Florida. Now that is good news.

A week of interviews . . . I wonder if Kitty Dukakis feels like I do—so sick of talking about myself.

One good thing happened from all the interviews: Maeve Binchy, the Irish author, read that I loved her book "Light a Penny Candle" and sent me "Firefly Summer."

. . . I have never seen anything like the trashing of Dan Quayle. He is a fine choice, but I honestly believe that the liberal press are so eager to beat George that they are beating Dan to death. He is certainly as well qualified as Geraldine Ferraro, Spiro Agnew and I could go on and on. I might even suggest Mike Dukakis! The real truth is that Harry Truman, who will go down as a great president, was thought to be a "little man from Missouri." Some people rise to the occasion—others don't. Harry did. I cannot watch the tube. The leaning towards the "Bad Duke" gets me down.

. . . ABC Poll: 50% BUSH—47% DUKAKIS

. . . *The Scholastic News*—never wrong in last 25 years—57% BUSH—43% DUKAKIS

. . . Tulsa, Oklahoma. Went to Children's Medical Center for emotionally disturbed, abused, drug recovery children—ages from babies to 17½ . . . started out the door and there were the little 11- and 12-year-old boys I had read to. One child, Dudley, who they said suffered from lack of self-esteem, asked if he could hug me good-bye. Another little voice said, "Don't forget me." I was so touched, and the next thing I knew I had an armload of little boys. Willis, my (Secret Service) agent, mumbled as we walked out, "They can forget all those expensive programs and just give them a little love." But sad to say, we can't forget all those expensive programs because they don't get the love.

. . . Boarded a commercial plane for Los Angeles. Had a little nap. At one time during the flight was awakened when the pilot announced that "If we looked out the right window we could see the four corners. If you got down on all fours, you could be in four states at one time." So, of course my traveling companions suggested a campaign stop. What a photo op!!

October 12—Anniversary of Robin's death—or was it the 11th? Time does soften death. It was 35 years ago. Hard to believe that our little angel would be 39 years old!

October 13—Awakened early. The pressure mounting on the debate this afternoon. George seems relaxed. 26 more days to go. Awakened to a new ABC–*Washington Post* poll: BUSH, 51%; DUKAKIS, 45%. If the election were held today it would be a landslide for George, but we all know that numbers go up and down.

Dan Quayle announced this week: "No more handlers." I am thrilled as the handlers have gotten too important (as if it is perception that counts, not substance)—as have the press (how many times we see the press interviewing each other?)—as have the spin artists (why not let the viewer decide what they just heard or saw?) I read that one station is now claiming that this is a "Bush ploy," getting Dan to speak out. I can vouch for the fact that this was a surprise!!!

I was led into the (Los Angeles) debate surrounded by friends: Governor Sununu, Gloria and George Deukmejian, Henry Kissinger, Gayle Wilson, the Darmans, Mosbachers, Bobby Holt, Al Simpson and on and on. I sat between Neil and Jeb. On they came. Same podiums, same mound. Incidentally, this time Kitty, looking beautiful in a bright red dress, came right over to shake my hand. I met her before she got to me. (At the first debate, I had asked Pete DuPont to take me over to her and introduce us.) Then the debate started. George was relaxed and confident and funny. The questions were asked by Bernard Shaw, Ann Compton, Margaret Warner and Andrea Mitchell. Jeb got so excited over his dad's answers. Neil, as always, was thrilled. All, if not almost all, gave GB a big win. George was a clear winner. We'll see when the national polls come out.

. . . Drove to a large rally at Loyola University. Drive was long and so we called George W. to see how he liked the debate. (He is the son who pulls no punches and tells it like he thinks it is.) He confessed that he and Marvin had gone to the movies as they couldn't stand the pressure. Marvin told me that George sent him out about 12 times to call friends and ask them how it was going. They then went home and were watching a taping when we called. George W. said that the late evening news was good.

October 14—Visiting California School for the Deaf . . . A warm welcome. Big crowd that all wanted to touch me. They were such a gentle group, tiny little noises to get my attention. They touch. It was like walking through a bunch of butterflies. I loved them. Some are also slow. Many of them are truly beautiful. I walked through the school where they live 5 days a week and go home for weekends. Each child grows up literate and with a vocation. On into a TV station where a precious girl interviewed me. She was part of a team: cameraman, director, lights, etc. All children, all without words. I was put in a chair, with an interpreter, and interviewed live. Michelle had moved into the house when she was 12 and for the first time in her life "felt important." So sweet. Imagine being in a regular school and not hearing a word. She was articulate, bright and warm—very strong in her beliefs. She asked me not to forget people like her, and I won't. When we got through, the whole crew rushed together and said: "You did it, you did it!" to each other. It was their first live interview. Michelle shone like a light. Her mother and father were there to share this glorious day with her. I left full of love.

. . . Flew back to George. We walked over to Chasen's with Tommy Lasorda and Jerry Weintraub. We were joined by Jane Weintraub, Tony Danza and wife, Tommy's wife, Jo Lasorda, Peter O'Malley (owner of the Dodgers), and Jerry's lawyer. In the next room, Gloria and Jimmy Stewart, Barbara and Frank Sinatra, Jane Dart, and Stevie and Iris Dart (Iris wrote the book that I so adored, "Beaches"; Jane's husband, Justin, had been a member of President Reagan's "kitchen cabinet") were dining with Fleur Cowles. We had a nice visit. Fun, relaxed evening. Polls all day look good for George.

October 15—Dodgers won in the 9th!

October 16—(Denver) GB read the papers. Darling front page picture of Neil with Lauren and Pierce . . . Endorsement by Rocky Mountain News. I finished my diary and called Jean Becker of *USA Today*. It is hard to write for a week and then pick out a few incidents to put in the weekly news article. I keep a daily diary, pick out what I want to use for the week, talk to Jean, she sends the final back, I okay it and off it goes. I had to tell her that I would not write one after the election. She says that Kitty has agreed to write one. I think it would be too hard on the loser, and the winner will be too busy. Either way, I said, "No." (When I was approached about writing the column last summer, I was told that Kitty had agreed to it; therefore my office felt I should, too. I wonder if the same gimmick was used to get Kitty to write one?)

October 17—George and I didn't' sleep well at all. Highway too close to room. At times thought that trucks were coming into window. I think we are both beginning to believe that he might win—and then there will be so much to do. George is not letting himself think that way, but you can't keep your mind from churning. So we got up at 5 a.m.

On plane flying home . . . a lovely black lady who worked for United Airlines came up and said: "I want you to know I made up my mind to vote for your husband this weekend. Let me tell you what decided me. It was the death penalty. We must stop this killing. People just have to pay. It may be a deterrent." She also said that she never thought that she would say that. I feel the same way. We just have to stop these killings.

October 18—55% to 38%, new ABC–*Washington Post* poll. 17 points ahead. Too good to be true. Do we believe it? No. We are scared to death that people will stay home. The Teamsters endorsed George yesterday, but not Dan Quayle.

October 19—Spent day in Missouri. Then flew to NYC and was greeted by news the Stock Market went wild with rumors about an exposé The Washington Post was doing on George's "romance" with Jennifer Fitzgerald. The market plunged. Ugly campaign tactics. How do you defend against that which isn't, wasn't and never will be? It got so bad that Ben Bradlee (Washington Post) put out a statement that no story was coming out or being worked on. We must be doing better than I thought for this kind of ugliness.

October 20—AL SMITH DINNER in NYC
. . . Mike Dukakis came up and apologized to George for something a "low level" staff member had said about George. He should have. [This refers to Donna Brazile, who had made a crack to the press about the above rumors. She was fired.]

October 22—Marvin Bush's 31st birthday.
. . . Chase Untermeyer, John Sununu, Jim Baker, George and I had lunch outside in the garden in the sun (a little crisp, but our last chance.) These men are working on the transition team. Very interesting. *Both* parties are working on transition. The day after the election, the transition team must be in place and ready to go, about 95 people that first week.
. . . George spoke to Jim Baker about being Secretary of State and John Sununu about Chief of Staff. I am assuming that Jim said yes. George

told me that John said he wanted to talk with (his wife) Nancy. Two very big jobs. Ridiculous to talk about jobs when you haven't won, but very necessary.

. . . Nap

. . . Walked

. . . We went to the annual Italian American Dinner. They honored former Prime Minister Craxi, Liza Minnelli, Peter Rodino who is retiring after 40 years in Congress, and an Olympic skating star—all from Italian backgrounds. George passed me a note during the evening saying that the M.C. was "dangerous near the mike." How true! It was a very long evening. I sat next to our old friend PM Craxi, who is a very big man. He suffered under the TV lights and kept moaning about the heat. He was right. The speeches went on and on. I finally showed him George's note, and he laughed. I talked Spanish and he spoke Italian and we did pretty well. At one time in the evening, as a speaker was going on and on, he leaned over and said very clearly in English, "Very dangerous man."

The "Bad Duke" came during the dessert, sat through the speeches and then gave his talk (well done) and then GB (better), and we went home.

October 24—George was in Connecticut, Maine and Vermont. He saw Doro. I asked him if Doro was upset by all the protesters. He said there weren't many and why would I ask? I told him that the evening news had said that there "were more of them than us" at the meeting. George was surprised and said that was just not true. No wonder we feel down on the press. Mike Dukakis called George a liar and a racist today. Nice campaign.

October 25—In Illinois . . . met President Reagan's teacher. That's right, President Reagan's teacher, now Mayor of Jacksonville, Mayor Helen Forman. I said that could not be as I just went to his 77th birthday party. She taught Ronald Reagan when he was at junior high school, and it was her first year of teaching. She is 84 years old and fit as a fiddle. She also told me that she taught him English—not government—and she thought he was very good at English.

October 26—13 more days to go. Decatur, Illinois. I awakened in the middle of the night. Can't keep my mind from racing over problems. I probably even make up some problems in the middle of the night . . . new polls show George with a double digit lead, but I just can't believe them.

October 27—California . . . Jim Baker called and said the polls are showing a little slippage to MD.

. . . Lots of speculation over who will hold what job in the Bush administration. Hard not to begin to believe that we are going to win. But "It ain't over until it's over" is very true. You can go down just as fast as you go up. Mike Dukakis is blitzing the airways with talk shows and media. It may be paying off.

October 28—California, Nebraska.

October 29—Call in the middle of the afternoon that my brother Jim Pierce had an emergency operation in Orlando, Florida. Tried all the numbers that I was given and finally after dropping G.'s name, I got his nurse. He was in great pain, but they had given him medication. Margie must be very worried. I am.

October 30—One of the nicest days of campaign '88. First of all, the overnight tracking looks good . . . We flew to Philadelphia with George P. for church with retired Cardinal Krol. We were very touched when George P. fell in behind the Catholic nuns and took communion.

. . . George and I went to Bob and "Big Z" (her name is Teresa but no one calls her that) DeAngelis' house in Norristown for lunch with their pregnant daughter, Paula, and son-in-law. This was a campaign tradition that we started in 1980 and have loved. They are a great family and besides that, "Big Z" is the best cook ever. Their neighbors were on the street, and I found Tommy Lasorda's three brothers in the crowd and brought them over to meet George.

October 31—(Halloween)

Nervous time . . . Barbara, Jenna, Laura and George W. went to South Bend with George. The girls went in costumes. Jenna was a package of Juicy Fruit and looked just like it, and Barbara was a vampire, or "Vampora," some character they all seem to know.

. . . This is the last week of the campaign. It has been ugly. Dukakis, or his supporters, have called George a racist, liar, and adulterer, silly and effeminate. I truly believe that George has run on his record, and Dukakis has run away from his. When George talks about Dukakis' record, they cry foul.

[The best example is the now infamous Willie Horton incident. Under Governor Dukakis, Massachusetts allowed weekend prison furloughs. One weekend, convicted murderer Willie Horton raped a woman and stabbed a man in Maryland. George used this heinous incident to illustrate that Dukakis was not tough enough on crime. Then a pro-George independent committee—not our campaign—decided to turn the example into a campaign ad, using the image of a sinister-looking Willie Horton, who was black, as the focus. We got blamed for dirty politics and racism. Baloney. The ad was not ours, and the truth of the matter is, Willie Horton should not have been out of prison. The victims' families campaigned for George, they were so angry with Dukakis. Roger Ailes, who was in charge of our ads and did a great job, was unfairly blamed for the controversy. He had nothing to do with it. I still miss seeing Roger on the "Today" show, where he was brilliant yet devastatingly funny while knocking the Democrats.]

The negative ads on both sides are bad. We ran one on defense weapons that ends by saying that (Dukakis) thinks by riding in a tank he can make us forget what he is against, all the while showing that silly scene of him riding around in a tank with that silly enormous helmet on his head. Poor man, he looks ridiculous. Some staff person must be cringing. They thought this would be a marvelous photo op!

. . . How do we cope with the pressure? I guess George is right. "Faith, family and friends." All have helped.

. . . Lots of mail.

. . . Lots of people want to redo me. My favorite so far was the lady who took the LIFE magazine picture gave me a new haircut, new earrings, necklace, clothes, makeup, and sent me a slide she had taken of her work of art.

. . . Lots of people want to pass advice on to George.

. . . Lots of people have requests.

. . . Lots of resumes.

. . . Lots of people with ideas for projects for me. A large, orchestrated one for mental health. I sympathize with them all. And if George wins, I wonder, if while working to make America more literate, could I highlight some others?

November 1— . . . On plane Casey told me that she had gone to Williamsburg to hear Crystal Gayle, Peggy Sue and Loretta Lynn sing. She went to both concerts, 2 p.m. and 5 p.m. At both concerts she said that Loretta and Peggy Sue campaigned for George, and they were booed at the five o'clock concert. Crystal told the audience, "No matter who you are for, be sure to vote." How right she is. It makes me sick when I read the percentages of Americans who do not vote.

November 2—Flew to Rye, N.Y., for a Barbara Pierce Bush Day. It was fun. My family greeted me in the old family drugstore we used to go to, McCullough's, and then we marched the length of the village. So much has changed since I bought that Marshmallow Fluff and walked to the movies. A Hunan restaurant! When I was growing up we hardly knew where China was . . . The old movie theater is now the Town Hall. The mayor, Mary Ann Ilse, is a woman!

. . . On to Rochester, N.Y. . . . went to bed "too tired to think. Too fat to like myself."

November 3—Took off for Arkansas. When we return to VP House, we will know if we have won or lost.

. . . On to Baton Rouge.

. . . Bumpy plane ride to Cincinnati.

November 4—Raining off and on all night. Amazing volunteers worked all night setting up for a big rally. They hung painted sheets out windows, great political signs, built big platforms and stands for press and performers.

Big rally. George and Doro came in on a fire truck, covered with confetti. On stage with George Voinovich [now governor of Ohio] and baseball great Johnny Bench. George spoke to hundreds and hundreds of people who had been standing in the rain for 2½ hours. The rally ended with Moe Bandy singing "Americana."

. . . On to a big rally in Michigan.

. . . Newark, New Jersey.

. . . The sadness is that no matter what happens on Tuesday we lose our Secret Service. They go to other details. If we win, ours go to Dan Quayle and Marilyn. These have been wonderful men and women whose only job has been to keep us safe. They have been very much a part of our life during the past eight years. They know our children and grandchildren. They have worked, run, fished, laughed, driven with us. On the whole they are the finest, most decent men and women I know, and I will hate to say good-bye to the VP detail. I'll never forget the day when George was singing in the car, and just as we were getting out of the car a quiet voice from the front said: "If I were you, sir, I wouldn't give up my daytime job."

. . . I also have kissed my four advance ladies good-bye and thanked them: Nancy Pilon, Suzanne Rich, Andrea Raiford and Karen Gossett. What a job they did.

November 5—Did an event with (Governor) Tom and Debbie Kean in New Jersey.

Philadelphia . . . met by our most wonderful friend, Elsie Hillman, and our state chairman, Tom Judge. Elsie had been the most devoted Republican worker in the state and knows everyone. She also knows the joy of life. How they have worked.

. . . Great rally at Immaculata College. Both Senator John Heinz and Arlen Specter were there. John Heinz's polls show him at 80%.

. . . Flew off to Illinois, met by the governor, Big Jim Thompson. He is a fun campaigner, loves the push and the pull of a crowd . . . Enormous crowd in Chillicothe, Ohio.

. . . Flew to Colorado City. Doro and I hopped on a plane and flew to Los Angeles.

November 6—Casey brought me coffee at 5:30. Doro came in right after that, dressed with washed hair. She looked so beautiful. At 6:40 Jeb, Doro and I went to the studio to do "Face the Nation" with Lesley Stahl. I'm not sure Lesley knew what hit her. She went negative and attacked, but Jeb and Doro were superb. Back to the hotel and we called in our last *USA Today* column. Then to a 50-year-old church, St. Nicholas Church, in Encino, California.

. . . 20,000 people at a rally where we met up with GB.

. . . 2nd rally in Los Angeles, 10,000 people.

. . . Flew to Detroit, exhausted. Bed about 12:30.

November 7—One day to go! Polls look like they are holding. Nervous time.

. . . Can't watch TV. Dukakis ads are so bad.

. . . Big rally, Southfield, Michigan.

. . . Ashland, Ohio.

. . . Flying to Missouri. Cautious optimism on the plane.

. . . St. Louis rally at headquarters. Elizabeth Dole and Bucky Bush met us. Governor and Mrs. Ashcroft (John and Janet), and Senator and Mrs. Danforth (Jack and Sally) were at the rally. Get out the vote. LAST RALLY OF THE CAMPAIGN!!!

. . . Flying home to Houston. The "handlers" are all on the plane. They want George to do six television shows via satellite. He put his foot down. 4 big rallies in 4 big cities are enough. We are all tired, but George is dead.

. . . Lee Atwater is quiet. Thinks it will be 53% of the popular vote for GB. I wish he was making more noise. His quiet bothers me.

. . . Craig Fuller has been superb. Good and thoughtful. Not full of gloom and doom.

Jim Baker has been superb. George loves and trusts him.

. . . Houston arrival was great. George, Laura, Phil and Wendy Gramm at the foot of the steps. The Gramms have been so great, so supportive. They were so excited. We, because of the gloom and doomsayers, were very nervous. They were almost high!

The rally at the Galleria was unbelievable. Crystal, Loretta, Peggy Sue, Moe Bandy, wife and children were there. Marvin, Margaret and Doro were also there.

November 8—This is the day.

. . . Voted at 8 a.m.

. . . Went to GOP Headquarters, made a few calls.

. . . Went to Memorial Park to walk 5 miles. It occurred to me that they had closed the park to all car traffic for George.

. . . Lunch at Center Court with my great buddy, Marion Chambers.

. . . Got a massage, did mail, washed hair and went over to the Nebletts'. They had a perfect dinner, a repeat of Super Tuesday.

. . . In the late afternoon Jim Baker had walked in our room and told me we had won. A few minutes later we were down again. We walked into the Nebletts' feeling pretty shaky. At one time in the evening Jim bet Lee $5 that we would get under 53%. Lee paid him off halfway through the evening. All our friends thought we had it in the bag.

At 8:16 CBS reluctantly announced George the winner. We went back to the hotel with our family. We watched the news and we went from a "squeak" to a big victory—42 states and 54% to 46%. We continued to watch the tube. First Lloyd Bentsen came on, congratulated George and said he was honored to serve as the senator from Texas again. He raved over Mike Dukakis and that was that. Mike Dukakis called George and then went public. Funny that Lloyd went public before Mike. I thought that was a breach of protocol.

. . . Down to the Convention Hall, where thousands and thousands of Texans and friends from all over the country were cheering my George. It was so touching. George gave a healing speech.

. . . G talked to the President, Margaret Thatcher, the King of Saudi Arabia and others.

. . . All five of our children's states went for George. We were so happy for them as they worked so hard.

. . . We went to bed in shock. Think of all the people who should have been here, who would have been so proud and said: "I knew it all the time." Neil Mallon, Marvin Pierce, Herbie Walker, Pres Bush, Bill Steiger and Jimmy Allison, for starters.

Well, it's over. How do you thank the people for all they've done? The advance people who literally worked all night and day? The staff who stayed in Washington and worked with none of the fun? The staff who traveled, who not only had the fun, but lost their luggage, slept five hours a night if they were lucky, constantly were asked to change speeches and survived on junk food; volunteers, the backbone of the campaign, who give hours and hours of time, who gather votes and money, spend hours on the phone, drive motorcades and on and on? How do we thank our brothers, sisters, and cousins by the dozens? And, especially, how do we thank our children and grandchildren for putting their own lives on the back burner for us? We will never be able to say thank you adequately, but will try our darndest to do right and be honest, good, caring people.

November 9—I awakened this morning with the President-elect of the United States of America.

16

"Please Guide and Guard Us"

George wanted to begin his first day as President-elect by going to church. It seemed the natural thing to do since we both were fortunate enough to grow up in families where God played an integral part.

So at 7:45, before we left Houston for Washington, we went to St. Martin's Church for a service of thanksgiving and guidance. Our present and past Houston ministers, Claude Payne and Tom Bagby, offered prayers, and Bishop Ben Benitez read the lesson. They were all wonderful, but the prayer that our son George W. gave touched us deeply:

> Our Heavenly Father, we thank you for your many blessings:
>
> We thank you for our health and safe passage during the past months.
>
> We thank you for our country and the freedom to exercise our free will.
>
> And we thank you for our greatest gift of all—your Son.
>
> We ask, Lord, that you open our hearts and minds to you:
>
> Many of us will begin a new challenge. Please give us strength to endure and the knowledge necessary to place our fellow man over self.

We pray that as we face new challenges, we understand that through you we can clear our minds and seek wisdom.

We ask that you open our hearts and minds to prayers so we can feel the solace of your gentle love.

Please guide us and guard us on our journeys—particularly watch over Dad and Mother.

We pray that our lives be beacons to you by remembering the words of David:

May that which I speak and that which I have in my heart be acceptable to thee, oh Lord.

The plane back to Washington was jammed with exhausted but happy staff and family. George's twins were wild. At one time they stuffed the toilet with paper, and I was up to my elbows pulling it out. I couldn't help but wonder if any other First Lady–elects had spent their first morning unstuffing the toilet.

It all seemed so sudden—the election was over and we had won. I can't explain it, but there was a difference in the air; a difference in how George—and I—was treated. Everything had changed.

After a big rally at Andrews Air Force Base, we drove to the White House, where President Reagan and Nancy greeted us. George, Laura, the twins, and Marvin's wife, Margaret, were with us, and the girls were thrilled to have their pictures taken with the President and Nancy in the Oval Office.

George then went to his office and I went home. Laurie Firestone and the stewards had decorated the house with WELCOME HOME signs; red, white, and blue bunting; and balloons. Paula and Millie were there waiting, too, and we all had champagne. It was so touching and warm. George came home that night absolutely exhausted.

A few days later we flew to Gulf Stream, Florida, and stayed with our dear friends Sarah and Will Farish. Will Farish was George's very first aide when he went into politics, and twenty-eight years later, before we left the White House, his son Bill also would serve in that position.

On this visit, their children stayed in a motel down the road to make room for us, which was pretty amazing in itself. It should have embarrassed us, but didn't, we're such good friends. I think it was there I learned just how different things were going to be for us. The press was everywhere, and even walking on the beach was impossible.

At one time I dove off a boat that was a half mile off-shore and saw a picture of the dive in the paper the next day. But we still managed to relax. George played some golf, and I read, answered mail, and swam. We went to church at Hobe Sound with Mom Bush on Sunday and had lunch with her and our great friends and supporters Elsie and Henry Hillman. We saw Nancy and Sandy Ellis, George's sister and brother-in-law, and John Sununu came down to fly back with us. George soon was going to announce his selection as chief of staff.

One of the first things on my agenda was a literacy conference that Susan Porter Rose had organized to be held November 15 at the White House, followed by an honors dinner that night. I had been bugging Susan about some money that had been given me for literacy, and I was worried about not having a place to put it. She finally had to tell me that this money was going into a new foundation—which was supposed to be a surprise—and that the dinner was not only to honor seventeen "learners of the month," but also Barbara Bush. "What if George had lost," I asked Susan, "and we had to go through an evening of being brave?" Susan said then it would have been a celebration of eight years of literacy work. Believe me, it would have been hard.

For the conference, Susan brought together literacy leaders from across the country. To be fair, I'll quote from my diary:

Bill Clinton from Arkansas (Governor) was a star, Mayor Wilson Goode of Philadelphia was terrible. I think I felt that way because under his leadership, Philadelphia was actively working to be a more literate city. I had expected him to be a better speaker, but I should judge by actions, not speaking ability. Robert Winters, CEO of Prudential, was the best. Harold McGraw, Peter Waite (of Laubach Literacy), Jinx Crouch (Literacy Volunteers of America), Jim Duffy (ABC), etc., all good. Susan Porter Rose gets all the credit for putting together a great conference.

The dinner was put on by ABC, PBS, and Prudential. There were so many stars that evening: Peter Jennings was the host; Pearl Bailey and a group of beguiling children sang a song about teaching children to read; our close friend Loretta Lynn sang "Coal Miner's Daughter" and then shared with us the fact that she had had four children by the time she was seventeen and reading had not been easy for her. There was a sensational film about the seventeen "learners of the month," all of whom had worked hard to learn to read.

It also was the birth of the Barbara Bush Foundation for Family Literacy.

The next day Susan brought over a very high-powered group of people, all concerned with the problems of illiteracy and all willing to help form a foundation. It was decided that the focus should be the entire family, to try to break the intergenerational cycle of illiteracy. We wanted to make literacy a value in every single home in America. The foundation officially was announced in March 1989 and to date has awarded fifty-two grants totaling $2 million to literacy programs all over the country. I'm especially proud of the foundation's extraordinary volunteer board of directors, all of whom are busy professionals and leaders in their fields, and of Susan Porter Rose, who was so instrumental in putting the foundation together and has now joined the board (see Appendix B).

⌁ This was a very busy period for us, for making new plans and saying some good-byes, too. At the end of November, the Ladies of the Senate had an informal luncheon for me, ending a happy time in my life. I loved those women and had faithfully tried to attend their Tuesday morning meetings. They gave me a beautiful gold watch from Tiffany that I will wear to the day I die.

Our house was constantly buzzing with many friends and politicians calling on George. Tip O'Neill came by one morning, and George invited him to be our ambassador to Ireland. We all got a little teary when Tip told us that he had always wanted this post, but just could not say yes at this time. He was so sweet as he told George that he and his wife, Millie, were now of an age when their health was not so great and they wanted to spend time with their grandchildren. Eventually, George offered the Irish post to our great friend Dick Moore.

Tip also gave George some good advice. He reminded him that Jim Wright, the new Speaker of the House, had greatly admired former Speaker Sam Rayburn, who had been very nonpartisan, and that George should remember to remind Jim of that whenever the two had problems. I thought it was also interesting that Tip said the three brightest men he had worked with were Tom Foley, who became Speaker of the House when Jim Wright was forced to resign on ethics violation charges; John Brademas, a former Democratic congressman from Indiana who had been Majority Whip; and Wilbur Mills—all three men whom George respected. We both admired and loved Tip. He may have been on the opposite team politically, but he was a decent, fair man. We were thrilled when he agreed to serve on the Board of Trustees for the George Bush Presidential Library Center. The nation suffered a great loss when he died in January 1994.

We spent a quiet, restful Thanksgiving in Kennebunkport and saw Doro and her family. George had talked to Mike Dukakis and offered to drive down to Boston to call on him, but Mike was not ready for that yet. However, he did come to Washington in early December for a visit. He and George had a pleasant talk, and then George called me down to say hello. I told Mike that Millie was going to "write" a book to raise funds for charity and that she had a chapter on famous people she knew. Could we get their picture together? He said yes but didn't move, so I picked Millie up to bring her to him. I heard him mumble something like "I never liked dogs" just as the picture was taken. He must have realized how ungracious he sounded and went on to explain that as a child he had delivered newspapers and every dog in town attacks the paper boy. I could certainly understand that. Dan Quayle also met Governor Dukakis during that visit and was very gracious, considering the awful things that had been said about him during the campaign.

Campaigns *are* hurtful, and George already had started the healing process by having a small dinner at the house with Lloyd and B. A. Bentsen, Nick and Kitty Brady, Helen and Bob Strauss, Bob and Betsy Teeter from our campaign, Kansas Senator Nancy Kassebaum, and Alec Courtelis, one of our National Steering Committee members. It could not have been an entirely comfortable evening for the Bentsens, but Bob Strauss made everything easier. He is absolutely the most amazing politician. He is everybody's friend and, if he chooses, could sell you the paper off your own wall. This was the second time that Lloyd and George had faced off; we had been opponents in 1970 when Lloyd beat George for the U.S. Senate. Both he and B.A. are nice people, and my admiration and affection for her knows no bounds. She is a great lady.

On December 6 we had a "December 7th" party for the press, in honor of George's Pearl Harbor gaffe. We had become quite fond of our traveling press corps during the campaign. However, I believe that 1988 was the beginning of great discontent on both sides of the political spectrum with the press and their "pack mentality," and if there had been a three-way vote among Republicans, Democrats, and the press, the press would have been the big loser. "The Capitol Steps" sang and were very funny. This is a group of young men and women who work on Capitol Hill and get together to sing very clever songs that poke fun at one and all.

All this time George was working hard at putting together his cabinet and the rest of the administration. Although my job was less daunting, I also had a staff to hire. I felt very lucky, for I already had a nucleus, tried and true for eight years, headed by Susan in the office and Laurie Firestone in the house. Both women agreed to continue on, thank heavens: Susan as chief of staff and Laurie as social secretary. Julie Cooke had been my number two in the Vice President's Office; she took a leave of absence to be a full-time mom, and then came back for the campaign. She agreed to be my director of projects, which included overseeing my involvement in literacy and numerous other interests. Julie is a very conscientious, thoughtful person who has great judgment. We still call to ask her advice.

Shortly after the election Susan asked me about hiring a press secretary. I had not had one for the eight previous years, although Sondra Haley of my staff had stepped in and acted as press secretary during the campaign. I wasn't sure I needed one now. Obviously I had not yet realized how much had changed and that everything I said and even thought would be news.

For as long as George had been in politics, he had asked his chief of staff or office manager to hire minorities. Although neither of us believes in quotas, we believe strongly in equal opportunity. So I asked Susan, who was in charge of putting my team together, to look for someone who qualified. As Yogi Berra once said, we found ourselves "with insurmountable opportunities." There were many attractive, bright, experienced people to interview. Early in the search, Congressman John Miller from Washington called to say he had the perfect person, a woman named Anna Perez. "Hurrah," I said, "a Hispanic." He said he didn't think so; he was fairly certain she was African-American. I told him it didn't matter; just have her call me. (As it turns out, her grandfather was Venezuelan). Anna became not only my press secretary, but also my constant companion for four years. She is bright as a whip, tough, fair, fun to be with, and has great judgment. She now works at Creative Artists Agency in Los Angeles, and like all the others, we stay in touch.

Susan did a great job of putting the team together, and for four years they all worked long hours—whether they traveled or stayed home in the office—to keep up with a very busy agenda. George used to tease me that I was a chauvinist—no men in my office. Not true. We had one very good man, Jay Suchan, who had worked with Anna on the Hill and I suspect deserved credit for keeping Anna organized and on time (see Appendix A).

In the middle of the transition, Christmas plans and packing, the Gorbachevs came to New York for a summit meeting. Once again I was struck by how much things had changed. I wrote in my diary on December 7:

Flew to NYC on the biggest plane—discovered that it was Nancy Reagan's. She had gone to NYC the day before for a dinner party that was being given for her, and the plane was going back for her. It was such a treat as I normally went on commercial flights. I went with Sondra Haley (SPR thought that I needed a press person), so there were the two of us and four Secret Service men. Silly. They did have the best pictures of George and our family in the picture-holders. Before I got off, I suggested to the flight attendants that they change back to Reagan pictures. Somehow or other I did not think that Nancy would be amused by Bush pictures all over the plane. We got to NYC very early, and the traffic was not bad at all. People had been warned not to bring their cars into the city and evidently they believed the warning . . . I asked to go by Tiffany to have the band on my new watch adjusted, and Mike Young (head of my new Secret Service detail) said that was fine, and we buzzed right over to the store. There were rope lines everywhere and people were dying to see Raisa Gorbachev and the General Secretary. They had arrived the night before and he was to speak at the U.N., lunch with the President, Secretary General of the United Nations and George and then sight-see. The crowds were kind and seemed to recognize me. I went into Tiffany through the crowd and found the watch repair department, and never have I seen people so accommodating. I asked if I could leave my watch and they could mail it to me. They said, "But what will you wear today?" (Showing me that they all knew that I was having lunch with Raisa and Nancy.) I assured them that I could go "naked-armed" to the lunch, but they said that the watch would be finished in fifteen minutes if I had the time. So I walked downstairs to window-shop to find that we were surrounded by people watching us ogling the diamond and sapphire necklaces. It was a little scary when I realized that they might think I was really shopping! So up we went to the repair department and signed about fifty autographs. I am beginning to realize that George is going to be President of the United States and that my window-shopping days are over. On to the luncheon with my beautiful watch fitting just perfectly!!

. . . Marcela Perez de Cuellar, wife of the Secretary General, met me and took me upstairs. I was greeted by an old friend who said, "We did it, Barbara darling, we did it! We've worked so long for this." I did not remind her that she was for Ronald Reagan in 1980 and that I'd read in the paper that she had supported Dole, Kemp *and* Bush financially in 1988.

. . . Guests were Barbara Walters, Carol Sulzberger, Estee Lauder, Matilda Cuomo, Drew Heinz, "Suzy" (the columnist), and many others including those wonderful henna-haired East Europeans or Soviet Satellite ladies who stand around and look uncomfortable. Mrs. Gorbachev arrived early, so when Nancy arrived on time she seemed late and rude. This is a small game that Mrs. R and Mrs. G play. So far the score is Mrs. G—2; Mrs. R—0. (In Russia she had Nancy in the wrong part of the museum and then told the press that her guest was late!) They barely spoke before the sparks were flying between the two ladies. Nancy felt that Raisa was being critical of the openness between our two countries because she kept saying, "I thought we were open," and Nancy would say, "What do you think we are doing now?" (I asked Nancy on the plane about this and she told me that President Reagan's speech was all about our new open relationship.) Barbara Walters came over and repeated the conversation and asked me what it meant. I had no idea. These two ladies just have a competitive thing. Mrs. G is or has been rude, and Nancy just plain does not seem to like her.

We did lots of pictures . . . they do want me in the pictures. What a difference an election makes!

We went in to lunch, many round tables. Marcela sat between Nancy and Raisa, then me, Maria Pia Fantani from Italy, Matilda Cuomo, Obie Shultz, the wife of the President of the General Assembly, and back to Nancy.

There were three courses, the first being a crepe filled with a poached egg and mushrooms all tied up to look like a sachet. It looked pretty, and Marcela cut into hers and I cut into mine and, of course, the yellow yolk ran out. Mrs. G took one look and put her fork down and never even pretended to take a bite. The second course was red snapper and Mrs. G waved the waiter away and finally Nancy said, "Aren't you going to eat anything?" Raisa answered, "I would, but I don't know what it is." We told her, she took some and ate not a bite. She did eat some of the dessert, a raspberry dish. Nancy said to Mrs. G after she had had two bites of dessert, "You are like my husband. He loves desserts." At that Mrs. G put down her spoon and fork and that was that.

Matilda Cuomo (wife of the governor) saved the day. She had been to Russia and spoke of the day-care centers that she had visited and the different ladies she had spent time with. Raisa would give a rote answer: "Oh, yes, Madame So-and-So is one of our national treasures." Although Raisa does speak some English, all the conversation comes through an interpreter. [I remember feeling so sorry for Marcela Perez de Cuellar. She had planned such a nice luncheon and it resembled a sparring match.]

At 2:10 Mrs. G got up, announced she had an emergency and rushed off. That was the day of the tragic earthquake in Armenia where some 24,000 died (final death toll was estimated to be 55,000) and the G's cut their trip short to rush home.

The stories continued to come out of Armenia about the thousands of homeless people in the freezing cold. On December 23, Jeb and his son, George P., flew to New York City, helped load a plane with food, toys, and medicine, and then flew on Christmas Eve to Armenia on a cargo plane with AmeriCares. They toured the totally wiped-out city of Spitak and went to a hospital in Yerevan, where George P. gave out toys. I wrote in my diary:

We saw them on TV. At one time Jeb was trying to comfort a woman who had lost her husband and two of her children and was trying to save a remaining child that they saw in the hospital. We also saw Jeb and George in a church praying. When our precious Jeb stood up he wiped a tear from his eyes. [Several years later Mikhail Gorbachev told George that tear did more for Soviet-U.S. relations than we ever will know. It showed the Russian people we cared.]

Jeb called from NYC on the 26th and said that George P. was

wonderful . . . I think it was just too much pain for a 12-year-old to see and feel. The stories were horrifying. One mother or grandmother fed her child by pricking her finger and the child sucked it for eight days. They saw the child.

In retrospect, I think it was probably very good for George P. We all take family, medicine, food, and water for granted. I was very proud of our Florida family—not only those who went, but Colu and the other children, who willingly had a lonely Christmas at home without their dad and brother.

George went on his annual post-Christmas hunting trip. He used to tease me about packing my bag early. This year he was so excited he was packed a week ahead of time.

We spent New Year's Eve at Camp David thanks to President Reagan's generosity. George finished Edmund Morris's book about Theodore Roosevelt; I read Ishbel Ross's *Grace Coolidge and Her Era,* and eventually read Morris's wife Sylvia's book about Edith Roosevelt. George met with quite a few people, and we both talked to our good friends Penne Korth and Bobby Holt, who had taken on the enormous task of putting on the Inauguration. We were trying hard to keep it as open as possible and stay within budget. Not only did we not go into debt, but the Inaugural committee had some donated money left over. Bobby was kind enough to ask me for some charitable suggestions, and one of the things we did was donate $5,000 to two libraries in each state, chosen by the American Library Association. The letters we got back were very moving. Most of these libraries were in small communities with very tight budgets and the donations made a real difference. In one New Mexico town, the amount of the donation was higher than their entire annual budget!

After Bobby and Penne left, I wrote in my diary:

(They) have organized an extraordinary five days, starting with a big Mall opening for thousands on Wednesday and ending with an ecumenical church service on Sunday at the National Cathedral. We hope that churches across the country will ring their bells at twelve noon after a service of prayer for our nation. This is symbolic of our belief that we are truly one nation under God. We must get back to faith, family and values. Our children need food, shelter *AND* love, faith, stability, family—they surely need someone who cares—they need God.

I also want to give credit to Senator Wendell Ford of Kentucky, head of the Inauguration at the Capitol. He and his staff not only did a wonderful job, but were very easy to work with.

    ⟅⟆ At one time during the campaign I had given George a list of things I really wanted to do someday when he got out of politics—things like take a barge trip with all the family through the French wine country, go on a cruise, and so on. Since we had won, the only one we could tackle now was to have puppies, so shortly after the holidays we sent Millie off to Will and Sarah Farish's Kentucky farm, where she married "Tug."

With everything else going on George managed to plan a surprise for me on our forty-fourth anniversary, a small dinner at a restaurant in Washington. I met him there to find Andy Stewart, Dick Moore, and Johnny Bush. The weather was so bad that other guests were stuck in airports and couldn't make it, but we had a great evening, ending with a play at the Kennedy Center.

On January 11 I did see the upstairs at the White House. Of course I had seen it many times before, but this was a complete tour of all the rooms, giving me an opportunity to decide where to put some of our personal furniture. Unlike past (and future) years, the visit was not covered by the press—Nancy met me upstairs instead of outside. That may have been why the media assumed Nancy had not shown me around. Actually, she showed me everything, including the laundry rooms and upstairs kitchen after I asked. I needed to see them so I could tell Paula about her living and work space. I was lucky that Nancy had redecorated the White House so beautifully. We needed to do very little. We turned one room into our family room, bringing our own furniture from the Vice President's House and the curtains that matched, although we had to add some material so they could fit the huge windows. I was amused four years later when I was informed that I could not take those beautiful drapes with us because "they belonged to the White House." Well, half was theirs and half was mine and I couldn't help but wonder who would want chintz curtains that matched my chairs and couches?

On January 18, we moved out of our home for the last eight years and into Blair House. Saying good-bye to the stewards—Rommy Cruz, Rudy Arca, Angel Paroan, Herman Capatti, and Danny Ibanez—

was hard, and I drove off in tears. I also was sad to say good-bye to Mike Xander, Beth Becker, and Barbara Marshall, who had taken such good care of the Vice President's grounds. As we drove up to Blair House, there were Betsy Heminway, Sandy Doubleday, and Doro and Neil cheering from the Inaugural Parade viewing stands. They must have sensed that leaving would be hard for me.

The Inaugural festivities opened with a ceremony at the Lincoln Memorial, just as they had in 1980. It was a wonderful night. Grandchildren Sam, Ellie, and Lauren danced away to the Gatlins, Sandi Patti, the Beach Boys, Up With People, and others, ending with Lee Greenwood singing "I'm Proud to Be an American," fireworks, and thousands of people lighting small flashlights representing a Thousand Points of Light. Our little children went to bed and our big children went off to one of three dinners. George and I went to all three briefly.

The next day was the Tribute to the First Lady at the Kennedy Center. Since the tickets to this event are fairly inexpensive, it is always well attended and they have to use three theaters. Mr. Scaasi insisted that I have a new suit for this, and I loved it. It had a pretty flowered blouse, and the jacket was lined in the same silk. Now that is the height of luxury because you can only wear one blouse with a suit like that—the matching one. Marilyn Quayle introduced me in each theater, which was nice. There were many, many entertainers. At one point we got slightly behind schedule. Our Noelle, age twelve, and her first cousin, Alexandra Schmitz, sang with a mariachi band in one of the theaters. Everyone was told the exact number of minutes they could perform, but the bandleader got carried away and each time they ended, they'd start the whole thing over again. Noelle and Alexandra would start in singing, dancing, playing the violin and guitar one more time. Nobody dared "put the hook" on the grandchildren of the President-elect. The girls looked adorable, dressed in high red boots, Mexican costumes, and enormous hats. I must add that I was mightily surprised that Noelle could do all that.

On Thursday night we went to a dinner that Kitty and Nick Brady had for our family and very close friends. We never would have seen anyone if they hadn't done that. Then we all raced off to the gala. Our four oldest grandchildren were allowed to go, and that made it even more special for us.

Finally it was Friday, January 20. It was a lovely, sunny day. We got up early, and I tried on my hat. It was dowdy-looking, and I decided it was my big day—no hat! We began at St. John's with a family church service with Tom Bagby from our church in Houston; John Harper, rector of St. John's; and the Quayles' minister taking part. We were surrounded by family and a few friends.

Then it was time to go to the White House. The atmosphere was much more relaxed than it had been eight years earlier. It was, after all, a "friendly takeover." I suspect it also was easier for the Reagans in 1989 than it would be for us in 1993. They were leaving the White House under very different circumstances. George and the President rode together, and I rode with Nancy. The streets were lined with people waving, smiling, and cheering.

It was so exciting with George's mother and so many of our relatives there, including five of the older grandchildren. To this day, my impressions are very vivid: lots of friends, beautiful singing, miles of people. It was thrilling.

Billy Graham gave the invocation and the benediction. I got many phone calls about this, people telling me that Inaugural ceremonies always included a man representing each faith. I explained that this was not true. We had researched this; plus, we considered Billy to be representative of all religions, a man of God. It wasn't just friends and strangers who got into the prayer act. One of our very distant relatives who had just been ordained let it be known to my office that she would come only if she could give a prayer. We turned her down and guess what? She came anyway.

Alvie Powell, a soldier in the U.S. Army who had performed for us before, sang "The Star-Spangled Banner."

Then it was time. Justice Sandra Day O'Connor swore Dan in, and Chief Justice William Rehnquist swore George in. (Although we considered Bill and Nan close friends, we badly missed Potter Stewart.) I held two Bibles: the one George Washington had held two hundred years ago when he was sworn in, and the one the House and Senate prayer group had given George, opened at the Beatitudes. I have used a different Bible at each of George's swearing-ins—one for the United Nations, one for the CIA, two for vice president, and one for president—so each of the children may have one.

As the oath was given, I felt as if we were standing still in time. In one awesome moment George Bush became President of the United States of America.

As I sat listening to his speech—which I had not read ahead of time—I remember thinking it covered many of the same concerns I had, things like education, the welfare of our children, and other issues. I was never so proud of him or what he stood for.

Then suddenly it was over and we were leading the Reagans to their helicopter. It was sad telling them good-bye, although he should have felt great, leaving with a very high approval rating and the affection of the nation.

After a marvelous—but too long—lunch, the parade began. George and I got out and walked at different intervals during the trip down Pennyslvania Avenue to the reviewing platform outside the White House. It is amazing how many of your friends you see along the route. I spotted Willard Scott and ran over and gave him a kiss. Unbeknownst to me, he was live on the air at that very moment. I think I left him speechless! How he has teased me about that ever since. The parade went on and on—a record three hours, forty minutes—but George and I stayed until the end. Our children and grandchildren ran in and out of the White Houe, and by the time we got there, they had reported on every room. George's mom was comfortably settled in bed in the Queen's Bedroom and had already had a visitor, Billy Graham.

We all dressed in our best new ball gowns and black ties, and one by one went by to see Mom and be inspected in our finery. I had a beautiful Scaasi blue velvet dress with a satin skirt, a stole, and a glorious Judith Leiber blue satin bag made of the dress material with a rhinestone clasp and shoes dyed to match. Knowing that I would wear the shoes only once, I bought a pair for twenty-nine dollars. They were absolutely the most uncomfortable shoes I ever owned, in addition to which, the blue dye came off on my feet and was almost impossible to get off. The dress, the stole, the bag, the shoes (good riddance to bad rubbish), and the pearls later went to the Smithsonian. That night, after fourteen balls, every inch of my body ached, as did George's.

This is what I wrote about the next day in my diary:

Saturday the 21st we opened the house to the public at 8 a.m. People waited all night long. Amazing. Some people said: "I saw you come in last night!" After a half an hour, George went to work and I went upstairs to start finding things. (Our bags had been unpacked but who knew where things were?) Imagine this house had all 10 of our children, all 10 of our grandchildren, Mom, a doctor, a nurse, Paula and two nannies. All during the day we saw tourists streaming through the White House and out the front door. Once Jenna and I went to check on Mom and found her sitting up in a chair at her window waving at the tourists who were looking up and waving. When they saw Jenna and me they yelled "Come on out." We waved and said we couldn't and tried to look sad so they'd know just how badly we felt. (When we tried going downstairs, the tourist line came to a standstill. It just didn't work.) There were about 85 people out by the North Portico and spontaneously they started to sing "God Bless America." We couldn't help but weep. So tender. [By now you've discovered we weep more for joy than sorrow.]

Later in the day we went to check on Mom again and she was outside shaking hands with the tourists in her wheelchair. She was such a sweet lady. Several of the children spent a lot of time shaking hands also.

At noon that day we had all our relatives and our children's in-laws for lunch. As the group was growing by leaps and bounds I made a rule that no girlfriends or boyfriends, just fiancées. George said that I was going to cause many engagements. The office had called one day in a panic and said that one of our relatives had called and said that she wanted to bring her fiancé and *her* name was so-and-so. The office asked what they should do. I said: "Say yes." Then there were those who asked us if they could break the rule and bring their best friend. The answer was: "Sorry, no." There are more last minute things to solve at a time like this. After all was said and done, about 250 family came to lunch.

That afternoon the children, girls and I went to Constitution Hall to see a play, "George to George." It was fine, a little too old for the really young ones, but they behaved.

Back to the White House and dressed for yet again another Ball, in fact two. The Texas State Society Ball was jammed and filled with friends. The Young People's Ball—Marvin and Lee Atwater in charge—was loud R and B. Lots of fun. Dreadful music. It was like being at an aerobics class.

We ended Inaugural Weekend by attending a service at the Washington National Cathedral on Sunday. It was truly beautiful. That cathedral has special meaning for us: Neil, Marvin, and Doro went to the cathedral schools; the boys were confirmed there; George's mother had made one of the needlepoint pillows; we had said the final good-bye to many of our friends there; it was one of my favorite places to bring visitors; Bishop John Walker was a friend. So we felt very much at home.

Memories of the weekend are many. I think we sat down to eat together only once, and as I looked around at the table, Barbara and Jenna were not anywhere to be seen. I mentioned it to their mother, and one of the butlers spoke up and said that they had just telephoned the kitchen and ordered sandwiches to be delivered to the bowling alley. The bowling alley! We put an end to that before it started, and they ate with us.

One of the sweetest sights of the week was Marvin and Margaret's little Marshall asleep on the Lincoln bed. She looked big as a minute. Neil and Sharon's son, Pierce, learned that if he rolled over on his back at the top of the ramp by the solarium, he could slide to the bottom. He would pop his hands over his head with his stuffed monkey and buffer his stop.

Then one by one our children left, leaving George and me alone in that wonderful house with literally the weight of the world on his shoulders.

17

The First 100 Days

That first Monday George went off to work at seven A.M., and I set about getting settled in. I especially wanted to unpack some of our personal pictures to set around on the tables so this great big house would feel more like home. One thing I did not have to worry about were paintings for the walls. The White House has the most glorious collection of art, and I pretty much got to choose just who I would like to spend the next four years with: Glackens, Twachtman, Winslow Homer, Cassatt, Monet, Cézanne, Potthast, Lilla Cabot Perry, Remington, Russell, Thomas Sully, Metcalf, George Healy. We also brought with us from the Vice President's House a borrowed painting from the Houston Museum of Fine Arts, *Passing By,* by E. Martin Hennings, a Taos painter. I even found a Grandma Moses to go in the room I set aside for visiting grandchildren, not that those little monkeys ever would notice.

Every day I was struck by how much things had changed in our lives. I expressed a desire to use a smaller car rather than a big black limousine, and on out-of-town trips, to travel by train or commercial airline. Susan Porter Rose and Mike Young, head of my Secret Service detail, agreed to the smaller car, but they said I really could not travel commercially since the number of threats against the First Lady is higher than that for the vice president. That's just the nature of the "job." But what really persuaded me was learning that if I flew commercially, the flights sometimes would be delayed while the agents thoroughly checked out the plane, luggage, and so on. I reluctantly also gave up on the train. To inconvenience so many others was not reasonable. We nicknamed the plane I flew on "Bright Star," for the leukemia foundation George and Hugh Liedtke founded after Robin died.

Another big change occurred when Millie came home to her new life. We were so glad to see her, but there was a big difference between opening the door at the Vice President's House (where there wasn't a soul around) in your bathrobe and letting the dog out at six A.M. and throwing on your warm-up suit at the White House (where the morning crew already was hard at work), waiting for the elevator to take you down two floors, racing down a long corridor through the Diplomatic Reception Room and out to the South Grounds. Gradually the butlers took over that job. I really enjoyed those morning walks, but it also was nice for George and me to be able to enjoy coffee in bed and share the newspapers. We read all or parts of five papers every morning, discussing the news as we went. This is still my favorite time of day.

On February 1 we had our first big formal White House party, a white-tie reception for the Diplomatic Corps. This had been a tradition of many years which the Carters stopped, the Reagans reinstated, and we continued. For many ambassadors and their wives, it provided their only opportunity to see and speak to the president. It was always a colorful event for they came dressed to the teeth, often in native costumes. As for me, I decided to wear my Inaugural gown one more time before sending it to the Smithsonian.

I wrote in my diary about the evening:

Just before we were to go downstairs, George suggested that we invite Willie and Ulla Wachtmeister, dean of the Diplomatic Corps and our very close friends, to come up and march down the Grand Staircase with us. They were followed by our Chief of Protocol, Joseph Reed, and his wife, Mimi. Millie bounded up to her friends, the Count and Countess. Ulla was in a glamorous black velvet gown, soft and feminine, with a lovely diamond tiara. She looked like the fairy godmother in Cinderella, if not Cinderella herself. As they leaned down to pat their old friend, Millie turned her back, walked a few feet and quietly threw up. George led the horrified guests into the living room saying, "She has never done that before. It must be *evening* sickness!" Joseph Reed kept saying, with hands fluttering, "Perfectly natural, perfectly natural," in his very eastern accented voice. What an introduction to the Diplomatic Corps for Millie.

I might add that it was certainly an interesting start for wonderful Joseph, who turned out to be a fine protocol chief.

Almost every day we experienced a "first." On February 9, George gave his first State of the Union Address, and although I had been to many, many before, this was very different. I wrote in my diary:

It is so funny not being the wife of the Vice President. I used to sit in a single seat on the side, sort of like a step-sister. I invited Marilyn Quayle to sit with us, no closer, but just not isolated. I had Marvin, me, Doro, Marilyn, Ann Simpson and Corinne Michel. When I walked in, I got a nice ovation. It is customary, but it still pleased me. I felt that they had great affection for George who, after all, had worked with many of them. He walked in to much applause. I thought he gave a wonderful speech. He was interrupted some fifty times. He showed warmth, caring, wisdom and humor. So much to do!

The day after the speech we went to Canada for a meeting with Prime Minister Mulroney, stopping on the way home for a weekend in Kennebunkport. There we discovered yet another change that is true to this day. When we walked from Walker's Point to downtown one morning, the crowds around George were enormous. A large press corps kept asking questions, and the people in cars almost drove off the road because of rubbernecking. After I left one of the stores, the press went in to ask what I bought and how much I'd spent.

It wasn't much better back in Washington. I wanted to show our friends Don and Adele Hall from Kansas City the newly renovated Blair House, which is right across Pennsylvania Avenue from the White House. As we started to cross the street we found ourselves surrounded by the press asking questions, which gathered a crowd. At first George and I tried walking to Blair House or to church, but it was just so disruptive, bringing traffic to a standstill. We decided it would be more thoughtful to ride, thus giving up one of our great pleasures—another fact of life that took a while to accept.

〜 It wasn't long before George was earning his nickname, "Perle Mesta" (she was a famous Washington hostess during President Truman's time), which had been given to him during his UN days. I had known for years about George's flair for entertaining—after all, he had brought ten Yale classmates home for our first Thanksgiving dinner—but the White House staff was in for a shock. I wrote in my diary on February 16:

Yesterday was a great funny day. George awakened full of it—whatever that means—and decided to have a dinner party that night. He decided on fourteen. Laurie (Firestone) told me that the chef said, "I am used to having two weeks notice." How funny. We were lucky that he had given us twelve hours notice.

The next day I flew to Denver to visit the Food Bank of the Rockies, which worked with Second Harvest. This is a marvelous national program that feeds many hungry people with food that ten years ago would have been dumped—cans that were dented but perfectly good, two-day-old bread, and so on. Then I went to visit grandchild number eleven, who had been born February 7: Neil and Sharon's Ashley Walker Bush. She is a beauty. I had a quick visit with her older sister and brother, Lauren and Pierce, and was then going to go by Lauren's classroom. The Secret Service suggested that I not go as that would highlight where she attended school, creating a security risk for Lauren. It was another tough change we'd have to get used to—and our children and grandchildren, too.

I got home that afternoon to discover that George must have felt "full of it" again: He had forty coming for an informal, light buffet supper upstairs and a movie downstairs in the White House theater.

⌒ A week later we left for our first major trip abroad. First stop: Japan, to attend the funeral of Emperor Hirohito, followed by quick visits to China and Korea. I wrote in my diary:

I am so confused about the time we spent in the air. I know we left from the White House at 5:45 a.m. (Wednesday) and arrived in Tokyo at 1:10 p.m. They say it is Thursday here. Who knows?

. . . We drove straight to our residence, absolutely *NO* cars on the road. (Roads cleared for foreign arrivals.) George went right to bi-laterals with other foreign heads of state, starting with lunch with President Mitterrand. During the talks George invited him to visit us in Maine in June when Boston University, celebrating its 150th birthday, was giving both Presidents (and me) honorary degrees. [Later that year, BU also gave Helmut Kohl of Germany an honorary degree. I was in mighty fine company—which is the world's greatest understatement.]

. . . We were waiting to hear about John Tower's confirmation hearings from Washington. The FBI says he is clean and yet allegations continue to come. I guess we'll know tomorrow. George told me that John asked to see him alone on Tuesday and said he was grateful to George for standing by him. George said that he had tears in his eyes as he told GB that "he would be the best Secretary of Defense that this nation ever had."

February 24—Today is the funeral for Hirohito, now known as Showa. (As in China, the emperor's name changes after death.) So the last 60 years are now known as the "Showa Era."

. . . It is raining.

. . . Dressed in black shoes, stockings, dress, coat, hat, veil, gloves and even black earrings and pearls. Pretty grim and ugly. George and Jim Baker in their rented morning suits. (National Security Adviser Brent Scowcroft and John Sununu did not don theirs.) Off we went in a big black limousine with American flags flying in cold, drizzly weather. We arrived in about ten minutes and were led immediately to a front row seat. I sat next to President Kaunda of Zambia, a darling man whom we had visited in 1981 or so and who had returned for dinner with us at the V.P. House. At our dinner he and his lovely wife sang a love song duet that I will never forget. He also played the guitar. I remember that he was a Christian and that they had a picture of the Last Supper over their dining room door at his palace. George sat next to the President of the Federal Republic of Germany, and next to him was François Mitterrand. Down the row from us sat many "royals," the King and Queen of Belgium, the King and Queen of Sweden, the King and Queen of Spain (we had a private dinner with them at the Okura Hotel, seated on the floor; I am not sure His Majesty enjoyed either the food or the seating arrangement, but we laughed a lot—they are delightful people), the King and Queen of Togo and many others. I did not see any of the top Russians or, for that matter, the Chinese. [All in all, fifty-five heads of state, eleven premiers, and fourteen members of royalty attended the funeral. For some, including George, attending the funeral was somewhat controversial because of Hirohito's role in World War II. However, George and the other heads of state felt strongly it was part of the healing process. And certainly most Americans trusted their president's judgment on this: After all, he had been shot down during the war by the Japanese!]

. . . In front of us was a black cloth curtain. We were seated in a big black and white tent and were given small lap robes and there were small heaters. In spite of all that we were cold. I enjoyed seeing all the ladies in their fur coats and hats (can't touch fur if you are an American politician's wife.)

. . . After several announcements and quite a little time, the curtains opened in the middle and the procession came marching in, monks carrying the bier, and then the delicate little royal family walking slowly, the ladies in black coats and gowns to the floor and veils that came way past their shoulders. The new Empress walks like a ballet dancer, and she reminded us of a beautiful black swan with her graceful posture and lovely long neck. The men in morning suits and top hats in their hands. The Imperial family paid homage to the fallen Emperor, bowing quite a few times. The new Emperor spoke as did the Prime Minister, the heads of the Diet and the Chief Justice (a cold damp wind blowing all the time).

. . . There was much carrying of (the Emperor's) personal effects, including his microscope. They were carried in and out of a tented, draped pavilion. Reminded me of the Egyptian or Chinese Tombs where treasures were buried along with the body. Some very weird chanting, and the curtains closed and opened. This all had to do with the separation of church and state, I believe. It ended with the foreign dignitaries going up to the bier, bowing to the Showa, turning and walking towards the royal family, stopping, bowing again and walking out. The whole ceremony took about two and a half hours and was really freezing. Having said that, I wouldn't have missed that for anything.

. . . A word of praise for the Japanese protocol. Everything went like clockwork. There was no waiting. That is amazing when you think they had to orchestrate 120 motorcade arrivals and departures.

. . . George had bi-laterals all during this visit, including one with Cory Aquino that was set up at the last moment. She at first said that she had no time for a meeting. I couldn't believe it. No time to meet with the President of the United States, but she had a change of heart. I sat quietly in on the short meeting with GB, Jim Baker, Brent Scowcroft and John Sununu. Cory had four people. One of the things she mentioned was needing the name of someone to talk to to facilitate the AID (Agency for International Development) money they needed. What nerve! Too busy to meet, but not too busy to ask for money! She is an attractive-looking woman. (George said in the car that we had to understand that she had enormous pressures from the left. There were also rumors that she held the Reagan/Bush administration responsible for her husband's death and this attitude was a holdover from that.)

Next stop was China, where I couldn't believe the changes:

We drove past thousands of people and many, and I underline many, new buildings. Many brighter winter clothes including several children in bright fur coats! Still thousands of people on bicycles, still people pulling loads on bikes, but so many more cars, buses and trucks. People say that the traffic jams are enormous! (The roads were all cleared for us.) When we got to Tiananmen Square there were hundreds and hundreds of people. We stopped and had pictures taken. We waved to the people and they all waved back. They used to just stare. Chairman Mao's picture still over the big outer gate, but Lenin, Engels, Stalin and Marx gone. The trees have grown around the Great Hall of the People. The Chinese and American flags on telephone poles or light poles everywhere. And the wonderful red and white banners hung across the road for visiting heads of state. I certainly never thought when we lived in the PRC that we would see this welcome for George. It was great to be back.

. . . President Yang Shangkun hosted a banquet. He did the nicest thing and gathered many of our old Chinese friends at a reception before the dinner.

. . . We went to our old church to discover that they had moved into a much bigger church and the crowds were overflowing. We did see the three ministers who had led our services 19 years before. They gave us such a warm welcome back to our Peking church family. It was very moving.

. . . Deng Xiaoping hosted a warm, intimate luncheon. This fascinating 85-year-old man was just as sharp as he could be and looked very well. He only smoked one cigarette during lunch. That was amazing as in the old days he chain-smoked.

. . . We gave our return dinner at the Great Wall Hotel. George thought that it would be fun to have a Texas barbecue for the Chinese. It was not one of our better ideas for the Chinese didn't seem to understand ribs and beans, and the beef and chicken in the PRC is not the same as ours. But the idea was fun and the room looked pretty with red-checkered tablecloths and flowers.

Usually when our president goes to a foreign country, he will meet privately with the dissidents or opposition. Both George and I believe strongly in human rights. But our ambassador, Winston Lord, invited dissident Fang Lizhi to our banquet, which made it almost impossible for the top Chinese leadership to come. This caused a big flap even before we arrived. For a smart man (Lord), this was an amazing act, and hours were spent trying to find a solution to this gaffe. The night of our banquet we still did not know if the leadership would attend or not. After quite a wait, they did arrive. During the dinner, George, thinking that dissident Fang was in the banquet hall and fearing that there would be a scene, mentioned that he hoped this had not caused too much of a problem. The answer he got was very noncommittal. It wasn't until the next day that we discovered that Mr. Fang had been prevented from attending the dinner. He had been stopped twice by the police and buses were kept from picking him up.

... The other unpleasant thing that happened was that the Chinese security got way too rough with the press on a visit back to my beloved Forbidden City. I should have stopped the tour and told our hosts that unless they lightened up, the tour was over. It wasn't until Carol Powers, the superb White House photographer who had been assigned to me and a true friend, got socked so hard that her jaw was dislocated, that I did stop and lay down a few ground rules. To her extraordinary credit, she did not make a scene, and it wasn't until we got back to the guest house that she went for help. [To save money I had not let the office send a press advance person on this trip and so I must take the blame. I tried so hard to save money and was rarely, if ever, successful.]

In Korea we were entertained by President and Mrs. Roh, and George addressed the National Assembly. The two things that pop into my mind about that trip are the beautiful ladies in their glorious pastel-colored dresses, which one of the men in our party said made them all look pregnant (I thought they were lovely), and the tight, tight security in the country due to a strong anti-American sentiment at that time. We went everywhere by helicopter instead of motorcade.

On the plane coming home I wrote in my diary:

The whole trip has been overshadowed by the Tower vote. The committee finally voted on a partisan basis: 9 for; 11 against. George is on the phone talking to Joe Biden, Chris Dodd, Lloyd Bentsen and others, asking them to please not make up their minds until he gets back and talks with them. We have just seen Bob Dole on CNN and he says he cannot understand Sam Nunn. No proof that the innuendoes are true. This is truly a character assassination.

The accusations against John ranged from alcoholism to questionable dealings with defense contractors—none of which could be proved and none which George felt were true. The Senate eventually voted in March, 47 for and 53 against. We were heartbroken for John and thought it was unfair.

By the way, the Tower hearings marked the end of any "honeymoon" period between George and the Democratically controlled Congress, and the press heralded it as a major political setback for the new president. That certainly sounded familiar as Bill Clinton struggled with many of his appointments.

෴ All during this time I was trying to determine exactly what my agenda would be. I had told Susan Porter Rose and others in the office that each day we should do something to help others. I didn't want to waste the great opportunity before us. Julie Cooke, in charge of projects, took this to heart. I trusted her judgment on everything, and she scheduled many events that either highlighted a need, helped encourage volunteerism, or focused on literacy.

We didn't waste any time. On January 31, I visited Martha's Table in Washington, where they have enormous soup kitchens, staffed in most cases by volunteers, and also a highly professional team of child-care staff to tutor and love homeless children after school. I had visited this remarkable place before, and would return several times in the next few years. Three days later we visited the United Community Ministries in suburban Virginia, which also feeds and clothes the homeless. During the next four years, I sent them many boxes of clothes—always anonymously. I wasn't sure how they would feel knowing they had the President of the United States's clothes!

We did literacy programs in Philadelphia, Chicago, and the Bronx. There we visited a multigenerational program that was in the heart of a tough poverty area. The Secret Service were concerned because several of the students had criminal records. I said not to worry; that was the whole point of the visit, to encourage them to get their lives back on track. When we arrived at the top of ninety stairs to visit one of the classrooms, there was the lovely Brooke Astor. She was bordering on her nineties herself and was concerned about *my* having to walk up so many stairs. She is a great supporter of libraries and literacy, and I am her greatest admirer.

We helped celebrate Black History Month in Anacostia, a poor area in Washington. We hosted Reading Is Fundamental on the South Lawn for their annual celebration of books, and I attended and spoke to both the United Way and American Newspaper Association conventions about literacy.

We went to the hundredth anniversary of the National Zoo, and Doro and I welcomed to Andrews Air Force Base the Armenian children, victims of the earthquake, who were brought here by PROJECT HOPE to receive medical care.

But of everything I did, my March visit to Grandma's House in Washington certainly received the most attention. This is a wonderful place where babies with AIDS are housed, treated, and loved by a fine professional staff and caring volunteers. There I held a precious baby who later died. Unbelievably, this photo made news because, even then, people still thought that touching a person with the virus was dangerous. Along with Burt Lee, George's doctor, I also met with a group of adults with AIDS. It was a wrenching visit. Besides having trouble finding housing and medical care, they all had personal problems. I especially remember a young man who told us that he had been asked to leave his church studies when it was discovered he had AIDS. His parents also had disowned him, and he said he longed to be hugged again by his mother. A poor substitute, I hugged that darling young man and did it again in front of the cameras. But what he really needed was family.

∝ I always felt George took a bad rap on the AIDS issue. He closely followed the progress being made at the National Institutes of Health through Dr. Tony Fauci. During the Bush administration, funding for AIDS doubled to nearly $5 billion. Of course, it was not enough. But there also is not enough money for cancer, heart, stroke, or many other kinds of research either.

I took some pleasure from the fact that the AIDS virus was isolated through leukemia research. Money spent for cancer research affects AIDS and other autoimmune diseases, and when we find the cure for one problem, we find the cure for others.

Every year we put candles in the White House windows to commemorate AIDS victims, and George and I both visited various hospitals and clinics involved in the fight against AIDS—but it never was enough. Members of Act-Up, a radical gay group, hounded George during his presidency, after drowning out the more reasonable voices speaking out about AIDS.

This is a sickness that can be helped by education. We have got to teach the young that there is no such thing as safe sex, although maybe there is safer sex. I also think there's nothing wrong with reminding our youth of the moral aspects of promiscuous sex and drug use. Certainly we must teach them they are not invincible.

⤷ The best way to explain how I felt about my "job" as First Lady" is to share with you a letter I wrote during my first year in the White House but never sent. Donnie Radcliffe of *The Washington Post* had written an unauthorized biography about me which was very kind. But Liz Carpenter, who had been Lady Bird Johnson's press secretary, wrote a scathing review—not really of the book, but of me. She felt I was letting women down by not speaking up on issues, even if it meant disagreeing publicly with my husband. I said I didn't care what she said, but obviously that was not true, for I woke up one morning and wrote a letter to Liz, whom I knew and liked:

> Dear Liz,
>
> I read with interest your review of *Simply Barbara*. I know how you feel about me. How did you like the book? Well, I know how I liked the book and I also know that I like you, and I thought that just for fun, and because I am learning how to use a computer, I'd write you a *personal* letter explaining just how I see life these days.
>
> Long ago I decided in life that I had to have priorities. I put my children and my husband at the top of my list. That's a choice that I never regretted. If I had any regrets, and who doesn't, I wish I'd taken more time to listen a little longer, look a little deeper and spend even more time with our children. Having said that, they all grew up and "my turn" came and I did the same thing. Unconsciously at first, and then with great purpose these last few years, I set priorities—my priorities.
>
> After spending several months pondering over exactly what cause I would take on if George got elected to "high"

office, I realized that a more literate America would benefit every single thing I worry about: crime, unemployment, pollution, teen-age pregnancy, school dropouts, women who are trapped into welfare and therefore poverty, etc. You name it, I worried about it. Incidentally, we hadn't heard about AIDS, the homeless or hunger at that time as major crises. So I made my major a "More Literate America," with several minors all related to better education. I have not regretted it for a minute. Abortion, pro or con, is not a priority for me. ERA is not a priority for me, nor is gun control. I leave that for those courageous enough to run for public office. Educating a young girl early that she has a choice to wait before she has a relationship with a boy is a priority for me. Teaching that all people are equal is a priority for me. Feeding the hungry and housing the poor is a priority for me. Keeping kids in school is a priority for me, and I could go on and on. I do not want to defuse or confuse my top priorities.

Incidentally, I may have learned this from one of my heroines who said not so long ago:

"It would be sad to pass up such a bully pulpit. It's a fleeting chance to do something for your country that makes your heart sing . . . and if your project is useful, and people notice it, and that reflects well on your husband . . . heavens, that's one of your biggest roles in life." (Lady Bird Johnson from an article in *USA Today* on First Ladies.)

Even though I never mailed the letter, I sure felt better after I wrote it, so I really owed Liz Carpenter a thank-you.

✍ I tried hard to stay out of George's business for all of the above reasons. Needless to say, I did not succeed. George barely had gotten into office when I agreed to do some press interviews, and Terry Hunt of the Associated Press got me again. (He's one of the reporters who got me into trouble over the Geraldine Ferraro incident.) He asked me if I favored enactment of laws banning the sale of military assault guns to the public. I, of course, answered "Yes," never dreaming it would make big news. But the press interpreted this to mean I disagreed with my husband! It seemed so clear to me that there was absolutely no need for anyone to have an assault weapon, and frankly, I assumed it already was against the law. Apparently it was not. My wonderful brother Jim and my husband were both against gun control. Among their reasons: There already are many laws on the books that only law-abiding people keep, and gun control would be one of them. We had an honest disagreement about gun control and probably still do. However, in March, George did expand the ban against importing assault weapons, including the AK-47, which had been used in California to kill five schoolchildren.

About that same time I also hosted a luncheon at the residence for several members of the White House press corps who had been asking for interviews. This was the first of several I would hold over the next few years, and I enjoyed them very much. For the most part, I liked the reporters and found the lunches stimulating and fun. But I never got off scot-free. I always made news even though I swore I wouldn't. I must say, however, I found it was interesting that the fact George and I agreed on 99 percent of the issues never made the news!

⤚ All during this time George and I were discovering the wonderful pleasures of living at the White House. Even the simplest daily routines could suddenly become almost magical. On January 30 I wrote in my diary about, of all things, lunch:

I ate in the West Hall Sitting Room at a little game table. I ate off President Cleveland's white china with touches of navy blue and gilt, made in England, I believe. It was lovely. Duck soup, smoked trout, delicate salad and peaches and passion fruit! Glorious. The food is so special that you cannot believe it.

The butlers loved trying to make me guess whose china I was using. Imagine being served a meal on dishes that Abraham Lincoln ate from! For a while my favorite was the china of Rutherford B. Hayes. It was so ugly. Each serving looked like the food that was to go on it: a plate shaped like a fish for the fish course; oysters for oysters; and snow-shoe–shaped dessert plates.

The White House staff constantly amazed me. By this time I had lived or visited many places but never had seen a household where every living human's only concern was to make us, our children, and our guests happy. Actually, that's not entirely true. Their first concern was taking care of the People's House—your house—and they do it with great pride. I also was impressed with the fact that they do not gossip about previous tenants.

I decided to make the tiny sitting room next to our bedroom into my office. It is a lovely sunny room on the southwest side of the house with the magnolias that Andrew Jackson planted right outside the window. However, in the spring, I moved to the north side of the house into the beauty parlor. The southwest corner was really too hot in the summer sun, and I needed a room that I really could use as an office. The other room was just too pretty. But this one, with its wonderful northern light, was perfect. Pat Nixon had made it into the White House beauty parlor, and I know that it always irritated Nancy Reagan that she "got credit" for putting it in. I don't care who did it—it was a needed addition to the White House and all First Ladies used it. The carpenters made a nice little desk for me and I could spread out my papers, computer, and printer and be right at home. And yes, I also had my hair done there.

There was one problem with the office: My window overlooked Pennsylvania Avenue and Lafayette Park—a great, fun distraction. I would like to share with you some of the observations I would record in my diary in the coming months:

It truly is like looking at a Norman Rockwell Saturday Evening Post cover. It gives me a seasonal view of Washington. Much of what I see is for my eyes only as I alone am the only observer. The people on the first floor have too many barriers (trees, etc.), and most rooms on the second floor look over the South Grounds. How disappointed the protesters would be to know that only one person sees them.

. . . This past Friday a small, but persistent protest was held across Pennsylvania Avenue. For the first time I could really read the signs held up by a small hard knot of people. On two long banners stretched out and held through drizzle and rain was writing that said: *STOP MADMAN MILO SEVIC NOW* and *STOP GENOCIDE IN KASOVA*. There was a small group of people marching up and down carrying both the American flag and a red flag with a black figure or seal in the middle. Now that is sad. My own little protest and I don't know what it is all about. I, the only observer, did not know who Milo Sevic was. [Little did we know then how newsworthy

Milosevic, a Serbian leader, would become as the painful breakup of Yugoslavia dominated world news.]

... I saw a school bus pull up the other day and a group of school children got out holding cardboard signs, made in school, I'm sure, and then one group holding a large sheet on which was written *SAVE OUR RAIN FORESTS.* They marched up and down and after twenty minutes reboarded the bus and took off for school. These children are being taught "peaceful protest." Pretty nice.

... In the winter I often see people come and feed the pigeons and squirrels. There is one person, I have never figured out whether it is a man or woman, who comes and dances with the birds. It is a modern kind of crazy dance as he or she flings out seeds to the birds and darts around throwing arms and legs in odd gestures. It always amazes me that passersby seem to take it all for granted and do not look surprised.

... This morning I was talking on the phone to Arnold Scaasi when I looked out the window and saw a bride and groom posing across the street for a wedding photo with the White House in the background. I was flabbergasted to see the bridesmaids dressed in black. The bride—in white, thank heavens—had a big bustle on her back and a great floppy hat. I loved it and called Doro, who was visiting, to come and take a peek. Arnold told me that he is often asked to design black bridesmaid dresses!

... I love looking out. I know that eventually I'm going to see everything. The other day an extra long white stretch limousine drove up and stopped on Pennsylvania Avenue in front of the White House. The top was slipped back and slowly a big cowboy hat appeared and then a head. The head turned our way, a picture snapped and the head and hat slowly disappeared again. The car rolled off as the trap door, or whatever you call those things on the top of the car, closed.

I worked at my desk (when not looking out the window) about three hours a day. Wonderful Chris Emery in the usher's office became my computer guru, and after years of keeping handwritten or audio diaries, I turned high-tech. Like millions of Americans, I quickly developed a love/hate relationship with my laptop, but without it I'm not sure this book would exist.

The mail especially was brutal. In the first hundred days alone I received more than 30,000 pieces of mail, and my yearly average was roughly 100,000 letters. Most of the mail was positive, which was very nice, and sometimes it was about the silliest things—such as George not liking broccoli! I also heard from many people hoping I could help solve their problems, which personally I could do very little about. But we referred more than 12,000 letters over the years to various government agencies that possibly could help. Fortunately, I had the wonderful Joan DeCain, in charge of my correspondence, and her staff to keep my head above water. On the other side of the White House, Shirley Green was doing the same for George, whose mail volume averaged 3.4 million pieces a year. Shirley was a good friend who had been with us for years; she was the prefect person to trust with the mail.

Neither during the vice presidential or White House years did I have an office in the Old Executive Office Building (part of the White House complex) or the East Wing, traditionally where the First Lady's staff works. As it was, my staff was jammed in on top of each other, including our marvelous volunteers, without whom we could not have gotten through the work load. I always suspected my staff appreciated my staying out of their way. Lucky for them, I couldn't even do a "surprise" drop-by: Millie always preceded me by about two minutes, announcing my arrival.

Another thing I loved about White House life was having George so close by. If he needed a break, he'd call and say, "Do you want to take a spin around the South Grounds?" or "Can you pop over to the Oval Office to say hello to so-and-so?" Sometimes he would suggest that I give the guest a tour of the residence. I suspected at times he just wanted to get rid of them and get back to work. Or he might call and say, "How about joining me for lunch?" or "How about me joining you for lunch?"

One day very early in the administration he called and said, "What are you doing? Look out your window, you'll see a friend." I walked over with the phone in my hand and there looking out of the Oval Office was Danny Rostenkowski paying a courtesy call on the new president. We waved. He and George had served together on the House Ways and Means Committee, and although they had many political differences, they were good friends.

Right after Millie's son, Ranger, moved in with us, Danny and his wife, LaVerne, came to the White House for a visit. We were sitting in the West Hall Sitting Room, and Ranger got so excited that he promptly wet—just a little—on Danny's shoe. We still remained friends.

Another time Danny sent me some shampoo that he said was made especially for people with white hair. A well-known cosmetics firm is based in Danny's district, and he often passes out shampoos to members of Congress and other friends. The first day I used it, several people mentioned my hair looked different but I thought nothing about it. When George came home, he not only mentioned it, he suggested that maybe I'd added a little color. We went out in the light and, lo and behold, I had a definite platinum blond look. It was not a shampoo for me and, as it turned out, it was not for Millie either. When I shampooed her with it, she became a brown and slightly yellow-haired dog. I never dared tell Danny that he had given me the wrong shampoo.

At this writing Danny is under fire, accused of financial wrongdoing. We certainly wish him well. With George and me, friendship counts and we always will remain Danny's friends.

∽ By March Millie's expected pups had become big news. One of the local Washington papers had a "Millie Countdown," and my press office was getting calls from all over the world. One Australian reporter insisted on a full report on how Millie felt. He apparently didn't understand he was inquiring about a dog.

The White House carpenters made Millie a large nest with a presidential seal that fit in my office/beauty parlor/birthing room. We were hoping that she would have her babies there. Even I was amazed at how big she was getting. Her veterinarian predicted a large litter, scaring me to death about all the bad things that could happen. I asked him over and over again for his night number.

The vet taught me how to take Millie's temperature, explaining that when it went down two points, the puppies were on the way. What he did not tell me, however, was that a dog's normal temperature is 102 degrees. So when Millie was at 98 degrees on March 17, I was very disappointed because she seemed to be trying to nest, both in and outside the White House. Temperature or not, I was sure the time had come. That night we were hosting a group for dinner and a movie, so Paula sat with Millie during the meal and I skipped the movie. Around 9:15, Millie sat up, panted several times, and lay down to deliver her first of six babies. I wondered if Dr. Lamaze watched animals give birth before he came up with his natural birth concept involving panting and relaxing? It was a miracle to me. Millie knew exactly what to do and so did the pups. They were nursing almost before they were cleaned by their mother. I called George at the theater to tell him the good news, and he asked me if it was a boy or a girl. I told him that I didn't know as it was too soon to tell. He slipped out of the movie to see the third pup born. We stood watching our little Millie deliver and got quite teary. She had five girls first and then had her only boy, Ranger. They weren't too young after all to tell the difference.

Millie's puppies were a joy. They were absolutely the dearest, sweetest little ones and a pleasure to the whole White House. My office had more visitors and drop-in trade than I could believe. Millie was a perfect mom. She knew exactly how long she should sleep with them, and after about a month she moved back in with us. I have wondered so when I read about parents abusing their children: If a dog's natural instincts are to protect her young, why, oh, why wouldn't we humans do the same?

∾ Not all the animals at the White House were quite so beloved. One Sunday in April we were having a relaxing family afternoon, and I decided to swim laps. This was one of the great habits I had gotten into during the first hundred days, to take advantage of the White House swimming pool and do laps every day, rain or shine, summer or winter. I swam with a snorkel and mask, and it was very relaxing.

On this particular day I first had to shoo away a pair of mallard ducks who were having a little rest and swim. Millie was beside herself with excitement, barking and running around the pool. I finally got started and had just swum half a mile (twenty-four laps) when a great big rat went right in front of my face mask. Believe me when I say that this fella did not resemble Mickey Mouse. There was nothing cute about him. I flew out of the pool screaming all the way. George and Don Rhodes, who were throwing horseshoes at the time, came running to my rescue and took care of that nasty little devil. I was through swimming for the day and had to force myself to go the next. You can believe I checked every drain before entering the pool.

In addition to swimming, I played tennis at the crack of dawn several mornings a week with friends. It took a while to learn to concentrate on my game, the view was so awesome: either the White House or the Washington Monument was in the background.

George immediately had a horseshoe pit put in and opened it by inviting about twenty world champion players to the White House to inaugurate it. They and their spouses were so excited to be there.

That was the beginning of the White House Horseshoe Tournaments, which started with sixteen teams from all different departments and eventually grew to thirty-two, I believe. Marvin and George teamed up, playing the nurses, the groundskeepers, electricians, housemen, military aides, and on and on. At lunchtime we often would hear the clink of shoes as people practiced. Although women were certainly welcome, only two played—one was a nurse who beat almost everyone, and Nancy Mitchell from the usher's office. It was such a good way for us to get to know the folks who made our lives sing. The finals brought some of the families together for soft drinks, or hot chocolate if it was cold.

 Soon after taking office George called a meeting in the Oval Office that included the Vice President; Boyden Gray, a trusted friend and George's chief counsel for twelve years; the Chief of Staff, John Sununu; Burt Lee, good friend and the President's doctor; Susan Porter Rose; and myself. The purpose of the gathering was to discuss the Twenty-Fifth Amendment to the Constitution: what would happen if George got ill, what the law was, and what we all should do. It is a dreadful thought, but one every president must think about and face. George led the discussion, and I remember two things very clearly: Dan Quayle sitting quietly, saying not a word; he was in a most sensitive position. And Burt Lee saying that the people in that room would be the most likely to notice a change if George were ill and must be ready to declare him unable to continue to be in charge. What an awful burden for a friend—not to mention a spouse. I am glad that we never had to face that issue. I think George wanted this meeting early on so that the performance of the Wilson administration would not be repeated, when the President's illness had been hidden from the public for months. We all promised George that we would be honest and responsible, no matter how hard. Boyden explained the legal side to us. That settled, we decided that we would never talk about this meeting since any discussion about the president's health starts rumors.

A few weeks later I read a small squib in the paper about the meeting, and the unnamed source said that Marilyn Quayle had spoken up a lot. She was *not* at the meeting. It was so unfair to her. Probably someone in the meeting innocently discussed it with a spouse or a friend, who then told someone else, and so on. This is how many leaks happen, through thirdhand sources, and the facts almost always get twisted in the retelling.

I don't think the average American realizes just how important the president's health is to the whole world—or maybe I was the only one who didn't. If the president of the United States hiccups, the world trembles.

When George had his annual physical, the press wanted to know absolutely everything. George is very healthy, and I always questioned the press's right to know things about his body that had nothing to do with his ability to govern. We all remember the grim and minute details of Jimmy Carter's hemorrhoid operation. We were told more than we wanted or needed to know about that miserable, painful procedure.

❧ As for me, I had never felt better and I was thrilled because I was losing weight—easily. I convinced myself that was because I was eating smaller portions and working so hard. However, I was having some problems with my eyes, and Dr. Lee insisted I get some tests run. I wrote in my diary on March 20:

> I am now driving back from Walter Reed Hospital having had all sorts of tests and drinking some radioactive stuff that makes all the alarms go off at the White House. All this testing has to do with my eyes. They started acting up the week before the Inauguration. I thought it was a makeup problem, allergy to makeup, etc. But it didn't stop. They are red, sort of tearing all the time, itch, are puffy and I see double. After a visit to Bethesda and Walter Reed hospitals, they think I have a thyroid gone berserk. Frankly, it is a little scary. I don't want pop eyes.

Eventually I was diagnosed as having Graves' disease, caused by a dysfunctional thyroid. (It doesn't mean you'll go to the grave; it's named for the doctor who diagnosed the ailment.) As it turns out, it was the disease causing me to lose weight, and once we started treating it, that ended. Since it is not life-threatening if treated, we decided to go public immediately.

Needless to say, the press made a big deal of it and there were endless articles about Graves' disease, which probably was good. However, I didn't realize just how seriously some people were taking my illness until April Fool's Day.

George and I were going to attend the annual Gridiron Club Dinner, an evening where members of the press put on little skits at the expense of politicians but all in good fun. Their motto is "We often singe, but never burn." It's supposed to be off the record, which means you can count on reading it in *The Washington Post* the next day.

When I saw the dinner on my schedule, I decided I had to play an April Fool's Day joke not only on our hosts, but also George. So I came out of our bedroom that night dressed to the nines for the black-tie dinner, and wearing a strawberry-blond wig. So much had been made of my white hair, I thought this was the perfect joke. George was flabbergasted, saying, "You are not going to wear that thing, are you?" I loved it, however, and away we went. But it really almost backfired. Several people asked George if I was really sicker than what was reported and was I wearing a wig to cover hair loss, etc. Some people thought that I hadn't come at all and wondered who the woman with George was. Some people just never even mentioned it when they talked to me. That was one April Fool's Day joke that many people just did not get.

꼭 Later that month we hosted three black-tie dinners for foreign visitors; the Mubaraks from Egypt; the Shamirs from Israel; and King Hussein and Queen Noor of Jordan. Interestingly enough, the Israeli ambassador and his wife came to the Egyptian dinner and the Egyptian ambassador and his wife came to the Israeli dinner.

The Mubarak visit was the first, and George took Hosni and his son over to Baltimore to see the baseball Orioles' home opener and throw out the first pitch. So when Prime Minister Shamir came several days later, George felt that he should do something special, and they went to see a film at the Air and Space Museum. Then of course he couldn't let our old friend, King Hussein, be without a special event, so he took him to Mount Vernon. George told me that sometimes these private trips really allow for a more informative, relaxed exchange of ideas than the official talks.

Audrey Hepburn attended the Israeli dinner and came to call on me the next day to talk about her work with UNICEF. I had met her once before in Rome at a luncheon when George was vice president. Audrey felt passionately about two things, both of which mattered to me also: She loved children and became an advocate for young people in distress around the world; and she adored dogs. She had read *C. Fred's Story,* and after that first lunch she disappeared and returned in a few moments with her two small dogs in her arms. I loved that; it was so human. When she came to call in 1989 she played with Millie's puppies, and I was slightly surprised that Millie let her pick them up without even a small protest.

How the world admired that lovely creature! She was famous as an actress—who will ever forget *Breakfast at Tiffany's?*—but I think she will live forever in the minds of the world as a lover and protector of children, for whom she traveled to the most desolate spots in the world. Shortly before her death in January 1993, George awarded her the Medal of Freedom, but she was too ill to attend the ceremony.

The dinner for the King of Jordan and Queen Noor caused a small crisis in the kitchen. We had checked with the State Department for any special menu requirements and were told no shellfish or red meat. (The King probably remembered that we had dropped a steak in his lap in Houston.) So we settled on duck. They had been marinating for some time when we got the word that the Queen would prefer white meat. Laurie called and asked what we should do: Should we change the menu? I said absolutely not. After all, the Queen was, in truth, just an American girl (Lisa Halaby) who married a king and she certainly would understand. I am glad to report that His Majesty wolfed down all his duck.

He is such an extraordinary man. I remember years ago attending a state dinner for His Majesty that Richard Nixon gave. In his toast President Nixon said something like: "Your Majesty, when you took over the throne, there were many people who said that you would not last. Well, sir, you have outlasted three American presidents." Well, that was six presidents ago and he is still going strong despite the many problems he faces. In spite of major differences of opinion during the Iraq crises and Desert Storm, George and I both respect and have genuine affection for Jordan's King.

During the next four years George and I would host thirty-two state dinners, most of which were part of an official state visit that always began with a very impressive, formal arrival ceremony. Both this event and the dinner gave the visiting heads of state an opportunity to be seen in their homelands with a world leader; both events had so much dignity; and both gave the leaders and their aides an opportunity to talk with Americans they might want to see. For example, people who do business in a particular foreign country often were invited to that state dinner to encourage more exports. The dinners also were a wonderful opportunity to showcase American hospitality, cuisine, and entertainment.

All the dinners were special, but one that stands out in my mind was for Australian Prime Minister Bob Hawke. To begin with, Bob and Hazel are warm, open people and great fun. We had invited Leontyne Price to sing and were so lucky that she was free for that night. During dessert, she gave us a little preview of what was to come later in the evening. While the strolling violins were playing "As Time Goes By," we suddenly heard the most beautiful sound. It was Leontyne at George's table singing along, low at first and then louder and louder. It was so special and sweet—a magic moment of pure beauty.

Of course not everything always went perfectly. There certainly were gaffes here and there, but at the dinner for the Antalls from Hungary, almost everything that could go wrong did. I wrote in my diary:

George said during the music after dinner that we needed to tighten up a bit. I'd say so! . . .

1. There was nobody waiting at the door to take her coat.

2. When we got to the top of the stairs, the door leading into our private residence was locked.

3. Nobody kept us on schedule.

4. Nobody told us what positions to be in for the flag ceremony.

5. Nobody gave us names in the receiving line.

6. There were four blank seats at the P.M.'s table because of the storm. (The weather was so bad that several guests from the New York City area were still sitting at the airport. I had to signal somebody to bring others over to our table.)

7. Violins came in too late and George thought they were too long.

8. (Concert pianist) Van Cliburn was superb, but considering our guests' jet lag, too long.

9. When George glanced at his cheat cards so that he could thank our talented good friend Van, he noticed that they had Frank Liszt on his cards. He caught it and so did say Franz Liszt (Hungarian composer) and not Frank. Yikes, could you see the next morning's papers if he had gone with what they had on the card?

We almost had a real crisis during the dinner for the new president of Mexico, Carlos Salinas. The pastry chef had described the dessert on the menu as "Mexican Fantasy." Just as the platters were leaving the kitchen to make a dramatic entrance into the State Dining Room, Laurie noticed that the chef had constructed an adobe house out of edible sweets, filled with ice cream and surrounded by a fence and flowers. It was stunning. BUT, leaning against the wall of the house was a little candy Mexican boy taking a siesta with a sombrero over his eyes. Just the unfair image that this young bright Harvard graduate was trying to (and has) erased about Mexico. So as each platter went by, Laurie plucked off the sleeping boy. It would have been insulting. She saved the day for her country, but the next morning had to face the pastry chef who had labored so long over that glorious dessert.

Then there was the dinner when the popular and talented Harry Connick, Jr., was to perform. He was very unhappy (to say the least) to discover that his date, model Jill Goodacre, was not sitting with him at dinner. I should explain that we never put couples together at social functions; we always split them up. To complicate the situation, Mr. Connick wanted us to change the seating when most of the guests already were in place.

Still unhappy after dinner, he threatened not to perform and went to his dressing room. It wasn't until he walked into the East Room and sat down at the piano that we were sure the crisis was over. That said, he gave us a knockout performance.

Certainly one of the people who always helped smooth out such problems was Laurie Firestone's very able assistant, Cathy Fenton. She is truly a beautiful young woman whose gentle touch made every crisis seem not so bad.

On April 25, I wrote in my diary:

Monday was George P.'s 13th birthday. Imagine having a teenage grandchild!

. . . George and I were up at the crack of dawn and flew by helo to Andrews Air Force Base and from Andrews to Norfolk where we went to the memorial for the 47 crew members who died on the Iowa.* It was the most moving ceremony and made more so by the audible sobs of the wives, children, families and friends of the dead. The ceremony was held in a large, damp hangar. The captain of the ship spoke and I thought he was very moved and moving. George spoke and was wonderfully comforting. He cracked at the very end and just barely got through it. We walked down the line and spoke to the immediate families. Almost impossible to know what to say to a young woman who has lost her husband or to a mother or father who has lost their only son. You can just hope that they believe in God and that they know that God loves their child, husband, brother and loved one even more than they do.

We were so very busy those first few months but always made time for friends and family. Our children and grandchildren were in and out of the house and made life seem more normal. My friends were pretty good about calling. I say "pretty good" because most friends don't want to impose. My advice is to impose, as it can get to be pretty lonely in that house. Thank heavens for Andy Stewart, who spoiled me by calling or coming over every day. I was so lucky to have her.

For the most part weekends were spent at Camp David. George and I worked out a wonderful schedule. He had his office at the lodge called "Laurel," and I had one in the president's cabin, "Aspen." We both got up very early and worked all morning. We did this whether or not we had guests, giving each of us time to answer mail, think, work on speeches, and generally get caught up. (Although the president *never* gets caught up.) Our guests were on their own with a world of things that they could do, and then all of us would meet at lunchtime. In addition to family members, "Perle Mesta" invited people from all over the country to spend the weekend, and sometimes aides or advisers would come up to brief George and then stay for lunch before heading back to Washington. We also had a number of foreign visitors, including Prince Charles, who had dinner with us. Women

---

* An explosion in the U.S.S. *Iowa*'s gun turret had killed forty-seven sailors on April 19 while the ship was participating in naval exercises near Puerto Rico.

always oohed and aahed to me when they heard that, which I found so funny. After all, he was the age of our oldest son, although I liked to tease George W. that the Prince was much better dressed and considerably more polite!

◅ The first hundred days ended April 30. It's a term made up mainly by the media to "judge" whether the new president is doing a good job. Quite honestly, I don't remember what they said about George. What I do remember is that it was an unbelievable but exhilarating whirlwind. As close as I can count, I hosted either alone or with George: eighteen receptions, sixteen dinners, twenty-four coffees or teas; nineteen lunches; and two breakfasts. I visited nine states and four countries, conducted twenty-four press interviews, and participated in forty-two "doing and caring" events and forty-one other types of events. We had fifty-one different overnight guests and fed 5,825 people.

And it was only the beginning.

18

Whirlwind First Year

By this time I knew one thing for sure: I had the best job in America. Every single day was interesting, rewarding, and sometimes just plain fun.

In May George W. invited me to Dallas to see the grandchildren and throw out the first pitch for a Texas Rangers baseball game. He had been part of a group of investors who had bought the team and was chosen to be one of two managing general partners.

I had another important task that trip: deliver the first of Millie's pups to leave the nest to Jenna and Barbara. The girls named her after their favorite baseball payer, Scott Fletcher. Fortunately, they named the dog "Spot Fletcher," for "Scott" was traded to another team shortly thereafter.

George W. had planned the best evening for me, and I was really touched. I wrote in my diary:

We started with a reception for the wives of the players, wives of the owners and some key women in the management. We had pictures taken and everyone was darling. On to the game and I was so excited. George knew every living human, almost seemed like all 38,000! He introduced me to the "best groundskeeper in the major leagues"; the "finest ticket-taker in any park"; and the "fastest hot dog vendor." He knew them all.

(George W.) had Reading Is Fundamental posters everywhere and on everything. Jimmy Dean was there, and they ran our RIF (public service announcement) on and off during the whole game. George gave away 1,000 tickets to kids participating in the RIF program and handed out bookmarks with Texas Rangers on one side and RIF on the other to every single person who came. The ball I was to throw out had been signed by all the players and by the coach. Below their names they put their favorite books. I was crazy about Bobby Valentine, the coach. While waiting in the dugout, he and I talked. He told me that he always thought the greatest thing that could happen to a man was to throw a ball to his son. Then he said that was not true. "The greatest thing that could happen to a father is to sit with your arm around your son and read." He went on to tell me that he and his son, Bobby, are reading The Wizard of Oz series. He tells me that he rushes home after practice and reads to his 5-year-old before the game. I loved that talk.

There is a footnote to the story about the signed baseball. Several weeks later I attended the Literacy Volunteers of New York's annual fund-raiser. One of the participants was Larry McMurtry, and his *Lonesome Dove* was one of the books that had been written on the baseball (by a baseball player whose last name also was McMurtry, I might add). I had planned to make a little game of this and throw the ball to Larry during my speech, but when I saw his Coke-bottle glasses, I thought better of it! I handed it to him instead.

➶ One of the greatest pleasures of my job was the luncheon the Ladies of the Senate give the First Lady at the Capitol every spring, and the reciprocal luncheon she gives at the White House. I missed my friends on the Hill and really looked forward to this event every year. The first year, the whole enormous Caucus Room was decorated like a schoolhouse and filled with children's books, which later were donated to District of Columbia schools. Nothing could have pleased me more.

The next year they decorated the room as a Maine seacoast city because they knew how I loved Kennebunkport. Everyone received an autographed copy of Anne Morrow Lindbergh's *Gift from the Sea,* and mine had a personal inscription. I was thrilled. The next year the theme was "Texas," which they knew was our real home, and the last year, it was a "Secret Garden," as they had seen pictures of me working with my flowers. They were all happy occasions, and I have never lost my affection for those marvelous women, Democrats and Republicans.

My first luncheon for them was June 5, just as China was in turmoil over the brutal put-down of protests in Tiananmen Square.

We were very upset over the suffering on a personal level, and officially, it was a huge concern for George. A day with my friends was just what the doctor ordered. And to make it even more special, Betty Ford and Lady Bird Johnson, former presidents of the Ladies of the Senate, attended. After a lovely lunch, the Harlem Boys Choir sang— the first of several times they would entertain for us at the White House. They are thrilling singers and excellent students as well. In future years I would have the New Visions Dance Theater perform, young handicapped children who were beautiful and graceful; the two-man comedy act Greater Tuna; and the cast from *Conrack.*

When lunch was over, Betty had to rush off, but Lady Bird and her daughter Lynda, married to Senator Chuck Robb of Virginia, accepted my invitation to join me upstairs:

The reminiscing was fun for me. (Lady Bird) remembered the Mary Cassatt, the Winslow Homer (Proutt's Neck) and several other paintings that friends of theirs had donated to the White House in their name . . . when Lady Bird got to the Thomas Eakins portrait of little Miss Ruth Harding,* a grumpy little girl with a big bow on her head and a turned-down mouth, she told the story of showing off the White House to a small group. When she got to the Eakins, she said: "Have you ever seen a grumpier little girl?" A voice from the back of the group said, "You'll be glad to know that she grew up to be a grand person. I married that little girl." Lady Bird was always a joy, and she brought the White House to life even more with her happy stories.

I continued to be spoiled by life in the White House. One wet morning when I was supposed to play tennis, I got up at 6:00 A.M. to walk Millie around the South Grounds. I noticed that although the rain had stopped, the tennis courts were soaked and had puddles of standing water, so back to bed I went to read awhile. At 7:30 I got a call saying that my tennis-playing friends were waiting at the court. I couldn't believe it, but threw on my clothes and ran down. There, in a wet world, was a bone-dry court. The groundskeepers had squeegeed the court and then blown it dry with giant blowers.

Another time I was not so lucky. During the whole four years we

---

* Ruth Harding was no relation to President Harding. She was the niece of Jennie Dean Kershaw, the fiancée of Samuel Murray, who was Eakins's favorite pupil and closest friend.

were in the White House, the exterior was undergoing renovation, which included being scraped down and painted. That first spring the south side of the house was wrapped with a canvas covering with only small openings for the windows. One morning I got up and walked Millie at 4:45 A.M. under leaden skies. I was dressing for tennis as George left for the Oval Office and at 7:00 A.M. was on my way out the door when George called and suggested I look out the window. It was pouring. Because of the wrapping around the house I hadn't noticed. To everyone's amusement and amazement, I went out and swam instead. My theory is that you can't get any wetter than wet.

I was having a tough year tennis-wise, and after my matches, the ushers and other members of the staff would ask how I'd done. Each time I had to confess that I had not been on the winning team. Until . . .

On the 25th I played tennis with Jean Douglas (Mrs. Leslie) against Andy Stewart (Mrs. Potter) and Aileen Train (Mrs. Russell). For once I was on the winning side. Of course, my partner, Jean, is really good. Having lost so many times I came into the house dancing. When I sat down for lunch that day I had a bouquet of flowers on the table with a small tennis racket and a note tucked in the center of the arrangement, "Congratulations from the White House Staff." No wonder I am so happy in this house.

But with the good came the bad. My trip to Kennebunkport later that month, always a cause for joy, began with much heartache instead. Security had to be tightened at Walker's Point, which included adding a large chain-link fence; a helicopter pad was put in; and a small house was built where the doctor and military aide could stay. To accomplish all this, they had to cut down a number of trees, which really hurt since Walker's Point is built on a rock ledge and every tree had taken years to grow. Suddenly we looked like a prison instead of a beautiful summer home. It all made me cry. I'm not too proud of that, but it hurt to see a ten-foot-high fence when we rounded the drive instead of the ocean. (The security people eventually agreed, and forty feet of fencing came down.) In retrospect, the Secret Service and everyone who worked on the Point tried their hardest to keep George safe and to respect our wishes and privacy. But that first view was a shock.

We were especially eager for the Point to look pretty and be ready for the visit from François Mitterrand and, at the last minute, his wife, Danielle. Many preliminaries go into a visit from a head of state, and

Doro agreed to meet the French advance team and show them the rooms where the two Presidents would meet; where Jim Baker and their Foreign Minister, Dumas, would meet; and where the enormous support staffs would sit and wait.

It had been decided that the Mitterrands would stay in George's mother's bungalow. This wonderful little house had been given to her as a wedding present some seventy years before and enlarged about thirty years later. I don't believe that other than being cleaned and used hard every summer, it had been touched since. Doro said all went well on the walk-through until they got to the bungalow. Even the most beautiful summer cottage that has been unopened for eight months looks dirty and feels damp; Doro said Mom's looked even worse. Her tiny little hospital bed especially seemed shabby, but Doro told the French not to worry: We would rent a large bed for the President. The advance people were so kind, but even they looked shocked when they glanced into the bathroom and there was a "riser" on the toilet for Mom. One man turned to Doro and said in total horror, pointing with a disdainful finger, "Wat is dis?" Poor Doro. She lived through it, but said it was so embarrassing.

Several days before the visit I arrived with a small army to open the big house and Mom's. We cleaned morning, noon, and night. My aide Casey, Paula, even Carol Powers the photographer pitched in, and by Friday we were ready. I must say that when the rented bed appeared it was horrible, and what's worse, I think the rental people bought the ornate brass monstrosity especially for the visit. It would have looked more at home in a French bordello. I wonder what François thought? Maybe better not to know.

On Friday George had Secretary of Defense Dick Cheney and the Joint Chiefs of Staff for a working lunch on our deck, and in the afternoon, Walter Curley, our Ambassador to France, and his wife, Taitsie, our close friends, arrived along with Jim and Susan Baker, Brent Scowcroft, John Sununu, and Jody Bush, who is George's brother John's wife. She came because she speaks fluent French, we love her, and George thought it would make François feel more at home. Dinner that night was such fun as we were surrounded by dear friends.

It had been decided that during the visit I had to take the ladies sight-seeing since every inch of the Point would be used for meetings. At the last moment I called Doro, who worked for Maine's Department of Tourism, and said, "You are Mrs. Tourism. Please find a restaurant in Portland with a view of the harbor, tell me what boats are available, and see about dropping in on the museum."

I was so touched by the job she did. First of all, there was no moaning on her part. She was so burdened by her own life—holding down a full-time job with two young children—and she took this on with joy. She quickly called me back and said, "No such restaurant. But Mom, Betsy Hunt has a wonderful house on the bay that overlooks the islands and she is eager to have you. We have a great boat, and the museum is ready." All this with three days' notice.

On Saturday, May 20, we awakened to a lovely, bright Maine day, walked down to the new helicopter pad, and met François and Danielle and their party. Quickly the men went into meetings, and shortly the ladies took off for Portland. Danielle and I had with us an interpreter and the French ambassador's wife, Hélène de Margerie.

Danielle is a fascinating woman who has an agenda of her own. We no sooner got in the car than she started talking about her foundation and the plight of the Kurds. For forty-five minutes she talked and we listened. She talked about the Kurds' flight from Iraq and Iran and also a lot about the Turks. I confess I began to feel a little drowsy, which is not too surprising considering our five days of hard work and late nights combined with the warm car ride. I found myself praying that I would not fall asleep or, worse, say something like, "Tell me more about the Turds." Fortunately, I didn't, and Danielle certainly opened my eyes to the suffering of these poor people, which continues on today. I was and am impressed by her fervor and passion.

Dinner that night was at two round tables of eight in our dining room with a roaring fire. I wrote in my diary:

George's table had a rather lively conversation about religion. I wasn't there, but I understand that Danielle told them that she did not believe that intellectuals believed in organized religions, life after death, etc. Susan Baker and George defended strongly. I guess that it got a little heated at their table. Our table, on the other hand, was fun and François was amusing and warm and cozy. I never saw him after that that he didn't mention the fact that we had had him in our home. I believe that 24-hour visit was the beginning of a great relationship between the two men. George was and is devoted to François.

After the dinner ended I announced that our little church was having an early morning service for us and that the vans would leave from both the

Point and the hotel at 7:45. I thought that it was funny that George was trying to shush me and Jim Baker, who was at my table, was asking me to repeat the announcement. George thought that Jim and I were needling Danielle. Not at all. We just hadn't known that their table had had that strange conversation.

The next morning many of us, without the Mitterrands, went to our First Congregational Church for an early morning service. They kindly put the service ahead an hour to accommodate our departure for Boston University to celebrate their 150th year.

It was a relaxed yet productive visit and the beginning of many heads of state coming for informal visits to Maine. Brian and Mila Mulroney and their four marvelous children came from Canada several times, and John and Norma Major of Great Britain, to whom we felt very close, came with their two children. The Kaifus came from Tokyo with their son and a charming, bright interpreter. We were thrilled when the two later married. They said the romance started on that trip, so I guess more than foreign affairs were advanced on those Kennebunkport visits. Our old friend Poul Schluter, the Prime Minister of Denmark, came on his honeymoon. His new wife, Anne Marie Wessel, was a lovely former ballet dancer and director of the Royal Danish Ballet.

One summer the King of Jordan and Foreign Minister Saud of Saudi Arabia came by for separate meetings (more about that later), and the Rabins came from Israel and spent a weekend in the summer of 1992. Yitzhak and Leah had been friends for many years as he had been their ambassador to Washington during our early years in the capital.

Shortly after the Mitterrand visit George and I took a quick trip to Italy, Belgium, Germany, and England. Our main destination was a NATO meeting in Brussels, but we stopped on the way in Italy to celebrate Memorial day at Anzio, where so many Americans gave their lives in World War II. George gave the most beautiful speech and had me in tears. The streets were lined with hundreds of cheering people, and it was interesting to note that many of them were older and obviously remembered the sacrifice that so many Americans had made for them.

In Belgium, Queen Fabiola and I made a lovely visit to a village where mentally disabled people live independent, productive lives.

The Queen and I had met several times before, and she is such a caring, spiritual person. She and her husband, King Baudouin, were childless and seemed to have such a gentle, close relationship. It is hard to know what other people are feeling and thinking, but I truly felt that this quiet lady had an enormous faith in God and a strong drive to help others.

The reports in the papers about the NATO meeting were stunning. They raved over George—his knowledge, his ability to persuade, just everything about him. George told me that Jim Baker and Brent Scowcroft deserved a lot of the credit because they had been through some very difficult negotiations on nuclear weapons and other matters. Even the papers at home were very kind and called the meeting a great success.

We flew from Brussels to spend a day or two with the Kohls in Germany. Hannelore is an old friend and a bright, charming lady, so it was an easy visit. We did many things, but the most fun was flying over much of Germany in a helicopter. I couldn't get over just how clean West Germany was. There were absolutely no old used cars or farm equipment left around to rust and no garbage. Where did they send it?

We also took a beautiful boat trip on the Rhine River from Oberwesel to Koblenz. I wrote in my diary:

Listened to a great men's singing group, went by the famous Lorelei Rock and finally at 2:30 or 3 o'clock went into a marvelous buffet lunch. All the time we were passing castles and lovely old towns, great looking trains went by, people waved from windows and streets, boys rode bikes down the bike path waving all the time, people waved American flags and flags hung from their homes and we went by old forts and on and on. It was a joy. The day was bright and sunny, a dream day. I sat next to Helmut Kohl. It was here that Helmut made my day by saying: "It's great to see a lady with a lusty appetite." Now why doesn't George Bush say something romantic like that?

. . . We flew on to London on a crest of good feeling over the great success in Brussels.

. . . Went off to Number Ten Downing Street to meet up with George. He was talking with Margaret (Thatcher). Denis met us at the door and kissed my hand. The press asked him to do it again. He didn't, so I picked up his hand and kissed it on the spur of the moment. Yikes. Will I never learn? That picture went around the world. George and Margaret appeared, and we went to Buckingham Palace for lunch with Her Majesty and Prince Philip.

The Queen and Prince Philip greeted us, and while the Prince and George reviewed the Scots Guard, Her Majesty and I chatted. She had just returned from a visit to Sarah and Will Farish's farm, Lane's End, in Versailles, Kentucky, and said that she'd had a lovely time. I asked her if she had seen my little puppy. (The second of Millie's pups to leave the nest went to Will and Sarah.) She said rather coolly that we'd talk about that later, and I thought, "Oh my, you are not supposed to ask the Queen a direct question or something."

. . . After lunch Her Majesty led us over to a table with her picture and his in lovely, silver frames. She presented them and then turned over a leather frame and gave it to me with the biggest smile. There was a signed picture of Her Majesty with "Pickles." I was so thrilled that I almost cried. There was our sweet little puppy. She looked so big. Nothing could have made me happier.

One other funny thing happened at that lunch. On the gift table was a small silver bowl with three little feet. George looked at it and asked what it was. The Queen answered: "I don't know. *You* gave it to *ME*."

That spring our grandson George P. spent some time with us in Washington. He showed no enthusiasm and seemed to have lost all energy, and I worried about his attitude. I shouldn't have wasted the time. He is a marvelous, bright, serious young man. But at the time I worried. I guess that it showed, because after he went to a Baltimore baseball game one night with George, and Dick Darman and his son, I received the most marvelous thank-you letter from Dick. It put everything in perspective and explained my thirteen-year-old grandson to me:

Your grandson is, of course, a great kid. Like boys of all ages he's part of the mystical brotherhood bound together across the generations by bubble gum cards. But what's most remarkable is this: You know how a child's face can seem totally blank at times—and then all of a sudden, it can switch to an open, bright smile that not only transforms the child's face, but seems to capture the very heart of life at its best. It's almost a trap. Just as one is wondering how to get through the blank stare, one is totally drawn in and engaged with spirit transformation.

Our kids have perfected the blank face and the transformation—and I am always vulnerable to the trap, surprised and delighted each time.

But the most dramatically delightful version of the transformation I've ever seen is that of George P., when he goes from the essence of non-communicative blankness to that fantastically engaging smile. I bet it gets you every time. It sure got me.

I have read over the years some not-too-nice things about Dick Darman, who was George's budget director. I also have read that he won me over. He certainly did. I also loved his wife, Kath, and I loved his relationship to his own boys. Like John Sununu, he does not suffer fools gladly either and that does not serve him well. But among the many nice things he did was to remind me that thirteen-year-old boys live a life of their own. How could a mother of four boys have forgotten so soon?

Thursday was my 64th birthday. I swam a mile as I did every other day this week . . . It is a well-known fact that I detest birthdays (mine, that is). If you are in public life everyone feels they have to remember. That darn Willard Scott mentioned my birthday on the "Today" show—and I'm not even 100—so I spent the day thanking people and answering the phone. I did talk to all our children, including Jeb from Indonesia. I sat down to a quiet lunch with a book, and when my dessert came in, it was an adorable little chocolate present, wrapped in a candy ribbon, sitting in a sauce. Below the present were some musical notes and when hummed:

You got it—Happy Birthday to you! So sweet. I could kill myself. I was too dumb to take a picture!

Every year we were in the White House something happened on our birthdays to make them hard to ignore. The next year, I got a phone call that really amused me. The White House operator told me that she had a call for me from a Mr. William Wright. Normally if I didn't know someone, I would not take the call and ask her to transfer it to the office. However, I decided to take this one as his name sounded familiar. This nice voice said that it was his birthday, too, and he just couldn't believe that I had accepted his call. He said that he was a history teacher who called the White House often, only to be told that "the First Lady and the President were busy." I thanked him for calling and wished him a happy birthday. Once again he said that he could not believe that I had accepted his call. I explained that normally I wouldn't have, but I wanted to wish him a happy birthday. He said, "You're kidding." I repeated, "Happy Birthday," and hung up. I'm afraid that I left a very confused man.

I believe that was the same year that George gave me the most unusual present. I had mentioned in passing that although there were hundreds of different kinds of athletic shoes, it was really hard to buy Keds, the old-fashioned sneaker. The next time I'm going to say diamonds, for on my birthday George dragged in a bag of twenty-four different styles, colors, and patterns of Keds. He had written the company president and asked him to send what he had. So, just to tease George, I divided them into three lots for Camp David, Kennebunkport, and the White House, but did not match up the pairs. So I now wear the purple with the black or the pink with the orange, and so on. I love watching children's faces as they poke their mothers and point.

In July we celebrated a truly important birthday in Maine: George's mother's eighty-eighth. Mom seemed so much better. She was stronger than she had been and came to us from the bungalow for cocktails. The family—all forty of us—sang "Happy Birthday," and then George, who was sitting next to his mother on the couch, reached over and said, "Mom, you've had eighty-eight birthdays. Tell us about the best." And she said, quick as a wink, "Well, of course, today, George. I am sitting here holding the hand of my son, the President of the United States of America." That was a precious moment; one that you want to hold on to forever.

∝ A few days later we left for our first G-7 Economic Summit, held that year in Paris. First, however, we stopped in Poland for a thrilling visit. We could not have chosen a more exciting time to be there.

The Solidarity party had just won an overwhelming victory in the first free elections under Communist rule. Two years earlier, General Jaruzelski had told George that Solidarity was dead. Now they were on the verge of taking power. The General himself seemed more relaxed, and his wife, Barbara, seemed much thinner than I remembered and spoke better English.

We hosted a lunch at the ambassador's residence in Warsaw that was memorable for several reasons. First, it was hot as the dickens and was held outside. George immediately suggested that coats be removed, and everybody seemed thrilled with the idea. When General Jaruzelski arrived and was told to remove his coat, he seemed hesitant. But then he retired into the back room and came out in his shirtsleeves. Later, when they insisted that he give a toast, he confessed that he had removed his suspenders and was afraid to give too long a speech in fear that his trousers might fall.

The second thing I remember is sitting between the General and a Solidarity leader, Janusz Onyszkiewicz, who had spent many years in jail. Tension seemed at a minimum, considering the circumstances.

Also, the Polish people, men and women, smoked all the time. It smelled terrible.

The next day we flew to Gdansk, where we first visited Bishop Goclowski. He gave us a quick tour of the six-hundred-year-old Oliva Cathedral with its beautiful panels of the kings and an amazing organ that has extraordinary carved wooden figures that move.

We went right from there to the home of Lech and Danuta Walesa, which was new for them. Before the election they and their eight children lived in only half of the house; the other half was headquarters for Solidarity. Now they would have both halves of what was a rather small duplex. They were so excited. We were led into a small room with a table that could hold eight people. Each place was set with six different glasses, and we were fed enormous amounts of food and drink while Lech talked a mile a minute through an interpreter:

He is bewitching. For starters, he began this monologue with all the things George had been going to say to him: that they must have economic reform, etc. During the course of the conversation he talked about his responsibility as a Nobel Peace Prize winner, an obligation to do something for his country. I also remember him saying that when this all started he couldn't have dared ask for free elections, an elected Parliament, etc. He said that they just started by asking for bread and it went from there.

. . . Danuta is shy and quiet, but when she smiles it is a joy.

After lunch the four of us drove to the shipyard. The roads were jammed, and as he looked at the crowds, Lech spoke his only English, saying over and over, "Oh, my God, fantastic." As we got closer, he said, "Ten times more than Margaret Thatcher." The Polish estimated the crowd at 250,000. I looked out over an ocean of people and saw ABC's Peter Jennings, up on a press platform, surrounded by people as far as the eye could see. Imagine my surprise when I read in the White House press summary that he had started out his program that night asking, "Why has President Bush had such disappointing crowds?"

We left Poland on a real high. It was so exciting to see democracy coming—slowly, painfully—but coming.

From there we went on to Hungary, where we were met in Budapest by Interim President Straub and his wife, Dr. Gertrude Szabolcsi. They were both charming scientists who spoke English well and were familiar with the United States. He was an interim president only because the Hungarians were in the middle of trying to write a constitution and deciding what kind of government they wanted.

Although we arrived in a terrible thunderstorm, the streets were lined with waving, cheering people. We arrived at Kossuth Square to find 25,000 soaked people. They had spent hours waiting. I am terrified of lightning and could not believe that these dear people braved that storm to see the President of the United States. That was the only thing that got me out on the platform as the storm had returned and lightning and thunder were raging again along with torrents of rain:

A Secret Service agent took off his coat and made George put it on. (I had an umbrella.) President Straub gave quite a long speech and when it came time for George to speak he tore up his talk and spoke briefly from the heart. Then George plunged into the crowd to shake as many hands as he could. There was an elderly woman in the front who looked cold and was literally dripping wet. George whipped off his coat and put it around the woman.

When we got back in the car, I scolded him for giving away the coat. He looked offended and said, "We have so much, Bar, and she looked so cold." Right he was, but he had just given away someone else's coat! He looked shocked and then we all burst out laughing. He sheepishly confessed to the agent and later replaced the coat.

The next day I visited a home for blind retarded children, run by nuns whom I consider close to saints. I then joined George for a fascinating discussion with a group of students, and then went to the Transylvanian Refugee Center at Tahitotfalu. This was a marvelous camp where the community had taken 110 families into their homes and now were helping them build their own on donated property. The refugees came from Transylvania, which was being brutalized by Romania. I visited one of the finished houses and thought it looked like a small Swiss chalet. To them, it looked like heaven. This was the most positive, hopeful refugee camp I had ever visited.

That night our able ambassador, Mark Palmer, and his wife, Sushma, a biochemist, had a large reception at their residence for George. We had a receiving line at the top of the garden and our dear protocol chief, Joseph Reed, stood and greeted the guests and then passed them on to George, saying in the most formal way, "Sir, let me introduce you to the President of the United States and Mrs. Bush." George and I got the giggles. We knew our names. It was theirs he was supposed to pass on. So we shook hands with a stream of officials and never ever knew a name.

After the receiving line, we were about to walk down some stairs into another part of the garden to join an even bigger group when the announcer said, "Ladies and gentlemen, the President of the United States and Mrs. Bush." At that very moment, the Palmers' dog—a big bulldog named Fred, if I remember right—slowly started walking down the stairs. The timing could not have been more perfect. The Palmers were so embarrassed; everyone else loved it.

The next morning we left for Paris and the Economic Summit, which had been planned to coincide with the French Bicentennial Celebration. We went immediately to Place du Trocadéro for the simple but very elegant opening ceremony, followed by a full afternoon:

. . . The spouses lunched in the beautiful heretofore unseen Morny Apartments. About sixty wives of Chiefs of State or Heads of Governments attended this luncheon, so I saw many old friends from around the world. I sat next to Madame Mitterrand and a bright young man who is in charge of the big ceremony on the 14th. He is praying for good weather. So am I. I ate every bite and Danielle nibbled—as she did at every meal. I'm afraid that I didn't change my pattern either, but it is all so good!

I opened the new wing at the American Hospital and back to the embassy to change quickly into a short cocktail dress for a night at the Opera. This was the opening of the new Opera House. I didn't like the building at all, but certainly it had many pluses. The acoustics are marvelous; every chair I am told has a full view of the stage (there are 2,000 seats); the depth of the stage gives amazing versatility to the producer. The minuses to me were that first of all it is ugly, and the stairs going down from the balcony are shallow, steep and there is no hand railing. I found them frightening. The pluses outweigh the minuses. We went on to the newly redone Musée d'Orsay (the old railroad station and now a 19th century museum). We had a great, but slow and late dinner. Home late . . . long after we were in bed we heard fireworks. Danielle Mitterrand told me that they went by to see the people dancing in the streets. After all, they were celebrating 200 years of independence—we know how that feels.

The next morning, July 14, was relaxed, and I had a good visit with Taitsie Curley. Then we went to the Bastille Day Parade and I sat with the spouses. Protocol put me with France, Bangladesh, Egypt, Ivory Coast, Zaire, Mali, Greece, and Uruguay for almost every event:

I sat next to Mrs. Bangladesh and her 6½-year-old little boy who never left her side. There were three of us and two seats. As the parade went on and on he got very restless and bored. He sat on my lap half of the time which was okay with me as, frankly, I got bored also.

We went to the Ministry of Foreign Affairs building for lunch where we stood around for almost an hour and a half. Hannelore Kohl, Margaret Thatcher and I were talking when we noticed that there were hundreds of people outside in the garden having a great time. We saw loads of our friends like Carlos Ortiz de Rozas and his wife Carmen from our U.N. days, and so the three of us escaped to the outdoors to visit. We enjoyed the breeze and friends. I went back to get George, but (someone from) Protocol grabbed me. I think they were panicked that all the captives inside would rush outside—and they were right!

Another great meal. The French certainly live up to their reputation. However, the lunch was 1 hour and 5 minutes late. The number of people being accommodated at all events is amazing—32 different motorcades with police escorts. This of course will end tonight and then the Economic Summit starts.

The leaders from the G-7—the United States, Japan, Great Britain, Italy, Germany, Canada, and France—all went to a working dinner, and the rest of us went to the Hôtel de la Marine for supper. After dinner we all came back together to watch the celebration, a very big dramatic show that we could hardly see through the bulletproof glass and certainly could not hear. We turned up the TV monitor and that helped a lot. The highlight of the evening was when Jessye Norman came out dressed in a flowing blue, white, and red gown, like the French flag, and belted out "La Marseillaise" as you have never heard it sung!

I found all of this very interesting: Jessye was born in Georgia and now lives in Westchester County, New York; the new Opera House was designed by a Uruguayan who now lives in Canada; I. M. Pei, an American, did the Pyramid; and a New Zealander restored the Musée d'Orsay. I think this shows the French have a lot of confidence. I believe that we would feel that we must have an American do all these things.

The minute Jessye finished we took off for our beds. George was exhausted. He had been running from meeting to meeting for two days. When we got into bed, the skies exploded, and I got up and watched the most beautiful fireworks. George never heard a sound.

Here are some of the things I wrote in my diary about the many people we saw during the French Bicentennial:

... I had a nice visit with Benazir Bhutto, who truly looks pregnant.

... Mila and Brian Mulroney are surely the most attractive couple. She is tall and wonderful. Speaks English, French and some Slavic language. Everyone loves her. Very chic. He is warm as you get to know them.

... I am very fond of Suzanne and Hosni Mubarak. She had a Welsh mother and is truly a lovely looking woman, 47 years old, trim and happy looking with two grown sons. He is a dark, handsome man who had a hard time following Sadat, but now seems secure and respected.

... I am very fond of Hannelore Kohl, she is bright and full of warmth and outspoken.

... Margaret Thatcher seems to be out of sorts with the men both at NATO and the Economic Summit. She is having trouble at home. She is kind to me and I like her and have enormous respect for her.

. . . I really enjoyed President and Mrs. Hillery from Ireland. He has a wonderful job—goes to all the ceremonies and doesn't have the worries of a Head of State. He is a fine, warm, funny person and so is she. Both are medical doctors.

. . . We have enjoyed President and Mrs. Sanguinetti of Uruguay. She has sat at my table and is charming.

. . . Sally Mugabe of Zimbabwe and her husband, President Robert Mugabe, seem to be warm, nice people. They have had many sad suffering times. Both sons died and she had a bad kidney problem.

. . . Elizabeth Diouf of Senegal and her gentle seven-foot-tall husband, Abdou, are highly respected.

. . . Mário Soares from Portugal is charming, very chic.

. . . Corazon Aquino was one of three women who were heading their delegations. She was in France on a state visit on the 12th and 13th and just stayed on. On this visit and all succeeding visits she was warm and friendly.

. . . Marie-Thérèse Houphouet-Boigny of the Ivory Coast was a large, friendly woman.

. . . I was sorry that I didn't get to visit with either of the Gandhis. They both look well. Rather amazing that both India and Pakistan are now headed by the children of assassinated leaders. They are neighbors and enemies and now, getting better, I hope. I like them both so much.

. . . The Greeks, Efrosine and Christos Sartzetakis, newly elected, are unknown to me. I sat at his table, but far away and he hardly spoke.

. . . Mrs. Cameroon, Jeanne Irene Biya, very dignified, quiet and I did no more than greet her and smile at her.

. . . I don't know the name of the President of Bangladesh, but I sat with one of them at every meal. She became a challenge to see if I could wipe the frown off her face. Her little boy appeared at 11 p.m. to see the parade . . . he let us all know he was tired, irritable and couldn't see.

I read a great deal on the trip. This time it was *Foreign Student* by Philippe Labro, suggested to me by Virginia Governor Jerry Baliles. I loved it. I also read *The Dinner Party* by Howard Fast.

೭ I spent a lot of time in Maine that summer. George's mother was frail and I wanted to be nearby, and although I was feeling wonderful, I still suffered from double and sometimes triple vision and had popping, watering eyes, a result of Graves' disease. George came when he could, but he had a lot of problems:

August 3—G. started out west on a three-state visit, but came home after one stop in Chicago. Lt. Colonel William Higgins, who has been a hostage for months, was rumored to have been executed yesterday. It is very complicated, but the Israelis kidnapped a sheik last Friday because of a terrorist Arab attack on Israel which they claimed was because of an ambush attack on the Arabs earlier, which they said was caused by etc. The extremists say that until the sheik is freed they will kill a hostage daily. Poor Pop has the weight of the world on his shoulders.

The children came and went with their children, and they all were wonderful and continued to be a joy. Noelle at twelve years old took painting lessons and was producing some pretty sweet watercolors. She was wonderful with her younger girl cousins, who looked up to her at all times. One of the younger girls found a mini sanitary napkin and asked Noelle what it was. She didn't know what to say and, thinking fast, said that ladies put them under their arms to stop perspiration. The little girl then wore them under her arms the rest of the day—until she ran into her mother.

Noelle struck up a great friendship with her cousin Wendy Stapleton, and when George and Laura's twins arrived, they dogged the two older girls all the time. Noelle and Wendy spent some time trying to hide from their seven-year-old cousins. Then Neil and Sharon's Lauren arrived, and she wanted to do everything that Jenna and Barbara did and they tried to hide from her. It never changes.

All four of the older granddaughters slept in the dormitory, a large room on the third floor of our house that has five beds.

One night I went up to put the little girls to bed and hear their prayers. As we all knelt, Barbara said the Lord's Prayer, and Jenna made up a sweet personal prayer. Five-year-old Lauren thought very carefully and finally thanked God for flowers and little animals. So cute.

George finally came to get some R&R and spent a great deal of time on his boat fishing. With our boat, the press boats, and the Secret Service and Coast Guard boats, we were a small armada. Unfortunately, George was not having much luck. One of the Maine papers ran a "Day 1—No Fish" column with a picture of a fish with a line drawn through it. The press showed up at the Bush/Mulroney press conference with the logo on their T-shirts, which George loved. We got up to "Day 14—No Fish." That day, as George and I left on the boat, a small delegation headed by Betsy and Spike Heminway and made up of our children, grandchildren, and the staff carried homemade posters encouraging George to catch a fish. They thought they were so funny—and they were.

> *September 4—.* . . Now is truly our last day.
>   . . . it has been a great summer.
>   . . . George's mom has been a beautiful, uncomplaining wisp of a thing wandering around trying to dump her nurses and enjoying being with her children and grandchildren. She is the most selfless person and a joy to be with.
>   . . . On Saturday we had our big press picnic on the Point. We served only hamburgers and hot dogs with all the trimmings. They came with their families and it was loads of fun.
>   . . . On Sunday morning George went to the annual church breakfast, met us at church where he spoke and then with Marvin, Brent Scowcroft and I took off in the boat for Boone Island. We hadn't been out five minutes when George saw a lone gull diving and announced that we would slow down and troll for a minute. With Marvin at the wheel and three rods in, George announced that he had a fish and, lo and behold, he did! The press charged over on their four chartered boats and pictures were gotten by all. Then they all blew their horns. It was so sweet. I believe that they were all pulling for him.

Shortly after we got back I received an honor that had been a long time coming. I did not earn it, nor did I deserve it, but when Smith College gave me an honorary degree, I was thrilled. It meant a lot to me as my Dad would have been so pleased.

I did a lot of traveling that fall for literacy programs all over the country and was lucky enough to return to Midland to dedicate the George Herbert Walker Bush Elementary School, the first in the country to be named after him. How we teased George, for the school board vote was a "landslide"—three to two in favor. Now I must

Playing pool with the boys at Cranston Senior Center in Rhode Island.
(Carol Powers)

Please notice that no one is driving the boat while George points something out!
(Susan Biddle)

Watching *Marine I* land at Kennebunkport was too much for granddaughter Ellie LeBlond's ears. (Carol Powers)

Three of my boys: George, George W., and Jeb. (White House photo)

George gets some ribbing from family and friends about his inability to catch a fish. (David Valdez)

ty-five years after dropping out of Smith College, I finally get my gree, even if it is just honorary. (Carol Powers)

Making a new friend during International Literacy Day at the United Nations, September 1989. (Carol Powers)

Goofing with the grandchildren outside the White House. (Carol Powers)

Attending convocation at Morehouse School of Medicine in Atlanta, October 1989. (Carol Powers)

One of many friends I made while First Lady. (Carol Powers)

You can see who's getting all the attention during this visit to a nursing home in Washington, D.C. (Carol Powers)

Reading to a group of children in New York City. (Carol Powers)

One of those moments in the White House you never forget—showing Rosa Parks the original Emancipation Proclamation in the Lincoln Bedroom. (Carol Powers)

Sorting through a new shipment of books for the grandchildren. (Carol Powers)

At Wellesley College with Raisa Gorbachev, June 1, 1990. (Carol Powers)

Millie and Raisa Gorbachev get acquainted while I drive the golf cart
at Camp David. (Carol Powers)

Horseshoe diplomacy between
George and Mikhail
Gorbachev, May 1990.
(David Valdez)

Taking a break from a working weekend at Camp David. From left: Secretary of
State James Baker; Barbara Bush; George Bush; Raisa Gorbachev;
Mikhail Gorbachev; Soviet Foreign Minister Eduard Shevardnadze; Brent Scowcroft,
head of the National Security Council; and Marshal Sergei Akhromeyev of the
Soviet Union. (David Valdez)

ping for *Millie's Book* in
tember 1990 on the Fox
orning Show with anchor
Lark McCarthy.
(Carol Powers)

George gives Margaret
Thatcher a taste of the
Wild West at the Economic
Summit in Houston, July
1990. (Carol Powers)

Hard at work, August
1990. (Carol Powers)

Welcoming President Gampy to Kennebunkport, August 1990. (David Valdez)

Can you believe this outfit someone sent Millie? (Carol Powers

One of the perks of being First Lady, throwing out the first pitch during a 1990 World Series game. (Carol Powers)

I can't remember the story I was telling Prince Fahd Bin Salman of Saudi Arabia, but he was nice to laugh. (Carol Powers)

Thanksgiving Day 1990 in the Saudi Arabian desert with our troops. (Carol Powers)

Katharine Hepburn gets a standing ovation at the Kennedy Center Honors, December 1990. From left: Katharine Hepburn, Dizzy Gillespie, me, our daughter-in-law Margaret Bush, and Dan and Marilyn Quayle.

Rubbing noses with a young cancer patient at Children's Hospital in Washington, D.C. (Carol Powers)

George (second from right) and Secret Service agents pull me back up the hill after I broke my leg, January 1991. (Carol Powers)

You can see how worried everyone was—George and Arnold Schwarzenegger back on the slopes. (Carol Powers)

Getting a free ride from my aide, Peggy Swift, in the Oval Office. (Carol Powers)

Watching George tell the nation that Desert Storm has begun, January 16, 1991. With me are our daughter, Doro; my press secretary, Anna Perez; Millie; and Billy Graham. (Carol Power)

Sharing a tender moment with a young soldier at Fort Campbell, Kentucky. (Carol Powers)

orge takes a "power walk" with the omnipresent media in Kennebunkport. (Susan Biddle)

Caught sleeping again, this time on *Air Force One* with grandson Sam LeBlond. (Carol Powers)

ing very silly with me of my staff and cret Service agents luring a late-night flight home. (Carol Powers)

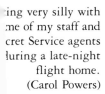

Queen Elizabeth and the
"talking hat," on the White
House lawn, May 1991.
(Steve Purcell)

A royal White House evening
(Susan Biddle)

A little quiet fishing in the
Black Hills of South Dakota
with the President.
(Carol Powers)

quickly add that they had to break the rules for George—you were supposed to be dead to have a school named for you in Midland County.

I soon got used to waking up in hotel rooms and sleeping in strange beds. One morning I was up early having a cup of coffee and listening to a local radio station for the news. Much to my shock the phone rang and it was the same "live" radio talk show. I said that Mrs. Bush was ASLEEP. They rang a little later and once again asked for Mrs. Bush, and I said, "Not available." I got the giggles, for I had gone out over the airwaves twice, both times sounding really grumpy. I suspected the bellboy who had brought the coffee had slipped his friend the room number.

I visited so many wonderful programs, from the restored Majestic Theater in San Antonio; to the Cal Farley Boys Ranch outside of Amarillo, Texas; to Eugene Lang's "I Have a Dream" classes, where a person, family, or group adopts a class and promises to help them go to college IF they will stay off drugs and stay in school; to WOW (Wider Opportunities for Women), a national program which helps get women off welfare and achieve economic independence. I attended the United Nations International Literacy Day, hosted a coffee for the Second National Adult Literacy Congress, and taped tributes for "Disney Salutes the American Teacher." I was on "Sesame Street" and "Oprah Winfrey" and marched in Chicago's Columbus Day parade—and much, much more.

One of the most important events of the fall was the Education Summit held at the University of Virginia in Charlottesville. It was attended by almost all the governors and many of their wives and George's entire cabinet. He had made education a top priority, and this meeting was an important step. They all divided into working groups, rolled up their sleeves, and came up with some very good guidelines which eventually became part of George's America 2000 program, his blueprint on how to improve education in our country and which is still being used today. I was very impressed to learn that Clinton's Secretary of Education, Richard Riley, decided it was not necessary to "reinvent the wheel."

As part of the summit, we hosted a dinner in Monticello, the home of Thomas Jefferson. What a house. Hours could be spent studying this extraordinary man and his home, where he lived with fourteen grandchildren. That in itself made him special. I wrote in my diary:

We had a reception in the house and then went to a lovely dinner in a truly beautiful tent. I sat next to Terry Branstad (Governor of Iowa and chairman of the National Governors' Association) and Bill Clinton (Governor of Arkansas) who went out of his way to be charming. I wouldn't be at all surprised if he runs in 1992. He is very attractive and seems to have analyzed both Carter and Dukakis pretty thoroughly.

The next morning the cabinet and governors split into three groups: "Choice and Restructuring"; "A Competitive Work Force and Lifelong Learning"; and "Post-Secondary Education: Strengthening Access and Excellence." We visited all three groups and heard their recommendations. George sat at the table, and I sat with the spouses behind them.

After the early morning session the spouses all retired to another hall, and I called on several wives who had said they would be willing to share with us projects they were involved with. It was fascinating:

One who had expressed an interest in sharing was Hillary Clinton from Arkansas, who gave us a good rundown on her program H.I.P.Y. [Home Instruction for Pre-School Youths]. This is a program that goes right into the home and works with families. She has modeled it after a program that was started in Israel and also is being used in Florida and a few other states. She is a lawyer and very bright and articulate. I noticed that they, the Clintons, were the last to appear for everything. [Shades of things to come?]

I called on Sue Ann Thompson from Wisconsin. She is a sixth grade teacher and read a wish list of things she wanted in schools. I noticed that people turned off pretty much over that. Typical. The only one who had practical experience and people were turned off. She is one really bright, nice lady.

Julie Mabus from Mississippi has put a lot of energy and focus on literacy in her state and done it in a very professional way. I liked her very much.

Martha Wilkinson from Kentucky has "Martha's GED Army." She has made it "chic" to get a GED.

Lynne Cheney spoke as a cabinet wife and as the chairman of the National Endowment for the Humanities and urged that we train teachers for the arts along with the sciences.

Then I asked Jeannie Baliles, wife of the Governor of Virginia, to tell us just how she set up her state's private-public sector foundation to work with literacy. She is a ball of fire and has done a real job in her state and shown great leadership in the field.

I spoke about the Barbara Bush Foundation for Family Literacy.

At the luncheon the sharing continued. Shirley Bellmon from Oklahoma told us about her Cottage Industries program that she started. Her project has allowed women to stay in the home, be with their children, continue their education, gain in self-worth and on and on.

I called on Susan Bayh from Indiana, wife of the youngest governor, Evan Bayh. Susan has taken literacy on in her state with a capital L. Evan was a classmate of Marvin's at St. Alban's. I knew his mother and father well.

Bea Romer from Colorado shared a brochure with us on The Year of the Reader, the Library of Congress initiative.

Matilda Cuomo also shared with us her mentoring program in New York State. It seems many states are getting into mentoring—a big brother, big sister concept.

Pat DiPrete talked about Rhode Island's plan to put all children through college.

This session gave us all a lot to think about.

I remember thinking what an incredible group of women they were, and I was impressed by their significant contributions to their states.

So many momentous things happen in the daily life of a president that it is hard to know what to comment on. The fall of 1989 was no exception:

George got a capital gains tax reduction—a victory.

Hurricane Hugo devastated several southern states.

There was a failed coup in Panama.

A tremendous earthquake rocked San Francisco. I found myself thinking: Does it ever stop?

And on a personal level, Bishop John Walker died. He was a friend besides being the bishop of the diocese of the District of Columbia. We went to the service at the National Cathedral, and when we got home, George sat down and wrote John's children the most wonderful letter. I was amazed and felt guilty that I hadn't thought of doing the same thing.

We took District of Columbia Delegate Walter Fauntroy to the cathedral with us, and while we were waiting in the car for George, he told me that he was mad at the President. His wife had seen George holding a drug baby and had said, "Walter, you spend your life going to foreign countries helping other people. From now on we are going to help Americans. You and I are going to adopt an abandoned crack baby." At the time of the funeral they were going through an eight-week indoctrination course and eventually they got their baby. At fifty years of age, that was quite a commitment for Walter and his wife, Dorothy. George and I were both thrilled by that story.

~~~ There also were dramatic developments in Eastern Europe as the Iron Curtain literally fell open. The world was changing right before our eyes, and every day George faced a new challenge. I wrote in my diary:

November 11—This has been the most extraordinary week. Turmoil around and across the world. Deng Xiaoping in the PRC has stepped down. The East Germans have opened their borders and people are pouring out. The Soviet Union, which is sitting on a time bomb, is not objecting. The longest ruling dictator in Eastern Europe (Bulgaria) has stepped down. "A new breeze is blowing" and the people of the world really do want freedom. Every now and then this week I have wanted to shout: "Why are we doing our regular thing? Why aren't we dancing in the streets and singing and rejoicing?" I guess because as each new thing happens we also see so much to be done and we may well be looking at chaos. George certainly is President at the most interesting of times. His job seems to be putting Humpty Dumpty back together again without endangering the rest of the world.

. . . I heard him on the phone yesterday talking to Helmut Kohl. Helmut had been in Poland on a visit, but raced back home. Imagine people flooding into West Germany. Not just families being reunited, but food, housing and jobs to be found. Many people were overwhelmed, filled bags with oranges and rushed back over the border to East Germany. They had not seen an abundance of food like that for forty years. The stories were so moving.

We really got laughing for some people were not so pleased with the wall coming down. But the man we liked best was the guard at the wall. He said that he didn't like it one bit as that meant he'd lose his job. He has a point. No wall, no job.

Later that week we greeted Lech Walesa at the White House, accompanied by Lane Kirkland, president of the AFL-CIO, and Mrs. Kirkland. The East Room was jammed with the cabinet and members of the United States labor unions. These people had been supportive of Solidarity, the labor movement in Poland, and it was right and proper that they be there when Lech Walesa received the Medal of Freedom, the highest honor our president can bestow on a foreigner. This surely must have been one of the most moving ceremonies that we held in the White House. Lech stood there with tears in his eyes and gulped several times while George gave an inspired speech and the citation was read. Lech suddenly represented "every man" who ever had lived behind the Iron Curtain. There was not a dry eye in the room. Lech Walesa truly changed the course of the world. He said over and over again that he "couldn't believe that he was in this great land of the free."

We had a receiving line that took forever because everyone wanted to shake his hand. Unbeknownst to those of us in the line, there was a small drama happening in the State Dining Room. As this was a very special reception and was late in the afternoon, we had a heavily laden dining table covered with many trays of food, candelabras, and beautiful flower arrangements. One of our larger guests backed up to our lovely antique table and rested against it—well, really put a large amount of his rather large body on the table. The table broke in the middle and food, candelabras, and flowers crashed to the floor. The staff coped with it all and by the time the receiving line ended, all had been propped up and the guilty guest had slipped out never to be seen again. The table was gone for three months undergoing repairs.

George very kindly invited me to join him for four small, working dinners in November that gave me a front-row seat to everything that was happening:

One was with President Nixon, who had just returned from China. Nobody is more interesting when it comes to world affairs.

The second was a dinner with Henry Kissinger who also had just been in China. Deng Xiaoping told Henry that he still believed in all the things he believed in before—reaching out to the world, modernization, etc. Deng asked Henry why we were so shocked over Tiananmen when the Cultural Revolution was going on when we opened relations with the PRC. He pointed out that surely that was much worse. He had a point.

And the third dinner was with Lech Walesa. It was such a great evening. He is such a charming man. I truly felt that I noticed a big difference from last July. I think he is beginning to see the world as it is and not as he wanted it to be. He is also beginning to think of Poland as part of the whole. He mentioned that Germany must not be united again. (This did not come as a surprise because we found that most Europeans felt the same way. They remember German occupation and those memories are not pleasant.) Lech also mentioned that the stories of the East Germans being overwhelmed by all that fruit did not surprise him. He said that they were better off than most people in Poland. We Americans take so much for granted.

The fourth dinner was when our dear friend Prime Minister Brian Mulroney and Joe Clark from Canada came to debrief George after their trip to the Soviet Union. The fall of 1989 George was under criticism for not acting and for being "prudent" when it came to pushing for change in Germany and Eastern Europe. The dinner was fascinating. First of all they had spent hours with the leadership. They said 10 hours with one leader, 5 hours with Gorbachev and 8 hours with another man. They must have been dead tired as their whole trip was very short. Gorbachev asked many questions about George. He is scared to death of Germany reuniting. Brian quoted Gorbachev as saying several times, "One can be poisoned by eating unripened fruit." I think that meant: "Don't push us, we're not ready." Who knows? Gorby seemed to be sending a message to George that they were not going to be coming to the table with any flamboyant gestures. They all agreed that the Soviet economy is absolutely the worst. Amazingly enough Brian and Joe got the feeling that Gorby was relaxed about his future and his worries were Germany's reunification and not about putting bread on the table. Brian said that he acknowledged his domestic problems, but did not want a handout, but did want loans. Our side (Jimmy Baker, Brent Scowcroft, Bob Gates and our ambassador to Canada, Ed Ney) all agreed that the Soviet Union had to stop spending 5 billion dollars in Central America and Cuba before we could start giving them loans.

. . . The press is all over George for not taking immediate action. Gorby is getting a great welcome in Italy today where he and Raisa are on a state visit. She is also. George says to remember what our aim is—democracy to take the place of a dictatorship. Well, that's what's happening in Eastern Europe. We are getting what we want. They may not be yelling "George, George," but we are getting a freer world. He is so wise.

Just when I thought this life of our was going to overwhelm me, something would happen to remind me "real life goes on." I wrote in my diary on November 30:

Doro called and said that she went to a teacher's meeting and the teacher said that Sam (age 5) was a very bright boy, but that he was in cahoots with two other little boys. When the teacher asks a question Sam will raise his hand and when called upon will say, "Toilet," and then the two other boys burst out laughing. The teacher asked for help. She also said that Sam and the two other boys blow on their hands and make "fart" noises and then die laughing. Hard on the teacher, to say the least. Doro went on to say that Sam came home, opened the door and said, "Any calls?" Doro said, "Why would anyone call?" No answer. Then Doro said, "Sam, I won't scold you, but why would someone call?" He said, "I said a bad word." Doro tried to find out the word and he wouldn't tell. He finally said that it started out, "nnnnnnn." Well, finally Doro had to ask as she did not know any "nnnnn" words. It turned out that Sam said "naked body." Funny boy. History repeats itself every generation, doesn't it?

In early December George was scheduled to meet with Gorbachev on Malta, off the coast of Italy. We all agreed that it would be better if I stayed home. I had written Raisa and invited her to meet me in Florence while the men were in Malta. She very politely turned me down by saying that she had been to Florence. Sad to say, I hadn't and still haven't.

The men truly had a fascinating meeting. George tells me that it was pleasant with no friction. The earlier briefings by Andreotti of Italy and Mulroney of Canada made it easier. As George spoke first, he could make suggestions without Gorbachev having to ask. The suggestions were mutually beneficial to all of us. He had a short, pleasant visit with Mrs. G. . . . George said he adored his time on the ship rolling around out there. I would have hated it.

While George was gone the annual Kennedy Center Honors came and went. It is one of the most exciting, fun evenings of the year. The honorees that year were Alexandra Danilova, Harry Belafonte, Claudette Colbert, Mary Martin, and William Schuman. I wrote in my diary:

George, of course, would have done the honors, but it worked out very well. We would have all preferred to have him where he was—making a kinder and gentler *AND* more peaceful world . . . It was a star-studded evening: Helen Hayes, Dina Merrill and her new husband, Ted Hartley, Marvin Hamlisch and his new bride, Terre, Larry Hagman, Leontyne Price and her brother General George Price, Gloria and Jimmy Stewart, Sidney Poitier, Don Ameche, Lynn Redgrave, Isaac Stern, Kelly McGillis, Gregory Peck, Bernadette Peters, Van Cliburn and his amazing mother Rildia Bee . . . it was three hours of joy, great music and dance. The show opened with the Red Army Song and Dance Ensemble. It was a rousing opening and so appropriate with the "non-summit" that was going on in that rough Mediterranean at that very time. Bishop Desmond Tutu came to honor Harry Belafonte for his work with UNICEF and the oppressed in South Africa. That got a great ovation. The evening ended with the Soviets singing "God Bless America." It was so unbelievably moving . . . I raced backstage to thank them all before I left. There were such good vibes running around the room. It was a very special evening. We did not stay for dinner. Those other poor people had dinner at 11 p.m.!

Christmas in the White House was a joy. Planning had begun from almost the minute we moved in. I thought Nancy Clarke and Gary Walters were teasing me when they came to talk to me about the Christmas theme in February. But the decorations are all made in-house, and the ribbons and other materials have to be ordered early. We settled on a Story Book theme, which seemed appropriate to my interest in reading. Down in the bowels of the first floor the flower shop worked all year. Often when I would drop by I would see figures appearing that looked like Aladdin with smoke coming out of his magic lamp, Babar and Miss Rumphius, a favorite of mine by author Barbara Cooney. Sometimes I met several women who were volunteering their time to make doll costumes, bows, and so on.

We started celebrating Christmas early, on November 27, when Marshall and I rode the cherry picker to the top of the National Christmas Tree to put on the star. After that, we did something almost every day:

December 5—I went to Mazza Gallerie in Washington to shop, but more to make a statement about the Salvation Army. I read in the paper that many malls across the country had banned the bell-ringers. Who can think of

Christmas without the Salvation Army bell-ringers? So we let the press know that I was going shopping at the Mazza Gallerie because they permitted the Army to stand outside with their pots and bells. I dropped $11 in the pot with the press watching. The response was immediate and good. Georgetown Mall immediately permitted them in. [We later heard from the Salvation Army that that small gesture truly had filled their coffers.]

December 6—An 18-foot Fraser Fir from Spartansburg, Penn., was delivered on a horse-drawn wagon.

December 7—I flew to Houston to do many events and while there dropped by St. Martin's Church to pick up a crèche that they made for us. I went dreading it thinking that although it would be great to see our dear church family friends, it would be a homemade job. Not at all. What a surprise. It is absolutely magnificent. I have never seen such beautiful work. It is enormous, more than 5 feet. Along with the kings and shepherds there are some 50 pieces including C. Fred, Millie, Bevo (the University of Texas long-horned steer mascot) and an armadillo all done in the most beautiful needlepoint adoring the baby Jesus. I felt ashamed that I thought that I was doing a kindness to tuck in a visit to see my friends.

I was to fly from Texas to Andrews Air Force Base and then drive up to Camp David to join George, who was flying in several hours earlier from some other part of the country. We heard that the weather was closing in and that although George could fly in a copter up to Camp David, I might have trouble driving up later because of icy conditions. George opted not to go on the chance that I couldn't make it. Thus bad weather gave us one of the very nicest experiences we had in George's four years as President: watching the Christmas decoration go up.

When I got home at 1 a.m., Dennis Freemyer, a young White House usher, gave me an early morning tour of the State Floor and already it looked wonderful. George and Millie were sound asleep. For years volunteers had been invited to come help decorate. They arrive a week ahead of time, working in a warehouse and then moving to the White House the final weekend to put up all their finery. They decorate all the rooms and, of course, the big tree in the middle of the Blue Room. These wonderful people come during their vacations and at their own expense. Many of them have come every year and are an enormous help.

We awakened to discover our family tree was up in the Yellow Oval

Room, a glorious 14-foot tree. It had been put up the afternoon before by some White House elves. It was covered with thousands of tiny white lights, decorated gingerbread Christmas cookies that Paula makes, and our own decorations collected over the years. George and I went down and met the volunteers and invited them to come upstairs to see our family Christmas decorations and the new crèche. I am constantly amazed at how little it takes to make other people happy. In any case, it made us very happy to show off our lovely house, Lincoln Bedroom and all.

Saturday night we sneaked off and took our children to our favorite restaurant, the Peking Gourmet, that Marvin had discovered in Virginia. When we came home, the staff and volunteers were putting snow on the 17 large trees in the front entrance and the grand cross hall on the State Floor and this had disintegrated into a snowball fight.

December 10—We attended the "Christmas in Washington" program that NBC puts on every year at the Pension Building. The stars were Olivia Newton-John, Diahann Carroll and her husband, Vic Damone, the flutist James Galway, Take 6, the Eastern High School Choir, the United States Naval Academy Glee Club and the United States Army Band Herald Trumpets. George invited the guests back for a drink and a preview of the decorations. We ended by singing Christmas carols around the piano in the East Room.

What a treat for us. Vic Damone told George that he had read that George yelled his name when he threw a ringer in horseshoes. True. George does yell "Vic . . . Vic Damone" when he throws a ringer. Short, of course, for victory. Olivia Newton-John is a lovely looking young woman and very nice.

December 11—We had the press preview of the first floor. The tree in the Blue Oval Room is covered with 80 storybook characters.

That same night we began two weeks of holiday receptions with the Congressional Ball. Every member of Congress is invited with his or her spouse. Laurie Firestone told me that any event with Congress was a hassle. They want to bring several guests or bring a staff member. When Laurie stood firm, they would try to appeal directly to us. Some just plain showed up with the uninvited. There are 435 House members and 100 senators, so the potential for this party is well over 1,000. George and I stood in a receiving line for several hours that night and almost all the nights following.

We held "'eclectic" receptions, with a mix each night of cabinet members, the Supreme Court, the staff, the Secret Service, the press, and friends. It was much nicer for all, we felt, and we kept the tradition all four years. George and I would stand in front of the tree in a receiving line, have pictures taken with those who wanted them, go into the East Room to enjoy the entertainment, and then after several hours head back upstairs with aching knees and happy hearts.

During the public tours during the day, groups of singers, choirs, or bell ringers came from all over the country to entertain. We often would open the door to the private residence at the top of the Grand Staircase just to hear the music. As the grandchildren arrived for the holidays, they sat on the steps and listened. Neil often took his children down and talked to the tourists. It is such a special time.

On December 12 I had the Diplomatic Children's party, sponsored by THIS (The Hospitality and Information Service, kind of a Welcome Wagon for foreign dignitaries). It was a mob of little ones, each with a camera. We asked the cast of *A Christmas Carol* from Ford's Theatre to come and do a little scene. I was to sit on the floor surrounded by children, and I spent the whole program wondering how I was going to stand up again. I could see the pictures of me crawling around trying to get up. As it turned out, a nice military aide stepped up and gave me his hand. Marshall Bush loved the whole afternoon and ran around being a little hostess.

On the thirteenth I went to the Central Union Mission in Washington to help give out Christmas bags to the children. The mission has a wonderful program where different groups—such as employees at the FBI—are given information about a specific child so they can fill a bag with toys, clothes, books, and other gifts for that child. I was supposed to read from Luke, chapter 2, verses 1 through 20, which is the story of the birth of Jesus. I took one look at those preschool children and realized that they were way too young and talked to them about the birth instead.

George lit the National Christmas Tree on the fourteenth. Willard Scott once again came to our rescue and dressed like Santa. Loretta Lynn and her daughter Peggy sang, and Tommy Tune sang and danced.

In the midst of all this activity George flew to St. Martin in the Caribbean for a brief meeting with Mitterrand.

Then our children and grandchildren started to arrive for our first Christmas in the White House and life became really wild.

The girls and I took the granddaughters to *The Nutcracker*. Ellie and Marshall were a little young. At one time one of the girls leaned over to the other and said, "Say peepee." Fortunately both girls were sitting on my lap, so I stopped that immediately. (Guess which little girl had picked up bad habits from big brother?) Sharon was not so lucky. One night she took the children to the President's Box at the Kennedy Center to hear carols, and in a quiet moment (one of the little boys) said in a loud voice, "My penis hurts." Sharon raced him out and brought them all home. Poor little guy, it turned out his suspenders were too tight. It makes me giggle just to think of that.

Then we had two parties that we had started in the Vice President's House that were really fun. On the seventeenth we had what we called our family brunch. This started out to be a few friends with their children and some of the Houston friends that our children had grown up with. Thank heavens we had moved to the White House, for by 1989 we had grown to 170 people. Our friends' children had gotten married, and grandchildren had gotten married and they also were having children. We loved that party, and had George been reelected, we might have had to rent a larger ballroom. We started out in the East Room, where we had entertainment for the children, and then moved upstairs to the second and third floors for a buffet lunch. (In case you're wondering who paid for this, the answer is "George Bush." It's a very good question. At the White House, if the event is business or official, you, the taxpayer, pay for it. If it is personal, the president pays for it. The staff is very careful about keeping track of which is which.)

Finally, for the last party, we invited all the household help and their families. It was fun to meet the spouses and children of all the people who worked so hard, not only at Christmas but all year round, to keep the People's House as near perfect as possible. We watched their children grow over those four years.

December 23— . . . Well, here we are at Camp David after a busy two weeks of Christmas parties at the White House. People raved over how the White House looked and it was true, but I have to say that every year I have gone away thinking "This year was the most beautiful." Well, *this* year was the most beautiful!

. . . We had catastrophe after catastrophe. I guess that happens when you have 11 children together. Little Jebby got a fever. George P. cut his chin while ice-skating and had to have five stitches. Jenna got the flu. Noelle hurt her wrist and had to go to the hospital nearby. It was not broken as Burt Lee was afraid, but was sprained. WOW!

. . . There was lots of action in our house all week, really from Sunday on. Brent Scowcroft, Jim Baker, Colin Powell, Dick Cheney, Bob Gates and John Sununu were in and out of the residence. On Tuesday night after our Christmas reception, the crowd gathered upstairs again and George told me after they had gone that we were invading Panama the next morning, December 20th, at 1 a.m. He stayed up until 4 a.m. He called many heads of state to tell them what we were doing.

. . . This past week has been a real history-maker. On Wednesday morning George sent troops into Panama for many valid reasons. #1. They had elections several months ago and Noriega was beaten three to one and yet he overturned the people's vote and took power. #2. He declared war on the USA and then a Marine was murdered. #3. His troops harassed a Naval officer, beat him and his wife and sexually threatened his wife. #4. We have thousands of American citizens in Panama. #5. They have violated our treaty. Sad to say, Noriega again was not caught, but his government is out of power and the duly elected government is now in power. We are praying that he will be caught right away. We lost 24 American men and are heartbroken about that. It is hard being president.

George reported to the nation the morning after the invasion at 7:15 a.m. The support is pretty universal across the country.

Then during the week there were rumblings in Romania and the impossible happened. Ceauşescu fled last night and at this moment chaos is in charge. The sad part is that Ceauşescu had really torn the country apart and there is no structure left. Their son is under arrest, but they escaped by helicopter to an unknown place. What a world. A new breeze is blowing. I was really shocked to hear that when Gorbachev announced the overthrow or the falling apart of the dictatorship, the Russian Congress cheered.

December 24—George flew down to the White House to have a press conference and back again. When he got back he went over to see the boys play Wally Ball. While there he got the phone call saying that Noriega had sought refuge in the Embassy of the Vatican. Finding Noriega made our Christmas.

December 25—We had 30 for lunch that first Christmas at Camp David.

December 26—We awakened this morning to see pictures from Panama showing the people cheering the Americans.

Ceauşescu and his wife were captured, tried, found guilty and executed on the spot. It certainly brought back many memories. Imagine people we had dined with not so many years ago are now dead.

After Christmas George made his annual trip to Beeville, Texas, to hunt. He called me from there to tell me that Sandy Ellis, George's sister Nancy's husband, had died. God bless him. He was a darling brother-in-law who after a series of strokes had faded away over the last few years. Sandy was the first of us to die.

I barely had hung up when George W. called me with the best news: Charles Walker Bush had been born and was waiting for Marvin, Margaret, and Marshall to come pick him up. Marvin and Margaret had been wanting to adopt another child for some time and were thrilled. There was something sort of mystical about this, a death and a birth.

On New Year's Eve, the last day of the year and the decade, George and I flew to San Antonio to visit the wounded from Panama. We went immediately to a church service on the base, and then visited the troops:

We went on to Wilford Hall, where we saw about 21 or so of the wounded. There had been 200 in all to begin with, but so many of them had gone home or been transferred to hospitals nearer their homes. After Wilford Hall we went on to the Brook Burn Hospital and saw 11 more. It was one of the most moving experiences. First of all we were warned by the General who met us that they were an unusual group and it had been a privilege to doctor them. . . . They were all proud of what they had done and, he said, they all wanted to go back.

. . . They had horrendous wounds, from head wounds to the feet.

. . . They had members of their families with them. I saw several rooms where the mother, father, and stepmother and stepfather were all there together reflecting, I guess, the new world.

. . . There were mixed marriages . . . many. A very handsome black man with two beautiful boys and a lovely Filipino wife told George, "I couldn't have better care if I had all Donald Trump's money."

. . . In one room were two very young boys who had been in the same unit . . . they both had "fragment wounds," which I believe meant that something blew up around them. Both boys had families with them. The first boy had a tube in his nose and looked scared. We had been told that both boys had colostomies. . . . I said to the scared boy, "You know there is a life after a colostomy. Our son has one and plays wonderful tennis, jogs, and has a beautiful wife and a family." The mother from NYC whispered to me, "Thank you for saying that." The boy in the next bed was a 20-year-old with a mother, wife and fat little baby girl. He said that the first thing they told him was that our son had one. Marvin would be pleased to hear that.

. . . There were about six paraplegics, and they were amazing. One boy with a big loving Hispanic family had just heard that two of his buddies had died. He had read their names in a national magazine and was in tears when we walked in. He had the most awful head wounds besides everything else. I could tell from his mother's eyes that she knew what lay ahead for him. I felt so sad for her and for him.

. . . The most adorable Italian boy from New Haven almost jumped out of his bed when he saw George. "The most exciting day of my life." Since he felt he couldn't hug George, he asked if he could hug me and, of course, I hugged and kissed him and he kissed my hand. To think this darling boy will never walk again.

. . . The most moving moment came when a paraplegic said as we were leaving, "Sir, I wanted to give you this flag. It represents my buddies in Panama. We're proud of you and back you." [That flag was on George's desk in the Oval Office until we left on January 20, 1993, and is now on his desk in Houston.]

George told each of them that we were proud of them and that we wanted to thank them. Amazingly enough, many of them tried to stand for their Commander in Chief. Many thanked him for what he was doing, quite a few wanted to go back with their buddies. George asked each one where they had gotten their wounds, and they seemed pleased that he was familiar with the scene and the fighting in Panama.

This was one of the hardest days in George's presidency.

Finally, after the first of the year, it all ended. On January 7, 1990, I wrote in my diary:

The past few days have been dramatic to say the least. I am constantly amazed by GB's stability and ability to keep things on an even keel. All during the week after Christmas and early into the next week the press and the Congress were starting to get on GB's case about Panama. In fact, on January 4th, *The New York Times* had two articles on the editorial page suggesting that the Panama attack had been a failure as we did not have

Noriega. They evidently put their paper to bed early as Noriega turned himself in to American authorities on the evening of January 3rd . . . the Vatican had sent a special emissary to negotiate with Noriega. Thousands and thousands of people had gathered outside the Vatican Mission in Panama City and were calling for the Vatican to give them Noriega. I overheard George telling Brent that anytime during the night he would be ready to hear the news if anything happened. I was working after dinner when George rushed through my office and said: "We got Noriega and I am going over to the office to make a statement." . . . We learned later that the Vatican had told him that he would be granted refuge until noon the next day and then he must choose between the USA and Panama. Had he chosen the latter, I believe that they would have torn him limb from limb . . .

Today, Noriega is in an American prison, and the people of Panama have a duly elected, democratic government.

19

Flying Chain Saws

Despite the excitement over Noriega's surrender, 1990 did not get off to a great start. On January 7, I wrote in my diary:

> Pop (George) came into lunch today and said that Neil had called. He is worried to death. The group investigating the Savings and Loan scandal are investigating Neil because he was on the Silverado Board (as) an outside director. They came to Neil and said that if he'd sign a paper saying he'd never be on a bank board or have anything to do with a financial institution for the rest of his life, they would move off his case. He rightly said, "I've done nothing wrong. I am 33 years old and I won't sign that paper." His whole problem is that he is our son.

At the time, we thought that the fact they were investigating Neil was unfair but that it would come to little or nothing. How wrong we were.

Neil became the poster boy of the S&L scandal, despite the fact he was just one of literally hundreds of outside directors of failed savings and loans. He was investigated by the government *and* the press, who decided Neil was guilty before he even had his say. We particularly felt that NBC's "Dateline," hosted by Jane Pauley and Stone Phillips, took an unfair shot when they aired a piece on Neil in September 1992—long after Neil's case was settled but right in the middle of George's reelection bid.

Eventually, Neil did not have to sign that piece of paper, but he lost all his savings, his business, his house, and most important, for a while, his reputation.

The whole family suffered for Neil. Jeb told me a story that was so painful that when his partner, Armando Codina, tried to tell me again, I stopped him. It just hurt too much to hear it twice. Jeb and Armando were trying to put a business deal together, and the banker they were talking to said that they just couldn't work with the "Bush boy." Jeb and Armando, who had established a reputation in Miami for integrity and honor, were appalled. The bankers thought Jeb was Neil. Poor Neil. First, he was being judged guilty without an opportunity to defend himself; now his brothers were suffering because of name association.

Marvin told me a story of a friend of his getting in a verbal fight with two men he overheard talking at the airport. One said, "I hope they don't let him off just because he is the President's son." Marv's friend turned around and said, "I know him and there is not a dishonest bone in his body." Then a fight started.

George was heartbroken over what was happening but couldn't even talk to his son about it because a government agency was investigating him. He was especially disappointed in some members of Congress who professed to be friends, but who let politics get the best of them. Henry B. Gonzalez of Texas, whom George always liked, took out after Neil with a vengeance. (Henry later also filed impeachment papers on George during the early days of Desert Storm.) Congressman Frank Annunzio, who always told me how much he liked and respected George, suddenly found himself opposed in his Chicago district and attacked Neil unmercifully. And if Pat Schroeder from Colorado wasn't crying about some other cause, she always could use Neil as a daily kicking bag.

On the other end of this spectrum, we were touched, and so was Neil, by how family and friends rallied around him. Once more Lud Ashley, who had left Congress, came to the rescue and helped raise money to pay Neil's legal fees. When Neil moved from Denver to Houston, his longtime friends there welcomed him with open arms. And Neil's wife, Sharon, although she suffered horribly with her husband, stood by him like a rock.

In May of 1991 I wrote in my diary:

For the last few months George has talked privately like a man who is not running for office. I know he has the children on his mind. He is consumed with worry about Neil and a guilty feeling. He knows that Neil never would have been in this trouble if he hadn't been the son of the president.

I will say no more about this, but what happened to Neil took up more than its fair share of my diary for the remaining White House years. I couldn't help but think of former Secretary of Labor Ray Donovan, who, after being accused of wrongdoing and then exonerated, simply asked: "Where do I go to get my good name back?"

ᗍ In early January we held the first of five Presidential Lectures, one of the best things we initiated at the White House. Nan Ellis suggested it after she heard David Donald, a Pulitzer Prize–winning author, speak about Lincoln. We loved the idea, and invited Professor Donald to kick off the series. Standing below George Healy's portrait of Lincoln in the State Dining Room, he chose to speak about the sixteenth president's life in the White House, rather than his role as politician, diplomat, or commander in chief. I wrote in my diary:

(The professor) was amusing, fascinating, warm, scholarly and so interesting . . . Boy, oh boy, we think we have problems. When the Lincolns moved into the White House, it was not furnished, there was oilcloth on the floor in the State Rooms because of the overflow from the spittoons, people could roam freely in and out of the house, there was no fence, we were at war with ourselves, Mrs. Lincoln had brothers and brothers-in-law fighting on the "other side" from her husband and government. Washington insiders thought she was a spy and a country bumpkin. They lost a beloved child while at the White House. Mary Todd Lincoln was depressed much of the time and hardly left her room. They had no friends. Their (political) party was new and so he had no proven party members to count on. The President's offices were on the same floor as the family residence. They had soldiers bivouacked on the South Grounds, etc. Professor Donald did a marvelous job and it was a splendid afternoon.

Through the next few years we had lectures on Theodore Roosevelt and Harry Truman by Professor David McCullough; Andrew Jackson, by Professor Robert V. Remini; and George Washington, by Professor Gordon S. Wood. The White House came to life for us during these lectures and things were certainly put in perspective.

I think that we were aware of Lincoln's presence more than any of our other predecessors. His anguish was such that it almost could be felt, especially in the room he used as his office, now known as the Lincoln Bedroom. We could stand and look out the same windows he did. However, we never saw or believed in the famous ghost, nor did Ranger and Millie. (Winston Churchill and Queen Wilhelmina of the Netherlands were among the believers. During separate White House stays, they both reported seeing Mr. Lincoln. Also, the Reagan's dog, Rex, reportedly refused to go in the room.)

Some of the more interesting stories about life in the White House came from people who once lived or visited there. The little sitting room off the Queen's Bedroom had quite a lot of history. Lynda Robb told me that she served Chuck dinner there one night since they could not date in public and maintain their privacy.

Another night we had a small dinner for Susan Eisenhower and her nice fiancé, Ronald Z. Sagdeev. I couldn't help but think how much the world had changed: Imagine President Eisenhower's granddaughter marrying a Soviet! We had David and Julie, Anne and Susan Eisenhower, and a few others. I loved the reminiscing as we walked through the rooms that David sometimes stayed in from 1952 to 1960, and later, Julie and David stayed in during the Nixon years:

David told me that my little office—beauty parlor—puppy birthing room was the room his grandfather painted in. He said that he used to come into the room and talk to him while he painted and he always wondered if he was saying what his grandfather wanted him to say. I believe that Ike would be very proud of him. He has written a superb biography of President Eisenhower. Julie verified that the tiny sitting room off the Lincoln Bedroom was the room that her dad had chosen as his upstairs office. The Eisenhower ladies talked about riding their tricycles on the ground floor, and Anne told me that her grandparents had one of the first built-in-a-wall television sets in the West Sitting Hall and later sent me a picture of it. Pretty big and ugly. They are such a nice family and it was a relaxed, fun evening. David and Julie are truly thoughtful, nice, bright and easy.

Later in the year, Ed and Tricia Cox also visited us in the White House, and Ed told us that he studied for his bar exam in the White House solarium. I remember thinking at that time how sad it was that the White House had become almost a prison for the Nixon family during the difficult Watergate period.

⮑ My diary entries from the first few months of 1990 reflect a wide range of activities in our lives—and thoughts in my head. I'd like to share just a few of them with you:

January 20—Just a year ago today George was sworn in as the 41st President of the United States. So of course this past week has been a rehashing of "The First Year" and marking George on his efforts. Doro called just thrilled by the *Boston Globe* poll: "In a nationwide poll of 1,002 people done for the *Globe* this week and last, more than 80% of those polled expressed a favorable view of the president, heady personal vindication for a man who just 18 months ago trailed Governor Dukakis by a wide margin in pre-election polling and was thought, even by some Republicans, to be virtually unelectable." I know and so does George that this is a very fragile thing. [Little did we know how fragile.]

February 2—Just back from the National Prayer Breakfast. Although it ran a little late, it truly was one of the best. Jimmy Baker was the reluctant main speaker and got me weeping a little as he shared his thoughts on faith and friends. He told a very meaningful story about driving to the White House one day and just as he was pulling into the driveway, he saw a former chief of staff walking all alone down the street—no driver, no security, no entourage—just all alone. He said that reminded him that all the trappings that go with power are fleeting. He went on to say that the only power that lasts is the power of God. He said, "Those people who didn't return my calls before I got these jobs, won't return them after I leave." He talked about the support that friends had given him. He certainly spoke movingly about his friendship with George. And, the thing I liked best was that he gave that near perfect Susan a lot of credit and showed his great love for her.

Jim did such a great job as Secretary of State that I suspect people are still returning his phone calls. He earned the respect of the whole world.

February 5—The hostages weigh very much on our minds. Not a night goes by that we don't pray for them.

February 14—One night several weeks ago George and I decided to walk Millie just before bed. We walked partway around the drive and saw two ladies looking through the Southeast Gate. George loves to visit with tourists and suggested that we walk over to say hello. The ladies kept saying, "Nobody will believe me when I tell them I met you" or "The others are going to die when they hear we talked to you!" One of the ladies told me that her grandmother was going to be 80 years old and would I drop her a note? I said, "Of course," and she gave me her name and address. The other lady asked me to drop her husband a note or otherwise he'd think she was lying. So I got her address. I did go right upstairs and write the two notes.

. . . Several weeks later I got a letter from Dottie Craig, who has taken on the task of raising money for the White House Endowment Fund . . . Among many things, Dottie's letter said: "You both made a friend who sounds as though she'd lay down her life for you when you talked with Betsy Sodano last Monday evening, the 22nd, through the W.H. fence, as I understand it. She is a cosmetician at a People's Drug Store in Maryland. I talked to her this morning because after she saw my name in a newspaper article about the fund, she called Earle's office to say that she wanted to help fund-raise in Maryland." That was so sweet. People are truly nice.

February 15—George, Jim Baker, Brent Scowcroft, John Sununu and Dr. Burt Lee left for the Drug Summit in Colombia . . . The dreaded trip was here. The press had been building up the danger for months. We got more letters and phone calls saying, "Don't let him go," from friends and strangers alike. I hardly slept at all the night before. George explained to me that we can't ask our Latin American friends to battle the drug cartel, risk their lives and then not go to the meeting because there were threats. He also explained to me that the security was going to be very tight. He was right, but it did not make me sleep any better that night or the next. GB called me when he left Colombia. I was so relieved. I cleaned my desk and then greeted George when he arrived at the South Lawn.

All during this time "the new breeze" of democracy was continuing to spread throughout the world, making it a very exciting time to be in the White House. One day in February, Jim Baker woke us up at 4:45 A.M. with the great news that Violeta Chamorro had upset Daniel Ortega in the Nicaragua elections—and by a pretty big margin. The press had been reporting that Ortega would win, which would mean a major defeat for George.

In March, the new President of Czechoslovakia, Vaclav Havel, and his wife came for a visit. When you realized that just four months ago this playwright-dissident didn't know if he was going to be jailed, exiled, or what, it truly was a momentous occasion. I had Olga Havelova for coffee and liked her very much. She had white hair and was a very chic, natural-looking woman. We had simultaneous translation as we visited, so I confess some of what she said was lost. But I did understand that she had been in jail several days and he for four and a half years. She told me that at one time they were given the opportunity to emigrate to the United States, but they refused. It would have meant not going back. I asked her if during the tough years, did she wish they had come. She looked shocked and gave a firm "No" answer.

Nancy Ellis came down from Boston to attend a dinner Katharine Graham of *The Washington Post* gave at her house for the Havels. All the Washington "in-group" were there and some administration types. Nan said that it was a good evening but that during dinner, Teddy Kennedy got up and asked Nick Brady to change places with him, thus putting himself between Nan and Kay, the hostess. The Havels gave Nancy a ride home to the White House since they were staying in Blair House, right across the street from us. She said as they were getting in the car, Teddy Kennedy came down and insisted that he get in the same car and take them to the Lincoln Memorial. They walked up the steps, and Teddy read the writings on the wall to them. Nan said that poor Mrs. Havel looked astonished and dead tired and clearly wanted to go home to bed.

We felt the "new breeze" again the very next day when we had a reception welcoming the National Symphony and especially its director, Mstislav Rostropovich, home from a glorious trip abroad. George had trouble speaking when he told the group about Slava having a chair brought up to the Wall in Berlin and playing his cello. It was so moving. But the highlight of the trip was Slava's return home to the Soviet Union. He had been exiled for sixteen years and had just recently had his Soviet citizenship returned to him. Evidently, when the orchestra played "The Stars and Stripes Forever" in Russia, the tears flowed on all sides. On top of all the other emotions at our reception, the symphony played "Linda Lou" for us, which really almost got us in tears again. Prescott Bush, George and Nan's father, had sung that song for years with his Silver Dollar Quartet. It was a wonderful hour.

Certainly one of the great privileges of living in the White House was meeting, seeing, hearing, and enjoying the best of the best our country has to offer. I know that for most people, getting to come to the White House and meet the president of the United States is an unforgettable experience, but many times we were much more in awe of our guests.

Another good case in point: In late February we held the annual Governors' Dinner, and the next day I invited the spouses to join me upstairs for lunch in the Yellow Oval Room. I had asked Helen Hayes to also attend and recite for us.

She started out by telling a story about two old ladies who met playing bridge at a club. As the party was breaking up, one said to the other, "I enjoyed being with you so much and would like to call you for a game sometime. I am so embarrassed, but I just can't remember your name. Would you give it to me?" And the other lady paused, thought, and answered, "Do you have to have it right now?"

Helen proceeded to tell us that she, too, sometimes forgets and therefore she had her glasses and a copy of the Benét poem that she recited. She only took a tiny peek. At almost ninety years old, she was amazing—a tiny, beautiful lady who stood straight as an arrow.

At the end of the lunch, Bill Orr, husband of Governor Kay Orr of Nebraska and one of our two male spouses, asked if he could give a toast. My heart sank, for it was time for the lunch to break up and I was afraid that his toast would be long and anticlimactic. Wrong—again! Bill told us that he and Kay had a ninety-eight-year-old friend. When they asked him why he looked so serene and untroubled, he said that he guessed it was because he had no peer pressure. Bill said, "Miss Hayes, you clearly have no peer pressure. In fact, you have no peers. You are the greatest lady of the theater." And then he made a toast to Helen Hayes and sat down. It was just so right and perfect, and another magic moment at the White House.

Both George and I loved Helen Hayes. Fifty-three years earlier I had gone with my fourth grade class to New York City to see a young, beautiful actress in *Victoria Regina.* That actress was Miss Helen Hayes.

She was a great lady. She campaigned for George, which was such a kindness.

∾ In March, while attending the funeral of Chappy Rose, Susan Porter Rose's father-in-law, George leaned over and said to me, "I'm afraid that I have done something that you are going to think is very bad." When I asked, "What?" he told me that he had invited the new Japanese Prime Minister, Toshiki Kaifu, to meet him at the Annenbergs' house in Palm Desert next week. I started to protest that he couldn't do that to Lee Annenberg, and he shushed me and said the funeral was starting.

Everyone was agog that George invited the Prime Minister with only seven days' notice and that the Prime Minister accepted. Usually there are months of preliminary meetings before the two principals meet. However, that just wasn't George's style.

Only the Annenbergs could have coped with a mini-summit with a week to prepare. George and I are very fond of both Lee and Walter. Lee was a former chief of protocol, and Walter was a former ambassador to the United Kingdom. They both did first-class jobs. There also was never a more giving couple. While we were at their house for the summit, George announced a gift of $50 million from Walter and Lee to the United Negro College Fund.

Their home, Sunnylands, was—and is—heavenly. At that time the main house was filled with the most glorious collection of Impressionist paintings, which they since have given to the Metropolitan Museum of Art in New York City. They hosted a beautiful dinner in the most spectacular dining room ever. But what impressed me the most was that Lee Annenberg herself made sure that all guests were well taken care of.

∾ One day in early March, Lee Atwater, who was doing an outstanding job heading up the Republican National Committee, fainted at a meeting. Eventually we learned that he had an inoperable brain tumor. We were stunned. This energetic, enthusiastic, bright young man was only thirty-nine years old, and he and his wife, Sally, were expecting a baby within the month.

Over the next few weeks I wrote about Lee in my diary a number of times:

. . . George W. came to Washington and had Lee Atwater for breakfast. They had a two-hour talk. Lee and Junior were great friends. ("Junior" was Lee's name for George W.)

. . . Lee's doctor gave him a fifteen-year reprieve. Burt Lee thought that he'd be lucky to have two years.

. . . Harry Dent came to Washington and spent the day with Lee. He is not only a hero of Lee's, but also is devoting his life to Christianity. Lee is seeking. (Harry, like Lee, is a native of South Carolina. He served in the Nixon White House.)

. . . I asked Lee how Sally was doing and he said that "she was as strong as horseradish." I reminded him to share with her and not to forget that she was frightened, worried and hurting also. He was sweet and said that he had awakened the other night and looked at her and realized that she was so vulnerable. The new little baby girl is due in two weeks.

. . . Bad news about Lee Atwater, went to NYC and doctor says he has 18 months to live.

Lee died March 29, 1991. He was one of a kind, and rose to the occasion in death as he did in life. He had nothing to apologize about, ever. George Bush truly loved him.

∽ There is another sad footnote to the spring of 1990: In April, Ryan White, the young hemophiliac who contracted AIDS through blood transfusions, died. He was at first ostracized by his school, but after a two-year court battle, won the right to attend classes. He devoted much of his remaining years to educating the public on how you get AIDS and how you *don't* get AIDS. He was a true hero.

Burt Lee and I flew to Indianapolis to attend the funeral. Burt had served on President Reagan's AIDS Commission and worked with AIDS patients at Sloan-Kettering in New York City. He also had met often with Jeanne White, Ryan's mother, so he asked to go with me.

Many celebrities had taken up Ryan's cause, including Elton John and Michael Jackson, who had been supporters and friends for several years and attended the funeral. I was most touched, however, when some of his schoolmates, an all-girl group, sang "That's What Friends

Are For." They stood in a semicircle, tears running down their faces, singing around the open casket where their tiny, eighty-five-pound, eighteen-year-old friend lay wearing his jeans and reflective dark glasses. It was so sweet.

⟩ One of the hardest tasks for me during the White House years was to decide which invitations to accept. My scheduling office received on the average one hundred invitations a day for various events, ranging from second graders who wanted me to come read them a story to major national associations who wanted me to keynote their conventions. Often attached to the invitations would be comments or suggestions from Susan Porter Rose, Julie Cooke, Anna Perez, and every now and then, someone from George's office who had a special interest. Almost all of them were for causes or events I would have loved to support or attend but didn't possibly have time for.

The problem was never more acute than during the commencement season. Every year, out of one hundred or so invitations, we could accept only a handful. Many of the schools wanted to confer upon me an honorary degree. We tried very hard to select those that would represent a cross-section of schools and regions. In 1990, for example, we accepted invitations to speak at Southwest Community College in Cumberland, Kentucky; St. Louis University in Missouri; Wellesley College in Massachusetts; Kennebunkport High School in Maine; and Dunbar High School in Washington, D.C.

At the last moment Walter Annenberg asked me to do the University of Pennsylvania as a favor to him. I believe that they had invited Vaclav Havel, and he had to turn them down at a late date. For Walter I would do anything, so at the last minute we added the University of Pennsylvania, which was celebrating its two hundred and fiftieth anniversary.

My staff and I had been working on *the* speech off and on all spring. We asked Ed McNally from George's speech-writing department to help, so he joined our brainstorming sessions, which included Susan Porter Rose, Julie Cooke, Anna Perez, Susan Green, Jean Becker, and Sondra Haley. We sat around and talked about the things I wanted to say and tried to choose the theme for this year. They reminded me that I always say, "You have two choices in life. You can like it or not. I chose to like it." That, of course, is very simplistic. I know that there are people in life who have so many troubles that their choices are nil. But I was talking about people who waste their lives complaining about things that cannot be changed, who don't appreciate what they do have, and who spend time wishing for that which they cannot have. I read someplace that Oprah Winfrey said something like: "I have been lucky. But I made my luck." I believe that. Incidentally, I believe that most of us would not think Oprah was "lucky" when hearing about her difficult childhood. She overcame and is a real heroine to me.

We talked about my dad and the things he told me that you can give your children and about how important it is to give them independence. George has been wonderful about that, and I think it has added a lot to our children's lives.

I suggested that we end with the marvelous story from one of Robert Fulghum's books about "where do the mermaids fit into a world of wizards, giants and dwarfs." I wanted to make the point that we're not all alike and we have to respect each other's differences.

We also talked about my feeling that in order to be happy, one does not need to be married, and if married, one does not need to have children. But if you do have children, *they must come first*. They reminded me that I always say that I am "the luckiest woman in the world." I am.

Somehow, out of all these ramblings, a speech began to take shape.

In early April, the Gorbachev visit to Washington was announced for the end of May and beginning of June, conflicting with my Wellesley College address on June 1. However, rather than cancel, Susan Porter Rose suggested that I ask Raisa if she'd like to give a joint graduation speech with me. I asked George, and he thought that it was a brilliant idea.

Next I called President Nan Keohane of Wellesley to be sure that it would be okay. She sounded absolutely thrilled. I asked her please not to tell anyone because I didn't want to put pressure on Raisa to accept. I also warned her that judging from past experience, it might take quite a while before I got a definite answer.

I then hand-wrote Raisa a note, telling her that I was so pleased that a date had been set for the summit and inviting her to join me at the graduation. I told her that we could fly up to Boston together and that I thought it would give her a chance to tell a marvelous group about her great country and her great hopes for Soviet women. Foreign

Minister Shevardnadze was gracious enough to hand-carry my letter to the Soviet Union for me.

A couple of weeks later, a handful of Wellesley girls began protesting my selection as their commencement speaker. According to them, "Barbara Bush has gained recognition through the achievements of her husband." Wellesley, they said, "teaches us that we will be rewarded on the basis of our own merit, not on that of a spouse." I should add here that the author Alice Walker was their first choice as a commencement speaker. When she declined, they invited me, the runner-up.

By the time my staff and I sat down for our second speech meeting, Wellesley had exploded into controversy. Although only 150 of the 600 graduating seniors had signed the petition, the protest had become big news. I told my staff that I did not want to make a special speech catering to Wellesley. I also did not want to complain, explain, or apologize in any way. By the end of the meeting, we had settled on three things I wanted the students to consider: You have to get involved in something larger than yourself; Remember to get joy out of life; Cherish human relationships. When I read my final draft to George, he suggested "Read to your child," and I added "Hug your child, love your child." Imagine my forgetting the most important and obvious things! We cut and pasted and were ready to start the graduation trail.

I gave a slightly different speech at Southeast Community College, located in Cumberland, Kentucky, the heart of the coal-mining country. These were truly a group of courageous students, many of whom were the first in their families to further their education beyond high school—and sometimes, elementary school.

Next was the University of Pennsylvania, where I gave *the* speech. I wrote in my diary about that occasion:

I followed Bill Cosby into the stadium and there was a great deal of cheering. He is funny. He wore dirty sneakers or running shoes and a gray sweat suit. There was some worry when he arrived, but he quickly robed up and all was well.

Then came St. Louis University, where I basically gave the same speech with some local color added in. At neither school did the speech get any national attention. I think you need controversy to make news.

All this time the Wellesley situation was boiling. Here are some of the things I wrote in my diary during the month of May:

I got the darndest support from people like Ellen Goodman, Barbara Mikulski, Cal Thomas, etc. There were letters to the editor, and I received letters from friends and foes alike. Just yesterday *The New York Times* ran a front-page story about it and my phone rang off the hook. Richard Nixon called me and was outraged. My brother Scott Pierce called and wanted to know if I was all right. Jessica Catto called from London and wanted me to know that she had written an op-ed page article and faxed it to *The Washington Post.* George Bush thought the whole thing was dreadful. I have to remind myself that *THEY* invited me. I sometimes feel as though they think I invited myself.

. . . I must say that I felt for the President of Wellesley. She knew that I might just cancel the whole speech. There goes the graduation speaker and much more important, maybe Raisa's first speech in the USA.

. . . I can't go anywhere that I am not asked about it. So although I am not going to change my talk, it is not as much fun.

. . . That darn Wellesley flap has taken on a life of its own. There are more editorials, more talk shows, etc. It's putting too much pressure on. I read in the paper this morning that we had sent someone to Wellesley to ask the girls what they wanted me to talk about. FALSE. We did announce that Raisa Gorbachev was going to Wellesley with me and would speak. (That, of course sparked speculation that I had invited her so I could hide behind her skirts.)

On May 30, the day before the Gorbachevs were to arrive, I wrote my brother:

Dearest Scott,

A million thanks for your letter. Don't worry about your old sister . . . at least for now. The Wellesley thing has become a bore. We are tired of answering letters . . . almost all defending me. I feel for the college as they are getting hate letters. I am trying to spread love, not hate, so this is not helping me any.

. . . This is the day before the big arrival and the papers are full of stories about things GB and I have done or thought. Funny how total strangers know what you are thinking. The truth about the invitation to Mrs. Gorbachev to come to Wellesley with me is that I wrote her long before the brouhaha, having sworn the president of the college to secrecy and gotten permission to invite her. I gave my note to Shevardnadze, their Foreign Minister, to carry home. Then a month or two went by with no answer. Now she has accepted and we are off the day after tomorrow for the speeches. It should be a fascinating three days. One thing I can promise you, I am going to love her in spite of anything she does or does not do. I am expecting her to be charming on this visit. She must have read Nancy's book. We have, of course, met before. The news about what is happening in their country is tough.

Love to all,
Bar

Also on May 30, I received a fax from Chris Bicknell, one of the young Wellesley women who objected to my being the speaker at the graduation. It was such a nice letter and really cleared the air. One of the things she said was: "I want to say thank you! *Thank* you for being the only one (it seems) to understand the reasons behind our debate—and thank you for saying so to the press."

I quickly picked up the phone and called Chris. I could hardly believe it, but the White House operator found her in her dorm room and we had a warm, nice talk.

The next morning we awakened to the most beautiful day in the world. I walked the dogs at 4:45 A.M., read the papers, swam, and got ready for the arrival ceremony.

Raisa looked so stylish and chic with her turned-up collar on a lightweight wool suit. After the receiving line, I walked her upstairs to have coffee in the West Sitting Room. My three "girls" came to join us—Neil's wife, Sharon; Marvin's wife, Margaret; and Millie. The latter seemed to bond to Raisa as we toured the residence. Raisa had interesting things to say about everything. At one point she gave us a small history of our previous meeting, what we said in the car, and so on. She told me that the Soviets think there are two great American Presidents: Roosevelt and Reagan. I showed her Ronald Reagan's portrait and said that we didn't like it. She, to her credit, said that she liked President Reagan very much. I quickly told her that we loved

President Reagan; we just didn't like the portrait. (Neither did the Reagans; it later was replaced.)

The state dinner that night was lovely, with the beautiful Frederica Von Stade singing for us.

Then it was Friday, June 1. The day had arrived.

The funniest thing happened on the plane going up. I didn't know what it meant, but it sure shook me up for a minute. Raisa and I sat and talked through her interpreter for a while, and then I told her that if she didn't mind, I thought that I'd go over my speech just one more time. I moved across the aisle and started to work. After about a minute, Raisa interrupted me and asked, "Barbara, are we both supposed to be giving a speech?" I couldn't believe my ears. We had worked out all the plans in advance through the Soviet Embassy, and it had been agreed that we both would speak for six minutes. We even had told the embassy we would help with her talk, an offer they declined. I told her that we had hoped she would speak for six minutes. She pulled out a tiny piece of paper and started to write away. In a minute she got up and went into the ladies' room. While she was there, I asked the interpreter if I had understood her correctly—was she telling me that she didn't have a speech? How could there be such a misunderstanding? He smiled, patted his pocket, and produced the translation. Was Raisa being funny? Whatever it was, I was glad that she was prepared.

From the moment we got to Boston it was thrilling. Governor Dukakis met us at the airport, which was very kind. At every street corner there were people cheering. This caused no end of trouble as Raisa wanted to stop and shake hands and thank people. I made a deal with her: *After* the graduation, we could stop whenever she wanted, but I was determined that we would be on time. She was just not used to people at home cheering them, so the Boston welcome was especially nice. When we got to Wellesley, she did not put on a robe. I longed to join her as it was so hot, but President Keohane had gone to the trouble to get my hood from Smith College. Raisa told me that they didn't robe in the Soviet Union; therefore, she couldn't here. She was very conscious of the "home viewer." I think she got criticized on her last visit for being so stylish. This time she was wearing a lovely, long-skirted, light wool suit that I got to know very well over the years. Thank heavens that it was very becoming, for she wore it everywhere.

When Raisa and I walked into the tent, the young women went wild. Doro had come down from Maine to give me support, which really touched me, and Susan Porter Rose told me later that tears ran down Doro's face when we came in. The buildup had been so big that there were five thousand people in the tent, and five thousand standing outside. The TV networks carried it live. Thank heavens I didn't know that at the time. George saw part of it in Washington.

Chris Bicknell gave the first speech, I was next, and Raisa was last. She gave a very dignified, very poised talk. It was a good length and was translated as she spoke. I was very proud of her. I can't imagine giving a graduation speech in Russia! (See Appendix C.)

How did I feel when it was over? The truth is, I did understand what the girls who had protested were saying. I had quit worrying about the whole thing once the speech was written because I felt good about what I wanted to say to them. I will confess that I was thrilled with the welcome they gave Raisa and me.

One thing did bother me, however: One of the young women who had been so vocal against my selection was from a South American country. I thought she showed very bad taste criticizing the wife of the president of her host country. I'm not sure why, but I thought it was okay for American citizens to protest me, but not our guests!

After the commencement, we had a quick laugh with Doro, then headed for the Boston Common to visit with a group of elementary students at the *Make Way for Ducklings* sculpture, based on the famous children's story by Robert McCloskey. The entire route was lined by schoolchildren and people waving and cheering. We got out of our car three times to shake hands and wave. We were on a tight schedule, and I had trouble keeping Raisa going. We finally got to the ducks, and there we saw our nephew and niece, Jamie and Sue Bush, and their children, Sam and Sarah. They were adorable. Raisa said, "You seem to have family everywhere."

We had a small ceremony around those dear ducks with students from the Mather School, then talked to the press for a few minutes. They asked me how we were getting on, and I answered, "Just fine. We are having a great time." When they asked Raisa the same question, she gave the same answer, but took hours. George would say that she is the kind of person you ask the time and they tell you how to build the clock. (He says that about me, too.) As we had agreed that we *must* be back in Washington for the signing ceremony, we started back to the cars. I shook hands, said good-byes, and arrived at the car only to find that Raisa had gone back for ten more minutes with the press. We finally got her into the car and took off for the airport. I honestly think that since they did not have such openness with either their people or the press, she felt it would be rude not to shake every hand and answer every question. As we drove by many houses on the way to the airport, I found myself wishing that we could stop, go up to a door, and go in. I think she would have been surprised to see how gracious Americans are.

At six o'clock, we all met in the East Room of the White House to watch the two Presidents sign a series of agreements concerning arms and trade. It was quite a meeting. Imagine sitting in a room with the two Presidents of the most powerful countries in the world—and being married to one of them!

We were due at the Soviet Embassy at seven-thirty for dinner. Raisa and I had had a big discussion about what she was going to wear, long or short, and she took forever to finally say, "Short." So I wore my bright pink, very short dress from Scaasi, and she wore a long-sleeved, black velvet suit. It was so hot. She looked pretty as a picture, but must have died of the heat. If so, she never let on. We had a receiving line and went right on into dinner. They had seven courses, but the memorable one, as always, was the caviar, which they passed twice. We got home fairly early but I was dead tired. I bet she was also. It was tiring to spend a day speaking through an interpreter, not to mention giving a graduation speech where there had been so much controversy.

On Saturday morning we flew by helicopters, the men in one and the women in another, to Camp David. It was such an interesting day. We flew over miles of residential areas, and I could see that all the Soviets were impressed with the homes. One Soviet security man couldn't believe it when a Secret Service agent told him that he lived down below in one of the lovely subdivisions. The Soviets seemed amazed by our private lives.

The men were scheduled to work all day, so Raisa and I decided to go for a long walk. We went right to our cabins, changed our clothes, and were ready to take off when I looked at her feet. Although she had on pants, she also had on very high heels. I tried to persuade her to let me get her some walking shoes. She assured me that these were her walking shoes. (Her interpreter said that for photos, she wanted to have heels on.) I decided we should tour the camp in a golf cart instead. We talked of lots of things. She asked me if our children owned their own homes. I said that yes, they did. She asked if we had helped them buy their homes. I told her that we hadn't. I explained that we put them through college and since the age of twenty-one or so, they had been on their own. She asked how that could be, and I explained to her that both husbands and wives worked, they saved enough money for a down payment, got a loan for the remainder from the bank, and then paid monthly installments on the loan. I also explained that over the years some of them had been able to "trade up." She told me that their only child, a daughter, had a doctorate degree, was a researcher married to a surgeon, and that they could not afford their own apartment. So with their children, two girls aged three and ten, they lived with the Gorbachevs. She seemed genuinely interested in how much things cost in our country. For example, in the Soviet Union, all lipsticks cost the same—imported name brands and cheaper ones. The government subsidizes things at a great cost. She asked a million questions about the free enterprise system.

After a long golf cart trip around Camp David, we returned to the house for lunch. The men had been on the patio at the main cabin working all morning. It was fascinating as they were all wired up to two translators who were repeating every word as it was spoken. We had a very good lunch and then planned on a nap until three-thirty. But George's aide, Tim McBride (one of the finest young men we know), came running in early and said that the Gorbachevs were on the terrace, so we hurried out. I had noticed before lunch that Raisa's poor feet looked raw. We really hadn't walked at all and yet she had large blisters. She came back after lunch in black mules. The men went outside again, and Raisa and I talked in the living room. Later in the day Raisa and the men threw a few horseshoes. Mikhail threw a ringer on his first or second throw and was thrilled. George had it mounted and presented to him at our informal dinner that night.

It was during our long talks at Camp David that Raisa suddenly became a person to me and not just this woman who had done all her homework (although, as always, she had).

She was the first wife of a Soviet leader who was in the public eye. There were no rules for her. She had no staff of her own. People from the Foreign Office did help her with invitations, and people from another office helped her with the mail, but she was blazing a new trail and it was not easy. I think that she had been hurt by the criticism about her, and she asked me why I was so popular. I told her, as honestly as I could, that I felt it was because I threatened no one—I was old, white-headed, and large. I also told her that I stayed out of my husband's affairs. We both agreed that we put our husbands first above all else. I liked her a lot and felt very sympathetic. I also liked him. He was a strong, very able person and also quite charming. United Nations Secretary General Pérez de Cuéllar had said once: "He is either the world's greatest actor or is sincere." George and I agreed that he was sincere. He was smart, fast, and had a great sense of humor. We couldn't understand how he could keep his spirits up, there was so much turmoil at home. But he seemed confident. Someone said to me during the visit, "He's a small man, isn't he?" I was surprised. I didn't think of him as small at all.

          We had another historic visit later in June, when Nelson Mandela came to call on George. I wrote in my diary:

On Monday morning I swam and was working in my office when George called and asked if I could rush over to the Oval Office. I said, "Yes," and raced into clothes and ran over, jamming on lipstick, pearls and earrings as I went. I had gotten the word from two sources that Mrs. Mandela would not be with him, but she had come unexpectedly. The minute I arrived, Nelson Mandela came right over to greet me. He is not as tall as I thought. He is in his seventies and stands straight as an arrow. He is a kind-looking man with a real presence. Winnie Mandela was in native costume. She is a big, smiling woman. Both were charming. After a few minutes of talking we walked out to a press conference and both men spoke. George did a beautiful job. Mandela spoke without notes. As I stood there next to her, I kept thinking that this smiling woman is the lady who allegedly has those "bully" boys who beat people and who ordered them to "necklace" people (pouring gasoline on rubber tires and putting them over people's necks). All done while her husband was in jail. I also had read that she built an enormous personal house. What to believe? [The Mandelas have since separated.]

. . . Mandela's welcome in this country, NYC, Boston and Washington, D.C., has been overwhelming. Jesse Jackson has stuck to him like glue. He attacked George in his introduction of Mandela. Much to my disgust, (Washington) Mayor Marion Barry, whose (cocaine) trial is ongoing, appeared with him last night and got a big applause. Is there no one to protect this fine man (meaning Mandela, not Barry!)?

Earlier that spring, another VIP visitor came to the White House—Michael Jackson. Now you might wonder why I would mention a pop star in the same context as men who will be remembered for changing history. Because it always amused me what a huge ruckus the appearance of celebrities caused at the White House—sometimes more than the history-makers. You could tell from the number of staffers who left their desks to sneak a peek who was hot and who was not. Michael was definitely hot. I wrote in my diary:

He was honored this week as the Entertainer of the Decade by the Children's Museum. I went over to G's press conference announcing the Gorbachev visit and met Michael in the Oval Office, where he was talking to George and having a "photo op." He wears the darndest clothes, skin-tight black suit with at least two big medals on his chest, and this day he had on four belts, red leather with big silver buckles. One belt was around his waist and the other three were around his left leg, two above the knee and one below. He has straight, long black hair. You really have to listen to him as he has the softest voice, almost a whisper. He was very pleasant and genuinely wanted to see the upstairs at the White House, especially the Lincoln Bedroom. So I walked him over to the residence and was just amazed by the numbers of normally sophisticated people who suddenly appeared to be walking by, gaping and staring. He does like crowds, and I can certainly understand that. After we saw the Lincoln Bedroom we went across the hall to the Queen's Bedroom with Millie and Ranger at our side. The dogs jumped up on the window and looked out at the tourists leaving by the North Portico. This was a great fun thing to do because the tourists always take one last look back and when they spot the dogs and sometimes me, they wave and take pictures. This day I asked Michael to join us at the window. I have never seen such excitement. People literally jumped, laughed out loud and waved. I wouldn't have been surprised if they had done cartwheels and somersaults.

I was delighted when George asked me to head the U.S. delegation to the inauguration of the President of Costa Rica. So in early May, Nancy and John Sununu; Jeb (Columba was supposed to come but little Jebby got sick at the last minute); the former governor of

Puerto Rico, Luis Ferré, and his wife, Tiody; and Roger Ailes, our great friend, who had run the successful campaign of President-elect Calderón, headed for Costa Rica.

A couple of things stand out from the trip:

The Calderóns were among the most gracious people you could wish to meet and had the most attractive, charming children. The morning of the inauguration, they had us over for a long relaxed breakfast as if they had nothing else to do.

At the inauguration, as our delegation walked into the stadium behind our flag, we got a standing ovation. I don't believe that anyone other than President Calderón got the same. The Costa Ricans love the United States, and we love them. I felt so proud knowing that the cheers were for the USA.

Of the 29,000 people there, John Sununu was probably the only person who wore tails. His comment: There were 28,999 badly dressed people there! I overheard him say to Roger Ailes, "You and I look as though we are going as two sofas." How I love John and his sense of humor.

        While all of this was going on, I still was trying to keep my pledge to do something every day that would make a difference. I unveiled a literacy billboard in Miami, visited a library in Los Angeles and a veterans' hospital in Kansas City, attended a fund-raiser for an adult literacy center in Cleveland, played pool at a Boys and Girls Club in Washington, gave out books in an Iowa elementary school, and so much more.

The summer especially was very busy since George and I were going to host the annual Economic Summit in Houston. One might question the wisdom of choosing our hometown for a summit in July. But not to be deterred, the city picked the summit slogan, "Houston's Hot," and went to work.

It was hot—and got hotter—but it also was wonderful. For six months a group of five thousand volunteer citizens worked on cleaning up our city. They didn't just clean the route that the delegates were going to use, but the whole town (and it's held up very well since then). George asked Jack Steel, who had been our loyal good friend since the first campaign in 1964, to sign on as special adviser, and Ben Love and Ken Lay coordinated the business community.

In Washington, Susan Baker, Kitty Brady, and I got together and talked about what we could do for the spouses that would be fun. We couldn't possibly compete with the canals of Venice or the castles in France, England, or Germany, but we did have one thing that, although not unique to the world, was pretty special: Texas hospitality. We decided to take them to San Antonio for a quick tour of that beautiful, historic city and to ask friends to host meals in their homes. Two very dear people came to our rescue: Betty Liedtke, wife of George's former partner at Zapata, agreed to have a dinner in Houston; and Joci Strauss said she would love to host a luncheon in San Antonio.

Such nice things happened. Everyone wanted to help. The Garden Club of Houston, to which I belong, planted the most beautiful giant pots around the university. Houstonians volunteered everything. For example, the press who came from around the world had free food in the convention hall, thanks to the hotels and restaurants.

On the evening of July Fourth, right before the summit, George flew to London for a quick NATO meeting. He is the strongest man. He arrived in England on Thursday morning, worked all day, had dinner with Her Majesty, spent the night with Henry and Jessica Catto at Winfield House, worked the next morning, and flew to Houston, arriving in time for dinner with me and then to bed early. I was tired just hearing about it.

I wrote in my diary about the week:

Saturday George had a one-on-one meeting with P.M. Kaifu of Japan. He is a new breed of Japanese. To begin with, he is young. He is tiny—not that that's new, but really tiny. He and his nice wife are happy-looking people. She, Sachiyo, is about 50, speaks English and is literally the tiniest little person I have almost ever seen. Mila Mulroney and I look like GIANTS next to her. They are both very agreeable. I think he is tough to deal with, but who isn't? I feel that all over America there is a big anti-Japanese feeling. Americans are very worried about the Japanese "buying up America."

. . . At 3:30 Saturday afternoon we took 6 Japanese, including the Kaifus, and Baine and Mildred Kerr, Marion Chambers, Charles and Sally Neblett and the President of Rice and Mrs. Rudd to the Opera House at the Wortham Center to see "Carousel." It was a glorious presentation and I got teary. I had forgotten what a sad play it is. There is not a bad song in the musical . . .

Sunday morning—Early 8 a.m. church at St. Martin's with Denis and

Margaret (Thatcher). It was wonderful. Usually we have a smattering of people at that service. It was jam-packed.

. . . G. had one-on-one with Brian Mulroney. I swam and we had lunch with Mila and Brian at the Health Center.

. . . Raced over to the Rodeo. We got there early so that George could meet with Jacques Delors, president of the European Community. Then we had a reception which was attended by Japan, England, EC and Canada. All the Heads of State wore their big cowboy hats. I was sort of glad that Mitterrand had not arrived as it was a long evening for people suffering from jet lag. We went into a mini-rodeo and a mini "Grand Ole Opry," featuring among others, Minnie Pearl, the Gatlin Brothers, Loretta Lynn, Charlie Pride, the Judds. These friends have been there when we needed them over and over again. It was a fun evening. Like "Carousel," this was put on especially for the Summit. I am so proud of Houston.

July 9—George went to one-on-ones with Chancellor Kohl and President Mitterrand. In the middle of the day we went to Rice University to greet the delegates in reverse protocol order. The European Community came first, followed by Japan, Italian Republic, Canada, Federal Republic of Germany, the United Kingdom and France. We had a small reception and then were led out for the ceremony. It was hot. All seven anthems were played, the Colonial Fife and Drum Corps marched, cannons went off in salutes, etc. GB gave a two-minute welcome, and then the spouses went off to do their own thing. I came home and read Scott Turow's BURDEN OF PROOF.

George went to a G-7 dinner at Bayou Bend, Miss Ima Hogg's home in River Oaks, now a museum. The spouses went to Hugh and Betty Liedtke's house for a perfect dinner . . . the house looked beautiful, and all the guests said that they loved being in a private home. We had the spouses of the Heads of State, the Foreign Ministers and Economic Ministers. It is so much nicer to have Susan Baker and Kitty Brady with me. Betty had some little children playing chamber music during the dinner in the library and after dinner the most attractive young couple singing. It was just right. Because Denis joined us, Betty invited her husband, Hugh, Baine and Mildred Kerr, and her brother-in-law and our old friend, Bill Liedtke, to join us. Denis is a stitch. Suddenly, in the middle of a conversation about Russia, he says in a very loud voice and his British nasal voice, "Am I boring you?" The truthful answer is, "No."

Danielle Mitterrand sat on my right. She is a fascinating woman. Difficult, as she speaks not a word of English. She wears absolutely no makeup and is very good looking, I think. Protocol puts us next to each other at all times.

July 10—Hot, but not as bad as I feared. I went out to Ellington Air Force Base and met each group as one by one they arrived in their motorcades and we took off for San Antonio.

The spouses' side of the Summit was headed by Melinda Farris, her staff, plus many volunteers. They were efficient and calm and we did not have a hitch.

. . . We were met by Mayor Lila Cockrell and other dignitaries and put on a large air-conditioned bus . . . On the bus was a Mr. Henry Guerra, "the voice of San Antonio," who gave us the history of San Antonio as we drove to the Mission of San Jose.

. . . Lunch at Joci Straus's glorious cliff-hanging house with its bright colors, high ceilings and spectacular views. At my request Joci invited Flo Crichton, Patsy Light and the two Straus daughters, all of whom I love. On her terrace she had ladies making little tortillas which we filled with butter and cheese. There was music. The lunch was a delicious acorn squash soup, a plate of the best marinated beef and lovely tiny black beans, lettuces and other delicacies.

Back on the bus and on to the Majestic Theater that Joci had restored and I visited last year on the day of its reopening. They had about 900 children who are participating in a summer program in the audience and a half-hour program that reflected local talent.

On to the Alamo, where the Mayor made us all honorary mayors.

. . . We had our joint dinner with the men and many local Houstonians at the Museum of Fine Arts. It did us proud. The collection is superb and has grown so since we got into public life. They had a wonderful John Singer Sargent, a Mary Cassatt, a Bellows, a Frieseke, etc. in the reception hall. At the top of the stairs was the Remington that they had lent us at the Vice President's House. Speaking of the Vice President, he and Marilyn flew down for dinner bringing Nancy Sununu and Clayton and Jeanne Yeutter and others. The flowers were lovely. The food was delicious, and the tables looked spectacular. The entertainment was wonderful. Cicely Tyson was the M.C. A favorite of George's, Michael Davis, a juggler—now don't stick up your nose—was hilariously funny and François sitting next to me really roared. George was dying to get him to do his juggling act with chain saws, but nobody (except GB) liked the idea of buzzing chain saws flying all over a room with seven world leaders in it. Randy Skaggs and his wife sang some country music and were followed by Marilyn McCoo, a glorious black singer who is a joy to behold and hear, and that darling Frederica Von Stade, the opera singer with the voice of an angel. It was a special night.

July 11—The spouses went early to the Texas Medical Center, where we had 19 different tours. We had asked the spouses their interests and sent them off on their own tours. We take second place to no one in the medical field. Dick Wainerdi, head of the center, arranged everything. We ended the tours with a very informal buffet.

We went to the Brown Convention Center, where we heard George read part of the joint communiqué, said good-bye to our foreign friends, toured the dining facilities for all the press, miles of free gourmet food, and George went to his press conference.

The last thing we did was go to the campus of the University of Houston, where we had a "Thank You, Houston" party to which everyone was invited. It was enormous and had entertainment and tent after tent of food. This was a small thank-you to everyone in the city who had made the Economic Summit of 1990 so very special. [Jack Steel later told me that after all the bills were paid, $600,000 was left over. The money was given to the Convention Center, the museum, the Houston Clean Committee, and other groups that helped us so much.]

In mid-July we flew to California for the opening of President Nixon's library. George invited Tricia and Ed Cox and their son, Christopher, to come to Washington and fly out with us. We gathered the White House staff who had been there between 1969 and 1974, about nineteen in all, so they could say hello to Tricia.

The library is a lovely, very bright, graceful-looking building surrounded by beautiful gardens, a reflection pool, and masses of flowers. President Nixon and Pat led us on a tour of the building and the grounds. The house that Richard Nixon was born and grew up in was a tiny house that was ordered from the Sears, Roebuck catalog. It had one bedroom on the first floor and one upstairs that was hard to stand up in. Dick showed us the fireplace and bookshelves that his dad added. I wondered what those grandchildren who are growing up on Park Avenue and in the suburbs in Pennsylvania were thinking.

The opening also was attended by President Ford and Betty and President Reagan and Nancy. Everyone was so excited and pleased to see Pat Nixon, who had suffered a stroke several years earlier.

The actual ceremony was outdoors, and the reports in the papers varied as to how many people were there, but it was large. I saw so many faces of old friends that I was dying to talk to and thought we would have an opportunity to afterward, but didn't. After everyone had said a few words, President Nixon spoke without a note and gave a very upbeat speech.

During the lunch, Ronald Reagan told funny joke after funny joke. I think that George was sort of glad. He had worked for all three of the former Presidents—and now here he was, the sitting President. It made for a rather strange situation.

    It amazed me when George was President how there was "always something." For example, on July 20, Justice Brennan resigned out of the blue from the Supreme Court. I asked George if they had been thinking about a new justice just in case one resigned. He said: "Of course." In fact, he told me that within a month of taking office, he had met with a group of people and asked them for a list of qualified candidates. This was one of a million reasons why George was President and I wasn't.

A few days later George nominated David Souter for the Court. He came by for a quiet drink with us and became one of the people whom I liked immediately.

Also in July, George signed the landmark Americans with Disabilities Act, one of the pieces of legislation he was most proud of. For 43 million Americans, this bill meant an end to employment discrimination and access to all public buildings and transportation. More than two thousand people were on the South Lawn to witness the signing, making it one of the biggest events ever at the White House.

I'd like to share with you parts of a letter George received in 1993 from Evan Kemp and his wife, Janine D. Bertram, concerning this legislation. The letter touched both of us deeply.

> We are not sure that . . . you really take the credit for the great and revolutionary thing you did for this country when you fought [for] and then signed the ADA into law . . . as 43 million Americans become more integrated into society, you deserve all the credit.
> . . . On March 17, 1989, you first invited us to the White House for a small dinner in your residence . . . Each

subsequent year, you invited us to a Christmas party. We were informed by the Secret Service that you had to personally approve Janine's attendance at these events because of her record . . . as you know, Janine was caught up in the Vietnam era, became an "urban guerrilla" and served 52 months in prison for bombing and bank robbery. Clearly, she wasn't your average Republican.

. . . Your openness to include Janine gives her and others the knowledge that people can change, they can grow up. After they grow, the President and First Lady, the highest office holders in the land, may include and accept them.

. . . (Evan) graduated at the top of his class from the University of Virginia Law School. Yet, after 39 job interviews, he could not get a job because of his disability. Fifteen years ago, Evan was told by the federal government that using a wheelchair made him incompetent to supervise two people. Yet, you, Mr. President, didn't bat an eye when you named him Chairman of the Equal Employment Opportunity Commission.

You, Mr. President, encouraged disabled people, convicts and all other Americans to set aside our "victim" status. The ADA was one such policy. Your fight against quotas on the Civil Rights Act of 1991 was another.

Never forget what a great contribution you made to our nation.

That summer was a tough one for Millie, who had been limping and crying. At first her veterinarians thought she maybe had lead poisoning from the scraping of the paint off the White House walls. I was heartsick. It was obvious she was in pain, although she was, as always, undemanding and remained my shadow. Eventually she was diagnosed as having lupus and put on prednisone. She showed immediate improvement and has continued to take the medicine and to feel very fit.

When her illness became public, Millie received 382 get-well cards; then she received 122 notes on an article in *Good Housekeeping*. This was shades of things to come. Eventually, Millie had to have her own volunteer, Jean Richards, in the White House mailroom to answer her letters. She also got a tremendous amount of presents and even portraits.

The summer was worrisome for me, too. All year I still had been having problems with my eyes. They were puffy, swollen, teary, and I still saw double a lot of the time. (I still do when I'm tired, but am so used to it that I hardly notice it anymore.) By August I was weaning myself off the prednisone which I had taken for my eyes, and it was very painful. I also was taking therapy to try to strengthen my muscles. In layman's talk, it was explained to me that the prednisone I took killed something in my right hip and caused muscles to weaken, especially around my knees and hips. I confess I was in a lot of pain that would last through the fall. I couldn't wait for August to come and some R&R in Kennebunkport.

It was not to be, however, a very restful vacation.

On August 2, Iraq shocked the world when it invaded its tiny neighbor, Kuwait. At the time, George was in Colorado with Margaret Thatcher. Several weeks later, Margaret would say to George: "Now is not the time to go wobbly, George." George always loved that, and wobbly he did not go.

20

The Storm Before the Storm

August 7, 1990—George said this morning it has been the toughest week in his life. Fortunately he has kept the door open to world leaders and has talked to them often during the last year and a half. So when the Iraqis moved into Kuwait, George was able to get worldwide support. Earlier this week an amazing thing happened. Jim Baker and Shevardnadze denounced Iraq at a joint press conference. Who ever would have believed??? (George) had to send troops to Liberia to evacuate American citizens there this week to help them escape the escalating civil war. This morning troops were sent to Saudi Arabia. There are troops on the Saudi border. Based on gloom and doom reports all over TV, gas prices have soared. God bless my George.

There was much discussion about whether George should spend any time in Kennebunkport during the Gulf crisis. He felt strongly that he could stay in touch from Maine, and he didn't want to appear to be held hostage in Washington. However, it certainly changed the texture of our "vacation."

During one weekend he spent with us, I walked into the kitchen for a cup of coffee and heard *"Bonjour, François."* Other times I overheard "Good morning, Your Eminence" or "I just wanted to keep you abreast of what is happening and to ask your advice and assistance." Brent Scowcroft told me George talked to Hosni Mubarak while fishing out on his boat, *Fidelity*.

To show you just how difficult the balancing act between "real" life and worldwide politics was during this very difficult time, I'd like to share with you my diary entry from August 16:

This was an extraordinary day. Mrs. Bush's brother, John Walker, had an emergency operation in the night and George, knowing he was ill, went over to the hospital around 5:45 a.m. to check on him. He arrived a few minutes after he died. Johnny might be everybody's first choice as "the most remarkable person" any of us ever knew. He was a great athlete and a surgeon who around 1950 had polio and lost most of the use of his arms. The eldest of their five children died several years later, also of polio, and later they had two Down's Syndrome children, two little girls. That is almost more than any two people can bear, but bear it they did. Never a word of complaint from either John or his extraordinary wife, Louise. John had a great sense of humor, a loving heart, interest in everyone else, and always good advice *IF* asked.

George called me from the hospital and asked me to go over and tell his mother. The fact that he had gone to the hospital was sure to make the news and he did not want Mom to hear it on the radio or television. She looked so beautiful and seemed to understand very well. We shed a tear or two and both agreed that Johnny had been a saint. Later I went back to be sure that Mom was all right and to suggest that maybe she'd like me to push her down to see her sister, Nancy, also bedridden, who has a cottage on the other end of the Point, to tell her. She said that she had already done that and that Nancy understood. I could hardly believe her story and asked the nurse and, yes, she had done just that. Sometimes both ladies seem absolutely oblivious to all that is going on around them and at others, they seem really alert. They always rise to the occasion.

Meanwhile we had all the little kids cleaning out their rooms, straightening their drawers and then I had room inspection. We made a picnic lunch and sent Ellie, Sam, Jebby, Barbara, and Jenna to the beach for the day, I hoped.

. . . At twelve noon His Majesty King Hussein (of Jordan) arrived with an entourage at the helicopter pad. George and I walked down to greet him. He was an old friend and was very warm and friendly, although he had been anything but in the press. He softened his approach in the press later. The group of 12 had a lunch of half a lobster, chicken salad and muffins, blueberry pie and ice cream. George said that they ate it all.

Twenty minutes after the Jordanians left, another helicopter arrived with His Royal Highness, Prince Saud al-Faisal of Saudia Arabia, their Foreign Minister, with his entourage including our esteemed friend Prince Bandar, Saudia Arabia's very able ambassador to the United States. They stayed almost two hours and left.

Meanwhile the grands all came home from the beach. They were kept riding their bikes and playing down by the helo pad. They wanted to see and meet a real live King and Prince. We had a few lessons on shaking hands firmly, looking into the eye and speaking politely. This almost immediately disintegrated into "Good afternoon, Your Royal Hiney," and other such funnies. When the big moment came they all behaved.

We went in the evening to a fund-raiser for Dick Snelling, who is running for governor of Vermont.

We ended that very long day with the arrival of Laura and George. Their girls were glad to see them—and so was I. (The truth is their girls are so easy and fun to be with.)

George returned to Washington several times to brief Congress and consult with advisers, especially when the crisis would escalate. On August 20, for example, the Iraqis took thirty-five Americans hostage and placed them near key military or other strategic sites. The stock market plunged dramatically. We were on the verge of a war, a hostage situation, and a recession. It was an incredibly tense time for us and the country.

Once when he came back to Maine, George brought with him Cardinal Bernard Law of Boston and his assistant, Monsignor Timothy Moran. The Cardinal is very interested in world politics, and I remember he suggested to George that "some good just might come of all this bad," such as a solution to the Lebanon and Palestinian problem. At the time I didn't see how, but I certainly thought of the Cardinal's prediction on September 13, 1993, when the leaders of Israel and the PLO shook hands on the White House lawn.

Despite everything else going on, I managed that summer to read Kitty Dukakis's book, *Now You Know*. I wrote in my diary:

It was a shocking book as advertised, but not for the reasons I heard from friends. She writes with great frankness about being a manic depressive and an addict. What an enormous burden for Mike and herself. I am no doctor, but the agony they must have gone through was horrible. My gut feeling is that this book will be a comfort for people who have mental problems. They will certainly feel they are not alone and maybe it will encourage them to get help.

During the time that he was in Maine, George and I would go over to Mom's bungalow to catch the evening news. He would sit on the couch and hold his mom's hand as they watched together. She hardly ever said a word. I know that was very hard for him.

Billy and Ruth Graham spent the last weekend with us in Maine, staying in Mom's bungalow. He spoke at both our winter and summer churches, First Congregational and St. Ann's. It was such a comfort to have him there. He has been very dear to our family through the years, and we are grateful to him.

༄ The very next weekend we flew to Helsinki, Finland, for a mini-summit between George and Mikhail Gorbachev. (Only George would consider a trip to Finland as a "weekend trip.") It was my first flight aboard the brand-new *Air Force One.* I wrote in my diary:

George told me that he couldn't wait for me to see the plane. He said that I wouldn't believe it and I don't. It is tremendous. The President's Suite has two rooms and a bath with a *SHOWER.* A large bedroom with oversized single beds at an angle like a ship's cabin. We can touch hands, but not feet. There is also a two-man desk with pivot chairs, a raised TV set, along with lights and shades that can be controlled from the bed. In GB's study there is a large partners table and a covered couch that would seat five very comfortably. And then there is a conference room down the hall a bit. Other planes this size hold 400 people. This plane holds 93. The galley is five times as big as Doro's kitchen. It is a very grand plane and a joy. We put on our night clothes and slept like babies. George got up and took a shower. I didn't dare for fear that I would soak my hair.

I spent the first day in Finland sight-seeing with Virginia Wein-mann, wife of our ambassador, Jack Weinmann, who later in the administration became Chief of Protocol. She took me to Porvoo, a lovely old town filled with warm and friendly people. Imagine my surprise when I heard someone call out, "How's Millie?" Don't ever underestimate the power of CNN.

That evening we dined in a restaurant while George had dinner with another old friend, Finland's President Koivisto. It was there that I discovered just how expensive everything is in Finland. I had been told that a Big Mac cost $8, a beer $5, and a massage $150. I ordered a delicious meal, trying to go by the lowest price, and it cost $70.

I wrote in my diary other observations of Helsinki:

It is the beginning of fall here, and the trees are beginning to turn right outside our window. Because we have been here on the weekend, we are seeing all the half million people who live here out on the streets. I am beginning to think the native costume is the running suit. Everyone, every age, has one.

The next day the spouses all met at the Koivistos' for tea. Raisa arrived wearing the exact same suit that she had worn for the Welles-ley speech. I think she was sending a message home again. We sat around a round table: Raisa, Mrs. Koivisto, Rebecca Matlock (wife of our ambassador to the Soviet Union, Jack Matlock), Virginia Wein-mann, myself, and several other ladies. Raisa did most of the talking, focusing on the problems that her country was having. You could tell she felt very strongly. From there we went to visit the library at the University of Helsinki, which had as much Russian history as Finnish. Hundreds of people were waiting across the street, and before the bus stopped, Raisa asked me to go greet the people with her. She took my hand and away we went. She made a little speech thanking the people on her behalf and my behalf. I now had a new spokesperson! I was very amused by the whole situation. Raisa could not pass up a crowd without making a little speech, and I was touched she included me.

After the library visit, we went to our separate embassies to freshen up and then Raisa was to host a tea at the Soviet Embassy. She appeared in a much more stylish outfit—it was closed to press and there would be no TV cameras. At the last moment we were told that except for me, all the other ladies we had spent the day with had been uninvited to the tea, including the wife of our host, the President of Finland. It was to be just the two of us and our interpreters. I wasn't sure why Raisa did that.

Although we had just finished lunch, Raisa served a full tea, starting off with both black and red caviar in a small pastry and some sort of smoked fish on toast. We moved into kiwi soufflé (more like a mousse) and a blueberry tart. This was served with a red wine, which both of us drank just enough of to wet our tongues, and a red fruit drink that tasted very much like cranberry juice. She talked at length about their troubles again. She did ask me about how much two pounds of caviar would cost in the United States. I told her that I did not know, that we did not deal in two pounds when it came to caviar, but that I guessed that it would cost around $500. Our interpreter said that she thought that was correct. I told her that George and I both loved caviar, but never felt that we could afford it. She was still very interested in how much things cost. She had no inkling how the free enterprise system worked, nor do I think she understood our work ethic. I asked her about their politics and where their troubles were coming from. She said that people were impatient. They had only one political party, but that within the party there was competition. She said that shortly they were going to have quite a few political parties. I told her that a two-party system worked well, but more parties made it almost impossible to get a consensus. (I confess this is not my field of expertise, but this is what I told her.)

Each visit with Raisa made me like her more and understand her a little better. She clearly loved her country and husband and wanted to be a part of the solution. At times, their customs and traditions seemed so different from ours that I felt we might as well be from different planets; at other times, we were very sympathetic to each other.

Later, when we joined our husbands for their joint press conference, Raisa was back in her famous well-worn suit. Both Presidents seemed relaxed. The communiqué was very clear and united on the issue of Iraq. George came away from the summit thrilled with the results: Now almost all the world was united against Saddam Hussein's invasion.

After we returned from our trip, *Millie's Book* had its official coming-out at the Pierpont Morgan Library in New York City, followed by several weeks of a media blitz. One day I taped all three network morning shows: the "Today" show with Deborah Norville; "Good Morning America" with Joan Lunden; and "The CBS Morning Show" with Paula Zahn. I wrote in my diary: "All three ladies are beautiful blondes and I began to mix them up in my mind. They all three seem chic, stylish, bright and very nice. And they all three asked the same questions."

I also wrote in my diary about two magazine covers Millie and I appeared on: "In both . . . it looks as though I had forgotten to iron my face."

I had a wonderful time writing the book and was hoping sales would be good enough to raise a little money for my literacy foundation. What happened shocked everyone: It made its first appearance at number 1 on *The New York Times* best-seller list. All fall I signed and signed and signed books. My great friend Sally Neblett from Houston designed bookplates that I could autograph, which at least kept me and my staff from having to lug heavy books with us everywhere.

Over the years Millie sold more than 400,000 books and raised more than $1 million for the Barbara Bush Foundation for Family Literacy. Eventually the book came out in paperback and was printed in German and Japanese. Millie found out that being the President's dog had more than one perk. George liked to joke that it just wasn't right: He was President of the United States and his dog made more money than he did!

Also that fall, the very creative nonprofit Children's Literacy Initiative in Philadelphia invited me to read stories aloud on the radio. As a result, we launched "Mrs. Bush's Storytime," beginning with an ABC call-in program with Peter Jennings about literacy. For sixteen weeks, a host of celebrities, cartoon characters, and I read children's books, broadcast on ABC radio stations all over the country. The idea was to get families back to reading together and to spread the message about the importance of reading aloud to your children. The second year, the stories were made available on cassette tapes through Western Publishing Company, and we tucked into each one a how-to pamphlet with hints on reading aloud to your children. I often wondered if anyone listened, but as I write this in the fall of 1993, the fourth year of "Mrs. Bush's Storytime" is soon to begin on Thanksgiving Day and even will be broadcast to Shanghai, China.

Over the years people have told me just how much they enjoyed the stories. I usually ask if they listened with their children. They sometimes say yes, but almost as often would say, "Oh, no. My husband and I listen going to the market on Saturday mornings."

∽ The launchings of *Millie's Book* and "Mrs. Bush's Storytime" were nice beginnings to what otherwise was a difficult fall. For much of the year, George and his team had been working hard to get a budget through Congress that also would include a five-year plan to reduce the deficit. Finally, he almost had a deal with the Democrats when Newt Gingrich, a Republican congressman, got in the middle of it all and the compromise fell through. George agreed to raise taxes *if* the Democrat-controlled Congress would agree to cut spending. As a result, George was clobbered by members of his own party and the media. One New York newspaper ran the headline: READ MY LIPS: I LIED. Ugly. I wrote in my diary:

> Everyone wants to pile on, but I don't worry. George IS doing the right thing. We just have to get the deficit down. I find myself in the funniest mood. I truly feel that George is doing what is responsible and right for the country and to heck with politics. There is a life after the White House and both of us are looking forward to it.

Eventually there was a compromise that seemed to please no one. I really felt it was a disgrace the way Congress—Democrats and Republicans alike—played politics with such an important issue.

George also was wrestling with Congress over a Civil Rights Bill. He did not want to veto the proposed bill, but the wording made quotas a possibility and that was not acceptable to him. George felt strongly about equal opportunity; he did not like imposing quotas. Again, it appeared they had an agreement worked out with Teddy Kennedy, the sponsor of the bill, but then the Democrats broke their commitment. It was apparent they did not want to give George a bill he could sign before the midterm elections, coming up in November.

And always hanging over George's head was the crisis in the Persian Gulf. I wrote in my diary on September 16:

> Over the weekend George talked to François Mitterrand and told him how great it was that he had sent troops to Saudi Arabia. That dreadful man Saddam Hussein had sent troops into the French Embassy and scared their people to death. The more troops we get there from other countries, the happier I am. I love to hear George talk to his foreign friends: *"François, mon ami . . ."*

A wonderful, great thing did happen to George that fall: He got his own dog. Marvin and Margaret gave Ranger, Millie's only male puppy, back to us. George and Ranger had bonded early on, and for months he had been calling Margaret to invite Ranger up for the weekend at Camp David. Then he started suggesting that she bring Ranger over to the White House on Thursday nights so he would be sure to be there in time to leave for Camp the next day. Then he suggested that we return him on Monday morning instead of Sunday night. When he started asking that we keep him until Tuesday, Marvin and Margaret suggested that we keep him at the White House for Marshall, whose dog he really was. I was so glad for George to have that sweet and very amusing dog during these tough times. However, he immediately changed our sleeping habits: Ranger got up at five A.M., an hour before Millie.

But he was worth it. A big, bouncy puppy, he could leap straight up into the air and his handsome face made us laugh. He charged around Camp David in the snow and the rain, and he wandered the White House, knowing no strangers. He loved to curl up by George's side, and was everything in a dog George wanted.

Ranger made so many friends that we suddenly noticed that he was growing by leaps and bounds—out, not up—and George had to send out a memo requesting people *not* to feed Ranger:

IMPORTANT ANNOUNCEMENT
February 6, 1992
THIS IS AN ALL POINTS BULLETIN FROM THE PRESIDENT
SUBJECT: MY DOG "RANGER"

Recently Ranger was put on a weight reduction program. Either that program succeeds or we enter Ranger in the Houston Fat Stock Show as a Prime Hereford.

All offices should take a formal "pledge" that reads as follows:

"WE AGREE NOT TO FEED RANGER. WE WILL NOT GIVE HIM BISCUITS. WE WILL NOT GIVE HIM FOOD OF ANY KIND."

In addition, Ranger's "access" is hereby restricted. He has been told not to wander the corridors without an escort. This applies to the East and West Wings, to the Residence from the 3rd floor to the very, very bottom basement.

Although Ranger will still be permitted to roam at Camp David, the Camp David staff including the Marines, Naval personnel, All Civilians and Kids are specifically instructed to "rat" on anyone seen feeding Ranger.

Ranger has been asked to wear a *"Do not feed me"* badge in addition to his ID.

I will, of course, report on Ranger's fight against obesity. Right now he looks like a blimp, a nice friendly appealing blimp, but a blimp.

We Need Your Help—All hands, please help.
FROM THE PRESIDENT

We also were thrilled that fall when Doro and her two children, Sam and Ellie, moved from Maine to Washington. She got a job she loved at the National Rehabilitation Hospital, a state-of-the-art medical center where exciting things were happening in medicine. We loved having them so close that they could just pop in and check on us.

For me personally, it was an even busier time than usual. Besides campaigning for the midterm elections, I tried to keep up with my other causes and interests, which included both traveling and hosting teas and receptions at the White House. One reception that I especially remember was for the Craniofacial Foundation. This is one of Cher's favorite causes, and she arrived looking smashing. She is so trim and elegant and has the most beautiful complexion. I told someone how great I thought she looked and they said that she has had every kind of plastic surgery known to man. If that is the case, then we all should line up for the knife. She truly looked lovely. The wonderful part was that she knew all the kids by name. Many of these children were so deformed that it was hard to even look at them. She hugged them, held them, and played with them. I believe that Cher got involved with this group after she made the movie *Mask,* about a child with a deformed face.

Another distinct memory came during a trip to New York City, just after I had finished a visit to a day-care center for homeless children. I wrote in my diary:

As we drove up to the hotel, the Waldorf, I could not believe my eyes. There sitting in a wheelchair on the corner of Park Avenue and 50th Street was Jean MacArthur (wife of General Douglas MacArthur). I jumped out of the car to run over to give my dear little friend a kiss and say hello. That darling, chic lady said that she was just out getting some sun and air—as if she was out in the countryside instead of on a busy street corner in NYC. One of my traveling companions said, "Look at Mrs. Bush, kissing a homeless person." Some homeless person. Jean has made the Waldorf Towers her home for many years.

At the end of September we went to New York City for the United Nations General Assembly meetings. The reports coming out of Kuwait of rape and plunder were dreadful. We were very grateful that George's cousins' child, Sandy Clement, was in the United States with her Kuwaiti husband, Charles Haddad, and their five children when Saddam Hussein invaded. There was much hope then that the worldwide show of strength against Iraq and the air embargo would let our troops come home without firing a shot.

While in New York, I met with Queen Noor of Jordan. I wrote in my diary:

She is a glorious-looking person, from a country that is overburdened with problems and has come out on the wrong side of the Iraq problem. They desperately need money for their refugees and it is hard to raise. She started out on her mission by saying that we must remain friends. I agreed. Then she talked about how we had made mistakes and that this was an Arab problem that must be solved by Arabs. I explained to her (which she already knew) that we had been invited into the region, as were 23 or 24 other countries, by Arabs. I also explained to her that if Jordan had been invaded we would have come to their aid also. She talked a lot about Israel and the weapons that they had that were illegal. I feel very sorry for their country, but must admit I was very glad to see the beautiful creature go. I like her so much, but truly feel that they are very wrong. The world can no longer sit back and watch one country, a member nation in the United Nations, invade and take over another, also a member state.

George spoke very movingly at the General Assembly and afterward we stood in a receiving line with Jim Baker and greeted several hundred people. We saw Eduard Shevardnadze from the USSR; our old friend Richard Akwei from Ghana, whom we knew both during our UN and China years; Ambassador Bishara from Kuwait; a delegate from Albania, which I mention because I don't believe that I had ever met an Albanian before, much less touched one; and the representative from North Korea, who looked George directly in the eye and said that he had listened carefully to George when he spoke about both Koreas being in the United Nations and he would pass his message on to Pyongyang.

During those several days George started early in the morning and went late into the night having bilateral meetings with other leaders. It took a tremendous amount of work to continue building, and then maintain, the coalition forming against Saddam Hussein.

The next night I had the great privilege of attending the opening of the Metropolitan Opera, with Plácido Domingo singing the leading tenor role. It truly was a glamorous evening:

The other honored guests were Prince Rainier and Prince Albert. The former was a dear, gentle man and the latter was the same. Very polite and kind. The Prince and I sat together the whole time and the minute the lights went out, the Prince went out. His head fell against his chest and he very quietly snoozed, awakening only when the audience clapped or his own snoring awakened him. Then he would clap away, saying, "What glorious tones. How marvelous, etc." as though he had heard it all.

I had another brush with royalty in early October when Princess Diana, in the States to raise money for several charities, came for tea. Just like when Michael Jackson came, I couldn't believe the number of staff who turned out to stare. And they had plenty to stare at. She is absolutely lovely-looking, and also bright and funny.

Margaret and Marvin had attended a gala dinner with her, and our dear friend Jenny Acland, wife of the British ambassador, put Marvin next to the Princess. They had great fun together, teasing and laughing, until Jenny asked Marvin to please invite the Princess to dance. He refused, saying that he had injured knees. All those years at dancing school gone to waste! Princess Diana told me at the tea—with a twinkle in her eye—that Marvin had behaved disgracefully. George later sent her a photo from that evening, which she signed for Marvin and sent back. He displays it with pride.

ʙ In early October, the budget crisis boiled over when both the Democrats and Republicans voted down the budget that had been worked on for months. George had granted a budget extension the week before but said he wouldn't grant another. So, without a budget, he was forced to shut down the federal government. Only people who were considered essential personnel could work, and no one was allowed to volunteer their time. The entire White House staff was let off except those crucial to the security of the government. And all the poor tourists who had come to Washington found the doors locked at the museums and monuments.

During the shutdown, we had the swearing-in ceremony for

David Souter to the Supreme Court with 250 of his best friends. Standing in the receiving line, both George and I were impressed by the true affection people felt for David, and he for them. He gave us a very modest thank-you. I wish I could remember exactly what he said, but it was something like, "I will never be able to thank you all, but I can promise that I will pass it on to someone else." He said it so beautifully, slowly and with real feeling. We had no refreshments because we had no staff, but everyone seemed to understand.

During all this I was working hard for Republican candidates running in the midterm election. Without counting the days, I know I slept more nights in a hotel room than in my own bed, spending day after day on the road. I went from Connecticut to Texas to California, all the way to Hawaii, back to California, to Maine, to Florida, to Illinois, to Ohio, Kentucky, Georgia, back to Texas and on and on.

The funniest thing—at least we thought it was funny—happened to Jean Becker on the Hawaii trip. She and Sondra Haley were deputy press secretaries in my office and also advanced almost all my trips. They always had great stories of the things that happened to them on the road.

Jean was standing in a phone booth in Hawaii trying to talk to the office back in Washington when a pickup truck with a bunch of guys pulled up. They were playing the radio so loud Jean couldn't hear, so she politely asked them to please turn it down. A few minutes later Jean heard a funny noise, turned around, and one of the men was relieving himself on the side of the phone booth. She hung up and found another phone down the road. So much for the glamorous life of traveling.

We were traveling so much we didn't know where we were, and neither did anyone else. While I was in Maine I got a phone call from Jody Bush, my sister-in-law. She was calling from the cabana by the White House pool to find out if she could go for a swim. I said certainly—but where in the world did she think I was? It turned out she thought I was upstairs in the White House.

That reminds me of the great luxury of the White House operators. Besides being the world's nicest women, they can find anybody, anywhere, any time. But you had to be careful—you never knew where the person was you were calling. Once when George asked them to find Carla Hills, the U.S. Trade Representative, they woke her up in a Switzerland hotel room. I was in Houston campaigning when the phone rang at five-thirty in the morning and I heard that much beloved voice say, "How's the big guy?" I answered, "George Bush, I don't know how your dog is, nor do I know where you are, but I am in Houston, Texas, and it's only five-thirty!" He said, "Oh, my gosh, I thought you were in Washington. I'm in Minnesota."

The moral of that story is that we were working too hard *and* the White House switchboard could find us anyplace.

While on a campaign swing in Dallas, George W. asked me to go to the Institute for Aerobics Research Gala. Before I went, I told George (the father, not the son) that I was going to tell them that I bet I was the first speaker they ever had whose body was made up of 33 1/3 percent fat. He bet me I wouldn't say it. I did, and there was sort of a stunned silence and then a large laugh. It was the leanest, trimmest, healthiest group I had ever seen.

A great bonus that night was seeing George and Laura's twins dressed up for their school's Halloween Carnival. I wrote in my diary:

Jenna went as Miss Halloween and looked so beautiful despite the fact that she had skeleton earrings and all sorts of ugly things on her costume. Barbara had on an all-green body suit and was covered with purple balloons—she went as grapes and won third prize. Both girls were heavily made up and I could see shades of things to come. They are truly going to be great beauties!

Another campaign stop was Portland, Oregon, which is one of the most beautiful cities in America and home to some of the finest, nicest people. Unfortunately it also seems to be the home training base for the state-of-the-art protesters. I went out to do a fund-raising breakfast for our friend Mark Hatfield, who was in a battle for his Senate seat. When Mark got up to speak, two protesters—one after the other in different parts of the room—started screaming very ugly things, making it impossible for Mark to be heard. The audience immediately stood and clapped and clapped until the protesters were removed kicking and yelling from the room. Antoinette Hatfield, Mark's wife and a great friend, is always so positive. Her response to all this was: "Look at it this way, Bar. They both paid to get in and the campaign can use the money."

In 1992 I went to Portland to do a fund-raising dinner for George. On the way to the hotel we passed some men and women in black body suits with masks on their faces. Some were holding signs that said: KILL THE PRESIDENT. Since George was elsewhere, that didn't bother me too much until I spotted a large poster that had a familiar-looking white-headed cartoon character with the words OFF WITH HER HEAD written in bold black letters. After the speeches had been given but before the dessert, the Secret Service strongly suggested we leave because of a bomb threat. We drove past a large crowd of protesters being held off by mounted police. By the time we got to the airport we heard via car radio that seventeen people had been arrested and some people slightly hurt in the fray.

Unfortunately, being the target of such things is a part of public life, but I'm not sure you ever get used to it. On a similar note, a friend sent me an article in which Joan Rivers quoted me as saying the most vulgar, disgusting thing I had ever read. When I let George see it, he said, "When did you talk to Joan Rivers, Bar?" He was just teasing, because he knew I had not talked to her at all. I distinctly remember forgetting what she said I said, but it was so ugly. Public life!

⟅⟆ I stopped campaigning long enough in October to fly to Ottawa, Canada for the International Conference on Literacy and Corrections. Mila Mulroney introduced me, and I gave a speech that Susan Green, the wonderful, talented, funny woman (and closet Democrat) who had written my speeches for years, had worked on really hard. We all agreed that it did no good to keep men and women in prison and send them out having learned only how to be better criminals. I kicked off the conference, got back in the car, and flew home. I don't think I ever got used to in-and-out trips like that. On this particular day, I was home in time to have a 2:30 P.M. reception for the Victory Awards, which were sponsored by National Rehabilitation Hospital. Every year they honor people who have demonstrated great courage in the face of adversity.

A few weeks later we hosted the presentation of the Congressional Gold Medal to Andrew Wyeth in the Roosevelt Room. It was such a treat. He is a great painter and comes from such an amazing family— his dad, N. C. Wyeth; his son Jamie Wyeth, who designed his father's medal; and his sister, Wyeth Hurd, who painted Pat Nixon; all of whom are outstanding artists. His sons called him Daddy and kissed him, and I couldn't help but think that if more people did that, we'd have fewer problems.

 ⌒ Unfortunately, these bright spots were rare. I had trouble reading the papers, so was thrilled to find Ken Follett's *Pillars of the Earth*. George also enjoyed it—although he didn't give up reading the papers.

I wrote in my diary on October 24:

Discouraging week for G.B. The budget talks have folded. The Civil Rights Bill had to be vetoed and the papers this morning are saying that "Republicans are running, not walking away from" George. He has worked so hard and he is right. It certainly is hard. Two more weeks until the election and G. says that it will get worse, not better.

I am having to work on myself to not be bitter about those members of Congress who are acting gutless, and there are so many on both sides of the aisle. What I should be thinking about are those valiant few, like Bob Dole and Bob Michel, Al Simpson, Orrin Hatch, Strom Thurmond and really so many more, who are helping George. I also have to remember that he will have to work with them all again.

. . . George has just called from Hawaii, where he was campaigning and attending a summit of 12 Pacific Island nations. It is 8 a.m. there and somebody has told him about a nice article in *The Washington Post* by Donnie Radcliffe about me. How kind of him and how kind of her. He says that his trip is going well, that his budget has passed the House and will get through the Senate. Amazing! Finally!

Just before the election I joined the cabinet wives for lunch. I think we really needed each other that day. I wrote in my diary:

Kath Darman had been feeling very low and Nancy Sununu should have been for the press had been beating both these women's husbands up for a fare-thee-well. I had heard rumors going around that I was pushing George to get rid of both of these men. As Sam LeBlond would say: *NOT!* Tom DeFrank of *Newsweek* called Anna Perez and told her that he was going to go with that story and just wanted to verify it. I was so grateful to him for calling that I called him back myself and told him how much I admired both men and that I thought George was well served by his staff. For a reporter to check on a story is a pretty rare thing these days. *Newsweek* did not print that story.

There are always some mischief-makers in Washington who are trying to make trouble for reasons known only to themselves. Patty Presock (George's wonderful assistant) told me that two masked/voice-altered people appeared on Pat Robertson's program who claimed to be staff members fearful of reprisals who said that George was being taken over by liberals. That started rumors about just who they were, and that wasn't healthy. I believe that they were two recently fired staff members, but that doesn't matter. They didn't have the courage to let their faces show. They should not have been given air time.

In all honesty, George's administration was freer of rumors than most. Gossip and rumors are the food that Washington insiders live and thrive on. When reading a newspaper, you should suspect it's rumor if it reads something like this: "A high White House official, who spoke with the agreement that he would not be named, said . . ."; or, "A source close to the President, who spoke off the record, said . . ." George refused to give off-the-record interviews, which did not always endear him to the press. I remember once when James Reston of *The New York Times* canceled an interview because George wouldn't do it "off the record." Many people plant leaks to get the word out or to send up a trial balloon to get public reaction. Some people do it feeling they then can get better press for themselves. That just wasn't George's style.

⤎ On my final campaign swing, I stopped in Salt Lake City for Genevieve Atwood, a bright, enthusiastic candidate for Congress who in her rally speech gave an unusual endorsement for George. She said that she was for George Bush "right down to his underwear." I don't think that is why she lost, but she did.

My staff and I were so exhausted when we finally got home November 1 that we cheered when the plane landed at Andrews Air Force Base. We had campaigned for thirty-three candidates in twenty states and twenty-nine cities. I wrote in my diary the next day:

I have just talked to Peggy (my personal aide) and she is feeling blue. I know the feeling. The press is so anti the GOP this morning. I think the hardest part of campaigning is the waiting. Now people need to get out the vote. They don't need me anymore, so I invited the children to come for dinner tonight. Andy (Stewart) will come for lunch. I give a literacy speech tomorrow and then fly to Texas to meet up with George and vote on Tuesday.

George and I went to rallies in Tyler and Waco, Texas, with Clayton and Modesta Williams. He was running for governor against Ann Richards and despite all the bad publicity he got, I liked him.

Election Day arrived and I sunk myself into some new reading thanks to Kath Darman. She had discovered that Rosamunde Pilcher, author of *The Shell Seekers* and *September,* had written several books before these best-sellers and they were now out in paperback. They saved my life and I read away. I just could not watch the news.

The election was something of a downer. We lost governorships in Texas, Florida, Nebraska, Rhode Island, and Kansas. We were thrilled when John Engler won Michigan; Jim Edgar, Illinois; Bill Weld, Massachusetts; Pete Wilson, California; and George Voinovich, Ohio. We lost Rudy Boschwitz's Senate seat in Minnesota, but Mark Hatfield won his seat easily in Oregon. All in all, it probably wasn't as bad as it felt. On an off-election year, the party who holds the White House traditionally loses twenty-four seats. We lost eight in the House, one in the Senate, and came out even on the governors' races. So it was not the wipeout that we kept reading and hearing about. My own track record was not great: twenty-three lost; ten won. While I sat and felt badly for everyone, George, naturally, was on the phone calling winners and losers alike.

꩜ It had been an exhausting two months since Labor Day, but certainly there was no time to rest. George signed two major pieces of legislation in November. The first was the Head Start Bill, which gave this program its biggest boost since it had been founded in LBJ's administration twenty-five years earlier. George's goal was eventually to make Head Start—which gives low-income and at-risk children a running start at a good education—available to every eligible child.

And he signed the landmark Clean Air Act, the first overhaul of that program since it was passed in 1970. He specifically targeted urban smog; acid rain; and cancer-causing emissions. Getting the bill through Congress had required some tricky negotiating between business interests and environmentalists. Bill Reilly, George's head of the Environmental Protection Agency, John Sununu, and many others had done a great job.

Then, on November 16, we left on one of the most important overseas trips we took during George's presidency. Before coming home, we would visit six countries; George would join other world leaders for a historic summit in Paris; he would meet face-to-face with a man who long had been considered an enemy of our country; and most important, we would have our best Thanksgiving Day ever.

I wrote in my diary the first day, as we headed for Czechoslovakia:

The trip over takes 8 hours and 15 minutes with a 6-hour time change. George has travel down to an art. We, of course, fly at night so that he will not miss a day's work. Now with this beautiful new plane it is so easy. (Before we left) George called at 4:30 and suggested a 6 p.m. dinner at the house. So smart, because if you wait until the plane, it takes at least an hour before they can get everyone settled and served after takeoff. So the ushers called Pierre (Chambrin) in for a light supper of eggs and bacon, a favorite of George's. What a laugh. We had the softest eggs in a wonderful puff pastry, bacon, and a side plate of smoked turkey and salsa. Pierre does not know light, but he does know good!

The ambassador's residence in Czechoslovakia, where we stayed, was a beautiful, graceful home with a fascinating history. It had been built in 1928 by a member of a very old wealthy philanthropic family, the Petscheks, whose members were spread all over Europe. In 1938 the family told the household staff they were going out to the country for a few days. They never came back. Other members of this great family did the same thing on the same day, leaving other European capitals. Imagine my surprise to find that my darling friend in Washington, Annelise FitzGerald, whose husband, William, succeeded Dick Moore as ambassador to Ireland, was one of those who left. She, her mother, and sisters escaped through England, Portugal, Argentina, Cuba, and finally New York City, where the entire family rendezvoused. Her dad came through Canada. Her aunt and uncle had built the residence we were staying in. At various times the house had been owned by the Nazis, Czechs, Communists, and now the United States, who obtained the house for debts owed us. And yet it still retained needlepoint pillows and other furnishings from the day the owners walked out.

The U.S. Ambassador was our old friend Shirley Temple Black, who with her husband, Charlie, worked as a very effective team for the United States.

Olga and Vaclav Havel met our plane, and she and I immediately went to visit a hospital for mentally retarded children. It was a grim institution and had "that" smell. The directress said they were hoping to enlarge the already huge place, and Olga spoke up immediately and said: "Oh, no. We want smaller institutions, more family atmosphere." In the car Olga told me that the directress was from the Communist regime, as are so many others, and that they will have to learn the new ways. Change is hard. She also told me that 80 percent of the women were in the work force and they would like to see that lowered. Like us, they worried about families staying together.

We stopped at a school, where the children came in just for the visit since it was a Saturday, and then we walked across the Charles Bridge, built of wood in the twelfth century and then rebuilt of stone in the fourteenth century. The view of Prague was spectacular. In fact, it was the best place to see the city, because close up, everything seemed dingy, gray, peeling, and crumbling. At one time during the day we were in the car with the Havels and passed the railroad station. George asked Vaclav how the railroads were, and Vaclav's answer will remain with me forever: "Like everything else in the country, George, old."

Later that day, we went to Wenceslas Square to celebrate the one-year anniversary of "The Velvet Revolution," so called because not a shot was fired. I wrote in my diary:

No words can describe this ceremony. There were one million people there all waving American and Czech flags. It was on this place that the revolution took place a year ago. Vaclav spoke and then George spoke. The response was overwhelming. . . . After the speech we walked out into the crowd to shake hands and then walked up on an unprotected platform to sing "We Shall Overcome," which has become the theme song for freedom around the world. It was so moving. I could not believe the crowd and the emotional feeling.

En route to Paris, we made a brief stop in Germany to visit the Kohls. When we got into a helicopter and flew over German forests and the Rhine River Valley, I couldn't help but think that it is still the cleanest country I have ever seen. I wrote:

The Kohls took us to Ludwigshafen, their home, where we indulged in the best and biggest meal anyone has ever eaten. It is so flattering to be taken to one's private home. The food was good, but the conversation was better. . . . Helmut agrees with George: We cannot allow naked aggression. He felt that Saddam Hussein does not understand the strength we have in Saudi Arabia and he felt people should tell him this. George felt that Saddam should be told himself and the message should not be relayed by one of his people. It is known that he has shot people who have told him things he does not want to hear. He is crazy. There was some discussion that he watches CNN and is getting a distorted picture of what our people are thinking at home. CNN, of course, shows the dissidents and not the supporters. The polls all show overwhelming support of George. Half the people who don't support him just think he isn't doing enough. I'd hate to be president!

On the way there Hannelore told me the problems of unification of the two Germanys. East Germany has no telephones (12 percent have phones), very bad roads, no idea of competition, no cars (now that they can buy a car, they don't know how to drive), no hospital beds, no social security, no health insurance and on and on. She was not discouraged, feeling that they can solve their problems.

We flew on to Paris, where George went to dinner with François Mitterrand and I had a cozy dinner with three dear friends: Susan Baker and our most able ambassador and his wife, Walter and Taitsie Curley. (I should note that Taitsie went by her given name, Mary, while living in France. Since our last two ambassadors' wives' names were Bootsie and Honey, she thought she'd make it easier for the French.)

We were to be in Paris for three days for the Conference on Security and Cooperation in Europe. It was a historic meeting of all the leaders of Europe and the United States and Canada, and many people considered it the official end of the Cold War.

The first day the spouses had a rather eventful lunch at the Trianon Palace:

It was a large lunch, and many wives of heads of state, heads of governments and international organizations were there. I was on Danielle's (Mitterrand) right; Poul Schluter's ballet dancer new wife was on her left. At the ends of the table sat Mila Mulroney and the directress of Le Grand Trianon, Madame Simone Hoog. Across from me were Hannelore Kohl, Mrs. Vassiliou from Cyprus and Raisa Gorbachev. The latter looked just fine. She did not take the tour and arrived a little late for the lunch.

The press came in before lunch with little or no discipline and in the shoving and pushing, one photographer's camera swung and hit Hannelore Kohl in the neck and she had to leave the lunch. We all worried about her.

The lunch itself was quite funny. Raisa made quite a few toasts. It seemed a little strange because no one else made a toast. (Obviously a difference in customs again.) Later, teasing, I told Mila that it was like an old Russian movie and it began to look like she was trying to drink us under the table. I heard Mrs. G. tell Mila that she had seen all the troubles that they are having in Canada with Indians and French-speaking people, etc. After she went on for quite a while about all the ills of Canada, to save my friend I said that the television often showed the controversy and very rarely the good. Mrs. G. said that they had a saying in their country, "Where there's smoke there's fire." I said that we also had the same saying, but that sometimes the press made it into a forest fire when it was only a bonfire. She countered with, "There must be something there." Danielle Mitterrand said that sometimes you wondered if the press wanted to put out the fire or make it into something bigger. When Mrs. G. wanted to speak, she would interrupt Mila, who was talking to Anne Marie Schluter, and say, "Mila, excuse me, I'm talking," and then give another toast or start talking. She had a very good interpreter who spoke both French and English and, of course, Russian. Danielle Mitterrand, who is innately polite, realized that her luncheon was getting out of hand, and so she told a slightly risqué story to Mila and the rest of us. I watched Raisa's face as her interpreter struggled to explain the story to her. As it was a play on words, I guess it was difficult. We were all laughing and Raisa never cracked a smile. I was so proud of Mila. She never told Raisa that she had seen all *their* troubles on the tube. We all have and, even if the press is exaggerating, they are dreadful.

We were going to have one night off in Paris, and George asked Walter Curley if just the four of us could go out to a Paris restaurant and have dinner. Walter later told us that the Secret Service and the

Paris police laughed at him when he suggested different places. If we had dinner on the river in a boat, they would have to close five bridges. The Eiffel Tower restaurant could be done, but we would have to walk up and down, and so on. In the end, George had President Gorbachev for a working dinner.

The next day the spouses went to see the magnificent Picasso exhibit. I wrote in my diary:

> Neither Hannelore Kohl nor Raisa came. We have heard that the former hurt her second vertebra. The latter said that "She had seen a Picasso show before." We all had, but it was like visiting old friends—you always notice or learn something new *AND* our hostess had invited us. It was a fascinating tour. I was amused by Anna Perez, who had advanced the exhibit. The press was set up in strategic places around the museum for photo ops. Anna sidled up to me at one time and said when you get to the next room, just walk on through. *DO NOT STOP* and talk to the press. Evidently there were some pretty graphic pictures on the wall where they wanted me to stop.

The politics taking place while we were in Paris were almost unbelievable. For example, the French Premier, Michel Rocard, won a confidence test by just four votes. The very next day, Mrs. Rocard hosted a luncheon for the delegate spouses, which would have been very awkward if her husband had been ousted the night before.

But the major political storm was in England, where Margaret Thatcher—while attending the meeting in Paris—was in a fight for her political life. She also was facing a confidence vote that she had to win by a majority of votes plus 15 percent. She fell short by five votes of winning on the first ballot, so now we had to wait until the next week to see what would happen. She must have felt lonely away from her family at this difficult time, given this terrible insult by her own party. She had lost support mainly because of her poll tax and her opposition to a unified Europe.

On Tuesday night, President Mitterrand hosted everyone at a dinner at Versailles Palace. I wrote:

> The arrival at Versailles was so beautiful. The palace was lit from top to bottom and the drive was lined with soldiers. The minute we got there we ran into Margaret. She is a gutsy woman. I gave her a big hug and told her that we had been waiting all day for the news. She said, "Not to worry," and

went on to say that she'd get it on the second ballot. George and I took Margaret by the arm and ran the gamut of the press. The first person I saw after we went through the receiving line in the Hall of Crusades was Hannelore Kohl in a neck brace. She had been hurt.

After a short reception we were led into the Opera Hall, where we saw a very short selection from three ballets. The theater was exquisite. I sat next to George and President Gorbachev. Walt Curley said that he counted 520 seats. It seemed hard to believe. There were three balconies, one-person deep, I'd say. It was so nice.

Then we were led into the Coronation Hall, which was glorious, and had a refreshment and an opportunity to "wash our hands." (Stylish port-a-cans were brought in for the occasion.)

And then we went into the Hall of Mirrors, where I sat next to President Mitterrand and President Gorbachev. Thank heavens that I had Daisy Richardson to interpret for me. Daisy is married to a foreign service officer. She was born in Poland and speaks some Russian, beautiful French and, of course, English. President Gorbachev's interpreter spoke only Russian and French. We were seated at a long, long table that held 200 people with mirrors lining all the walls. They reflected chandeliers, the candelabras and the beautiful flowers. We were all in our very grandest gowns and it was the most glamorous evening—a fairy tale evening. George sat across from me and next to Danielle and Raisa. I noticed several times during the evening Raisa and Mikhail raising their glasses to each other and exchanging affectionate glances.

The next day, after the historic signing of the CSCE treaty calling for the reduction of conventional weapons in Europe, we went on to Jeddah, Saudi Arabia, where we were met on arrival by a very gracious King Fahd.

While George had a men-only working dinner, I went to the Royal Palace for dinner with Princess Jawhara. It was a fascinating evening and gave the Americans a glimpse of the Arab culture:

The palaces are made of marble, they look well made and are very clean. We arrived at the Palace and there was a screen at the door—thus preventing the men from seeing the ladies. Princess Jawhara was inside the door to greet me and introduced me to several of her sisters and sisters-in-law and one chubby eleven-year-old niece dressed in a long elaborate gown. The Princess is a pretty lady with black hair and eyes . . . she had on a beautiful silk dress with a beaded jacket and the darndest pearl necklace and bracelets with diamond and emerald clasps. They were so exquisite and beautiful. We went into a large hall whose walls were lined with chairs. I stood and shook hands with every guest, 400 ladies. The first through the line were the King's sisters. They all looked like him and wore a black net or veil pulled tightly over their hair and several had covered faces. They all had on fabulous gowns and the most beautiful jewelry. Margaret Tutwiler* whispered to me that now we know who buys all that beautiful jewelry that we see in stylish ladies' magazines. There were many young women who were great beauties. Almost all the Arab ladies were related in some way. I had been well coached, and so I knew I was to drink the Arab coffee, which is slightly medicinal in flavor and quite pale, maybe weak is a better word. I rather liked it. It comes in a tiny little cup, you drink it down, shake your cup from side to side and it is picked up. After the receiving line, the Princess and I sat and talked through an interpreter for a few minutes and then many of the women were led up to sit, talk and tell me what they do. And they do a lot. During the last 30 years the Arabs have started to educate their women. Quite a few of the women I met were married before they started college and got their doctorates. I met medical doctors, many university professors and some ladies who have formed a group to do good works (an Arab Junior or Service League?). They are very proud of their latest project, which is taking care of and working with Down's Syndrome children. Her Highness at one time leaned over and squirted my hand with scent that is pure essence and lingers on through many washings. She also gave me a great malachite and gold house. When I opened the double doors I found a lovely little working clock. This beautiful clock will be in the George Bush Library for all to admire. We did not go into dinner until 11 o'clock. The food was unbelievable and delicious. After dinner we retired back to the same room, where the coffee and incense came in again. I waved the incense towards me as is the custom and then to my shock my skirt was lifted slightly and the whole incense burner was tucked under my skirt. I was panicked. I was sure that my brand-new Scaasi gown was going to go up in flames and I with it! It was an evening never to be forgotten by me or any of the Americans who were lucky enough to be there. Besides the women who were traveling with us there were the wives of American businessmen and foreign service officers, mostly from the Consulate corps.

* Margaret was Jim Baker's spokesperson and usually attended working dinners, but could not, since she was a woman, so she came with me. There was "discrimination" at our dinner also: My Secret Service agents were left outside; a woman agent had to be brought in.

The whole evening did remind me that we have a lot of learning to do about the customs of our foreign friends and they about us.

Thanksgiving Day, 1990—The best we ever had.

Our day in the desert with our men and women in the military was a highlight of George's presidency. What a privilege it was for us to share their Thanksgiving Day.

That morning we slept until 6:45 and then had to race for a 7:35 departure from the guest palace. Our first stop was the air base in Dhahran, where we visited with the U.S. and Allied troops. George spoke, and then we plunged out into the crowd while somebody tried to keep order. Dhahran was the hottest stop. Every single serviceman and servicewoman seemed to have a camera. I was asked to sign pictures of their wives, husbands, babies, and dogs. We posed for as many pictures as possible and hugged and clasped hands.

We took a chopper to the Army Tactical Location, and repeated the speech and plunge. This time we also went through the chow line and got a Thanksgiving plate, which we then ate at two different tables with darling young people. A woman named Lisa at my table told me that her husband had gone last year to Panama and now it was her turn. They were so very young.

We choppered out to the U.S.S. *Nassau* for a short and very moving Thanksgiving Day service on the stern of the ship. We worked the crowd as best we could. The men were hanging from the rafters, and those on the upper deck were too far away to talk to.

Our final stop was the Marine Tactical Location, where we also saw the Seabees and the Brits. The spirit was amazing, and we spent quite a little time there.

Our guide for the day was General Norman Schwarzkopf, an amusing, big bear of a man. He was an expert on the Middle East and understood the customs of the Arab world. He was very deft at avoiding political land mines as well as military ones. He exuded confidence that day and expressed gratitude to George about having all they needed to get the job done, instead of having "his hands tied behind his back" as they did in Vietnam.

Flying over those miles and miles of desert we occasionally saw tracks that were made by trucks. We did see some roads that were bulldozed out of the sand. We also saw patches that were from underground water, and as the winter season comes on, they become boggy and impassable for cars and tanks. But for the most part you can drive anywhere in the desert. Every now and then we would fly over a pipeline that you can clearly see from the air. That worried me, as it seemed so easy for the Iraqis to blow up. The General told me not to worry, that our air power was so superior. We saw an occasional Bedouin tent, and if we looked hard, we could see camels in a two-mile radius of the tent. The camels dig down and find some root, and therefore graze in the sand. The General told me that every inch of the desert belonged to someone. Amazing.

The only disappointment of the day was that we learned Margaret Thatcher had resigned. This was quite a blow to us, although we were prepared for that possibility. Margaret had been such a rock. George called her from our last stop to express his regrets. After a hard fight, John Major from Margaret's Conservative party beat Michael Heseltine and became the new Prime Minister.

I hated leaving those brave men and women in the desert, and George and I both were thrilled when they got a special treat in December: a visit from none other than Bob Hope. At age eighty-eight, it was quite a feat that this remarkable man put together yet another USO show for American servicemen and servicewomen abroad at Christmas. George and I love Bob and Dolores, and they have been more than kind to us over the years.

∽ We went on to Egypt, showering on the plane to get rid of some of the sand and dust. While there, I visited the Egyptian Museum with a dear friend from our days at the United Nations, Eglal Abdel-Meguid, whose husband was now the Foreign Minister. Suzanne Mubarak, who has worked so hard raising money for neighborhood libraries, took me to visit the Children's Library of Cairo. I wrote about my observations of this great city:

Cairo matches Prague when it comes to pollution. And Cairo is the only city that I have ever seen where the buildings seem to be crumbling from the top down. They have added a new overpass for cars, and as you drive over the city it is dreadful to see the tops of beautiful old houses crumbling. Our friends Sadri and Katy (Prince Sadruddin Aga Khan and his wife, Princess

Katherine) told me a story of a friend of theirs who lives in an old restored house. She was sitting with her mother when they heard the most terrible sound. They thought that a bomb had been thrown. Then the air filled with dust and covered everything. They ran choking out on their balcony to see that the house next door had literally fallen down and was gone. No bomb at all, it just fell.

. . . As Suzanne and I were driving past all those crumbling houses, she said: "I don't know what happened to us, Barbara. Once we were the leaders of the world and look at us today."

She also pointed out to me that every other person we saw had a baby in their arms. She told me that they cannot get their people to cut the birth rate. Katy told me that Cairo was a city built for 1 million people and now 13 million live there. Katy was born in Cairo, and she and Sadri have a lovely old house in the old district that they have restored. Such a beautiful, old, crumbling city. The people look amazingly happy when you consider all their problems.

On the way back to the States, we made a nonscheduled stop in Geneva, where George was going to talk with President Assad of Syria. It was a controversial move on George's part. The papers were full of stories of the Israelis being upset by the visit, but George felt he must try for peace in every way he could. I wrote of Assad: "He looks like a warm friendly man for such a villain."

We got home very early in the morning on Saturday, November 24, and after a restful weekend, took a quick, marvelous trip to Mexico to visit with Carlos and Cecilia Salinas and their family. Carlos truly has been a great president for a country that has so many problems. I was shocked when Carlos told George that because of terrible pollution—a problem he is vigorously fighting—the children of Mexico City paint the sky gray, not blue, and without stars, which they've never seen.

Jeb and his family and George and I had a lovely visit with them in their family home in Monterrey, and they once spent an evening with us at Camp David, where Colu and her sister Lucilla joined us. At one time during the evening one of those very shy, quiet young women looked right at Carlos and said that she wanted him to know that he made them once again proud to be of Mexican heritage. It was said with such sincerity and feeling that I know Carlos was pleased and touched.

In December I plunged myself into getting ready for our second Christmas in the White House, but it wasn't so easy with the Iraq situation dominating everything:

December 2—This has been some week. Needless to say, the whole time, before, during, and since we returned from Mexico, has been spent worrying and thinking about Desert Shield and our troops there. Thursday the U.N. had their vote and they have given permission for any means to get Saddam Hussein out of Kuwait after January 15th. Then on Friday, George announced that he would meet with the Iraqi Foreign Minister in Washington and Jim Baker would meet with Saddam Hussein in Baghdad afterwards. This is not to negotiate, but to be sure that Saddam understands that we mean it and that we have the ability to wipe them out. The papers are full of urging for the latter move . . . the U.N. vote will make it much easier for George to deal with Saddam Hussein. As often is the case, the rest of the world backs George more than our own (Congress) or press. The House and the Senate have been having hearings. Many of the Congress members have plenty of criticism, but no solutions. We awakened this morning to Sam Nunn saying something like, "Of course, I am for stopping Saddam Hussein, just not in this fashion." We waited, but no solutions followed. Incidentally, I was amused to see that Sam resigned from Burning Tree Club because they have no female members, and I was told he also has changed his opinion on abortion. Guess who is running for president!

December 5—The Congress is hearing all sorts of witnesses on the Iraq situation. They are rapidly making it impossible for us to get Saddam to believe that we are serious. Oh, God, I feel sorry for George. Meanwhile Kuwaitis are being raped and plundered right and left.

December 15—Although we have done a million things this week the Iraq problem is still foremost in our minds. All the American hostages were released this week and we closed our embassy in Kuwait.

Many people are criticizing and prophesying that it will be a bloody war. There are stories about 50 thousand body bags that will be needed to bring our military home. This is very tough on the families that are left at home.

The message has come back . . . Saddam says that the first moment he can meet with Jim Baker is January 12th. He wants to get closer to the U.N. deadline and then who knows what shenanigans he will come up with? In a press conference yesterday George said that he found it difficult to believe that Saddam couldn't meet with Jim Baker for two hours when he met with people like Muhammad Ali, John Connally, Ted Heath and Ramsey Clark on the spur of the moment. Quite a few people let themselves be used by Saddam, but I did not expect it of John Connally, a fine former governor of Texas, who in contradiction to U.S. policy went to Iraq with (Houston businessman) Oscar Wyatt. He must have felt silly when he got there to find that it had already been announced that the hostages would be freed. He and Oscar brought back a half-empty plane of hostages and took credit. I could believe anything of Oscar Wyatt, but I found it hard to believe that John Connally would crassly put financial gain above honor. [I want to add here that we love John's wife, Nellie, and George had great respect for John when he was governor of Texas. George was very disappointed when he made the trip with Oscar, who had business dealings in Iraq.]

Amazingly enough, life went on. The Christmas season was fast upon us and we made all the usual calls on hospitals and schools, had all the Christmas parties, and took presents to Toys for Tots. This is one of my favorite programs. Marines collect new toys for underprivileged children and see that they are delivered. I went to help pack toys, but mostly to help get the word out that they were desperate for more new toys, plastic bags for packing, and volunteers. If you are reading this near Christmas, I hope you will remember the Toys for Tots program in your hometown.

Earlier in the month we also had hosted the reception for the annual Kennedy Center Honors. This year they honored Jule Styne, Katharine Hepburn, Dizzy Gillespie, Risë Stevens, and Billy Wilder. All were great stars, but Katharine Hepburn got the most attention for a lot of reasons. First, she is a great actress; second, she is slightly eccentric. She came to this black-tie event in a black turtleneck, a black trench coat, black pants, a white scarf, and black sneakers. Her marvelous hair was piled on top of her head in a rather helter-skelter fashion that was beguiling. She seemed feisty and immediately tweaked George on his antiabortion position. She allowed as how she wondered why she had come. Then having said that, at the awards ceremony itself at the Kennedy Center, she seemed very moved by her tribute, which showed scenes of her with Cary Grant, Henry Fonda, and Spencer Tracy, the love of her life. She stood with tears in her eyes and said, leaning over the balcony, "I never saw that scene with Spence before. They were all remarkable actors. I was lucky." She was lucky—*and* she was good. I was amused to see that after the intermission was over, she started back to her box and by mistake took the wrong door and ended up one box away. Instead of going back out into the hallway to come through the right door, she just climbed over the railing.

We also entertained visitors from England. The new Prime Minister of Great Britain, John Major, came up to Camp David with his wife, Norma, on the twenty-first. We found them both very likable, and we struck up an immediate friendship. George put great trust in John and valued his advice.

As always, the White House looked spectacular, this year with the theme "The Nutcracker." The parties were fun, but the one that stands out was when Sondra Haley and Ann Brock—my delightful director of scheduling—brought their "star dates." Since they are both huge fans of the soap opera "All My Children," they decided it would be fun to invite two of the male stars to be their dates to the Christmas party. They got "Yes" answers from "Tad Martin" (Michael E. Knight) and "Will Courtland" (Patrick Stewart). It wasn't too hard to tell who were soap fans at the party, and there were many. The girls and their dates brought the house down.

⮞ All our children came home. Their in-laws were marvelous about letting us have them every year George was president. I think that they knew that George needed them. He needed their support, their jokes, and their love—this year, more than ever. And we did have a wonderful Christmas, with all the usual noise, excitement, and constant motion of typical big families.

Nevertheless, 1990 ended on a tense note. It was as if the whole world was holding its breath.

Desert Storm

The line had been drawn in the sand and so we waited. An ABC/*Washington Post* poll showed that the majority of Americans backed the President, but of course there was still controversy. I wrote in my diary in early January:

The Congress wants to position themselves on both sides. It takes guts to be George Bush . . . I asked George the other day how he could read the papers and listen to the news. It is so slanted and filled with things that didn't happen that I feel my stomach churning. He said calmly, "I know what I am doing, I know what I have to do and I don't worry about what they say." I wish I could feel that way. He is at peace with himself. That is not to say that he enjoys all this, but he can look at the big picture.

. . . The press has a disproportionate part to play in this battle of waiting and nerves. As an example, Dick Cheney and Colin Powell came up to the Residence to see George after their trip to the Middle East and reported that we were ready for anything, everything was in place. Then a member of the press reported that they had said we were not ready. Think of the message that sends to Hussein, not to mention our allies! I could make a case that this might keep Saddam Hussein from obeying the U.N. Resolution and costing many Americans and Iraqi lives. Once this rumor got out, then every paper, TV station, radio, etc., picked it up as the gospel and it went like waves across the country.

We spent our forty-sixth wedding anniversary at Camp David with Nick and Kitty Brady. A friend told me once that if she could come back as anyone, it would be Kitty Brady. I can understand that. She is smart, laid-back, naturally nice, and sensational-looking.

We returned to Washington early Sunday afternoon and George went immediately into meetings with his military and diplomatic advisers. I invited the wives to come talk with me. We all needed to be together during such a difficult—and sometimes ugly—time.

Protesters constantly picketed the White House and kept up an incessant drumbeat. We could not hear them in our bedroom or George's private study upstairs, but I could from my office. Vietnam-era protesters Daniel Ellsberg and the Berrigan brothers resurfaced, and some of their group went through the White House on the public tour and tried unsuccessfully to throw red dye in the fountain. Another person chained himself to the fence.

The protesters were very much in the minority, but I hoped that all Americans realized their president did not want war. No one did.

We were all hoping for peace on January 9 when James Baker and Iraq's Minister Tariq Aziz met in Switzerland. After six and a half hours, Jimmy came out and told the world, "I regret to tell you I heard nothing" that would end the crisis. He said Aziz refused to talk about Kuwait, just wanted to talk about a Middle East conference. Hopes for peace were put off again.

I was trying hard to keep up my regular schedule. One morning in early January, for example, I met with members of the National Federation of the Blind. They were so fascinating I visited with them much longer than scheduled. Their spokesperson was a young blind woman who was a Yale Law School graduate and a court trial lawyer. She showed me how she took notes with a pocket Braille device that looked like a ruler. They told me that only 25 percent of our blind children are taught Braille; the other 75 percent are locked into second-class citizenry. The group was petitioning to have Braille education made available to all children. I had never thought about this before, but everyone must know how to read—whether it is by sight or by feel.

On January 10 I flew down to Charlotte, North Carolina, to do a public service announcement with the darndest group—several basketball players with the NBA's Charlotte Hornets. They ranged from Tyrone "Mugsy" Bogues, five feet three inches, to Ralph Sampson, seven feet four inches. Together we visited Piedmont Open Middle School to help promote the NBA's "Stay in School" program. Mugsy, the shortest man in the NBA, told the students if he could attain his goals, so could they. The players also told the students that even if you're good at sports, the number of college kids who get on a professional team is so minute that if you don't have the backup of an education, you have nothing. Ralph Sampson told us that he was offered a professional basketball contract after high school and every year he was at the University of Virginia. Yet, he turned down the big money and stayed in school so he could have his diploma. What role models these young men were, and what a breath of fresh air in a world of worry.

On January 13 Congress was set to vote on whether George had the right to use arms in the Persian Gulf to back up the United Nations resolutions that had been passed against Hussein's aggression. There were many senators and representatives who wanted to usurp the powers of the President as Commander in Chief. This is a problem almost every president is forced to address. George feels strongly there are many times that the president must be able to act and not have his arms tied behind his back. In the end, after much debate and many dire predictions of hundreds of Americans killed in a ground war, the House and the Senate passed a joint resolution backing George. Regrettably, much of the Democratic leadership fought and voted against it. Can you imagine what Saddam Hussein's gleeful reaction would have been if Congress had not supported the President?

The UN Resolution gave Hussein until January 15 to get his troops out of Kuwait. The last hope for peace came when Javier Pérez de Cuéllar, the UN Secretary General, went to Iraq.

Again, failure. Saddam was rude to the Secretary General and kept him waiting for four hours. I remember feeling so frightened for our men and women who were there *and* for all the civilians in Iraq. George felt that if Saddam Hussein were to die, people would dance in the streets as they had in Romania when Ceaușescu fell.

All during this time we invited dear friends up to Camp David; people who had no agenda and with whom George could relax. George mostly worked, but the moments of exercise and rest helped. Betsy and Spike Heminway came one weekend, along with Arnold Schwarzenegger, Maria Shriver, their thirteen-month-old daughter, Margaret, and a nanny. Doro and her children and Margaret and her children came also, along with Marshall's close friend and playmate Abigail Meyer. I know it sounds like a crowd, but Camp David can handle it. It was tremendous fun as everyone in the group was very competitive and willing to try just about anything.

Maybe just a little too willing.

After a great snow, everybody got out the toboggans, saucers, and sleds. It was so much fun that unused sleds were at a premium. After church on Sunday, Betsy and I hurried and changed our clothes and raced out so we could get some sledding in before the crowd hit.

I wrote:

I jumped on the saucer and was the first down. During the night there had been a little thaw and then a big freeze. The hill had become thick ice and the ride was so different. I went spinning around and around so fast that I can still feel the fear that I felt. I knew that I should fall off, but I just could not seem to let go. Luckily, I hit a tree with both my legs and not my head, which might easily have happened. I was shaky, but not hurt—I felt. George had just come out on Aspen Terrace and was yelling "Bail out! Bail out!" and he and the agents rushed down that slippery hill. I said I could walk up, but was quickly forced to lie on a toboggan, and they pulled me up. That feeling of being out of control is the worst. The doctor insisted that I go to Hagerstown and be X-rayed. As Betsy and I were leaving in the ambulance we saw George, Arnold, Spike and Maria and all the grandchildren sleighing. They were smart enough to "bail out." The X rays showed that I had a thin fracture of the fibula. Minor, but a bore. Poor Arnold. For weeks afterwards I claimed in my speeches that the last thing I heard before crashing was Arnold yelling "Break a leg!" and therefore I was never going to invite an actor for the weekend again.

January 16—For the last twelve hours I have known something so dreadful that I can't even imagine it. I have the feeling that I'd like to go to bed and pull the covers over my head and stay there for six weeks, and then peek out and see if it is all over. If it isn't, I'd like to crawl under again. The day had a dream-like quality. George told me last night that they decided that it would start tonight. God knows they have given Saddam every chance.

. . . All America is praying and we are, too. George told me last night that it is always on his mind. As we said our prayers and as he read the message he is going to give to the American people tonight, his voice cracked and his eyes got misty. I know that those innocent children get to him. That darn Hussein, he is putting all those children at risk. George has been praying for the children all week, which led me to believe that unless Saddam met all the U.N. conditions we would have to attack and liberate Kuwait. I asked him over coffee in bed this morning as he read through tonight's message who wrote the speech and he said that he had. I had wondered how it could have remained a secret if it had been written by the speech writers. (This is not to cast aspersions on the speech writers, but once you tell a secret—it is no longer a secret. I had to bite my tongue all day. I wanted to share with Andy, my dearest friend, but I knew I couldn't tell. Too many American lives depended on secrecy.*) George told me that he might come home and have lunch with me and take a nap. I guess that sleep did not come too well last night.

. . . Susan Baker called. Neither of us said a word about the attack, but each of us knew that the other knew. We had a cozy, comforting talk and she told me something that someone had told her. "For Jesus, peace is not the absence of struggle, but the presence of love." That's nice.

We invited Billy Graham to spend the night with us because, unbeknownst to him, we wanted him to conduct a church service the next day. He did not know the war was to begin.

That evening Billy and I sat in our small sitting room watching TV. We saw Bernie Shaw of CNN talking from Baghdad. He said that CNN had given their reporters an opportunity to leave and though some had opted to stay, he said he was leaving on a plane that was being sent for him at three A.M. Baghdad time. I thought to myself: Oh, no, you are not leaving at dawn tomorrow, for in thirty minutes the bombing will start. I like Bernie and his wife, Linda, a lot, but I also must confess that I thought: Darn you for not leaving when your President asked you to. I know that Marlin Fitzwater, George's press secretary, called CNN president Tom Johnson twice to warn him to get his reporters out before the bombing started.

We, like the rest of America, watched the war begin on CNN. Three of their reporters were on the air for fourteen straight hours.

---

* I know that this is not relevant, but on the subject of secrets, for just the above reason, I am dead convinced that there was no one "Deep Throat" during the Watergate crisis. Had there been, it would have come out. Secrets, once known by one other person, come out eventually. I am not saying that Bob Woodward and Carl Bernstein made him or her up (although I wouldn't put it past them), but "Deep Throat" probably was a composite person, and I suspect they used a little literary license to make a better story.

They would say: "We hear planes, but can't see them and the anti-aircraft obviously can't either." The reporters described hiding under tables to get the news out. Because of our capability to have "surgical" bombing, our planes managed to avoid hitting any shrines and highly populated housing.

George slept fitfully and called the situation room off and on all night. The morning reports were great: no planes lost. Later in the day, it was not so great: We had lost three planes; the Brits, two; and the Kuwaitis, one. Saddam answered the attack by aiming SCUD missiles at Israel, hoping to draw them into the conflict, which might have resulted in Jordan's and Syria's entering on Iraq's side.

Congress and the vast majority of the American people supported George, but the protests continued outside. At one point they said we should expect 100,000, but the turnout was much smaller.

Nevertheless, when George talked to our allies, they all asked about the terrible protests taking place in America. George had to explain that they were seeing only the 20 percent who were against and not the 80 percent who were backing him. Incidentally, I want to emphasize that I didn't for one moment question the motives of the protesters. They were doing what they thought was right. However, I was very grateful one day when I heard a great cheer and looked out my office window to see about one hundred supporters of the administration marching. That was refreshing.

I could easily understand people like our friend Mark Hatfield and various religious leaders who are morally opposed to war in general. But I cannot understand sitting back and letting one country invade another and ravage its people. The reports coming out of Kuwait were so nauseating and brutal that after reading about ten pages of the Amnesty International report, I had to stop or get sick.

January 21—Several of our captured pilots have been paraded across the screen. Saddam Hussein says that they will be put in targeted strategic places, so if we bomb we will be bombing our own people.

January 22—Yesterday Bernard Shaw came home from Baghdad and came by to see George. It was fascinating. My feeling is that he feels guilty about something and is not quite sure what. There seems to be some feeling that CNN is being used by Saddam Hussein. Whether it is true or whether it is jealousy on the part of the national networks, I don't know.

... the former PM of Singapore, Lee Kuan Yew, and Madame Kwa

Geok Choo came by for tea. They are old friends from the UN days and both are bright, very interesting people. She had water with no ice and he had hot water . . . saying that tea was a diuretic to him. I had to laugh, for a few minutes later he was talking about some world leader that they both thought looked badly and he mentioned that "he had some small operation—piles," he thought. He can't be faulted for not telling it like it is! He reminded me of Sadat during our visit to Egypt many years earlier when he shared with us his views of the world. Lee Kuan Yew sat telling George, Brent Scowcroft and Bob Gates just how he saw the world . . . I was thrilled to sit in on such a discussion. He told George that he thought the coalition was brilliant and he hoped that George would share the glory when victory came.

January 23—I watched the war on CNN and saw Israel attacked by SCUD missiles and this time they hit. We watched people panicking. I thought of the children in Israel and the children here in our country. Recently Ellie ran into my room and said: "Ganny, we are being bombed. I'm scared." I thought, I hope parents are monitoring what their children are seeing on the television and helping them over this brutal time.

I had a call from Shelley Winters, the actress, who wanted George to make some war act that would forbid the press to "tell all." She was outraged about the way they talked to our briefing generals. She felt they were aiding and abetting the enemy. I tried to explain to this extremely agitated woman that if the President were to do as she asked and put a ban on the press, the hue and cry from one and all would be deafening. She was inconsolable and I sicced her on to the heads of the networks and big newspapers. Good luck, Shelley. I do know the frustrations that she felt. The press is just trying to do their job, although they are just making ours much harder.

. . . During the crisis I met with a Pentagon group who gives support to the families of the soldiers in the desert. I was amazed about how much had been put in place before the war. This military has thought of everything.

On January 28 I received a nice break from the tension when I flew to Boston to visit a Commonwealth Literacy Corps program at the United Electric Company. The new Massachusetts Governor, Bill Weld, met me there and we toured together. When this company discovered that 50 percent of its employees spoke a foreign language and were illiterate in English, it set up English as a Second Language courses right in the workplace. It also encouraged its employees to submit suggestions on how to make better use of time and space and how to make the plant safer and more efficient. Believe it or not, the company soon was saving hours of workers' time, making their work space more efficient and increasing the production rates with fewer errors. It also had happier employees and employers. By the way, it *exported* to Japan. I loved the great pride I felt at that plant.

That night I attended an I Have a Dream banquet sponsored by George's nephew Jamie Bush. He and his wife, Sue, had adopted a class of children, guaranteeing them a college education *if* they met certain requirements: stay in school, stay off drugs, and make reasonable grades. This is Eugene Lang's program which I've already talked about, which is popping up like mushrooms across the country. Jamie and Sue have proven that you don't have to be rich to accomplish this. But you do have to work very hard to get the money needed and to find people who are willing to serve as mentors and role models.

February 4—George got up early and flew to three military bases. We saw him live on CNN and I had tears watching him. He was speaking to home bases of some of the Desert Storm troops, and their families and buddies were there. The reception was great, flags and much cheering. He met with some of the wives and families of those who are missing. I could see it was tough. They kept saying on TV that he was fighting a cold. That was no cold. He was just so moved.

Every single event at the White House was affected by what was happening in the Middle East. At the annual Governors' Dinner, for example, Gary Morris was the entertainer, and he sang "Bring Him Home" from *Les Misérables,* and ended the evening with "Amazing Grace." It was so beautiful and moving.

The next day I was to speak at the spouses' luncheon. I teased them that when I was the host of this annual event, I provided entertainment, but when they were the host, they made me speak! However, this year, I had something very special to share with them, a telegram George had received:

Dear Mr. President,

I am the wife of Lt. Commander Scott Speicher, the pilot of the FA-18 from the USS Saratoga which was downed last Thursday. I cannot pretend to know how it feels to commit our country to war. But it must have been a painful decision. I

know you have an awful lot on your mind, but I want you to
know that I feel the same way now that my husband and I felt
when he was deployed last August. We supported you then,
and I support you now with all my heart. Someday my children will be old enough to understand that their father went
away to war because it was the right thing to do. Rest assured
that all my children and I are well and I wish to maintain as
normal a routine for them as possible, free of press and television cameras. The Navy is helping tremendously in that respect.

God Bless you and all of our men in uniform.

Joanne Speicher and Antonio Salazar
Lt. Commander U.S. Navy
CACO CLAW 1 NAS CECIL FIELD
JACKSONVILLE, FLORIDA 32215

George's answer:

January 24th 1991

Dear Mrs. Speicher, Dear Joanne,

You sent me a very moving telegraph. Barbara and I read
it together and we shed a tear for your very noble husband.
And we said a prayer that God give you the continued
strength and courage that you have now.

I have read about Scott. He must have been "Mr. Perfect," for he was loved by all.

Sometimes God acts in strange ways . . . ways we do not
understand right away.

The fact is your husband gave his life not simply so a
small country could once again be free, but so those kids of
yours will have a better chance to grow up in a world more
peaceful, more just.

Give your kids a big hug from Barbara and me. We
know what family and faith can do to lift you up when you
are hurt. And clearly those kids have a mother who loves them
and whose courage will lead them.

I am proud of your wonderful husband and I will never
forget him.

George Bush

George suffered over each and every casualty and their families. I love this woman for her telegram to him.

          ⁓ We received many wonderful letters before, during, and after the war. I want to share a few more with you that touched me deeply. The first came from a young woman in the Air Force, stationed in the Saudi desert. She wrote in part:

> Today I sit outside my tent. I see a land I do not claim as my own, but out of respect and compassion for those who do, I am here. We share a common friend—peace. We see a common enemy—terrorism. When we speak in these terms, all boundaries cease to exist. I am afraid of what it might cost. But *far* more afraid of what it would cost if we elected not to invest at all.
>
> I wanted you to hear that, for what it's worth, straight from me. A woman, a professional of 19 years, someone who is proud of what we, the United States of America, believe in.

The second letter is from a mother:

> Dear Mrs. Bush,
> This letter is from one who loves her country and wishes to express a few thoughts with someone who also needs our support.
> I am a 38-year-old mother of two. My son, who is 19, is serving in the Army Reserves in the Persian Gulf. . . .
> I just wanted you to be able to tell President Bush that even though my only son is away, due to war, that he has my support as well as that of our whole family.
> I know that he feels deeply about God, country, and family, as do we all. Sometimes people forget that he is and was before he was President, a man and a father.
> . . . We pray that God will give him guidance and wisdom in these troubled times . . . I am proud to have President Bush representing our country in the world's leadership. May God Bless my son and our servicemen and women; our

country; and may God Bless our President and his family.

February 8—The war drones on. It is the darndest war, fought over the tube. CNN covers everything and tells us that they are only able to show us what the Iraqis want us to see and hear. Then they show civilian killings and residential bombings. (Although they have told us, we believe our eyes and forget that we are only seeing what they want us to see.) We know that Saddam has put weapons on residential roofs and in residential sections. We have been hearing that they have five-story underground bunkers. Yesterday (former Attorney General) Ramsey Clark was in Iraq with Peter Arnett saying that we were killing civilians and little children and was beyond the pale. He is an outrage to his country and has been for many years. (I can hear George saying: "Why don't you tell us what you think, Bar.")

The White House has been closed to tourists since the beginning of the air war. I miss the tourists. They bring the White House alive, they make it truly the People's House. I am surprised that I feel this way.

. . . In early February we awakened to see a bomb shelter filled with children and old people in Iraq that had been bombed. Saddam Hussein is an animal. It was a command post and he put those old and young people there. He does not care about human lives. It is extraordinary to me. This is a targeted war on our side and their SCUD missiles just hit helter-skelter. I think we forget that war is not nice.

One of many side effects of the fighting was America's sudden fear of flying because of possible terrorism. On Valentine's Day, I was scheduled to fly to Indianapolis to visit a Veterans Hospital as part of National Veterans Hospital Week. George and John Sununu asked me if I'd mind taking a commercial flight to make the point that the airlines were safe. I said not at all. The press was alerted to the trip and came with me on the nearly empty plane. Fortunately, the trip got good news coverage, and the airlines said that people responded.

That morning as I got into the car to leave the White House, there was a little bag with a valentine in it and a Texas Instruments Thesaurus/Spell Checker (just the right size for my traveling bag) waiting for me on the seat. Although I say that George and I don't need to give presents, and heaven only knows that we have everything under the sun and more, I was thrilled.

After visiting the hospital I flew to Grissom Air Force Base, my second base visit in a week. (The first was Griffiss Air Force Base in Rome, New York.) First, I talked with the families of those who were in the desert—many of the spouses had been gone since August—and then walked out into a freezing cold hangar for a rally with about 2,500 men, women, and children connected to the base. It didn't matter what I said; they cheered. We worked the rope line and shook as many hands as possible. I was saddened to hear that quite a few of the young enlisted men held down second jobs so that they could support their families. The commander told me that when the men went overseas, this added income was lost and the families had to go on food stamps. That is dreadful! The same support group that I met with at the White House and that Joanne Speicher mentioned in her telegram was helping as much as it could, providing services such as financial planning programs and counseling for the children.

One of the most heartwarming visits we made during the war was to the Raytheon Missile Systems plant outside Boston, where they make the "SCUD-buster," the Patriot missile that was such a hero in the war. It saved thousands of lives by knocking Iraq's SCUD missiles out of the air.

For years this plant had been criticized for making weapons, and it was exciting to see what pride the workers had in their product and their work as they heard about their success night after night on TV. George toured the plant, and then we went into a giant rally of about three thousand workers. It was jammed, and men and women literally hung from the rafters. It was so much more emotional than I expected, and I was reminded of World War II and Rosie the Riveter. Patriotism flooded the room, and I must confess that tears ran down my cheeks. They cheered for their country, for their own work—and for George.

After the visit we drove up to Maine to spend two nights in the three cozy rooms that are winterized in the house. We read, took long walks, and watched movies. That Sunday morning we went to our winter church that we love. When Pat Adams, our minister, called for prayers for people who are sick or in need, a well-dressed stranger jumped to his feet and asked us to pray for the thousands of innocent children who were being killed every day in Iraq. He really got warmed up, and then Pat thanked him for his words and asked him to sit down. On and on he went—babies being slaughtered by gas bombs, and so on. Suddenly the congregation rose to its feet and started singing "God Bless America" to drown him out. One amusing moment in this nightmare came when he said, "I can speak. I am a member of this church." Mary Philbrick, the matriarch of our church, said quick as a wink, "Oh, no you aren't," in a clear, loud voice that even he didn't dare to question. Eventually he did sit down and was quiet for a while, only to jump up again to get louder and uglier. In the interim the police chief had come in and sat next to him, and he and another policeman dragged him out at the request of the church deacons. (The Secret Service do not remove protesters unless they threaten the security of the President.) It was the most unpleasant happening, and I felt shaken and sick at heart that we had brought this on our friends. During the coffee hour, we apologized and they reassured us it was okay. In fact, I think we all felt even closer than before. The next day we read in the paper that the man was a frequent protester associated with the Berrigans.

On February 20 the Queen of Denmark, Queen Margrethe II, arrived with Prince Henrik for their long-planned visit. At age fifty-one, she was six feet tall and looked just like what a fairy-book queen should be. She appeared for the arrival ceremony in a stunning plum-colored coat and a marvelous sort of winged-looking hat. Had she flown off, I wouldn't have been surprised. I joined George; Jim Baker; Brent Scowcroft; our ambassador, Keith Brown; and all their counterparts and Her Majesty and the Prince for coffee and an interesting discussion. She is an artist, and Laurie Firestone and I later went by the National Women's Museum to see a Danish exhibit that included some of Her Majesty's work.

We had an interesting group of guests for that dinner. Staying with us was a baseball hero, Texas Ranger pitcher Nolan Ryan, and his beautiful wife, Ruth, and our good friends Maggie and Armando Codina, who are a great Cuban refugee success story.

I wrote:

The State Dinner was one of our best. The food was absolutely delicious and Frederica Von Stade sang. She ended her program with "The Star-Spangled Banner" and it was so beautiful and moving. The Queen wore the most glorious diamonds—tiara, necklace, and brooch, all big with many large pearl drops. She wore a red velvet gown and looked very queenly. George said that she was a very good dinner partner.

There were many guests, but the hit of the evening was Melanie Griffith. She came with her husband, Don Johnson, in a tiny dress that hardly covered her sensational body. Laurie had put Marvin at her side thinking that she would enjoy a young person and it might encourage Marvin to come again. He turned us down for almost all White House events. He really did not like to be in the media spotlight. All during dinner the butlers, who loved Marvin, slipped him notes saying things like, "Keep your eyes on your plate, your mother is watching" or "Eat your dinner and stop ogling the lady next to you."

In any case, we had a nice visit with Melanie and Don upstairs before they left to go to their hotel. Several weeks later I received a letter from Melanie that said something like when she was a little girl, her mother told her if she had good manners and obeyed her, she might grow up and be invited to the White House. She said that her dream had come true. Then she said very nice things about the evening and thanked me for both of them.

Then there was this P.S., which I loved: "I just wish my mother had told me what to wear when I went to the White House."

Melanie will probably never read this, but if she does, I want her to know she looked beautiful and adorable and certainly added to the evening.

⌒ The next night, George and I had planned two events in the residence for the same time. I was having a small reception for the Barbara Bush Foundation for Family Literacy Corporate Committee, a group made up of corporate CEOs and headed by Red Poling of Ford Motor Company and Martin Davis of Paramount. George was having a group coming for a light supper and then they were going to see the Ford's Theatre production of *The Black Eagles*. George generously suggested that we join forces, which made for an absolutely fascinating evening for me and my guests. We gave them all a drink and sat in a semicircle in the Yellow Oval Room. George's group included the Supreme Court Justice David Souter; Air Force Chief of Staff, General Merrill McPeak; and Dr. Benjamin Payton, President of Tuskegee University. George first thanked my group of CEOs for all the help they had given to the foundation and said that I had reported they were doing a superb job. We then talked about the economy and the Persian Gulf. George asked General McPeak to tell us about the surgical bombing and other aspects. I took a chance and said, "You know, General, my husband is under tremendous pressure from his four sons. They all say, 'Tell 'em you're going to bomb all bridges and hotels where you know they have strategic equipment and communications. Give them a set number of hours and then do it.' " I was fascinated, for Ben Payton spoke up and said that he agreed with our sons, then the others joined in, too. I really do think that's what most Americans were feeling.

As I kissed George good-bye, I told him that without my asking for anything he had raised $1 million for me that night. Wrong. Within the week two of those men pledged $1.5 million to the Barbara Bush Foundation for Family Literacy.

That same evening I flew to Arizona with Jimmy Symington, former Democratic congressman from Missouri and a former chief of protocol. Jimmy and his wife, Sylvia, are two of Washington's most attractive inhabitants. We were going to do a breakfast for his cousin, Fife Symington, who was running in a special election for governor. (He later won.)

While there I visited with the Arizona Air National Guard and their families and then had the usual rally. This visit was slightly different, however. I had very private visits with four families: one whose son/husband was a prisoner of war; one whose relative was missing in action; and two whose relatives were killed in action.

People always ask me how I handled these visits. I can't answer that, but I liked to be alone with the families and let them set the pace. They were always kind to me, and I never had an unpleasant experience. There was a lot of listening, a lot of tears and hugs. They all mentioned the strong help they were getting from their peers and support groups.

The first family was the family of Lt. Colonel Clifford Acree, the POW that we had seen on the tube, led in looking doped and beaten early in the air war. I visited with his wife, mother, father and aunt. I was so proud of the wife. She had organized a POW/MIA support group and seemed to be doing well. They all spoke well of George and it was a very moving visit. The darling mother was teary and I couldn't blame her. [He came home safely.]

The second meeting was with a Hispanic family of a KIA (killed in action). We had the whole family there, darling grandparents, an aunt who had a boy there herself whom she hadn't heard from in weeks, a sister, an uncle and a fiancée. The latter didn't fit the picture at all. She was very young and dressed to the teeth and very sensual looking. The others were all so warm, teary and darling and she seemed sulky and did not speak. I was shocked that the family seemed to shun her. Later Anna Perez told me that she had been paid a lot of money by a national magazine and was furious when the base would not let their reporters and cameras in the room while we were visiting. She had arrived separately from the family with two very Caucasian-looking people with cameras, saying they were "family." Anna said that it was very sticky, but they were kept out of the room. No wonder the family shunned her. We hugged, had tears, talked and promised to try to get in touch with the first cousin whom they had not heard from.

. . . Next was the wife of an MIA. She was so adorable and had such faith that although she had been told that the chances of his being alive were slight, she believed he was. I certainly hope so. [She was right; he came home!]

. . . The last visit was really sad, a Native American family, a very young widow and mother with her sister, brother-in-law and two young children. The baby was being taken care of by the sister, who seemed to love the precious child. I had trouble sorting it all out in my mind as the widow showed no affection toward the baby, the daughter of the dead Marine. I don't know if it is the stoic Indian culture or if the wife was in shock, which certainly would be normal. It was so sad. I was so glad that she had that nice sister. We did offer to help her find affordable housing. My heart broke for all these families.

From Arizona we flew on to Campbell Air Force Base on the Tennessee and Kentucky border. We had been warned that this would be an "uptight" visit, for many of the 28,000 troops that had been deployed from this enormous base were on the front lines and, with a ground war on the horizon, they were frightened. I walked out to the largest, most enthusiastic rally ever. Lee Greenwood, that great patriotic country singer, was there and they loved him. So did I and so does George Bush!

February 23—The deadline came and went and (Saddam) did not withdraw. We are going to have an early dinner at Camp David and fly down to D.C. There George will announce that the ground war has started—8 p.m. our time and 4 a.m. their time. George had spent the day working at his office and talking to leaders around the world, Senate and House Leadership and all the former Presidents. It is a terrible, awful decision, but certainly had to be made. That madman has set over two hundred oil wells on fire in

Kuwait and is continuing the killings. Dear God, let it be quick and let there be few deaths.

February 24—The ground war did start last night. George went immediately to the Oval Office. He made a short announcement on the ground war. Dick Cheney gave a short announcement at the Pentagon and then took some questions. . . . He has done such a good job. He seems so steady and no nonsense. Before we went to bed John Harper of St. John's Church was called. He had offered to help in any way that he could. He said that we could have an early morning communion service at church. So Patty Presock got on the phone and so did I and invited as many people as we could reach, making it clear that it was not a command performance. Many of the staff attended. I only saw Anna from my office. I was touched that both Doro and Marvin went with us at 7 a.m., which means that they got up at 5:30. It means a lot to have your children there. It was a lovely service. John gave the best sermon, I thought. It was sincere and sweet. We have been friends for a long time and that made the service even more special.

. . . At church Dick Cheney passed George a note telling him that "Norm says things are going well." There was a hard knot of drummers outside the church. When we saw them they were really odd looking and only about five people.

. . . George and Marvin gathered a crowd for lunch with horseshoes before: David and Ann Bates and their three children (David used to work for George and is like a son to us); Steve Quamme; Marvin, Margaret, Marshall and Abigail Meyer, Walker; Doro, Sam, Ellie, and Sam's friend Carlos, plus Doro's new friend, Bobby Koch (pronounced Cook). With Pop and me that made 18 for hamburgers, hot dogs, French fries, cherry pie and ice cream. I swam a mile while they were throwing shoes before lunch. I wonder what Bobby Koch thinks of this nutty family: a fat old mother swimming in the middle of the winter outdoors; and a father who plays horseshoes like it is the most important game ever while running an international war thousands of miles away that will affect the world for years to come.

By afternoon we got the word that we had lost twelve of our people. George was so sad. I didn't know how to console him.

February 26—We awakened this morning to a defiant speech by Saddam Hussein. He said that he has asked his troops to withdraw from Kuwait, but was by no means surrendering. He may not be, but his troops were surrendering right and left. George has stood firm and has resisted all pressure to accept the Russian or Iraqi plan. I am so proud of George. He has worked up a superb team and coalition.

February 28—Yesterday was a big day in the life of our country.

. . . George called and told me that he was going to give a talk to the nation at 9 p.m. I told him that I was out for dinner and would be speaking at the time to the National Foundation for Depressive Illness Foundation Benefit Dinner. He asked me if I couldn't speak before the dinner and get home in time for his speech, which is exactly what I did. I went over, gave my speech and got back and was sitting on a chair in the Oval Office when George announced that 100 hours after the ground war started (42 days after the air response to Saddam's invasion of Kuwait), he was calling for a cease-fire *IF* Saddam Hussein accepts unconditionally all 12 U.N. resolutions. It is so thrilling. All the pundits said that it would be a long war, that we would have thousands of dead, that it would cost billions of dollars more than it did, and on and on. We awakened this morning to hear Saddam declaring victory. It makes you want to go in and bomb the whey out of him. The reason we didn't go all the way into Baghdad was that we never wanted to devastate Iraq. We just wanted to get him out of Kuwait and cripple him militarily. We are assured that has been done.

I was a little surprised to hear the drums going the day after the war ended and must say I wondered why. I suspect that they are now protesting our having gone at all.

The next day I went to Baltimore to help cut the ribbon at the International Book Bank. The Governor and Mayor were there along with many dignitaries. Governor Donald Schaefer, a longtime dear friend in the literacy world, said such nice things about George. He said he was proud to be an American with a president like this, that he felt a "quiet pride" in our country. Anna Perez and I talked about it and decided that he was right. We felt a "quiet pride," not only because we had won the war, but in the way we won.

From there, I visited Fort Meade in Maryland. The trip was originally planned as a rally to cheer the troops on, but instead it was a celebration of the cease-fire and victory the night before. It was so touching with flags and such cheering. Unfortunately, the wives and children were thinking their husbands and dads would be home immediately, but I knew there would be a lot of peace-keeping and mopping up.

March 2—I wish I could freeze the newspaper columns in a time capsule. They are raving over George today. It won't last, but nobody thought that a war could be fought like this and won in this manner. I am so proud of him and his team that I could burst. Dick Cheney, the Secretary of Defense, is as competent as they come. He seems very laid back and reassuring. He does not have a Dr. Strangelove image that so many of our Secretaries of Defense get, whether they deserve it or not. Colin Powell, Chairman of the Joint Chiefs of Staff, has been superb. These two, along with Norm Schwarzkopf, Commander of the Allied Forces, have been strong, reassuring and have made *NO* mistakes that I can see. Jim Baker, Secretary of State, has done what he does best, which is diplomacy, the very best. And I can't leave out Brent Scowcroft and Bob Gates. They worked hard behind the scenes. They are two of the finest public servants. They are wise and good. George Bush has been well served.

I want to add here Dan Quayle, who was at George's side, loyal and supportive in every instance. I also don't want to forget to mention that we were really part of a worldwide team, just one of thirty countries in a coalition that stood and fought together.

That weekend George invited Al and Ann Simpson to join us at Camp David. Al was having a hard time in the press for a statement he had made about Peter Arnett of CNN being an Iraqi sympathizer. George wanted to show his support for Al, who, besides having an unbelievably good sense of humor, is a true, loving friend. We were joined by Fred and Martha Zeder and Jack and Bobbie Fitch, friends from Texas.

About that time I learned that *Millie's Book* was going into its eighth printing—400,000 copies—and was on *The New York Times* best-seller list for the twenty-third week. In fact, the book was climbing back from number 7 to number 5. Nobody could believe it, but I couldn't help but wonder, "Could it have anything to do with the fact that George is 91 percent in the polls?"

I continued my base visits, especially since most of them had been scheduled before the war ended. On March 6, I headed to Jacksonville, Florida, to visit the Mayport Naval Air Station. I wrote:

First I spoke to some members of the families of those deployed in the Gulf. I said a few words and then invited discussion. Of course the first question they had was when was their husband or wife, father or mother coming home? To that I could say soon. In regular service life they are at sea for 6 months and then home for 6 months . . . The only sour note was one

male spouse who asked me when Congress was going to update the laws . . .
when was a reservist who gives up a high-paying job going to get compen-
sation for being called back into the service? They asked the wrong person
that because I feel so strongly that if someone has been in the reserves for 9
years, getting their education or accepting pay for their training and then
gripes about serving when called, they are wrong, dead wrong. Before I could
answer the woman standing next to me said, "Do you mean you can't live on
what we have been living on for years?"

Next to the USS *Forrestal* (aircraft carrier) where we made the most
dramatic entrance coming up on the plane elevator to find 4,000 troops lined
up on the flight deck. I was led to a mike, introduced and invited to speak.
To hold that speech and pray that my dress would not blow up was no mean
feat. After a few words of thanks on the windiest deck, I walked the lines and
shook hands and smiled at those I could not touch. It was amazing. They had
just been told that they were not going to be deployed and were so disappointed. Isn't that funny? They, too, wanted to be part of the action!

I had run into the same thing at an earlier visit at Quantico
Marine Base near Washington. They were sad they weren't in the
desert. Somehow I suspect their families felt differently.

༨ On March 7, Margaret Thatcher, now Lady Thatcher, visited us at the White House, and George bestowed on her the highest
medal a foreigner can receive from the U.S. government, the Medal of
Freedom. We had heard that Margaret was crushed about her recent
defeat, but she seemed her old self. I wrote:

We sat in the Oval Office with John Sununu, Brent Scowcroft, the two
she called "Tweedledee and Tweedledum"—Bob Gates and Larry Eaglebur-
ger, Sir Antony Acland and several of her people. She hasn't changed much.
She is still on top of the world situation and still seems to do most of the
talking. She does have a lovely voice, is a joy to hear and we were very glad
to see her looking so well. Denis doesn't say much. I am crazy about him.
What a rock he is for Margaret.

After a receiving line and reception, we all retired upstairs for a small
dinner of 60 in the Yellow Oval Room. As Denis and I walked into the
dinner, he asked me if he could ask a personal question. He said: "I have met
Dan Quayle several times and I found him bright and very nice. Why doesn't

the press like him?" I had to tell him that I did not know as Dan was all he said and much more. At that moment Katharine Graham (owner of *The Washington Post*) walked up to our table and I suggested rather facetiously that he ask her. I should have known that Denis would, and he did. He came back and reported that Kay had said that Dan was "superficial" and she didn't like him. She also told Denis that she didn't know him.

. . . George made a nice toast to Margaret, and Margaret answered—at some length. Denis said in a loud stage whisper, "Don't go on, Mum." Then George stood up and invited others who knew Margaret and loved her to please feel free to speak. He turned and said, "Bar, you start it off." I should be prepared but never am, but stood and toasted dear Denis and sat down. Denis stood and said, "As Anthony said to Cleopatra as he walked into her tent, 'I did not come to talk,' " thanked us and plunked down. George told me later that it reminded him of Henry the VIII saying to his 6th wife, "I won't keep you long."

March 10—We attended the annual Ford Theatre Gala. This year country music was featured and George was, to use a little country music lingo, in "hog heaven." Some of the entertainers were Randy Travis, Alabama, Clint Black, the Statler Brothers, Tammy Wynette, K. T. Oslin, Ricky Skaggs and Pendley and Wolz. The hosts were John Ritter and Teri Garr. Morgan Freeman did the tribute to Lincoln and ended with "Thank you, Mr. President," looking up at the box where Lincoln had sat the night he was shot. He then turned with the most loving expression, looked George right in the eye and said, "And thank *YOU*, Mr. President." It was a moment of great emotion.

Later that week George took a trip to Ottawa, Martinique, and Bermuda to meet with Brian Mulroney, François Mitterrand and Margaret Thatcher, in that order. I headed to Houston for several days of rest and exercise. Since the trip was strictly personal, I flew down and back commercially. I wrote:

People were so nice to me on the plane. They smiled and sent me notes, asked to have their pictures taken with me, etc. When they were asked to stay in their seats until the "unnamed VIP" unloaded, they clapped. It was *NOT* for me, but GB. Everyone I met or spoke to raved over George and told me just how good they felt about themselves and our country.

We ended our trip on a real high. Peggy (Swift) and I were sitting talking in the car when . . . a man in a yellow beat-up truck drew up beside me at a red light. He glanced at me, recognized me and his face broke into the biggest, most handsome smile. I smiled and he rolled down his window and said, "I didn't think you stopped at lights." I said that I did. He asked for an autograph. I handed him one that Peggy had in her bag that I had signed before, and as he drove off, he was shaking his head saying, "Nobody will believe this. God bless America." It was so sweet.

As you can see, this was almost a euphoric time for us. However, there was something bothering me deeply. In March, at our annual meeting to decide the theme of this year's graduation speech, I said that I wanted to talk about tolerance, doing unto others as you would have them do unto you. It seemed to be needed that year more than any other; the papers were filled with terrible stories about racial and religious intolerance. I felt so strongly that we could not let our troops come home from the Gulf War to any racial problems. All races and religions had worked side by side in the desert; I felt we must do the same at home.

I did talk about intolerance last year, but without the controversy that had surrounded my Wellesley speech the year before, my remarks did not get as much media coverage. And sad to say, as I write this in early 1994, our papers are still filled with stories of intolerance. It's a part of America I despise and pray so fervently we one day will overcome.

 In the next few weeks, the cease-fire was signed, and slowly but surely our troops started coming home. On June 8 we had a huge celebration in Washington with an old-fashioned parade and supposedly the biggest fireworks display ever in Washington. But the beginning of the day is what touched me the most:

We went early in the morning to a wreath-laying service at Arlington Cemetery. It was a most glorious day. It was warm, but not too hot. As we drove to Arlington we could see people walking toward the parade route in shorts and comfortable shoes, often carrying picnics and folding chairs. They waved and cheered when they saw George. The service at Arlington was very moving. We first marched up that long stairway in front of the Tomb of the Unknown Soldier. George laid the wreath in a solemn ceremony. So far in this war there are no unknowns. Then on into the Amphitheater, where

George went with Generals Powell, Schwarzkopf, and Streeter (commanding general of the local military district), Secretary Cheney, the Ambassadors of Kuwait and Saudi Arabia and some other military men to the stage. I was with several of the wives to the side. From where we were sitting we could see the faces of the families who lost loved ones in the war. They were dear sweet faces and many had smiles with tears. It was so tough to look at them. My heart ached for George as I know he feels these deaths as though they were his own children. The service was filled with beautiful music and prayers. George spoke as did the Ambassador of Kuwait. After the last song George came over, took me by the hand and led me down to the families. We hugged, had pictures taken and shook as many hands as possible. We would have stayed longer if they had let us, but all those people had to get to the parade. We did feel that they personally deserved our thanks.

As a footnote to Desert Storm, we went to Kuwait in March of 1993 as guests of the Kuwaiti government. It was an extraordinary trip, and I wish all those families who lost loved ones could have been with us. The gratitude toward the United States was overwhelming. People waved American and Kuwaiti flags for mile after mile every-place we went, and the Arab women made that wonderful trilling sound as a welcome. They stood for hours just to catch a glimpse of George, whose face was everywhere on posters, flags, and billboards.

We saw such devastation and heard tales of horror and just plain meanness. We met with families whose sons and husbands were still hostages or MIAs in Iraq. We saw museums that were burned the last two days of the war. We heard of rapes and visited a hospital where the handicapped were thrown out on the streets and babies in incubators were put on the floor so the machines could either be broken or taken as loot. We visited the blackened oil fields where eventually over seven hundred wells had been set on fire as the Iraqis fled the country. Everyone we met had a death of a family member to report.

However, nature and the human spirit are amazing. We saw rebuilding going on everywhere, including the Bayan Palace, where we stayed. There were patches of green shooting through the thin layer of oil and I even saw some yellow wildflowers. I was told the oil on the ground actually was holding in what little moisture they have, thus the growth.

We went one morning to visit with the families of the POWs and MIAs and they gave George an antique door. As we approached we were so moved to see that they had inscribed on the door in gold the names of the American men and women killed freeing Kuwait. The inscription read:

> When a man gives you the key to his home, it means that you are the best and most valuable friend to him; and when a man gives you the door of his home, it means that you are one of his family.

This beautiful old door symbolized to us more than anything their gratitude, and it will be forever on display at the George Bush Presidential Library Center in College Station, Texas, for all to see and honor those courageous Americans who died.

22

Of Cabbages and Queens

After the war ended, it was nice to settle back into a somewhat normal, although busy, routine. Springtime brought, among other things, the commencement season, and George and I both had a full schedule often taking us in opposite directions.

So I was very happy on May 4, a Saturday, to find myself on *Air Force One* with George headed for the University of Michigan, where he was to give the commencement address. Three congressional friends from Michigan—Guy Vander Jagt, Carl Pursell, and Fred Upton— also were on board, and they warned George he could expect some protests during his speech.

We were taken immediately to a huge stadium filled with seventy thousand people, and despite the dire predictions, George got a great reception with the exception of a very small group with megaphones who yelled "Bulls—t" the whole time George spoke. At one point, when he was talking about the importance of freedom of speech, he stopped, looked over at them and said: "When I wrote that, I didn't know you guys were going to be here!" He got a huge laugh and applause. I do not know how he got through that speech, but he did—and did it well—and said he hardly noticed the protesters. Everyone was thrilled, including Governor John Engler, who had worried that the protesters would ruin the day.

We flew back to Camp David, bringing with us Bob Teeter, an old friend from past campaigns, and his wife, Betsy. Craig Fuller, George's chief of staff from the vice presidential years, and his wife,

Karen, also drove up from Washington to spend the night. We all separated to do our own thing: I went to ride my bike and swim laps; George to nap and go for a jog; and the Fullers and Teeters to ride bikes and take walks.

Halfway through my swim I was interrupted and told that George was in the dispensary. I was told not to worry, that he just had a little shortness of breath while jogging. I put on a robe and went to find him hooked up to a cardiac monitor and with an IV in his arm. He told me that he had felt exhausted while jogging and had to stop and walk several times. When he finished his run, the doctor suggested that he stop in the Eucalyptus Cabin (the very appropriate name for the medical cabin) to be examined. They discovered that his heart was out of sync. Simply stated, the upper chamber was pumping at a different rate than the lower chamber. It was fibrillating.

George, of course, was joking about the whole thing. When I walked in, he took one look at my face and said: "Remembering how sympathetic I was when you broke your leg, I know you'll be caring." That was a family joke, as I had kidded him about continuing to sled while I went off in the ambulance to be X-rayed.

Meanwhile, Dr. Mike Nash, the White House doctor on duty, and John Herrick, assistant to the press secretary, were attempting to get a protesting George to Bethesda Naval Hospital. I was so impressed with how everyone worked so efficiently and calmly. George suggested that I stay with our guests, but that was out of the question; they were our friends and would understand.

We got on the helicopter with the monitoring machine and the needle still feeding something into his vein. The latter was there just in case he went into cardiac arrest; they could shoot a stimulant into his system immediately. It was necessary, but hardly comforting to an amateur like me.

George, on the other hand, opened his briefcase and worked the twenty-minute trip to the hospital as though he felt fine. In fact, he was bemoaning the fact that he had complained in the first place. As I sat there, the most dreadful thoughts ran through my mind: Dear God, this wonderful man must not die. A little later, as he worked away, I thought: Don't you dare die. I'll never forgive you. Hardly courageous, but that's what I thought.

Before leaving Camp David, I asked the Secret Service to please let our children know that we were headed for the hospital but they should not worry. Their father was making jokes and we were going just as a precaution. The message was passed on right in front of me, but it must have gotten garbled in transit, because all of them heard it from friends or television. We hated that, but it was just one of those things.

While the doctors ran their tests, I sat quietly with George in the large presidential bedroom at Bethesda. Again, he was quite funny and very regretful that he had even mentioned feeling tired. He said that he'd rather be at Camp David. We both got more respectful, however, when the doctors told us that when the heart stops fibrillating and kicks back into sync, there is a danger of blood clots shooting through the body and causing a stroke. I noticed that George stopped talking about going back to Camp David.

I spent the night in the hospital, going home the next morning to change my clothes and bathe. When I went back for lunch with George, Doro had brought Ellie and Sam over to see their grandfather. He loved that.

At one time during the afternoon George got up to go into the bathroom, which was complicated since he was still attached to an IV. He came back and got into bed, and we were watching TV when we suddenly heard a voice say, "We caught a glimpse of the President at the window a minute ago." Immediately a picture of George appeared on the screen. You could tell it was taken from far away, but it was definitely George. Little did they know what they had just filmed. I peeked out another window and there on a hillside, a hundred yards away, was a little knot of press with their cameras aimed at George's bathroom. What a dreadful job. I don't often sympathize with the press, but a lot of their lives are spent just sitting and waiting.

After George was settled down for the night I went home. I did this partially to reassure the world and our own children that it was not serious. I was promised that the doctors would let me know if there was any change. Before I got to the White House they called to say that his heart was back to normal.

He came home Monday and went right to work, although he continued to be hooked up to the cardiac monitor. A few days later, George was diagnosed and treated for Graves' disease. What a peculiar illness—it attacked my eyes and George's heart. It is unusual for a husband and wife to both have this problem, but not unheard of. I received several letters telling me of other couples who shared our same disease. I also heard from people who weren't as lucky as we were. They were not diagnosed as quickly and really suffered. I have to give credit to the doctors at Bethesda and Walter Reed hospitals for jobs well done, and later, to the doctors at the Mayo Clinic.

Not surprisingly, the press began to speculate on George's health, and rumors ran wild—some, I suspect, started by political opponents. One day, the rumor that George had lupus swept across the United States and the stock market dropped forty points. I loved setting people straight: THE DOG had lupus; George was fine. George W. heard the rumor and called from Dallas to say we could end all the talk if his dad and I would just stop drinking out of Millie's bowl.

Then story after story appeared about the fact that George, Marvin, Millie, and I all had autoimmune diseases. There was much speculation about this, one sillier than the next. Some suggested that we received bad rays when we lived in China, and then the water supply at the Vice President's House came under great scrutiny. We probably will never know the answer. I remember once asking a doctor why a terrible illness had afflicted a darling child, and he said: "Barbara, our body is made up millions of cells. All it takes is for just one to go bad. The miracle is that more of us aren't sick."

Actually, we're still searching for answers. In December 1993, George, Millie, and I gave blood to Dr. Jonathan Jaspan at Tulane University to be tested for a possible common virus that might be responsible for our autoimmune diseases. A virus conceivably might trigger one type of disease in George and myself (that is, Graves' disease), and another type in Millie (lupus). If such a virus is found and proved to be the cause, it will be an important breakthrough.

As much as I hated George's illness, some very sad things happened that spring that made it seem quite insignificant. Our very dear friend Bill Liedtke died of cancer. He was one of our first friends in Midland, and he and his family have been very much a part of our lives ever since. Then Senator John Heinz was killed in an airplane accident. It was a double tragedy, as a helicopter and plane crashed over a school yard and two little boys on the ground also were killed, along with five in the air. John was a wealthy man who well could have sat home and never lifted a finger in his life. He chose to serve his country. He was young, bright, and caring. The very next day, our dear friend John Tower was killed in a commuter flight with his daughter Marian. Then later that year Dean Burch died after a long and horrible fight against cancer. George had a special rapport with Dean and will miss him always. And Lee Atwater died in March. It was a very difficult period.

But of course many exciting things were happening, too, and that's what we chose to focus on. In April, as chairman for the 75th Anniversary Celebration of the National Park Service, I had the pure pleasure of seeing the Grand Canyon for the first time.

In early May we had the Second Annual Great American Workout at seven A.M. led by Arnold Schwarzenegger. Arnold gathered many great athletes for this event, and at his own expense visited all fifty states to urge governors, schools, and parents to help get our nation into shape. All statistics show that exercise not only prolongs life but improves its quality.

Also that spring we dedicated the ecumenical chapel at Camp David, with leaders of all religions taking part in the ceremony. Among those attending were Adele and Don Hall, who, along with many others, had helped raise the money to build it.

I was continuing to travel to promote literacy. One trip I particularly enjoyed was to the Martin County Literacy Council in Stuart, Florida. George's cousin Shelley Jansing was a volunteer in the day-care center connected to the literacy program and had urged me to come. About three hundred volunteers were tutoring nine hundred students, six hundred of whom were prisoners. I was very impressed with the program, and proud of Shelley for her commitment.

One night I came home very late from a trip to be met by a White House electrician. He asked me if I wanted to know where everyone was sleeping. I was exhausted and said, "No," then went to bed and lay awake wondering just who "everyone" was. George Bush hates an empty bed.

Back home I had a reception for the Washington Parent Group Fund to celebrate its tenth anniversary. I had been involved with it almost from the beginning. Founded by lawyers, businessmen, parents, and educators, it had grown from helping nine schools in 1981 to more than seventy schools in 1991 through 515 different programs. One of this program's strengths is that it insists on parental involvement. Family is the answer to so many of our problems, and the sooner we accept responsibility for our own children, our own neighborhoods, villages, and communities, the better off we will be as a country.

We had several foreign visitors that spring: President Lech Walesa and his wife, Danuta, from Poland; President Violeta

Chamorro from Nicaragua; and President Turgut Ozal of Turkey and his wife, Semra.

However, the visit all of Washington was talking about was the Queen of England's state visit in May. As the date approached, excitement ran high. Finally the big day came, May 14. I wrote in my diary:

She arrived on the Concorde from London this morning and we had the arrival ceremony at 11 a.m. People were really excited and started gathering on the South Grounds 1 to 2 hours ahead of time. It was muggy! Several people fainted. Her Majesty looked lovely in a purple linen suit with a smart straw, purple, black and white hat. She is sweet and has a nice sense of humor. Thank heavens, as the podium step was not pulled out for her to step up on and she looked, according to the press, like a "talking hat." You literally could not see her face as she spoke; just the hat bobbing up and down.

We had a quiet lunch with HM Queen Elizabeth II, HRH the Duke of Edinburgh, the British ambassador and his wonderful wife, Antony and Jenny Acland, George and Laura and Will and Sarah Farish. Nan Ellis, George's sister, breezed in at the end of the lunch and joined the group. I jokingly told Her Majesty that I had put our Texas son as far away from her as possible at the table and had told him that he was not allowed to say a word to her or, for that matter, to our only daughter's beau, who was coming to the dinner that night. She asked him why that was. Was he the black sheep in the family? George W. allowed as how he guessed that was true. (Not true at all.) Then she said, "Well, I guess all families have one." George W., of course, asked her if their family had one and who it was. She laughed and asked me why I thought him so dangerous. I told her that he said what he felt and besides that, he threatened to wear cowboy boots in the evening to the State Dinner. I told her that they had Texas flags on them or GOD BLESS AMERICA. She asked him which pair he was going to wear that night and he said, "Neither. Tonight's pair will say GOD SAVE THE QUEEN."

And as for Doro's beau, she has four brothers who love her and tease her all the time. They constantly were threatening her that they would ask what her dates' intentions were, etc. The Queen laughed. Incidentally, when George W. came through the receiving line at the State Dinner, Her Majesty, with a smile, looked down and without a word, he pulled his pants' leg up to show her his boots with an American flag on them.

After lunch we retired to the Rose Garden, where the Queen presented

George with the Winston Churchill Award. It was truly miserably, burning hot and George jokingly said that he had a 45-minute speech and in the interest of good sense and because he did not want to cook Her Majesty, he would just say thank you. Which he did. I only mention this as the next day I read that he had torn up a 45-minute speech. Of course he wasn't going to give a 45-minute thank you!

The Queen and George replaced a tree that her father had planted and that had fallen over in a big storm last fall. And then she went off to place a wreath on the Tomb of the Unknown Soldier. Joseph Reed, our unique Chief of Protocol, told me that the Queen saved the day when out of the blue the heavens opened up and the queen whipped a tiny umbrella out of her pocketbook. Otherwise, Joseph said, we would have had two faux pas in one day.

The State Dinner that night was lovely with tables covered with white peonies with dark centers and lavender and pink roses. . . . The British ladies all wore varying degrees of tiaras, the Queen's being the largest and right on down to an adorable one that Jenny Acland wore. I sat next to the Duke and General Norman Schwarzkopf. The latter is a warm funny man who happens to be great. He is so new to the political world that he needs a keeper. He is in demand, his upcoming schedule is awful, and he has yet to learn that you do not have to accept everything. This morning's paper had him apologizing for some politically incorrect thing he had said. The world of politics is a tough one.

The Prince is charming and I gave him Libbie Reilly as his other partner. Her husband, Bill, was president of the World Wildlife Fund and now heads the Environmental Protection Agency. Libbie is a great beauty, very bright and has the singing voice of an angel.

Jessye Norman sang for us after supper. One of the many joys of living in the White House is that great entertainers generously come to perform. Often you can sneak down in the afternoon and hear a dress rehearsal. Jessye Norman's voice in an empty East Room is magnificent and fills the room and the house.

The next morning I picked Her Majesty up at Blair House, and we rode out for a visit to the Metropolitan Police Boys and Girls Club. On the way people waved and cheered. I waved back very enthusiastically until I realized that, number 1, they were waving at her; and number 2, after watching her, I realized that ladies do not almost fall out of the car waving. They do "The Light Bulb," which she has made so famous. All the Brits had on their hats and gloves. I didn't own a hat, but I did wear my gloves.

The program we visited is another excellent one in which the police mentor children and keep them in school and off the streets. The children put on quite a show for us.

From there we went to visit the Marshall Heights Community Development Organization to meet with three first-time homeowners. This area had the most dreadful reputation for guns and drugs, and the good people of the neighborhood started their own patrol and took back their streets.

In the first house, a wonderful woman named Mrs. Alice Frazier got so carried away that she just put both her arms around Her Majesty and gave her the biggest hug—the hug that went around the world. It was so sweet and the Queen's smile was a joy. Mrs. Frazier had spent the whole morning cooking and of course we could not stop for one bite. But her house smelled wonderful.

Hundreds of schoolchildren, several bands, and lots of just plain people were crowding the streets. It was a rousing welcome for the Queen. Even though it was very hot, she plunged into handshaking, didn't flick an eyelash, or even glow (a ladylike term for "perspire"). She, poor soul, went on to several more events, including a garden party at the British Embassy for some 1,800 people.

That night the Queen and Duke joined us for a helicopter ride over to see the Baltimore Orioles play several innings of baseball. Her Majesty told us the garden party had turned into a large crush, but that she had a lady-in-waiting who puts her elbows up and charges into a crowd, making a path for the Queen. This same formidable lady also carries a parasol with a point on the tip. If the crowd gets too close, she pokes the ladies on the instep. They jump back, never knowing what happened to them. We all got the giggles, with Her Majesty leading in the laughter.

There was some reluctance on the part of the Secret Service and Scotland Yard to have the Queen go out onto the playing field. However, George talked her into it, and they went out through the dugout. She received a tremendous ovation. We left after two long innings and I was glad that they could get home and to bed.

The next morning the papers all had pictures of the podium with only the talking hat showing. When the Queen addressed a Joint Session of Congress, she opened by saying, "I do hope you can see me from where you are sitting." She had them in the palm of her hand from that moment on. The speech was only twelve minutes long. The fascinating thing is that she can only speak words that the elected government has okayed or written.

That night we went to the beautiful return dinner at the British Embassy, and then the trip was over. Both Her Majesty and the Duke were warm and gracious, and we enjoyed the visit very much.

᠆᠊ Summer began with a great fun event for us. During a visit to California, Jerry and Jane Morgan Weintraub gave a party for us at their lovely house in Malibu, Blue Heaven, named for one of the songs that Jane made famous. They have been loyal friends of ours for years and stuck with George through thick and thin. It wasn't always easy, especially in 1992, when much of Hollywood backed Bill Clinton.

We had a receiving line in the house and then went into a tremendous clear plastic tent covered with "A Thousand Points of Light." I wrote:

The guest list was a moviegoer's dream: For starters, Mr. and Mrs. Johnny Carson, Don and Barbara Rickles, Gloria and Jimmy Stewart, Danny DeVito and Rhea Perlman, Tom Hanks, Chevy Chase, Olivia Newton-John, Goldie Hawn, Sally Field, Raquel Welch, Sylvester Stallone, Dinah Shore, Angie Dickinson, Merv Griffin and Eva Gabor, Julie Andrews, Billy Crystal, a very pregnant Demi Moore and her husband and George's friend, Bruce Willis, Janet Jackson, Clint Eastwood, Richard Gere, his girl with the mole, Cindy Crawford, Bernadette Peters, Jon Bon Jovi, Warren Beatty, Steven Spielberg, Sidney Poitier, Arnold Schwarzenegger, another great friend of ours, and his wife, Maria Shriver (also very pregnant), and her parents, Eunice and Sarge Shriver, Lod and Carole Cook, our great friend and head of ARCO and many, many more. George sat at the table with Goldie Hawn and Sally Field and found them both captivating and fun. I sat next to Warren Beatty, Sidney Poitier and later Richard Gere. They were all very nice. I remember telling Warren Beatty that I had loved *Reds* and he suggested that I might be one of the only people who had seen it. Not a success, I guess. It was a most glamorous night and to top it all off I danced with a very bright Sylvester Stallone and a very attractive John Travolta. That was great fun and I had my picture taken with them both. I was thrilled as I wanted to send the picture with John to Mildred Kerr. In 1978 she and I had taken her daughter-in-law Mimi and some other young friends to see *Grease* after they helped me address some political mail that I was sending out for George W. We loved *Grease* so much that the next afternoon we took in *Saturday Night Fever.* The latter film turned out to be filled with words that embarrassed us and especially embarrassed those young women with us. Unfortunately the same words are used today almost as common words, but not by us.

(The Weintraub party) was the most glamorous night ever and such fun. Jane has the most beautiful voice and she once again came out of retirement for us. Fortunately I now have a disc of her songs and so can hear her year-round.

On July 1 in Kennebunkport, George announced the appointment of Clarence Thomas to fill the vacancy left by Thurgood Marshall on the Supreme Court. Clarence arrived in Maine at lunchtime with John Sununu, White House Counsel Boyden Gray, Deputy Chief of Staff Andy Card, and Attorney General Dick Thornburgh for the announcement. They sneaked him past the press, stationed across the bay from the Point in a van with tinted windows. We had a quiet lunch and then walked down to a press conference where George made the announcement.

The press had gone mad speculating on who the nominee would be. I was told that Rita Beamish with the Associated Press had been on the phone to possible candidates and if they were at home, she knew they were not the one. Great ingenuity on her part. I should add we liked her a lot. I believe that George surprised them.

We were touched when Clarence choked up when talking about his family. He is the most extraordinary man. He talked about how he came from a very poor family in Pinpoint, Georgia. After his father abandoned the family, he was raised by his mother, grandmother, and grandfather. He never dreamed as a child he would even see the Supreme Court, much less be nominated to it. "Indeed, my most vivid childhood memory of the Supreme Court was the 'Impeach Earl Warren' signs which lined Highway 17 near Savannah," Clarence told the press. "I didn't quite understand who this Earl Warren fellow was, but I knew he was in some kind of trouble." He went on to tell us that he had attended an all-black Catholic school taught by white nuns and that his mother, grandparents, and nuns all were adamant that he make something of himself. It was very sweet.

⌒ The Fourth of July was spent parading, literally. Returning Desert Storm veterans were being honored across the country. We started in Marshfield, Missouri, a darling little town that has had a Fourth of July parade for 110 years. They march everything by: at least two sanitation trucks, loads of horses, with or without riders, trick dogs, Boy and Girl Scouts, trucks, fire engines, farm equipment, bands, and of course many, many Desert Storm troops. We were accompanied by Governor John Ashcroft and his lovely schoolteacher wife, Janet, and both of Missouri's senators, Jack Danforth and Kit Bond. John told us how thrilled he was by the Clarence Thomas appointment. They had worked for two years in the same tiny office for then Attorney General of Missouri Jack Danforth. John said and still says that no finer, more decent man exists than Clarence Thomas. And of course his former boss, Senator Danforth, was a huge fan. In light of what happened to Clarence later, this is interesting.

Our second parade was in Grand Rapids, Michigan, with Governor John Engler and his bride, Michelle. It was huge, but the same good feeling ran through both communities and it was heartwarming to see. That night we got home in time to see the fireworks from the Truman Balcony. We invited Marilyn and Dan Quayle and their family to come watch with us. Marilyn and I went upstairs and watched the show from the catwalk on the roof with many of the children. It was wonderful, even when it drizzled. Umbrellas were brought up and we looked like a group of Mary Poppinses. The South Lawn of the White House and the whole Mall were filled with families on blankets. It was a sight to behold.

July 8—Tough times . . . going to lift the sanctions on South Africa, Israel causing trouble and we have the MFN [Most Favored Nation] vote on China. Then you add to that the tough time the Senate is giving our wonderful friend Bob Gates, G's nominee as Director of the CIA, and Clarence Thomas, G's nominee for the Supreme Court. I asked Bob how his kids were doing with the awful attacks being made on him. He said that their friends were great, they all have rallied around the children, but that several of the teachers have said ugly things. How outrageous! Clarence is also being raked over the coals. They are saying he is "anti-Israel, pro-life, a white man in a black man's skin." The women's group NOW and the Black Caucus have come out against him and on and on.

On July 13 we left for the annual G-7 Economic Summit, this year to be held in London, but we stopped en route in Rambouillet, France, so George could meet with François Mitterrand. During a formal arrival ceremony in the courtyard of the chateau, George presented General François Roquejeoffre with the Legion of Merit medal for his leadership during Desert Storm.

While the leaders met, Danielle Mitterrand and their charming granddaughter Justine gave me a tour of the lovely summer home of the President of France, open to the public when they are not in residence. We took a walk through the grounds and toured the Shell House and the Queen's Dairy. They are both made to look like one thing and then turn out to be another. We walked up to a tiny cottage covered with a thatched roof, walked in, and found an exquisite room all decorated from head to toe with shells. They were beautiful. I have seen only one other like it and that was in a marvelous villa at Gasparilla Inn in Boca Grande, Florida. Another tiny room was painted in the fashion of Versailles. This incredible place was a playhouse built for Marie Antoinette. It took ten years to build and they said she rarely, if ever, visited it. The dairy was equally grand when we went inside.

When we arrived in England, we went almost immediately to Number 10 Downing Street for dinner with John and Norma Major:

. . . The security is unbelievable. But remembering the bomb that had gone off about four months ago in the tiny backyard of Number 10, I was pleased. George gave the Legion of Merit to General Peter de la Billière, who led the British Troops in Desert Storm. After the ceremony we went into dinner with Norma and John, just the four of us. They are the most attractive couple. He seems well in command of his role and she seems very less intimidated by the job than she did at Camp David, in fact very comfortable. They took us upstairs to their residence for after-dinner coffee. The only thing I remember is that they had a painting by Winston Churchill. He was a much better painter than I thought. The men talked at length about what must come out of this Summit for Gorbachev (he had been invited to come at the end) and the world.

Once again we stayed at Winfield House, this time with Ambassador Ray Seitz and his wife, Caroline. We heard good things about both of them from everyone. Ray is a career Foreign Service officer, and George appointed him for that reason and for many others, including ability. He felt that the State Department needed the appointment of one of their own—as opposed to a political appointee—to this illustrious post for morale purposes.

It struck me as funny that right in the heart of the city and on this elegant estate we were awakened early in the morning by the cock-a-doodle-do-ing of a rooster who lived nearby!

Norma Major had planned a lovely tour for the G-7 spouses, including a boat ride and lunch on the River Thames, and a visit to Kew Gardens, which was founded in 1759 and is now three hundred acres and exhibits thirty thousand different species. We walked in the gardens and the roses were absolutely at their glorious peak. That night we went to see *Carmen Jones* in the Old Vic Theatre while the heads of state met. The next day we visited a Spinal Injuries Center at Stoke Mandeville Hospital, followed by lunch at Chequers.

That evening Queen Elizabeth and Prince Philip were hosts for a state dinner at Buckingham Palace:

(It was) every little girl's dream and maybe the dream of some not so little girls. . . . We got dressed in black tie and drove to Buckingham Palace with Jimmy and Susan Baker and Nick and Kitty Brady. We were met by HRH Prince Philip and a Lady-in-Waiting. It amused us that François Mitterrand beat us to the party. I'm afraid that he had heard reports that he was always late to everything. Protocol-wise, we should have preceded him, but he came early this time. We were met in the Blue Room by HM the Queen. She looked lovely in a yellow silk gown. No tiara! There were 64 participants, all the regulars and the Prince and Princess of Wales, the latter looking so beautiful in a one-shoulder, many-colored chiffon dress. The young prince seemed so sad. I feel sorry for them as they should be the happiest people in the world. Three former Prime Ministers were there— Heath, Callaghan, and Margaret Thatcher. I sat next to HRH Prince Philip and Former PM Callaghan. Both more than pleasant and charming. The minute the Prince was served he started in, down goes the food and then his plate was whisked away. Hard on Callaghan as he was in what we called "starvation corner," last to be served, and HRH was sitting waiting for the next course. I said: "Don't put your fork down, Sir, or your plate will be taken." He laughed, put down his fork and away went his dinner! Hardly a bite eaten. After dinner our numbers swelled and we had coffee with the new arrivals. George was talking to a group of people when a woman turned to him and said: "Peter, how are you?" and went right on talking to him. He quickly realized that she thought she was talking to somebody else and said: "I'm George Bush, the President of the United States." Needless to say, she was humiliated. A rather humbling experience for my truly humble husband. How we teased him. He later sent her a picture of himself with Ranger and on it he wrote: "I enjoyed meeting you. I'm the one on the left." He hoped that she would think it was funny and that it would put her at ease. Obviously it did not, as he never heard back from her.

Her Majesty then said she had a surprise for us. We went outside on a balcony that overlooked the courtyard. No words can tell how exciting it was. We were led out in the exact middle of the courtyard and stood under an arch. The view in front of us was three great arches into which troops marched, the Air Force, Marine and Guard Bands, about 250 of them. At one time they were joined by about 24 bagpipers. The pièce de résistance was James Galway, the flutist. When he played "Danny Boy," it was, I believe, the sweetest sound I ever heard. They had a laser beam show that out-Disneyed Disney. At one time they flashed the names of the G-7 countries on the far walls and then flashed something symbolic of that country. In our case it was the Statue of Liberty. At the same time they played "God Bless America." It was most generous of Her Majesty. Then came the most amazing fireworks, shooting from the chimneys, rooftops and balconies. Remembering how singed everything gets at Walker's Point after fireworks, I wondered the next day just what Buckingham Palace looked like in the morning. In any case, Her Majesty gave us a storybook evening.

The next morning Princess Diana came by Winfield House with her sons, William and Harry. The two boys were absolutely like any others their age and were very excited to see *Marine One,* which was tethered on the lawn under guard. They asked all the right questions and had a twinkle in their eyes. We asked them if they wanted to see *Air Force One,* the giant Boeing 747, and they rapidly agreed that they did. So we sent them out to Heathrow Airport. I later heard that Danny Barr, the President's pilot, gave them a first-class tour of the whole plane, although I think they were a little disappointed he didn't give them a spin.

Meanwhile their mother and I went to Middlesex Hospital/Hospice to visit the AIDS ward. It was a very moving morning. We met many patients and talked a little about their concerns, one of which was visiting the United States, since our country was not issuing passports to anyone who tested HIV-positive. They didn't specifically ask me about changing the policy; my impression was they wanted to make sure I was aware of it.

I have visited hospice programs twice with Princess Diana and feel that I have learned from watching her. She is so warm and loving to the sick. Their faces light up as she takes time with each person, and she seems to know the right questions to ask.

Before we left London, George and Mikhail Gorbachev had a joint press conference. It was an accident waiting to happen. The press advance team changed their minds three times about the location of the conference, and the White House communications team had to work all night to set up the cables. As it turned out, the wires got mixed and the two leaders' statements and answers were broadcast into their own countries in the other person's language. Now it sounds funny; then, it was very embarrassing. Nevertheless, it was an exciting conference. It was announced that we would visit Russia at the end of July to sign another weapons reduction treaty.

From London we flew to Athens, where we were met by our old friends, Prime Minister Konstantinos Mitsotakis and his wife, Marika. The second morning of our visit, we took a walking tour of the Acropolis. I was so glad I had worn sneakers, for it was very hot and slippery. (Out of respect for our country, you'll be happy to know, I wore matching ones!)

Next stop was Crete, where we toured the Greek ship *Limnos* and the U.S. naval vessel the U.S.S. *Dewert*. The men on the two ships had one thing in common—they were young. Later George told me that he saw the ships tied up stern-to-stern and remembered that in his talk he referred to them as tied bow-to-bow. He corrected it in the speech and sent it back to the writers with a note that said, "The pointy end is the bow."

We went to the Prime Minister's house and were greeted by Marika Mitsotakis and the children. They lived in the most heavenly house high on a hill overlooking the harbor with a view of the mountains and room for the whole family, including four children and nine grandchildren. Although it was beautiful, the best part is being invited into one's home. That is the greatest honor that can be bestowed on a person. It does not matter if the home is large or tiny. I remarked to the Prime Minister's daughter that the house was lovely and she said: "Yes, the house is beautiful, but my mother is the house. It is not the same when she isn't here." A nice tribute to a very nice friend.

We finished our visit with a big evening reception in Athens given by our very able ambassador and wife, Michael and Estelle Sotirhos, and an early-morning greeting to the American community at the U.S. Embassy. This was something we did—or at least tried to do—in every country we visited, to greet the American community, particularly those serving in our embassies, and let them know how much we appreciated their hard work and dedication to their country.

We flew on to Ankara, Turkey, where we renewed our friendship with President and Mrs. Ozal. We were represented there by one of the wisest and most senior of our diplomatic corps, Morton Abramowitz, and his wife, Sheppie, who were retiring after a long and distinguished career, and there was a medal ceremony upon our arrival honoring them.

I have to mention one of the banquets we attended while in Turkey. The table was set with very old gold ware that was not in great condition, but was very beautiful with filigree work. We discovered that it came from the Ottoman period. There was a gold plate in front of each of the 150 guests. I read in the paper that Semra Ozal had bought the plates for our visit. The writer in the paper suggested that they were so ugly (they weren't) that he wouldn't be surprised if she sent them back to France, where she bought them. When you think that Nancy Reagan took so much criticism for china that was given to the White House in her name. Imagine the stir if she had bought gold plates!

Semra and Turgut took us to the beautiful old city of Istanbul, where we toured the Blue Mosque, St. Sophia Cathedral, and Topkapi Palace. It was all too fast, but worth every minute. We saw many Ottoman treasures, an exhibit of whirling dervish dancers, and a small concert using ancient musical instruments. We had lunch during a boat trip on the Bosphorus, almost reaching the Black Sea. I wish we could have. I hadn't realized Turkey is literally in two continents. We had a nice lunch facing Asia, and then the boat turned and we were looking at Europe. This is a beautiful part of the world.

Turgut Ozal was a courageous leader who backed the United Nations Coalition against Saddam Hussein, his very threatening neighbor. He and George were on the phone to each other a lot, and George respected his judgment a great deal. We last saw him in Houston shortly after George left office. The four of us had a cozy lunch and a nice visit. When he died just a short time later, we and the United States lost a good friend.

꙳ A few days after we returned home, George signed the National Literacy Act of 1991. Needless to say, I was thrilled. Secretary of Education Lamar Alexander, Secretary of Labor Lynn Martin, and several congressmen and senators were there. Most had very legitimate reasons for attending, like Senator Paul Simon and Congressman Bill Goodling of Pennsylvania, who have been champions of literacy. As for some of the others, I wasn't sure what their role had been. I was amused to see that when George invited the members of Congress to stand behind him when he signed the bill, there was a lot of elbowing and they all got as close as they could.

I must say that I got more credit than I deserved. I had heard that George was going to give the pen to me, but before he could, Senator Simon spoke up and said: "That pen ought to go to Barbara." I have donated it to the George Bush Presidential Library Center. In the end, however, it's not pens and pictures that count; it's the National Literacy Act that *really* counts. It was the first piece of legislation—and to date, the only one—ever enacted specifically for literacy, with the goal of ensuring that every American adult acquires the basic literacy skills necessary to achieve the greatest possible satisfaction professionally and personally. But even more than that, the act seeks to strengthen our nation by giving us more productive workers and informed citizens.

That summer Joseph Reed announced his resignation as Chief of Protocol. He certainly is one of a kind. He cared for the Diplomatic Corps as though they were his babies. He entertained them at Blair House and made all our foreign guests feel most welcome. He treated the doorman the same way he treated the King of Spain, and that's pretty nice.

⤻ We were barely home when it was time to turn around and fly to Moscow for the treaty signing. We arrived very late on July 29 and went straight to Spaso House, the ambassador's residence. If ever I saw a house that needed a face-lift, this was it. It suddenly looked very shabby and run-down. We were greeted by Ambassador Jack Matlock and his wife, Rebecca, who also were getting ready to retire after years of service.

The next morning we were received in St. George's Hall at the Kremlin. It is large and impressive and very dramatic. Raisa and Mikhail greeted us and after the ceremony was over, Raisa and I went for a tour of the Kremlin:

Just before we went on our tour Raisa took me into a little room and changed her shoes. Much to my amazement she changed from very high suede shoes to very high leather heels. Remembering how her feet got blistered at Camp David in stilts, I thought that she would put on walking shoes. But no—beauty first. We walked to and into the Annunciation Cathedral, by the Cathedral of the Archangel, past the Czar's cannon and bell and into the Armory to see a small portion of the gold, jewels and diamonds. The diamond coronation crown and necklace of Catherine the Great put all the Ottoman Empire jewels to shame. They were so delicate and beautiful with their double-headed eagles.

Back to the Palace for tea. There were loads of tourists. Raisa still loves to plunge into crowds. It is fun.

In the afternoon we went to the Novodevichy Park, where we presented a *Make Way for Ducklings* sculpture to the children of Moscow from the children of the United States. It is an exact replica of the sculpture Raisa and I had visited in Boston Gardens. This was an idea that was thought up and executed by Susan Porter Rose. It took an unending amount of planning and fund-raising to do. The artist who sculpted the original statue, Nancy Schon, offered to duplicate it, and she and her husband were there for the unveiling, along with Robert McCloskey, who had written the book fifty years before. We also brought with us copies of the book in Russian. The setting was perfect, on the Moscow River across from the Novodevichy Monastery and right by a duck-feeding station. Susan literally did not leave a stone unturned: The cobblestones from Boston were surrounded by the black stones from Moscow. Everyone said that the workmen from both countries worked well together. It was a happy and lovely gift. I got the credit and did not deserve it; Susan did.

We met the Gorbachevs at the studio of Zurab Tsereteli, the artist who made the magnificent statue of St. George that is on the United Nations grounds in New York City. This is the most remarkable man, who paints a picture a day just to keep his hand in. Every inch of his studio was covered with paintings, many of them just finished, as George's personal aide, Bill Farish, can testify. Bill had backed up to let us by and had a nice flower on his jacket for the rest of the day. We were led into a back room where the artist unveiled two bronze models of Columbus. He invited us to pick one out, explaining with great enthusiasm that the actual statue would be larger than the Statue of Liberty and would go on the tip of Roosevelt Island, where it will be seen from the United Nations. I know George's heart sank. Who was going to pay for this? Then we were told that it was privately funded. I could see the relief on George's face. We loved that visit and the magnificent artist.

That night the Gorbachevs had a lovely dinner for us in the Kremlin:

We started in the Garden Room, then into the Hall of St. Vladimir for a receiving line—In they poured. Some we knew like Dwayne and Inez Andreas (he is head of the Archer Daniels Midland Co.). Mrs. Yeltsin came through, but no husband—until the very end of the line. We were about to break up the line when in he came, bigger than life. He is outrageous. He wanted a "photo op" with George and Mikhail with himself in the middle, but Mikhail would not turn around, but kept his back to the press pool. "Gorby" moved him on to me and Raisa. Raisa seemed very welcoming—for the press, I guess. Jack Matlock had told me that Yeltsin had criticized Gorbachev in the Parliament and had ended by saying that "besides all other complaints, he was sick of having four telephone calls a day from Raisa Maksimovna Gorbacheva." As everyone had gone into dinner, Boris Yeltsin offered me his arm and said, "As I am going to sit by you at dinner, please let me take you in." I started in with him and then thought better of it and went back to ask Raisa what I should do. She suggested that we all go in together and kept me from making a mistake. I sat between the President of Russia and the President of the Soviet Union. Both men were charming. I must confess that I thought that Boris was using me to needle Mikhail. Evidently they need each other right now, but it is clear that they don't like each other.

The dinner was held in the Palace of Facets—one of the oldest rooms in the Kremlin, built in 1472 by Ivan the Great. It served as a throne room and a reception hall by Ivan and his successors.

The next day we went to a dacha in the countryside where the men talked and Raisa took me for a boat ride on the Moscow River. I loved every minute in the tiny little speedboat. There was a driver and a security guard in the two front seats; Raisa and I were directly behind them; and her interpreter and Jim Sloan, the head of my Secret Service detail, were behind us. Raisa had a small parasol with her and, to her credit, she did offer it to me. I turned it down. It must have been a funny scene as the poor interpreter had to lean forward to hear Raisa and took a chance every time she turned her head that he might lose an eye. All along the way we saw families having a swim in the dirty river and sitting on bare dirt patches, which Raisa called beaches. I couldn't believe the bathing suits. The biggest men and women were in tiny little strings of suits. I got the giggles thinking of how shocked they'd be by my bathing suits with skirts.

Later that day George and President Gorbachev signed the START treaty, another step in ending the Cold War.

That night we had a reciprocal dinner at Spaso House. Almost everything was brought from the White House kitchen. For the first time we produced something really bad—a watercress soup that normally tastes wonderful. If we hadn't been the hosts, I almost would have enjoyed it, since the faces of people as they had their first bitter sip were so funny. The rest of the meal was delicious, but the evening was made because the wonderfully talented Isaac Stern offered to come and play the violin for us.

The next morning we left for Kiev, a city which touched me deeply. It is beautiful and old but with so many problems. I rode in the car with Mrs. Antonia Kravchuk, the wife of the Ukrainian leader and now the President, Leonid Kravchuk. She was the nicest young woman, a math teacher who had absolutely no interest in politics. The crowds along the way were tremendous, so we slowed the motorcade down to enable the people to see George, who was riding in the car ahead of us. We waved and talked all the way in:

Mrs. K. told me some of the awful consequences of Chernobyl that is only sixty miles away. It was and is dreadful in a real sense. They know the ground is contaminated for miles around. They no longer can go into the really lush green forests we passed on the way into town for berries and mushrooms. They don't plant vegetables and wheat anymore even though this Kiev is known as "the breadbasket" of the Soviet Union. Their other main source of income was from tourists, but who would want to come here now? They don't know what will happen to their children and babies. It is so much bigger than I thought.

We and many other countries have sent teams in, but it is all so new. The ghastly part is that it did not need to happen. (The Soviet scientists) were sloppy.

Our last stop before leaving Kiev was a very moving visit to the Babi Yar Holocaust Memorial:

The Germans occupied the Ukraine for two years. When they saw the war was ending, they lined the Jews up, marched them to the field, had them dig trenches, strip and fold their clothes, put their jewelry in another spot and line up by the trenches and they shot them. They killed 33,000 people at the end. I sat next to some of the survivors. One lady was twelve at the time. Her brother and sister were killed. One lady had a baby in her arms, she fell into the trench protecting her baby with her body. When it was all over she pushed her way out through the dead or dying and she and her baby lived. One lady near me had hidden a Jewish family for two years at great personal risk. It is inconceivable to us. What horror—what courage.

Soon after returning home I took off for Maine and the grand-children. I loved how they loved seeing each other, their great-grandmother, and their cousins, the Stapletons. George and Noelle spent hours with Walker and Wendy Stapleton, the children of George's much younger cousins.

Like the summer before, however, this was not to be a real vacation. It all started on August 19:

George and I were going to play golf at the crack of dawn with (Boston Red Sox pitcher) Roger Clemens and his wife, Debbie. Roger was to bring a group of Red Sox players, and the wives and I were going to play after the men. BUT everything was against this game. First of all we were called in the middle of the night and told that there had been a coup in the Soviet Union and that Mikhail Gorbachev and Raisa were under house arrest in the Crimea, where they were on vacation. Our host for some of the trip we recently took, Vice President Yanayev, is now in charge. He is a hard-line Communist. We are seeing tanks in Moscow on the tube. My heart goes out to our friends the Gorbachevs. To his credit Boris Yeltsin is working hard to bring Gorbachev back. When John Major talked to Boris he said, "I only have a few minutes left." He was in his office at the Parliament building and was under siege. We knew it was tenuous at best, but this is such a shock. Rumors are running wild. We heard that Gorbachev was "undergoing treatment." That he has been "put on a ship in the Baltic," that he was "taken to a military base," etc. There are so many questions. Is Raisa with him? I hope so because they are so devoted. It is so frightening. Will the new group keep the recently signed agreements? And there are so many more questions.

Then Hurricane Bob came roaring up the coast and if the coup hadn't cancelled the game the weather would have. The Red Sox came by with tons of souvenirs for the grandchildren and nephews and nieces. The house was like a madhouse. George and Brent (Scowcroft) were on the phone between cups of coffee, the builders had run over to board up our house against the hurricane, and plans were being made for George and Brent to return to Washington. Everyone departed the Point and we who were left spent a quiet day putting away all the porch furniture, toys and the children's tent. In the afternoon the Secret Service said that we must all evacuate. Before we could go we had to move George's mom and aunt to a safe place and then Colu, little Jeb, Paula and I went up to Blueberry Hill, Jane and Jerry Weintraub's beautiful old farmhouse, and settled in for a nap. Noelle and George went to their cousins' house. The winds and rains were fierce and the electricity went out on the farm. The eye of the hurricane went by at 5 p.m. and high tide came at 8 p.m. and so we were lucky. We went back home at 6 p.m. and the swell of the waves in the cove was absolutely magnificent. At 8 p.m. the cousins returned with the other children and we all stood out on the deck and marveled at the sea. George checked in every few hours and all was well with us. Not so great on the Soviet front.

George returned on the 20th.

We awakened to pouring rain. We are getting tired of being damp. They say we have had more rain this August than any other August in history. I really think that 18 inches came down in two or three days.

G. spent the morning on the phone with Yeltsin. He sounds fairly assured or at least not hopeless. Brent and George say that this is the most important day. We will know whether the coup will be overturned. Two of the eight who headed the coup are "ill" and have been removed.

. . . Our house is like a circus. Doro and Colu alleviated some of the strain by taking the three little kids, Sam, Ellie, and Jebby, to the movies . . . we ended up by being 11 at the table. In the middle of it all Pop called me into the bedroom and told me that he was talking to Mikhail Gorbachev. It was very exciting. The coup had failed and we were thrilled. There were so many ramifications if the coup had succeeded and the hard-liners had taken over—back to the days of the Cold War. What would have happened to the Mideast talks? The weapons treaty that was signed just a few weeks ago in Moscow? The giant steps that the Soviet Union had taken towards democracy? . . . Both Gorbachev and Yeltsin thanked George profusely for his statements and for not recognizing the insurgents.

In September I received a letter from Raisa, responding to a letter I had written her. We had heard and read that she suffered greatly during the coup. Among many things she said:

> Those three terrible days were a severe trial for us all. However, we are deeply convinced that such values as freedom, democracy and human dignity, in the name of which perestroika was initiated, have already become irreversible. It makes us happy and inspires optimism.

How relaxing was the rest of the summer? Here are a few excerpts from my diary:

Walter Cronkite and Betsy came by for dinner with an old friend, Bill Harback, and his wife, Barbara. They were cruising up the coast.

. . . Jimmy Dean, the sausage man, came into the river in his boat *The Big Bad John,* named after his big song hit.

. . . G. had a meeting at the house with (Bob) Teeter, (Dick) Darman, (Andy) Card, (John) Sununu . . . Jim Baker just back from talking to NATO Foreign Ministers. He had interrupted his vacation in Wyoming for the meeting.

. . . Arnold and Winnie Palmer came for a few days.

. . . Brian and Mila Mulroney arrived with their four children.

. . . G. had a briefing from Bob Strauss, Dick Cheney, John Sununu, a Russian expert, Bob Gates and Brent Scowcroft. [Bob Strauss had just become Ambassador to the Soviet Union when this all happened. Talk about timing! He did a great job.]

On the 28th Norma and John Major arrived with their children, Elizabeth and James. They are very relaxed guests and eager to sunbathe and walk. The men, of course, talked business.

. . . George had a great tennis match on Thursday afternoon with Jeb as his partner against Craig Stapleton and (Maine Senator) George Mitchell. We had a small group at the house (Nick and Kitty Brady, Speaker Tom Foley, Senate Majority Leader George Mitchell, our family and the Majors) for a drink and then down to the River Club for a Clambake with a larger group including the governors of Maine, Vermont, New Hampshire and Massachusetts. Frankie Hewitt of the Ford Theatre gathered the disbanded cast from *Forever Plaid* who had acted in the show in Washington and we went across the street to the Casino for that great musical. It was a perfect evening.

Before leaving Kennebunkport for the summer I decided, almost as an afterthought, to take the advice of Craig Stapleton, who, after Hurricane Bob, suggested that perhaps I should remove fifty years of scrapbooks and photo albums from the house. He had seen them in our bedroom the day after the storm and just thought maybe they would be safer somewhere else. So Peggy Swift and I boxed them up and shipped them to Washington to be put in storage. Considering what was to happen to our home in a few months, Craig saved those scrapbooks, which I definitely needed to help write this book.

We ended the summer by going home via Lewiston, Maine, where George, Lamar Alexander, and Maine Governor Jock McKernan kicked off America 2000 for the state. A week later I was doing the same thing in Maryland with Governor William Donald Schaefer, Undersecretary of Education David Kearns, and many others, including Lou Sullivan, Bill Reilly, and Jim Watkins from the cabinet. America 2000 was an innovative, bipartisan effort to improve education in our country, and I would attend several more state kickoffs in the coming months. I always loved the enthusiasm and dedication to our children that I found, whether I was at the huge Arsenal Technical High School in Indianapolis or in tiny, rural Winona, Mississippi.

At all the kickoffs I shared with the participants one of the more amazing statistics I had come across. Did you know that if a child never misses a day of school from first grade to twelfth grade, he or she would have spent only 9 percent of his or her life in the classroom? The other 91 percent is spent in the home or out in the community. We cannot expect teachers and the schools to solve all our children's problems.

September 13—This week we have been involved with three black men; three amazing black men. Clarence Thomas, whose mother could not care for him and whose grandparents took him in, sent him to parochial school, expected him to do well, and he did.

Then yesterday at a brown sack lunch at the Dept. of Education I heard Dr. James Comer from Yale University speak on the Comer Schools, a system he created that is being tested in the public schools and it seems to be doing very well. It has a lot to do with getting input from parents, having a strong principal, a strong social aid, great expectations along with a good academic course. Empowering parents seemed to make the big difference. His mother, a housemaid, went through the seventh grade; his father, a laborer, went through third grade. His mother made up her mind that she would marry a man who had the same values that she had. She knew that she would never go to college, but her children would get an education. She had five children who between them got THIRTEEN degrees. Amazing.

Then the third man we saw was Stan Scott, an old friend of ours from the Nixon days. Stan was born into a newspaper family in Atlanta, Georgia. He remembers his grandmother sitting in the back of the segregated trolley listening to him conjugate verbs. She felt that he had to learn to speak correctly to move to the front of the trolley. Stan was one of the first black writers for a white paper. He was nominated for a Pulitzer Prize because of his coverage of Malcolm X's assassination. He worked for Nixon, Ford, Philip Morris and then bought a Miller's Beer franchise which he has just sold for a lot of money. Stan has three children and a magnificent wife, Bettye. He also is riddled with cancer. We saw Stan at a dinner in Washington where the money will go to set up a scholarship in his name at the United Negro College Fund. Stan gave a talk filled with love and gratitude. What a man! [He died April 4, 1992.]

All three of these men had something in common—someone who cared for them, a family member who urged them on.

. . . I read Hume Cronyn's book *Terrible Liar: A Memoir.* I so admire both Hume and his truly talented wife, Jessica Tandy.

. . . I taped thirty-six introductions for the Disney Channel's "Salute to the American Teacher." It is such a worthwhile program. This series runs for nine months and it recognizes excellence in teaching.

September 18—Dee Jepsen (wife of former Senator from Iowa) came by one morning this week to brief me on The National Coalition against Pornography. They are keeping their focus on things that are illegal and those things where children are concerned, so all those disgusting magazines like *Hustler,* etc., are out of children's first strike zone. I am eager to help them as it does have something to do with a healthy child and we have already decided that a child must be healthy in order to learn. (America 2000's first of six goals.) The sexual exploitation of children must be stopped!

. . . I visited the Baptist Senior Adult Ministries Adult Day Care Center. This is on the edge of the University of Maryland and is a wonderful place where older people, retarded adults and people with Alzheimer's can go for the day, 5 days a week, thus giving the caretaker a little relief and not costing what a home or a hospital would cost. I took Millie with me thinking that they would like to see her. I think they did.

I did lots of other programs. Too many to mention.

. . . Joseph Reed gave a lunch for the King of Swaziland. The King came with one of his seven wives. He must marry one lady from each of his tribes. He is twenty-three years old. His wife asked Anna Perez just how old she was and how many children she had. Anna told her that she was forty and that she and Ted had three children. Her Majesty asked Anna what was the matter with her. Anna was nonplussed for once!

Also that fall I did a little work for Childhelp USA, a wonderful group of people who help abused children. Childhelp was founded by two dynamic women, Yvonne Fedderson and Sara O'Meara, who are absolute stars. They also have a star-studded group of Childhelp ambassadors, including Cheryl Ladd, Florence Henderson, Jane Seymour, Dionne Warwick, and Efrem Zimbalist, Jr. I attended the dedication of their new residential treatment facility near Culpeper, Virginia, which means they will have places for children to get help on both the East and West Coast.

At the end of September, George and I spent several days at Sea Island, Georgia. This was our first trip back since our honeymoon forty-six years earlier, although we had planned to return every year. There were people along the route into the Cloisters with signs saying HAPPY ANNIVERSARY, MR. PRESIDENT. It wasn't our anniversary, but it was sweet anyway.

Former Attorney General Griffin Bell arranged golf games for both of us. George played with Griffin, Bill Jones, and Jack Lumpkin. My game was and still is poor, but after a hiatus of thirty years, I had taken it up again and was loving it. I like to play in a twosome right after George's foursome for two reasons: He plays so quickly that he clears the way for me; and I love to see him having fun with his friends. Since he has left office we play a lot together. I can't give him any competition, but I am the only one who will play at 6 a.m. with ten minutes' notice!

Griffin arranged a foursome for me with Louise Suggs, one of the first great professional women golfers who started the women's golf tour. Now a teacher in Florida and Sea Island, she hits the straightest, longest ball with absolutely no effort. He also lined up two other ladies, Fran Green and Carolyn Carter. All three were so much better than I was, but they were a lot of fun and very nice. I think that they were surprised that anyone who played as badly as I did was eager to play the second day. But out they came. Louise took me over to the practice tee and gave me a mini lesson before the game.

We were there for two nights and got a great rest. I only hope we don't have to wait another forty-six years to return.

꩜ We had some fascinating visitors during the fall of 1991. King Juan Carlos and Queen Sophia of Spain came for an overnight at Camp David with their friends and ours, Bob and Georgette Mosbacher. Her Majesty and I visited the National Rehabilitation Hospital. It is such a wonderful place that I loved taking foreign visitors there—and besides that, our Doro was working there.

Another treat for me was that Maeve Binchy, an Irish writer and one of my favorites, came to the White House for lunch with her very nice husband, Gordon Snell. She has written *Light a Penny Candle, The Lilac Bus,* and many others. I invited several of my friends whom I thought would enjoy her: Flo Gibson, who reads books on tape for the blind and others; Nan Ellis, George's sister, who happened to be in

Washington; and, of course, Andy Stewart. I also included Maeve Gallagher, the wife of the new Irish Ambassador. We laughed our way through the meal.

Also that fall, as part of the upcoming five-hundredth anniversary of Columbus's discovering America, the "Circa 1492: Art in the Age of Exploration" exhibit came to the National Gallery. This extraordinary show was a cross section of the world's great art at the time of Columbus. There were many treasures that had never been seen outside their own country. The centerpiece for me was the Leonardo da Vinci *Portrait of a Lady with an Ermine* (Cecilia Gallerani). Now I have seen all three of his ladies, the *Mona Lisa* in Paris and the National Gallery's *Ginevra de' Benci*.

We lost another friend that fall. Nan Rehnquist, wife of Chief Justice Rehnquist, died after years of fighting cancer. It was so sad. Many people did not even know Nan was sick.

And we were agonizing through Clarence Thomas's confirmation hearings. Our whole country suffered, and it was awful to watch the disgraceful procedures on television:

October 11—Clarence Thomas and his wife (Virginia) came over to see George. They are in shock. They cannot believe what is happening. All the women's groups are up in arms and the hue and cry for Clarence's blood can be heard from every side. It is setting a picture that anyone can testify if he or she wants and cause doubts.

Sexual harassment is wrong. Let's hope some good will come of this. Women will now testify if, in truth, they are being harassed.

The question is: Is this woman telling the truth? It is Clarence's word against Anita Hill's. I do not mean to sit in judgment, but I will never believe that she, a Yale Law School graduate, a woman of the 80s, would put up with harassment for one moment, much less follow the harasser from job to job, call him when she came back to town and later invite him to speak to her students at Oral Roberts University. It just makes no sense at all. It also makes no sense to me that this was all publicly aired on television. We are talking about reputations here and a good man was smeared.

October 15—Clarence Thomas's nomination was passed by a 52 to 48 vote.

. . . It is becoming very obvious that the 1992 campaign has already started. George wanted a Civil Rights Bill, a Crime Bill, Tort Reform, a

Capital Gains Tax reduction, the Line Item Veto, Health Care Reform and many more things that the country needs and wants. None of which will happen because the election is a year away. [He did get a Civil Rights Bill later that fall.] I mentioned to George that it had been a sad and ugly week and he said, "Every day is ugly in my life." I hated that. I think I got him when he was very tired.

October 28th—As the election year creeps up on us things get tense. It isn't just the Democrats that knock George, but the press is all over him. It is interesting how they can slant a story by using an ugly word, a qualifier. Like: "Last night a WEAKENED president"; or "The IRRITATED president said."

In late October I flew down to Atlanta at the invitation of Rosalynn Carter to speak at a luncheon for one of her causes, Project Interconnection, a wonderful program that houses mentally ill homeless. After the lunch we went out to visit the Carter Center. It is a glorious seventeen-acre compound that consists of a library, museum, and a center that serves as an umbrella for President Carter's various projects and is connected to Emory University.

We had a minute to visit with the former President, who was gracious and pleasant. I sometimes find Rosalynn to be a complicated person. She is very partisan and not comfortable with me. Earlier in George's administration, I had asked Rosalynn for lunch at the White House, which would have been her first opportunity to see their portraits on display. I told her that we had revived the White House Endowment Fund that had been started under their administration but died during the Reagan years. Her answer: "Good. Republicans have all the money." Huh? Since when have the Harrimans, Roosevelts, Rockefellers, and Kennedys all been Republicans?

I get the feeling that she is a nice lady who loves her husband very much and is not as happy and content as she should be. I could well be wrong and I certainly hope I am. Both President Carter and Rosalynn have made a large contribution since leaving the White House, working for the good of others, housing for the homeless, and so forth.

The next week I went to Dallas to visit George W., Laura, and the girls while George went to Spain for the beginning of the Middle East Peace Talks. One night, while having dinner at the home of Elvis and Joan Mason, we watched George and Mikhail Gorbachev open the talks.

It was so thrilling to watch what was going on in Spain. It was such an amazing group of people sitting at the same table—Israelis and Arabs—who harbored so many ancient animosities. Just the fact they had sat down together was a miracle.

The next day I visited the Scottish Rite Hospital, where they are doing marvelous things for children with learning disabilities, and then on to Brian's House, where Laura works with AIDS babies.

That afternoon I was working away on my computer when Peggy Swift and Jim Sloan came into my room looking very serious. As George was just returning from Spain, they scared me. They quickly reassured me that he was okay, but said that a terrible storm was raging in Kennebunkport and it looked like we had lost our house. There were thirty-foot waves at Kennebunk Beach. Thirty feet! The agents had to abandon Walker's Point, but our longtime agent and friend, Tom Clarke, was watching from a safe house and reported seeing waves breaking over the three-story house. It was so hard to believe. We had to wait and see what the next high tide would do in the middle of the night, but they could see horrible damage already.

I called George. I needed to talk to the one other person who cared as much as I did—even more, if possible. George had gone into a meeting before the agents could brief him, so I was the one who broke the news to him. He said he would call me right back. When he did, he told me that everything I had heard was true, but that I must not worry. It would be all right. It was such a comfort to talk to him.

I called Laura and George W. Then Doro called me "just to check in" and I had to tell her.

That night I went to a dinner honoring Ralph Rogers. What a remarkable man he is. He founded Texas Industries, and then, in 1970, helped found PBS and later the Children's Television Workshop, which does "Sesame Street." At this time he was working hard on a preschool children's program, P.E.P. He has been a great contributor to many community programs. I love Ralph, but I don't know how I got through that evening.

After the event I flew to Houston, where I was to meet George and spend the weekend. Neil met me at the airport and, yes, I had to tell him. I hated being the one having to deliver all this bad news. What a Halloween! More trick than treat. It was a dreadful night.

Early in the morning George called and told me that the house was standing, but the damage was extensive. Unfortunately, we had several agonizing days of commitments in Texas, but George's thoughtful brother John went to Maine immediately and reported back. He said it was awful, that among other things, our first-floor bedroom was a wreck. I asked him about the bookshelves (where our scrapbooks and photo albums had been up until two months ago!) and he said, "What bookshelves, Bar?" At that point we decided we had to cancel the weekend in Texas and go to Maine.

We couldn't believe what we saw. The deck was totally ripped up, the stone walls were down in many spots, the Wave was ripped off its foundations, and the porch was gone. I had just redone the Wave, a little guest house, and I just could not bring myself to even look in the door. I should have, for after it had been moved, propped up on blocks, and moved back onto a new foundation, we discovered that only one glass had been broken. Lamps, books, and china had stayed put, and the little bedroom looked spic-and-span.

That was not true of the big house. The living room walls were gone, and with them, every stick of furniture. It looked like a ball-room. The whole downstairs was either broken or demolished or gone. Forty percent of the dock was gone. The dock, the stone walls, and the house had been there since 1902. Now all eleven acres were strewn with our books and belongings.

Betsy Heminway had dropped everything and driven to Kenne-bunkport to help. Our nephew Billy Bush and our cousin's child Jay Field came down with two other boys from Colby College and worked alongside us shoveling sand, rocks, broken glass, and china out of the downstairs rooms. Amazingly, the second and third floors had not been touched.

I ran the gamut of emotions. What did I feel about the house in Kennebunkport? Of course I had dark moments. It had meant so much to George and his whole family and, in all honesty, to me. But for some reason I also felt so fortunate, so loved, and so surrounded by family and friends. Then I would remember my little garden, our beautiful living and dining rooms that Mark Hampton had helped decorate, and I would feel like weeping again. Then I would think about the many people up and down the coast who lost everything and who didn't have George Bush and great kids and I would realize how lucky I was.

That Christmas our cousin Susue Robinson suggested to all our relatives that this might be a great year to give us something that plugged into the wall. Just think about what we take for granted: lamps, toasters, waffle irons, washing machines, dryers, irons, ovens, TVs, refrigerators, dishwashers, and on and on. George, of course, replaced big kitchen appliances. Susue offered to coordinate the gifts to be sure we didn't receive ten toasters. All this was unbeknownst to us. Our Christmas was a large surprise, and needless to say, we were very touched.

Our builders, the Philbricks, started work immediately and did a great job working under the worst conditions. George's mother once again gave us the tennis court as a present. (It had been a joint birthday present in 1980.) Then I traveled to High Point, North Carolina, to the furniture store of Edgar Broyhill, the son of the former senator and our friend Jim Broyhill, and I picked out materials and ordered couches, chairs, tables, and some odds and ends for the first floor. As much of our old furniture as possible was repaired by a superb refinisher in Maine, John Dickinson. By May we were in our finished and furnished house thanks to the hard work and generosity of many friends.

As I write this in January of 1994, I feel very lucky all over again. The people of Los Angeles are digging out from underneath a horrible earthquake and parts of the East and Midwest are suffering from one of the worst winters on record. Mother Nature can be so brutal and unforgiving sometimes, and I hope and pray that all those hurting now will find the same love and support we did.

━━━━

⌒ In November we went to the opening of the Reagan Library, which is in a most glamorous setting on a hillside in the Simi Valley. Lady Bird Johnson, Dick and Pat Nixon, Jerry and Betty Ford, and Jimmy and Rosalynn Carter also came, and it was a nice reunion for us all. Now we have seen the libraries/museums of all the living former presidents and a few of the others.

All the presidents spoke briefly. Jimmy Carter was very amusing when he said that the Republicans were getting four times more speaking time than the Democrats. He also went on to say that he was the only person on the stage who had never met a Democrat president. (He has now, darn it.)

President Reagan gave a marvelous speech which brought back

great memories of that lovely man. There was one sad thing. Pat Nixon did not look well at all. She was very frail-looking and through her smile you could see that she was in great pain and having a terrible time getting air into her lungs. She and Dick did not come to the lunch, but quietly slipped away. This gentle lady died in June of 1993. She was a wonderful person and First Lady, and my memories of her are all good.

Also in November we took a quick four-day trip to Italy and Holland. In Rome, while George attended NATO meetings, I of course got to have all the fun. First I visited the Capitoline Museum, then went to Valentino's thirtieth anniversary show of unbelievably beautiful dresses, many loaned by their owners, including Audrey Hepburn, Jackie Kennedy, and Brooke Astor. The money from the show, which also traveled to the United States, went to benefit AIDS. Next I went to Boys' Town, a home for boys from seventeen foreign countries, including political refugees. Many Americans support this community, including Pete and Joan Secchia, our ambassador and his wife, who had planned this marvelous trip for me. Monsignor John Patrick Carroll-Abbing, the founder, took me on the tour.

Something very funny did happen there, which shows how quickly—and innocently—you can get into trouble. They asked me to get up and say a few words to a school assembly, which was difficult since I didn't know Italian and few of the boys spoke English. At one point during my talk, I used sign language to say "I love you." As it turns out, a slight variation of that gesture has an obscene meaning in Italy! At least one Italian newspaper mentioned it the next day.

Before leaving Rome, we had a nice visit with the Pope and the American community. His Holiness, a true man of peace, was most generous with his time. We then flew on to the Netherlands, where we were happy to see Prime Minister Ruud Lubbers and his wife, Ria. We had dinner with Her Majesty Queen Beatrix at the Noordeinde Palace, and I sat next to the Prime Minister, who told me an interesting piece of trivia.

I was asking Ruud about the beautiful lady who was on the wall looking down at us. He said that she was a Russian princess with very extravagant tastes, a Romanov. After ten years of marriage she ran out of money and wrote her father, the Czar of Russia, to please send her some. He said that he would, but that she had some pictures that he would like in return. Thus the beginning of the incredible Hermitage Collection—which explains why they have so many Dutch and Flemish masters' paintings!

༄ Shortly after we returned home President Carlos Menem came for a state visit from Argentina. He is a charming man and George told me he really was working hard at privatizing his country and making a democracy. He and George struck up a real friendship and over the years had fun playing tennis both in Argentina and the United States.

All that fall the press was swirling. It seems to me, looking at my diary, that both sides were making mistakes, and the press was waiting to pounce. Senator Bob Kerrey of Nebraska, and a Democratic presidential candidate, told a filthy, insensitive joke about lesbians to Bill Clinton and a live microphone picked it up. Then Dan Quayle's press secretary, Dave Beckwith (whom I like very much), made a tasteless remark about that and had to apologize. Mario Cuomo called Dan Quayle "Danny boy" in a most denigrating way, and yet when Dan called him Mario, the Governor said that it was an ethnic slur. John Sununu attacked Ann Devroy of *The Washington Post* and that caused great excitement. She had been attacking him for weeks in the paper and that was okay, but he got clobbered for retaliating. I guess along with never putting on a hat or a helmet for the cameras, one of the first lessons someone in public life must learn is: THE PRESS HAS THE LAST WORD.

The pressure was mounting on John, who had come under criticism for a variety of things, including misuse of government planes. On December 1 he turned in his letter of resignation. He had been such a great friend and it hurt, but he knew best. He has gone on to great things in the private sector, including appearances on CNN's "Crossfire," where he makes the conservative argument with humor and sanity.

The day George was having a press conference to announce John's replacement and his campaign team, I tuned in to TV to watch:

I sat watching CNN and suddenly realized that they were not going to leave the Willie Smith rape trial for George's press conference. I finally found him on C-SPAN. He announced Sam Skinner as his new Chief of Staff, Bob

Mosbacher as campaign chairman, and Bob Teeter, Fred Malek, Mary Mata-lin, Rich Bond, Charlie Black and George W. as the team.

The Willie Smith trial is dominating the news . . . I'm not sure that this should be on television. It is such an intrusion on both the accused and the accuser.

On December 7 we flew to Hawaii for the fiftieth anniversary of the bombing of Pearl Harbor. What an emotional day that was:

We went by launch to the USS *Arizona* Memorial. Many of the fleet was in port and sailors were lined up saluting their Commander in Chief as he went by. I had expected to be moved, but never as much as I was. There were survivors there and families of those who to this day are below in the sunken ship. Within sight of where we were sitting we could see the hull of that enormous ship itself just below the surface of the water, and every few minutes a dot of oil from the ship popped up and a tiny shiny oil slick appeared for a moment. After all these years it was still leaking. Eleven hundred men were entombed right below us. Pearl Harbor must have been much as it was that morning fifty years ago, beautiful, sunny, calm and peaceful when those planes came over. An 89-year-old Congressional Medal winner introduced George. He was not only moving, but visibly moved. We kept silent at the infamous moment when the raid started—7:55 a.m., I believe, and then taps were played, a flyover, and George and I dropped leis into the hole where one looks down to see the hull. I know that this day brought back many memories for George. One man yelled out to George and said: "George, San Jac!" George turned around and looked at the man and said, "Frank, how are you?" Frank said, "You have a great memory," and George said, "I read your name tag, but I certainly remember you." I asked him in the car if he really remembered Frank and he did—forty-seven years later. Amazing. I thought that George looked younger than anyone else we saw there. At one time during the day we went over to the enormous *Missouri* and George did some tapings, which were then played during half-time of the Army-Navy game. Think how the world has changed in these fifty years. Then we did not have TV for civilians, and now George can be seen in a football stadium in Philadelphia when he is in Hawaii.

We returned home to a totally decorated White House. This was our prettiest Christmas of all, I believe. It was a needlepoint Christ-mas: The tree was covered with needlepoint ornaments, plus a town, a Noah's Ark with all the animals, and of course the crèche—all of needlepoint.

December 8—I have just returned from the press showing of Christmas at the White House. I think they all agreed that it looked spectacular. There are 26 trees on the State Floor. It took 40 volunteers approximately 1,600 hours to do the decorating. They started on December 2nd and finished on the 8th at 3 p.m. More than 100,000 people will tour the White House between now and December 29th. The State Dining Room has the 22nd Gingerbread House made by Hans Raffert with Hansel, Gretel, the witch and this year Millie. Hans was careful to explain that the reason Ranger wasn't there was because Millie was the "First Dog." It's in the eyes of the beholder, I guess, or maybe Ranger's forays into the kitchen were not always welcome. More than 500 people contributed to the needlepointing, 314 Saintly Stitchers from St. Martin's Church in Houston and another 290 people including White House staff, friends and relatives. (Even Skip Allen in the Usher's Office needlepointed a jack-in-the-box.) There are 1,370 pieces. (Florist) Nancy Clarke, who truly is an artist, made most of the patterns and organized the whole project. She estimates that 150,000 working hours were spent on this year's decorations.

What really made that Christmas special, however, was that all the hostages finally came home! Terry Anderson, Thomas Sutherland, Joseph Cicippio, Alann Steen, and Jesse Turner helped George light the National Christmas Tree on the Ellipse and then came to the White House for a reception. How good it was to see those fine men home and with their families.

All our children with the exception of Jebby and his troop came for Christmas. We missed them badly, but talked often.

On Christmas Day President Gorbachev resigned and the Soviet Union ceased to exist. It was not a shock—the country had been unraveling ever since the August coup as one republic after another declared its independence. And yet, it was a shock. Suddenly, the Cold War truly was over. The country that had been our enemy most of my life no longer existed. We were excited at the prospect of democracy coming to all these new republics—including Russia—but still nervous at the uncertainties ahead.

And we felt great sadness for the Gorbachevs. He was, after all, the one who introduced perestroika and glasnost, which eventually brought freedom to his country. He was instrumental in ending the arms race and the Cold War—and now he was out of power. I wondered about Raisa, whom I had grown to like very much, and whom I knew loved her country and husband deeply. A new wind was blowing . . .

  ❮ Speaking of which: Exactly one week before Christmas, I flew to Concord, New Hampshire, on a cold, snowy day and officially filed the papers declaring George a candidate in the Republican New Hampshire primary. Pat Buchanan had just thrown his hat into the ring, challenging George from the ultraconservative right wing of the party.

  It had begun.

23

"Back & Forth and Ups & Downs"

Our New Year began on the other side of the world—literally. We landed New Year's Eve in Sydney, Australia, the first leg of a trip to the Far East. We immediately cruised out to the Admiralty House Dock, where we walked into a reception and watched New Year's Eve fireworks with Prime Minister Paul Keating and his wife, Annita, and Governor General Bill Hayden and his wife, Dallas.

When this particular trip had been planned, Bob and Hazel Hawke were in office, and she had sent me a letter saying she was looking forward to our visit. Suddenly they were out and the Keatings were in. We did see the Hawkes, whom we liked very much. Like Margaret Thatcher, they were beaten by a challenger from their own party, which is not much fun. We knew that we had Pat Buchanan to look forward to when we got home, and we were reminded of the new breeze blowing. At that time, I didn't think that George and I would be caught in it.

We immediately liked the Keatings, too. Annita, a lovely, slender native of the Netherlands with long curly hair and a great smile, had met Paul when she was working for Alitalia, and he courted her all over the earth.

Accompanying us on the trip were Secretary of Commerce Bob Mosbacher and a group of American businessmen, most of whom were connected to the auto industry. George had invited them to join us to promote American exports abroad since trade issues were a prime focus of the trip.

446

I should note here that soon after returning home, Bob Mosbacher left Commerce to go to the campaign. Barbara Franklin, an old friend and a very smart businesswoman, became the new Secretary, joining Lynn Martin and Carla Hills in the cabinet, the first time three women served at the same time.

We flew on to Canberra, the capital, a beautiful new city which we have watched grow over the years. When we got off the plane for the arrival ceremony, I noticed that George's military aide's back was covered with flies. Suddenly, I realized that I was, too. This is sheep country, and we came right during the fly season. We were teased about how quickly we learned the "Australian wave" because you just have to keep fanning your face to keep the flies away. We stayed with our Ambassador and his wife, Mel and Betty Sembler. They are a magnificent couple from Florida who started STRAIGHT, a very successful drug rehabilitation program. Betty had a fly "zapper" right in the kitchen.

There is so much that is lovely about Canberra that helps you forget those darn flies. The buildings are magnificent and the vistas lovely, and the people of Australia are warm, relaxed, and very much like Texans, the biggest compliment I can pay anyone.

One night we had dinner with the Governor General and Dallas Hayden. Their house and the view through the park in the back were glorious. We saw kangaroos jumping about, which I loved. I suspect that they are like our deer, who eat our gardens and generally are a pain.

Next stop was Singapore. Our Ambassador was the former Governor of Indiana, Bob Orr, and his wife, Josie, had done a stunning job of redoing the temporary residence, all in black and white.

That night, President and Mrs. Wee Kim Wee gave us a grand dinner. George, as usual, put a lot of pepper on his food, and the next morning he awakened feeling fine but with a black tongue. I went for Burt Lee, who took one look and in amazement said: "Holy Cow!!" I told Burt that that was hardly comforting from your doctor. They were not sure if it came from medicine that George was taking for his fire ant bites that he got while hunting in Beeville, Texas, just before the New Year, or from the pepper, or from all the octopus we had been eating. We told George not to stick his tongue out and all would be well.

We flew on to Korea, where our Ambassador, Don Gregg, and his wife, Meg, met us. When George was vice president, Don was his National Security Adviser. We were thrilled to have a chance to see them again and stay in their home.

A small group of us had a beautiful Korean dinner with President and Mrs. Roh Tae Woo, after meeting their children and two of their grandchildren. They were living in a new official residence, the Blue House, named for the blue titles on the roof. The old house was built by the Japanese when they occupied the Korean peninsula before and during World War II, and the Koreans hated it for that reason. I noted in my diary that in Australia, Singapore, and Korea I found real distrust of the Japanese—if not hatred. It always amazed me that you still can find the same feeling today in Europe about Germany.

The next night, at the state dinner, the Rohs (pronounced "Nohs") had an enormous cake wheeled in to celebrate our forty-seventh wedding anniversary. I sat next to the President on my right and the Chief Justice on my left. I asked the latter if he spoke English, and his exact answer to me was: "I cannot communicate with you." And he didn't. It could have been worse. I remember another Korean dinner that went on forever where neither partner spoke a word of English.

We left Korea the next morning for a marvelous day in Osaka and Kyoto, Japan, with our old friends former Prime Minister and Sachiyo Kaifu. They are such a nice, positive couple. Yuko Kojima, newly engaged to the Kaifus' son, was there and interpreted for me on the whole trip. We toured the Kyoto Imperial Palace and ate lunch in the famous Tsuruya Restaurant, sitting on pillows on the floor. It was exotic and very good.

We went on to Nara to visit a recently opened Toys "R" Us store, which was a real breakthrough for American trade.

Then on to Tokyo, where we stayed at the Akasaka Palace, the Japanese guest house. It was as I remembered it, the grandest, most ornate palace I have ever seen, copied from the gilded European Victorian era, I believe. The service was the same, the very best. The next morning we had the official arrival ceremony in the courtyard of our Palace.

. . . The Emperor and the Empress were the official greeters. She, Michiko, is a lovely, graceful, thin lady. She was a commoner, the first. We were told by PM Miyazawa that her mother-in-law made her life miserable.

We loved her gentle ways. On this trip we discovered that she quietly goes to the U.S. Embassy to play duets with Bonny Armacost on the piano. The whole Imperial family is musical. The Crown Prince Naruhito is very attractive and not married. He must marry a girl who is willing to give up her job and live a secluded life. We keep hearing rumors that he is in love with our friends the Owadas' daughter, who is at their state department.*

. . . We climbed into a car and went to pay a courtesy call on Emperor Akihito at the Imperial Palace. We sat in the same room where we had talked with his father and where we had met with this Emperor and wife when he came to his father's funeral in 1989. The exchange of gifts was embarrassing. We gave them a quilt. Granted, it was pretty, but I did not feel very appropriate. [I think the State Department thought it was a very "American" gift to give.] They gave us a big painting, a lovely plate and a box. They will go to GB's museum.

Mrs. Miyazawa (wife of the Prime Minister) and I visited the American Trade Fair in the Mitsukoshi Department Store, their Bloomingdale's. We saw everything from cars to electrical appliances.

I think by now most of us know how that day ended:

At 3:20 I went and took tea with the Empress and her daughters-in-law and the young prince. We watched George and our Ambassador, Mike Armacost, play and be beaten in tennis by the Emperor and the Crown Prince. After tennis we went back to our rooms and George told me he didn't feel very well, but not too bad. He saw the doctor and then took a nap for several hours, after which we rushed to a dinner that the Prime Minister was having. We stood in a receiving line for quite a while and then George asked to be excused. I thought he had been called to the phone. Not true. He had been violently sick to his stomach.

This was a big dinner, mostly men, the two Cabinet members, Nick (Brady) and Bob (Mosbacher), the businessmen who were traveling with us, a lot of George's traveling squad and many Japanese businessmen and officials. We were in a long thin room with a balcony at the far end where several cameras were set up. I do know that our hosts had been very strict about no aides hovering about. There was a head table and three long tables going the length of the room. Not another living human could have been seated and left room for waiters to serve.

* For once, rumors were right. He married Masako Owada in 1993.

It was a beautiful meal and all seemed to be going well, but George certainly did not look well. I noticed that Rich Miller, the head of George's Secret Service detail who was seated halfway down the room, never took his eyes off him. George was seated between the PM and his very nice wife. Suddenly he leaned over and told the Prime Minister and me that he wasn't feeling well and thought he better leave—the next thing you knew—he passed out, his eyes rolling back in his head while getting sick. The PM caught him and held him. I was so proud of our Secret Service and medical team. They were there in a second. It all happened so quickly. A large agent charged down the middle aisle and the PM said in a firm voice: "You stand there and guard your president." I believe that he meant for him to stand between George and the cameras. That big man did not move. We all learned later, one camera was left on and unattended and that's how the word of George's ailment was instantly seen around the world. I hated that because Doro saw it as she was getting dressed to go to work.

George came to immediately, realized where he was and said: "Maybe you better roll me under the table, let me sleep and you just go on with your dinner." They had pushed a stretcher down one side of the room and Rich Miller told George he was going to help him walk to it. George said absolutely not. He would walk out of that room by himself. He asked for his tie, which they had removed, and put it back on lying on the floor, which in itself is no mean feat, and walked out smiling and apologizing after asking me to give his toast. He looked awful, and, I guess, felt the same. How I wanted to go with him, but I felt I must stay or people would think he was really ill. You are not trying to fool the public or press, but you don't want to panic the world either unnecessarily. Once again I was really scared—was he really sick? That was one long dinner!

Prime Minister Miyazawa made a friend for life in me. He held George with such care before Rich Miller tried to stretch him out on the floor. I can remember Rich saying to Dr. Roberts, who was on duty that night, "I can't lift him," and the quiet voice of Kiichi Miyazawa saying, "You have my leg." No wonder he couldn't lift him. That's quite a load, a president and a prime minister at the same time.

I also remember Nick Brady saying "Give him air." I had night-mares about the fact that I hadn't moved to my precious husband's side. Several weeks later I was relieved to see a series of TV pictures that showed me wiping George's face and trying to help and then stepping back to let the medical team in. Once again, it reminds me that eyewitness accounts are not always true. I could have sworn that I had not touched George and that really worried me.

I do not know how to explain what happened later during the toast, but I do know that whatever I said must have worked. Sometimes somebody up there just leans down and the right thing happens. I remember making a joke about George being such a poor sport for losing his tennis game that afternoon. I later apologized to our ambassador for making a little fun of his tennis game and blaming him for the whole incident. His response: "That's what ambassadors are here for."

When we got home from our trip we had lots of mail about George's sickness, but the letter that I liked best said:

> Dear Mrs. Bush,
> Tell Mr. President not to be embarrassed that he threw up on international TV. I once threw up on my dog.
> Love,
> Jennifer

The next morning I kept my regular schedule while George slept. By the afternoon he was feeling better and was able to hold his meetings and get back on schedule.

(I went to a) luncheon hosted by Bonny Armacost at the U.S. Residence. Bonny is a lovely person who does her country proud as does her fine husband. Hanae Mori, the great dress designer, was there, a concert pianist and other ladies who all star in their fields. One of the Japanese ladies gave us a second day of lectures on male dominance in Japan. This came up because many wives had not been invited the night before to the dinner. She elaborated on her life in Washington, saying that Japanese men did not include their wives even in the District of Columbia.

That night we went in black tie to a beautiful dinner that the Emperor and Empress had for us. The Emperor and Empress were waiting for us at the door. They led us upstairs and introduced us to their family. There were about ten members there. The brother of the late Emperor, his son, etc. Then into dinner. Their Highnesses had shortened the evening by an hour, which was most kind. The most thoughtful thing of all was that Her Highness had a special dinner cooked for George that the four of us ate, bland and pureed food. It was delicious and just what he needed. I did see several of the wives that had not been invited the night before.

. . . I sat next to the Empress and the Crown Prince. He studies medieval transportation, especially as it relates to travel on the Thames River, I believe. He was a great dinner partner. Because they live such restricted lives, so to themselves, they must develop interests in order to survive. The Empress told me that their tiny lovely little princess daughter studies the kingfisher.

. . . We are reading that the trip was a failure. That is not true. It was a trade trip and many of the things we went for, we got. We are trying to get a level playing field for our manufacturers and workers. Many restrictions were lifted.

Unfortunately, George's illness, which was blown out of proportion, put a shadow on the trip. I was disappointed to learn that many people in the traveling party—including press—had come down with the same flu, but that was never reported, so rumors about George's health started again.

    ∽ We came home to plunge into New Hampshire and the first primary, while still trying to carry on real-life duties. The experience was so different from previous years. First, Iowa was not a factor. Since one of their senators, Tom Harkin, was in the race on the Democratic side, and because on our side Pat Buchanan was concentrating on New Hampshire—partially because the economy was getting better in Iowa—there was just no race there.

On the other hand, the economy was bad in New Hampshire and the other New England states. During previous campaigns, I was told their kids were dropping out of high school as soon as the law would allow (age sixteen) because they could make $9 an hour in fast-food restaurants at the mall. Every window would have a Help Wanted sign.

This year, there were no jobs, malls were closing or had boarded-up stores, and kids were staying in school. Was that the silver lining in a very black cloud?

On February 17, the day before the primary, I ate an early lunch and took off for one last day of speaking and shaking hands in New Hampshire. It was sort of sad after twelve years.

While campaigning hard for George, I was watching the five Democrats flail away at each other. The one thing they had in common was George, and they were really bashing him, to say the least.

In a state that small it was hard not to cross paths. On that last night, I was at a Manchester TV station at the same time as Bill Clinton and Jerry Brown. We didn't see the former, but Jerry and I ran right into each other. He stuck out his hand and said, "Hi, I'm Jerry Brown." I said, "Hi, I'm Barbara Bush." We smiled, shook hands, and went our separate ways.

The final vote in New Hampshire was Bush 58; Buchanan 40. The original estimates were that the vote would be much closer, so we were pleased. It was interesting to me that George got much of his vote from women. The gender gap had narrowed, at least in this state. The exit polls also showed that the higher the education, the more people voted for George.

⌒ Of course there was no time to rest and, in fact, George was already campaigning in the Super Tuesday states. Earlier in February he had gone to Orlando, Florida, to attend the National Grocers Convention:

He saw the newest state-of-the-art device for checking out. It is not on the market yet, but the press all had a week of fun acting like George was "out of touch" and had never seen a checkout scanner. They knew darn well that this was new and revolutionary. The author of the original story, Andrew Rosenthal of *The New York Times,* hadn't even been there, but just wrote (his story) from the press pool report.

Eventually some of the press did write about how the story was blown out of proportion, but not until after media all over the country had picked it up and the damage was done. Columnists used it right up until Election Day.

What's almost even more frustrating, however, is that nearly two years later, we're still hearing about this erroneous story. I was watching "60 Minutes" on January 16, 1994, when I heard Andy Rooney refer to the fact that George was "out of touch." His proof: George had never seen a grocery store scanner. Baloney! Once these stories get into the computer systems, they never die, even if they are not accurate.

I did wonder sometimes in the White House if it was worth awakening every day to the abuse that opponents and the press give the President. I knew that George was the best. I could not have survived without that knowledge. AND, I could not have survived without friends. Andy Stewart, of course, was the very best, but Betsy Heminway and Phyllis Draper were also so great about checking in and coming by when they were in town. And my 90th Club ladies were all supportive. I also knew that I could call Mildred Kerr, Betty Liedtke, Bobbie Fitch, or Marion Chambers in Houston.

       🖎 In February George asked Doro to head the U.S. delegation to the Winter Olympics. The rest of the delegation consisted of Don Johnson, Melanie Griffith, Nancy Ellis, and George's friend from Andover and Yale days, Osborne Day. Ossie had been in the ski patrol during World War II and had skied in the very place where the Olympics were to be held, Albertville, France.

For the last year or so Doro had been getting back into the mainstream of single life. It was not easy to date, however, when you were the daughter of the President. It was a job sorting out who liked her for herself and who liked her for being George Bush's daughter. She is so funny and kept us laughing about some of her experiences.

For example, she had learned not to accept a date for cocktails *and* dinner. Instead, she would say, "I can't have dinner, but I'd love to meet you for a drink. You see I have to get home to my *two children*." That immediately cut the list down. Then, if they stayed on board, she would meet them for the drink and if she liked them, she could say that if they still wanted to have dinner, she had gotten a baby-sitter after all. I can't remember that she ever got beyond the drink with many men. I do remember that one time she went to meet a man whom one of her cousins felt she must meet. They barely had sat down when he said: "Let me tell you what I don't like about your father . . ." Doro jumped up and explained that she had just come by to tell him that she couldn't meet him after all—a crisis at home!

But by February of 1992, Doro had met a man who seemed very

nice and it was becoming apparent to her father and me that she was getting serious. While Doro was on her Olympics trip to France, Bobby Koch called and asked if he could come up to Camp David to talk to George. He told George that he wanted to ask Doro to marry him when she returned home. Bobby worked for Dick Gephardt, a Democratic congressman from St. Louis who as House Majority Leader often attacked George, sometimes pretty viciously. Bobby told George that it was time for him to change jobs and he would before the marriage, if she accepted. George would not have asked him to do that; Bobby offered.

I could hardly stand it when Doro got home from Europe. I so wanted to tell her, but I didn't. On the fifteenth of February she called in tears to tell us that she was engaged. Bobby had taken Sam, Ellie, and Doro out to dinner and proposed to all three of them. Doro said that Sam's reaction was: "Oh, yeah!" He gave Doro a lovely ring with three beautiful diamonds, one for each of them. We instantly adored Bobby. When your children are happy, everything seems better.

February 23—I had a nice quiet morning yesterday. I did my mail and rode the stationary bike for an hour and read Margaret Truman's *Murder on Capitol Hill*. That's fun. I recently had finished Maeve Binchy's *Circle of Friends* and hated to see it end.

. . . I went over to thank the volunteers who sort and answer my mail. They say that I am still getting over 100,000 letters a year. I only see a sample of my mail. They claim that I see the bad with the good. I do get letters from people who are hurting. Darn this economy. There is just no reason that it does not pick up, interest rates are down, inflation is down and there are signs that things are moving in the right direction.

. . . Walked over to see the most wonderful show at the Corcoran Gallery, a picture of the black world called "Songs of My People." It is very powerful and moving.

George and I traveled, separately and together, to campaign and do fund-raisers, from Florida to California, Texas to Colorado, back and forth and up and down.

One afternoon I flew to Peoria, Illinois, and spoke at the Annual Washington's Day Birthday Dinner with and at the request of the Minority Leader of the House, Bob Michel, and his wife, Corinne. What a rock Bob had been for his president. George always knew he could count on him. He will be missed by his country when he retires, as he is not running for reelection in 1994.

We visited the Reagans in their beautiful new house in California.

We had a Drug Summit in San Antonio attended by the presidents of Mexico, Colombia, Ecuador, Bolivia, Peru, and the Minister of Foreign Affairs from Venezuela.

In Houston I helped dedicate the Barbara Pierce Bush Elementary School. Now that was exciting—I had my own school. I couldn't help but wonder what my father would think. This past Christmas (1993), I went to hear their choir sing and they were very, very good—of course!

As we toured the country I met more hairdressers than I could believe. I never traveled with a hairdresser, either at home or abroad, but instead found someone locally. They all were nice, some better than others, but they all were willing to come at the crack of dawn to comb out my hair. Some looked so teased up or disheveled themselves that I would give them my head with fear and trembling.

One morning on the campaign trail I walked into Peggy Swift's room to have my hair done and there was a middle-aged man who had brought his wife with him, thank heavens. This poor man seemed nervous, but that was normal in little towns. Often people were nervous when they had to do the hair of the wife of the president. What wasn't normal was that the poor fella had not zipped up his trousers. As he did my hair I could see his wife notice the omission and begin to try to catch his eye. After he was finished, Peggy brought the photographer, Carol Powers, in to take my picture with the couple. I took pity on the man and asked them to wait one moment while I put on my pearls and lipstick. While I was gone the wife took care of the problem, but I bet they have had fun telling that story and I hope they had a laugh. We certainly did.

On a trip to England a young man came dressed from head to toe in black leather, had an earring in his left ear, long stringy hair, and what looked like a week-old beard. He was late because the Secret Service was reluctant to let him up to the room—and he wondered why. I sort of mentioned that he did not look like your run-of-the-mill hairdresser and asked him why in the world did he want to look like Arafat? He said that he looked like Don Johnson. I quickly told him that I knew Don—in fact, had just seen him—and he was clean-shaven. The next morning he came without the beard and told me that his "mum" was thrilled.

Another hairdresser told me that he had hung his picture with me in his salon and a fellow worker had torn it to shreds. I noted in my diary that I guessed we should put that man down as doubtful!

∽ I didn't write much about the Democrats in my diary in 1992. I will confess, however, that I wrote over and over again that Bill Clinton did not have a chance. The American people would never vote for him. I wrote him off from the start. I am such a bad politician that I thought that Senator Bob Kerrey would be the hardest to beat. He seemed to have so little baggage and he was a Congressional Medal winner for heroism in Vietnam. If it comes to politics and you want to know who is going to win, ask me. Then go the other way!

The week before Super Tuesday George won South Carolina with 67 percent of the vote to Pat Buchanan's 2 percent and David Duke's 7 percent. Then George swept the Super Tuesday states by hefty margins. I should also note that 166 of 167 Republican congressmen had endorsed George. It was obvious that his party was solidly behind him.

However, Pat Buchanan claimed victory during the evening by saying that he beat David Duke ten to one in Texas, three to one in Louisiana, and so forth. But the thing I loved best was he said that he might not be winning many votes, but that he had "won the hearts of the American people." Huh?

Anna Perez told me during the campaign that she felt Pat was a racist, that he was saying all the "code" words that tell her that. I think her exact words were "a mean-spirited racist." Certainly his speech at the Republican Convention later that year sent the message loud and clear. I worried about some of the racist things I was hearing. Whether they were specifically racial or not, the perception was there. Mildred Mottahedeh, that brilliant businesslady who reproduces some of the most magnificent porcelains from around the world and who has been so generous to the White House, wrote me in a letter: "The USA is really a prize concoction of the world and that's what makes us so special." George and I both believe that, and to feel our country fragmenting off into more defined racial pockets was and is of great concern.

⮷ In March we took Sam LeBlond with us to Arkansas to meet another "Sam"—George gave "Mr. Sam" Walton the Medal of Freedom. Mr. Sam was the founder of Wal-Mart, which had grown from a little store in a small Arkansas town into a national retail giant. Mr. Sam, who died a short time later, gave George a Sam's Club card that day, and little did we know that we soon would become regular shoppers in Maine and Texas.

March 27—I cut the ribbon on the Smithsonian Exhibit of First Ladies. They are no longer showing just the gowns and furnishings of the time. This new exhibit will also show the lady herself, her political involvement, her writings, her interests, etc. I thought it was well done until I came across Mrs. Kennedy's and Nancy's. There, prominently displayed, were Kitty Kelley's books about both ladies. These were both ugly books written by someone who did not know either woman and both books were largely discredited. Somehow or other I thought the Smithsonian was better than that [and mentioned it at a later date to Roger Kennedy, the director of the National Museum of American History. He agreed and I hope they are gone].

We tried hard to keep up with noncampaign events. In late March, for example, we attended Joe and Pat Gibbs's Youth for To-morrow Gala at the Kennedy Center. This is a great program for kids at risk which is run by Joe and Pat with the Washington Redskins taking an active, personal interest. America is filled with good and caring people.

In April I had a luncheon for the Morehouse School of Medicine and a few days later a reception for Tuskegee University. I went to a lunch given by my 90th Club ladies and attended the Congressional Club's annual luncheon for the First Lady on April Fool's Day. As a joke, they had the room decorated like Christmas Day. But they also gave a donation to Christmas in April, a marvelous program that started in Midland, Texas, and has now spread across the country. I visited Covenant House in New York City with Nancy Dickerson Whitehead and met the wonderful, loving Sister Mary Rose. I spoke at a fund-raiser in New York City for Boston College, where Doro got her degree, and I visited various literacy programs.

I also would like to tuck in here a luncheon I went to for Elayne Bennett's Best Friends program. Elayne has done the most marvelous job gathering prominent black women to mentor young girls. The goal is to keep them in school and off the streets, to prevent teenage pregnancies, drug abuse, and so on. The program has spread to several junior and senior high schools.

But the most fun of all was planning Doro's wedding, which was coming up in June. Arnold Scaasi was designing a lovely soft peach chiffon gown with a lace top for our very happy, beautiful daughter.

⌒ Like past campaigns, I was having trouble watching or reading the news, so I was reading a lot on the plane and at night. I read two books that I loved in April, *To Dance with the White Dog*, by Terry Kay, and John Grisham's third book, *The Pelican Brief*. I still liked his first book best, *A Time to Kill*.

At the end of April we invited John Grisham and his wife, Renee, to a state dinner for President and Mrs. von Weizsacker of Germany. I sat between the President and John. One of the perks of being the hostess is that you can invite and sit next to whom you want. During the dinner John asked me what I thought of the verdict. I asked him what verdict, and he said the beating in Los Angeles involving Rodney King. He told me the jury had found the police officers involved not guilty. NOT GUILTY? How could that be? We had seen the tapes, like everyone else. John and I discussed that we hoped the city would not riot. A few days later I wrote:

Los Angeles had two days of burning and looting. There were breakouts in Atlanta and San Francisco, but things are calming down. I know it can't be compared, but I thought of Lincoln. Imagine being President when your country is at war with itself? How awful. There are undercurrents that are ugly. Blacks turning on Koreans. Blacks pulling whites out of their cars and trucks and beating them. Over fifty people got killed. I kept thinking of all those families and what suffering they are going through. I thought of all those black mothers and how do they explain a "not guilty" verdict. I wondered how we would explain it to our own grandchildren when we don't understand it ourselves. [I know that I am being judgmental and I don't really approve of that, but this is what I put in my diary.] George was in touch at all times. At first the Governor and Mayor did not want federal aid in quelling the riots, but finally they asked for it and got it immediately. One of the saddest hours in our four years.

George went to California . . . The thing that really bothered him was what happened to the Koreans. Over 2,000 small businesses owned by the Koreans were burned. Could some in the black community be racists?

Here is a sampling of some of the other things we were up to that spring and of the thoughts going through my head:

May 3—I do not know whether George will survive this political year or not, but I do know that he is the only stable person running. He has the Congress, top labor leaders and the press against him. They smell blood. There is a life after politics. My only concerns are for the country and I'd hate for George to lose for his sake. Think how good it would be for our children. They could get on with their lives.

May 15—The Gorbachevs, who are on a whirlwind speaking tour of the country, came for dinner with us, the Bakers, Brent and George W. On this visit they brought their tiny pretty daughter, Irina. She was just as peppy and bright as she could be, this Ph.D. mother of two little girls. Raisa looked tired, but who wouldn't be on a trip like the one they are on—14 cities in 12 days . . . Mikhail was careful not to criticize Boris Yeltsin too much and then Raisa would speak up because she thought he was not being tough enough. That reminds me of me sometimes. I am often not as generous as George. It was a fascinating evening and good to see them again.

I gave the graduation speech at Marquette University and George at Notre Dame . . . heard on CBS that George had had a lukewarm reception at Notre Dame. It worried me. When he got home and I asked and then told him about the report—he was shocked. He said it was really very warm and enthusiastic. He later got a letter from the president of Notre Dame saying that he could not believe the "lukewarm" report. He said that they were very enthusiastic. I wish he'd told the world that.

May 18—Did Literacy Volunteers of NYC annual fund-raiser, I believe my favorite fund-raiser. This year the readers were Arthur Miller, William Styron, Gwendolyn Brooks, Anna Quindlen and Amy Tan. Each year it gets better and this year was another great evening. I love the readings and I must confess that I love not having to sit through a long dinner.

May 20—Had Mary Pohlmann and Debbie Stafford for lunch. (Two young friends that I had gotten to know and like so very much from Iowa.)

I had not seen Andy Stewart for several days and asked her to join us. As she was playing tennis, she said that she might come in tennis clothes. I said that was fine, but she must be there by 12:30 as I had a full afternoon and I was sure that the others did also. She came running in on time, but in a state of disrepair, if there is such a word. No necklace, no earrings and two *LEFT* shoes, one a wedge heel and one plain. We all laughed until we cried. How I love Andy and how she brightened my life.

May 21—LSU Graduation speech . . . What a gentle part of the country. (Louisiana State University in Baton Rouge)

. . . Flew from Louisiana to Kennebunkport. The Nebletts from Houston spent the weekend with us. I was so excited to see George's face when he saw the house. He thought it was perfect. I am so happy.

June 5—The trips are good. The press is bad. Margaret brought the children by for a swim. I know our children are worried about us. Margaret, Marvin and Doro come by often just to be sure that we are all right. How we love our children! Andy came by. All is well.

Pop arrived Sunday night from California. He said he had a great trip. . . . I might as well write it now because it caused me great unhappiness. He had a great trip, but Evans and Novak wrote the most damaging article saying that our campaign was in such disarray that Pop didn't even meet with his State Vice Chairman, state Sen. Ken Maddie. In fact it said that the senator refused to meet his plane and that the senator was an authority on farming and that George met with farmers that the senator didn't even know. The fact is that the senator met the plane, spent the day with Pop, knew all the farmers and even came back and toured the plane with him. How can we fight that?

. . . On June 2nd I flew to San Antonio, Texas, to speak to the AARP Convention at 8:30 a.m. I was followed by Ed Bradley of "60 Minutes" fame. After my talk and as I was walking out of the convention hall I heard Ed Bradley saying, "Do you think if Kuwait's main product was bananas instead of oil this administration would have risked the lives of our young men and women?" I wanted to march back in and tell him, "You bet oil made a difference, but so did standing up against brutal aggressors." I also would have asked him if he knew what would have happened if 29 other U.N. member countries hadn't formed a coalition and stopped Saddam Hussein? He probably would have sent his army into Saudi Arabia. All the world would be dependent on Iraq for energy. We would have high inflation, long lines at the gas stations, high unemployment and on and on. I wanted to ask him if he remembered that one country invaded another, raped the women, killed, stole and burned. We are not to interfere in the internal affairs of a country, but when one of our member nations gets invaded, we are obligated to go to the rescue. As long as I stayed in the building I could hear Ed Bradley trashing the administration. I hated that.

. . . John and Norma Major came for the night at Camp David. The men talked and the ladies walked. Sometimes we all did both.

One of the happiest things that happened to us that spring was the birth of the ducks. This has happened before at the White House, but this year we made an effort to save them from these hideous black birds that had been seen swooping down and carrying the babies off. After the ducklings hatched, the mother pushed them out of the nest and then led them to the water in the fountain on the South Grounds. It was the cutest sight to see her waddling down the lawn with her ducklings following. After the first raid by the black birds, the White House carpenters made a little cage that fit into the fountain, then herded the mother and the babies into the cage to remain there until the babies were old enough to fend for themselves. The father, a beautifully colored male mallard duck, swam and hovered outside the cage, would then leave and come back for visits. We ended up by having two families in two cages. Mallards could teach humans a lesson about monogamy. Anyway, George and I walked the dogs down to the fountain several times a day to see those darling little ducklings.

⟳ On June 11 we left on what promised to be one of our more difficult trips abroad, to attend the UN Conference on Environmental Development—known as the Earth Summit—in Rio de Janeiro. En route, we were going to stop for a visit in Panama. We fully expected protesters in both countries. I also knew the wives of the heads of state in both countries were in their twenties, so I worried about not having much in common with my hostesses.

First stop, Panama:

The hot air blasted us as we stepped off the plane. Silk is not the material to wear in this part of the world. The humidity must have been at 98%! President Endara, a heavyset 55-year-old man, and his very exotic

25-year-old Chinese/black wife, Ana Mae, were awaiting our arrival, as were our Ambassador Deane Hinton and his wife, Patricia. He has been a great troubleshooter for his country.

After coffee with Mrs. Endara and a large lunch, we went to a big rally at the Plaza Porras put on by the dynamic Mayor of Panama City, Mayin Correa. Sad-to-say an American soldier had been killed yesterday by terrorists and so the security had to be tight. The death breaks our hearts, but George says that we cannot let terrorists rule our lives . . . I sat in on the briefings so I know that 80% of the people like us. The drive to the rally was wonderful, streets lined with crowds waving American flags and cheering people. The plaza was jammed and enthusiasm ran high. We barely got there when a few students started throwing rocks and what we thought were firecrackers. It turned out that the Panamanian police panicked and what we thought were firecrackers was tear gas and it was ghastly. The poor people in the plaza with babies could not get out and the gas was so painful. We finally had to leave the platform. My eyes still feel burned. We were thrown into our cars and took off. It was heartbreaking for the crowds on the streets who were still waving, cheering, but some had tears flowing down their faces. It was so sad that the few can ruin it for the many. If you have never been around tear gas, it is just impossible to stand. It burns your eyes, throat and lungs. It is truly unbearable.

We arrived at Rio at twelve midnight. The next morning a very nice military wife came to comb out my hair. She says that they cannot walk the streets with even a wedding ring on because of the crime. We heard that from everyone. Evidently for the Conference they cleared the streets of bands of young boys and the street people and trucked them out to the country. It is so sad. These are the children who leave home or are pushed out because their parents can't feed them. [These are the same children who are being gunned down in 1994 to get rid of them.]

. . . The view from our hotel window was sensational. Right out front were big rocks and a tremendous surf breaking. With the doors open the sound was lulling. On the side we looked over a tremendous pool and three tennis courts and if you looked slightly further you saw a hillside favela, which I believe means a slum. It was a slum. There is no running water and it reminded me of the ride into Caracas, Venezuela, from the airport, but the proximity to this luxurious hotel made the contrast even more noticeable. Further off in the distance we could see a glorious beach, but we were told that it is unsafe to swim as the water is so polluted. What a tragedy!

Libbie Reilly, Peggy Melton, the wife of our ambassador, and I took a thirty-minute drive to Ramoa de Mattos Duarte Orphanage, run by sisters. I loved it and wanted to take most of the children home with me. The drive was lovely. For some reason the hills surrounding the city reminded me of Kweilin in China. [I'm beginning to feel like Miss Marple in the Agatha Christie stories. Everything and everyone reminds me of something or somebody else. Old age, I guess.]

After a lunch we went into the Conference Hall to hear George speak. It was very interesting. Things were running a little behind schedule and I got to visit with Shirley MacLaine, Bianca Jagger and Seymour Topping (of *New York Times* fame) and his wife, Audrey. They were all very pleasant and all, I'm sure, against us. I saw Castro from a distance.

Castro got a lot of applause which made a lot of news. But why not? He was advocating enormous environmental changes for the Third World which the developed countries would pay for. As the Third World so outnumbers the developed countries, their cheers were deafening. At the same time Senator Gore was at the Conference advocating a policy that would have cost the U.S. taxpayers billions of dollars and many thousands of jobs. It, too, sounded great, but the consequences to our people would have been earthshaking.

We went by a rain forest close to town. It was beautiful, lush and so thick that I don't think we could have walked through it without a machete. It had been a plantation until 130 years ago, all cleared and planted. Then the owner had six slaves plant two hundred thousand trees which today is this amazing jungle. It is never too late. We must continue our tree-planting program in the United States that George initiated.

We had dinner that night with President and Mrs. Collor at the Palacio Laranjeiras. This is a really beautiful palace that the governor lives in. It was built by a private family about 80 years ago. They must have been very rich! I sat next to Fernando Collor, an extremely attractive young man whom George liked and we had such great hopes for. [He left office abruptly, accused of corruption. Sad.]

The Tuesday after we came home the Yeltsins arrived for a state visit. It was a historic occasion—the first state visit ever of a *Russian* president. It was the most beautiful day and the ceremony was magnificent.

We had the usual tea for the ladies and then Naina Yeltsin and I went to visit Martha's Table to make sandwiches, stir the soup, and play with the children. They had moved since my last visit and are in a much better, bigger place. They feed nine hundred people in five parks and in four locations; they tutor adult literacy students; and they have a place for children to come after school. How I love this place and the wonderful people who run it, Veronica Park and Olivia Ivy. They also have seventy volunteers a day and they could not exist without them.

Naina was great. She listened to everything and said exactly the right thing to the press. I already had grown to like her very much. She and Boris had come to Camp David in February for an informal visit. It was freezing but she never complained. She wore pants as requested and two very pretty sweaters. There is just something about her that is warm, cozy, and relaxed. Late in the morning Doro arrived with Ellie, Sam, and Bobby Koch. They came bouncing in, pink cheeks and all. When I introduced Ellie, she went right over and gave Mrs. Yeltsin a great big hug. Naina is that kind of woman; you want to hug her. During our talk she told us some of their troubles: Those in the old regime will not give up the power; the President has passed new laws, but they won't conform to them; the press does not print what happened. We all laughed, as we hear that all around the world. She went so far as to call them a third party. She told us that one of their problems was that the family was disintegrating. I remembered thinking that we have so many of the same problems.

Anyway, on with the state visit:

Ranger, Millie and I were down visiting the ducks when I looked up and saw George and Boris walking down to also see our ducklings and the tennis court. Boris prides himself on his tennis game, but George tells me that "the ranking committee" (an imaginary group known only to my husband, our sons and his brothers) says that he is not very good. George gave him a tennis ball machine. We looked at the ducks and the court for a while and then Boris went off to his luncheon and George came home for a little chicken salad à la Pierre. It was a joy to have George home for lunch—alone!

At the State Dinner for the Yeltsins Naina seemed dear, but nervous. She told me the next day that she had been running late, rushed in to turn on her bath and the shower poured down on her hair. What a good sport. She brushed it back in a hurry and came on as she was. She is the most unselfish woman. Rather than make us wait, she came with a damp head. I must say she looked lovely and no one noticed.

. . . The dinner itself was truly superb. I sat next to Boris and Bob Allen of AT&T. Two easy dinner partners. I put Robin Gerstner (whose husband now heads up IBM) on Boris's right. She is so pretty and such fun. During dinner Boris leaned over and said, through an interpreter, "Barbara, I don't know the protocol, but what should I do if a woman has her foot on my foot?" I looked over at Robin Gerstner and said, "Oh, dear, I don't know what to tell you." Just then Boris lifted his leg and up came mine! We both burst out laughing. I was, in truth, stepping on his foot. Heaven only knows if I had been grinding his foot into the ground! He then told me that in Russia that meant that the woman loved the man. I quickly told him that was not true in our country. We did laugh.

When the violins came in Boris asked me to dance. I told him that I *DID* know the protocol to that, "Protocol demands you dance with the woman on your right." He had been teasing me all night about protocol, saying that he was a "bad boy" and did not go by protocol. Well, he grabbed Robin Gerstner and they spun around to music in the State Dining Room. It made the party more fun! He has a great twinkle in his eye and really seems to like people.

When we left the State Dining Room and headed down the hallway, Boris and I did take a spin in the hallway to the violin music. He is fun.

    The next day I hosted a lunch at Mount Vernon for Naina with the gracious help of the Mount Vernon Ladies Association. We had a wonderful meal on the veranda with a sensational view of the Potomac River.

The men signed seven more treaties that afternoon—including an agreement that eventually would lead to another drastic cut in nuclear weapons—and then we went to a return dinner given by the Russians. I asked Boris to sign my menu, and he wrote: "Barbara, remember it was you who stepped on my foot and you know what it meant. I feel the same way. Boris."

George and I were home in bed early that night. The Yeltsins told us that they only need three and a half hours' sleep a night; George and I need six to seven hours. The Yeltsins came back for breakfast and we waved them off.

Only one thing marred this wonderful visit. Our good friend George Bell died and we had to miss the funeral. How I wanted to be with my friend Bertie, but it just could not be helped.

Immediately we went back to the campaign. George left that same day for California, and I went the next day to Dallas to give the keynote speech at the Texas Republican State Convention. That night I went to a private dinner and saw many old friends. Dallas was a problem for us, as some of our big backers and friends were neighbors of Margot and Ross Perot. I got the impression it was hard to live in Dallas and be for George Bush, especially since it appeared Ross held grudges.

. . . A *Washington Post* article this morning says that Ross has had investigators looking into our boys and Hugh Liedtke for years. It is sick. Ross also tells a story about visiting us in Maine back in the 60s and going out in the boat with George when the motor failed and George "almost cried." That is the craziest story I ever heard.

I barely remember the visit to Maine, but I know that George *never* came close to crying. All this from a man who offered George a big job when he left the CIA in 1976. Thank heavens he didn't take it. I confess to liking Margot and the children very much and will resist saying all I feel about Ross. Some of his quotes are truly off the wall, such as this "quote of the week": "When I go to a meeting and they open with a prayer, I put my wallet away and leave. I know all they want is my money." I'm reminded of what people used to say about a man in Houston: "If he didn't have all that money, he'd be the most disliked man in town." I wonder if that applies to Ross?

June 24—Poor Dan Quayle got into the worst thing. It could have happened to anyone . . . especially me (I am the world's worst speller). A teacher handed him a cue card with POTATOE written on it and then Dan asked a little kid to spell "potato." Dan tried to make the child put an "e" on the end as his misspelled card had it. The press and all the comedians had a field day with this. My heart ached for him. My heart should have ached for the teacher who made the mistake, but it was Dan who got the blame and for days this very important mishap wiped out other unimportant news like the signing of the weapons treaties with Yeltsin.

. . . During the past week I kicked off the Summer Quest Reading Program in a public library and another time I visited one of the Boys and Girls summer programs. Both do a great job and need all the support they can get.

On June 26 we had Bobby and Doro's rehearsal dinner at the White House. The Kochs wanted to give the party, but the children wanted privacy, which we could guarantee only at the White House. I should apologize right now to Marlin Fitzwater, George's press secretary, who gave Anna Perez, my press secretary, a very hard time about the wedding. He just could not understand why Anna was being so closemouthed about something as simple as a wedding. Anna was doing exactly what I asked: "No press about the wedding, please, not one word." That's what Bobby and Doro wanted and Anna kept her word.

The White House was abuzz with excitement, and so many people volunteered their time to make this a spectacular wedding. We had to limit the rehearsal party to seventy-four people and tried to be sure that Doro and Bobby had their friends. Of course all our children came and brothers and sisters and spouses. Bobby's family turned out en masse and were so nice. Bobby's parents, George and Helen Koch, are absolutely the best, the easiest, and most relaxed people. The dinner was in the State Dining Room and it looked wonderful. The whole White House did. There were lots of toasts, all loving, mostly funny, but the one I liked best was the rap song that Sam, Ellie, and Doro had worked on for days to sing to Bobby:

> *We're Doro, Sam, and Ellie,*
> *And we're making a toast,*
> *To Bobby Koch, who is the most,*
> *Extraordinary person we ever met,*
> *He'll make a great family man, you bet!*
> *Tomorrow is the big day we become a family,*
> *When Bobby Koch joins us three.*
> *We'll have a great life, that we know is true,*
> *But the message of this rap is: We love you!*

The wedding itself was to be held the next day at Camp David. Laurie Firestone really put on this wedding. She can make magic and knows the right way to do anything and everything. All the off-duty White House butlers volunteered to serve as a present to Doro, and although George paid for the flowers, Nancy Clarke, Wendy Elsasser, and Dianne Barbour from the florist shop decorated the chapel and the tables on their day off. White House chefs Pierre Chambrin, Franette

Dancing with Sylvester Stallone at Jerry and Jane Weintraub's house. Look at that smirk! (Susan Biddle)

Floating down the Thames River in London with friends. From left: Hannelore Kohl of Germany; Mila Mulroney of Canada; Norma Major of Great Britain; and Sachiyo Kaifu of Japan. (Carol Powers)

Meeting the future King of England, Prince William, along with his mother, Princess Diana; Caroline Seitz, the wife of the American Ambassador to England; and Prince William's little brother, Prince Harry. (Carol Powers)

Cruising the Moscow River with Raisa Gorbachev. (Carol Powers)

Relaxing with a friend. (Carol Powers)

George gets a phone call from Mikhail Gorbachev that the coup has ended and he and Raisa are safe, August 1991. (Susan Biddle)

George and his mother in
Kennebunkport. (Family photo)

Strolling in Kennebunkport with
two of my favorite friends, Mila
Mulroney and Millie.
(Susan Biddle)

Sharing a thought with my husband during the Reagan Library dedication, Novemb[er] 1991. (David Valdez)

Everybody at the White House had to wear ID tags including Ranger. (Carol Powers)

Volunteering at the Goodw[ill] book sale in Washington, [DC]. (Carol Powers)

Topping the National Christmas Tree, one of twelve times I did the honors.
Helping out are grandchildren Lauren and Pierce Bush and Joe Riley,
chairman of the Pageant of Peace. (Carol Powers)

randson Walker Bush checks out the train
under the White House Christmas tree,
December 1991. (Joyce Naltchayan)

A Christmas tree covered with needlepoint
ornaments. If you look hard, you can find the
Raggedy Ann and Andy dolls I stitched.
(David Valdez)

Bundling up with Naina Yeltsin at Camp David, February 1992. (Carol Powers)

Getting tips on how to use the computer from some young experts in
Winona, Mississippi. (Carol Powers)

Millie meets with some of the fourth graders touring the White House. (Carol Powers)

Heading to Kennebunkport with granddaughter Ellie LeBlond, Millie, and Ranger. (Carol Powers)

"Sure, I can take your picture with the President." (Carol Powers)

Doro is absolutely radiant; please don't look too carefully at what the father of
the bride is wearing. Neil and Sharon are at left, and behind them are my
brother Jim and his wife, Margie. (David Valdez)

Naina Yeltsin meets some young
Americans outside Martha's Table in
Washington, June 1992.
(Carol Powers)

Sharing a laugh with Boris
Yelstin, June 1992.
(David Valdez)

The family whoops it up on first night of the Republican National Convention, Augus 1992. (Susan Biddle)

The clan gathers for the Republican National Convention in Houston, August 1992. Sitting on the floor are, from left, grandchildren Jenna, Marshall, Ashley, Lauren, Ellie, and Jebbie. Second row, sitting down, from left: Laura, Barbara, Pierce, me and George, Sam, and Jeb and Columba. Back row, from left: Marvin holding Walker, Margaret, George W., Sharon, Neal, Doro, Bobby, George P., and Noelle. The only one missing is our thirteenth grandchild, Robert, who was still nearly a year away. (David Valdez)

George P. addresses the conven surrounded by his family. (Susan Biddle)

The last night at
the convention.
(Carol Powers)

Actor Gerald McRaney
keeps me dry during a
campaign stop in
Florida. (Carol Powers)

Making a new friend in
Louisville, Kentucky.
(Carol Powers)

Millie tries to explain to Larry King why George Bush should be reelected president. (David Valdez)

The Bush women campaign te[...] from left: Doro Koch, me, No[...] Bush, Nancy Ellis, and Marga[...] Bush. (Carol Powers)

Our son Marvin hams it up on the campaign trail, Halloween 1992. I never knew we looked so much alike. (Carol Powers)

Whistle-stopping toward the end of the campaign. Sam LeBlond and I huddle to keep warm. (Carol Powers)

The White House staff bids us good-bye as we head to Houston for Election Night. I'm about ready to hug James Selmon. (Carol Powers)

Telling Hillary Clinton how wonderful life in the White House is.
(Carol Powers)

Oh, good. Santa Claus didn't forget me on our last Christmas in the
White House. (Carol Powers)

One last walk around the White House grounds, January 20, 1993. (Susan Biddle)

Welcoming the Clintons to the White House, January 20, 1993. (Carol Powers)

Three women with two things in
common: We've all been married to
the Vice President of the United
States and we all showed up in
purple. (Susan Biddle)

Houston, we're home!
(David Valdez)

McCulloch, and Roland Mesnier made a beautiful cake and cooked a lovely buffet supper, including an enormous fresh salmon that Ted and Cathy Stevens had sent us straight from Alaska. I wrote in my diary:

The guests arrived at 4 p.m. and were taken to Laurel to freshen up and have a cold drink or tea. At 4:30 the father of the bride showed up to change into his clothes and asked what people were wearing to the wedding. I told him his navy blue suit would be just fine. I couldn't believe it when he confessed that he hadn't brought a suit. He said that he thought it would be informal! He did come up with a blue blazer, a white shirt and some 20-year-old white summer pants with a thin blue stripe which the boys call his "New York Yankee" pants. Bobby Koch had given him a wedding tie and that added to his look. How I love that man. He thought it was informal! Wait until he gets his Scaasi bill!

The chapel looked so beautiful with peach roses, and there was music in the balcony. The groom walked in from the back of the altar followed by Sam and his three brothers, P.C., Danny and Monte Koch . . . All four boys had on blue suits and the ties Bobby had given them. Bobby was so dear to have Sam at his side. (This was Sam and Ellie's second wedding in two months. Their dad had gotten married in April and they were in that wedding, also.) Everybody was in place and then to great trumpets down the aisle came Ellie LeBlond in a floor-length lavender gown holding a miniature nosegay like her mother's. Her face was literally beaming. Behind them came my precious George with Doro on his arm looking incredibly beautiful. She looked exactly right. Chaplain Jonathan Frusti led the service. George W. read a passage as did a friend of Bobby's. The little church choir, made up of several service personnel and some of their wives, sang three lovely songs (our young chaplain leaves the altar to join the choir). Their voices are clear and sweet. Sam and Ellie wiggled a lot. It didn't seem to bother Doro or Bobby. Doro put a loving hand on Ellie every now and then. When Doro and Bobby knelt to be blessed there was a BUSH/QUAYLE sticker on Bobby's soles. His brothers put it there. Neither George nor I noticed. I suspect we were praying.

After the wedding we walked back to Aspen and took a lot of pictures; the bride and groom formed a receiving line. The parents mixed and mingled and had fun. Everything about the wedding was happy and we will forever be grateful for all who made it so perfect.

. . . All during the weekend George had been on the phone with other heads of state about the problems in Yugoslavia. I heard him talking to Major,

Kohl, Miyazawa, Lubbers, Cavaco Silva (of Portugal) and Mulroney. Then we awakened the morning after the wedding to find that California had suffered another dreadful earthquake. All this on his mind and a wedding, too.

We flew back to the White House and I took Ellie to see the ducks. We still have seven. Then Ellie and I went up on the Truman Balcony to read books. I got so tired that I took her into my room and we both climbed on the bed. She read aloud to me and did a great job. I sat up and looked and SHE COULD READ! She had broken the code and could really read. Hurrah, another grandchild can read! Ellie is going into first grade this fall. She could read because she was read to by her mother and baby-sitters. Seeing a child read is such a miracle.

The next morning we were back on the campaign trail—George to New York City and Detroit and me to Nebraska and on and on and on.

We were back in time to have Luciano Pavarotti for lunch on Tuesday. It was such fun as he has an air of joyous energy that fills a room. We talked about Italian politics, a subject he seems to love.

That night we had our annual diplomatic picnic, and for the second year in a row, the heavens opened up and the rain crashed down. I guess I deserved that because after Doro's glorious weather I had said, "I don't care if we have hail or sleet from now on, if we can just get through the wedding." Luckily, the staff moved everything in quick as a wink.

On July 5 we left for the annual G-7 Economic Summit in Munich, Germany, stopping in Warsaw en route. We had a rousing welcome all the way from the airport to the Royal Palace. It was nice to see Lech and Danuta Walesa again. She is a great beauty and looks very young despite the fact they have eight children, ages six to twenty-two, and are grandparents. They say she is a very steadying influence on him.

On this trip we officially returned the remains of Ignace Paderewski to the Polish people. A great composer, concert pianist, and statesman, Paderewski had died in New York City in 1941, when his country was occupied by Germans. His dying wish was to be buried in his homeland—but not until it was free. So he was entombed in Arlington National Cemetery until we took him home in 1992. It was a very moving ceremony.

Afterward George spoke in Castle Square to a tremendous crowd. Lech Walesa told us only the Pope had drawn that many people.

That evening in Munich, while George went to a working dinner with François Mitterrand, I had a quiet dinner with Kitty Brady and Susan Baker. I then intended to crawl into bed but instead got all involved in Wimbledon. I was so excited because Andre Agassi won the men's singles. Hurrah!

Several years before, George had invited Andre to play tennis at the White House. Although his manners were great, his clothes and appearance were not. It was pouring rain, and I told him that he was darn lucky because I wouldn't let him play in those awful clothes on the White House court. He was very funny and promptly gave George one of those strange psychedelic-colored pants with those even stranger underpants hanging down. How we all laughed at the thought of George wearing them. It wasn't long after that he was in another Wimbledon when he *had* to wear all white. I sent him a telegram wishing him well and telling him I admired his costume and that now he could play on the White House court. When he returned he came by to see George at the Oval Office and brought me the shorts and shirt he had worn! Pretty cute. Another time Andre and Wendy, his girl of many years (he was twenty-one at the time, and he told me that he had known her since she was eight), came to spend a night at Camp David for a little tennis and golf. I was very touched when both of them showed up in church at 9 A.M. and he had a well-worn Bible in his hands. I wrote at the time:

Thank heavens he has shaved. He still has the dyed stringy, long blond hair and the earring. I cannot criticize another part of him, having been so bad about his clothes. He wore whites at Wimbledon and here at Camp David. He was telling us about the house he is building in Las Vegas— instead of a dining room he will have a pool table, instead of a formal living room he will have pinball machines and penny arcade games. He is just a little kid, but a nice little kid.

And now he had won Wimbledon. I was thrilled for him.

The first day in Munich the spouses all met at the Seehaus Restaurant, known for its good food, atmosphere, and beautiful English gardens. Hannelore Kohl was our hostess. While at the luncheon I got a note from Anna Perez:

> Danielle Mitterrand's motorcade was bombed in Northern Iraq this a.m. Potential 4 deaths, 12 injured, children involved. Mrs. Mitterrand's safety has been confirmed. Info is sketchy. Will get more to you later. Anna.

One of the ladies said: "What in the world was she doing there?" I said I was sure that she was trying to help the Kurds. It was criminal what was happening to those poor children and people. Saddam Hussein just would not leave them alone.

We later learned that a car bomb had detonated as the motorcade drove by. Three security people and a ten-year-old girl had been killed.

After lunch we got into a bus so fancy it was impossible to see out the windows with ease. We headed for the Glyptothek Museum:

> We hadn't gone one moment when we came to a bridge and, believe it or not, hit the bridge. Poor Hannelore, she had planned everything so carefully. The explanation was that the driver had pushed a button to raise the shock absorbers and thus raised the level of the bus! We were able to back out, but it meant missing many of the sights that were planned. So the tour was, "If you could see, you would have seen a pavilion . . ." It was funny, but not to our hostess. The truth was that by the time the charming man, Professor Everding, who was guiding us, told us about a building, we had long since passed it. From then on the afternoon was fine.
>
> That night we saw a performance of "Carmen" which I enjoyed enormously . . . Roger Porter (of George's staff) thought the production was more sensual than any he had seen before. I must say that the TV and everything is more sex-oriented here than even in the USA. Rose Zamaria went for a walk across the park and came upon a man with absolutely no clothes on walking her way. (I would have loved seeing Rosie's face.) She also saw another man in a cut-off tee-shirt and nothing more riding a bike. That is evidently OK in Germany although it does not sound very comfortable to me!
>
> The next morning we went by helicopter to Hohenschwangau and then by horse-drawn carriages up a hill to Neuschwanstein Castle. This was a fairy-tale castle built by Ludwig II. It was described to us as "a monument to Wagner." Poor old Ludwig II was engaged briefly, but broke the engage-

ment. It was intimated to us that he was in love with Wagner (the composer), who did live with him. This castle was enormous. We walked up miles of spiral staircases. There was a glorious chapel, a music room and a grotto right in the castle. Every inch of the castle was carved, painted, gilded and on and on. . . . Poor Ludwig II got dethroned because of the money he was spending on this castle and shortly afterwards drowned—whether by his own hand or another's is unknown.

The next day President and Mrs. von Weizsacker hosted a luncheon, and I sat between him and Boris Yeltsin. The latter is so easy and funny. He constantly teased me, including reminding me of the foot incident at the state dinner.

We went on to Finland in the late afternoon—although it was hard to tell what time of day it was. At that time of year, sunset was around 11 P.M. and it came back up by 4 A.M. Very confusing. We stopped in Helsinki to attend the CSCE (Conference on Security and Cooperation in Europe).

While we were there Bill Clinton announced that Al Gore would be his running mate. Again, I showed just how politically astute I am:

I can't understand him picking another southerner from a small state. Al has a good military record and a very nice family. He is a liberal and a demagogue. Neither he nor Clinton have ever been in the private sector. They are just professional politicians. They have made their living in politics. Amazing.

Tellervo Koivisto, the wife of the Finnish president, had planned a wonderful program for us which included a luncheon cruise and museum visits. I was very pleased to see that she carried the lovely Judith Lieber bag that I had given her. While at the White House I gave these exquisite little bags as gifts to the heads of state's wives. They are made in America, they are beautiful, everyone loves them, and I know and love Judith.

⤳ We went home to Maine for the weekend, and I noted in my diary that the planting on Walker's Point was coming back from the Halloween disaster:

The bayberry and rosa rugosa are pushing up through the rocks and are looking pretty good. I am thrilled. I guess I should have trusted God a little more.

George's mother seems so much better. At church on Sunday as part of the children's service, Jack Allin said: "Pussy Cat, Pussy Cat, where have you been? I've been to London to visit the queen. Pussy Cat, Pussy Cat, what did you do there?" And before a child could answer a loud clear voice said, "I frightened a little mouse under the chair." And it was our precious mom. We almost cried, it was such a sweet moment. It is so amazing. Mom is just floating in and out so gently.

George left for California, and ended up fishing in Wyoming with Jim and Susan Baker during the Democratic Convention. I stayed in Maine with the grandchildren and Mom, resting up for the big push ahead.

24

The Campaign

This is a most painful chapter to write. The weeks leading up to Election Day almost seemed like a game we played as children where we'd take one step forward and two steps back.

July 17—There is a new poll out this morning that shows Bill Clinton 23 points ahead of George. Pretty frightening. Somehow or other it seems impossible for George to win, a Congress that bucks you on every turn, a tough press corps, 5 Democrats, 1 Republican and 1 Independent, all railing against him for months. AND THE ECONOMY! It just seems impossible to me, but we will do our best.

. . . I am hiding my head like an ostrich. It hurts too much to see George and the children so lied about. Only 3½ more months to go.

Yesterday morning as I was driving out to play golf I heard Ross Perot on the radio saying that he would no longer remain in the race. The fact that he chose this day for the announcement came as a surprise. This was the last day of the Democratic Convention and should have been Bill Clinton's day. Whether Ross did it on purpose or just did it we will never know. I'm tempted to think that he did it without thinking of Bill or anyone else. He seems to be extraordinarily self-oriented.

July 21—The political picture could not be any worse. Clinton came out of the convention 25 points ahead.

. . . George is being trashed by one and all.

. . . George spoke to the National League of Families (of American

Prisoners and Missing in Southeast Asia) in Crystal City (Va.). He got booed. Darn that Ross Perot. He has really hurt these people by making them think that their loved ones are alive and that their government has not done everything they can to find them. The government is absolutely convinced after years of intelligence that they are still not holding our men. What purpose could it possibly serve to lie about this?

Lest you think I was obsessed with the election—and of course we actually were—I'd like to share some other diary entries from that time period.

I flew down to Washington on July 22nd for the Medal of Arts Luncheon where Marilyn Horne, for one, was honored. She is a great lady with a glorious voice.

Winnie Palmer and her daughter and three granddaughters and one grandson came for iced tea. We walked down to see the ducks. The baby ducks have grown so much that they could now be released. Nice Dale (Haney) had waited for me to come home, and he cut the cage while the Palmer group was standing there. Dale (one of the groundskeepers) is so dear to all the animals and takes Ranger for walks while he does his chores. (He invites Millie, but she is a mother's girl.)

I visited Martha's Table while I was home and read one of my favorite books, *Amazing Grace,* to thirty bright little kids. They all sat on the floor and listened and entered in while sitting next to or on a volunteer's lap. . . . One child spent the whole time softly rubbing or feeling a volunteer lady's hair. It was very sweet. These little ones are from the homeless shelters or the worst public housing projects. They were bright-eyed and smart. These are the kids we are losing, and it must not happen.

I went to Boston for a RIF (Reading Is Fundamental) event and on to the Thyroid Foundation luncheon. As we stood in the receiving line and doctor after doctor came through the line, I wondered what in the world I was doing being their speaker? You may be sure that I did not speak about the medical side of Graves' disease! I went on to Maine to be with George W., Laura, the girls and their houseguests, Jimmy and Debbie Francis.

When George joined us in Maine for a short weekend, he told me that people around the country, Republicans included, were calling for him to dump Dan Quayle from the ticket. Even a former president called and advised giving Dan another job. The pressure was enormous.

I'd like to go on record right now as saying that Dan Quayle was a superb vice president. He is loyal and smart. There is no question that he had a perception problem, and it was politically chic to kick Dan around. It was darned unfair, and how he and Marilyn kept their cool, I will never know. When I think of the ridicule Dan got for talking about family values in 1992, and now hear our opponents talking about them in 1994 without ridicule, it hurts me for the Quayles. Dan was right, you know. So many of our problems stem from dysfunctional families. And our welfare system locks people into poverty and discourages two-parent households. We give incentives for all the wrong things: not working and having more children.

⤵ Once again, friends came to my rescue. Andy Stewart drove over from New Hampshire and we had two days of terrible golf and lots of laughs.

After taking political trips to Baltimore, New Jersey, Ohio, and Florida, I flew back to Maine to be with our gang and my dear friend Bertie Bell. She's another one of the group of close friends who made my life at the White House such a joy. She hung in and stayed in touch.

The Prime Minister of Israel, Yitzhak Rabin, and his wife, Leah, came to Maine on August 10 to spend a night. We had known each other over the years and it was nice to see them again. In fact, many years ago, Leah and I had played tennis in Washington with Jessica Catto, whose husband, Henry, was then Chief of Protocol.

The men worked all day while Leah and I went to have a delicious lunch at Jerry and Jane Weintraub's Blueberry Hill farmhouse, where they generously let us pick blueberries every summer. Leah wanted to go antiquing, but because there was a very radical Jewish group in town protesting the visit, Security didn't think it was safe. This group rented a boat and sat off the Point yelling ugly things about the Prime Minister over a loudspeaker. The men broke for dinner, but then worked all through the night.

The next morning an agreement was announced that we would give Israel $10 billion in loan guarantees, but they agreed to curtail building settlements in the occupied territories. This had been a source of tension between the United States and Israel for some time, so the agreement was an important announcement.

At the end of the news conference, CNN's Mary Tillotson asked George the most scandalous question about a story that had run in one of the New York City tabloid newspapers. There was not a word of truth in the story, which concerned an alleged affair that had been looked into for years. Yet, it dominated the news, burying the real story about the agreement with Israel. Marlin Fitzwater later told me that he asked Mary why she had done that, and she said that her boss ordered her to ask that question.

Jim Miklaszewski of NBC told me that the Clinton people had blasted him because he had said during a panel discussion that their campaign was calling around trying to get reporters to go with that ugly story. I asked him if, in truth, they had done this, and his answer was "Absolutely." That's definitely playing hardball.

About this time the campaign took a definite turn for the silly when *Family Circle* magazine decided to sponsor a chocolate chip cookie contest between me and Hillary Clinton. I can't speak for Hillary, but my office knew nothing about the contest until it came out in the magazine. And to make matters worse—it wasn't even my recipe! As it turns out, *Family Circle* had found the recipe in a 1986 *McCall's*, which got it from a chef who worked at the Vice President's House. *My* chocolate chip cookie recipe was one that Patsy Caulkins had given me years ago when we were housemates at Yale. Just to make sure all of you got the right one, here it is:

Mix:	*1 cup butter*
	1 cup granulated sugar
	1 cup brown sugar
Add:	*2 eggs and beat*
Sift and add:	*2 cups flour*
	1 teaspoon soda
	1 teaspoon salt

Add:	2 cups quick-cooking rolled oats
	2 teaspoons vanilla
	1 12 oz. package chocolate chips

Bake:	Drop by tablespoons onto ungreased cookie sheet and bake for 10 minutes at 350 degrees.

This silly contest popped up all over the place during the conventions and the campaign and even prompted some serious columnists to write about it as "anti-feminist." Yikes. And then on top of everything else, *I lost*.

Actually, this story reminds me of a true scandal in my office, which I don't think ever has been revealed before: Let's call it "Recipegate."

My office got hundreds of letters requesting recipes for cookbooks, articles, and other publications, and we had a select few that we sent out. Then a woman wrote in inquiring if I was trying to kill George: Most of my recipes were loaded with fat and cholesterol. (Please keep in mind that back when I cooked for my family, we didn't worry about such things.)

A volunteer in my office, a wonderful woman named Alicia Lee, who also happens to be a great cook, took it upon herself to make my recipes "politically correct," substituting margarine for butter, egg whites for eggs, and so on. Finally she gave up and started sending out some of *her* favorite recipes.

I knew nothing about this until a woman told me one day how much she loved my bean recipe. Bean recipe! My bean recipe was to open a can. What on earth was she talking about? So there it is. There are cookbooks all over the country with "Barbara Bush's favorite recipes" that I've never seen before. I just hope they're good.

༒ Finally it was August 17, time to head to Houston and the Republican Convention at the Astrodome. The first stop was a huge rally where we saw all our children and grandchildren and many dear friends from across the country. We called on the Reagans, and then went to the Houstonian, our home away from home, to get ready for the big week ahead.

Unfortunately, before we even left the plane, the convention was off to a bad start.

There was a pro-life plank in the Republican party platform (which is decided by a platform committee and not the President) and some very specific judgmental words about homosexuals that did not reflect George's views at all, and that set a bad tone for our convention. I believe that a platform should set *broad* guidelines and that religious beliefs should not be in the political arena. Unfortunately, I made that view known in an interview just before we arrived, so the "Barbara Bush is pro-choice" rumor ran wild—exactly what I had tried to avoid for years.

Let me say again: I hate abortions, but just could not make that choice for someone else. And contrary to the platform plank, which was opposed to *all* abortions, George was against abortions with the exception of rape, incest, and where the life of the mother was threatened.

The very first night I went to the convention and heard Pat Buchanan and Ronald Reagan speak. I wrote in my diary:

(Buchanan) endorsed George strongly after cutting him to ribbons for month after month and was very extreme. It is hard for me to accept his kind of campaigning . . . I hate "gay bashing." I sat next to (his wife) Shelley, whom I remember from the Nixon White House and like. I noticed all through the campaign that his sister, Bay, walked next to him and that Shelley walked behind them all the time. That made me think of George's mom, who always noticed if the husband waited for the wife. She gave Ron Reagan high marks for being thoughtful to Nancy. She would have given Pat very bad marks. I remember one time we were with the Reagans at some ceremony or another. We were briefed and told that the Reagans would walk through the door followed by George and me. When the door opened and they started through, Ronald Reagan stopped, stepped aside and said, "After you, Barbara." He is innately polite.

Speaking of Ronald Reagan, he gave a very good speech, vintage Reagan, and had a great reception from the delegates.

⁀ The next day I had the most unbelievable schedule: Along with our grandson George P., I dropped by a "Black America Salutes the First Family" breakfast; did a ton of press interviews; toured the American Spirit Pavilion, where they had every kind of convention and other souvenirs you can imagine, including *Millie's Book*; and attended a fund-raiser for a local candidate. But the most fun of all was a reception that evening at the Museum of Fine Arts. The Ashmuns, Kerrs, Fitches, Nebletts, and Liedtkes had gathered family and friends, which was our only real opportunity to see them since everyone was so busy.

I left the reception with such a wonderful warm feeling and went to the Convention Hall, where the first stop was the PBS booth and an interview with Judy Woodruff:

It was truly unbelievable—starting out with a hideous editorial from the *Houston Post* (against George) and fast moving into "politically incorrect" things said by speakers at the Convention, at least according to the press pack. It was so combative that I finally said, "Stop. Where were you at the Democratic Convention? Were you asking these questions? How come it is OK for them to allow only a pro-choice person to speak and you do not say a word or ask a question? Be fair. We have pro-choice speakers and pro-life speakers and we all have one thing in common—we're all pro-Bush. We showed our congressional people and they showed NONE. And you asked no questions! Be fair." She cut it short. I felt abused.*

You can't beat the press. They always have the last word, and the next morning I turned on the tube to see a panel discussing how badly *I HAD ABUSED JUDY WOODRUFF!* If George hadn't been running for President that might have been funny!

Secretary of Labor Lynn Martin, who is pro-choice, keynoted the convention that night and did a superb job. She is a bright, enthusiastic, energetic woman. As she spoke, I remembered sitting in a living room in Rockford, Illinois, twelve years earlier and listening to this young woman, a single parent of two girls. She was running for the congressional seat that John Anderson was vacating. Since that time, Lynn and I had campaigned together a lot, sharing long bus rides and marching in freezing parades, and here she was keynoting the convention and sitting in the President's cabinet.

* I probably should explain this diary entry. The Democrats refused to let Pennsylvania Governor Robert Casey, who is pro-life, or any other pro-life Democrats, speak at their convention. Also, their senators and congressmen had little or no role in the convention since the Democratically controlled House was in the middle of the Post Office scandal.

Mary Fisher also spoke and was magnificent. She has tested HIV-positive and is dedicating her life to the research, prevention, and the cure of AIDS. Mary is the daughter of our friends, Max and Marjorie Fisher, and is a single mother of two young boys. She believes passionately in what she is doing. We have kept up our interest in her work and value our friendship with her immensely.

Jack Kemp and Phil Gramm also spoke Tuesday night and did well, I thought. It was interesting to hear them, knowing that both were probably thinking ahead—four years ahead, to be exact. But now they were 100 percent behind George.

The next day was as crazy as the first. I visited the Texas Children's Hospital, met George at the huge Republican Gala, rushed home to do more press interviews, practiced my speech, which was coming up that night, and then had dinner with all our family, seventy of us. I ate with my brothers and their wives, and George ate with his. Both our families have been so supportive during George's political career.

Unfortunately, George P. and I had to leave early to change clothes and head for the convention and our big night.

We were preceded on the program by six of the most amazing "Points of Light" recipients, and then Marilyn Quayle spoke. She is a great wife and mother and a very bright woman. Unfortunately, her speech did not convey her warmth or caring and she was very much criticized for it. The work Marilyn has done with breast cancer is far-reaching, and she got little or no credit for that. She started the "Race for the Cure" in Washington, and has raised millions of dollars for the fight against this dreadful disease that needlessly kills 46,000 American women every year.

Then it was my turn. In all honesty, I can't remember a word that I said, but the highlight of my talk came when I called the family out and ten children and twelve grandchildren appeared. I asked George P. to speak for the family:

Among other things, George read a letter that his grandfather had written him after his trip with AMERICARES to Armenia after that devastating earthquake several years ago.

George P. gave a loving endorsement of his grandfather, ending with a last minute addition of "VIVA BUSH," which resounded through our trips for the next few months. "P" wrote his own speech and delivered it so well.

He stood straight and gave that beautiful smile that Dick Darman mentioned several years before. He made us so very proud [see Appendix D].

One thing that happened gave me the giggles. George came out after our little talk and was immediately rushed by the grandchildren—as primed by the handlers. Jenna and Barbara were very enthusiastic and at (age) 10 were like big puppy dogs. They charged their grandfather and for a moment I feared that he might buckle under their weight. Now that would have been a photo op!

The next morning we attended an early-morning prayer breakfast at the University of Houston with Jim Baker. George spent most of the day working on his speech for that night. I would not have been able to sleep if my speech had not been finished the day it was to be given!

At noon the Harris County Republican women hosted a Tribute to the First Lady. I was very touched. Representative Olympia Snowe, Senator Nancy Kassebaum, Ambassador Carla Hill, and cabinet secretaries Barbara Franklin and Lynn Martin all attended. Jane Morgan Weintraub sang, and not only looked sensational but sounded like an angel. Rich Bond, Janet Steiger, and Jeb Bush all spoke. Every one of them lied about me and I loved it! They had a film narrated by Charlton Heston that made me sound like a saint. I knew better, but loved it also!

That night I raced to the Convention Hall so I could hear Jerry Ford speak. He and Betty were so great to be there and he gave a marvelous speech. Jerry had campaigned hard for George, and they had been very generous with their words and time. He was followed by Senator Jack Danforth, Dan Quayle, and Bob Dole, who in his very commanding yet funny way, introduced George.

Of course I think George was great. But I wasn't the only one. He was interrupted so many times that his thirty-five-minute speech took almost an hour.

. . . The place went wild. We went up to sit behind the stage to listen to the end. There were all the little grands, full of it, and dying to get up on that stage. They had had a taste of applause the night before and liked it, I guess. I joined George and then all the family did. They had an overkill of a balloon drop. If any more had come down we would have been buried! All the kids loved it and they all looked adorable.

So a convention that had started out on rocky footing ended on a very high note for us. The polls showed that the gap between George and Bill Clinton had nearly closed, and we felt ready to go.

⁓ I spent the first three days traveling with George, which was fun, and despite terrible weather, we felt a rush of excitement and high hopes.

August 21—We flew to Gulfport, Mississippi, to the biggest hottest rally ever. It was there that George and I saw a sign that we loved: "George P. for President in 2024!" From there to a fund-raiser where we had some of the "sweatiest" pictures ever taken with supporters!

On to Branson, Missouri, where we went to a rally of 17,000 people in a theme park. There were Glen Campbell, Loretta Lynn and Moe Bandy, all great supporters, working up the crowd. One forgets that these poor people have stood there for three hours in some cases. It was truly a great start. We went that evening to Moe's theater for a wonderful show . . . He is giving the proceeds of the night to literacy and that is just great! So ended Day One of the official 1992 campaign.

August 22—Up early. Flew to Woodstock, Georgia, a town of 3,500, and there we were greeted by 25,000. . . . It was the darndest thing you have ever seen—it poured rain and people stayed for hours. It was drizzling when we arrived and several times it poured again. I was under an umbrella. Paul Coverdell and Newt Gingrich were there. On to Birmingham, Alabama, where exactly the same thing happened. It rained and 17,000 people stayed. We were with Helen and Governor Guy Hunt and Ray Scott, a fishing pal of George's.

In every town we did a fund-raiser. The people who come are always so fresh and eager and we are always so tired and rushed. It hardly seems fair to them. They are so generous and deserve more than they get.

We went from Alabama to Dallas, where we had supper with George and Laura and then George spoke at a Baptist meeting. So ended Day 2 of the 1992 official campaign.

August 23—Day 3 of the campaign was spent at church and the State Fair in Illinois with (Governor) Jim Edgar and Brenda. I could not get over the numbers of people who met us at every stop . . . It was amazing. In Georgia and Alabama they stayed through the rain, and in Mississippi and Illinois through intense heat. I know that George is going to win.

*August 24—*71 more days.
. . . Other things are happening in the world. At this very moment Miami, Florida, is being hit by the big hurricane—big. Our children (Jeb and Colu) have been evacuated from their home. I can't wait to hear that they are all right.

. . . Woody Allen and Mia Farrow are having a disgusting public separation.

. . . "Fergie" is all over the news with pictures of her swimming topless with some young man other than her husband and her children standing by.

George flew to N.J., Connecticut and right to Florida. He declared the area a disaster. He says that it is the worst devastation that he has ever seen, 250,000 homeless. Horrible.

. . . I watched from Los Angeles and Hurricane Andrew is the worst in our history. It also ripped through Louisiana. I have just seen G. there on the TV.

Later I went with George when he toured both south Florida and Louisiana again. It was so hard to believe. This hurricane didn't cut a swath through an area, it absolutely demolished everything as far as the eye could see. The one bright spot was seeing the volunteers from the Red Cross and religious groups, victims of Hurricane Hugo, medical teams from all over the country, the National Guard, and other military units, all setting up day-care centers, medical clinics, soup kitchens, and centers for dispensing water and for helping people with their insurance. Not only did the hurricane victims lose their homes, schools, and hospitals, but in many cases their places of work and therefore their jobs.

The campaign went on and on. It seemed like endless meals one week—and none the next. I rediscovered that all pillows at hotels and motels feel like rocks and everyone wakes up with stiff necks. The windows don't open and the heat or air-conditioning is never adjustable, so you cooked or you froze. Sometimes you would get lucky. Doro and I once were put in honeymoon suites. Right next to my bed was a big bathtub for two, and from the bed you could see the toilet. What happened to the blushing bride? There is a generation gap.

We felt rushed all the time and very grateful to all the people who were working so hard.

Despite the long hours, it was exciting to meet so many interesting people and hear their stories. Many of our experiences were wonderful. One great example is when Gayle Wilson, wife of California Governor Pete Wilson, and I visited a Hispanic housing development in Los Angeles. The locals had taken charge of their own area and were crime free. As we were walking out of this truly humble housing project, a young girl came up and said, "Mrs. Bush, I go to Phillips Exeter Academy." She told me that another girl from the same complex also goes there. She said, "I want you to know that we don't only bring up gang members here." I was so touched and wondered how these two young women felt among so many children from considerably more comfortable backgrounds in that cold, cold New England climate. Exeter should be proud. I am sure that this girl will do well in life because she not only earned, but also was given, this opportunity.

In North Carolina a man gave me a check for $100,000 in response to George's plea for the American Red Cross and their Hurricane Andrew relief work. Later I heard that the Red Cross got 53,000 telephone calls pledging more than $4 million in response to George's message. In addition, the government of Kuwait gave $10 million.

Actor Gerald McRaney of "Major Dad" fame spent a day campaigning with me in Florida. The people loved him and he was a great campaigner.

In early September, George and I had lunch with the Roy Harris family in Asheville, North Carolina. Several months earlier, Mr. Harris had been in the audience during a Rose Garden interview George did with "CBS This Morning." After asking George a question, he thanked him for asking him to the White House and invited us to his house. Well, we took him up on it and went for lunch with the whole family, including his wife, Diantha, and their two daughters, Stacy and Lisa. Their community all had pitched in and they had a delicious spread. The family was involved in their church, the Girl Scouts, the schools, and so on. It was another bright spot.

The very next day we went to Louisville, Kentucky, to attend a Triple A baseball game with Will and Sarah Farish and Dan Ulmer, one of the owners of the Louisville Redbirds, and his wife, Helen. Everyone who came brought a can of food for the hurricane victims. We got a huge standing ovation when we walked out onto the field for the singing of "The Star-Spangled Banner," and then George threw out the first ball and got another standing ovation from 20,000 people. We did not see one bad sign or hear one boo. We were thrilled and surprised when George got yet another ovation when we left.

While we were at the baseball game, Bill Clinton was at a car race in South Carolina, where he got booed badly. Almost all the press reported it except for our old friend David Broder of *The Washington Post*. His column said that George threw out a ball at a baseball game where his people expected him to be booed, and Bill Clinton went to a car race where there were 100,000 people. Period. Not one word that George was cheered or Bill was booed. I just could not understand that. Many years before we had established a friendship with Dave and Ann Broder with the full understanding that they were Democrats and politics would be put aside in our friendship. I respect Dave, but this article was so blatantly partisan and untrue. That was a dark spot.

On Labor Day we walked the four-and-a-half-mile Mackinac Bridge in Sault Ste. Marie, Michigan, an annual event that brings out about 100,000 people, with Governor John Engler and Michelle. Then it was on to Milwaukee, where we attended a Labor Day picnic with Wisconsin Governor Tommy Thompson and Sue Ann Thompson, and then back to Michigan for the Hamtramck Polish Festival Parade.

Despite the great events we were doing, I wrote in my diary about this time: "I am back to my bad feelings and feel discouraged about winning these days. The crowds are great, but the playing field is not level. It is hard to run against the world!!"

George and I rarely traveled together, which I hated. He was great about calling and checking on me. Most of my campaign trips were built around big rallies, then smaller fund-raising lunches or dinners. Anna Perez and I worked on two talks: one to be given at the rallies, and since I am not a rah-rah speaker, these were not easy for me; and a second warm and cozy talk for the smaller groups. I much prefer the latter. George, meanwhile, was doing his job *and* speaking around the country.

Between speeches we managed to tuck in visits to literacy programs, which I loved. In Lexington, Kentucky, I helped dedicate the Carnegie Lexington Literacy Center, which Will Farish had supported. They have a wonderful, big-picture approach to literacy: in-house poets and writers, classes for new learners, writing classes, children's story hours, state-of-the-art computers.

We often visited shopping malls to shake the hands of shoppers, and I would stop in the bookstore to promote "Mrs. Bush's Storytime" and read to a group of children. Sometimes local campaign staffs would point out to my staff that children couldn't vote, so maybe I shouldn't take the time. Ridiculous.

In Louisville, Kentucky, Sharon Darling, who is a member of my foundation board and is director of the National Center for Family Literacy, took me to a great family literacy program, Parents and Children Together, where the mothers spend their mornings studying and the afternoons working with their children:

They are the poorest group of women, all have several children, some as many as four, no man in the household, most, if not all, dropped out of school early, black and white, and all felt alone and forgotten. There was an outpouring of gratitude for the program and the most amazing feeling of "sisterhood." We talked about what they hoped for their children. We talked about sex and the fact that there was something worth waiting for IF THEY GET THEIR EDUCATION. I was touched—one shy lady asked me to hug her and the whole visit turned into a hugging, crying time. Then we went into a class with the mothers and their children. Each one of my new friends wanted me to see her child or children. This is what I mean when I talk about family values.

In Barberton, Ohio, near Akron, I visited the Decker Family Development Center. The entire community supported it, including the hospital, local university, and service clubs, and they received funding from the federal, state, and local governments. I was so impressed with all the services the center offered the entire family—and under one roof—that I suggested that they apply for a grant from the Barbara Bush Foundation for Family Literacy. There was an awkward silence and then someone told me that they already had received one! Now that was embarrassing. We also visited another impressive foundation recipient in Denver, the Bishop Richard Allen Center.

⮑ On September 17 I logged in my diary that in one week I had visited eleven cities in seven states. My events had included the ceremonial receiving of the Olympic Flag in Atlanta for the 1996 games (which George also attended); eight fund-raisers; five school, library, or literacy events; two cultural centers; three rallies; and one fair. Yes, I was exhausted. Several times during September I noted in my diary that both George and I feel very good on the road and discouraged when we get back to Washington. The reception on the hustings was great, but bad press "inside the Beltway" got us down.

September 28—I am flabbergasted by this campaign. We are allowing the Clinton campaign and the press to walk all over us. George Bush has been a great president. Interest rates are at a 20-year low; inflation ¼th of the 1980 levels; the U.S. is the world's number 1 exporting nation; George negotiated a North American Free Trade Agreement (NAFTA) with Canada and Mexico which will open more markets for U.S. goods and create more jobs; overall drug use is down by 13%; more assistance in drug crop destruction; tougher law enforcement against drug dealers; net farm income at record levels and government supports have declined; a transportation bill that will pump millions of dollars in the economy, create hundreds of thousands of jobs and strengthen the infrastructure of our country; the first Clean Air Act in a decade; 1990 Child Care Bill; a revolutionary Americans with Disabilities Act; a Civil Rights Bill with no quotas; on George's watch the Cold War and the nuclear nightmare have ended and he won the release of the hostages in Lebanon; he helped bring about the end of the civil war in El Salvador; he restored a democratically elected president to Panama and the victory in the Persian Gulf made us all proud; he vetoed 33 bills that would have cost the American public billions of dollars. He did all this with the Congress bucking him on every positive program he sent to them. The Congress, Democratically controlled, on the other hand, has been found to be filled with corruption, check kiting, drug and sex scandals. It has all been swept under the rug, covered up. I do not understand it!

As you can see, I was frustrated. So we would just get back out there on the road and try harder.

One of the most fun, exhausting, and interesting things we did was take train trips across the Midwest and later in the South. The first one, in late September, began in Columbus, Ohio, and included five scheduled stops and one impromptu. We learned right away that after every rally stop, we had to get back on the train and wait twenty minutes while the press corps reboarded. There were around two hundred traveling with us, and they had quite a distance to go to get back to their cars. As the train pulled out of the station we would go back to the caboose and wave:

Then I thought I would work on my computer. Not at all. People lined the tracks at every intersection waving and cheering. We ended by standing on the back of the train and waving for hours. It was exhausting, but fun. If the crowd was big we were sad that we couldn't stop or slow down. There were some Clinton/Gore people out, not many, and they were friendly. There were two who mooned us. I thought that was quite funny and certainly different!! One man, who was on a pickup truck in the middle of a field with several children, dropped his pants and mooned us while his wife took pictures. Great example for the kids. The train tracks in Ohio and Michigan go by many attractive homes. Many families were having picnics and waving flags as we went by. There were "Where's Millie?" signs. Many people ran along the track or rode bikes alongside of the train until the road ran out. People stood on hilltops with flags as we went by. All along the 130 miles people put pennies on the track and the minute we went by children were collecting the flattened pennies as souvenirs of the Presidential train. The leaves are beginning to change and we love the beauty.

On a smaller scale, I took several bus trips with Nancy Ellis, Doro, Margaret, and Noelle. We each would give a short talk and then work the crowd. I spoke first, introducing Nan, who spoke as a sister and then introduced Margaret, who spoke as a teacher and daughter-in-law and then introduced Doro, who spoke as a daughter and then introduced Noelle, the cleanup hitter, who spoke as a granddaughter. We had great crowds every place we went in Illinois, Wisconsin, Ohio, Pennsylvania, and New Jersey.

October 3—This morning I am absolutely convinced that George is going to lose. It is wrong, but all the press are printing such negative things. I will miss the White House life, but I can already feel a little splurge of excitement about going home to Neil and Sharon, friends, to play golf, and to setting up a home in Houston. I could die for my George, who has been a superb president and will go down in history as a great leader for the free world. The momentum is so strong against him.

October 8—Great news. The *Weekly Reader* Poll came out and George wins 55% of the vote. They have never been wrong since Ike's day. The only good poll I've seen. Gosh how I hate all this!!

October 11—23 MORE DAYS TO GO!
. . . This morning George said to me, "The hill may be too high to climb." I don't like to hear him say that, but I certainly have felt that he was going to lose. I have this terrible feeling that he is worrying about me. He needn't. Wherever he is, I will be happy. I will just hurt for him.

In October, there were three debates among George, Bill Clinton, and Ross Perot, who had jumped back into the race. They all run together in my mind. My memories are of lots of tension on all sides, lots of advice, and great relief when they were over. We always felt George did well. I also felt that it was a crime to let Ross Perot be there. He had not gone through the primary process, but had just bought his way in, and out, and back in. The morning after the first debate in St. Louis I wrote:

I can still hear (Perot's) voice: "Those people sit up there in Washington with their pointy little heads and don't do anything. Send me up and I'll set up my town meetings and by Christmas we'll have things going." Bill Clinton sat there smiling and loving all the cutting down Ross was doing of George.

The Richmond, Virginia, debate was the toughest for George. The audience was chosen by a polling firm but didn't seem to represent a cross section of our country. As far as we could tell, there were no businessmen or -women or any small businesses represented:

It was a funny set-up. Carole Simpson, the moderator, asked George to answer first every time and then gave no rebuttal time. The questions were things like "Mr. President, do you care? Do you really care about people?" As George is not too great about tooting his own horn, he did not hit this one out of the ballpark and I think he knew it. Generally speaking we thought he won that one, also. But then we always thought he won.

Something very touching happened right before the Richmond debate. Earlier that day, while I was visiting a bowling alley, a Vietnam veteran gave me a poem and his medal and asked me to give it to George to carry at the debate that night. That touched George. He did carry it, and after the election sent it back to the owner. I know that he felt that he let this veteran and all others down when he lost the election.

The next morning after the debate George P. and I left to campaign together in Texas. On the way down he worked on his talk, and Anna Perez suggested that he add something personal as he had done at the convention. We didn't know what he had come up with until the first stop and we heard his talk:

> Last night at the debate someone asked my grandfather if he cared. He cares all right. Once when I was playing baseball someone yelled "Get the *spick* off the field." That really hurt, and I told my dad. He told his dad and my grandfather cried. He believes you judge people for themselves and not for their skin.

It almost killed me to hear that story and yet think of how many children of all heritages have had that same thing happen.

I went to the third debate, in East Lansing, Michigan, with Jeb and Marvin. The only thing I really remember is that Ross Perot accused the Republican party of investigating his children. That is not true. He also had accused us of trying to ruin his daughter's wedding by doctoring some pictures of her. That's just plain nutty. Margot and his children always have been friends, and for them to even suggest that was wrong, and I told Ross that after the debate. He didn't answer me.

He continued his accusations during a "60 Minutes" interview later in the month, then he said the next morning that he had no proof. NO PROOF! After spending part of the debate and twenty minutes on "60 Minutes" talking about nothing else!

There also was one vice presidential debate, and we thought that Dan Quayle was great. He was very relaxed and called Al Gore several times on untruths. It was a good debate and exchange between two good men. Politically, I do not agree with Al Gore, but I would agree that he is a fine, decent man. I am afraid that all Americans remember that debate because it became apparent that retired Admiral Jim Stockdale, Perot's running mate, was physically not in shape to run for public office. I had much respect for this man, and it was a shame that he was put in that position.

While all of this was going on, we also were celebrating a very important event in Washington: the two-hundredth anniversary of the laying of the White House cornerstone. Curator Rex Scouten and his staff, who did such a superb job taking care of the White House and preserving its history, headed up the celebration, and we had a variety of interesting and educational events.

One of my favorites was the "Very Special Arts" art exhibit. Disabled students from across the country were told about the White House, and then asked to draw their impressions. The winners from all fifty states and the territories came to the White House and had their art on display. Some of the pictures were very good; some were very simple. But they all were special. Many had pictures of Millie, George, and me. My favorite was of a state dinner. In the middle was a little black girl surrounded by a king and queen and then George and me. The artist had made herself the guest of honor. It was so sweet. Another little girl explained to me that her painting was of a dance at the White House. George and I were there, along with Barbie and Ken, and several of her other heroes. I asked who the person was with her back to the front, and she said it was she. When I asked why she had not let us see her face, she answered, "I was looking at you."

On October 13, we buried a time capsule to be opened in one hundred years. George wrote a letter, and I put in *Millie's Book*.

Also that fall, Julie Cooke of my office was spearheading one of my favorite projects: inviting fourth grade students in District of Columbia public schools to the White House for special tours. We actually had begun this program in January of 1992, and before it ended, well over nine thousand students came through. Even though some of them lived just blocks away, they had never visited the People's House, and we were thrilled to give them this opportunity.

A lot of thought and volunteer hours went into this program. Before they arrived, for example, the classes were sent a packet to help them prepare for their visit, including a video. United Bus Owners of

America and Gold Line Tours provided free transportation for the students, and Merrill Lynch donated books about the White House to each school's library.

We set aside Monday, the day the White House is closed to the public, for the tours. The students arrived through the "front door," the North Portico, and when they reached the Grand Foyer, the Marine Band played "Hail to the Chief." National Park Service guides then ushered the students through the State Floor. Each room was set up to illustrate a different White House function. In the East Room, for example, students participated in a mock bill signing. Boys and girls were chosen to play the parts of White House characters, such as the president, a congressman, a press person, and so forth. I remember that the Red Room had some hidden things the children were supposed to look for, and the State Dining Room had two tables set as they would look for a state dinner. The "President" and "Head of State" toasted each other.

We learned the hard way to give the students their chocolate chip cookies as they were leaving the White House to go out to the South Grounds. Millie, Ranger, and I sometimes caught up with them there. They took home with them a booklet of interesting facts and games.

Some lucky classes got to witness actual White House events. For example, one class witnessed a signing ceremony in the Rose Garden with President Bush, and several groups of students watched the helicopter land on the South Lawn.

Many of the kids wrote us letters after their visits. They talked about how great the guides, band, and cookies were. Comments on the music ranged from "wonderful" to "cool" to "the best I have ever heard." The cookies rated "quite good," "very, very, very, very good," to "MMM-MMM good." Many thanked *me* for baking them. One boy knew better. He said, "Never fire the cook."

Here are some of my other favorite lines:

"Thank you for inviting us to your humble home. Maybe Mr. Bush can come over and play Nintendo."

"You keep the grass a nice length."

"Do you pay rent?"

"You have a nice dog. She is as beautiful as you are."

October 22—Marvin Bush's birthday.

12 MORE DAYS TO GO.

Such a sad day. Our truly precious friend Betty Liedtke died. This breaks my heart for Hugh, for their children and all of us—her friends. Betty was the best kind of friend. I hurt for Mildred (Kerr), Bessie (Liedtke), Sidney (Hover)—and me. I can hear her saying, "Say, Bar . . ." and then something funny. After much discussion it was decided that Pop would go to the funeral. He wanted to be there for Hugh. I thought about Betty all day and smiled. When she came to the White House for a State Dinner she wore a large, maybe 3 inch by 4 inch, obviously plastic diamond on a ring around her neck. When I kidded her about it she said, "Oh, you like it? Why then I'll wear the bracelet that goes with it." And she did. I wondered all night what the people sitting with her thought!! She laughed at everything and yet was loving and caring all the time.

October 25—The polls look bad, but I just know that when the people get in that booth, they will vote for George. Look at the alternate choices.

I feel guilty. George is on the trail and will go until the end. I went out to see Sam play in a baseball game. I was so impressed with the feeling of good sportsmanship we saw. Both teams were going to have a picnic after the game. It was a great family feeling. I couldn't help but think that just a year ago Bobby Koch was not engaged—and now he is married, coaching a baseball team, father of two, having a baby and voting for a Republican for president. What a joy for our family.

. . . George got home last night around 10:20. He was dead. He signed 33 bills and did some mail. He tried to stay awake to the end of the (World Series) game. Toronto won in the 11th. That's good news as a Republican wins when the American League wins. He fell asleep before the end of the game. He feels good about the campaign.

. . . People are pulling back from George—(Terry) Considine in Colorado and (Senator) D'Amato in NYC. It is so ugly. He understands it. I don't.

Just when I thought the pressure and long hours were unbearable, something would happen to break the tension and make me feel better. I'll never forget when I did the Larry King show. Larry and I talked a while, then we took calls. The first four callers were anti-Bush, and I said to Larry, sort of kidding, "Where are the Bush people?" The next two callers were pro-Bush. I should have asked sooner! Millie went along with me and lay quietly at my side the whole time. Larry asked me if she was always that good, and as the camera focused on a sleeping dog, I said, "Always." When we left the studio, Peggy Swift and Anna Perez were in hysterics, for Millie had thrown up the minute the camera turned away from her. How awful for whoever found that little gift!

Toward the end of the campaign Marvin traveled with me quite a bit, which was a lifesaver. He is such good company and kept us laughing. And for a guy who truly hates politics, he is a great campaigner and speaker. During one of my interviews I looked up and there was Marvin in a Barbara Bush rubber mask. It was such a thing of beauty.

We worked mall after mall and shook thousands of hands. People waited hours to see us. I found myself thinking again: I just know he is going to win.

Then Margaret told me that Marshall's teacher called to ask if she could help prepare Marshall for either contingency, win or lose.

The last week we literally crisscrossed the country and ran into family and friends everywhere we went. I did unending radio, TV, and print interviews.

October 30—5 MORE DAYS TO GO!!!

. . . In New Jersey a reporter told me that the CNN Poll said we were within a point of Clinton.

October 31—I met up with George in Wisconsin finally and he had a dreadful cold. Several of his group have had the worst flu. He has had both. I thought he had a fever, but he had to get up and do a live Larry King show for an hour and a half.

. . . He did a superb job in spite of the darndest allegations from the Walsh Committee, the independent prosecutor's second indictment of Cap Weinberger, and some suggestions about George. There is nothing new, but it feels as though it has brought our momentum to a halt. The Congress has already spent 42 million dollars looking into the "Arms for Hostages" deal and found absolutely nothing wrong with George and yet new allegations are brought up the Friday before the election? Now come on!! George had the Congressional Report of 1987, which is open to the public—the whole testimony—nothing new. This was looked into by the Tower Commission, the Congress and the Walsh Committee.

This dreadful man finally handed in his report in January 1994 after spending a reported $100 million of taxpayers' money. He went out swinging at everything and everyone in sight, but with absolutely no proof of wrongdoing. There was none to find.

❧ I spent the Monday before Election Day campaigning with Marvin in Iowa, North Dakota, and Colorado, then home to Houston and George. It was over.

I wrote that night that I did not believe we would win, but I'm not sure I believed it. George woke up on Election Day and said that he still thought he was going to win. I must say that I thought he would, too. All that gloom and doom in the diary was just a way to protect myself. I know this all sounds mixed up—and it was. I just could not believe that when people got in the booth they wouldn't look at the three men and vote for George.

We voted early, then I visited with Jack and Bobbie Fitch for a while. I exercised, napped, visited with the family. In late afternoon, George W. told us, based on the exit polls, it was over; we would lose. Election evening dear Bill Moss had a buffet supper for family and friends. It was not easy.

Later that night we went to the hotel for George to make a concession speech. It was short and generous. When we saw all our dear friends who had been loyal for years, it really hurt. Our boys had killed themselves for us. I was glad that all their states had gone for George. George W. and Jeb had devoted almost full time to their dad. Marvin also worked hard, but he is more like me and couldn't stand to watch the news. Neil, all the wives, Doro, and Bobby all had worked. Noelle and George P. had actively campaigned. It was hardest of all on Neil and Sharon, who had longed to campaign but had to keep a low profile because of the vicious and untrue attacks on Neil. Margaret and Doro could not stop weeping. It hurt.

The week before the election Doro told me that a little classmate had said to Ellie, "Your grandfather is going to lose." The teacher told Doro that five-year-old Ellie just stood there shaking, fists clenched, and then she took her paintbrush, raised her arm, and starting at the face, painted the girl red with one big swipe! The teacher said that

Ellie looked so frustrated. I knew the feeling. How I wanted to get my hands on a paintbrush.

⟋⟍ Why did we lose? George Bush says it was because he didn't communicate as well as his predecessor or successor. I just don't believe that.

I think we lost because people really wanted a change. We had had twelve years of a Republican presidency. The Cold War was over, and now it was time to turn our attention toward the home front and the many problems that were and are facing our country. People were worried about jobs and the economy. There was an impression that George was more interested in foreign affairs and did not have a domestic program, which was not true. He had accomplished so much, and still had so much he wanted to do. But that was the impression.

For more than a year, George had been attacked by five Democrats, one Republican, and one Independent. I think people began to believe what they heard.

And the press. I honestly believe that most of them wanted Bill Clinton to win. He was one of them—baby boomers. Many of them had shared experiences with him, including the Vietnam War protest. David Broder told *The Los Angeles Times* after the election: "The feeling was that a second Bush term would be boring . . . for a lot of reporters of (Clinton's) generation, there was a sense of anticipation: 'Our folks are going to be in charge.' "

An excellent example of what Dave was talking about is Strobe Talbott. Strobe and Bill Clinton were college roommates at Oxford. They were friends. His wife traveled with Hillary during the campaign. That was okay, but Strobe also was an editor at *Time* magazine. Today he is the number two man at the State Department.

Another example was the "MacNeil/Lehrer Newshour," where Mark Shields represented the Democratic side and David Gergen the Republican side. I would listen in shock, waiting for Dave to speak up in George's defense. He hardly ever did. It turned out, of course, that David Gergen, who also was an editor at *U.S. News and World Report*, announced after the campaign that he voted for Bill Clinton and was not a Republican but an Independent. He also said that they had been friends for years, having met at the annual Renaissance Weekend held over New Year's. Today he is a senior adviser in President Clinton's White House.

And then there was Rick Kaplan, who produced ABC's "Prime Time Live" while helping advise the Clinton campaign, according to *Los Angeles Times* reporter Tom Rosenstiel's book *Strange Bedfellows*.

It all added up to some very lopsided reporting at times, which simply was not fair. I recently heard ABC's Brit Hume say on C-SPAN that the media greatly exaggerated the state of the economy during the election; he called it a "dark chapter in the recent history of the American media."

A study conducted by the University of California at Irvine found that campaign coverage of George in the three major news magazines from May 1991 to November 1992 was 17 percent favorable, 75 percent unfavorable. For Bill Clinton, coverage was 60 percent favorable, 34 percent unfavorable.

Yes, many reporters did do a fair job of covering the campaign—in fact, too many to mention. But I will be honest in telling you that the overall experience has left a bad taste in my mouth about the media, and makes me question what I read. I hate that. I respect and like many members of the press. I just wish I could respect more of what they do.

25

"One Last Time"

The trip home on Wednesday was sad. The three grandchildren who were with us, Marshall, Ellie, and Sam, watched movies on the plane. The Secret Service and the staff were sweet and didn't quite know how to act. George worked all the way back, writing notes, making phone calls, and generally cheering everyone up. It might have been easier if he had kicked somebody.

Our helicopter landed at the Pentagon and we drove to the White House, with Marvin and Margaret in the car with us. As we crossed Memorial Bridge, two military men who were jogging stopped and saluted when they saw the car. For the first and only time, I saw George's face crumble. He slammed his fist into his palm and said a few profane words. I knew that he felt he had let down the men and women in the military. We felt his anguish and were crushed.

By the time we arrived at the White House he had recovered. The Quayles met us at the bottom of the South Lawn and we walked up through a crowd of supporters and staff. They were very dear to welcome us home, but it wasn't easy to go through that. George, as usual, tried to be funny. When the cheering died down, he went to the microphone and said something like, "Haven't you guys heard? We lost."

Brent Scowcroft and Jim Baker came upstairs to have a drink in the West Hall Sitting Room and saved the day. They told us that Ross Perot had called them both because he wanted George to know that he had led "his people" in three cheers (hip, hip, hurrahs) for George on election night. He felt that George wouldn't have seen it because it happened at the time he was giving his concession speech. What an amazing, insensitive man!

Everything we did after the election had a "this is the last time we will ever do this" feeling. It also was an extraordinarily busy period. The mail was tremendous—we tried hard to answer it all—and our phone rang nonstop:

. . . Many Heads of State are calling in and George is assuring them that Bill Clinton will be great. I'm not so sure.

We have seen pictures of Saddam Hussein dancing in the streets of Baghdad and former Prime Minister Shamir (of Israel) is rejoicing and says that George deserves it. He blames his defeat on George.

. . . Goldwater says that it was the worst campaign that he had ever seen. He should certainly know. His campaign in 1964 was a lulu!

But Jimmy Carter takes the cake and I quote the Atlanta/Reuters Report: "Jimmy Carter said that he would not accept a 'permanent position,' such as a Cabinet job in Bill Clinton's administration. But Carter said that he would be willing to accept an 'ad hoc' advisory position in a Clinton administration, perhaps on foreign policy issues. Carter said he considers Clinton's victory more a rejection of President Bush than an endorsement of Clinton, who won with a minority of the popular vote"!! I'm sure that endeared Carter to Clinton! George wrote under that clipping in a note to Brent Scowcroft: "Brent, Jimmy Carter is one gracious fellow, managing to p.o. both Clinton and me in one sentence!"

. . . Nancy Reagan called to assure me that the Cindy Adams column saying that she was going to vote for Ross Perot was not true. (Hadn't seen it.)

The first weekend after the election we went to Camp David with family and friends. George's brother Johnny and his wife, Jody, came, and we watched movies and relaxed. Colin and Alma Powell came for one night with two of their children, a daughter-in-law, and one grandson. He and George talked of many things. One conversation that I remember was about homosexuals in the service and how difficult that would be for Colin. He was opposed, as was George. This is part of the generation gap that I think was one cause of our defeat.

It was interesting that Bill Clinton's first pronouncement was on this issue, when he said they should be allowed into the military. In fairness, I suspect that he was asked many things in a press conference and this one answer was highlighted. Should homosexuals be denied the right to serve their country? There are many pros and cons, but like Bill Clinton, I have never been in the service and so have little to base my judgment on.

Later, when it came time to deal with the issue, General Powell, a good soldier and a great man, obeyed his Commander in Chief.

George spent a lot of time on the phone that weekend thanking people for their help and comforting them. I hated how everyone was attacking and blaming the campaign and George for the loss.

Exactly one week after the election we attended the Senate Republican Dinner on the Hill honoring George and Dan Quayle. Senate Minority Leader Bob Dole, a great war hero and certainly a congressional hero of the Bush/Quayle years, was the host and had us very close to breaking down. No man ever served his president more loyally or with more grace under very difficult circumstances. With the Democrats controlling both houses of Congress, every piece of legislation was an uphill battle. We saw many of our friends who had started out with us in politics, and now it was time to start saying good-bye. It was an emotional evening.

The very next day we left for a long weekend on Gasparilla Island in Florida with Will and Sarah Farish and Sarah's great parents, Mary and Bayard Sharp. We golfed, fished, and most important, spent time surrounded by good friends. Millie and Ranger went, too, and we took glorious early-morning walks on the beaches and golf course.

I went directly from there to Houston and looked for the perfect house for two old retired people. I stayed with Bobbie and Jack Fitch and saw twenty-two houses in a day and a half. They were either too grand, too expensive, or not what we wanted. The long and the short of it was that we decided to build a "patio" house on our own property, a tiny lot that has great neighbors. This was the same lot everybody had been saying for years was too small to build on, so there was something sort of fun in doing just that.

On November 19 George flew up to Greenwich, Connecticut, with Doro to see his darling mother, who had slipped into semiconsciousness. They sat and held her hand for several hours and told her that they loved her, which she well knew. No mother has ever been more loved than Dorothy Walker Bush by her children—and her in-laws, I might add.

That afternoon Hillary Rodham Clinton came by the White

House for her tour. She was very easy to be with and, I believe, we had a good visit. We talked about the office, the mail volume, and Chelsea. I suggested that she might bring a cousin or a best friend to spend the first year and go to school with Chelsea. It's a big lonely house for one little girl.

Then I went downstairs to join George on the State Floor while he received the credentials of the new ambassadors and I had tea with their wives and children. Upstairs, Hillary was going through the White House with Chief Usher Gary Walters and two or three people who were going to help her with decorating.

At the end of the credentials ceremony I was slipped a piece of paper saying that George's mother had gently passed away. I am so glad that he had been with her that day.

The next day I flew to Atlanta to campaign for Paul Coverdell, who was in a run-off race for the U.S. Senate. Paul had been our campaign chairman in Georgia in 1980, and he served George as director of the Peace Corps. He and his wife Nancy were good friends, so even though I had sworn off politics for life, I couldn't say no. Nor did I want to. He did us proud by winning that race and has been a fine addition to the U.S. Senate.

I headed straight for Camp David, where George had planned a big weekend, including a Vespers service with Amy Grant. He had invited five Republican governors and wives who had been such good friends and worked so hard for us: Bill and Susan Weld of Massachusetts; Tommy and Sue Ann Thompson of Wisconsin; Jock McKernan and Olympia Snowe of Maine; Carroll and Iris Campbell of South Carolina; and John and Janet Ashcroft of Missouri.

In addition we had the Sununus, plus Bruce Willis, Demi Moore, and their two children. Amy, her husband, mother, and baby made up the rest of the house party. Where they all slept, I do not know. Amy and her wonderful guitar-playing husband, Gary Chapman, performed with the Camp David choir. John Ashcroft, then the Governor of Missouri, got up and sang a great, rousing gospel song. George also invited an additional fifty or so people—all good friends and people who had worked hard—to come for the service. Frankly, I had dreaded the weekend. I was tired with a deep fatigue from defeat, death, and the uncertainty of getting out of the White House on time. As usual, George had done all the planning and all the work and the whole weekend turned out to be a joy.

That Sunday afternoon at the White House we had our last "National Literacy Honors" evening that ABC-TV has sponsored for several years, and later that week we announced at a White House luncheon the latest Barbara Bush Foundation for Family Literacy grant recipients. This was not the last such announcement, of course, since the foundation would go on, but it was our last time at the White House.

On Monday we had the happiest, most loving funeral for George's mother, surrounded by family and friends of this magnificent woman. It was a beautiful day as we laid her to rest by her beloved Pres and our little Robin.

All our children with the exception of Sharon, who had another commitment, came to the funeral. The boys were wonderful and kept us laughing and crying on the plane going up and coming back. John Bush gave me an envelope with George's name on it that had been found in Mom's safe. In it were a group of letters that George had written his mother and father over the years. Everything George is, is so much a part of his Ma and Pa.

Ten years before her death Mom had written her children a letter "to be opened at her death" describing in minute detail her very modest funeral plans. Her last instructions were: "Let us after the benediction rise and sing gaily, as we depart, that lovely hymn we sang at Pres' service, 'Hark, Hark My Soul.' "

November 23—The third quarter growth figures were announced today. When George announced that the growth would be 2.7%, the Clinton campaign said that George was doctoring the numbers and guess what? When the figures came out for the third quarter the numbers were 3.9%, better by far than George said. Every time George suggested that things were getting better he was accused by one and all of "being out of touch."

Having said that (and feeling better because I said it), we are both looking forward to getting on with the next phase of our lives. I *AM* panicked about getting out of here on time, but I will.

George, Brent, and I went to Kennebunkport for Thanksgiving. It was a quiet, reflective weekend, and although it was cold, we three plus Kenny Raynor, our dear friend and the golf pro at Cape Arundel Golf Course, ran around the course every day playing eighteen holes of golf. And I mean ran. I was so flattered to be included, but then just how many nuts do you know who would drop everything and run around a wet, cold golf course with five minutes' notice? As the club was closed, the dogs were allowed to come with us and ran miles.

We went to our little winter church on Sunday, and as George walked to the door, the whole congregation came to its feet clapping. I could hardly walk in and had trouble controlling my tears.

It wasn't long before we were in the thick of the Christmas season. On December 1, Marvin and Margaret's little Walker joined me and Joe Riley, chairman of the Pageant of Peace, to put the star on top of the National Christmas Tree. I should have gained a place in the Guinness Book of Records as this was my twelfth year to do this.

On Sunday we hosted our fourth and final Kennedy Center Honors reception and then attended the celebration. This was always an evening of great pleasure and performances. So many superb members of the entertainment world have been honored on this evening in the past. This year's honorees were Lionel Hampton, Paul Newman, Joanne Woodward, Ginger Rogers, Paul Taylor, and Mstislav Rostropovich. Lionel and Slava Rostropovich were very dear to us, so this was a happy "last time" for us. At the very end, Master of Ceremonies Walter Cronkite gave a lovely, kind tribute to George.

George had such fun that week planning a surprise for the White House staff. He invited Dana Carvey, the funny "Saturday Night Live" George Bush impersonator, to go to the Kennedy Center Honors and then spend the night with us. He then called a White House–wide staff meeting for 9 A.M. Monday, which set the East and West Wings to buzzing. What was going to happen? Was he going to resign early? You name it, they thought of it!

The staff all gathered in the East Room, and at the appointed hour, the Marine Band played "Hail to the Chief" and in marched that tiny Dana Carvey. The room broke up. What followed was an hour of Dana imitating George and George imitating Dana imitating George. It was very funny, and really helped break the tension that had permeated the place since the election.

Later that morning we officially opened the Christmas season with the traditional showing of the decorations to the White House Press Corps. The theme was "Gift Givers," and the geniuses in the flower shop had dressed about ninety sixteen-inch dolls in authentic costumes of gift-givers through the centuries, starting with the Magi.

As usual, I prayed that I wouldn't make any news when talking to the press. I only made a little when I told them that they have no sense of humor and I thought they made up some of their sources who "wish to remain anonymous." They of course argued with me. I do think one easy way to improve reporters' credibility would be if they all agreed not to use anonymous sources. Only people who are willing to stand behind what they say should be quoted.

I went to my last Toys for Tots party, and was so surprised when General Walt Boomer, the assistant commandant of the Marine Corps and the general who had shown us around the Saudi Arabian desert on Thanksgiving Day, met me at the door. He had such kind words about George, which I appreciated very much.

While all of this was going on George was still consumed with the duties of being President. He had announced the previous week that in cooperation with a United Nations resolution, he was sending American troops into Somalia for "Operation Restore Hope," to help end the starvation there. The food we had been sending to those desperate people had not been getting through, and hundreds of thousands of people were starving or being killed. Before he made his decision, George first consulted with Bill Clinton.

It was around this time that I decided I would write my memoirs. Our lawyer, Terri Lacy, came to Camp David to talk about the future, and I sort of panicked when I realized what was ahead. There is no government money for any expenses of a former First Lady—as there shouldn't be—and I wondered how I was going to manage to answer my mail and cope with public appearance requests. What to do? An answer sort of fell in my lap. I got several very generous offers for my book and also some speech requests, which would help me pay for a couple of helpers. But then I worried how to give speeches, write a book, travel with George, build a house, run a house, play golf, be a good friend and a mother, grandmother, and wife all in one lifetime? Terri assured me that it would all work out, and it has. My troubles were minute compared to the ones George faced: paying for a new house and keeping up Kennebunkport, answering huge stacks of mail, a demanding speaking schedule, and so on. They, too, have worked out, thanks to George's amazing energy and his staff.

December 11—MEDAL OF FREEDOM AWARDS. Johnny Carson, wife and sons stayed with us. They are so nice. I later heard that Johnny said that the Lincoln Bed (an overlong double) was the closest he had slept with anybody in years. I'm sure that other guests feel that way, but like Johnny, are so thrilled to sleep in the Lincoln Bedroom, they are willing to forgo the sleep.

. . . Blair House. This party was to be a surprise thank you for Brent and it was. It was also a surprise for George Bush. I think that Jon Howe got them both to agree to come to honor each other. Then Admiral Jonathan Howe, the quiet gentle No. 2 at the NSC, gave a great talk and we were very moved. He said that General Sherman said about Lincoln that which he would say about George: "Of all the men I ever met he seemed to me to possess more of the elements of greatness combined with goodness than any other." I loved that. Because, God knows, George Bush is all that and more.

On December 13 we attended for the last time "Christmas in Washington," the marvelous star-studded annual NBC event that benefits Children's Hospital. Spike and Betsy Heminway came from Greenwich, Connecticut; Ken and Linda Lay from Houston; and Reverend Pat Adams from Kennebunkport for the evening. We also invited for dinner George's respected friend Jack Welch, head of General Electric, and Bob Wright, CEO of NBC. It was so much fun to share that great house with friends, and we just wish now we had shared it with even more. (I can hear the White House staff laughing—George kept the house pretty full.)

John and Norma Major came to spend a night at Camp David, along with two of his top aides, Stephen Wall and Gus O'Donnell, and Brent Scowcroft and his daughter Karen. We are devoted to the Majors, and it was a warm farewell to two great friends.

We hosted the usual evening Christmas receptions, which took on an even more special meaning. We knew so many of the staff would scatter around the United States.

Then we took our whole little family to Camp David for one last Christmas. Not so little, I guess. We had two grandchildren when George was elected vice president, and we had grown to twelve in 1992. It was a very, very happy time. These wonderful children look forward to being with their cousins, and this year they once again put on a play written by Jenna and Barbara. Six-year-old Pierce, Neil and Sharon's son, played Santa in a glued-on beard and a Santa cap. He has the dearest, smiling face, reddish hair, glasses, and the deepest voice that you ever have heard on a little boy. As in so many things in life, the planning was almost as much fun as the actual doing. Several days were spent in secret play rehearsals, costume and prop preparation. Then there was the well-known snowball fight where George got a black eye from a snowball that had a tiny piece of ice in it. The guilty party was so upset that George swore her to secrecy and he, in turn, never told on her. She didn't do it on purpose! Santa was good to us all.

George went hunting in Beeville, Texas, and I really started into some serious packing and sorting, although most of the work was done by the White House staff.

On January 1 George went to Somalia to visit the troops, and I joined him in Russia for the signing of the START II treaty, the broadest disarmament pact in history, according to the press. Among other things, it barred all Intercontinental Ballistic Missiles, the dreadful rockets that had scared the wits out of generations of kids all over the world.

We stayed at Spaso House and I am happy to report that repairs have started. It is still ugly, but they have started. Our guest room was the same, horrid brown curtains. It did look cleaner. I must say that brown sheets turn me off a little. Having said all these mean things, the water was piping hot, we had plenty of blankets, the beds were comfortable, I couldn't see the sheets (when my eyes were closed) and we slept like logs.

As Yogi Berra would say, "It was déjà vu all over again." We went to the Kremlin to the same building that the Gorbachevs had entertained us in. Naina and Boris met us at the door and we marched up that enormous red carpeted staircase past those very elite blond soldiers who stand with their noses up in the air, knees locked and their bodies leaning stiffly forward. They follow with their eyes the Head of State, looking down their noses all the time. Fascinating.

Same reception room, receiving line and on into that beautiful Facet room. This time I noticed what looked like delicate wrought iron chandeliers, but turned out to be solid silver that had blackened with time. I sat next to Boris and the mustached Vice President (Aleksandr Rutskoi), who I understand is giving Boris a very hard time.

. . . Sad to say they did not serve caviar as they did in the old days when you just shoveled it out on your plate. Boris talked mostly to George, which was all right as that was what we had come for. He did tap my foot just to remind me of our little game. He did tell George that he'd like to come to Kennebunkport. We said that we'd love to have him (and we would), but that it had to be a private visit.

Naina, Susan Baker, and I toured a little more of that beautiful Kremlin and then joined the men for the signing of the START II treaty. I know that George felt a personal satisfaction over that signing and it was a thing of pride for me.

On the way home we stopped in Paris for a few hours to say good-bye to François Mitterrand. The men talked and then had a press conference which both François and George handled with humor and warmth.

. . . On into cocktails. My, but the French do it well. Their canapés look and taste delicious, small, bite-sized, and they manage to avoid the plastic look that we have perfected. Dinner was even better, ending with the lightest, most delicious dessert.

. . . François was very funny and relaxed. He told several stories about his being a prisoner during WWII. He also told us a story about how Margaret Thatcher asked Ronald Reagan why she had not been invited to the 200th anniversary of the Revolutionary War Victory at Yorktown. I don't know if the story was true, but it is funny.

Good-byes are never easy, but when François said: "Good-bye, my dear friend," I was very moved.

That word *good-bye* hung over our heads for the next few weeks; it became a part of everything we did.

(On January 5th) George spoke at West Point. I was so glad that I had decided to go with him. By the time we got there it was a sunny bright day at that glorious spot on the Hudson River after a dreary start.

We ate in the most tremendous dining room with the whole corps— 4,000 great-looking kids. We walked to General Graves's house for dessert and coffee and stood on the porch and watched the "Long Gray Line" march by to go to the auditorium where Pop spoke. The speech was well received. Brent went with us, as did Col. Larry Mohr, one of the White House doctors. When Brent went to the academy, the Corps was half its present size. It was such a happy, impressive day.

The next day was our anniversary, and after a full day of official events, we came upstairs for dinner with Marvin, Margaret, Doro and Bobby. All four grands came and ate in the kitchen. They are wild and enjoy each other. How I love them and how I am going to miss them!

. . . Then one of those magic moments happened. Marvin asked us to go to the first floor with him and there was the "President's Own," the Marine Band, all ready and they played and the household staff sang "Happy Anniversary to you." They had stayed all that time while we had dinner. It was so sweet, private and personal. The grands danced, and George and I were very touched. I wonder if our grandchildren will remember that they danced at the White House on their grandparents' 48th anniversary with the Marine Band playing for them? They passed champagne. It was very thoughtful, and I suspect Gary Walters thought of it. In fact I'm sure he did.

. . . Kitty Brady had the cabinet wives for a final time on the 12th of January at the Treasury Department. This group of ladies have really bonded. I shall miss them a lot.

Marvin and Margaret and their friend Lloyd Hatcher, and Bobby and Doro and all their children, came to Camp David the weekend of January 9 for the last time.

We had very teary good-byes with Doro and Margaret. Doro took her little family to Florida to stay at Betsy and Spike Heminway's. Marvin went to Hawaii with his family to get out of the first strike zone of the Inaugural festivities. I'm afraid that I took for granted those wonderful children and their grandchildren. The drop-in trade at the White House had been a joy. I would hear those little voices around the pool or on the South Grounds and go out to find Sam, Ellie, Marshall with her sidekick, Abigail Meyer, and our little Walky Talk, Walker. I mention Abigail for she adopted us as her "Ganny and Gampy" also and we love her. Marvin, who hates politics, was wonderful about popping by quietly to check on his Dad and be sure he was all right. We will really miss them. That's the bad news. The good news was that we were leaving Doro happily married to the world's nicest man with a great big loving family. And the very best news was that while we were moving away from those children we were moving closer to Neil, Sharon and their children and George, Laura and Barbara and Jenna.

Esther and Dick Moore came up on Saturday night with Andy. It is all so final.

. . . Meanwhile down in Houston, the Fitches, Paula, Barbara Patton, Jack Steel, Don and Ariel are working away trying to make some sense out of all those boxes. What to send to storage and what to unpack. Many phone calls back and forth. Were any two people luckier than George and I? We certainly have good and loyal friends. I am beginning to really look forward to the move.

. . . I had a tea for my staff. So many of them have been with me for twelve years. I get a very heavy feeling in my heart when I think of them, how great they have been and what fun we had all working together . . . I wonder if I still have a brain. We'll certainly find that out and very soon! [I wrote that because I had become so reliant on my staff.]

On January 13 George gave the Medal of Freedom to Ronald Reagan. It was a real reunion of the Reagan White House. We were eager to have a lunch, but they really wanted a large crowd and had to fly back to California that day, so 280 came for the ceremony and refreshments. That was probably just as well:

. . . Saddam Hussein was violating the U.N. sanctions and at 1:20 p.m. British, French and American bombers were going to retaliate and hit missile sites. How we hated to see this happen during our last week, but that, of course, was exactly why it happened. (Saddam thought he could get away with it during the transition.) We just could not let this go by. Needless to say, George consulted with Bill Clinton and got total approval. I later saw Henry Kissinger on the tube and he said that Bill Clinton should be very grateful to George Bush for doing this for him. I also saw people like Donahue who said that George was just trying to regain some of his glory! Baloney!!!

Although all the weeks after the election had been emotionally draining, the last was the worst. I don't know what touched us most, but sometimes the love and support came from very unexpected sources. Shortly before we left, George received a phone call from actor Chevy Chase, whom we knew only casually and who was in town for the inauguration. He told George that although he had not supported him, he felt that George had served his country with honor and he wanted to say "thank you." That really touched George; it was a phone call Chevy didn't have to make.

Certainly anything that had to do with the military hit the tear button as George loved those young men and women. So you can imagine how difficult it was when we went to Fort Myers in Virginia on January 14 for the "Armed Forces Salute to the President."

Doro went with us. When George reviewed the troops for the last time I was almost overwhelmed with emotion. The speeches by Dick Cheney and Colin Powell were absolutely the most warm and touching. I'm not even a member of the bawl team and the tears flooded. Colin's speech:

"Mr. President, there comes a time every so often in a soldier's life when he has to say good-bye to an especially honored, respected and revered leader.

"It is always a profound and emotional moment. Anyone who has ever worn a uniform understands the ties that bind a great sergeant-major, or a ship captain, or a squadron CO to the men and women he leads.

"A loyalty grows in the unit—the loyalty of family—and the heart and soul of each member of that family is touched when the time comes for the leader to depart.

"For the over two million of us who serve in the Armed Forces, such a time has come for us today.

"To be sure, you have been the leader of the *ENTIRE* nation, in all its glorious and trying complexity. You have met the diverse challenges of an historic age and been equal to all of them.

"And yet, sir, despite the breadth of your cares and accomplishments for all Americans, a generation of American soldiers, sailors, Marines, airmen and Coast Guard will always think of you and regard you affectionately above all as *their* leader, *their* president and *their* Commander in Chief.

"That's because you have been unstinting in your faith in us, your pride in us, your respect in what it is we do for the nation.

"You have lived by the code we set for ourselves as warriors: dedication to one's troops, moral integrity, judgment, tenacity, courage . . . and to put it in military terms: DUTY, HONOR, COUNTRY.

"You have sent us into harm's way when you had to, but never lightly, never hesitantly, never with our hands tied, never without giving us what we needed to do the job.

"Your deep concern for the lives and sacrifices of those who serve in America's Armed Forces and their families has been felt in every barracks, on every flight line, in every berthing space of every ship.

"We have fought under your leadership for true and noble causes . . .

". . . In the Cold War, where the enemy was a hostile way of life . . .

". . . In Panama and Iraq, where the enemy was brutal tyranny . . .

". . . In Bangladesh and South Florida, where the enemy was nature's violence . . .

". . . And in Somalia, where the enemy is chaos and unspeakable human misery.

"History will remember you as a stirring leader of this nation in war and in crisis.

"History will remember you well for your leadership in peacetime . . . for your steady efforts to build a strong and capable military . . .

". . . For your steadfast support of the men and women who stand guard day and night, in every far-flung corner of the world, even when the glare of the world's attention is focused elsewhere.

"In 1981 you helped President Reagan begin to correct what the long, neglectful 'hollow force' days of the 70s had done to the spirit and sinews of America's military.

"Under your leadership our weapons have been the best, our magazines full, our training the most demanding and sophisticated in the world. Our leaders from the very top on down understand the use of force and the priceless value of our young men and women.

"America's revitalized forces shall be among your most honored legacies, Mr. President. They shall be the pillar of America's trusted power that you bequeath to the world.

"They shall be one of the tokens of greatness that you leave in tomorrow's history books.

"We are here today to honor you as a leader whom we have served with great pride.

"But no matter how heartfelt I try to make my words here, no matter how stirring this ceremony, no matter how warm our hearts, the honor we can offer in this hall cannot match what's written on the faces of our troops all around the world . . . the faces that America and the world see on their TV screens . . . the faces of courage, professionalism, compassion and hope . . . the bright faces of America's future.

"In their faces is written the highest and truest testimony to your leadership. And for that, Mr. President, the entire nation owes you its most sincere and profound thanks."

This was followed by a ceremony with singing put on by the combined services, and then a representative from each branch came forward and remembered something very personal about George. It was almost more than I could stand. So tender.

That night George's cabinet had a going-away party and presented him with his cabinet chair, his third. George was in the cabinet as UN Ambassador, Vice President, and President of the United States. The chairs are now in his office in Houston and are very handsome. I believe that George would tell you that he was served very well by the distinguished men and women in his cabinet.

. . . Everthing is sort of emotional and "last time." Yesterday we left the White House "for the last time" in a helicopter. In like manner we arrived at Camp David for "the last time."

Our last weekend at Camp David was very touching—and very hard. We had become so close to the service families who lived there, and we had many good memories with friends and family. For four years we jokingly had called it "Camp Marvin," since he had complained in jest one time that if President Eisenhower could name the camp for his grandson, why couldn't we change it in his honor.

As usual, we had a campful. Brian and Mila Mulroney and their children came from Canada to say good-bye. George planned one last Vespers service and asked George and Norma Strait and their son Bubba to come participate, and we also invited the Joint Chiefs of Staff and Supreme Court Justices and their spouses; and the heads of both transition teams: Vernon Jordan and Warren Christopher for the Clinton team, and Andy Card, who once again had come to our rescue and headed ours. When it came time for the service, the back of the chapel was filled with young Marine recruits.

We had to start the program without George and Brent Scowcroft, who were on the phone with François Mitterrand, John Major, and other world leaders about the situation in Iraq. George Strait had us laughing when he got all our guests to join in singing "All My Ex-es Live in Texas." Whoever thought that we'd see the members of the Supreme Court and Joint Chiefs singing that funny song. He sang my favorite, "A Father's Love," and ended the program with a song dedicated to George, "The Cowboy Rides Away." I'm sure that it will come as no surprise that we all cried.

The Mulroneys left the next morning after our last church service at the chapel. We said good-bye to Chaplain Jon Frusti, the choir, and all the little children. We had shared so much with them all, and I honestly feel that they are the true meaning of loving families and abiding faith.

George and Norma Strait were scheduled to leave early in the morning, but we found out that they were leaving just so Bubba and George could race home in time to see the football play-off games.

George is a rabid Dallas Cowboy fan, as is George Bush, so we persuaded them to stay on for the games and watch on our big screen. Between games Bubba and his dad played Wally Ball. For a very big star—George pulled in a record 87,000 swooning fans at the Houston Astrodome last year—they are the most natural, unspoiled family. George reminded me of our boys.

There was yet another teary good-bye with the Camp David personnel in the helicopter hangar. It was a surprise ceremony with a short speech by the wonderful Commander of the Camp, Joe Camp. (Yes, that's his name.) When it came time for George Bush to speak, he couldn't. I am sure that the Straits wondered just what they had gotten themselves into—a tear-soaked weekend, that's for sure.

On Monday night we had Al and Ann Simpson, Lud Ashley, and Fred and Martha Zeder for dinner. They told awful jokes and everything seemed funnier.

We ate dinner our last night in the White House with Pres, George's older brother, Johnny and Jody Bush, Billy and Ruth Graham, and Bobby Koch. Then we went to bed "one last time" in that glorious house.

26

A New Beginning

There is life after politics! Hurrah!

George and I quickly settled into our little rented house on West Post Oak. We were taken back into the community as if we had never left, and the "welcome home" still continues a year later. Houstonians truly have been loving and kind.

At 7:30 A.M. on January 21, George went to his new office on Memorial Drive to settle in and sort out, among other things, how in the world he was going to answer all his mail. A skeleton crew headed by Rose Zamaria came down with us, and a small army of volunteers—many of whom had helped George with his first congressional campaign—appeared to deal with the seven hundred letters a day that poured in.

I was getting reacquainted with shopping, cooking, and driving after twelve years of living a grand life. George took me out to buy a car and I had lots of fun shopping for the color I liked. Thank heavens he went with me to see that I also got a good car—American made, I might add. As it turns out, driving is something you do not forget.

Now, cooking is a little different. I never loved cooking, just eating. Why is it when people see someone who is a tad overweight, they assume she loves to cook? I don't. I can turn out a meal for fifty, but you would never go home afterward and say: "WOW! What a cook!" But I can light the fire and throw something on it. I can bake a potato and cook vegetables. So while we didn't starve, we did have some pretty lean meals. George lost two pounds without even trying; I, of course, didn't.

Just a few days after we moved home George W. and Laura and Neil and Sharon came for dinner. George W. was running the next day in a marathon and requested pasta for dinner. I made a tasteless dish of leftover turkey with a sauce to put over the pasta and served it up. The children kept straight faces, but George couldn't resist and said that he liked his pasta rare. It was just plain undercooked. The next day we watched George W. go racing by mile 19 of the 26.2-mile race and he finished in better than average time—in spite of my cooking.

Another afternoon Lauren, our nine-year-old granddaughter, came over after school. As she is a vegetarian, I decided to show off and use a new juicer we had been given. We cleaned a few carrots and jammed them into the machine along with some celery and a piece of tomato. All seemed well at first, but then suddenly food shot out of the juicer and reached as high as the ceiling and as low as the floor. Lauren couldn't control herself and got the giggles, and so did I.

Sharon came for Lauren just as George walked into the house to find me scraping carrots off of everything. He said not to worry, he had brought dinner home. He had made his first foray to Sam's Club and bought the world's biggest jar of spaghetti sauce and some spaghetti. While he watched the evening news, I continued to clean up my mess and start dinner. I turned around and in my haste knocked off the jar of sauce. Ugh, now I had sauce and glass mixed with the rest of the mess. That was the night George and I made an amazing discovery: You can call out for pizza!

We *were* having a lot of fun taking care of ourselves. We had all the modern equipment and our needs were not great. Paula, our house-keeper of thirty-four years, no longer was living with us, although she still was coming for a few hours every day to help out, and dog-sat when we were out of town.

We both longed to become truly private citizens, but that, I guess, is not to be. We live on a quiet, horseshoe-shaped street, and the tourists are a menace. On the weekends there is a steady parade of cars. Several amusing things have happened, however. There are two other springer spaniels that live on our street. Sometimes they are tied in the front yard, and people will see them and jump out and have their pictures taken with dogs they think are Millie and Ranger. That makes me furious, as they are not as handsome as our dogs and because I don't want anyone to think that I would chain our dogs to a tree in the front yard!

Another morning I was walking the dogs in my jogging suit and stopped to talk to our neighbor and friend Jack Fitch. We saw a small bus appearing around the corner and I immediately went and stood behind Jack's brick wall. A woman got off the bus and said, "I hope I'm not imposing, but I have a busload of British tourists. Can they get off and take pictures and talk to you?" Jack told her that she *was* imposing and that she also was breaking the law. She took off fast!

To solve this problem, which was ruining our gentle little street, the neighborhood got together and petitioned for state legislation and a city ordinance that allow us to gate our street. The revised Texas statute says cities can "regulate and restrict access to streets, avenues, alleys and boulevards in the municipality on which the dwelling of a former president of the United States is located, including the installation and maintenance of fences, gates, or other structures." Since there are very few "former presidents," the law does not affect many people. Barbara Patton, a beautiful volunteer in George's office and a neighbor and friend, along with Cassandra Manley, the head of our street association, and Jack Fitch joined forces with the help of many others to get this done.

George and I also changed our house plans to include a six-foot-high brick wall around our tiny drive-in courtyard.

I know that people don't realize how miserable they make the life of people who have been in the public eye, including actors and athletes. Some are kind and courteous, but others can be just plain rude. I have tried hard to get back to real life and am driving and shopping on my own. I know it is out of affection, but to be asked for your autograph, grabbed and hugged, or have your picture taken when you are racing to buy your groceries, or, even worse, something personal in the drugstore, is a little much. Sometimes when someone sidles up to me in a store and says, "Aren't you Barbara Bush?" I answer, "No, she's much older than I am," or sometimes I'll say, "No, but I am mistaken for her all the time," and march on. Often in my wake I can hear a voice say, "See, I told you that wasn't her!" My own grocery store is so used to me that I can shop pretty much like other people.

George, on the other hand, is much nicer than I and would never do that. Eating out can be especially hard at times. He stops eating, stands up, and is polite to everyone. He and I both love Sam's Club and are dangerous shoppers when we go there. We come out with stacks of paper napkins, office supplies, and huge jars and boxes of everything. However, it takes George hours to shop because he is mobbed.

～ On February 13 George and I flew to Miami for a much needed rest. He surprised me with something we always said we wanted to try, a cruise. We went on the *Regal Princess*, one of the "Love Boat" ships that advertises on TV. We were met by Captain Cesare Ditel, along with the TV captain, Gavin MacLeod, and the director of the ship company, who had come all the way from England. (The last two did not go on the cruise.) Something incredibly touching happened as we left the harbor: Earlier, George had visited a submarine that was in port, and as we passed by, the sailors were up on deck, saluting their former Commander in Chief.

Our ship had 1,600 guests and 900 staff. We fast learned that we could not walk out the door of our room without George's being swamped with requests for pictures and signatures. But the wonderful Italian captain invited us to use his deck up on the flying bridge during the day and to eat our dinner with him in his quarters. He was charming and we enjoyed that very much.

We worked out early in the gym. I rode the stationary bike and kept my head down reading a book; George jogged around an open deck with a large following. One morning George went into the sauna after his jog and came out stark naked toweling off. There stood a persistent photographer who asked George if he could take his picture! For the first time in his life George Bush said, "Absolutely NOT!"

We got off the ship in San Juan, Puerto Rico, where Governor Pedro Rosselló and his truly beautiful, vivacious wife, Marga, had a dinner for us in a tent under the stars at the Fortaleza. It was one of those magical nights with a cool breeze blowing from the harbor. They kindly let us bring the ship's captain with us. They gathered about seventy of our Puerto Rican friends, including several from the States.

We jumped ship in St. Martin, as planned, and flew to Miami to see Jeb and Colu and their three children. The next morning we went to Deering Bay, a marvelous development that Jeb's great friend and partner, Armando Codina, founded. George played golf with Jeb,

Arnie Palmer, who designed the course, and Joe DiMaggio, who loves golf. Both men are amazingly unspoiled after years of being loved by their fans. After a light lunch the Palmers dropped us off in Jacksonville. Arnold pilots his own Cessna jet, and we love how he makes announcements just like an airline pilot.

George and I had a cozy dinner with June and Dan Jenkins. Dan is a sportswriter who also has written several best-seller books. His latest, *Bubba*, is very funny—I would call it men's humor. Since reading it I sometimes refer to George as "Bubba." Bubba's dad would always come home, plunk down in front of the TV, and then mumble and talk back to the screen. I have occasionally found George Bush doing just that. I myself could be called "Mrs. Bubba" because I don't mumble at the screen, I yell gentle things like "IDIOT" or "FOOL," and feel better for it.

We had come to Jacksonville so I could attend my first meeting of the Board of Trustees of Mayo Foundation. Rochester, Minnesota, is the home base for the Mayo Clinic, but there are satellites in Phoenix and Jacksonville, where this particular meeting was being held.

I was thrilled when they invited me to join such a prestigious board, but I quickly realized how much I had to learn. The other members represent the worlds of business, education, law, media, and, of course, patient care, healing, treatment, and research. Then there's me. I'm afraid that so far I only have brought a good name—my husband's. The Mayo Clinic certainly is one of the best health care facilities in the world. During this time of medical care reform, they not only are on the cutting edge of patient care, but also have kept costs 20 percent lower than the national average while constantly striving to make medical care better and accessible.

When the meeting was over, I caught up with George in Albany, Georgia, at Nilo Plantation, the home of Gene and Evie Williams. George went to high school with Gene and we have known and loved both of them since then. Their plantation is lovely, with enormous live oaks covered with Spanish moss, green fields, ponds and lakes, pine and magnolia trees. There is every kind of wildlife you can imagine: horses, mules, swans, peacocks, ducks, cranes, deer, and so on. George had a great time hunting quail.

∽ This was sort of typical of our first year out of office. There were so many friends we wanted to see, so many things we wanted to do, but we seemed to race from place to place.

In March, for example, we went back to Florida for spring training with George W.'s Texas Rangers and the Houston Astros. We went to games, played golf in the pouring rain with an old Andover and Yale classmate of George's, Bill Howe, and his great wife, Joan, and visited with Mary and Bayard Sharp, Sarah Farish's parents. In May George went to the Kentucky Derby with Will Farish, now chairman of Churchill Downs, and fishing in the Bahamas with Nick and Kitty Brady.

And in April we took the thrilling trip to Kuwait, which I already have shared with you. One thing I did not mention, however, was the planned terrorist attack on George which was thwarted. Fortunately, we knew nothing about it until we returned home.

In between the traveling we were working on our house in Houston, which was going up just two doors down from our rented house, and we were redoing Mrs. Bush's bungalow in Kennebunkport, which we had inherited by default. It had to be overhauled from stem to stern without losing the essence of the house that the family grew up in. In all honesty, both houses were a joy to work on as everyone wanted to do a good job for George.

And both of us were trying to write books. George and Brent Scowcroft are working on a book about the seven dramatic changes in the world during the four years of the Bush administration. Since they both are speaking and doing so many other things, the book has been slow going for them.

George, for example, became chairman of the Eisenhower Exchange Fellowship, a group that tries to identify young people from abroad with leadership potential and brings them to the United States for six weeks. We went to Philadelphia to meet about thirty fellows who were finishing their tour and had been all across the country meeting with our leaders on every level in every field.

This is just one of the many causes that we are trying to support, including leukemia, the Crohn's and Colitis Foundation, and Boys and Girls Clubs. We both have become involved with M. D. Anderson Cancer Hospital in Houston, and George has gone on the Texas Medical Center Board. He also has become active in the Greater Houston

Business Partnership, and I have accepted the job as Ambassador at Large for AmeriCares. We are encouraging volunteerism and want people to try to take back their own communities by being responsible, supportive, and interested. In short, we are trying to live up to George's Thousand Points of Light credo: "From now on any definition of a successful life must include service to others."

I will be honest and tell you we also have learned to say no. We are trying to keep a balance and stay focused on just a few causes.

For me, of course, my number-one cause is still literacy, with emphasis on the Barbara Bush Foundation for Family Literacy. With Benita Somerfield at the helm as executive director, we have many exciting plans for the future as we continue to raise money for literacy programs. We still strongly feel that focusing on the family is the best place to start to make this country more literate, and I still feel that being more literate will help us solve so many of the other problems facing our society.

∿ In the spring my older brother, Jim, who had been in bad health for many years, began to fail rapidly. His problems made Job's troubles seem light in comparison. Just everything was wrong with his body. I flew up to see him at the hospital, and although he was in considerable pain from cancer, he maintained a great sense of humor, optimism, and courage. That was a privilege to see. We talked intermittently, when he could. He told me how much Dave Peake's loyalty had meant (Dave was a childhood friend who now lives in Houston); what our brother, Scott's, great love and strength had meant to him; that our sister, Martha Rafferty, had been there for him through thick and thin; and above all just how much he loved and depended on Margie, his wife. He said that she was everything to him, and that is so true: My sister-in-law has been the greatest wife and mother.

Jim Pierce was unique, to say the least. I'll never forget when George was vice president and he showed up for a visit dressed in blue jeans and riding a motorcycle. I loved him. He died in a bed in his living room holding Margie's hand and looking out a window at a redbird in a magnolia tree.

I was very proud of what the editor of *Sports Afield* and Jim's boss, Lamar Underwood, wrote after his death: "Jim Pierce made hundreds of close friends and served the interests of sportsmanship everywhere.

His magazine leadership and influence transcended traditional editorial/advertising lines to achieve reader reward. Jim was always on the front line in the battle for editorial integrity and useful, illuminating editorial coverage."

But as is so often the case when there is a death, there also is a new life: Robert Patrick Koch weighed in at ten pounds, six ounces on May 20. Doro and Bobby, along with Sam and Ellie, were thrilled.

We had another great sadness that spring: Our poor Ranger died of cancer. George, along with Don Rhodes, was devastated. I truly believe that George, who had not let us see him mourn the election or the loss of his mother, let his grief for all come out when his dog died. I really did not know how to help him, but it was very touching how Millie tried to take Ranger's place. Then George got a note from Fred Zeder that said, "Sorry. I've just heard Ranger's gone paws up." That brought a smile.

It was one night about this time that I absolutely couldn't sleep, and I got to thinking about what I have learned in life—sometimes the hard way—and the advice I'd like to give my precious children, if I could or would. I found myself at my computer composing a letter, which I never sent but would like to share with you now:

> . . . Faith, Family and Friends.
> Try—and oh boy, how hard it is—to find the good in people and not the bad. I remember many years ago that I wasted so much time worrying about my mother. I suffered so because she and I had a "chemical thing." I loved her very much, but was hurt by her. (I am sure that I hurt her a lot, too.) Grace Walker said to me once, "Think of all the lovely things about your mother . . . all the things you love and are proud of about her." There were so many that I couldn't count them all. I think that I expected her to be perfect. Nobody is perfect. Certainly not me. So LOOK FOR THE GOOD IN OTHERS. Forget the other.
> Clara Barton, founder and president of the Red Cross, was once reminded of a wrong a friend had done to her years earlier. "Don't you remember?" the friend asked. "No," replied Clara firmly. "I distinctly remember forgetting that." Not bad advice. Take a lesson from your dad. He says when I remind him that someone has been hateful, "Isn't it better

to make a friend rather than an enemy?" He's right, too.

Don't talk about money ... either having it or not having it. It is embarrassing for others and quite frankly vulgar.

DO NOT BUY SOMETHING THAT YOU CAN-NOT AFFORD. YOU DO NOT NEED IT.

If you really need something and can't afford it ... for heaven's sake call home. That's what family are all about.

Do not try to live up to your neighbors. They won't look down on you if you don't have two television sets. They will look down on you if you buy things that you cannot afford and they will know it! They are only interested in their possessions, not yours.

Be sure that you pay people back. If you have dinner at their house or they take you out, have them back, but remember you don't need the expensive thing. You can make the best spaghetti in the world. People love to come to your home. Plan ahead and it will be fun.

Value your friends. They are your most valuable asset.

Remember loyalty is a two-way street. It goes up and down. So be loyal to those people who are loyal to you. Your dad is the best example of two-way loyalty that I know.

Love your children. I don't have to tell any of you that. You are the best children any two people ever had. I know you will be as lucky. Your kids are great. Dad and I love them more than life itself. I think you know that about your dad. I do also.

Remember what Robert Fulghum says: "Don't worry that your children never listen to you; worry that they are always watching you."

For heaven's sake enjoy life. Don't cry over things that were or things that aren't. Enjoy what you have now to the fullest. In all honesty you really only have two choices; you can like what you do OR you can dislike it. I choose to like it and what fun I have had. The other choice is no fun and people do not want to be around a whiner. We can always find people who are worse off and we don't have to look far! Help them and forget self!

I would certainly say, above all, seek God. He will

come to you if you look. There is absolutely *NO* down side. Please expose your children and set a good example for them by going to church. We, your dad and I, have tried to live as Christian a life as we can. We certainly have not been perfect. Maybe you can! Keep trying.

In early May we headed for Kennebunkport and a glorious summer in Maine. We were barely there when Esther and Dick Moore and Hugh and Anne Sidey spent the weekend. It was cold but fun. They were the first of 177 different overnight houseguests, counting our children and grandchildren. I would remind you that is 344 sheets and 344 pillowcases. I dread to think of the towels we washed!

One of the most fun groups we had come up were the six military nurses at the White House who had taken such good care of George. To explain this weekend I first have to give you a little background: When they had treated George for shoulder spasms with hot packs and deep heat therapy, they played music, and Art Wallace brought a Roger Whittaker tape (he is a famous British balladeer) which they all loved. As these things happen, they formed a Roger Whittaker Fan Club. Kim Siniscalchi became the president and George became the recording secretary of the club. The other four were Paula Trivette, Mary Jackson, Debbie Beatty, and Ellen Tolton.

Just before we left office in January, George made the nurses promise they would take leave and come to Maine for a weekend. He then tracked down Roger Whittaker through his agent and called his home outside London and talked to his wife, Natalie. I would have loved to have seen her face when she picked up that telephone. (I bet she checked on the authenticity of the call.) They accepted for the weekend of June 12.

I raced around getting the Point ready for its first big weekend of guests, and George had more fun planning the visit. He had big pins and polo shirts made that we all were to wear that said "Nurses Weekend; Roger Whittaker Fan Club," with the dates and the club slogan: "More Roger in our lives."

The Whittakers arrived and turned out to be fun-loving, ready-for-anything people. We raced them out to the golf course as Roger loves golf and got back to the house just in time to greet the nurses' minivan. They poured out of the bus all wearing T-shirts with blown-up pictures of Roger on one side and themselves on the other and "MORE ROGER IN OUR LIVES" underneath. They had left Washington at 5 A.M. and driven all day, and every time they stopped, people asked them about the club. When they got to our gate, the guard who checked them in looked at their shirts and said: "I never heard of this guy until today. He's up at the house now." So George's surprise was a surprise until the last minute! Thus began a weekend of golf, tennis, walking, biking, and lots of singing. It was a treat.

In July the George Bush Presidential Library Foundation Board of Trustees came to Kennebunkport for a meeting. The majority of the people, about one hundred strong, stayed at the Colony Hotel, a big beautiful old wooden hotel, but Will Farish and Walter and Lee Annenberg stayed with us and were our first guests in the refurbished bungalow. Lee and Walter were so great. The room they stayed in was about the size of the closet in their guest room when we stayed with them in the desert. To hear them talk you would have thought we'd put them up in Buckingham Palace. Peddie, the preparatory school that Walter attended and to which he had just made a large donation, sent a big banner which we put outside their bedroom door on the side of the house.

The trustees, along with officials from Texas A&M University, came from as far away as California and Puerto Rico. Former Governor Don Luis Ferré and his wife, Tiody, attended. (He turned ninety in February 1994 and George was thrilled to go to the party.) I believe that George was as moved by the numbers of people who have wanted to help with the library and who came to this meeting as by anything that ever happened to him. We tried to show them a good time. We brought all the guests to the Point for cocktails by trolley in the evening and then took them back to the Boat Club for a Maine dinner. Dick Cheney, Tip O'Neill, and Dick Jackman spoke, after which Jane Morgan Weintraub sang. Dick Cheney gave a very warm testimonial, and Tip was so dear and funny. Dick Jackman, a vice president at Sun Oil, has helped George out many times and is not only really funny, he also is motivational. He starts out rather seriously and then sneaks up on you and you realize that here is one funny man.

The next morning after breakfast we met at the Colony Hotel to discuss the library. The presentation by Texas A&M impressed everyone: They are the third largest university in the country, rank fifth in the number of Merit Scholars and eighth in research. Walter Annenberg announced that when he went back to college for his Ph.D., he thought he'd go there.

Several universities wanted George's library, but I believe the A&M spirit was the deciding factor. When it opens in 1997, the entire complex will include the library and museum, administrative offices, a teaching and research facility with classrooms, meeting rooms, and conference facilities. The George Bush School of Government and Public Service will offer a master of public administration degree, and George looks forward to teaching and working with the students.

The lunch crowd and drop-in trade were pretty heavy all summer, including President and Mrs. de Klerk of South Africa, who came for lunch. We feel that he is trying to set his country on the right road as peacefully and fairly as possible without ripping it further apart.

One day I wrote in my diary:

Very few people would believe our yesterday. We had the "Book Group"* for lunch; three Cardinals: O'Connor from New York, Law from Boston, Baum from St. Louis and now the Vatican, and Father Murphy from Boston. They are at Proutt's Neck for a few days' rest. They mentioned that they knew Jack Allin, former President Bishop of the Episcopal church and our summer minister at St. Ann's by the Sea. George got on the phone and invited Jack for lunch. At one time Wendy Stapleton came in with our grandchildren Marshall and Walker and some little boy who is staying at the Stapletons'. (Wendy was baby-sitting our grands while Margaret went to the airport to pick up Marvin.) Then Johnny Walker (GB's first cousin and a federal judge), his wife Katharine, their baby little Katy and Kimba Wood, the judge who was put up for Attorney General, then so unfairly caught up in "Nannygate," dropped by in the middle of the lunch. (She was an attractive young woman and seemed very nice.) Griffin Bell, Marlin Fitzwater, Wick Sollers and Boyden Gray appeared. Margaret came back with Marvin, Chrissy Evert, Andy Mill, little Alex and a nanny. A few minutes later Don and Adele Hall drove in. At four eight of us rushed out to the golf course and got in thirteen holes and had to quit on account of darkness and the fact that Paula was going to kill us. Suddenly instead of eight for dinner we had four Marvin Bushes, four Mills, three from the Griffin Bell group as Boyden left

* These are the people helping George and Brent Scowcroft on their book: Condi Rice, provost at Stanford University; Ginny Lampley and her husband, Robb Mulberger; Arnie Kanter; and Flo Gantt.

and two Halls. Paula told me it would all work out and it did. It was a case of the fishes and the loaves.

We were so busy and hectic that I can't believe what I did one day. For weeks I had looked forward to Phyllis Draper's coming for lunch with four Smith classmates. When the big day came I was just sitting down to lunch with George when they called from the gate to say that they were on their way up. I had totally forgotten. George suggested that I tell them I thought they would like to see the town and that we would have a cool glass of something and then I'd take them to Mabel's Lobster Claw, made famous by the press during our presidential years. I confessed, and they all were kind. We did have that cool drink and I did show them our favorite eating spot in Kennebunkport.

We did some great whale-watching that summer, a new sport for us, and we are kicking ourselves that we did not discover this sooner. Some of our guests I'm sure wish we never had, since they got seasick bumping around out in the ocean. About forty porpoises raced along-side our boat and dove and played when we were out looking for whales with little Jebby one day. They are hard to find, but well worth the search.

One day George let Sam and Jebby, both ten, take our tiny dinghy out on the sea. The little outboard motor quit and they could only move whichever way the wind blew them. Their mothers and I watched out the window with great fear as they bobbed up and down on the waves; George laughed at their plight. Finally, a lobsterman took pity and towed them in.

So George decided that the grandchildren needed a bigger boat, which they will have for the summer of 1994.

And, of course, we did not stay home all summer. In August, thanks to Trammell and Margaret Crow, who gave us their beautiful boat, *Michaela Rose*, we took a cruise in the Mediterranean. Noelle, now sixteen, went with us along with George's young cousins Craig and Debbie Stapleton and their sixteen-year-old daughter, Wendy. Included in the adventure was a visit with King Hassan II of Morocco, where George played golf. We cruised to Gibraltar and up the Spanish coast and had a fabulous time. It was a dream trip.

∝ On September 13 George was standing on the South Lawn of the White House when Prime Minister Rabin of Israel and Yasir Arafat of the Palestinian Liberation Organization signed a peace accord. I also had been invited, but just wasn't ready to go back yet. However, it was right and proper that George be there. The signing would never have taken place without George. Ronald Reagan also must get credit for rebuilding our defenses and keeping us strong. If George hadn't held firm against the pressures to make immense loan guarantees to Israel without an agreement from them that they would not build in the occupied territories, the Arabs would not have come to the table. If George had not formed and held together the coalition to free Kuwait, the Arab world would not have come to the table in Madrid. Many friends, domestic and foreign, called to congratulate George after the signing.

George met with Arafat and said he was charming. Amazing! Who ever thought that we would recognize a sworn terrorist?! Let's hope something comes of this famous handshake as many, many people have worked years to get peace in the Middle East.

George stayed on in Washington to help show support for NAFTA, joining former presidents Jerry Ford and Jimmy Carter and President Clinton in the NAFTA push. The Clintons invited him to spend the night, and George said he loved seeing the White House staff. He also said that the house looked lovely.

We watched the NAFTA debate with great interest and I found myself on the same side with Al Gore and voting for him all the way. He showed great control, reason, and ability. He also showed Ross Perot to be devious. Ross made many damaging statements that night, but the things he said about Mexico alone would make him unfit for public office. It was so insulting to our friends and neighbors to the south. I can't imagine how hurtful those words were to them. It hurt us. George was very happy when NAFTA passed, as he truly feels it will be good for the country. Incidentally, more Republicans than Democrats supported Bill Clinton on this vote.

I did go to Washington with George for Colin Powell's touching, dignified retirement ceremony. There is no finer man, American, or friend, and we also love his wife, Alma.

We moved into our dream house on October 18. Every person who worked on our house did a splendid job, and we are so grateful to them all. It is everything anyone would ever dream of or want at our age. We are surrounded by people we love; we have every modern appliance we could ever want; every room is really bright and pretty; Imelda Marcos would be jealous of our closets, if not my clothes; we are handicap accessible. We are so happy that every day we awaken and say to ourselves: "How could we be so lucky?"

⌒ The answer to that is that we might stay at home a little more. We both gave numerous speeches in the United States that fall, and George went to Brazil, taking along Jeb; Cannes, France, Genoa, Italy, and Switzerland, taking along Margaret; and Puerto Rico, taking Doro and her friend Jodie Dwight. In November he and I took a trip to the Far East with Carole and Lod Cook, going to China, Hong Kong, and Taiwan, then stopping in Sweden and England before coming home just before Thanksgiving.

We had a happy holiday with Neil and Sharon and children and my two nephews, Jim and Scott Pierce, and their darling young families. Then on Sunday we once again joined Lod and Carole Cook and flew back to London for a fascinating four days. (Everyone needs a Lod Cook in their lives. He is one of the most generous people.)

John and Norma Major hosted a wonderful lunch at Number 10 Downing Street, where we saw many old friends, and Ambassador Raymond and Caroline Seitz also gave a lunch at Winfield House. But the highlight was going to Buckingham Palace for lunch with Her Majesty Queen Elizabeth II and His Royal Highness Prince Philip.

They received us in their private quarters and the four of us sat to have a glass of sherry. At one time the door opened and six Welsh corgi puppies came in. They were all well behaved and dear, smiling little dogs. Then Her Majesty said something like, "Before we forget we must do what we are here to do," and handed George two leather boxes. One held an enormous heavy gold chain with a big burst on the end. This "Collar" with enamel on one side and gold on the other literally came well past George's waist. It was very impressive. The other box held another big burst on a large ribbon to be worn across the chest, I guess. So much for ceremony. The actual title of the award is Knight Grand Cross of the Most Honourable Order of the Bath. George is the eighth American to receive it, the other seven being Ronald Reagan and six World War II generals.

We went in to lunch and had a lovely time. Both the Queen and Prince Philip know a great deal about the United States and the world, so it was a stimulating visit. I remember that we talked about what George had observed on our trip around the world; our mutual friends, Will and Sarah Farish, with whom the Queen has stayed in Kentucky; and our sons' races for governor: George W. in Texas and Jeb in Florida.

When we got home from the luncheon George's aide, Michael Dannenhauer, asked me to witness a paper that George had to sign. It said that if for any reason George withdrew from the order or became deceased, the collar would be returned. So, as long as George lives, the stunning collar—valued at more than fifty thousand British pounds—will be on display in the George Bush Presidential Library Center.

David and Carina Frost had a lovely dinner at their absolute jewel of a house with many friends. I loved it when we were talking to, and I quote them, "two lesser Knights" at the dinner and they asked if we had signed the paper.

Several months later, German Chancellor Helmut Kohl presented George with the Grand Cross, special class of the Order of Merit, to recognize his world leadership, and while in Kuwait, the Amir had presented him with the Necklace of the Most Excellent Order of Mubarak, which had been given only four times in the history of the country. These, too, will be on display at the library—forever.

In the middle of December I took a completely different kind of trip: I went with a group from AmeriCares to Croatia, carrying food and medicines to the people of Sarajevo. We were a crew of volunteers along with Nancy Huang, my new aide, and Ben Orman, my new doctor, and Dr. Larry Mohr, who was with us at the White House. We didn't know what to expect and were disappointed to discover that we could not take the supplies ourselves to Sarajevo. It just was not safe. Bob Macauley was determined to go, but the airport was closed and, I believe, eleven people were killed that day. So we flew into Split, where the cargo was unloaded and trucked to Sarajevo the next day.

We visited the refugee camps, one drearier than the next. These people are feeling hopeless. They want to go home. They have no jobs and nothing to do. They worry about their families and friends. They live in barrack-type rooms with two other families in many cases. Several things impressed me. The number one request that the doctors have is medicine for depression, which I was told time after time was their biggest enemy. They also constantly fight dysentery, and hepatitis had broken out just before our visit in one of the camps. The women all knit, but they don't have much yarn, so they make a garment, tear it out, and make another. The last camp we went to was the worst: one hundred people sharing four toilets and sinks and no showers. The smell was pretty bad. We were gone four days in all, and in a way, it was the perfect way to start the holiday season.

A quiet Christmas was spent in our new home with Neil, Sharon, and their family. Our other children spent Christmas in their own homes. We talked to them all, missed them, but were so glad that they had each other and were well.

So now we have come full circle. Nineteen ninety-four is upon us. I remember years ago saying to George when we were first married: "I can't wait for you to retire." He looked surprised and said that he couldn't think of anything worse and that he hoped he never would.

Well, I'm glad he still feels that way. There are so many more things to do. This new life is a beginning and not an end. This year alone has two gubernatorial races ahead, which we are very excited about. We are proud that Jeb and George W. have chosen to serve their country in this way. They have paid their dues: They both have been successful in business—met payrolls, paid taxes, and supported their families; and they both have been community activists, both socially and politically. They will make outstanding governors.

We have so many plans for trips and events and friends in 1994 that it boggles the mind. But I know it will be fun. Certainly it has never been boring.

George Bush and I have been the two luckiest people in the world, and when all the dust is settled and all the crowds are gone, the things that matter are faith, family, and friends. We have been inordinately blessed, and we know that.

Appendix A

It's impossible in one book to recognize all the people who have made a difference in your life over the years, but certainly there are two groups of people without whom I never could have accomplished one thing: our Houston volunteers, who stuck with George and me through victories and defeats; and my White House staff.

The volunteers I especially would like to recognize are: Marjorie Arsht, Betty Baker, Mary Stuart Baker, Susan Baker, Melza Barr, Kay Bruce Baxter, Taylor Blanton, Sarah Bergner, Dot Burghard, Flo Bruenig Carroll, Betty Lou Carter, Janet Cartwright, Bill Cassin, Kristi Cassin, John Cater, Roland Chamberlin, Marion Chambers, Nancy Cook, Nancy Crouch, Linda Dyson, Ida Fahey, Daphne Murray Gawthrop, Sarah Gee, Bebe Gow, Peggy Green, Sara Green, Ada Grundy, Pat Halla, Margi Jenkins, Mary Louise Knowlton, Betty May, Dossett McCullough, Ed McCullough, Betty Kyle Moore, Betty Ann Murray, Becky Orr, Barbara Patton, Caroline Pierce, Mary Sage, Helene Speights, Bill Spence, Nancy Spence, Jack Steel, Margaret Voelkel, Kris Anne Vogelpohl, and Jane Wainright.

✎ And the following were the members of my White House staff. Some of them were with me just a few months; some were with me for twelve years, beginning in 1981 in the Vice President's Office. They all helped make a difference: Susan Porter Rose, Julie Cooke, Laurie Firestone, Sondra Haley, Susan Green, Celeste Dorsey, Anna Perez,

Joan DeCain, Ann Brock, Cathy Fenton, Jean Becker, Peggy Swift, Sally Runion, Jane Moore, Jay Suchan, Kathy Steffy, Jeanie Figg, Anne Griffith, Diana Kellogg, Deborah Underhill, Diane Limo, Kim Brady Cutler, Catherine Coughlin, Casey Healey Killblane, Lea Uhre, Rosemary Gonzalez, Jean Wallace Leach, Aida Cipriani, Karen Connell, Ruth Mankin, Susan Hubbard, Deborah Scott, Courtney Dur, Don Mains, Elaine Speiser, Juanita Doggett, and Shirley Campolieto.

Appendix B

The mission of the Barbara Bush Foundation for Family Literacy is:

To establish literacy as a value in every family in America by helping every family in the nation understand that the home is the child's first school, that the parent is the child's first teacher, and that reading is the child's first subject.

To break the intergenerational cycle of illiteracy by supporting the development of family literacy programs where parents and children can learn to read together.

BOARD OF DIRECTORS

Dr. Joan Abrahamson, Chairman
President
Jefferson Institute

The Reverend Dr. Anderson Clark
President
READ America

Sharon Darling
President
National Center for Family Literacy

535

Dr. John E. Harr
Vice President, Office of Corporate Initiatives (Retired)
Capital Cities/ABC Inc.

Harold McGraw, Jr.
Chairman Emeritus
McGraw-Hill, Inc.

Sydney Olson
Director, Governmental Affairs
American Speech-Language-Hearing Association

Susan Porter Rose
Former Chief of Staff to Barbara Bush

Benita Somerfield
Executive Director
Barbara Bush Foundation for Family Literacy

Margot B. Woodwell
Vice President and General Manager
WQED

ORIGINAL CORPORATE COMMITTEE

Martin S. Davis, Co-chairman
former Chairman and Chief Executive Officer
Paramount Communications, Inc.

Harold Poling
Chairman and Chief Executive Officer (Retired)
Ford Motor Company

Joseph Antonini
Chairman, President, and Chief Executive Officer
K mart Corporation

Frank A. Bennack, Jr.
President and Chief Executive Officer
The Hearst Corporation

John J. Curley
Chairman, President, and Chief Executive Officer
Gannett Company, Inc.

Louis Gerstner, Jr.
Chairman and Chief Executive Officer
IBM

Thomas Murphy
Chairman of the Board (Retired)
Capital Cities/ABC, Inc.

Donald E. Newhouse
Samuel I. Newhouse Foundation, Inc.

Reece A. Overcash, Jr.
Chairman and Chief Executive Officer
Associates Corporation of North America

John J. Phelan, Jr.
Chairman and Chief Executive Officer (Retired)
The New York Stock Exchange, Inc.

Ralph Rossi
Vice Chairman
UST, Inc.

William A. Schreyer
Chairman and Chief Executive Officer
Merrill Lynch and Company

Appendix C

*Text of Remarks of Mrs. Bush at
Wellesley College Commencement
Severance Green, Wellesley College,
Wellesley, Massachusetts,
June 1, 1990*

Thank you, President Keohane, Mrs. Gorbachev, Trustees, Faculty, Parents, Julie Porter, Christine Bicknell, and the class of 1990. I am thrilled to be with you today, and very excited, as I know you must all be, that Mrs. Gorbachev could join us.

More than ten years ago when I was invited here to talk about our experiences in the People's Republic of China, I was struck by both the natural beauty of your campus . . . and the spirit of this place.

Wellesley, you see, is not just a place . . . but an idea . . . an experiment in excellence in which diversity is not just tolerated, but is embraced.

The essence of this spirit was captured in a moving speech about tolerance given last year by the Student Body President of one of your sister colleges. She related the story by Robert Fulghum about a young pastor who, finding himself in charge of some very energetic children, hit upon a game called "Giants, Wizards, and Dwarfs." "You have to decide now," the Pastor instructed the children, "which you are . . . a giant, a wizard, or a dwarf?" At that, a small girl tugging on his pant leg asked, "But where do the mermaids stand?"

The Pastor told her there are *no* mermaids. "Oh yes there are," she said. "I am a mermaid."

This little girl knew what she was. She was not about to give up on either her identity *or* the game. She intended to take her place wherever mermaids fit into the scheme of things. Where *do* mermaids stand . . . all those who are different, those who do not fit the boxes and

538

the pigeonholes? "Answer that question," wrote Fulghum, "and you can build a school, a nation, or a whole world on it."

As that very wise young woman said, "Diversity . . . like anything worth having . . . requires *effort*." Effort to learn about and respect difference, to be compassionate with one another, to cherish our own identity . . . and to accept unconditionally the same in all others.

You should all be very proud that this is the Wellesley spirit. Now I know your first choice for today was Alice Walker, known for *The Color Purple*. Instead you got me—known for . . . the color of my hair! Of course, Alice Walker's book has a special resonance here. At Wellesley, each class is known by a special color . . . and for four years the class of '90 has worn the color purple. Today you meet on Severance Green to say good-bye to all that . . . to begin a new and very personal journey . . . a search for your own true colors.

In the world that awaits you beyond the shores of Lake Waban, no one can say what your true colors will be. But this I know: You have a first-class education from a first-class school. And so you need not, probably cannot, live a "paint-by-numbers" life. Decisions are not irrevocable. Choices do come back. As you set off from Wellesley, I hope that many of you consider making three very special choices.

The first is to believe in something larger than yourself . . . to get involved in some of the big ideals of your time. I chose literacy because I honestly believe that if more people could read, write, and comprehend, we would be that much closer to solving so many of the problems plaguing our society.

Early on I made another choice which I hope you will make as well. Whether you are talking about education, career, or service, you are talking about life . . . and life must have joy. It's supposed to be fun!

One of the reasons I made the most important decision of my life . . . to marry George Bush . . . is because he made me laugh. It's true, sometimes we've laughed through our tears . . . but that shared laughter has been one of our strongest bonds. Find the joy in life, because as Ferris Bueller said on his day off . . . "Life moves pretty fast. Ya don't stop and look around once in a while, ya gonna miss it!"

The third choice that must not be missed is to cherish your human connection: your relationships with friends and family. For several years, you've had impressed upon you the importance to your career of dedication and hard work. This is true, but as important as your obligations as a doctor, lawyer, or business leader will be, you are a human being first, and those human connections—with spouses, with children, with friends—are the most important investments you will ever make.

At the end of your life, you will never regret not having passed one more test, not winning one more verdict, or not closing one more deal. You will regret time not spent with a husband, a friend, a child, or a parent.

We are in a transitional period right now . . . fascinating and exhilarating times . . . learning to adjust to the changes and the choices we . . . men and women . . . are facing. I remember what a friend said, on hearing her husband lament to his buddies that he had to baby-sit. Quickly setting him straight . . . my friend told her husband that when it's your own kids . . . it's not called baby-sitting!

Maybe we should adjust faster, maybe slower. But whatever the era . . . whatever the times, one thing will never change: fathers and mothers, if you have children . . . they must come first. Your success as a family . . . our success as a society . . . depends *not* on what happens at the White House, but on what happens inside your house.

For over fifty years, it was said that the winner of Wellesley's Annual Hoop Race would be the first to get married. Now they say the winner will be the first to become the CEO. Both of these stereotypes show too little tolerance for those who want to know where the mermaids stand. So I offer you today a new legend: The winner of the hoop race will be the first to realize her dream . . . not society's dream . . . her own personal dream. And who knows? Somewhere out in this audience may even be someone who will one day follow in my footsteps, and preside over the White House as the President's spouse. I wish him well!

The controversy ends here. But our conversation is only beginning. And a worthwhile conversation it is. So as you leave Wellesley today, take with you deep thanks for the courtesy and honor you have shared with Mrs. Gorbachev and me. Thank you. God bless you. And may your future be worthy of your dreams.

A Transcription of Mrs. Raisa Gorbachev's Remarks
at Wellesley College Commencement,
Wellesley, Massachusetts,
June 1, 1990

Dear Friends, I am pleased to be with you at this momentous and exciting day when you are leaving your college and entering a new life. I congratulate you on this important occasion. I am grateful to Mrs. Barbara Bush and to the college administration for this chance of coming to Wellesley during our stay in America. I thank college officials, professors, and all of you for your kind words and warm feelings.

I distinctly remember a similar summer day in Moscow. The years of my studies at Moscow University were over. We were then full of plans and hopes just like you are today. Being young is a marvelous time, a time of actions and expectations, of being confident of one's abilities, and sure that everything is still ahead. I wish that all your dreams of the future come true. The President of the Soviet Union asked me to convey to you his warm regards. He also wishes you happy roads in your life.

We know that people in America show great interest in what is happening in the Soviet Union, the land of Perestroika. This word, nowadays, sounds the same in all languages of the world. We associate with Perestroika the future of our country whose millions of people speak over 120 languages. Perestroika was conceived and is being implemented for the sake of the people, their dignity and equality. This goal is to make human ideals and values a reality. This vast and difficult task is a tough challenge, but we are confident that Perestroika will succeed. The guarantee of that is the patriotism and talent of our people, their tenacity, their strength, and their desire to overcome obstacles on the way on the road they chose.

In renewing our country, we want to make it open to the world. The Soviet people know the value of peaceful lives. We wish to have good relations with the Americans and other peoples. Of course all of us, [as] daughters and sons of our own countries and peoples, are different. The Soviet Union and the United States have different histories, traditions, and cultures. That, however, is not [a] reason for mutual estrangement and suspicion. People on both sides of the great ocean realize more and more clearly that our values bring us closer. Such values are love for one's own native country, love for one's relatives, children, the belief in what is good, and belief in solidarity to combat wars, violence, hunger, catastrophes, and other threats to mankind. These values are now more important than anything else. Hamlet's question, "To be or not to be," today confronts not only individuals or nations but the entire humanity.

So, what will our society be like? Not only the leaders of states, but the world community as a whole, share this responsibility. We women have our special mission. Always, even in the most cruel and most troubled times, women have had the mission of peacemaking, humanism, mercy, and kindness. And if people in the world today are more confident of a peaceful future, we have to give a great deal of credit for that to women who are active in advocating friendship, cooperation, and mutual understanding among nations.

You are entering a complex and multifaceted world. Your generation will soon assume the responsibility for everything that takes place on our planet. May good luck and happiness be with you. I wish you many good accomplishments. Thank you.

Appendix D

Text of Remarks Given by George P. Bush
to the Republican National Convention,
Houston, Texas,
August 19, 1992

Thanks, Ganny. I would like to talk about a member of the family that is not here tonight. You know him as the President, but I know him as the greatest man I have ever known. Despite the enormous pressures of his job, he always has time for his twelve grandkids.

In the presidential campaign, it's hard for people to get a sense of what makes a candidate tick. The family is what makes my grandfather tick.

I would like to read excerpts from a letter that he wrote to me after my dad and I came back from a relief mission in Armenia before he was inaugurated. I hope it gives you a better understanding of what my grandfather is all about.

He wrote:

Dear George P.,

A few days ago I met with the Deputy Mayor of Yerevan, in the Soviet Union. He was a stolid-looking guy and he came in with some people from Cambridge, Massachusetts, because Yerevan and Cambridge are sister cities.

He told me about how things were going back there in the U.S.S.R. He told me that the outpouring of generosity and caring from America had really meant a lot to the people there. And then he said this: "When your son wept, it was on every TV set in the Soviet Union and those tears said more than anything else about the decency of the American people."

My grandfather went on to say:

Men are not supposed to cry, says convention; but we do and we should and we should not worry when we do.

I cry when I'm happy and I cry when I'm sad, but when I saw you and your wonderful dad in that church in Armenia on Christmas Day I cried because I was both happy and sad. Don't ever forget what you saw there. Don't ever forget what you participated in. In less than two weeks I will be President of the United States. I know I will not forget what that little trip of yours meant to people all over the world.

You're a good man, Charlie Brown, and I miss you a lot.

Devotedly, Gampy.

This letter means a lot to me because it shows the heart of this man I love so much. I just wish people who see George Bush on TV or read about him in the newspapers could know him as I do. A man of enormous integrity and love for his family . . . and for all of America.

Thank you.

Index

545